JACKSONIAN AMERICA
Society, Personality, and Politics

The Dorsey Series in American History

JACKSONIAN AMERICA
Society, Personality, and Politics

EDWARD PESSEN

Distinguished Professor of History
Bernard M. Baruch College and
The Graduate School and University Center
The City University of New York

Revised Edition

1978 **THE DORSEY PRESS** Homewood, Illinois 60430
Irwin-Dorsey Limited Georgetown, Ontario L7G 4B3

ISBN 0-256-01651-8
Library of Congress Catalog Card No. 77–088295

Printed in the United States of America

1 2 3 4 5 6 7 8 9 0 ML 5 4 3 2 1 0 9 8

To my precious children,
Beth, Abigail, Dinah, Jonathan, and Andrew

PREFACE

When nine years ago I finished writing *Jacksonian America,* I had no thought of doing a future revision, regarding the book as my considered statement on life in the United States during the second quarter of the 19th century. The positive reaction of general readers, students, and historians to the book, with even its sharpest critics conceding its stylistic or scholarly virtues, also made me hesitate at the prospect of changing a piece of work I continue to be happy with. Of course I have changed my mind on a number of points, in some cases only hours after they first appeared in print, but I assume that such rethinking is characteristic of all but the most dogmatic authors and by itself would hardly justify a formal revision. What led me to undertake this task was the outpouring of new scholarly work during the past decade, work that it seems to me compels every serious student to modify his earlier perceptions of the era.

Chapter 3 of the first edition, for example, was entitled "The Less than Egalitarian Society" and its essential point was that the long accepted belief in Jacksonian equality of condition and opportunity was based on insufficient evidence. The recent research enables us to go beyond skepticism toward the statement of a new thesis concerning antebellum society and social structure, one that rests on substantial and in some instances massive data. An enormous quantity of good recent work has deepened our understanding of antebellum cities, medicine and public health, women, slavery, free blacks, "internal differentiation" within the Irish and other communities, voluntary associations, the professions, rioting and violence, and geographical mobility, among other topics. I have read and tried to absorb all this research, using its fruits to transform what I feel was my earlier random treatment of the social potpourri into something more searching and intellectually satisfying. In this age of "new histories," Jacksonian politics has by no means been neglected by modern researchers. My revised chapters have been influenced by the new quantitative studies, the controversial ethnocultural interpretation of politics, and the application of psychohistory to the personality and to the public behavior of Andrew Jackson. I have also given additional thought to foreign policy issues and to politics at the community level.

Let me give no false impression concerning the comprehensiveness of this book. While it does treat many topics that were and continue to be neglected in versions of the period that focus on politics as the beginning and end of wisdom, it makes no claim to telling it all. Perhaps I bypassed a discussion of social reform in the original edition the better to underscore my belief that Jacksonians contributed little if anything to it. If I have continued to say little about such matters as the great national reform movements and the life of the mind, it is because of my conviction that certain great themes are more sensibly left untouched than treated cursorily. If I have nevertheless ventured generalizations concerning these and other lightly treated subjects, it is not because of unusual boldness on my part but because I have read and thought about these themes for a long time. Further reflection has led me in some instances to delete passages that refer too laconically to topics, such as children, about which we continue to know too little. Perhaps because my consciousness has been raised, this edition omits the contemporary discussion of the beauty of American women that appeared in the original.

In view of the massive additions that have been made to the literature since the first edition was published, I have of course revised the bibliographical essay. The "Jacksonian [Historiographical] Controversy" that swirled about Arthur M. Schlesinger, Jr.'s *The Age of Jackson* has in the last decade been largely dissolved by new data and new preoccupations that relegate the famous national party battles at the heart of that volume to a place removed from the center of American life, as from historians' thinking about American life. Writing this revision has also afforded me the opportunity to read worthwhile older writings that I had earlier overlooked and to change my evaluation of several influential contributions. In the interests both of space and good sense, the new bibliographical essay is more selective than its predecessor, which I fear at times must have given the impression that I cited every single item I had read. If the new essay is nevertheless longer than the original, it is because I have had to assess more than a thousand new writings.

This preface also provides me with a welcome opportunity to pay back some old and new debts. The original preface neglected to mention the many dozens of hours of proofreading cheerfully contributed by Arnold Lepelstat—then a fine graduate student, now a fine teacher—and his wife Eda. I am delighted at the opportunity to make up for my forgetfulness toward them and to thank too Ellen Jacobs for helping to read proofs for this revision. I cannot begin to thank the many scholars whose criticisms and suggestions I have found invaluable as I worked on my new version of that marvelous period. (Those who are familiar with the original edition and with some of my recent work will know that if I think the era "marvelous," it is not because I find its achievements particularly praiseworthy but because I find them fascinatingly complex and endlessly suggestive.)

I must give special mention to my friend Samuel B. Richmond, master statistician and Dean of the Graduate School of Management of Vanderbilt University, who was kind enough to make himself available to check on the accuracy and good sense of my translations of esoteric statistical concepts into what I trust is clear prose. I have elected this approach for several reasons. This book is written for the general reader and the nonspecialist historian. I find something pretentious in flaunting thin knowledge recently acquired of a technique that is in fact unnecessary to use. And above all I believe that any historical subject can be discussed clearly and in the English language.

December 1977   EDWARD PESSEN

PREFACE TO THE FIRST EDITION

The time has come for a comprehensive reexamination of the Jacksonian era. A number of brilliant and provocative studies have in recent years illuminated the mentality and mood, the voting patterns and party conflicts, and the economic controversies that dominated the period. The newer interpretations have refined our knowledge and in some cases revealed hidden facets of that complicated quarter century between the Presidencies of John Quincy Adams and James Knox Polk. No one volume has been published, however, that would tie together the many modern contributions and, by supplementing them with earlier insights, attempt a new synthesis. The purpose of this book is to help fill the need for such a work.

*****

The book that follows is organized around topics and issues. Its method has been determined by its purpose, which is not to retell well-known political tales but rather to try to answer important questions concerning American civilization in the Jacksonian era. The politics of the time were important, but politics was not the whole of American life. For that matter, the era's political issues cannot be understood without reference to social and economic developments.

*****

I should like to give credit to some of the persons who were particularly helpful to me in preparing this book. In the seven years since I first began to think seriously about writing it, I discovered anew that librarians are the most cooperative species known to scholarly man. My graduate students in courses on Jacksonian Democracy at the City University and at the New School for Social Research were a marvelous audience precisely because they were never a passive audience. Their interest in ideas and their preference for a topical rather than a narrative treatment obviously made a strong impression on me. The late Ralph Harlow, with whom I worked for one year, and the great Edward Corwin, with whom I was privileged to hold several long discussions, gave me the benefit of their vast knowledge of the Liberty Party and of the era's constitutional issues, respectively. Professor Joseph Dorfman of Columbia University made invaluable suggestions concerning the economics section of the manuscript. Professor Adam Abruzzi was good enough to make suggestions concerning statistical issues relating to voting. Professor Hans Trefousse of Brooklyn College gave me the benefit of his critical reading of the chapters on politics. Professor Milton Cantor of the University of Massachusetts contributed an informed reading of the original chapters on society. Chancellor Irvin G. Wyllie of the University of Wisconsin went far beyond the call of editorial duty in helping me with every aspect of the book's preparation. Needless to say I alone bear responsibility for all errors.

A grant from the Research Foundation of the State University of New York for 1965–66 and a sabbatical leave for 1967, approved by the City University of New York, were indispensable. I am also in debt, immeasurably, to my wife and to my children, who have cheerfully and patiently permitted me to discuss the issues of the Jackson era at numerous supper tables and on long auto trips, with or without pretext.

CONTENTS

1

INTRODUCTION:
THE CONTINUING
FASCINATION OF THE
JACKSONIAN ERA

For history as for other human activities, fashions change. Subjects or issues that are all the rage one season fall into almost total neglect with the coming of another. Yet the Jacksonian era, resisting this rule of fickleness, has never lost its fascination to succeeding generations. While there can be little doubt that the modern resurgence owes much to the publication by Arthur M. Schlesinger, Jr., of *The Age of Jackson* in 1945, earlier historians had never ceased discussing the era nor had American readers lost interest in it.

Jackson was one of those personalities who stamps himself on an age. That the era was named after him is not simply another example of the tendency of Americans to oversimplify complex events. His striking weaknesses and his strengths, both in personal as in political matters, inevitably aroused the attention of contemporaries and later generations alike. He was a man of such force, so invincibly controversial, so widely believed to be either avenging angel or devil, that his own personality alone explains in large part the historical appeal of the era he seemed both to symbolize and dominate.

Other factors also account for the era's continuing appeal. Until recently it was almost universally believed that democracy came of age in America during the presidency of Old Hickory. Thus, Tom, Dick, and Harry won the right to vote and proceeded to take politics out of the hands of oligarchic caucuses, in the popular view. Socially and economically, too, the common man was supposed to have made great gains. The Jacksonian era reputedly witnessed the emergence of an unprecedented social equality. Foreign observers were bedazzled while Americans were split into hostile factions,

1

depending on whether they cared more for the masses or the classes.

Contemporary cynics and ultrarealists, however, refusing to take seriously what they derided as sham battles and opportunistic political rhetoric, delighted in exposing these pseudo conflicts for the humbugs they ostensibly were. Our modern historians of consensus were by no means the first Americans to be suspicious of the hyperbole employed by politicians. Without going into the relative merits of the views of the skeptics and their critics, it is obvious that if the former have a point, the reputation of the era is called into question. For if the great struggles for popular rights were more apparent than real, and if egalitarianism was only the reputation but not the rule, does it not appear that the era's importance has been overrated? Might it be that the attention of generations of Americans has been drawn to the age for the wrong reasons? Have our conceptions of the era been formed on the basis of the myopic judgments of its overwrought contemporaries, the mistaken analyses of gullible historians, and the cunning distortions featured by later Democratic politicians, eager to identify their cause with the allegedly democratic program of the Old Hero?

Even the name of the era is in question. One need not be an iconoclast to feel doubts about the aptness of such labels as the "Age of Jackson" or the "Jacksonian Era." For all his force of character, Andrew Jackson was President of the nation during an era of laissez-faire. National administrations in general and his own in particular had little effect on the social, economic, religious, and intellectual developments that were shaping American civilization. Even the political currents of the time were largely impervious to the will of one man. Such an important influence on politics as the startling expansion of the nation's transportation network had nothing to do with the personality, and little to do with the program, of Andrew Jackson. Thomas Cochran's advice to historians that they should discard the "presidential synthesis" in writing and teaching history has special relevance with regard to a multifaceted era that was little affected by the man in the White House, for all his undoubted verve.

And yet men of the period felt that Andrew Jackson was its dominating figure. This is attested by such varied sources as the novels of James Fenimore Cooper, the diary of Philip Hone, the journals of Ralph Waldo Emerson, the notes kept by scores of European travelers, and partisan newspaper accounts, whether by Jackson's supporters or his enemies. William A. Dunning several decades ago reminded us that in history oftentimes what people think is true is more important than what in fact was. God alone knows the actual reality; men only presume to know it, never accurately. It is clear that reality, as understood by Jackson's contemporaries, afforded him and his party starring roles. It is equally clear that the era's consciousness was itself a vital element in the life of the time. Part of the reality of the era was a belief—distorted though it might be—in the central importance of Andrew Jackson and of the campaigns he and his party waged in behalf of the common man.

The Dunning dictum is a wise one but its implications should not be misconstrued. While it directs the student of history to pay respectful attention to the ideas of an age, be these ideas foolish or wise, it does not go so far as to imply that whatever was thought was right. If Dunning's admonition is a useful antidote to the tendency to judge the past by the standards of the present, it does not follow that popular beliefs should not be subjected to critical evaluation.

The student of history continues to be under the obligation to check the accuracy of past beliefs against the ever more complex reality disclosed by historians as they uncover new data. That contemporaries were blissfully unaware of certain important facts does not detract from the importance of the latter. Historians, as George M. Trevelyan once observed, must "know more in some respects than the dweller in the past knew himself about the conditions that enveloped and controlled his life."

All of which is to say that if the Jacksonian era is to be understood, close attention must be paid to the recent disclosures that challenge traditional beliefs regarding its character.

The new evidence and modern interpretations compel us to rethink many of our ideas concerning the era and to reconsider even the appropriateness of the labels we have heretofore used in identifying it. Yet nothing about either the new data or the recent explanations of them seems to diminish the era's significance. Whether it was an age of democracy or seeming democracy, the common man or the uncommon, idealistic reformers or artful dissemblers, the era remains one of seminal importance. If it was in fact what it long seemed, then of course its reputation would be justified. If it was not an age of democracy or egalitarianism, the era if anything becomes more intriguing. For what is more interesting than the existence of a vast gulf between appearance and reality?

It has also become clear that the Jacksonian era was more complex than our earlier preoccupation with its political issues suggested it was. The vigorous economic developments, the unique society and culture, and the assertive and bold personality types which came to the surface fascinated contemporary observers and for good reason. They are likely to continue to fascinate future generations.

2

THE JACKSONIAN CHARACTER: A CONTEMPORARY PORTRAIT OF AMERICAN PERSONALITY, TRAITS, AND VALUES

The pursuit of the essential Jacksonian continues. The elusive fellow—and even such militant feminists as Harriet Martineau and Frances Trollope had the male rather than what the era regarded as the "female appendage" in mind when they reported the traits and values of Americans—has been interpreted as a child of the frontier, the democratic man, the product of equality, an entrepreneurial seeker after the main chance, and as a "venturous conservative" whose feet drew him irresistibly in the direction of speculative profit even as his mind held to "an ideal of a chaste republican order, resisting the seductions" of a dynamic capitalism. Nor do these explanations exhaust the list. These assessments have for the most part been arrived at through indirection, the nature of the man being inferred from the abundant evidence on his nation's behavior. The method is a sensible one and would in fact be the historian's only recourse were no other data available.

There does exist, however, a vast amount of evidence that throws a most direct light on the traits and values of Jacksonians. For not only did Americans themselves observe their fellow countrymen but an army of European, mainly English, visitors swarmed over this country during the Jacksonian era. They subsequently published hundreds of travelers' accounts in response to the great European interest in the young republic and an insatiable American curiosity about what the visitors thought of them. Covering almost every aspect of American civilization—its political, social and economic institutions; its intellectual life; the striking features of its climate and terrain—these reports by no means neglected customs and traits. Yet amazingly little has been done by scholars with this great storehouse of information on Jacksonian values and personality.

American historians have tended to avoid direct discussion of national character, evidently finding the subject disconcerting. If, in David Potter's phrase, they have accorded national character "a *de facto* but not a *de jure* status," their hesitancy has been due to the subjectivity invariably associated with discussion of the concept, the indistinctness and the overlap between traits of different eras or even of different peoples, and above all the dubious use made of national character by chauvinists. Aware, too, of the psychological ramifications of the subject, historians have modestly turned over its discussion to those whom they believe are the better qualified. For whatever the reasons, it is indeed a fact that "it has fallen to investigators in other, nonhistorical branches of learning to undertake a more searching and more systematic analysis of national character." A recent scholarly survey of important writings on American national character discloses that psychologists, sociologists, and anthropologists have done the lion's share of the work. Unfortunately, social scientists for all their acuity are not necessarily good historians. It remains the historian's task to apply to a particular historical context the useful insights into the nature of national character provided by his co-workers in the social sciences.

Certainly national traits and national character exist. At this late date it should not be necessary to show that they are not genetic in orgin. A unique history, nuances of institutional evolution, distinctive physical environment and physical separation from Europe, ethnic and religious heterogeneity, together with a memorable, if brief, career as independent polity—all combined to shape the American people into something different from all others. Their traits are worth knowing, for history is made not by impersonal forces but by people. Jacksonian life owed its special qualities to the kind of men who lived it.

When they have dealt with traits at all, historians have often done so in a curiously offhand manner. Perhaps because they felt the traits to be too obvious to warrant extended discussion, some scholars have alluded to them only briefly and generally, focusing instead on interpretation. They have sought that single illuminating factor, the key which at once opens the door to understanding. David M. Potter found it in abundance; George W. Pierson in the "M-Factor": movement, migration, mobility. Frederick Jackson Turner's well known version of an American molded by his frontier experience, it has been said, relied "for proof not upon descriptive evidence that given traits actually prevailed, but upon the argument that given conditions in the environment would necessarily cause the development of certain traits." Turner was perhaps a better empiricist than this criticism suggests, yet there is no doubt that he was far more interested in the interpretation of the phenomena of personality than in their description. An original intellect will of course be drawn to the interpretive or analytical, rather than to the merely descriptive, tasks of scholarship. Problems arise, however, when the soaring speculations of the creative theorist rest on insufficient or faulty evidence.

Turner had even less to say about American character than is generally thought. A passage at the very end of his famous paper on the influence of the frontier has been treated as though it were a discussion of the frontier's influence on American *character*. Actually, Turner was describing the influence of the frontier on the American *mind* or *intellect*. "From the conditions of frontier life came intellectual traits of profound importance," begins his last paragraph. The traits in question—"coarseness and strength combined with acuteness and inquisitiveness; that practical, inventive turn of mind, quick to find expedients; that masterful grasp of material things, lacking in the artistic but powerful to effect great ends; that restless, nervous energy; that dominant individualism, working for good and for evil, and withal that buoyancy and exuberance which comes with freedom"—are introduced by the phrase, "to the frontier the American intellect owes its striking characteristics." Turner then proceeded to name these characteristics—of the *intellect*.

Turner, who chose his words carefully, was not even purporting to write a list of traits of American character or personality. For a careful delineation of such traits we must turn elsewhere. And if our concern is with the traits of Jacksonians, we have almost nowhere to turn among the historians.

Nothing affords a better clue to the nature of the Jacksonian than the composite version of him that emerges from the contemporary accounts. That the likeness cannot be an exact one goes without saying, since the traits are always the traits as refracted through the eyes of the beholder. Observers were never completely disinterested, nor did such men as Philip Hone, George Templeton Strong, or Calvin Colton claim to be impartial. James Fenimore Cooper is a marvelous source for the Jacksonian era, both for such novels as *Homeward Bound* and *Home As Found,* and for his collection of essays *The American Democrat.* Published in 1838, the fiction and the commentary alike afford a wealth of detail on Jacksonian mores that attest to the literary craftsmanship of its assembler, as their flashes of insight bespeak his penetrating intelligence. An impartial intelligence it was not, however, since Cooper was repelled by so many of the new ways, emotionally drawn as he was to the old.

Foreign visitors faced special problems, as the more thoughtful of them well understood. Thomas Hamilton was aware "that the narrative of a traveler is necessarily a book of inaccuracies," the range of his observations "limited to those peculiarities which float . . . on the surface of society. . . . His sources of information are always fallible and, at best, he can appeal only to the results of an imperfect experience." Much of his "narrative must be derived from the testimony of others. . . . Details are loosely given and inaccurately remembered. Events are coloured or distorted by the partialities of the narrator; minute circumstances are omitted or brought into undue prominence, and the vast and varied machinery by which fact is manufactured into fallacy is continually at work."

Hamilton was alluding to the problems faced by the fairminded visitors. Not all of them were.

A number of English authors became famous or notorious precisely because their hostility was ill concealed. According to J. S. Buckingham, who came here to undo what he felt was the mischief done by some of his countrymen, they had sought "only for blemishes, and to turn even the virtues [of American life] into ridicule." Others had shown "a strong political bias, hostile to everything connected with the name of a republic." Since England was a political battleground during the era, many Tory sympathizers sought to provide political ammunition for the struggle against democratic reform at home by harsh accounts of its alleged unfortunate consequences for the America they visited. Buckingham also charged that some visitors had substituted fictitious and imaginary stories for facts, unjustifiably misrepresenting and caricaturing the American people.

Probably the most notorious as well as the most widely read traveler's account was Mrs. Frances Trollope's *Domestic Manners of the Americans*. Critics then as later were to explain the dim view Mrs. Trollope took of American ways by reference to a business failure she suffered in Cincinnati during her stay in this country. This is economic interpretation of human behavior with a vengeance, and is unjust to a woman of great integrity. As a snob of sorts, she simply disliked Americans—their principles, their manners, their opinions—and she frankly admitted as much. But that a given action was repulsive to her did not prevent her from reporting it honestly. If many Americans did not take kindly to her sour comments, a number of respected persons admired her forthrightness, believing it close to the mark. Mark Twain later compared her report to "photography" in its accuracy. She herself, in a reflective moment, conceded that "it is chiefly in the superficials that they [the Americans] are deficient." Her book was, of course, a detailed portrayal of just such unlovely superficials. For all its author's bias, it is indispensable to the student of Jacksonian manners. Charles Dickens and Captains Hall and Marryat likewise provide examples of visitors who, while heartily disliking much of what they saw, strained to keep their accounts free of the bias they were charged with by some contemporaries.

Visitors presented still other problems. Some could turn warts into beauty marks while others seemed blind to our virtues. The admirable Duke of Saxe-Weimar could give a most detailed picture of everything he saw, but he seemed utterly incapable of formulating a generalization about his experience. Michel Chevalier, on the other hand, seemed to have a penchant for large abstractions.

When it came to theorizing, Alexis de Tocqueville of course stood alone. While the brilliance and originality of Tocqueville's insights are justly celebrated, not least for how well they have worn, his reporting must be treated with great caution, as his own colleague Gustave de Beaumont, John Stuart Mill, and a number of modern students have warned. His interest was not in facts but in their meaning. America was to him a kind of generalized case study of *démocratie*, the civilization of the future. A nice example of the problem posed by Tocqueville as observer is his discussion of Americans and the law. Since, in this democratic society, "an offensive law of which the majority should not see the immediate utility" would not be enacted, it followed that the people respected the laws. This was good logic. Unfortunately, it did not seem to be borne out by the facts, which in their perverse way simply would not conform to Tocqueville's expectations concerning them. He made large assumptions which, while quite legitimate in a discussion of democracy in general, simply were not based on the complex and contradictory American example of that system. Fortunately, Tocqueville's eyes were not completely closed to the mundane facts of American behavior. When his own observations are borne out by his contemporaries, he invariably offers not only the most profound explanation of the causes and likely consequences of the phenomena under consideration, but the most memorable—because the most discerning—descriptions of them as well. He had "an intense sensitivity to men and events."

The contemporary portrait of the Jacksonian, then, was drawn by unavoidably fallible and subjective men and women. (Harriet Martineau, one of the most indefatigable of the visitors, had the additional burden of deafness, hearing only what was shouted into her ear trumpet.) In the following chapter, I note that foreign visitors invariably presented a distorted version of American *society*. Fortunately, they managed to describe American personality traits more objectively. It is easier to be an accurate reporter of personal behavior than to evaluate institutions, and one is more likely to manifest clinical detachment when engaged in the former process than in the latter.

The version that follows was put together by credible observers, for I have excluded the evidence of writers whose anti-American bias seemed to make it impossible for them to report accurately. Unless otherwise noted, the only characteristics included in the discussion are those alluded to by a number of observers. I trust that it is a sign of the reliability of the composite image that there was a large degree of agreement about its component features by so many and such unlike reporters.

Contemporary comments about Americans fall into four not always distinct categories: emotional traits or attributes of personality; mental or intellectual traits; manners, habits or customs; and values—themselves, of course, manifested in behavior. The notorious spitting done by males chewing tobacco is a nice example of a clearcut *habit* which is distinct from personality and mind, and can be related to values only by the too imaginative. Shrewdness, on the other hand, is a trait that cuts across all lines, reflecting personality, intelligence, and one's appraisal of the scheme of things. In any case the categorization emerged naturally from the observations of contemporaries.

The natural or unspoiled part of his person—precisely that aspect of personality least touched by the artificial or institutional environment that gave distinctiveness to his society—was the most admired feature of the Jacksonian. Dickens found that "by nature [Americans were] frank, brave, cordial, hospitable and affectionate." Marryat took time out from his censure to remark that "at bottom [Americans] are a very good tempered people." Captain Hall was amazed at how even-tempered they were, despite his faultfinding. Harriet Martineau found that westerners were the most pleasant people in the world, a judgment that George Combe would expand to include Americans from the other sections. Charles Murray believed the American people unusually hospitable and cordial, while Peter Neilson was impressed by the small but significant fact that Americans went out of their way to give directions to the traveler. Sir Charles Lyell, the great geologist, was interested above all in the country's rock formations, Cincinnati's "alluvial terraces," for example, attracting more of his attention than did its society. When he did glance up from the fossil flora, however, he noted admiringly that the human fauna behaved with propriety and a wholesome openness. A realistic note was injected by William Thomson, who observed that the polite and gentlemanly manners of the south could be construed as an effect of the duels so lightly entered into on the merest hint of offensive behavior. On the other hand, he found northerners equally polite.

American generosity was also applauded, if not always by the American people themsleves. New Englanders, Miss Martineau was advised in the nation's capital, "do good by mania." She was herself most favorably impressed by "the generous nature of their mutual services." America was the land of assorted benevolent associations, the leaders of which clearly were not themselves suffering from the abuses they sought to correct. Sophisticated critics of a later time might explain their charitableness as only neurotic do-gooding, brought on by emotional discord of one kind or another: it might be due to a too strong or a too weak father, or to the crisis following the disappearance of the traditional opportunities for their privileged class to play its accustomed paternalistic part in society. Jacksonian travelers, less inclined to be psychoanalytical, noted the absence of economic or tangible self-interest in the charitable activities of Americans, and applauded. They found the most "praiseworthy feature of the American character, their steady and liberal pa-tronage of benevolent institutions." American prison reform had aroused worldwide interest: the official purpose of the visit here by Tocqueville and Beaumont, after all, had been to study the Ameri-can penal system. Many visitors agreed with Hamilton that it was impossible "to praise too highly [the Americans'] . . . active benevolence which . . . takes so deep an interest in the reforma-tion of the objects of punishment."

If Miss Martineau experienced little impoliteness, a number of the visitors complained of rudeness shown by the Americans either to them or to others. Staring was characteristic and disconcerting. Requests that the plate be passed at hotel or boarding house table often went unheeded, as was true also of requests for removal of hats in theatres. A minister was dismayed to find a church service emptying before he "had scarcely named the text." He had not yet had time to be boring. Fanny Kemble, having been offended once too often by American women who unceremoniously interrupted a nap she was taking on a river boat for no better reason than to glance at the books lying by her side, exclaimed that "no person whatsoever, however ignorant, low or vulgar, in England, would have done such a thing."

The American was curious, sometimes excessively so, according to visitors who felt themselves badgered by incessant questions they not only had no wish to answer but which they considered bad form even to ask. "They cannot bear anything like a secret," was the conclusion of Marryat, one of whose confidants had advised him that the Ursuline Convent had been stormed more because of curiosity about the life behind its sealed gates than out of bigotry. A conversation between two Americans, strangers to one another, in which were put the following questions, all answered without hesitation: "what is your name? where are you from? where are you going? what is your profession? . . . how many dollars have you made? have you a wife and children?" indicates that Americans themselves took no offense at their frank and disingenuous curiosity.

Harriet Martineau was delighted with the "incessant play of humor [that] characterizes the whole people," but again she was in a distinct minority. Grund thought they did not laugh well, while Hamilton believed them to be humorless: in his opinion, Kentuckians were the only Americans who could understand a joke. Most visitors agreed in essence with Dickens who found the Americans to be a people whose "temperament always [was] . . . of a dull and gloomy character." Tocqueville offered a characteristic explanation of the excessive gravity of Americans: as social upstarts of a democratic community, they took themselves too seriously. It was "in aristocratic communities [that] the people readily give themselves up to bursts of tumultuous and boisterous gaiety, which shake off at once the recollections of their privations." Democratic men (having less misery to shake off?) preferred "silent amusements which are like business and which do not drive business wholly out of their minds." The Americans, who according to Marryat laughed at themselves after reading Mrs. Trollope's account of their foibles, evidently had minds free for things other than business. National humor is very much a matter of taste. Varied evidence, ranging from the tall tales published by A. B. Longstreet, the spoofs written by John Pendleton Kennedy, Seba Smith, and Charles A. Davis, and obscure memoirs kept by rural families describing a life that was "lively, full of fun and jokes," indicate not that Americans were humorless but rather that Europeans were unable to comprehend the fact.

The visitors also found Americans dull. Since the emotions of the people were too restrained, "there is little of what is called *fun* in America," mourned Francis Lieber. "A very grave people . . . woefully ignorant of the difficult art of being gracefully idle," was Hall's judgment. They "make a toil of pleasure." Mrs. Trollope found "Jonathan . . . a very dull boy." If the English were by "no means so gay as [their] lively neighbors on the other side of the channel," compared with the Americans they were "whirligigs" to whom "every day is a holy day, and every night a festival." She had never seen "a population so totally divested of gaiety . . . from one end of the Union to the other. [She knew New England only by reputation.] They have no fêtes, no fairs, no merrymakings, no music in the streets, no Punch, no puppet-shows." She spoke from her own limited experience but other observers registered similar complaints about a "funeral solemnity," "oppressive atmosphere," and a general absence of gaiety. "Americans are . . . destitute of the sense of pleasure," wrote Chevalier. To judge from American behavior at public meals, Dickens thought that "undertakers on duty would be sprightly beside them." Americans probably were not unhappy with the explanation given by Tocqueville and others that their alleged dullness was due to the absence of an aristocracy here. Small enough price to pay for so great a good. Hall's well-known plaint that he never saw a flirtation in this country was likewise probably admitted with pride by some of this highly moral population.

Many Europeans found Americans a cold people. Even Miss Martineau was offended by the apparent coldness and indifference she ran into. New Englanders were singled out. Although Combe found the people "essentially amiable," they were too "cold and reserved," giving "no greeting of welcome on arriving, and no thanking you and wishing you goodbye at leaving a hotel." Shirreff likewise found that "external forms of decency" were faithfully observed, but the "tactiturn, phlegmatic, and calculating disposition" of its people made them "objects of dislike." Admirable but not lovable, said Hamilton. The visitors were not sure whether Calvinism or other factors were to blame for this unattractive trait. Few blamed it on the weather, as did Beaumont, but many agreed with his verdict on the Americans: "cold as ice."

The cruelty displayed so often and by so many Americans was shocking. Whether tories or liberals, the visitors—with the exception of Lyell and a few others—were repelled at both the system of slavery and at white American attitudes toward Negroes, whether slaves or free. Joseph Pickering was horrified that a respectable crowd could watch, with feelings that ranged from indifference to enthusiasm, as a colored man was burned alive. In Hartford, according to Abdy, "to pelt [colored people] . . . with stones, and cry out nigger! nigger! as they pass, seems to be the pastime of the place." Europeans were dismayed not only by racism but at the cruelty shown unfortunates. Buckingham could understand neither newspapers nor their readers in treating flippantly poverty and misery "that ought to thrill the heart with horror or melt it with pity." Hangings or public executions of any kind attracted vast crowds of "respectable" or obviously well-to-do folk, as well as the other kind. William Dean Howells' father recollected that public hangings used to fill the taverns and grog shops, as thousands of people came from all over the countryside, most of them of "respectable appearance," drawn to the spectacle by "morbid curiosity." One visitor was appalled at the sight of young women cheerfully present at a hanging in New York City.

Violence was a much-observed trait, although it was reported mainly in the south and on the frontier. Personal quarrels occur everywhere but Americans seemed ready to mutilate one another for reasons that Europeans found incredible. In Kentucky one man came near to killing another for opening a coach window. As shocking as the ridiculous reasons for fighting were the extreme forms it took. Stabbing, shooting, gouging out of eyes, biting off of nose or ears were not uncommon. Frontier violence was not too surprising, but what amazed visitors was the proneness of "respectable men" of some standing to throw themselves savagely on someone who had inadvertently provoked them. Members of political parties which differed only slightly in programs nevertheless attacked one another brutally on election days, both in the city and the countryside. Ethnic and racial animosity provoked bloody riots in cities in every section of the country. In one notorious instance men killed one another in New York City over a dispute concerning the relative merits of two famous actors. Abraham Lincoln in 1838 warned against "the growing disposition to substitute the wild and furious passions in lieu of the sober judgments of the courts; and the worse than savage mobs for the . . . ministers of justice."

Less frightening if not more attractive was the selfishness of Americans. Tocqueville was aware that they could be public-spirited, but he found no one more dedicated to the gratification of his own physical wants than the American. (In his explanation, public-spiritedness was self-interest sensibly pursued.) The bad manners sometimes displayed at the dinner table were regarded by some as nothing more than the behavior of men so preoccupied with satisfying their own wants of the moment that they either ignored requests by others for food or else gave them inferior portions. Combe concluded that there was something in his training that led the American to the ignoble feeling that the purpose of life was nothing more than the satisfaction of "his own good pleasure."

Americans as individuals were wanting in self-confidence. The word "insecure" was not yet the vogue in those happy times but, if it were, it would have been applied to a people who, every day and in every kind of company, asked the visitor, "What do you think of us upon the whole?" Miss Martineau felt it was not a serious flaw but she admitted that like Captain Hall, she had suffered through innumerable variations on "the perennial question: 'How do you like America?'" Hamilton found this "restless and insatiable appetite for praise, which defies all restraint or common sense," one of the "most remarkable features" of the American character. Lieber, who came here to stay because he was so delighted with this country, reports being asked, "Do you think it as fine as the Rhine?"—"What, sir?"—"The Hudson." He describes his figurative gnashing of teeth, "when you enjoy on a hot day a glass of cool, sparkling cider of the best kind, and an officious acquaintance . . . seeing the praise of the liquid in the expression of your face, asks you: 'Now, tell me, is not it equal to any champagne?' The taste is gone at once." In Tocqueville's memorable words, the Americans "unceasingly harass you to extort praise, and if you resist their entreaties, they fall to praising themselves. It would seem as if, doubting their own merit, they wished to have it constantly exhibited before their own eyes." They were also insecure amongst one another, according to Abdy, whose explanation of their preoccupation with external appearance or conspicuous display anticipates the better known theories of Tocqueville and Veblen.

Americans were also notoriously thin-skinned. If, in Buckingham's words, "one of the most striking features of the American character (was) . . . the extreme sensitiveness of all classes to the opinions of foreigners," they also had a "peculiarly quick sensitiveness . . . to the censure" of these same foreigners. They hated criticism. So sensitive were they to it, that in Grund's striking phrase, they mistook praise for irony. Dickens was lionized during his visit here until it was discovered that he was planning to publish comments critical of America. Cooper was subjected to "frenzied villification" for writing a novel that lampooned American traits. In commenting on their unhappiness with Captain Hall's book, Mrs. Trollope observed that "other nations have been called thin-skinned, but the citizens of the Union have, apparently, no skins at all; they wince if a breeze blows over them, unless it be tempered with adulation." These words were written before the storm broke over her own volume. Subsequent visitors came to similar conclusions.

Marryat advised those who came after him: do not find fault with them if you seek their hospitality. Tudor referred to the "extraordinary sensibility to the slightest appearance of dispraise" as a "puerility" which had he "not witnessed on a thousand occasions (he) . . . should have believed utterly incredible." They *demanded* praise. "Such an unhappily sensitive community surely never existed in this world," wrote Fanny Kemble in her journal. An American woman had told her, "I hear you are going to abuse us dreadfully; cf course, you'll wait till you go back to England and then shower it down upon us finely." The prediction was not inaccurate, for Miss Kemble did in fact "shower it down" upon them, finely. It was hard to insult Americans, however, for as Dickens noted, they quickly cited their newness as a country as the excuse for all faults. When the occasion demanded it, Americans could display a very thick skin, indeed, which made them immune to insults, let alone faint praise. "This man [the American]," wrote Tocqueville, "will never understand that he wearies me to death unless I tell him so, and the only way to get rid of him is to make him my enemy for life." There is no better proof that when it suited him an American could make himself impervious to criticism than in the friendly reception he gave the book that contains those devastating words.

"The most striking circumstance in the American character," wrote Captain Hall, "was the constant habit of praising themselves." Insecurity and thin skin seemed to go hand in hand with boastfulness. Only a few observers mistook the latter trait for arrogance but almost all of them found it unattractive. Lieber, like Miss Martineau, believed that this "national contentment" was an innocent blemish, in part a simple response to the criticisms of foreigners. She did feel, however, that much of this boasting was absurd, and that combined with the insatiable hunger for flattery, was "the most prominent of their bad habits." It was agreed that Americans, in view of their achievements, had much to be vain about but need they be so wearisome about it? Americans of every sort, in all sections and of every social order, praised to the heavens their weather, their rivers, the speed of their railroads, their political system, their orators, even their roads—which were notoriously bad or at the least discomfiting to a normal human anatomy—and, of course, themselves. Only America had anything worth seeing, according to Mr. Wenham, a typical villager in Cooper's *Home As Found*. An Englishman, to his consternation, read in an American geography text that "the English tongue is spoken in greater purity of idiom and intonation with us (in America) than in Great Britain."

Americans could make a virtue of necessity. That a slaughterhouse was situated in the midst of a residential district, was praised to Mrs. Trollope as an example of the antiaristocratic quality of American society. If Marryat was right, that "Americans are the happiest people in the world in their own delusions" Tocqueville had a logical explanation for it. "As the American participates in all that is done in his country, he thinks himself obliged to defend whatever may be censured in it; for it is not only his country that is then attacked, it is himself. The consequence is that his national pride resorts to a thousand artifices and descends to all the petty tricks of personal vanity."

The boasters were also inveterate complainers. Harriet Martineau was amazed to hear complaints even against "the confoundedly prosperous" state of the country, not to mention every other variety of phenomenon—with the exception of land, the only thing exempt from abuse. They were particularly enthusiastic in denouncing the people of sections other than their own, invariably describing them to foreigners as the *real* culprits, whatever the ascribed fault. In Marryat's flamboyant description, easterners "pronounce the southerners to be choleric, reckless, regardless of law, and indifferent as to religion; while the southerners designate the eastern states as a nursery of over-reaching pedlars . . . ; Boston turns up her erudite nose at New York; Philadelphia . . . looks down upon both, while New York . . . . swears the Bostonians are a parcel of puritanical prigs, and the Philadelphians a would-be aristocracy." " 'Hatred' is not too strong a term for their sectional prejudice," concluded Miss Martineau.

In matters of the mind, the American was above all practical. In Tocqueville's view, his spirit was "averse to general ideas; it does not seek theoretical discoveries." In politics Americans were interested in men more than principles, immediate outcomes and success rather than long-range consequences or ethics. Anti-intellectualism (a value that will be discussed shortly) was due in part to an aversion for the nonutilitarian character of the speculative thinking that was done by the learned. Americans preferred newspapers to great literature and were more capable of mechanical invention than of theoretical scientific innovations. The New Englander only represented an exaggeration of a national quality in being "content when he feels a grievance to apply a remedy," or in dealing with "the business of common life [with] . . . practical good sense." Their "fertility of resource," in Martineau's phrase, clearly stemmed from their preoccupation with immediate and tangible problems. A rural editor in upstate New York asked, what need was there for reflective thinking? "The main thing is utility." A modern scholar concludes that the "vigorous, sustained interest in science" during the era was based primarily on "the appeal of social utility."

Americans were clever but not profound. Their minds were quick enough in dealing with a practical or a commercial issue, but ostensibly incapable of appreciating or coping with intellectual problems of a fundamental sort. Nurture triumphed over nature in this instance, since shrewdness was a characteristic of the American mind largely because it was so admired an ideal in the American scheme of things. The most sympathetic observers conceded not only that an unattractive cunning characterized their thinking, but that New Englanders, believed to be its arch practitioners, were generally admired for their gift. "Smart dealings" or a shrewdness which "gilds over many a swindle and gross breach of trust," were extolled, as was "every fresh display of low trickery." They smiled approvingly at a "clever villain's witty rogueries." "Commercial frauds" were "generally dignified by the name of intelligence." Pickering expressed a typical judgment when he said that "shrewdness was (one of) the . . . most striking features in the character of an American." The modern historian of the Land Office concludes that the success of men who absconded with public money "in retaining the respect of their fellow citizens provides evidence of the fact that the 1830s were a period of changing ethical standards," an era in which a thief "passed for an honest man."

If they were not profound, they pretended to be, according to Lieber. He was disturbed at the descent into "verbose and therefore unfelt" cant indulged in by Americans who pretended to a depth of feeling they did not truly have. Cooper and a number of the visitors felt they were shallow. Their skewed sense of values testified to this. "Hint to them that they eat peas with a knife, and they are highly enraged; tell them that their conduct to the 'niggers' is inhuman and unmanly, and they laugh in your face," reported Abdy. Tocqueville's conclusion was that their paltry concerns and preoccupations turned them ultimately into paltry men. "They strain their faculties to the utmost to achieve paltry results, and this cannot fail speedily to limit their range of view and to circumscribe their powers."

They were not gifted conversationalists. Urbane visitors and Americans alike were unhappy with a conversational style that was composed in part of bombast, swearing—if not in "the more polished circles"—a solemnity and dullness particularly ridiculous in view of the lightness of its content, and at the other extreme from their hyperbole, an incommunicativeness that was equally characteristic, particularly in the northeast. The laconic style was not a trait of the strong, silent man from the west but rather of a shrewd, selfish, opportunistic man of the city. Mrs. Trollope has given us a verbatim transcript of a marvelous conversation between two New Englanders she overheard while on a boat. It is a bravura example of an art of discourse in which the speaker reveals nothing of importance as he in turn darts questions, probing for weaknesses in his opponent's defenses:

> Well, now, which way may you be traveling?
> I expect this canal runs pretty nearly west.
> Are you going far with it?
> Well, now, I don't rightly know how many miles it may be.
> I expect you'll be from New York?
> Sure enough I have been at New York, often and often.
> I calculate, then, 'tis not there as you stop?
> Business must be minded, in stopping and in stirring.

"So they went on," she writes, "without advancing or giving an inch, 'till I was weary of listening." Miss Martineau was dismayed at questions answered with "solemn pedantry," and of such length that she "found it difficult to keep awake during the entire reply." Equally disconcerting was to be told that the weather lately had been "uncommonly mucilaginous." The harsh conclusion of a number of observers was that though Americans talked at great length they said nothing that was worth hearing.

Americans loved scandal and were quick to believe the worst. Hamilton was amazed that "no villainy is too gross or too improbable to be attributed to a statesman in this intelligent community." A distaste for aristocracy undoubtedly explained in part the delight in the exposure of foibles, actual or alleged. Hone's diary entry for September 22, 1837, reads "Libels. Everybody complains of the success which attends the publications of libels on private character; everybody condemns the depravity of the times in which, and the community by which they are encouraged. Everybody wonders how people can buy and read those receptacles of scandals, the penny papers, and yet everybody does encourage them. . . ." Cooper's fictional personification of this trait was Mrs. Abbott, a small-town widow, whose life was dedicated to gossip. She pursued her vocation with great success, possessed as she was of no scruples, a scorpion's tongue, and a reputation for deep religion. One envied her dead husband.

A well-known modern theory postulates as the characteristic type of the early 19th century, an inner-directed American, marching to his own music, living his life according to his own and his family's notions as to how it should be lived. Observers during the Jacksonian era saw a very different American, indeed. The American was a conformist, in the opinion of foreigner and native, to the sympathetic as to the jaundiced. In an essay in *The American Democrat,* Cooper wrote that " 'they say,' is the monarch of this country." His striking fictional creation in *Homeward Bound* and *Home As Found,* the Yankee publisher, Steadfast Dodge, who is a catalog of vanities, arrogance, cowardliness, demagogy, bad manners, envy, gossip, and slander—in a word, everything unlovely— would even have a ship's course determined by majority vote. Whether the phrase "tyranny of the majority" was too strong, as some of Tocqueville's contemporaries thought it was, there was no doubt that in small things as in large, Americans guided their behavior by the anticipated reactions of their neighbors to it. Grund was told that in Boston, "the habit of conforming to each other's opinion, and the penalty set upon every transgression . . . , are sufficient to prevent a man from wearing a coat cut in a different fashion, or a shirt-collar no longer *a la mode,* or, in fact, to do, say, or appear anything which would render him unpopular." A young man would not wear mustaches, since such a deviation would cost him his practice in law. An informant told him vehemently, "This is a *free* country, sir! Every man may do or think what he pleases, only he must not let other people know it."

Combe was struck that in matters of great moral significance, men feared to affirm what they knew was right, because of fear of majority opinion. In the realm of the insignificant, a minister of his acquaintance would not wear a cloak of novel design for fear of public opinion. This people was other-directed with a vengeance! Christopher Baldwin, the librarian of the American Antiquarian Society, in his diary entry for March 1, 1830, noted that had he stood for reelection to the school committee he would have been defeated because his religious beliefs were offensive to the majority. A traveler describes an entire coachful of passengers acquiescing in one person's singular misbehavior, evidently out of fear by each of doing something distinctive and therefore wrong. The American press, "less marked by independence of principle, and integrity of purpose," than any other, pandered to the consensus. A kind of "suburban religion" was detected by observers, then as now, who believed social coercion rather than inner conviction accounted for much church attendance in America. On the one hand, it was believed, this inordinate deference to majority opinion resulted in a sterile intellectual conformity. In this country, wrote Tocqueville, difference of opinion is "mere difference of hue." The other terrible effect was a sameness of personality. To Dickens, the Americans were "all alike . . . no diversity in character." Their "fear of singularity" accounted for what Miss Martineau believed to be their main fault: "a deficiency of moral independence." In this land of conformity, she wrote, "worship of opinion is, at this day, the established religion of the United States."

Related to the American's deference to the opinion of others, was his need to associate himself with them in every manner of activity. The Jacksonian was an inveterate joiner. His tendency to create organizations was often praised as an example of republican freedom and democratic self-expression. Cooper, however, was suspicious of it, while Mrs. Trollope noted sourly that the enthusiasms responsible for the coming together tended to fade quickly. They thus organized not out of deeply-felt conviction but from a rage to associate. Tocqueville conceded that the freedom to associate openly was an assurance that conspiracies would not arise. He was nevertheless concerned that "unrestrained liberty of association for political purposes," might augment the chances of anarchy. His interpretation of the phenomenon of associationism was as logical —and as arguable—as were some of his other evaluations of democratic man: since "all the citizens are independent and feeble, they can hardly do anything by themselves, and none of them can oblige his fellow men to lend him their assistance. They all, therefore, become powerless if they do not learn voluntarily to help one another." Less controversial is his charming description: "Americans of all ages, all conditions, and all dispositions constantly form associations. . . . religious, moral, serious, futile, general or restricted, enormous or diminutive. The Americans make associations to give entertainments, to found seminaries, to build inns, to construct churches, to diffuse books, to send missionaries to the antipodes. . . . If it is proposed to inculcate some truth or to foster some feeling . . . they form a society."

If few of the contemporaries would have agreed that the "M-Factor" was the American's most distinctive or significant trait, certainly a need to be constantly busy was noted as one of the American's characteristic traits, and a restless movement from one place to another as equally typical of his behavior. Bustle was the rule. New York City was "the busiest community that any man could desire to live in. In the streets all is hurry . . . ; the very carts . . . are at a gallop, and always in a brisk trot," Buckingham wrote. Chevalier thought Pittsburgh the world's busiest community. Marryat found "all is energy and enterprise; everything is in a state of transition . . . of rapid improvement." The explanation given by a visiting phrenologist was that American "air is drier than that of Britain—the habitual state of the American people . . . is (therefore) one of much higher mental excitement than that of the inhabitants of Britain." Whatever the causes, Lieber believed that "an American distinguishes himself . . . by a restlessness, a striving and driving onward." He "wants to perform within a year what others do within a much longer period." Thomson spoke of a "disease of locomotion," which carried children away from families, while Hall noted that "the passion for turning up new soils" meant they had no permanent attachments. Murray, who spent several years here, found that "the American agriculturalist seems to have little local attachment. A New Englander or Virginian will leave the home of his childhood without any visible effort or symptom of regret. . . . I have seen such repeated instances of this that I cannot help considering it a national feature." His explanation was succinct. The American farmer picks himself up "if by so doing he can make ten dollars where before he made eight." In one of his remarkable passages on American *wanderlust*, Tocqueville offers a more complex explanation, according to which, movement was pursued as much for "the emotions it excites . . . as for the gain it procures."

Mrs. Trollope's book had publicized certain uncouth American habits and customs. She was shortly to be immortalized, since subsequent visitors observed that the cry, "a trollope! a trollope!" went up from American audiences when one of their number happened to be caught in that public slouching that had so offended their critical visitor. Americans slouched in theatres, they slouched in church, they were even discovered slouching when attending sessions of the Supreme Court. At one theatrical performance, Mrs. Trollope had found "the bearing and attitudes of the men perfectly indescribable; the heels thrown higher than the head, the entire rear of the person presented to the audience, the whole length supported on the benches, are among the varieties that these exquisite posture-masters exhibit." Their subsequent attempts to police offenders indicate that Mrs. Trollope's description was not exaggerated. Like a famous statesman of more than a century later who used his shoe in part to show his scorn of the traditional diplomacy and the breeding associated with it, it seems fairly clear that some Americans slouched to political purpose, in their case to display indifference or contempt for the manners of an aristocratic society. Fortunately Mrs. Trollope's strictures had effect and Americans came to see ordinary civility as devoid of social implication.

Americans were great chewers of tobacco and, what was worse, notorious spitters. Poor Miss Kemble discovered that to her "profound disgust," gentlemen too did it. On board a boat, "it was a perfect shower of saliva all the time." Almost every user of public conveyances sounded variations on the theme. "Copious spitting" was the rule. In boarding houses and hotels after a meal, an orgy of spitting would commence—although less fastidious types did not wait for the meal to end. In homes, too, spitting "was incessant, the carpet serving as a receptacle . . . when boxes were not within immediate reach." Even among the upper classes, men of otherwise polished manners indulged themselves, although in all fairness, Boardman observed that the refined would not spit on living room floors. Dickens was amazed that even in the nation's Capitol, in law courts, and hospitals, "in all the public places of America this filthy custom is recognized." Senators and judges were adept in the art.

Americans even spit in their sleep. The visitors must have exaggerated for their comments seemed to indicate that spitting threatened to drown the country.

There was some difference of opinion as to whether or not they were drunkards but there was agreement that Americans drank to excess. "Why do they get so confoundedly drunk?" asked Marryat. Mrs. Felton's explanation was that Americans drank so much from the time of infancy on, that "by the time they arrive at the years of maturity they become . . . habituated to the practice." To Buckingham as to many others, the love of liquor was one of the great evils ruining the country. Liquor was to be found everywhere, and as Tocqueville noted, at most reasonable rates. He agreed with Hall that its prevalence here was due to the inordinate influence of the common man. Senators were thus afraid to tax so popular a commodity. Jacksonian candidates plied their constituencies with quantities of fiery liquid. Vigne believed that the absence of a law of primogeniture was a major cause of the evil, elder sons burying their disappointments in brandy. Attending a meeting of the Worcester Temperance Society, Baldwin was dismayed to find that all members "drank very freely of cyder . . . of the very worst sort." What must they have drunk in the privacy of their homes? Modern scholarship discloses that the visitors' observations were on the mark. For between 1790 and 1830 "Americans drank more alcoholic beverages per capita than at any time before or since," mainly whisky and other hard liquor, with each adult male imbibing on the average 17 gallons a year or more than one-third pint a day.

Drinking went hand in hand with gambling. Oliver found incessant gambling on river boats. Southern boat trips featured all night bouts of drinking and gambling. The latter custom was also closely aligned to speculation. The Jacksonian era was characterized by what Miss Martineau called a "speculative mania." It would not have been, had the American people not been ready to gamble on the prospects of great future gains. "Everybody is speculating, and everything has become an object of speculation," wrote Chevalier. Shirreff, who liked to believe the best of the Americans, discovered in the west that "speculators have . . . bought up, at high prices, all the building ground in the neighborhood." Back in the east, in 1836, "if two persons were seen conversing in the street of New York . . . in 19 instances out of 20, you would have overheard 'lots' and 'thousands of dollars' as the sole topics of their discourse." In *Home As Found*, Cooper includes conversations that appear to be satirical exaggerations of the speed at which the price of a lot could appreciate and speculative fortunes be made. A Hone diary entry for January 14, 1835, when the bubble was still short of the bursting point, shows that truth was the source of Cooper's fiction. Unbelievable appreciation of the price of real estate did occur.

America the land of plenty was admired but American eating habits were not. Observers held that most Americans were gluttons or something close to it. They were accused of eating huge quantities of poorly prepared food with the manners and perhaps the charm of certain barnyard animals. In fairness to the critics, they did concede that their evidence was based not on what went on in American homes but outside of them. There seemed to be a touch of sour grapes in some of the envious comment of the visitors. This country had an unbelievable abundance of the most admired foods, particularly meats, fowl, and dairy products, easily available to ordinary persons. The visitors copied down menus with great relish; in fact they reported nothing so fully or so vividly. Since Horace was not above reporting in some detail the menu at heroic Roman feasts, perhaps a detailed report on Jacksonian delicacies, as contemporaries observed them, will be forgiven.

Let us start with the morning meal. Vigne has left us the following graphic report of a breakfast aboard a Hudson River steamboat: ". . . to see 'bolting' in perfection it is necessary to go on board an Albany steamboat. [All wait for the bell to ring. When it does] the negro guards escape as best they can [since otherwise they will be trampled]. In less than one quarter of a minute, 150 or 200 persons have seated themselves at table, and an excellent breakfast of tea, coffee, eggs, beefsteaks, hot rolls, corn cakes, salted mackerel, mush, molasses, and so forth is demolished in an incredibly short space of time. The crowd then slowly reascends the staircase—and three fourths of them are quite surprised that they should be afflicted with dyspepsia! The music which usually accompanied the feasts of the ancients will never be received by the Americans."

Then to a noonday meal, this time in a New York City hotel with Boardman: "a table nearly long enough for a city feast, well covered with steaks, cutlets, eggs, ham, sausages, chickens fricaseed and barbecued; stewed and fried eels with delicious trout; add to these good things, rolls, cakes and an inexhaustible supply of excellent coffee. . . . This meal was only about 18 pence sterling each person."

Now on to Boston's famed Tremont House, regarded by many connoisseurs as the country's leading hotel, as Christopher Baldwin is greeted with the following bill of fare for Sunday dinner: "pea soup; broiled salt fish; cod's head; oysters [according to one of Grund's gourmet friends this was one food Americans knew how to prepare]; corned beef; corned pork; ham; tongue; turkey; chickens and pork; oyster pie; *anguilles;* mutton cutlets; fried smelt; stewed ducks and olives; hara coat mutton; curried veal; tongues; *macaroni a parmesan;* roast beef; pork; veal; leg of mutton; goose; turkey; chickens; partridges; puddings and pastry; dessert."

Late one evening Abdy arrives at a tavern in a small village in Connecticut and asks if he might have some tea and perhaps some eggs and bacon. The following snack was placed before him: "four or five large slices of toast, swimming in a pool of melted butter—a large dish of fried bacon—half a dozen boiled eggs—an apple pie— some preserved quinces—cucumbers in vinegar—currant jam— potatoes with butter—sweet cake—cheese—bread and butter—and tea with its usual accompaniments."

The overwhelming consensus was expressed in Murray's understatement that Americans did eat an "unreasonable quantity of food."

The quality of American cooking and food preparation came in for sharp criticism. New York restaurant food was judged "more excellent in point of material, than of cookery," the American table in general, "more remarkable for superabundance of food than skill . . . in preparing it." Buckingham was convinced that "one of the most valuable reforms that could be effected in America would be a reform in the culinary and dietetic system of the country." His countrymen's way with food provoked Cooper to an outburst in *The American Democrat:* "The Americans are the grossest feeders of any civilized nation known . . . food is heavy, coarse, ill-prepared and indigestible. . . . National character is, in some measure, affected by a knowledge of the art of preparing food. . . . It is certain that the connection between our moral and physical qualities is so ultimate as to cause them to react on each other." Verily Cooper seemed to believe that *Mann ist was er isst.*

Visitors were disconcerted most by the American style at the dinner table. Speed and silence were the rule. Huge amounts were swallowed at breakneck speed; woe to the man who dawdled. The "extraordinary rapidity" with which food was gorged or "pitchforked down" fascinated some observers, although Miss Martineau was disquieted at the "celerity" of the American attack. Even more depressing was the absence of that pleasant talk that gave charm to a table or, in the words of the ancients, turned feeding into dining. The stillness of death was one common metaphor used to describe the atmosphere at the American table; another spoke of animal gratification. Marryat expressed the popular belief that the American "eats his meals with the rapidity of a wolf," in order to rush to his business or practical affairs. And yet it was also noted that on some occasions Americans rushed through a meal in order to do nothing better than to lounge, chew, and spit in another room.[1]

The visitors' unhappiness with American eating was an important factor in the overall negative impression so many of them had of the American. That they reacted as strongly as they did to what was after all a natural act, tells us as much of observer in this case as of observed.

The consensus was that the American was unrefined. Murray found middle-class Americans "deficient in those lighter accomplishments" which constitute charm, while Cooper bemoaned American ignorance of music—"which elevates and refines human

---

[1] European attitudes may not have changed too much. Some years ago when I was at a southern university, I had occasion to take to lunch an English scholar who was visiting the campus to deliver a series of lectures. We had only enough time to drop in to the student lunch room. A juke box was blaring, the decor was indifferent, the food equally so. The visiting professor looked unhappy. Trying to put the best light on matters, I remarked that we Americans being a pragmatic people, did not make a fuss about food, regarding it essentially as fuel for the body, to be consumed quickly so that we might go off "to do the more important things." I shall never forget his quiet response: "Like *what* for instance?"

tastes"—and in addition found his countrymen "wanting in most of the higher tastes." They had no time for or interest in the amenities, drank standing up, did not know how either to relax or live well: "every class (was) occupied in getting money, none in spending it." The standard explanation was that this people was coarse not because their nation was youthful but rather because of their warped values. "In the United States there is no standard of values," wrote Vigne. He meant that there was no standard that he could approve.

High on the American's scale of values was his egalitarian belief that one man—particularly an American—was as good as any other, certainly that he should be treated like any other. White Americans simply would not be known as "servants." Those who worked in other people's homes would not be summoned by bells. The word "mister" was omitted from door plates. One visitor ran into a tailor who would not go to him to take the measure of a coat, insisting it was "not republican," and a carriage driver who complained that the travelers on his coach "had had private meals every day and not asked him to the table." A fastidious traveler discovered that since his landlord would not dream of carrying water up to his room, he would have to perform his toilet in the public yard. Dickens was impressed, as were others, that there was only one class of travel on railroad cars; the rule on coaches was also best seats to first comers. Lyell seemed a little disturbed that "the spirit of social equality has left no other signification to the terms 'gentleman' and 'lady' but that of 'male and female individual.'" Miss Kemble was startled both at the pride of ordinary people and their frankness in expressing it: a farmer told her "without a moment's hesitation," that while the eggs he sold her were good, "the *very* fresh ones, we eat ourselves." How could anyone know "who is who" in this infernal country of constant handshaking, asked Marryat? Thomson confirmed Mrs. Trollope's experience. Where she had been surprised at "the coarse familiarity of address" between all classes, he noted that men of any trade or description entered into conversation "on terms of perfect equality." Mackay was impressed that a western farmer and his help worked, ate, even slept together. (Fastidious Europeans were terribly embarrassed at the American custom of having "gentlemen" of all descriptions sleep in one bed.) While Lieber did not think Americans unusually democratic in their social relations—they are "no more angels than other people"—he believed that one of their best traits was their readiness to "make use of ability come whence it may."

Many European visitors and, for that matter, Americans, were not particularly charmed by the American stress on egalitarianism, believing as did Cooper and Hone that it was responsible for the sordid manners and mean quality of American life, or like Tocqueville, that because of it liberty was downgraded. They took a dim view of the glorification of that same common man whose traits they found so depressing. Other visitors also agreed with Cooper, John Quincy Adams, and other Americans that for all the lip service they paid to equality, Americans in fact practised the same forms of inequality as Europeans, the one great difference being that in this country money rather than blood divided men into rigidly separated worlds. In a word, Americans were hypocrites.

American hypocrisy toward Negroes and Indians was most severely censured. Buckingham's reaction was typical: "what makes (their) . . . affected horror of 'amalgamation' the more revolting is, that many of the very gentlemen who declare themselves to be so insulted and degraded by being placed so near the coloured people (in lecture halls) . . . have no scruple whatever to keep coloured women as mistresses." The violation of American promises to the Indians was also criticized. In Mrs. Trollope's words, she "might have respected them however much (her) taste might have been offended by what was peculiar in their manners and customs. But it is impossible for any mind of common honesty not to be revolted by the contradictions in their principles and practice." "You will see them," she continued, "with one hand hoisting the cap of liberty and with the other flogging the slaves. You will see them one hour lecturing . . . on the indefeasible rights of man, and the next driving from their homes the children of the soil, whom they have bound themselves to protect by the most solemn treaties." Americans understandably had grown accustomed to their own foibles, learning how to rationalize even the worst of them. Visitors, equally understandably, were horrified at the gulf between American theory and practice.

Americans had boasted to Captain Hall that they were a very moral people. He found them rather a very prudish people. In St. Louis, young women who waltzed let it be known that they were to be held at a point near the elbows, not around the waist. Female limbs were not to be exposed in dancing. *The Rape of the Lock* was regarded by some Americans as a too salacious title. Earlier described as a prostitute, after the 1830s a woman of the streets was increasingly referred to by the euphemism "soiled dove." For that matter, the increasingly negative attitude displayed by medical writers toward sexual pleasure, even when achieved in marriage, appears to have driven growing numbers of men into the arms of prostitutes. Nude models were not available to a young sculptor and when a nude sculpture was completed, viewers—who in some cases had to see it separately, according to sex—were likely to be advised she was thinking "sweet thoughts" or of Divine Providence. The sculptor Hiram Powers explained that it was not "the person" of his famous nude Greek slave that stood exposed "but her spirit." According to what one informant told Marryat, Cincinnati's best society had snubbed Mrs. Trollope because she at first had been traveling without her husband. American prudishness sometimes threatened health since "middle-and upper-class women often declined to consult physicians for gynecologic services, except as a last resort," during the era. When Mark Twain said that man is the only animal who blushes, he was thinking of an American.

The transcendent American value according to most contemporaries was materialism. The distinguishing feature of the American was his love of money. "At the bottom of all that an American does," wrote Chevalier, "is money; beneath every word, money." His sacrifices, when made, "are systematic and calculated. It is neither enthusiasm nor passion that unties his purse strings, but motives of policy . . . in which he feels his own private interests to be involved." His motto is, "Victory or death! But to him, victory is to make money, to get the dollars, to make a fortune out of nothing. . . ." On this point there was practically no disagreement. The love of money was nowhere greater; any means of securing it was considered praiseworthy. Men and things were judged according to a monetary standard. At a party, Hamilton was introduced to various personages, each introduction preceded by whispered instructions to him as to the wealth of the individual he was next to meet: "had I been presented to so many money bags of dollars . . . the ceremony would have been quite as interesting." Combe remarked that Americans were judged according to the "extent of their possessions." Miss Martineau concluded that "wealth (was) . . . the most important object in life" to the American.

Diverse evidence indicates that many Americans did indeed practice dollar worship. In a number of cities publications containing nothing more than lists of rich men and the supposed exact sums they were worth went through many editions. A not atypical newspaper editorial, in scoffing at abstract thinking, asked what it had to do "with the accumulation of wealth?" What, it continued, "has intellect to do with man, except in helping him to cast compound interest and loss and gain?" At a time when mountain men were an object of romantic curiosity to their eastern neighbors, the mountain man's behavior, according to his modern historian, showed that he was "not an alternative to the [materialistic] religion of Jacksonian America, but an idiosyncratic and extreme expression of its values." "The love of money is almost the universal passion," reported a New England minister, but he was speaking not of his region alone.

The love of money had dismal side effects. It corrupted Americans, preoccupying them with vulgar displays of wealth or, in Miss Martineau's phrase, a "mean love of distinction." Tudor felt that it discouraged an appreciation of nature. Grund was startled to find theatre audiences who on the one hand counted the house at a performance of *Othello,* and on the other applauded Iago's admiration of a full purse. Hall blamed the love of money for all manner of American ills, including their indifference to women! How could there be time, interest or skill for pursuing the amenities in "a country where all men are engaged in one and the same engrossing pursuit—namely, that of making money(?)" DeRoos was present when "a young lady, talking of the most eligible class of life from which to choose a husband, declared that, for her part, she was all for the Commissions." His friend, a major, beamed happily until he found out that she meant commission merchants. Since the love of money was actually a love for the material things that money could buy, Dickens advised that "it would be well . . . for the American

people as a whole if they loved the Real less, and the Ideal somewhat more." He agreed with Miss Martineau that nothing spoiled
the American character more than their vulgar materialism.
Dickens' strictures were mild when compared with Tocqueville's.

In a one-page chapter in his second volume, entitled, "How excessive care for worldly welfare may impair that welfare," Tocqueville
wrote an oblique but terrible indictment of American materialism.
On one level his words seemed to be merely sensible advice to
seekers after creature comforts, that the way to secure them was to
cultivate the soul, the angel in man, which "teaches the brute the
art of satisfying its desires." For a fortunate paradox prevailed, that
"whatever elevates, enlarges, and expands the soul renders it more
capable of succeeding in those very undertakings which do not
concern it." He concluded with the warning that, "if men were ever
to content themselves with material objects, it is probable that they
would lose by degrees the art of producing them; and they would
enjoy them in the end, like the brutes, without discernment and
without improvement." This was pragmatic advice to men already
more brute than angel, that their brutishness was endangering their
continued enjoyment of the very animal pleasures they lived for.

Other values and traits were related to materialism and to a
lesser extent to egalitarianism. If Americans were opportunistic, if
amoral behavior was countenanced and shrewdness applauded, it
was clearly because the worship of gain was such that, in Juvenal's
old phrase, it smelled sweet no matter its source or by whatever
means secured. Expediency was their guiding star, according to
Chevalier.

Americans were snobs, though this trait and value was manifested mainly by the better sort or those who pretended to be,
according to Miss Martineau. A New York female complained to
Abdy that the marriage phrase should be, "wilt thou have this *lady*,"
etc., while in Philadelphia, a sensible woman advised him that his
"report on American manners and customs would be discredited or
undervalued by his countrymen when it was known that [he] . . .
had travelled with stage-drivers and conversed freely with working
people." Great pains were taken by urban society circles to maintain
the separation between them and lesser groups. Marryat said of
Philadelphia, "one thing is certain, that in no city is there so much
fuss made about lineage and descent, in no city are there so many
cliques and sets in society, who keep apart from each other; and it is
often very difficult to ascertain the grounds of their distinctions.
One family will live at number 1, and another at number 2 in the
same street, both have similar establishments, both keep their carriages, both be well educated, and both may talk of their grand-
fathers and grandmothers; and yet number 1 will tell you that
number 2 is nobody and you must not visit there; and when you
enquire why? there is no other answer, but that they are not of the
right sort." For hilarious examples of the pretentiousness of northeastern urban elites, their pretended disdain for titles, their raptures

at being mistaken for English family, and their abject conformity and materialism, Grund's account is indispensable.

If those near the top were snobs, those below were social climbers. Vigne told a much-repeated tale: "The captain of a steamboat . . . happened to ask rather loudly, 'General, a little fish?' and was immediately answered in the affirmative by 25 of the 30 gentlemen that were present." Murray found "the tavern kept by a general, wagon wheels mended by a colonel, day laborers and mechanics are gentlemen." Lieber ridiculed the constant name changes that were designed to suggest a respectable origin. He believed that insanity was caused in America by "a diseased anxiety to be equal to the wealthiest, the craving for wealth and consequent disappointment which ruins the intellect of many." Poor persons did without necessities to make false impressions. Working girls here earned not wages but "compensation," Dickens reported. Cooper was dismayed that "the love of turgid expressions [was] . . . gaining ground." He perhaps knew that Pickering had heard a woman address her son as "Altamont." The good widow Abbott, of *Home As Found*, had named her children Orlando Furioso, Bianca-Alzuma-Ann, Roger-Demetrius-Benjamin, and Rinaldo-Rinaldini-Timothy. Another of Cooper's creations, the New York City parvenu, Mrs. Jarvis, who spent her days intriguing to advance her social position, tells her husband, "no one in New York has a right to think himself or herself better than ourselves." The common view was that this coarse social climbing was an offshoot of egalitarianism.

Inevitably materialists and champions of equality had no respect for tradition. Americans "have no love for anything merely because it is old," observed Thomson. They were "so mutable, so much given to change . . . . that [he] . . . had scarcely met with one who knew who his grandfather was." One visitor found something "cool and heartless," a sign of disrespect for the dead, in their funerals, performed in too great a hurry. Another was upset that the burial places of national heroes were so poorly kept. In Hall's indictment, "the unpleasant truth seems to be, that nothing whatsoever is venerated in America merely on account of its age, or, indeed on any other account. Neither historical associations, nor high public services, nor talents, nor knowledge, claim any peculiar reverence for the busy generation of the present hour." They were "ready to adopt whatever is proved to be . . . advantageous," according to Boardman. This explained their contempt for traditional usage, whether in language or other areas, and what Lieber called the "ludicrous" ease with which they changed their names. According to Tocqueville, a society marked by constant fluctuations produced men with a taste for novelty.

Their disrespect for tradition merged into disrespect for law. Europeans were startled to observe a jury munching on food, the foreman announcing a verdict with his mouth full. Vigne blamed the spirit of equality for a courtroom informality in which lawyers sat casually on tables while judges spat. As a result of the growing feeling of self-importance on the part of the people, Chevalier believed, "the reverence for the laws (was) . . . wearing out with the Americans." In the case of so selfish a population, "the laws had no force when they jarred with interest."

Americans valued neither learning nor intellectual accomplishment. The attempt to limit medical practice to the trained, was resisted by Jacksonians. Tocqueville believed that "in no country in the civilized world [was] . . . less attention paid to philosophy than in the United States." Others expanded the charge to include literature and learning in general. Miss Martineau found that American scholars were unhappy with the "superficial character of [American] scholarship . . . the non-existence of literature." (Although she was of that small minority which believed that intellect was "reverenced" here.) Most visitors agreed with Mrs. Trollope that pure learning held little attraction to the American mind, the "pursuit of wealth" drawing it in other directions. Grund had been told by businessmen in Boston, "we consider professors as secondary men." Able sons were trained for business; a "poor boy who is a little hard of hearing, and rather slow of comprehension, shall go to college." Scholars were held in low repute because they commanded low incomes, the results of their intellectual efforts having little market value.

Americans seemed to have contempt for life. They blandly acquiesced in terrible steamboat accidents caused by faulty construction—"What are a few hundred persons more or less?" Hone wrote sarcastically in his diary, after a particularly terrible accident. After a mournful visit to a hospital, he observed that "Americans are the most careless people on earth. They freeze because they neglect the proper precautions, they are blown up by blasting rocks, run over by railroads, scalded in steamboats, crushed by falling banks of earth, and fall from scaffolds because they disregard danger and do not keep out of harm's way." The lust for profits overrode all other considerations, according to him. Americans were accused of manifesting an "utter want of . . . sympathy for the sufferings of others." They seemed ready on the slightest provocation to shoot or stab, particularly in the west and south. "Should a stranger jostle an American by accident," warned Logan, "he runs extreme risk of being shot or stabbed." He cited many examples. Murder was often lightly punished by the law, as was lynching. Duelists, often fighting over ridiculous alleged slights to their honor, in fact dueled not to satisfy honor but to kill. Marryat was surprised at the intensive practice by the involved parties prior to a duel. In this sense, certainly, Andrew Jackson captured very well the spirit of the times.

Some observers found glaring contradictions between American lip service and practice or between their professed and actual values, recording their judgments in a series of trenchant summaries. Americans were thus ambitious but lacking in lofty ambition. They talked up liberty but restricted its practice. They talked of lofty things in the absence of lofty feelings. Grund had been told, "in the absence of enthusiasm, which would inspire them with natural eloquence, they seek to maintain themselves at a certain elevation by pressing hard on lofty topics; having no wings, they endeavor to support themselves in the air by a *parachute*." Their principles were high but "their civilization and morals fall far below." They spoke glowingly of equality but strained to demonstrate their own exalted station. They loved change but dreaded revolution. Their bodies were in constant motion but their minds were inert. They loved to talk but had nothing to say. They were avid readers but preferred newspaper gossip to literature. They were in a constant "election fever" but cold to political principles. They had appetites but no passions. And finally, they knew how to make money but not how to spend it. This mournful catalog was dubious tribute to a people who were regarded as something less than they seemed.

The portrait of the Jacksonian drawn by his contemporary observers is of a good-natured but essentially shallow man: clever but not profound, self-important but uncertain, fond of deluding himself, living almost fanatically for the flesh (although not knowing too well how), straining every fibre to accumulate the things he covets and amoral about the methods to be used, a hypocrite who strains at gnats and swallows camels, an energetic and efficient fellow albeit a small one, who takes comfort in—as well as his standards of behavior from—numbers. It is not a very attractive picture.[2]

---

[2] Compare it, for example, with Commager's version of the 19th-century American: [optimistic; materialistic; courageous; an admirer of hard work and hard-earned wealth; modest; pragmatic; practical; a quantitative thinker; resourceful; antitheoretical; politically mature; indulgent of intellectuals; nationalistic; industrious; democratic; "not inclined to look too critically at the means whereby success was achieved"; egalitarian; easy in his social relationships; intolerant of aristocratic display; possessed with manners that were "the delight of European democrats"; a child of instincts who nevertheless had a passion for titles—largely "an expression of (his) carelessness, good nature, and humor"; good natured, generous, hospitable and sociable; casual and careless ("those who did not know him thought him slovenly and rude"); versatile; restless; self-indulgent; inclined to challenge rules; no worshiper of profits—as shown by his respect for the rules in the games he played, almost the only rules he took seriously; disrespectful of laws but worshipful toward the Law; tolerant of dissent and nonconformity; individualistic and cooperative; moral; somewhat prudish; romantic and sentimental; humorous; eclectic in philosophy; guided by honor, fairness, learning, freedom, patriotism, work, independence, courage, sacrifice, and rectitude, as standards of conduct]: *The American Mind*, chap. i. There are some similarities between the two versions but they are very few indeed. True, Commager was writing of the American of the entire 19th century prior to the 1890's, but he himself has written that no significant changes were discerned in the American during the entire period; see his *America in Perspective: The United States through Foreign Eyes*, New York 1947, introduction, xvi.

In that introduction, he has also written that the accounts of foreign travelers "all added up to a flattering picture." (!) *Ibid.*, xx. Perhaps the difficulty can be resolved by his statement that "jaundiced criticism came from the second-rate commentators rather than from the magisterial ones. The most judicious, the most learned, the most perspicacious, the most profound

Of course it was not a complete picture. The commentators were aware that there were Americans of altogether different traits, habits and values. Cooper's Effingham novels contain somewhat romanticized versions of more attractive American types, embodied in fictional persons whose characters, behavior, and even their looks correlate almost perfectly with their occupations, status, breadth of learning and experience. Landed wealth, in the person of Ned Effingham (Cooper's notion of himself), is handsome, gentle, calm, selfless, trusting, pleasant, evergracious, of spotless character; while old mercantile wealth, personified by John Effingham, is handsome but saturnine, sardonic, brilliant, cynical, sophisticated, cosmopolitan, but does have one skeleton in the closet. Ned's daughter is not only beautiful but gracious, learned, modest, worldly and possessed of high standards of taste. The various seamen have sterling qualities: the naval officer (the young Cooper?) is brave, modest, intelligent and cultured; the deep sea captain is honest, humorous, earthy, brave and a keen judge of character; the fresh water commodore is honest, virtuous, dignified, a sensible fellow. Other admirable types—in contrast to the assortment of schemers, opportunists, speculators and snobs, who predominate—have breeding, wit, benevolence, wisdom and refinement. There *were* such people, in life as in Cooper's fiction, as many of the visitors to their satisfaction discovered. They were rare, however. Much more typical was the unlovely Jacksonian of our portrait.

What are we to make of him? There are several things he seems clearly not to be. This is no child of the frontier, neither his ways nor his values having much to do with Indian fighting. The people who lived in western towns imitated their eastern brethren, while the small minority living on the western outskirts of civilization, who were engaged in conversation by enterprising travelers, disclosed values very similar to those of their countrymen. This conformist was no inner-directed man. And there is little evidence that our Jacksonian, as he pursued the main chance, looked back longingly to a "chaste, republican" past. His thoughts were for today, while by a better he meant a wealthier tomorrow.

No monistic interpretation explains him. Possibly his materialism is his most significant characteristic, explaining as it does, not only

interpreters of America returned a verdict that ranged from sympathy to enthusiasm"; *ibid.* Obviously, if "jaundiced" criticism is treated as the work of second-raters, if sympathetic to enthusiastic criticism characterizes magisterial commentators, and the views of the second-raters are discounted, one emerges with Professor Commager's charming portrait. As I indicated earlier, in my own work I have discarded only those commentators whose reliability there was much reason to question. It is interesting that Tocqueville, author of what Commager calls "the most penetrating interpretation of the American character ever penned," takes a very dim view of that character. Like so many other observers, he marveled at American *achievements* in politics, technology, construction, transportation. When his work is examined closely for its views on character and personality, however, it discloses an American who is paltry, anti-intellectual, unattractively materialistic, boring, insecure, vulgar, boastful, snobbish, pompous, conformist, cold and humorless, whose optimism concerns low goals, whose egalitarianism is disquieting, whose gregariousness derives from his own smallness as an individual.

his goals but so many of his ways and other values. What better explanation is there of his disinterest in the idealistic and reform movements which, while they proliferated during the era, commanded so little actual membership? What did it matter that some women felt unfulfilled or that colored persons were everywhere treated as less than human? What was it to him that his society might maldistribute status, so long as it promised to provide tangible comforts?

His values and intellectual traits appear to throw some light on his political and economic choices. Bigotry, supplemented by cruelty and cupidity, better explain atrocities against Indians and Negroes. Vanity and boastfulness made it easy for him to believe that his country—which was himself writ large—was superior to all others and could do no wrong. That much-admired pragmatic temper which rendered his mind indifferent to theories or fundamental principles, when combined with his lack of respect for learning, seemed to have a number of political consequences. For looked at one way, it was child's play for shrewd manipulators who sought his vote to convince this hardheaded, unlearned fellow that politics was a kind of simple morality play: good leaders v. bad, honest men v. dishonest, the people's friends v. their enemies. The unique American major party that was born during the era—which is many if not all things to most if not all men, which avoids or deflects crucial issues rather than meet them—is perfectly suited to the man who has neither interest in "fundamental principles" nor the wit to perceive them. If, as Lee Benson and Richard Hofstadter, among others, have suggested, he voted for every variety of reason except to advance his economic interest, he may have done so precisely because he was not as bright as the politically sagacious man envisaged by Madison in his Tenth *Federalist*. That in the long run it may be "brighter" to be bland about politics, is after all not a truism but only an ephemeral value judgment made by a well-fed generation which has read Orwell and experienced both Hitler and Stalin.

Our Jacksonian's lack of intellectual sophistication may account for his blissful unawareness of the central banking, or any other complex function, performed by the second Bank of the United States, and help explain the enthusiastic support he gave to those who would rid the nation of the monster of paper money by destroying the institution that best restrained its unlimited circulation. On the other hand, a combination of lust for gain, shrewdness, and hypocrisy may have accounted for his zeal in overthrowing what he well understood to be the great obstacle to the speculative profits his dreams were made on. On a more general level, disinterest in the "principles" operating in his economy would help explain his indifference to informed criticisms of its weaknesses, while his penchant for social climbing spurred him on to try to get what he could for himself. Finally, his conformity would explain his acquiescence even in policies he might secretly disapprove of or about which he might have qualms.

Jacksonians liked to think that Americans were different from—
and of course better than—other people. Students of history, however, will have recognized many familiar traits, some of them manifested as long ago and far away as first-century Rome, whose gross
new ways were so decried by spokesmen of the old patrician order.
Robert Kelley has recently noted that Americans going abroad
during the era were shocked to find that materialism, excessive
seriousness, anti-intellectualism, and obsession with success flourished too in Britain. These were traits that sprang up where a
booming commercial economy was emerging. It is by no means
certain that there had been significant changes in this country from
Washington's era to Jackson's, significant, that is, with regard to
national character. Europeans, not having been here before, had no
way of knowing whether change had occurred. They did, however,
have that freshness of viewpoint that so often enables the foreigner
to see things the native overlooks. Nothing was too commonplace
for them, they took nothing for granted.

That the portrait they drew was not a very attractive one can be
interpreted in ways flattering to the American psyche. (Of course
such an interpretation runs the risk of itself being interpreted as a
modern example of the American refusal to accept criticism.) In
this country the mass of inhabitants, whether appealing or not,
were at least *visible*, downright loquacious, inevitably unattractive
to the urbane observers who wrote about them. My point is that the
European counterpart of the Jacksonian common man was comparatively powerless and inarticulate, no object of fascination to an
army of interested reporters. The American was sometimes admired, more often criticized, but in either case treated with a respect
that was the more meaningful for being unspoken. Like him or not,
he had to be reckoned with.

3

THE CHANGING POPULATION: ETHNIC, RACIAL, AND SEXUAL MINORITIES

The American people were distinctive not only in their traits and values. During the second quarter of the 19th century the population, already more diverse than any other in the western world, became increasingly heterogeneous as European, above all Irish and German, men, women, and children poured into this country in great numbers. Despite the closing off of the human trade from Africa early in the century, the black population also increased at a vigorous rate, for all the afflictions borne both by slaves and free blacks in this country. Since the new immigrants, unlike their predecessors, now came over primarily in family groups, the female proportion of the population also rose. What was unique about American women was not their numbers but their condition. Nothing throws more light on antebellum life than these groups, whose changing situation markedly influenced social developments, the economy, politics, and perhaps most significantly of all—if the most difficult to measure—the flavor and the quality of the civilization.

Population growth continued at the normal 19th-century rate of close to a one third increase every decade. Thus the population rose from slightly less than 13 million persons in 1830 to about 17 million in 1840 and roughly 23 million by midcentury. The rate of growth however was not uniform throughout the country. The New England and South Atlantic states languished, the one region because it was losing old settlers, the other because it was not attracting new. The most exuberant upsurge took place in the west, the south central states increasing their population by half while the population of the north central states more than doubled during the decade.

An increasing proportion of the population was not born in this country. America of course had been a magnet to emigrants from the time of its colonial beginnings. But about 1830 a Great Migration commenced, European immigration to this country attaining vast, altogether unprecedented, proportions. Where typically in the 1820s fewer than 15,000 Europeans came here each year, between 1832 and 1850 the annual number fell below 50,000 only twice, and was usually over 100,000. In the 1830s more than a half million immigrants from Great Britain, Ireland, and Germany arrived in New York City alone. A variety of factors, economic and noneconomic, combined to dislodge the more than 2.5 million Europeans who migrated to the United States between 1830 and 1850. Coming now as family groups rather than as individuals, they were attracted by the golden opportunities of American life: work for all, low taxes, freedom and opportunity, abundance of food, land, and the absence of both a ubiquitous gendarmerie and compulsory military service. Of every 15 newcomers, 6 came from Ireland, 5 from the Germanies and the remainder from other parts of Europe.

Traditional accounts emphasized the relative prosperity experienced by the Germans here, certainly when their lot was compared with that of the Irish. Farmers primarily, Germans settled on semi-improved farms and towns in the north central states, just south of the New Endlanders' western reserve. When they remained in cities, as many of them did, it was believed that their "clean and orderly" living habits, combined with an economic status much superior to that of their fellow immigrants from Ireland, enabled the Germans to live reasonably well. Recent accounts raise questions about this version, if they do not entirely discredit it. In the heavily German city of Milwaukee, in contrast to native Americans who held the more prestigious jobs on the "upper rungs of the ladder," Germans like the Irish were found in the menial and low prestige jobs near the bottom. In New York City too, where German Catholics alone numbered about 50,000 by the eve of the Civil War, Jay Dolan has found that four out of five Germans had "unskilled, semi-skilled, and skilled occupations," a distribution "remarkably similar" to that of the city's Irish. In view of this evidence one understands better why some of the more radical German newspapers in the United States denounced the American economic system.

Most of the German immigrants, however, were far from being social critics and appear to have retained their optimism about this country and their chances in it. The many musical, literary, and political organizations they founded were in some cases motivated by a strong nationalism which "would resist assimilation to the superficial, uncultured, puritanical Yankee." Their national pride, as well as their actual circumstances, encouraged them to feel that their situation here was a successful one.

The Irish were another story. While their experience here was more variegated than used to be thought, their lot was more dismal certainly than that borne by other white-skinned persons, native or immigrant. Too poor to buy land for the most part, they settled in the major cities along the eastern seaboard: New York, Philadelphia, and Boston, or in a great port such as New Orleans. Yet they flocked too to such a smaller city as Albany where, in the quarter century after 1830, their numbers swelled from 2,000 to more than 23,000 or from about 8 to 40 percent of the population.

Most of them lived in abysmal conditions in these cities. Their poverty, overcrowding, and backwardness, and sharp landlord practices turned their housing into slums, disfigured by filth, the absence of windows and toilet facilities, crime, prostitution, disease, and a high mortality rate. Archbishop John Hughes of New York City at midcentury described the Irish of the great metropolis as "the poorest and most wretched population that can be found in the world . . . the scattered debris of the Irish nation." In fact the city at that time was "beset by a flood of impoverished, disease-ridden Irish," its hospitals, according to John Duffy, "jammed with patients and epidemics of typhus, small pox, and cholera . . . periodically sweeping through" Irish neighborhoods.

Irish workers made a significant contribution to the antebellum economy but their conditions were hardly enviable. Typically the men worked on railroad and canal construction gangs, provided the cheap labor in foundries and forges, increasingly dominated unskilled factory jobs, and in northern cities at first competed with and after a while took over work that had formerly been done by blacks. Irish women almost invariably worked as domestics. In midcentury Kingston, New York, of 254 women for whom occupations were listed, 240 were servants, while the few others were seamstresses. A recent comparison of the wealth owned by the various European ethnic minorities in the antebellum United States reveals that the Irish-born were on the average the poorest. They were worth only slightly more than half as much as persons born in England, Scotland, or Wales, and between two thirds and five sixths of what persons born in Scandinavia, Switzerland, Holland, and the Germanies were worth. And yet the economic situation of Irish males was not unrelievedly grim.

If the immigrants almost from the first sent cheerful letters home extolling American life and if, even more significantly, the Irish continued to pour into this country in the years before the Civil War, it was because their economic situation here seemed infinitely superior to the starvation many of them had faced in the old country. And with the passage of time an ever greater number of Irishmen managed to move into jobs that if not on the very top rungs of the American occupational ladder were nevertheless some distance from the bottom. Even in 1830, when only between 10 and 25 percent of Irish Catholics were "substantial" enough to rent pews in New York City churches and four out of five of them were employed in manual occupations, the community was sufficiently diverse to contain numbers of doctors, professors, lawyers, priests, book sellers, publishers, and officeholders. By 1845 the baptismal register of the Transfiguration Church—which may or may not have been typical of the larger Irish community—indicated that only 18 percent were unskilled laborers, as many as 25 percent held nonmanual jobs, while "the large bulk fell in the middle categories of skilled and semiskilled occupations." The multiplication of Irish churches, hospitals, schools, private academies, and colleges charging high tuition pointed too to the increasing number of Irishmen who were not poverty-stricken.

Internal differentiation was also the rule in small cities. Slightly more than half of Albany's Irishmen in 1855 were skilled workers, with 6 percent of them "small businessmen," including peddlers, and 1 percent in the professions. As early as a quarter of a century before, the Irish community of that city contained an "aristocracy," composed of grocers, merchants, and professionals, in addition to skilled workers. In New Orleans, the Irish elite or the "mushroom aristocracy"—what according to Earl Niehaus a later generation would call "lace curtain Irish"—lived apart from the mass of their poorer countrymen, even wore their own expensive militia uniforms, and dominated the numerous charitable, social, and patriotic organizations of the general Irish community. At the same time however that larger numbers of Irishmen were escaping from the very lowest level jobs in the economy, placards at the gates of many establishments continued to offer the advice: "No Irish need apply."

Supplementing their grim material conditions was the hostility the older Protestant community directed toward them. Almost everywhere the Irish made a convenient scapegoat for disgruntled groups dissatisfied with one or another aspect of their lives. Western Protestant evangelicals loathed the alleged Irish habits of drinking, rowdyism, poverty, and voting Democratic. Many New York City residents, unhappy with the corruption and inefficiency of local government and oblivious to their actual complex causes, had no difficulty in fixing the blame on "foreigners," usually meaning Irish Catholics by the term.

Anti-Catholicism, never entirely dormant earlier, assumed more virulent form with the great influx of Irishmen after 1830. The so-called Protestant Crusade was led by a mixture of fanatical and unprincipled ministers and publicists. It was fed by lurid exposés of outlandish plots and Catholic misbehavior: an alleged papal plan to absorb the Mississippi Valley; alleged atrocities—mainly of a sexual nature—committed in monasteries and nunneries; and regular performance of perversions attributed to the secular clergy. Absorbing these fantastic distortions was a credulous, bigoted, uneducated, and lower-class Protestant public, some of whom were so ignorant of religious history as to accept the canard that Catholicism was opposed to the teachings of the Christian Bible. The burning down of the Ursuline Convent outside of Boston in the summer of 1834 was only the best known of a series of violent attacks on Catholic lives and property in the 1830s and 1840s. The bigotry was usually as much anti-Irish as it was anti-Catholic, for in the popular mind the two went together. Paddy was reviled both for his poverty and his popery.

The "better sort" were more likely to condemn the new immigrants on social than religious grounds. One young northerner of leisure observed that "America, ever since we were overrun by Irish and German paupers, is not fit for a gentleman to live in." In the midst of the cholera epidemic of 1832, the eminent New Yorker Philip Hone noted, in his diary entry for September 30, that "a large proportion [of the English and Irish] lower classes find their way into the United States, destitute and friendless. They have brought the cholera this year and will always bring wretchedness and want." In addition to being the carriers of disease, these immigrants were turning the United States into the "almshouse and place of refuge for the poor of other countries." Many European officials had in fact contrived to ship their indigents in wholesale lots to this country, creating difficult problems in some of the communities that received them. But the mixture of hatred and contempt shown Irish and poor immigrants in general did not seem to be due to these difficulties. George Templeton Strong's diary entry for November 6, 1838, cannot be explained by economic facts alone: "It was enough to turn a man's stomach—to make a man abjure republicanism forever—to see the way they were naturalizing this morning at the Hall. . . . the very scum and dregs of human nature filled the . . . office so completely that I was almost afraid of being poisoned by going in. A dirty Irishman is bad enough, but he's nothing compared to a nasty French or Italian loafer." Such animus against Irish Catholics seemed to consist as much of snobbishness as of religious or racial prejudice.

Lower class aversion to the Irish was a complex emotion, explained in part by the incessant propaganda of anti-Catholic bigots, in part by other considerations tangible and intangible. A number of modern historians emphasize unlike lifestyles as a key source of ethnic tensions, focusing on the Irish penchant for fighting and whiskey and their moral latitudinarianism as important causes of their difficulties with lower class white Protestants. Since many Protestant workers themselves loved to drink liquor both on and off the job, as labor historians have recently been showing, it is possible that the similar Irish habit merely provided their critics with a pretext for loathing them. For that matter, as Dolan has pointed out, "temperance became a crusading issue" to Irish community leaders, who regarded intemperance as "one of the principal causes of poverty." Opposition to heavy drinking in antebellum America was not confined to Protestant "evangelicals." As for the sources of the peculiar bitterness dividing Irishmen and free northern blacks, it was compounded of economic rivalry, the Irish community's hostility to abolitionism as to other reforms it appears to have identified with an anti-Catholic worldview, and diametrically opposed positions with regard to Jacksonian Democracy, among other things, with Irishmen usually adoring and blacks abhorring Old

Hickory and his party. Many of the riots that disturbed the urban scene of the 1830s and 1840s pitted Irish Catholics against working class Protestants, white or black, as latent tensions often exploded into open violence.

For all the economic hardship, low status, and religious bigotry the Irish immigrants suffered here, they were substantially better off than at least one other group. Blacks were the pariahs of American society. While the precise figures varied from year to year, for most of the period blacks constituted slightly more than 10 percent of the national population. More than nine out of ten blacks were slaves, the precise proportion actually increasing from 92 percent in 1830 to slightly more than 94 percent by 1860. Slavery will be examined in the section on agriculture; this section considers the situation of free blacks.

Free blacks represented a tiny segment of the total population. Between 1830 and 1860 their numbers rose from about 320,000 to 490,000, but the percentage increase was less than one quarter that experienced by the American people as a whole during the same period. The significance of free Negroes transcended their small numbers, however. In a sense their very existence served as an inspiration to their enslaved sisters and brothers, for all the bitterness that was associated with that existence. (My assumption, like that of the ancient Greeks, is that freedom, no matter how miserable, is superior to slavery, no matter how comfortable.) Free blacks were an important part of the labor force, particularly in the South. Their society and the subtle divisions that developed within it are fascinating in their own right and for what they reveal about the adaptability, the hardiness, and the creativeness of American Negroes. And the obstacles placed in their path and the cruelties inflicted on them by surrounding white communities on either side of the Mason-Dixon line provide valuable testimony to the operative values of the white community. America's treatment of its black minority was an indivisible part of antebellum society, at least as revelatory of its character and ideals, as was any other element in that society's development.

Slightly more than half the free black population lived in the South during the antebellum decades, with an unusually large proportion living in cities. They were far better treated in the Gulf ports and the states of the lower South (South Carolina, Georgia, Florida, Mississippi, Alabama, Louisiana, and Texas), where about 15 percent of free southern blacks lived, than in the upper South. In his recent comprehensive study Ira Berlin finds that in part because blacks there were so few in number, "nowhere in the Lower South did whites dwell upon the free Negro problem with the same intensity as whites in the Upper South. No Lower South state ever considered the kinds of comprehensive black codes demanded in Virginia and North Carolina and enacted in Delaware and Maryland." It is not surprising that in a white Southern society which depended heavily on slavery, identified that institution with Negroes, and dreaded any prospect of mass emancipation, free blacks should have been a source of nervousness if not fear. Their freedom was in fact so circumscribed that according to Berlin, "the free [southern] Negro's only right that escaped unscathed was his ability to hold property." A "Memorial of the Free People of Colour of Baltimore" complained that "though we are not slaves, we are not free." The practices as well as the laws of the antebellum South confirmed the accuracy of the complaint.

Even in the lower South, where they were dealt with comparatively leniently, free blacks were hardly treated as independent human beings. No matter how prosperous some of them might have become, they were required to take white guardians to supervise their affairs and represent them before the law. Post-Civil War treatment of freedmen was anticipated in antebellum black codes and forms of peonage that made a mockery of the rights of the "free Negro caste." In the years before 1860 every southern state moved to deny them free physical movement, political participation, the right to testify against whites or to hold certain occupations. Free blacks throughout the South had to register and carry freedom papers. And in times of crisis or unusual racial fear, as in the immediate aftermath of Nat Turner's rebellion in Virginia, many free blacks discovered that their few legal rights afforded slight protection indeed, as they were brutally beaten by roaming gangs of whites and forcibly dragged into slavery by white "manstealers." There is evidence that many whites sympathized with and befriended individual blacks. Southern "racial mores" compelled participants to confine such relationships to their private, not their public, lives. Berlin finds that "brothels were perhaps the most integrated places in the South."

Freedom for some blacks was tolerated by the white South largely out of economic self-interest. As an editorial in the Nashville *Republican Banner* put it in 1860, "the free negro (sic) performs many menial offices to which the white man of the South is averse. . . . If they are driven from the Southern States who will supply their place?" Actually free blacks held many jobs in addition to those of hackmen, draymen, messengers, and barbers that were singled out by the editorialist. True, the great majority of free urban blacks were unskilled laborers. As for the skilled and semiskilled, many Southern cities tried to confine them to what was called "nigger work." In Richmond this meant that blacks could be barbers, carpenters, plasterers, blacksmiths, bricklayers, shoemakers, and work at perhaps a dozen additional occupations, while in Charleston it meant primarily carpenters and tailors. In the nation's capital they worked at these trades and also as coachmen, porters, butchers, servants, well diggers, hair dressers, bootblacks, messengers, and chimney sweeps. The chief characteristic of their stigmatized occupations was that they were usually service trades that "required little capital and generally depended on white customers." Southern cities passed ordinances limiting the occupational opportunities available to free blacks, and where the law was circumvented, white workers petitioned and put pressure on white employers and at times resorted to violence to drive Negroes out of trades forbidden to them. And yet the lot of the free black worker in the South improved with the passage of time. Employers who felt they needed them were indifferent to legal restraints and the threats uttered by more expensive white labor. It may be too that "the growing complexity of the Southern economy also protected the freemen's jobs and enlarged their opportunities." On the eve of the Civil War, there was a larger proportion of skilled free blacks in the South than in the north. Black craftsmen, according to Berlin, "generally earned good wages and many achieved modest wealth."

Free men and women were in general lighter in color than slaves: where by 1860 four out of ten free blacks were classified as mulattoes, only one slave in ten had some white ancestry. (In many Southern states a person who had only one African great grandparent or great great grandparent—that is someone one-eighth or one-sixteenth Negro—was adjudged a black and therefore subject to the regulatory laws.) Many free Negroes were the offspring of slave mothers and white fathers, owing their comparatively elite status to their mixed parentage. As a general rule, the lighter his or her skin, the better off the free black. Lower South free blacks were lighter skinned than were their upper South sisters and brothers and usually better educated, more highly skilled, and simply better treated as well. A white Southerner wrote that most darkskinned free blacks were "an idle, lazy, indolent set of vagabonds, who lived by theft or gambling," in contrast to mulattoes, who were "industrious, sober, hard-working mechanics" of "considerable property." The lightskinned Negroes, he concluded, provided "a barrier between our own color and that of the black and in case of insurrection [were supposedly] more likely to enlist themselves under the banner of the whites."

The living and housing conditions, the wealth, and the status and influence of free southern blacks was also internally differentiated. If a minority seemed to do fairly well, the majority did not. According to Berlin, "most free Negroes lived on the countryside, where they squatted in shanties on scraps of land that no one else seemed to want." And in the cities, where more than one third of free blacks lived, "most lived in the poorer neighborhoods on the outskirts . . . in back alleys, dank cellars, factory lofts, and the corners of abandoned mill sites." Dorothy Provine finds that they "were packed indiscriminately in Goat Alley, Tin Can Alley, and other slums in the District of Columbia." There as in other Southern cities, however, poor blacks lived alongside poor whites, often Irish immigrants, in "integrated" neighborhoods, perhaps as a result of white fears that a racial ghetto "might unite blacks and serve as breeding grounds for insurrection."

As with Irish immigrants, class lines emerged and rigidified among free blacks in the South. In Washington, Wilmington, and other southern cities a lightskinned caste of wealth and status appeared, composed of 10 percent or less of the free black community. The wealthiest black families in antebellum Natchez themselves owned slaves in addition to valuable real estate, forming a "close-knit coterie," who, according to D. Clayton James, "rarely hob-nobbed with the lower levels of free Negroes and slaves." In the South as a whole, the mulatto socioeconomic elite aspired to and sometimes attained the style of living they associated with the white upper middle and upper classes. In the fraternal organizations that sprang up in the free black community as a whole, the elite, as in Charleston, organized exclusive "fellowship societies" that barred membership to *blacks*. Berlin observes that the very names of some of these organizations—the Friends of Order, the Perseverance Society, the Society of Economy and Mutual Assistance—suggest that the upwardly mobile free Negroes who led them "hoped to imbue all blacks with the values of hard work, frugality, and strict morality, values they believed characterized their own success."

While they inevitably reflected the heterogeneous ideals and social structure of free blacks in the South, the array of Negro voluntary associations were important mainly for the varied services they provided the black community. Offering assistance to the disabled, the elderly, the widowed and the orphaned, schooling to the young, physical protection against manstealing, insurance against disaster, companionship, and a sense of social solidarity to all their participants, as well as entertainments, fairs, parades, concerts, suppers, picnics, and dances, these indispensable societies indeed "supplied nearly every conceivable service to the black community." One of their central activities was the funeral, "one of the most important occasions in the social life of many black communities." Benevolent societies were organized to deal with all aspects of these occasions, ranging from buying plots to the hiring of bands. For in the black community, "rather than a somber occasion, the funeral became a joyous event," in part perhaps because the "deceased [was] escaping the oppression of this world." Attitudes toward death were shaped largely by the African church, without doubt the most influential institution in the black community.

Many of the free blacks' schools, fraternal organizations, and benevolent societies were auxiliary agencies of black churches. For the role of the African churches was not confined to theological or moral teachings. Opposed and feared by many influential whites earlier in the era, after 1840 separate black churches came into their own in the South. Composed of slaves and the rank and file of free blacks rather than the elite (who often "quietly purchased pews within white churches"), the black churches were great popular institutions devoted to the emotional as well as spiritual uplift of their congregations. Certainly they offered dramatic worship, against which the services held in most white churches seemed insipid by comparison. Eugene Genovese has tellingly depicted the central role religion played in maintaining the morale and the integrity of the slave community in the South. The black church appears to have been equally vital among free blacks. If self-taught slave ministers of commanding presence and personality became the most respected leaders of enslaved rural blacks, so the ministers of urban black churches became "the most important element in the [free] black leadership class."

Although blacks in the free states have been said to have "enjoyed a degree of liberty and self-expression unknown in the slaveholding states," the north offered the free Negro a life something this side of paradise. From the cradle to the grave he was cruelly treated, singled out for abuse, legal and extralegal, direct and indirect. Many states in the northeast and northwest enacted restrictions designed to limit sharply the entry of migrating blacks into their areas. As Eugene Berwanger has noted, if antebellum Ohio eventually repealed these restraints, Indiana, Illinois, and Iowa did not. Such bars reflected, among other things, whites' feelings of racial superiority, hostility, and fear that seemed little different from those of the most bigoted whites south of the Mason-Dixon line.

Writing in the Philadelphia *Journal of Medical and Physical Sciences*, a physician in the 1820s observed that the so-called "black races were substantially different" from and inferior to "the Caucasian in mental condition, as well as in bone and nervous systems, skull dimension, and internal bodily organs." A generation later, state legislators justified a statute that would remove dependent or poor "colored persons" from New Jersey communities, by insisting that their biased verdict that free Negroes were an "idle, slothful people" was a dispassionate scientific finding. Similar attitudes characterized the thinking of white America on all levels. During his tenure as Jackson's attorney general, Roger B. Taney in 1831 anticipated his Dred Scott decision of a quarter century later. When the British government protested the application to her seamen of a law empowering South Carolina to imprison and possibly to enslave free black seamen on vessels staying in that state's ports, Taney formally advised Britain that Negroes were "a separate and degraded people;" their nominal citizenship, in any state unwise enough to have granted it, rested only on the "sufferance of the white population" and could therefore be repudiated at will. Dubious techniques of "fact-gathering" produced an 1840 census purporting to show that the insane and idiocy rate among free Negroes was 11 times higher than it was among slaves. Such "evidence," with its strong suggestion that slavery was the condition best suited for blacks, only reflected popular white beliefs that were pervasive in antebellum America.

Suffering under a variety of political disabilities, free blacks in the North enjoyed something substantially short of equal political rights and first class citizenship. Defining a Negro as a person no more than one of whose grandparents need have been a Negro, the northwestern states barred blacks from voting, testifying against whites, and participation in militia service, a pattern that became equally the rule in the older states of the northeast. Some states formally denied the Negro the right to vote, naming his color as the reason. Others achieved the same result by indirection, as in the case of New York where in 1821 the Van Buren faction simultaneously removed the property requirement for white voters while creating one for black voters, that was certain to result in almost total exclusion of the latter from the ballot box. According to the New York *Commercial Register* of November 3, 1835, only 75 of New York's 15,000 Negroes were officially qualified to vote in that year's election. In Pennsylvania, as Tocqueville was told, and in a number of other states, no laws were necessary, custom or the threat of force sufficing to bar colored voters. In most of the northeastern states Negroes were effectively denied the right to hold office, serve on juries, or even bear witness in cases involving whites. By the end of the era the right to vote had been granted them in only four states: Maine, New Hampshire, Vermont, and Massachusetts. They made up a very small proportion of the population of these states, however, 93 percent of northern Negroes living in states which deprived them of the suffrage.

Then as now theoretical political rights were no assurance of fair treatment. Negroes were subjected to untold humiliations which complemented the political deprivation they experienced in most states and made a mockery of the political rights they had managed to attain in a few. The physical proximity of attractive Negro women, like that of Negro males or females who "knew their place," offended no whites. But in all other cases whites in the north went to great lengths to separate the races. Law and custom segregated Negroes in coaches, railroad cars, steamboats, lecture halls, hotels, restaurants, hospitals, schools, even churches and cemeteries, during the Jacksonian era.

Capable of skilled work, as many slaves had demonstrated in the South, the northern Negro was characteristically confined to low-paying, unattractive, menial jobs. Inevitably the Irish immigrants posed a threat even to this marginal economic status. A Negro newspaper, the *Colored American*, on July 28, 1838, charged that "these impoverished and destitute beings—transported from the transatlantic shores, are crowding themselves into every place of business and of labor, and driving the poor colored American citizen out. Along the wharves, where the colored man once done [*sic*] the whole business of shipping and unshipping—in stores where his services were once rendered, and in families where the chief places were filled by him, in all these situations there are substituted foreigners or white Americans." Desperately trying to maintain whatever less-than-exalted place they had managed to win in the northern economy, some Negroes referred contemptuously to the Irish as "white niggers," and urged employers not to overlook the violence and lawlessness of Irishmen in contrast to the typically orderly behavior of the law-abiding Negro. But it was a lost cause. In the nation's large cities in the decade after 1837 Negroes were rapidly displaced by Irish and to a lesser extent other European immigrants, even in the low-status occupations of hackney coachmen, draymen, stevedores, barbers, cooks, stewards, and houseservants.

Negro housing in the north, as might have been expected, was abysmal. A few Negroes managed to own fine houses in attractive neighborhoods but the vast majority lived in ghettos such as Boston's "Nigger Hill" or "New Guinea," Cincinnati's "Little Africa," or New York's "Five Points," that were marked by squalor, filth, overcrowding in windowless shacks and shanties, and disease. A white Philadelphia contemporary reported that while the "colored population are scattered all over the city," for the most part they inhabited the most unattractive quarters, "being, like all poor people in cities, crammed into lofts, garrets and cellars, in blind alleys and narrow courts, with no advantage of sewerage, gas, or water, and with not a pure breath of air from one week to another." The high Negro death rate was officially attributed above all to poor living conditions and malnutrition. Leon Litwack's reference to "the vigorous exclusion of Negroes from white residential neighborhoods [that] made escape from the ghetto virtually impossible, . . . the fear of depreciated property values . . . [overriding] virtually every other consideration," induces a feeling of *déjà vu*.

A minuscule portion of the northern Negro community had managed to accumulate the money that Garrison had advised all Negroes to try to get. While it earned them a degree of comfort, it fell short of accomplishing that "influence and respectability" which money ostensibly begot. For it turned out that the racism of white men was stronger than their dollar worship. The abolitionist minister who had remarked that Boston and New York society would accept " 'orangoutangs' [if they were] worth a million dollars each," did not appreciate the virulence of a racial feeling that subjected wealthy or eminent Negroes to the same insults as their lesser folk. Foreign visitors were amazed that a successful Negro barber would not service Negroes, unaware that were he to do so he would lose all of his white trade. The latter cared not whether the head to be shorn was that of a poor man or not. It was sufficient that it was black.

White attitudes seemed inconsistent and hypocritical. An African Colonization Society (whose leaders included such diverse political types as Andrew Jackson, Henry Clay, and Daniel Webster), though ostensibly in favor of the transportation of American Negroes to Africa in order to improve their lot, hit out against attempts to expand the free Negroes' political rights. Improve their lot and they would want to stay! The Negro was reviled for his alleged shiftlessness and incompetence, but he was hated and feared when he refuted these charges. He was forced to attend his own separate and inferior schools but when the attempt was made to provide a decent if separate academy for him, as at New Haven, the white community responded with fury, not resting till the plan was discarded.

Early in the era some articulate blacks reacted to the cruelties inflicted upon Negro children in white schools by urging the establishment of separate black schools. Blacks in Rochester, New York, in 1832 petitioned the state legislature to create such a school, arguing that under "the present organization," black children "are despised . . . and completely discouraged," while the energies of the "colored scholar were confined, his hopes are crushed, his mind is in chains, and he is still a slave." Within 15 years, however, Frederick Douglass, the great black leader, joined other antislavery figures in denouncing separate colored schools. The problem, as blacks in Philadelphia discovered, was that their own schools were not "educationally comparable to the white schools of the day." Black schools lagged behind white in funds expended, facilities, quality of teaching, enrollments, and most significantly of all in the learning accomplished by students. Only one in eight black children studied or were taught the "difficult skill of writing."

Violence against the Negro was by no means confined to the South during the Jackson years. Cincinnati, Philadelphia and New York, among other places, all experienced mob attacks against Negroes and their white abolitionist friends. Even some abolitionists referred to "kinky heads" and by other signs showed that they too were not free of the feelings that animated most of their countrymen. On the other hand, it was essentially only among abolitionists that could be found white Americans seriously concerned about the plight of the free Negro and determined to alleviate it.

Yet in New England no more than in other northern areas did free blacks enjoy equal treatment with whites. What could be more hypocritical than New England churches which, with the exception of the Catholic church, confined Negroes to "nigger pews"—if they even permitted them membership? Blacks were well aware that even in Massachusetts, where due largely to the efforts of William Lloyd Garrison and other abolitionists the pattern of segregation was broken by the era's end, equality in theory did not mean equality in practice. It would be an unreasonable cynicism, however, that dismisses as altogether specious the good reputation for racial idealism enjoyed by the Bay State and its leading city. Boston held a special place of honor among southern blacks, one of them later writing of the city that it "was foremost in advocating the Negro's cause and vouchsafing to him the immunities of citizenship." And as James Oliver Horton has recently shown, the great New England city provided a setting that was particularly congenial to black migrants from the upper South in their attempts to create a sense of community in their new home.

For all the difficulties and obstacles confronting them, blacks in antebellum Boston and elsewhere were not merely a passive population resigned to suffering or dependent on their high-minded white friends for improvement of their lot. Constantly moving about the city in search of jobs and a "better social and political climate," blacks seem to have been as amazingly footloose as Peter Knights has shown their white working class neighbors were. In the face of numerous walls of discrimination, blacks indeed turned inward, but neither destructively nor in a mood of despondent defeatism.

Denied access to the good things of the dominant white society, blacks in Boston, Providence, New Bedford, New York City, and Philadelphia created a network of relationships that provided them practical if modest self-help as well as moral sustenance. Black boarding houses not only afforded homes to migrants from the South but widened their circle of contacts and in some cases provided leads to jobs as well. An informal job network came to operate across the northeast, acquainting the unemployed with work opportunities for blacks. Black newspapers, reform groups, and fraternal organizations all played a significant role in creating a broader "social network" that proved invaluable to the northern black community. And the black church played as vital and diverse a part in the life of the free northern black community as it did in the southern. In addition to the distinctive "emotional crescendo" that was attained in their religious services, black churches were "social, political, and cultural centers," offering support to choral groups and glee clubs, on the one hand, and to temperance, antislavery, and social protest movements, on the other.

Although these black institutions represented a significant achievement, their accomplishments should not be exaggerated, in the face of the hostility of much of the white community and the power of that community. Theodore Hershberg has recently found that by midcentury, "all social indicators—race riots, population decrease, disfranchisement, residential segregation, per capita wealth, ownership of real property, family structure and occupational opportunities—pointed toward socioeconomic deterioration within Philadelphia's antebellum black community."

An ultimate explanation of the antebellum Negro's dismal lot may well require an emphasis on the economic considerations that undoubtedly prompted his forced migration to this country in the 17th century. But by the Jackson era economic motives had become intertwined with many other. The typical northern white, particularly if he voted for Andrew Jackson's party, was an implacable enemy of the free Negro not so much out of rational economic fears as out of an irrational racism. Having convinced himself to his own satisfaction that the Negro was subhuman, he had doomed him to an existence that Senator Hayne of South Carolina—in a little-known passage from his great debate with Webster—could describe as poor, wretched, vile, and loathsome. In the judgment of Leon Litwack, the leading modern scholar of the matter, the only significant advantage the free northern Negro had over the slave was his freedom to speak out and petition against his increasingly bitter condition—although "much of this agitation proved legislatively fruitless. . . ."

A number of the articulate women who threw themselves into the movements to abolish slavery and improve the condition of the free Negro were convinced that the situations of American women and blacks were similar in important respects. The belief that antebellum society mistreated its female members seemed not to be widely held, no more popular with most women than it was with men. Perhaps Americans took for granted the appropriateness of the prevalent attitudes toward, and treatment of, women. Interestingly, foreign visitors, who took very little about this country for granted, judging its practices against its own stated ideals, found much fault with American male behavior toward women, many of them agreeing with champions of women's rights that women here were treated as inferiors and subjected to a double standard. Varied evidence suggests that the critics had a point.

Sensitive observers seemed to be distressed as much by what they felt were the false values propagated about the proper place of women in American life as by the actual circumstances of women in this country.

Barbara Welter has told us a great deal about the ideal of womanhood that prevailed during the period. A cult of "true womanhood" flourished—"presented by the women's magazines, gift annuals and religious literature"—giving stability and reassurance to an age otherwise marked by flux. It glorified four great virtues: piety, purity, submissiveness, and domesticity. Its spirit is nicely captured in the symbolic meaning attached by one writer to a dried white rose: "Death Preferable to Loss of Innocence." Like her counterpart in early Victorian England, the American young woman's purpose in life was to marry. (Pickering found that a single girl of 20 was considered old, and at 25 she was an old maid. The not atypical young woman in charge of the establishment he boarded at had married at 14.) All of her experience and training prior to marriage were designed to prepare her for that ecstatic state. Education, for example, was not to be pursued out of a mistaken zeal for abstract learning or truth, on the one hand, or a utilitarian desire to master a skill, on the other. In common with other activities engaged in by young women, its *raison d'être* was to increase her marriageability, and the scope, purpose, and nature of education were all modified accordingly. After marriage, the ideal style of wifely behavior was equally obvious. The wife of a farmer or mechanic might be asked to work harder physically and perform tasks foreign to the experience of the wealthy woman, but their goals and orientation were essentially similar. The one important exception would concern Negro women. The female slave's purpose, to judge from the comments of southern whites, was to work hard and above all to breed. As for her white counterpart, the "Southern Woman" of legend and antebellum fiction, John C. Ruoff has recently shown that this ethereal being was a sexless creature of delicate beauty, charmingly mindless, who, when she attained the married state that she yearned for, vanished thereafter from public view, foregoing flirting and riding for the creation of magnificent repasts [and] numberless children.

Such attitudes were fortified by contemporary medical opinion proclaiming that women were too delicate to be anything other than mothers and good wives, if not mere adornments to men. "The female sex is far more sensitive and susceptible than the male and extremely liable to those distressing afflictions which . . . have been denominated nervous, and which consist chiefly in painful affection of . . . every part of the system," wrote a physician in 1827. In the words of Charles and Carroll Smith-Rosenberg, "physicians saw woman as the prisoner and product of her reproductive system." And that reproductive system supposedly confined the woman to the limited role antebellum society insisted she play. Otherwise—if she lived "unphysiologically," which meant reading or thinking to excess, working too hard outside the home, or living too high or too luxuriously—she would produce only "weak and degenerate offspring." The level of gynecological theory and practice during the era was sufficiently low to make childbearing a risky matter indeed and this at a time when the taboo against birth control doomed women to incessant pregnancies. Robert Dale Owen and his small group of followers might practice "moral physiology," and the sophisticated few might use other techniques of contraception. But not the great mass of women. If they did not die, women often suffered torn cervixes and a variety of uterine difficulties in the wake of childbirth. Tragically, medical ignorance about "female complaints" was itself abetted by the contemporary belief, shared by many physicians, that such complaints were matters of morality and "delicacy," rather than proper subjects of clinical medicine.

Not all articulate women by any means responded negatively to the cult of true womanhood. Catherine Beecher's *Treatise on Domestic Economy*, published in 1841, was a paean to domestic life. Putting forward the ingenious interpretation that, in the words of a modern critic, "women were restricted to the domestic sphere as a political expedient necessary to the maintenance of democracy in America," Miss Beecher produced a primer describing how women could improve their every domestic function, from the setting of a table to the management of young children. The premise of her how-to-do-it manual was that the life confined to hearth and home was fitting and proper for women. The popularity of such a periodical as *Godey's Ladies Book* testified to the widespread acceptance by American women of the place set aside for them in the dominant ideology.

It is easier to write about antebellum ideals of womanhood, which were after all limited in number and relatively clear-cut, than about the actual situation of women, which was inevitably diverse and complex. To some foreign visitors the American woman's life seemed emancipated, particularly when it was compared with her European sister's. The relative absence of chaperones here was a source of much comment, as was the assertiveness of American women. By Tocqueville's theory, American women should have been bold, independent, and forthright, and sure enough he found them so. So did the untheoretical Fanny Kemble, although she was sensible enough to realize that no simple generalizations could account for so large and diverse a female population. Tudor, like Miss Kemble, thought them uppity and was struck by the fact that a small number of young women in Auburn prison caused more trouble than all the men combined. The verdict of phrenology, given by Combe, was that the American female head showed unusual "moral and intellectual development."

A unique feature of the American situation was the relative ease of divorce here. In the South, the "general conservatism retarded the introduction of divorce," and in South Carolina it was not permitted at all. Elsewhere states developed their separate divorce laws. Observers as disparate as Captain Marryat and Miss Martineau found these laws unusually easy or liberal. To the feminist, of course, divorce promoted women's rights in the same sense that to the follower of Turner, the frontier's safety valve improved the lot of the eastern worker. In the one case as in the other, the opportunity for freedom or escape—whether acted on or not—had a salutary effect on would-be "oppressors." An even more important solvent however was the increasing opportunity for women to work outside the home. Unattractive and low-paying though factory work might be, it did take women outside the home, give them money for their efforts—the money that alone conferred status on labor—and not least, it proved "a boon" to the spinsters and widows who otherwise lived joyless, not to mention totally dependent, lives. If, as Gerda Lerner has recently noted, the professions continued to be largely closed to women, school teaching and industrial work were not.

The legal situation of the American woman was not what European visitors thought it was. A half century ago Arthur Calhoun observed that such "equality" as she enjoyed "was a stingy concession even though it may have looked large to European visitors." Legally her situation was one of strict dependence and inequality. Possessing political rights during the first years of the Revolution, commencing with New York in 1778 and concluding with New Jersey in 1844, one state after another deprived her of the suffrage. From the point of view of the American woman's political rights, then, the significance of the Jacksonian era is that it witnessed the completion of the retrograde and antidemocratic tendency that had commenced a half century earlier. To the sympathetic Harriet Martineau, one of this country's main features was the "political nonexistence of women." Carroll Smith-Rosenberg concludes that "women in Jacksonian America had few rights and little power."

The relative shortage of women, particularly in the west, the new economic opportunities stemming from the nation's growth, the liberalization that some observers felt was an inevitable by-product of the youthfulness or newness of American society, all seemed to enhance the position of American women. Yet Calhoun found that "in sharp contrast to those signs of promise," there were "many relics of medievalism that encumbered woman's status down at least to the Civil War." In a legal sense, marriage was "permeated with injustice." To all practical purposes the wife belonged to her husband. He "had a right to the person of his wife and hence the sole right to redress for legal wrongs against her person. . . . She forfeited all personal control over her property so long as the marriage lasted. Her personal property vested absolutely in the husband." He could reclaim her if she went away and could use "gentle restraint upon her liberty to prevent improper conduct." He could beat her within an inch of her life without being liable for prosecution. A woman who won a divorce because of her husband's infidelity, forfeited all right to property earned during her marriage, as well as to their home and children. Unmarried women were regarded legally as perpetual minors. The era's legal formula for the married woman was that "the wife is dead in law." As shown by the acquittal in 1840 of the murderer of Helen Jewett, a New York prostitute, a double standard of legal justice prevailed. On the other hand significant legal gains were registered in a number of states in the decades before the Civil War. The most important of these permitted women to retain possession after marriage of property that had belonged to them before.

Opinions differed sharply over the quality of marriages in this country, legal aspects aside. Some thought them as much matters of convenience as they were elsewhere, while others thought they were uniquely noncommercial and romantic and thus a sign of the greater respect accorded here to the individual female personality. Yet not all men had pure romance on their minds. George Templeton Strong, well-to-do son of an old New York City family, confided to his diary that he would abandon bachelorhood only for a young woman of sound education, by which he meant a smattering of "literary taste." Other necessary traits, according to Strong, were "piety"; a "talent for obedience and submission"; "agreeableness"; "personal attraction—A No. 1"; "music"; and "from $50,000 to $100,000."

Almost every observer conceded that wives were treated with every outward sign of respect and deference. But to such women as Frances Wright, Margaret Fuller, Abby Kelley, the Grimké sisters, and others of that striking band of feminist leaders who emerged during the era, public gallantry or deference was precisely the rub. Surface pleasantries, gallant tenderness, exaggerated politeness were one side of a coin, the other side of which inevitably was featured by the real subordination, even subjugation, of the sex so flattered. It was not admirers of Mary Wollstonecraft alone who held to this view of things, by any means. Both Miss Martineau and Mrs. Trollope were critical of a regime which compelled women to separate from men at social gatherings. In Mrs. Trollope's striking phrase, American women were "guarded by a sevenfold shield of habitual insignificance." The two English women believed that American marriages doomed women to insipid and meaningless lives, devoted to gossip, clothing, and often to no greater ambition than merely getting through the day. One reason females could throw themselves into religion with the abandon they did was that their usual routines were otherwise totally devoid of drama or significance. What Barbara Welter calls the "feminization of religion" was not a victory for women's rights. Based on a detailed recent study of upper and middle-class women, Ronald Hogeland finds that their common experience was epitomized by the declaration that women were merely a "female appendage" to the "central drama of male activity."

Discerning male visitors also found fault. Even Tocqueville, who so admired both American women and the treatment accorded them by society, granted that marriage confined them to a narrow circle and required "much abnegation on the part of a woman and a constant sacrifice of her pleasures to her duties, which is seldom demanded of her in Europe." Another of his criticisms was made from the standpoint not of a male who believed women should have a greater opportunity to flourish as full persons, but rather from that of the male who wanted his women more "delightful" for his own pleasure. Thus, he wrote, American marriages tended "to make cold and virtuous women instead of affectionate wives and agreeable companions to men." Hall found that for all the kindness shown women, there was no mutual understanding between the partners here. Grund, typically so appreciative of American democracy, was caustic in his evaluation of its marriage institution. If marriages here appeared to work fairly well, it was because so little was expected of them. Significant relationships between husband and wife were out of the question in view of the real inequality of the latter. For that matter there was little communication between them. If American women were reputed to be good mothers, it was due to the fact that they got so little attention from their husbands that they could devote their energy entirely to their children.

Southern women were a group apart, in practice as in theory. White women, particularly the wives of well-to-do planters or of the many who aped their ways even though they lacked their means, were very much exalted, of course, their virtue extolled, their charms and femininity praised to the heavens. According to Calhoun, however, this "was the gallantry of the harem. Nowhere in the world were women shown more surface respect than in the South, yet degradation of the sex was obvious." If they were prized, among other things, for their "delicacy"—the euphemism for their tendency to refrain from or be spared the earthy pleasure of fornication—this virtue was evidently due in part to the venereal disease that was believed prevalent in the section and the fear of contaminating women with it. President Madison's sister had said of southern white women, "we are only mistresses of seraglios." The evidence is great that southern white males, married and unmarried, had easy access to the quarters of female slaves and took full advantage of it. The Negro woman's marriage to a slave, if permitted, was often treated with contempt. If the South was spared the "free-love" associations that sprang up in more benighted places, in the judgment of some southern white realists it was due not to a keener sense of traditional morality but to the easy availability of slave women to white men.

The life of southern white women was concerned with more than racially inspired sexual fears. As Anne Firor Scott has brilliantly shown, the lady of the plantation typically put in a much more difficult working day than is suggested in the myth of her daintiness. And on the Missouri frontier, wives, whether squatters or more permanent settlers, worked hard and long hours with little recognition. According to Henry Breckinridge, French-Canadian women there would "not be considered secondary personages in the matrimonial association," giving advice and playing decisive roles both in weighty and lesser matters. American women were far more submissive, treated either as helpmate or servant, their place indicated by the fact that they "came to the table after the men and boys were served."

Tocqueville completed his chapter on "the equality of the sexes," with the remarkable statement that were he asked "to what the singular prosperity and growing strength of [the American] . . . people ought mainly to be attributed, [he] . . . should reply: To the superiority of the women." Harriet Martineau, on the other hand, believed that if the test of a civilization were its treatment of women, the United States would come off badly. In her view, American practice fell not only "below their own democratic principles, but the practice of some parts of the old world." Woman's intellect was confined here, she was subjected to a double standard that crushed true morality; she was made subservient and ignorant, unfit for life as for a truly admirable marriage; "indulgence [was] . . . given her as a substitute for justice." To Tocqueville the admittedly limited life that was the lot of most women was a mere vagary of a marvelously exciting civilization. It was hardly a serious flaw to a young man who shared in the common notion that woman was essentially an adornment. His criticism was directed only at a system of education that unfortunately made this delicious creature less attractive than she need be. Like Tocqueville, Miss Martineau also marveled at the wonders of this civilization. But unlike him, she regarded women as more than ornament or mere appendage to man. Invariably, contemporaries who shared her view of woman's worth and significance, found fault with American society, believing that it was seriously flawed by its maltreatment of roughly half its members. To agree with Miss Martineau is not to judge the past by the standards of the present but rather by the standards of its most sensitive contemporaries who, like John Quincy Adams, could ask: "Why does it follow that women are fitted for nothing but the cares of domestic life?"

It would be pointless or what historians call "ahistorical" to find fault with the people of an earlier time for living by standards that differ from those of our own day. The historian's first task is not to argue with the history he or she discloses but to understand it. Who would understand Jacksonian America must ponder the significance of the fact that, both in thought and in deed, it denied equal justice to women, and to racial and ethnic minorities.

4

THE "URBAN REVOLUTION" AND OTHER SOCIAL DEVELOPMENTS

The United States during the Jackson years was a civilization in flux. All eras, even those with reputations for quiescence, are in fact ages in transition, although in some cases it is change so gradual, muffled, or hidden beneath the surface of events as to escape the notice of contemporaries. But social change was palpable in this country during the second quarter of the 19th century. Fundamental institutions as well as the surface of life were being dramatically modified.

Great social institutions are not lightly altered. Important developments typically unfold unobtrusively, taking shape behind the scene, sometimes at a glacial pace. Owing little if anything to the election of this man or that party, the chronology of a significant social trend, if it coincides with the years of a particular presidential administration, does so fortuitously. Certainly the growth and the qualitative changes in American population, cities, and religion during the period of Andrew Jackson were not due to his election to the presidency. These were "Jacksonian" tendencies only in the sense that they occurred during an era we are fond of identifying with the seventh president. The product of varied, essentially nonpolitical causes, the great social changes largely shaped the outlines and fixed the essential character of American life during the era. They also vitally affected the nation's political life, feeding it new issues and fostering new tactics and mechanisms that were to give a distinctive cast to the party battles of the era.

An urban sociologist has defined cities as "relatively large, dense, and permanent settlements of heterogeneous individuals." The growth in the number of such "settlements" was one of the central social developments of the period. Most people, of course, continued to live in the country, at the era's end as at its beginning, for all the dynamic expansion in the nation's towns and cities. Yet, in view of their importance, it is not exaggeration to conclude that the quantitative and qualitative changes that overtook urban communities during the era constituted a revolution of sorts.

In the Jacksonian as in earlier years, cities continued to be centers of the nation's commerce, industry, finance, and wealth. They were centers too of art and learning, with painting, music, theatre, medicine, and schools flourishing in urban milieus above all. In addition to serving as political and administrative centers, cities typically housed the most prominent and influential political figures in their states. And they offered a distinctive way of life that contrasted sharply with life in the countryside. Local residents had to devise unique institutions to cope with the special features of the urban setting. These characteristics appear to have been as true of Jeffersonian as of Jacksonian cities. What was unique about the antebellum decades was the enlarged dimension and scope and the growing complexity of urban problems.

Urban population during the era increased twice as fast as rural. Where in 1830 not quite 10 percent of the people lived in towns or cities of 2,500 or more people, by midcentury the proportion had almost doubled. Older cities grew at an unprecedented rate, while newer towns sprang up in all sections of the country. The spurt in urban population was by no means confined to the northeast. While the great metropolises, New York City and Philadelphia, continued to be the most heavily populated by far, the population of the former leaping from about 200,000 in 1830 to more than 0.5 million by 1850, with Philadelphia in the same period going from roughly 160,000 to 340,000, the three other cities with populations greater than 100,000—Boston, New Orleans, and Cincinnati—represented each of the nation's geographical sections. Leonard P. Curry has recently shown that the South held its own in this regard: "Qualitatively and quantitatively southern urban development in the first half of the 19th century closely approximated national norms." As for such western cities as Cincinnati, Pittsburgh, and Detroit, their population leaps of between 350 and almost 2,000 percent far surpassed the national average. Truly the "urban revolution" was a national phenomenon.

New cities were built at a frantic pace. In Rochester it was said houses were put up so hurriedly that tree stumps still stood in the cellars. Older cities expanded in order to contain their soaring populations. New York opened up the "frontier" north of the Washington Square area (a section which today is regarded as in the southern part of the city), while in Philadelphia there was a "westward movement" to occupy the area away from the Delaware River, and

Boston not only moved into previously lightly-occupied areas in the southern part of the city but also reclaimed for residential uses lands lying under water.

The modern historian of cities on the Texas frontier reports that in Austin in 1840 "Indian fighting was probably the most important municipal activity." This was one issue clearly foreign to the experience of older urban centers on the eastern seaboard. Nor can there be any doubt that numerous other developments were unique to particular cities, matters of their peculiar historical backgrounds or their unlike size and locations. The amazing thing about antebellum cities for all their diversity, however, is the similarity not only of their problems but of the responses and solutions they worked out to these problems.

Their very growth—sudden, unprecedented, and unanticipated—lay at the heart of the problems besetting cities and towns during the era. Barely able to deal with the smaller and more manageable issues of an earlier, more leisurely time, the lightly-funded agencies and institutions of urban communities were ill-equipped to cope with the pressures resulting from their sprawling new populations. Massive Irish immigration exacerbated tensions, producing disorder in which the newcomers were ranged against blacks in some communities and against white Protestants in others. One reason for the ineffectiveness of the volunteer fire companies in antebellum Philadelphia and other cities was the rigid separation of these groups along ethnic and religious lines: Irish Catholic and Protestant fire companies fought each other with greater ardor than they fought fires. Ethnic rioting caused enormous damage to life and property in the 1830s and 1840s, in the process undermining the social harmony that, according to Sam Bass Warner and some other urban historians, had made the precommercial city an attractive and neighborly community. Nor was it just a matter of ethnically and racially motivated disorder. Violence involving town and gown in antebellum New Haven, the home of Yale, reached proportions unheard of before or after in the 19th century.

Their increased social heterogeneity further divided Jacksonian cities. Residents lived in neighborhoods confined almost exclusively to their own social and often their own ethnic and racial sort. (And, as will be noted in the next chapter, class lines became more rigid and the gulf between the social classes deepened during the period.) The "social problem" became more pressing as the numbers and proportions of indigent persons increased. New tensions coincided with and perhaps explained an unprecedented drinking binge by Americans in Jackson's time.

Some people detected a decline in the morality of cities. Taking a walk one October evening, the New Yorker George Templeton Strong recorded in his diary: "It's a pity we've no street but Broadway that's fit to walking an evening. The street is always crowded, and whores and blackguards make up about two thirds of the throng." In Boston, houses of ill-fame were said to be kept "without concealment and without shame." Suppressing them seemed almost impossible. An issue of greater concern to most city residents had to do with their physical security.

Safety was everywhere precarious. Local constabularies often hesitated to interfere with such gangs as the Plug Uglies, the Forty Thieves, the Swamp Angels, and the Slaughterhouse Boys of New York City, or the Killers, Bouncers, Rats, Stingers, Nighthawks, Skinners, Gumballs, Smashers, Whelps, and Flayers who infested the working class districts on the southern fringes of Philadelphia, "now and then venturing out to assault an unprotected female or knock down a lonely passenger." Crime went largely unpunished in view of the paucity and ineffectiveness of police personnel. A virtue was made of necessity in some cases, as the "aimless brawls" of poorer districts were not only tolerated but regarded as "sporting events," so long as they posed no direct danger to genteel elements in the community at large. Cities with populations of more than 50,000 depended on police forces characteristically consisting of a dozen or so men. The low pay for such work assured that early in the era police protection would be as wanting in quality as it was meager in quantity. And if the policing done by handfuls of "professionals" by day was inept, the protection at night came close to being a joke. The nation's great cities relied on volunteer watches to protect their life and property during the evening hours. A watchman worked from sundown to sunrise for between 50 cents and $1 a night and he was expected to apprehend criminals and bring them before municipal justices the following morning. Composed in part of "ne'er do wells," many of whom "were often asleep or drunk on duty," watchmen were incapable, fearful, and in some cases had to be bribed to arrest a thief. It was no wonder that the well to do in a number of cities paid for private police forces to protect themselves and their property.

The root of this as of most other urban problems was money. A Jacksonian mayor of New York in 1839 invoked lofty language to explain why in this country public order depended largely on community goodwill and cooperation. The modern historian of that city's police force drily notes that "the argument of citizen capacity was often employed by those whose major concern was fear of increased taxation." It was only when riots spilled out beyond the boundaries of the lower class wards, threatening the lives and property of the "better sort," that prosperous taxpayers faced up to the need for improved police protection.

Fires were perhaps a greater menace to life and property than criminals. "Scarcely a night passes without our citizens being awakened by the cry of fire," wrote Philip Hone in his diary. Fire watchers had a field day, while European visitors were appalled both at the regularity of the great conflagrations and how casually they were accepted. Business districts were ravaged by the flames as mercilessly as were the crowded slums, a kind of democracy in the pattern of disaster. Techniques of fire fighting were backward and remained so for all of the period. In New York volunteer firemen were the rule until after the Civil War. In Boston volunteer companies commanded great prestige, as rivals fought viciously to be first and to play the most conspicuous part at fires. More than glory was at stake, since cash prizes could be won by companies responding most quickly to alarms, while members of volunteer companies benefited by exemption from militia duty. Observers inferred a variety of contradictory traits from the American attitude toward fires, including fatalism, optimism, and contempt for the old. In some cities, such as Philadelphia, volunteer fire companies were dominated by criminal elements, in other cities, such as New York, they came to have great political influence. Stephen Ginsberg has shown that in the latter city after 1842 municipal authorities considered the firemen "too hot to handle." But nowhere during the period were fires dealt with effectively.

Cities everywhere fought a losing battle against dirt and disease. Their failure lay not only in their niggardliness but in this instance in their ignorance and ineptness, particularly in trying to cope with the typhoid, yellow fever, and above all the cholera epidemics that devastated urban America before the Civil War. Quite apart from these dramatic outbreaks, the swelling population of poor and indigent residents strained fragile urban health facilities beyond the breaking point. A modern scholar reports that "the urban South after 1830 raised intellectual barriers against the health reform movement sweeping through the increasingly industrialized centers of the North." It would be more accurate to refer to a health reform movement that ostensibly swept through the North, for it was a movement that despite the best intentions of its advocates had no discernible effect on deteriorating conditions. New York City passed so many ordinances in the early 19th century that "a mere scanning of the council's legislative measures on sanitation conjures up a vision of New York as aseptic as a Hollywood costume picture." And yet, as John Duffy has recently noted, "the true scene, unfortunately, was quite different." For all the advances made in the science of sanitation and environmental health and the beefing up of the city's public health agencies, health conditions "remained fairly stable during the first 45 years of the nineteenth century and then deteriorated rapidly," reports Duffy. And the great metropolis' efforts compared favorably with those of other cities.

Boston's declining death rate in the late 1820s was attributed in part to the atypically "systematic cleansing of the city" that was carried out after 1823. At midcentury, however, a Massachusetts sanitary commission report scorned Boston officials who placed "dollars and cents" above the needs of "human health and human life," oblivious to the needs of the poor.

Contemporaries believed that Southern cities were distinctively laggard in maintaining cleanliness and public health. Officials in Memphis, Atlanta, and New Orleans reported a "rising incidence of disease" in the 1830s and 1840s, attributable in large part to the failures of urban government. A Memphis editor wrote in 1836 that "Memphis is pronounced by all strangers visiting it the filthiest and most deathly appearing town in the Union." Not 20 years later an eminent Southern physician claimed that New Orleans rather "was one of the dirtiest, and with other conjoint causes, is consequently the sickliest city in the Union." The modern scholar John H. Ellis agrees, concluding that New Orleans' economic decline in the years just after the Civil War was due primarily to the city's high mortality rate. Even before the War, the yellow fever epidemic in the summer of 1853 ravaged New Orleans, with almost half the residents contracting the disease. Duffy observes that the city's leaders "never exhibited the degree of social consciousness" shown by their counterparts in New York City in responding to such catastrophes. Antebellum Savannah and Alexandria were admired for their unusually vigorous programs for street cleaning and garbage removal, but these wholesome measures were "selective in their application," confined largely to the "major business thoroughfares." In all sections class bias, whether in cleaning streets, removing sewage, or introducing a new water supply, meant that the heavily populated working class districts most in need of these improvements were the last to benefit if they received them at all.

Public health was obviously a crucial issue to an age whose garbage disposal was left largely to pigs rooting in the streets or to scavengers. While ordinances banning hogs were a commonplace, so was the constant violation of such ordinances. As one historian notes: "The city was caught in a vicious cycle: as long as garbage was tossed into the streets, the hogs flourished, and as long as hogs roamed the streets, it was much simpler to throw garbage into them." A contract system for washing streets had the expected result of contractors vying to receive "the highest compensation for the smallest discharge of duty." According to Caleb S. Woodhull, the patrician mayor of New York City, private contractors were concerned more with "clear profits than clean streets." They performed their services carelessly, spilling odious matter in their rush to make the largest possible profits. Streets in working class wards were filled with garbage, dead animals, and diverse debris, including fecal matter thrown up by overflowing privies and by the poorly built sewers of the era. Such neighborhoods were permeated by a stench that "made life almost unbearable for nearby residents." In Duffy's judgment, attempts to regulate and deal effectively with these and the related problems posed by the "noxious trades" of tanning, distilling, and dyeing, as well the offal and bone-boiling establishments. which were "both a menace to public health and an outrage to sensibilities," were "slowed down by Jacksonian democracy and the principle of laissez-faire." For whatever the reasons, municipal authorities in all sections dealt feebly with the public health problems that plagued them during the era.

If urban administrations nowhere solved their most pressing problems or came close to raising enough money to do so, during the latter part of the era they strived and to varying extents succeeded in improving on their earlier performance. In Cincinnati, for example, municipal expenditures of less than $50,000 per year before 1820 rose to about 25 times as much by a generation later, a rate of increase almost twice that of the city's population growth.

And where only about 10 percent of the earlier budget had been allocated to poor relief, education, and public safety, 60 percent of the later budget was set aside for such social services.

In Boston in 1837, New York City in 1845, and Brooklyn in 1850, important police reforms were enacted, upgrading and profession-alizing police work as well as strengthening its administration. Pre-vention of crime now was regarded as an important duty. Essen-tially modeled after the famous London Metropolitan Police Act of 1829, the American reforms also significantly increased the size and pay of police departments. Thus by the era's end some of the major cities had been compelled to take significant strides in the direction of enhancing the safety of their citizens. The vaunted "London Style" police forces proved to be no panacea, however, for policing was not done in a social vacuum. In view of the varied tensions and antagonisms that continued to rend New York City, for example, "inefficiency and instability characterized the police force of the 1840s and early 1850s" as it had plagued the metropolis earlier. New problems inevitably appeared as old ones were solved.

As was true of police reform, most urban improvement was erratic, piecemeal, and affected by realistic considerations. David Goldfield has recently noted that the leaders of Southern cities were "not eager to burden themselves unnecessarily." City governments "determined expenditure on a simple cost-benefit calculation. If the business and growth generated by the service outweighed the cost in taxes on the leadership, the service would receive appropriate fund-ing. Thus, police and fire protection, paved roads, and street lighting rarely extended beyond the business district." In Boston, too, the upper class gentlemen who traditionally ran things adjusted them-selves to the necessity of financing projects, such as an improved water supply, a new courthouse, or a railroad to the Hudson. But they hesitated to spend more money for street cleaning or to expand the sewer system in the poorer wards. Similarly in Philadelphia the working class areas at first did not benefit from the marvelous new system for conveying water to the city that so impressed its visitors. The records of other cities also abound with instances of the class bias that attended the introduction and improvement of so many urban facilities. And yet, as in Cincinnati, urban expenditures rose sharply precisely because of the special needs of underprivileged persons and areas. Slowly, grudgingly, but inevitably, large urban debts were run up as the taxpaying classes came to accept the burden of providing the minimal improvements and facilities neces-sary to public order.

Paradoxically, the very deficiencies of municipal governments helped bring about the luxuriant growth of one of the era's adornments—voluntary associations. The proliferation of these organizations, which had moved Tocqueville to a lyric out-burst about the American rage to associate, was a feature of urban life during the period. Americans, as Richard D. Brown has shown

for Massachusetts, were inveterate joiners even before the Revolution, creating almost 200 associations in that state between 1760
and 1820. The pace of organization quickened during the early
19th century, as voluntary associations by the thousands were
formed in large cities and small, along the western frontier as on
the eastern seaboard. In the face of governmental pennypinching
and incompetence, these private organizations in many cases assumed the most serious responsibilities confronting antebellum
urban communities.

Their goals and interests cover a wide spectrum. Poverty, illness whether physical or mental, the plight of blacks, illiteracy and
ignorance, vice and immorality, drunkenness, crime and prison conditions, meager cultural resources, inadequate public health facilities, and skimpy municipal amenities were among the maladies for
which social activists sought the cure. Themes of such significance
complemented, if they did not surpass in importance, the limited
tasks assumed by mayors, recorders, city councils, and boards of
aldermen before midcentury.

Of course not every voluntary association had a highminded or
lofty social purpose. Some of them brought together in celebration
persons of similar nationality, others pooled their funds to provide
self-help to their dues-paying members alone, and still others had
nothing more serious in mind than fun and frolic for their participants, usually persons of similar socioeconomic station. Exclusive
clubs of high initiation fees and dues payments such as the Tremont
in Boston, the Philadelphia Club in the city of that name, and the
St. Nicholas in New York City, obviously sought to confer special
prestige on, as well as provide a haven of escape to, the elite
eminences they attracted. More important were the associations
dedicated to one or another form of public uplift.

In view of their great importance, the socially purposive local
associations have in recent years drawn increasing attention from
historians. Some controversy has arisen concerning the motives of
the directors and managers of these groups. Since the organizations
characteristically disseminated conservative social propaganda to
supplement the more tangible benefits they might distribute to the
beneficiaries of their largesse, some scholars have concluded that
the chief motive of their leaders was "social control." My own reading of their private papers and other evidence leads me to agree
with the English historian M. J. Heale, that more often than not the
men and women who controlled these bodies were persons of mixed
motives. Altruism, religious zeal, the desire to imbue their mate-
rially successful lives with a sense of nobler purpose, noblesse
oblige, combined with other more mundane feelings to inspire the
leaders of the voluntary associations into action. Since most of them
came of families that had long been part of the upper crust of their
communities, their belief in such doctrines as the Malthusian teaching that the poor are the authors of their own misery or that failure
was due to individual fault rather than to social institutions, was
second nature to them. They inherited such social philosophy pre-

cisely as they inherited their material fortunes. They parcelled out limited social benefits, always admonishing society's failures and unfortunates that they must blame their plight on their own weaknesses alone. It seems to me they gave such advice not out of Machiavellian cunning but rather out of sincere conviction.

While the abundance of voluntary associations testified to the social conscience as well as to the penchant for social cooperation of their activist members, the fact remains that these organizations fell far short of solving the great problems they confronted. Their failure seems to have been due at least in part to the determination of their leaders not to pose a challenge to the prevailing social order. Slight amelioration of the lot of society's victims seems to have been the chief purpose of the era's reform associations. Far from threatening such institutions as private property and private inheritance, private benevolence if anything strengthened them by reducing even if slightly the gulf between haves and have-nots, by its revelation of the sense of social responsibility shared by society's leaders, and by its dissemination of social teachings stressing the inevitability of inequality.

Many voluntary associations sought to enrich the life of the mind of poorer urban residents. A lyceum movement flourished, above all in New England, hundreds of these associations springing up in the decades after the founding of the first lyceum in the 1820s. Charging no more than a dollar or two a year for membership, lyceums gave "farmers and mechanics" the opportunity to hear eminent speakers on a great variety of practical and theoretical subjects. Offering their listeners a cheap night out, lyceums, according to one student, were "an extraordinary agency serving the threefold purpose of education, enlightenment, and entertainment." Athenaeums, sponsoring both "public discourses" and libraries said to contain "the whole of the works, periodicals, or standards, that hourly issue from the presses of America and Europe," supplemented by private library associations, hoped, in the language of one of them, to accomplish the "moral and intellectual improvement" of the clerks and humble citizens who were expected to use them. As was true of the welfare associations, the era's library companies, lyceums, athenaeums, and "institutes" were almost always governed by men and women of the upper crust. In Providence, R.I., property owning "mechanics" joined with wealthy merchants to sponsor such activities. Unusually moralistic leaders, such as John Pintard in New York City, hoped that flourishing cultural and artistic institutions would "prevent the growth of vice and immorality" within the city. The practical men who controlled Cincinnati believed that the city's reputation for being "the intellectual as well as the hog center of the middle West," in 1838, "enhanced the wealth and power of the city." Upper crusts in all sections appear to have believed that academies and museums "symbolized elegance and refinement," which helped bring "needed capital into the city." Pragmatic notions of this sort combined with higher motives helped account too for the proliferation of "academies of fine arts," established and run by successful men of affairs who hoped "to improve and refine the public taste in works of art."

The most successful intellectual and cultural reform of the era was the movement to expand the educational opportunities of the children of the poor and improve the quality of instruction in the schools they attended. The chief reason for the success of public education was the diversity of support it attracted. Some idealistic reformers hoped that improved education, by implanting equality "in the mind, in the habits, in the manners, and in the feelings" of commoners, would promote too equality of material condition. Labor radicals believed that education would "remove the veil of ignorance by which the poor who suffer are prevented from penetrating into the mysteries of that legislation of the rich by which their sufferings are produced"; an educated working class would have their eyes opened to "the monstrous frauds that have been perpetrated" on them. Friends of social order hoped with Horace Mann that public education would be regarded as "the great equalizer of the conditions of men,—the balance-wheel of the social machinery," while advocates of the developing industrial order shared his expectation that an educated working class would be unusually productive. Thomas Cooper of South Carolina no doubt spoke for conservatives elsewhere when he suggested that "education universally extended throughout the community will tend to disabuse the working class of [the dangerous] notion" that "property or wealth ought not to be accumulated or transmitted." The objectives of the wealthy men who ran the school society of New York City, the voluntary association which "dominated the educational scene" there for the first half of the 19th century, were to "prepare for usefulness a large portion" of the population, "who might otherwise grow up in idleness, remain a burden on the community, and become victims of every species of vice and profligacy incident to extensive and populous cities." Through their efforts they sought to instill "feelings of independence . . . highly important to cultivate, and be promoted among poor and laboring classes." The similarly wealthy Philadelphians who were the prime movers of the 1834 law that transformed the stigmatized public schools of Pennsylvania, "in which the poorer children were forced publicly to make a show of their poverty," had similar social objectives in mind. Since tax supported common schools would foster among "the rich, the comparatively rich, and the destitute" a similar feeling of "perfect equality," it was "the duty of the State to promote and foster such establishments." Championed by so heterogeneous a coalition, the expansion and improvement of public education in Jacksonian America was an idea whose time had come.

For all its popularity, a well-financed public school system based on increased taxes was not universally acclaimed. Some editors feared that if mechanics devoted too much time to formal study, "most of the conveniences of life and objects of exchange would be wanting; languor, decay, poverty, discontent would soon be visible among all classes." A modern student notes that public education in antebellum Louisiana died of pennypinching. Sending their own children to private schools, the planters and wealthy merchants who pulled the purse strings "were more than indifferent toward public education; they opposed it." The view expressed by one of their spokesmen, that the school system was a "humbug" and a "useless drain upon an overtaxed people" that he "would gladly see . . . abolished," evidently won acceptance by most of the people of the state. Nor was the failure of public education confined to those states and communities which strongly opposed the measure. The burden of a number of recent studies of educational reform in New England and northeastern communities is that there too the success it enjoyed was more apparent than real.

In many New England and northeastern communities the public schools failed to attract or to hold their intended beneficiaries—the children of the poor. Working class parents often felt they could not relinquish youthful breadwinners to institutions whose instructional program seemed irrelevant to the lives of the poor. For the curriculum and the administration of what one scholar calls the "culture factories" of the era reflected above all the social philosophies of the elite who ran, rather than the needs of those who attended, them. Wherever and whenever it has been introduced, whether in Napoleonic France or modern Red China, universal education invariably reflects the social objectives of those who control it; it is no accident that Jacksonian public schools were administered in accord with the philosophical ideas of the property-owning elements who financed them. Yet this fact detracts little from the worthwhileness of the era's educational reform. That it might have been done better under different circumstances applies to every social change. As it was, the abilities and the opportunities of countless youngsters were enhanced by the new development, for all its deficiencies.

An important feature of antebellum urban life was what some scholars refer to as a "communications revolution." Technological advances in the 1830s made it possible—and profitable—for newspapers drastically to lower their costs and their prices, thus for the first time reaching a mass audience. Shortly after September 1833, when the New York *Sun* became the nation's first "penny press," its sales soared beyond those of every other newspaper. Selling at one sixth the price charged by its competitors, its readership was no longer confined, as theirs had been, to businessmen, professionals, and politicians. Within a decade papers in other cities had moved to imitate the *Sun*. While there seems to be no way of determining precisely who or which groups consumed the new journals, the fact that the rate of newspaper, magazine, and book production increased more than three times as swiftly as did population indicates that a new, previously untapped audience, far more plebeian in character than the earlier one, was now being reached.

A merican medicine followed a mixed course, its development affected by the era's political, social, and even its religious mood, as well as by theoretical and scientific influences. Attempts to regulate medical education and practice were almost everywhere a failure, in part because opponents charged that medical licensing represented an "aristocratic" restraint on the free practice of medicine. To the followers of Samuel Thomson, the era's champion of natural or "herbal" medicine, learned physicians were "oppressors of the poor," a privileged order "that made the rich— richer, the poor—poorer." Joining forces with opponents of mercantile and financial "licensed monopolies," Thomsonian demagogues attacked the "medical monopoly," paralleling the Locofoco slogan, "Every man his own banker," with their own war cry: "Every man and woman his [and her] physician." The pervasiveness of such attitudes is impossible to measure but there seems little doubt that quackery of this sort found favor with the more overwrought Jacksonians.

This was an age too in which scientific ignorance was complemented by strange notions, some Victorian, others medieval. As Richard H. Shryock and Barbara Welter have observed, under the influence of the prevalent romanticism, illness was sentimentalized and a well-known author of a textbook on obstetrics could withhold important gynecologic information from a patient out of a sense of delicacy. Cultivated as well as uneducated persons continued to believe that disease and serious illness were the wages of sin. The cholera that devastated much of this country in 1832 and again in 1849 was believed to single out not only the poor and the filthy— persons the benevolent activist John Pintard called "the scum of the city"—but those who "had infringed upon the laws of God." Charles Rosenberg, the historian of the cholera epidemics of the 19th century, notes that they were widely regarded as "a scourge not of mankind but of the sinner." Excessive drinking, gourmandizing, and above all sexual activity which "artificially stimulated" the reprobates who engaged in them were believed to leave the system of the sinner defenseless against the dread disease.

Not that contemporary medical thinking was very much more impressive. Calomel, the universally applauded cathartic, was prescribed in doses "fit for a horse," supplemented by massive bloodletting. Adventurous doctors thought that tobacco smoke enemas (!) were the best cure for cholera, while the president of the New York State Medical Society suggested that "the rectum be plugged with beeswax or oilcloth so as to check diarrhea." Recognizing the helplessness of the medical profession in treating cholera, an unusually frank physician predicted that "some future historian will record our folly and credulity in the same chapter of events with Salem witchcraft, divining rods, and animal magnetism." Convinced that cholera was "an exercise of God's will," inflicted on a nation "sunk in materialism and sin," the devout resorted to prayer, in 1849 prevailing on President Zachary Taylor to set aside a day of "national prayer, fasting, and humiliation." The well-to-do simply fled town, where the disease struck most heavily, sensibly repairing to the countryside.

The era's medicine was also poorly equipped to deal with lesser, more pedestrian ailments. The behavior of many Americans was unhelpful. Personal cleanliness was known to be a pragmatic deterrent to many illnesses, yet it has been estimated that perhaps fewer than one in ten persons bathed themselves even once a year. Mutton was extolled, while vegetables, particularly tomatoes, were damned and night air was to be avoided at all costs. Angelina Grimké Weld could assure a fellow reformer that his piles would be cured if he would carry a horse chestnut in his pocket. Nor were such ideas confined to the laity. Dr. Samuel A. Cartwright explained that an ailment he named Dyaesthenia Aethiopis or Hebetude of the Mind was a disease of free southern blacks which, when it overtook slaves, manifested itself in the latter group's attempt to "diet, drink, and exercise" as did free Negroes. More prosaic diseases ravaged the white and black South during the era, with summer for good reason feared as the "sickly season." A contemporary country doctor prescribed salt and pepper for malaria, a disease which numbered Jefferson Davis's wife of less than three months among its many victims.

New medical schools were established in most states during the era, conferring thousands of degrees each year. Attempts to confine professional practice to their graduates failed, whether attempted by the medical societies that had been founded by eminent physicians or by local governments. "Irregulars" in the form of Thomsonians, homeopaths, mesmerists, or other varieties practiced as openly as did university graduates, shrugging off the petty penalties prescribed for the defiance, in an atmosphere marked by increasing skepticism toward formal restraints or requirements of any sort. In the 15 years after 1830 penalties on unlicensed practitioners were repealed in almost all of the 13 states which had earlier enacted them.

Nineteenth-century medical schools are not admired by modern historians of medicine. Russell Jones notes that many of them were diploma mills, interested only in the fees they collected, while even the more responsible institutions lacked clinical instruction. In Joseph Kett's judgment, these schools were bad, "sometimes incredibly bad." Their own inadequacies and a "rampant charlatanism," that led to the disappearance of "the barrier between the educated physician and the quack," made the Jacksonian period a "Dark Age of the profession." And yet all was not lost.

True, American doctors in search of the best in medical training had to go to Paris—as earlier they had trekked to London and

Edinburgh. At a time when the Americans' scanty knowledge of physiology, pathology, and chemistry made them "little more than clever routine practitioners," the scope, rigor, clinical experience, and theoretical knowledge present in French medical education made it far superior to the American brand and, in Jones's phrase, "a model of what was needed in the United States." If they depended heavily on French teaching and practice, it is also true that many American doctors profited richly from their Parisian experience. According to Jones, they "learned to identify diseases, improved their skill with the stethoscope, acquired practical knowledge of obstetrics and of human anatomy . . . engaged in medical controversies . . . and through their [subsequent] practice, teachings, writings, and research they disseminated what they had learned in Paris to their colleagues, students, and patients at home." American physicians became devotees of empiricism, increasingly convinced that purely "speculative approaches were outmoded" in medicine.

Gerald Grob has portrayed 19th-century hospitals that, for all their class bias in treating patients, did on the whole a creditable job. David Rothman's sharp indictment of the social motives of the men who sponsored mental institutions and other "asylums" suggests that, beyond disseminating misleading statistics that gave a false impression of the number of cures they achieved, the era's hospitals accomplished little of medical worth. Interestingly, the most knowledgeable historians of mental health, Norman Dain, Jacques Quen, and Grob, disagree, noting that many of the mental institutions of the time performed remarkably well, whatever the motives of their founders and sponsors. Grob reports that by mid-century, mental hospitals "were organized in such a manner as to facilitate the creation of a therapeutic environment that would change [for the better] the lives and behavior of patients."

According to Shryock, the introduction of anesthesia in surgery was "the chief contribution of American medical men during the 19th century." If his judgment is arguable, there can be no doubt that the achievement was nevertheless a substantial one. For before anesthesia, surgery was an excrutiating experience, avoided if humanly possible and performed at great speed when unavoidable. Removal of a tooth and for that matter ordinary dental practice were forms of minor torture. While there remains some controversy as to who contributed most to "discovering" anesthesia in the 1840s, there can be no doubt that several Americans played the decisive roles. Credit belongs primarily to Horace Wells, a Hartford dentist, who, if unfairly neglected in his own country, was rightly honored by the Parisian Medical Society as the "Discoverer of Anesthesia."[1] (The theoretical scientific ideas upon which Wells and his contemporaries built had been formulated by Sir Humphrey Davy and earlier science.) A medical age responsible for so great a breakthrough could not have been totally "dark."

---

[1] See the first edition, pp. 72–75.

American religious life fascinated visitors because of its strangeness. If there was much continuity, in an institution that stressed the immutability of its central truths, there was much change too in the complex, heterogeneous religion that flourished in Jacksonian America.

Paradox was the rule. For on the one hand religion seemed all-pervasive here. Atheists were almost nowhere to be found. Frances Wright—"Mad Fanny," the "high priestess of Beelzebub"—was all the rage one season precisely because her [unatheistic] "infidelity" was so rare a growth in this hostile climate. One gets an impression that her physical charm, her great oratorical gifts and her notoriety were more important in attracting large crowds to her lectures than any great interest her audience had in theological matters. Sunday was observed in some American cities as nowhere else in Christendom. This was the land of thriving Bible societies, Sunday School Unions, tract societies, and all manner of missionary activities. Millions of Americans belonged to the denominations which disposed of properties worth tens of millions of dollars. Nor was it simply a matter of token memberships. Nowhere else was religious life more actively pursued than in this country. Church membership here "was a strenuous affair," demanding much more from communicants than weekly church attendance. "Friendly onlookers" greatly outnumbered actual members. Tocqueville remarked the great influence exercised by ministers over all manner of secular affairs, including politics. Paradoxically, the American clergy in "keeping aloof from parties and from public affairs," managed to attain a great power over the state through its control over morals. Religious zeal was strong here, accordng to Tocqueville, because it was "perpetually warmed by the fires of patriotism." Whatever may have warmed it, there was little question that it was strong. Even secular reform, in Europe traditionally associated with irreligious doctrines and individuals, was here led more often than not by Protestant zealots convinced that to labor for the overthrow of slavery or drunkenness was to labor for the Lord.

Yet there was another side which revealed Americans to be amazingly and increasingly disinterested in religion as doctrine or mystic insight. Tocqueville was not impressed with the spirit of religious tolerance in the land for he attributed it not to a wisdom gained from experience but to sheer indifference. Why persecute men for their beliefs concerning the insignificant or nonexistent? In Tocqueville's complex evaluation of American attitudes, they were sincere, true, "but even in their zeal there generally is something so indescribably tranquil, methodical, and deliberate that it would seem as if the head far more than the heart brought them to the foot of the altar." For "not only do the Americans follow their religion from interest, but they often place in this world the interest that makes them follow it." American ministers, even if unwittingly, preached not the glory of heaven but religion's utility in enriching or making more tranquil the earth: "it is often difficult to ascertain from their discourses whether the principal object of religion is to procure eternal felicity in the other world or prosperity in this." A contemporary New Englander proclaimed that a nations' prosperity was "proportioned to the sacredness with which it [kept] the Sabbath."

Others also observed that nowhere did adult males seem so unconcerned with *true* religion as here. Token participation or sometime church attendance seemed due to social conformity rather than to inner conviction. Mrs. Trollope had never seen or read of "any country where religion had so strong a hold upon the women, or a lighter hold upon the men." Middle-class women of her acquaintance in this country seemed to collect itinerant preachers—who were "all the rage"—in the same way and in the same competitive spirit that elegant London ladies collected fashionable poets. For all the undeniable force of the Christian religion in a country where, according to Perry Miller, "general consent to the principles of Protestant Christianity was taken for granted," the fact remains that at best the churches, according to their own estimates, never enlisted as much as 15 percent of the nation's population in their membership. Bertram Wyatt-Brown estimates that not one Southerner in ten was a "devout churchgoer" when Jackson became president. The actual religion of the country according to many people was pursuit of the dollar. Even in the "infected" or "burned-over" district of western New York, that hotbed of religious enthusiasms, young men early in the era were said to attend church "from a sense of duty or for social intercourse," while "their mothers, wives, or sweethearts prayed nightly for their souls." After the emergence of Charles Grandison Finney, however, church was attended in western New York and the other areas touched by his spark for other than social reasons.

Many important changes affected American religion during the era, but nothing was more significant and certainly nothing came close to being as dramatic as the emergence of the new revivalism, launched or catapulted into prominence by Finney. Like many western New Yorkers a child of New England, the young Finney had trained for the law and had begun to practice it when he suddenly had a mystic experience that he compared to Saul's on the road to Damascus. Lawyer-like logic now became part of the intellectual arsenal of the man who, more than any other, produced a second Great Awakening in the Jacksonian era.

The fiery language, dramatic oratorical style, and comprehensible, even simple, theology of revivalism were not new with Finney, of course, antedating him by at least a century in this country. Methodism, as Richard Carwardine has recently shown, anticipated several of his chief themes and techniques. The new evangelism was directed, however, at the urban America of towns and cities as well as at country folk, and at the skeptical and commerce-minded men who ran affairs. Emerging at a time when such Calvinist ministers as Timothy Dwight, Lyman Beecher, and Nathaniel W. Taylor were trying carefully to justify more permissive notions of predestination and were being sharply challenged by orthodox defenders of the faith, Finney's huge success helped turn the tide in favor of possible salvation for all, and the power of each individual, exercising free choice, to achieve it. The victory was a stirring one though it should be noted that Samuel Hopkins' "conservative" theology for the era countenanced the comforting idea that more than 99 percent of good Christians were likely to be of the elect. Finney's achievement was not so much that he opened the doorway to heaven to the relatively few men who otherwise were headed for hell, but that he spoke a language that in fact brought masses of men and women into church. Like other revivalists his forte was a vivid description of the hell that he believed in literally and that yawned beneath the feet of the unregenerate. His great accomplishment—achieved through his magnetic presence, forceful gestures, glittering eyes, vivid imagery, mastery of a "scientific psychology" that first opened the sinner's heart through a demonic emotional attack and then reached his mind through force of logic—was to win over and recruit persons to Protestant Christianity who had previously been impervious to its appeal. To many men the previously dominant version of Calvinism had been esoteric in substance, stately if not dull in utterance, and relatively gloomy in outlook. Hell with all its torments was a marvelous thing if it truly existed and could be avoided by an act of will! Like other great revivalists Finney made hell real to his listeners, thus confirming, far more effectively than any learned theological treatise possibly could, the reality of the Christian message. And after his audience was made to feel the very presence of hell, Finney and others like him then invited them to vote for salvation, calling them out by name to stand and walk to the "anxious bench," there to have remaining fears and doubts allayed. At midcentury, well after Finney's star had fallen, rural Methodist circuit preachers were still bringing "many a hardened old sinner to repent and come forward to the mercy seat."

As always in the history of religion, the devotees of traditional rites and the learned purveyors of subtle theology were dismayed at the upstart and his simple ways. Beecher, too, opposed Finney at first, before 1827, but he was compelled to give ground and by the early 1830s was cooperating with him. Beecher had himself brought a revival to Boston in 1825 in his war against Unitarianism. The victory of evangelism was achieved not by the merits of its argument but by the practical success of its methods. Inviting his learned critics to go to hell, Finney answered them not with rational argument but by a head count. He wanted no part of Princeton Theological Seminary, preferring to fashion his own theology. His success in conversion, he said, was the surest sign of his rightness. That this was so is of course open to question. But the signifiacnt fact is that his answer or manner of answering came to be widely accepted. As for the unglamorous task of preventing backsliding, Finney left that to local pastors.

Finney's way with his critics, like so many other aspects of evangelism, reflected the traits and some of the paradoxes of the American people, a congruence that no doubt explains the response of the people to the movement. Like the people, revivalism was intensely pragmatic and somewhat materialistic. Its goal was converts and the maintenance of a "steady rate of church growth." One of its tests for the genuineness of conversion was the willingness of the convert to give money to the church. Finney might employ logic in his preaching, deny the incomprehensibility of Christian teaching, or proclaim the union he had fashioned between religion and science—or at least "the laws of the mind." Yet revivalism remained anti-intellectual. It scorned complex theology above all on the ground that its ideas were not understandable to the common man. Revivalism's main attack was on the emotions rather than the mind of the sinner. It was intolerant. It was also shrewd, perfectly capable of toning down its methods when it left Rochester for New York City and Syracuse for Philadelphia. "Protracted meetings" which ran continuously, night and day, in small New York State towns, designed to bring life and business to a standstill, were reduced to continuous *nightly* meetings in the big city. Evangelism worshipped success, which it measured in quantitative terms and was largely amoral in trying to achieve it. Perry Miller found Finney peculiarly American among other things in his ruthlessness. Revivalism was invincibly optimistic and thus unavoidably appealing to a people who insisted on their own and their society's goodness and the attainability of perfection.

While paying lip service to his belief in predestination, Finney actually taught that salvation was up to the individual. Critics implied that Finney believed himself very close indeed to God. If true, seekers after salvation were hardly discomfited. Finney's optimism seemed to have no bounds. He wrote that 'if the church will do her duty, the millenium (sic) may come to this country in three years." This even before the Jackson era had run its course! There was a hint of shrewdness or competitiveness in such prophecy since William Miller had fixed a precise date in 1843 for the great event.

Above all the new movement was democratic. Evangelism brought religion to the people in language they could understand, took religion out of the hands of a trained and conservative clergy, stressed the significance of the individual, glorifying his powers of mind and conscience, permitted women to pray with men, brushed aside denominational barriers as it did traditional usages, and lifted the laity to the level of the clergy—a rising that was not as spectacular as it would have been earlier only because of the plebeian character of the new ministry. Since the great years of the new revivalism were 1825 to 1837, historians have not failed to note that the similar chronological outlines of the religious movement and Andrew Jackson's emergence first as presidential candidate and then to occupancy of the White House, were more than coincidental. According to Perry Miller, Finney's movement was "a mass uprising, a release of energy, a sweep of the people which made it an expansion of that energy we call Jacksonian America." Finney, invoking a metaphor sure to appeal to a people who were constantly in an "election fever," told them that conversion was the decision to vote for Jehovah's party and support His administration over Satan's. Finney was personally apolitical but the era boasted men, including Andrew Jackson himself, who interpreted secular politics in similar terms. Sin was to be defeated by majority vote.

Actually evangelism appealed primarily to men who were anti-Jacksonian in their politics. (Professor Miller's comment that in western New York, Finney's movement was "not necessarily confined to Democrats," is a large understatement in view of the overwhelming anti-Democratic feelings of the people who made up the area's electorate.) While the movement was undeniably democratic it was also ambivalent and paradoxical—as was its American audience. It was particularly successful with the young. It attacked money and the life of accumulation yet its appeal was very much to the monied: to "real-estate magnates, millers, manufacturers, and commercial tycoons [who] led the parade of the regenerated." The sinews of war to finance Finney's campaigns were provided by the wealthy merchants—Anson G. Phelps, the brothers Dodge and Tappan, and others like them. For as Bernard Weisberger has discerned, "revivalism had popular trappings . . . equalitarian slogans and . . . democratic implications [but] . . . like Finney himself it had a touch of conservatism at the core." Not only did it not "threaten the economic underpinnings of society," it stood aloof from the great movements for reform, particularly abolition, that captured the imagination of Protestant moralists in the era. The iconoclastic New Orleans Unitarian Parson Theodore Clapp denounced the new evangelicalism as a "popular delusion" indifferent to "the poor and the sick." Finney taught the boring and unlovely cliché that nothing impaired the welfare of slaves more than strenuous attempts immediately to improve it. His interest he said was in winning souls. His tragedy, as sympathetic historians have conceded, is that the "victories" he won were ephemeral. He himself came to doubt the true Christianity of the thousands he had "transformed." His brave new spontaneous methods themselves became tired ritual even before he put them down, mechanically, in primers for those who would emulate him.

Neither the beginnings in the mid 1820s nor the decline in 1836 or 1837 owed anything directly to political events. William McLoughlin has persuasively explained the "matrix" from which successful revivals generate as consisting primarily of a combination of religious and social tensions. The movement's decline was hastened by its own increasing mechanism and intellectual sterility, the depression that both created new political excitements and "pinched the purses" of religious enterprises, and the redoubtable opposition to evangelism by the great benevolent enterprises of American Protestantism.

Organized earlier in the century for the most part, the benevolent societies were a significant feature of the Jacksonian religious scene. Taking the idea from the mother country, the leading Protestant denominations had created the American Educational Society, the American Board of Foreign Missions, the American Bible Society, the American Sunday-School Union, the American Tract Society, the American Home Missionary Society and a half dozen others. Interdenominational for the most part, with the requirement that their officers be laymen, this loose "benevolent empire" printed and published the good word, at home and in the hinterlands, and set out to "elevate the moral condition" of Americans. The high-mindedness of its leaders was confirmed by their New England origins and their Presbyterian or Congregationalist predilections. Personal righteousness was to them an insufficient goal. The "trustees" of benevolence felt called on to bring the truth to others. Supplementing their zeal was the wealth of many of their leaders. These were wealthy as well as high-minded Calvinists, their ample resources playing perhaps as important a part in the activity of the societies as their undoubted zeal.

Sincere conviction clearly motivated most of the leaders; their primary and direct purposes were religious and moral. Their intense dislikes were those felt by prudes and zealots: for "immorality," "freedom of conscience," or "religious heresy." Lois Banner makes a convincing case that "social control," narrowly construed, was not their idea of the chief purpose of benevolence. In New York City missionary leaders simply threw themselves into ameliorating the conditions of the poor. Yet the antipathies of some leaders were nothing more than the animus of social conservatives. They viewed with suspicion "democracy" and a "licentious press." Even those scholars of the movement whose interpretations of it clash on other matters agree that the leaders of American benevolence were conservative as well as wealthy men. They taught the American version of the doctrine of the "contented poor," and the necessity of social harmony precisely because they "believed that they [themselves] would suffer if men playing lesser roles . . . did not respect their economic and social obligations." In their analysis, the "trustees" believed that religion was not the opiate of the people but the stern purveyor of plain if difficult social as well as moral truths. Benevolence, although a widespread movement, was not truly national in scope. Certainly it did not catch on in the rural South. For if, as Bertram Wyatt-Brown reports, missionaries complained of Southern indolence, drunkenness, fear of innovation, and hostility to education, southern "plainfolk" resented the aggressiveness and snobbery of the Protestant zealots.

During the era, what might be called the traditional sects continued to thrive, although inevitably the career of each was singular and problems arose to bedevil all of them. Where one school of thought stresses the social roots and aspects of the inner discord in the churches, noting, for example, the democratic or lower class character of the Hicksite reform movement within the Quaker church, another approach emphasizes the significance of purely religious considerations, attributing differences to unlike theological views or varying beliefs about church structure. At the end of the period, Methodists were clearly most numerous, followed by Baptists, Presbyterians, Catholics, Congregationalists, Episcopalians,

Lutherans, and literally dozens of other sects. Methodists and Baptists by 1855 accounted for almost 70 percent of Protestant church membership. While the former was increasingly successful in the cities and eastern states, in social terms both churches "appealed to the plain men of the period." Although the Presbyterian Church had less than one half the membership of the Baptist and one third the membership of the Methodist Churches, it exerted a greater social influence than either, in part because, in the words of a contemporary, it was "the religious form preferred by the industrial and commercial classes, by men of enterprise and initiative." Between 1826 and 1832 Presbyterian membership increased at a healthy rate but thereafter the statistics suddenly took an ominous turn. Between 1834 and 1836 the old church actually lost 27,000 members. The following year the conservative or "Old Lights" took drastic measures by kicking out the close to one half of their membership who made up the "New Lights" and also abrogating their "Plan of Union" which since 1801 had enabled them to cooperate with Congregationalists in spreading the Calvinist faith, particularly in the west.

Robert Doherty has shown that at least in Philadelphia the "new men" were much likelier than the old to be of prestigious occupation and standing. Where about three fourths of the new group were "gentlemen," businessmen, and professionals, these groups constituted only one fourth of the old school, most of whom came of the artisan and laboring classes. The New Lights stressed interdenominational cooperation and evangelical preaching, a revivalism having "more attraction for well-to-do sectors of the populace than it did for disinherited ones." The leading new school advocate in that city, Albert Barnes, "the outspoken pastor" of the first Presbyterian Church, characteristically rejected original sin and predestination, predicted hellfire for those who "passed through [his] revival unmoved," and defended the sanctity of private property. If old-fashioned divines charged him as a heretic, large property owners applauded him as a model religious leader.

In the South the Methodists first, in 1830, and then in 1832 the Baptists, split, the latter into "Old School" and "New School" factions. In addition to theological divergences, these splits were caused by slavery, or by such an issue as attitude towards nonsectarian missionary ventures. In the judgment of Timothy L. Smith, a division of clergymen, at midcentury, into the categories of "orthodox" and "liberal" would be a misleading oversimplification. Instead there were a number of "significant strains of thought and feeling [that] flowed freely across denominational lines," in some cases uniting men of unlike denomination into a closer relationship than obtained between High or Low Church members of the same sect, and in other cases separating groups such as Evangelical Arminians and Revivalistic Calvinists, for a variety of factors exclusive of creed.

Europeans were startled at this luxuriant diversity of sects in America. Only the Catholic Church among Christians was "exempt from the fury of division and sub-division" or what one unhappy onlooker called "the outrageous display of individual whim which every other sect is permitted." And yet, as Jay Dolan has recently shown for New York City, its greatest and most popular stronghold, antebellum Catholicism was itself not free of some internal differentiation, if not strain. Composed overwhelmingly of working people, German and Irish parishes were nevertheless led by "the upper levels of the occupational hierarchy," with skilled artisans, businessmen, and professionals serving as trustees of the church. In this sense, Catholics were very much like Protestants. Modern studies indicate that in both northern and southern communities, lay Protestant leaders of their congregations were typically of high status occupations and backgrounds. In the many churches in which pews were sold or rented, pewholders had inordinate influence over church affairs. The social distinctions of secular society were paralleled in the organization of Christian churches. For that matter the unusually good salaries and perquisites enjoyed by priests placed them in "an income bracket higher than their parishioners": one priest remarked that many of his colleagues were able to "live luxuriously." The priesthood denounced excessive drinking, at times sounding no different than did evangelical temperance zealots, but with no discernible effect on the Catholic rank and file. Nor were all Catholics ardent churchgoers; half of the community lived "on the fringe of parish life." For all its social homogeneity and despite the remorseless hostility some Protestants directed against it, the Catholic Church in the city flourished. Certainly it grew wealthier. Where in 1820 it owned two churches and very little other property, by the eve of the Civil War there were 30 churches and its landed wealth was surpassed only by the Presbyterian and Episcopalian churches. And New York City was not unique "but the most conspicuous example of what was taking place across the nation."

During the second quarter of the 19th century, new groups came into being and infant religious movements matured to add still greater variety to a religious picture already heterogeneous. The west—and not only the frontier—bred interdenominational or improvised forms which were bound by no previous rules or precedents. Shakers, Millerites (predicting the exact hour of the second advent in 1843), Perfectionists, John Humphrey Noyes and his fellow believers in complex marriage, Rappites, Mormons, Zoarites, and numerous other sects burst forth, in some cases to burn out almost immediately, in others to persist in one form or another down to the present day. Considered fanatical in the extreme for their aversion to traditional forms, their stress either on celibacy or free love—never, it seemed, were they in between—their opposition to private property and war, these groups attracted later attention more for their individuality than for their typicality, for the following of no one of them compared to the size of the larger denominations. Though branded irreligious by some of their critics, actually the zeal demanded of their members was far greater than that demanded by some traditional sects, not only in its intensity but also in its conviction that all human affairs had to conform strictly to the imperatives of a nonhuman ideal. Together their numbers were great enough to make clear that unorthodoxy and socially icono-clastic religion were a popular expression of the era, a response of the not significant minority of the zealous, the alienated, the dis-senters from the materialism and the propriety that were the secular religion of most of their fellow countrymen.

There is no way to estimate quantitatively the extent either of religious feeling or religious influence in Jacksonian America. One factor that perhaps slightly deflected the message of the zealous and interfered with its impact was American irreverence. For example, after the high-minded Gerrit Smith, in the throes of his temperance enthusiasm, warned against taking the cup, advising that Christ had been unaware of the harmful effects of alcohol, the equally high-minded Arthur Tappan, in the throes of his own passion, recommended frequent holy communion. To which a wit re-sponded:

> Arthur Tappan, Arthur Tappan,
> Suppose It Should Happen—
> Mind, I'm only *supposing* it should—
> That some folks in the Union,
> Should take your Communion
> Too often by far for their good.

A more significant obstacle was the unspoken secularism of this materialistic people. The wild enthusiasm and unblushing irration-ality some Americans displayed toward otherworldly visions con-jured up by evangelical zealots were traits that, in the judgment of some, indeed paralleled those shown by others of their countrymen toward the great political leader of the era and the paradise prom-ised by his party's crack word painters. Far greater numbers re-sponded to the latter appeal than to the former. Was not this so because the Jacksonian promise was of this world?

American society followed no clear pattern in the Jacksonian era. It is hard to make unifying generalizations about the period's social trends, since the latter were not all of a piece. Egali-tarianism can be detected in one of the great religious movements of the time, but its purpose was to equalize not the conditions or opportunities of men in society but rather their chances of attain-ing salvation. (A witty scholar once said, referring to the great decision of nearly 4,000 years ago that permitted Egyptian com-moners to achieve immortality, that in ancient Egypt "rights for the masses meant rites for the masses.") In Jacksonian America minorities fared poorly. Cities grew unevenly and often unhappily, in large part because of racial and religious tensions. Yet cities did move, even if erratically, to face up to their problems. Medicine too followed a zigzag but upward course. The society as a whole was uniquely changeable and in that fact there was hope, particularly to a determinedly optimistic people who believed that change moved only in one direction.

5

THE INEGALITARIAN
SOCIETY

From May 11, 1831, to February 20, 1832, two young French aristocrats visited this country, commissioned by their government to study the American prison system. Among the results of their brief visit was a valuable account they wrote of American penitentiaries that came out in 1833. They observed a good deal more than prisons, however. In 1835 the more thoughtful of the two visitors, Alexis de Tocqueville, published the first part and in 1840 the second of *Democracy in America,* one of the most brilliant and penetrating studies of a civilization ever written. Surely it is among the most influential, as well, for from that day to our own the period it described has been known as the Era of the Common Man or the Age of Egalitarianism, in perfect accord with Tocqueville's own evaluation of it.

Tocqueville was not alone in depicting the American society of the second quarter of the 19th century in egalitarian terms. Many contemporaries, native Americans and European visitors alike, observed—or thought they observed—the same fluid social scene discerned by the young French aristocrat. Their joint perception of antebellum society is Tocquevillean not in the sense that its central propositions were original with Tocqueville but rather because no one else formulated the egalitarian thesis so comprehensively, so lucidly, so logically as he. Tocqueville's social portrait is a model of internal consistency.

According to the egalitarian theory equality of condition prevailed in Jacksonian America. Unfortunate minorities aside, few men here were either very rich or very poor. For that matter our rich were rich only by American standards, their wealth not comparing in magnitude to the great European fortunes. The near if not perfect equality of condition left little opportunity for the accumulation by individuals of vast surpluses. While classes did exist here, the differences between them were slight and diminishing, the barriers between them easily breached. Material success was accessible to all men, whatever their backgrounds. What rich men there were in America were typically self-made, born to poor or humble families. Nor did they hold on to their wealth for long. Flux ruled this dynamic society: riches and poverty were ephemeral states in this kaleidoscopic milieu. The limited extent and the precariousness of wealth explained the dwindling influence of those who possessed it. At a time when the most liberal of European states was grudgingly permitting some wealthy bourgeois to share the suffrage with the great landholders, the United States was brushing aside all important restrictions on voting. The deference characteristic of politics in the era of the Federalists and the Virginia aristocracy had given way to the strident rule of the masses, as the beleaguered social elite turned their backs on a democratic politics permeated with vulgarity, opportunism, and other unlovely expressions of popular power. A tyranny of the majority prevailed over government as it did over manners and all other important institutions of American life.

If the beauty of this thesis lies above all in its logic and coherence, it took hold as deeply and enduringly as it did because it seemed to be true to the facts of American life during the Jacksonian era. It not only told Americans what they wanted to hear; it told them what they had little difficulty convincing themselves was the actual case. Certainly there seemed to be much evidence to sustain this charming social portrait.

In the very first sentence of *Democracy in America*, Tocqueville had reported that nothing struck him "more forcibly than the general equality of condition among the people." From his time to our own a chorus of diverse commentators has agreed that with the exception of a few pariah ethnic and racial groups, the American people enjoyed an enviable material abundance. According to Michel Chevalier, who was sent here to study American public works by the French government two years after Tocqueville's departure, the "one thing that strikes a stranger is the appearance of general ease in the condition of the people of this country." Paupers were nowhere to be found, "every man was warmly clad . . . every woman had her cloak and bonnet of the latest Paris fashion." Even after the Panic of 1837 had struck, Charles Lyell reported that he "met with no beggars, witnessed no signs of want but everywhere the most unquivocal proofs of prosperity." If it could be said that the eminent geologist was so uncritical an admirer of American society that he even attributed beneficent features to American slavery, that charge could hardly be levelled at Mrs. Frances Trollope. For all her dislike of the manners and vulgarity of life in Cincinnati, like Lyell she was impressed by the absence of beggars on its streets. Buckingham, more detached than either the pollyannish Lyell or the "waspish" Mrs. Trollope, saw the same happy sight as they, observing that "you do not see anywhere in the streets persons asking alms or labouring under any visible want of the necessaries of life."

The glad tidings were also discerned by Americans. The popular writer Catherine Sedgwick assured her New England readers that there was no poverty in the area that was "not the result of vice or disease." Edward Everett detected an exuberant prosperity in the nation's cities, while William Dean Howells' father recalled that the farm folk of the Ohio Valley "usually had enough to eat." When Emerson wrote that "things are in the saddle riding mankind," he was saying, among other things, that the United States suffered from excess rather than from deprivation of material comforts. A writer in the *Washington Globe* of April 29, 1836, agreed, proclaiming, "We are all too rich, that is the greatest danger our simple republicans have to contend with." In his farewell address the following year, Andrew Jackson could cheerfully report that the small "planter, the farmer, the mechanic, and the laborer," the "overwhelming numbers" who represented "the bone and sinew of the country," owned "the great mass of our national wealth," which was "distributed in moderate amounts among the millions of free men who possess it."

Other evidence seemed to confirm the accuracy of these perceptions. During the antebellum decades ordinary farm families began to use or bring into their homes articles and implements earlier enjoyed only by the well-to-do, commodities serviceable in function if lacking in decorative detail. Gourmets might be discomfited at its quality but, as has been seen, there was universal agreement that the quantity of food was more than ample. A recent study that savages what its author calls the neurotic Andrew Jackson's brutal Indian policy, concludes that "whites prospered on the whole in Jacksonian America."

Nor has a consensus been lacking for the other elements of the egalitarian interpretation. Reminiscing about social life in New York City during the 1830s, a member of the city's social and economic elite recalled that the "comfortable independence" that was ostensibly available to most persons, "assured cordial welcome by one class to another." Visitors were startled at the social democracy of a society in which "a coarse familiarity is assumed by the grossest and the lowest in their intercourse with the highest and most refined." In this country of easy, endless handshaking—which so complicated the assignment of those observers who were trying to fix the social standing of individual Americans—prisoners were even observed shaking hands with a warden. "Aristocracy was doomed" here, as were "artificial distinctions in society," mourned the influential businessman, Samuel B. Ruggles.

The contemporary notion that social fluidity prevailed here was so pervasive that even Karl Marx believed it, writing at midcentury that social classes in America were "in a constant state of flux." Tocqueville's assertion that most wealthy Americans had been poor and were destined to fall again was not original with him. In 1832 the Philadelphia *National Gazette* observed that in this country "the sons of the poor die rich—while the sons of the rich die poor." Chastising striking workingmen, a judge in New York State reminded them that "in this favoured land of law and liberty the road to advancement is open to all." The common man was constantly reminded that "the most exalted positions" and great wealth were accessible to men of humble origin, since "merit and industry" rather than "exclusive privileges of birth" determined the course of an American's career. This belief in social flux and in what Henry Clay called "self-made men," came close to being an article of faith, so widely was it subscribed to by publishers, ministers, businessmen, leaders in the professions and in politics. Even the skeptical James Fenimore Cooper, who questioned whether wealth was in fact equally distributed here, attributed inequality of material condition to the equality of opportunity that he thought prevailed: since men differed in their capacity and industriousness, some succeeded while others fell by the wayside; but the competition was a fair and open one in which all had an equal chance. Giving sustenance to such beliefs were the well-known careers of men like John Jacob Astor, William E. Dodge, and Andrew Jackson himself, vivid examples of the rise from rags to riches or from the humblest circumstances to great success.

Neatly complementing contemporary beliefs in the common man's prosperity, his high status, and the ease with which he achieved worldly success was the conviction that, in Tocqueville's words, "the people reign in the American political world as the Deity does in the universe." A series of reforms democratizing the politics of Jacksonian America seemed to provide a solid underpinning to this belief. The overthrow of property requirements for voting,— at least for white adult males—the increasingly democratic system for voting for presidential electors, the discarding of the caucus system for nominating political candidates and its replacement by popularly-elected nominating conventions, dramatically increased the common man's control of government. The spoils system, particularly Jackson's own rationale for it, stressing as it did the ordinary citizen's ability to perform the tasks of government, was further evidence that politically as in other ways the age belonged to the common man. The rise of Andrew Jackson and the other "new men" who came to the fore after the end of the Virginia Dynasty was a sign that common men—albeit men of unusual determination and ability—had ascended to the highest levels of government. That humble origins were all the rage in the era of "Tippecanoe and Tyler Too" was one more sign that the people would no longer settle for leadership by an elite. Tom, Dick, and Harry insisted on leaders in their own image. The many historians who interpreted the party battles of the era as a warfare over great social and economic principles, in which Jackson's victories ostensibly represented a great popular success, helped win acceptance for the idea that the era of Andrew Jackson was the era of the common man.

Does the egalitarian thesis offer an accurate interpretation of antebellum society? That is the question. The original edition of this book held that the case for egalitarianism was not a strong one. It was put together largely by visitors on the run, many of whom had foibles that seriously detracted from their ability to understand and evaluate American society, relied excessively on logic, had a flimsy "factual foundation," rested on a number of questionable assumptions, and was contradicted by varied evidence to the contrary. (A friend who read a draft of my original chapter remarked, yes, it did a nice job of exposing flaws in the egalitarian interpretation: "too bad it did not offer substantial evidence" of its own.) Massive research conducted by historians during the past decade in previously neglected sources has finally enabled us to put the egalitarian thesis to the empirical or factual test that it had been previously spared.

I had earlier written that "a strong case can be made . . . that not equality but disparity of condition was the rule in Jacksonian America." An even stronger case can now be made for Jacksonian inequality. For by probing tax records, inventories of the property of persons recently deceased, manuscript census schedules, and other unpublished sources we have been able to discover for the first time who or what groups owned how much or what proportion of the wealth in almost every kind of milieu in antebellum America. The evidence is startling, even to those of us who were prepared to expect the worst. A small group of wealthy taxpayers held an inordinate amount of the wealth of their communities early in the era and a still greater share, almost twice the earlier portion, at its end. In the great cities of the northeast, the top 1 percent of wealthholders owned about one fourth of the wealth in the mid-1820s and about half the property by midcentury. For the smaller cities in other sections and for rural areas the proportions were not very much different, if somewhat less skewed or unbalanced. In the small borough of Stonington, Connecticut, for example, where in 1831 more than half the householders owned some property, no matter how modest the amount, by 1851 less than one third of them continued to do so. In Harris County, Texas, the wealthiest 5 percent of male adults owned more than 50 percent of the community's property in 1850. By midcentury the majority of Americans were assessed for no property whatever. This does not necessarily mean that they were either starving or penniless; it does mean that tax assessors and census takers estimated that most Americans owned no personal wealth or real property having any market value.

During the Jacksonian years persons were taxed not on income but on their personal and real property, paying their taxes to local rather than to national government. Historians have been able to estimate the wealth of all individuals by consulting the tax assessments. Since assessors had to make estimates that depended heavily on the potential taxpayers' own evaluations of their wealth, the assessments are neither precise nor totally reliable. Taxpayers were no more inclined then than they are now to make full disclosures of their worth. If anything, the tax evidence underestimates the extent of inequality, since it was the greatest wealthholders whose property was most flagrantly underassessed. During the Revolutionary era wealth had been unequally distributed but not nearly so markedly as in the Jacksonian period. In the phrase of Lee Soltow, a student of the 19th-century census data, "the proportions of owner- ship" at midcentury "are shockingly low." During the so-called era of the common man, the mass of the nation's inhabitants, white Prot- estants as well as blacks and recently-arrived Irish Catholics, owned practically none of its wealth.

The persons at the top of the wealth scale, on the other hand, were very rich indeed. Many dozens of families were worth millions of dollars each at a time when the purchasing power of the dollar was anywhere from 7 to 20 times that of the mid-20th century dollar. The small river city of Natchez contained two dozen individ- uals each of whom was a millionaire several times over in terms of the present value of his property. Men such as John Jacob Astor in New York City, Peter Chardon Brooks in Boston, or Stephen Girard in Philadelphia had princely fortunes that rivalled those accumulated by the richest men in Europe. (Tocqueville came to his inaccurate conclusion that no truly great fortunes existed here from his equally inaccurate assumption that wealth was so equally distributed that there were no surpluses to speak of.) In every geographical section the families who constituted the rich of the New World lived lives which rivalled in opulence and material splendor the lives enjoyed by the upper crust of the Old World. The great American fortunes may not have been as old as European, but fed from the diverse streams of commerce, insurance, finance, shipbuilding, manufac- turing, landholding, real estate speculation, and the professions, they rivalled Continental riches in magnitude.

Detailed evidence on individual families conveys more forcefully than do statistical tables the vast differences in the lifstyles of American families of unlike wealth levels. According to the million- aire William B. Astor a regular income of $10,000 per year enabled a city dweller to live lavishly in a comfortable house with servants, fine furnishings, a good table, good wines, a plentiful wardrobe, the ability to exercise the appropriate hospitality, and to maintain costly quarters in the country as well. Such an income may have been beyond the imagination of 99 percent of Americans but it was a mere pittance to the mercantile magnates of the North and the great planters of the South. The mansions known as town houses owned by David Sears, William B. Crosby, Harrison Gray Otis, Henry Brevoort, and other leaders of the urban elite, like the coun- try estates of Dr. David Hosack or John C. Stevens, would have been adjudged magnificent anywhere. Corps of servants, impressive libraries, elaborate furniture, sumptuous furnishings, stores of the finest wines, and expensive artworks filled the interiors of the homes of the American economic elite. In the warm weather months they retreated to the delights of the Rockaways and other ocean resorts or to the waters of Saratoga and regularly traveled to Havre in ships blessed with luxurious accommodations and, in Philip Hone's words, with "every day as good a table as the most fastidious gastronome could desire." Their lives at home during the workaday year were enlivened by a constant round of expensive parties, dazzling balls, extravagant fêtes, and excursions. The great ball given by Henry Brevoort on February 28, 1840, excited widespread attention for its extravagance, yet much space in Hone's more than 10,000 pages of diary is given over to description of smaller scale but equally splendid affairs, graced by eminences from North and South. Theater, Italian opera, soirees, and musical evenings also occupied the elite. Fastidious foreign visitors might mock the pretentiousness of the American elite's high life, but there could be no denying its expensiveness. In 1836 Parisian society was amazed at the "style of princely splendor" maintained by the fashionable New Yorker Herman Thorn or at his expenditure of close to $10,000 on a single fancy dress ball given at the magnificent palace that was his Paris home. Yet though Thorn was a rich man who, according to Hone, talked "about hundreds of thousands with the air of a man who has been brought up in the midst of gold, silver, and precious stones," there were close to 100 families in New York City alone whose wealth surpassed his.

The great mass of Americans lived very differently. As Stuart Blumin has recently observed, much is said but little is known about the antebellum "middle class," whether about its size or its standard of living. Soltow's reading of the midcentury census is that "middle wealth groups held very little wealth in America." Most people during the era were farmers, an estimated two thirds or more of the American working population making its living in agriculture. There were of course farmers and farmers, with successful but highly atypical operators of huge farms and plantations at one extreme and a much larger number of slaves at the other. While the situation of slaves was, as shall be shown, diverse, it would be ridiculous to regard them as anything other than the most unenvied and poorest group in American life. The wages of white farm hands and farm labor were even lower than the low wages earned by urban workers. Most farmers and farm families worked their own farms. The income of such farmers is notoriously hard to come by. Since these were people who largely consumed their own product, income is not the most relevant clue to their standard of living. In view of the unrevealing nature of the census data for the early 19th century, we continue to rely on random impressionistic evidence for a sense of the quality of farmers' lives in antebellum America. Diaries and journals left by moderately successful independent farm families in different sections of the country suggest the monotony, the hard work, and the generally poor quality of life experienced by the nation's yeomanry during the era. Thomas Coffin's family in New Hampshire worked hard, lived frugally and had little leisure. Ridding the farm of vermin constituted an amusement or form of recreation for the young. A large farm that was regarded as "fairly well improved," located on one of the "better developed farm communities" in Iredell County, North Carolina, characteristically eked out a living, its "produce yielding only a small return for the work involved, while prices of necessities bought were high." Living conditions were indeed discouraging to men who found that their incomes from sales frequently only balanced their purchases.

The plight of numberless poor farm folk was even more grim. The recently unearthed diary kept by an upstate New Yorker, Henry Conklin, reveals the desperate poverty that dominated the lives of his family and their neighbors. His sister Ruth was a workhorse at age six while his brothers Julius and Samuel "were bound out" until they were 21 years old by a father who could not afford to take care of them himself. Coming of a family that was too poor to own a cow, young Henry never saw a piece of factory cloth, and it was not until he was 12 that he was presented with a new pair of shoes— "the first [he] had had in [his] life"—and his family finally got a "cook stove." For the six years prior to 1843 Conklin's family "had been so poor that we had only one suit of clothes to our backs and when mother wanted to wash them she had to do it while we were abed at night or undressed and go to bed in the daytime while she washed and dried our clothes." Wendell Tripp does not exaggerate when he observes that "the central theme of Henry Conklin's reminiscence is poverty." In Conklin's poignant phrase, his and most neighboring families lived "in poverty's vale" during the Jacksonian era. And American farmers appear to have believed that their status in society was low. The "agrarian myth" that romanticized rural life was either unknown to most farmers or disbelieved by them.

Lacking the resources that even poor agricultural families might fall back on, working people during the era lived lives of unparalleled precariousness. For the better part of the period, the artisans and mechanics who composed the bulk of the urban population put in a work day that rivalled the farmer's sunup to sundown. The spectre of unemployment haunted them, particularly in the cold weather months of short working days, when employers had to pay for the light that the sun gave freely during other working seasons. In view of their low wages, workingmen had little to fall back on when their shops closed down, as they often did. In the decade of inflation that preceded the Panic of 1837, workers discovered that their wages did not keep up with runaway prices. The depression that came on the heels of the Panic kept perhaps one third of the working classes unemployed for long periods in the early 1840s. Quite apart from the depression years, labor fared poorly during the Jacksonian era. Most modern studies indicate that real wages stood still during an otherwise exuberant economic surge in the 1830s, at best approximating what they had been at the turn of the century. Jeffrey Williamson, who disagrees with the contention of Paul David and Stanley Lebergott that real wages fell during the second quarter of the 19th century, concedes that the poorer members of the working class suffered a "double deterioration in their relative economic position," affecting both their income or wages of employment and their expenditures or the prices they paid for consumer goods: "urban inequality [became] worse in real terms." Writing in the New York *Daily Tribune* on July 9, 1845, at a time when the working classes were "probably as well employed as ever before" and the city was "enjoying an unusual degree of . . . prosperity," it was Horace Greeley's "deliberate estimate, the result of much inquiry that the average earnings" of the city's working people—"embracing at least ⅔ of our population"—was a "pittance," that "scarcely, if at all, exceeds $1 per week for each person subsisting thereon." The many dozens of journals constituting the nation's labor press painted an even gloomier picture.

The living conditions of the laboring poor ranged from dismal to abysmal. Andrew Jackson could repair to the 'Hermitage," outside of Nashville, and his political enemy Nicholas Biddle to "Andalusia," near Philadelphia, mansions similar in their opulence for all the seeming ideological differences of their owners. Working people lived very differently. According to Mathew Carey, the wealthy philanthropist, working-class families in Philadelphia were squeezed together, 55 families to a tenement, lacking "the accommodation of a privy for their use." Their houses, according to a recent study, "were strung along, side to side as boxcars . . . obscured from the street view. . . ." Their tenants typically had one room per family, living "huddled to the rear . . . victims of a parsimonious building policy which meant crowding, noise, inadequate sanitation, lack of facilities for rubbish removal." According to the labor press, the major cities of the nation abounded with dismal alleys, "the abodes of the miserable objects of grinding poverty." Official reports in a number of the nation's cities expressed horror at both the overcrowding and the lack of ventilation and sanitary facilities in working-class housing and the biased public policy which barred or delayed access to urban improvements to the working-class areas which most desperately needed them.

Glaring disparities were not confined to housing alone. If beggars were not readily apparent on the streets, they could be discerned in less public places. Bell had seen "scores of destitute homeless wretches lying on bulks or under the sheds about the markets of New York and Philadelphia." Fellow travelers claimed they saw as much poverty here as elsewhere. Statistical studies confirmed the rising rates of pauperism and of those too poor to pay a minimal tax. Nor does the evidence indicate that membership in these forlorn groups was swelled by the dramatic failure of eminent men. Rather some poor men became poorer. It was estimated that in Boston in 1834 more than 5,000 persons were "aided annually as paupers." Edward Abdy reported that not only was pauperism increasing in the nation's cities, but that there was "little reason to hope it [could] be checked by the judicious application of charity."

Americans were still being imprisoned for debt in Jacksonian America, accounting for the majority of those serving jail sentences in many cities. This practice was shortly to be outlawed, largely because its negative effects were felt by businessmen as well as by the poor. In that era, however, its main victims, estimated at 20,000 in New York, Pennsylvania, and Massachusetts alone, were men who owed debts of $20 or less. As Peter Coleman observes, "the poor were the chief victims." Imprisoned debtors had been "petty traders rather than merchant princes, farmers rather than planters, employees rather than employers, artisans rather than capitalists."

The burden of the impressionistic evidence as well as of the quantitative data that modern historians have brought to light is that not equality but a general inequality of condition among the people was the "central feature" of American life during the Jacksonian era.

We have also learned a great deal—if not nearly so much as we need to know—about social mobility during the era. I had originally suggested that while Tocqueville's assertion that most rich Americans were formerly poor might "yet turn out to be right," it should be treated skeptically, since it was "based not on substantial evidence but rather on his own deductions, largely from what one informant told him concerning the disappearance of the law of entail in this country." In other words, the verdict was out. The verdict brought in by the investigations of recent years is that this Tocquevillean notion is as false as is his belief in Jacksonian equality of condition.

Tocqueville's logic, as always, was excellent, for certainly it followed that in a dynamic social democracy, "the conditions of life are very fluctuating, men have almost always recently acquired the advantages which they possess [and] at any moment the same advantages may be lost." The United States and his ideal democracy, however, were two most unlike things. As Tocqueville admitted, he was discussing "the image of democracy itself," rather than the actual United States. In the words of a contemporary French critic: "Tocqueville describes America but he thinks of Europe." The English visitor, J. S. Buckingham, turns out to have been closer to the mark than Tocqueville, when he wrote that "the greater number" of wealthy Americans "inherit land, or houses, or stock, from their parents."

A recent examination of the careers and backgrounds of the 2,000 or so individuals who composed the northeastern urban rich reveals that some of the best-known among them did in fact have the kind of background ascribed to them by Tocqueville. The richest American of all, John Jacob Astor, came of obscure and probably humble parents, while his successful partner, Cornelius Heeney, migrated from Ireland apparently with less than a dollar in his pocket to become one of the wealthiest and most philanthropic citizens in Brooklyn. Several other stories of rags to riches matched Heeney's. If evidence is thus not lacking that some rich men had in fact been born poor, "the most interesting feature of such evidence is its uncommonness." Detailed information on about three fourths of the interurban rich reveals that the overwhelming majority of wealthy persons—slightly more than 90 percent—were descended of parents and families who combined affluence with high social status. Only about 2 percent of the urban socioeconomic elite were born poor, with the remaining 6 or 7 percent born into families of middling status: modestly successful ministers and professionals, petty officials, small shopkeepers, artisans who doubled as small tradesmen, moderately prosperous farmers. A recent study of ante-bellum Newport's elite of about 250 shows that their backgrounds were remarkably similar to those of the upper crust in the great metropolises.

Many of the era's richest men, while born into affluence, man-aged to carve out fortunes that far surpassed their original inheri-tances. Such persons were self-made only in a special sense, their careers hardly illustrating what publicists of the era meant by that term. That the children of wealthy or well-to-do parents, living in an age of dynamic growth, convert their original advantages into yet greater fortunes is not a sign of social mobility. A family whose adult heads had for several generations been among the economic elite of their city and community cannot be said to have experienced upward social movement because their inordinate wealth kept in-creasing.

The marked similarity in the wealth levels and social standing of the Jacksonian rich and their parents and grandparents is, in tech-nical sociological terms, a sign of slight *intergenerational* economic or social mobility. The Tocquevillean thesis that American fortunes were both scanty and "insecure," with wealth ostensibly circulating with "inconceivable rapidity" during the lifetimes of individuals rep-resents a belief in *intragenerational* social or vertical mobility. A modern economic historian writes that the Jacksonian period was "a highly speculative age in which fortunes were made and lost overnight, in which men rose and fell . . . with dexterous agility." As a friend of Henry Clay had observed, "money and property among us are constantly changing hands." Evidence on the alleged rise and fall of fortunes during the lifetimes of the northeastern rich does not substantiate this notion of intragenerational flux.

Since many contemporaries claimed that the careers of wealthy merchants and professionals followed an erratic course in this kaleidoscopic economy, a modern study investigated changes over short-run or five-year periods to determine whether northeasterners who started and ended the race for wealth strongly may have lagged in between. They did not. "Few new great families sprang up while fewer still fell away." Since the midcentury population had in-creased substantially, the enlarged ranks of the later rich neces-sarily had to be filled by many persons who earlier were not among the wealthy or the richest 1 percent. Yet these "newcomers" were "more often than not from *families* of great wealth." In New York City they were younger members of the Lenox, Lorillard, Bronson, Cruger, Remsen, and other families of similar wealth and distinc-tion. For New York City, Brooklyn, and Boston, the extent of an individual's early fortune was the major factor determining whether he would be among the rich later. Increases in wealth followed the rule: the greater an individual's initial wealth, the more likely was it to enjoy an increase and the greater the amount by which it was augmented.

The pursuit of wealth during the era was marked not by fluidity but by stability if not rigidity. Great fortunes earlier accumulated held their own through all manner of vicissitudes. The tax records disclose for example that the Panic of 1837 appeared to have no effect on the slight rate by which the mighty fell or the puny rose. In Boston, of the owners of the modest property evaluated at between $5,000 and $7,000 just prior to the Panic, less than 1 percent became significantly wealthier in its wake, while slightly more than one third were hurt seriously or compelled to leave the city. In contrast, only two of the nearly 100 Bostonians each worth $100,000 suffered substantial losses, with about 23 percent enjoying gains of $20,000 or more in the immediate aftermath of the crisis.

Nor were such patterns of social stability confined to the urban northeast. Alexandra McCoy's study of Wayne County, Michigan, for the latter part of the Jacksonian era, defines mobility as "the achievement of wealth by men of lower class origins," and finds very little evidence of the phenomenon. The economic elite of that important area were not self-made men. Like the successful men of a half century later, shown by William Miller and his students to be fortunate sons of wealthy fathers, Wayne County's rich seem to have "enjoyed an advantaged early environment to enable them to start a business in the west." Plebeians could not afford the five or six thousand dollars required. If the wealthy were born of the rich, they also tended to remain in that closed circle. "Those [in Wayne County] who were at the top in 1844 tended to stay there. Only one took a fall."

Social mobility is not confined to movement into or out of the wealthiest or most socially prestigious classes or categories. Technically, social mobility is movement from one social *position* to another. (In view of the continuing controversy as to how best measure position, some scholars emphasizing such tangible indices as wealth or occupation, others stressing the intangible "status," it seems sensible to avoid an abstract discussion of definitions. Here I am guided by what I regard as Robert A. Dahl's good sense in suggesting that "power" is a useful term so long as no attempt is made to define it.) For all of the emphasis by Tocqueville and other contemporaries on the rich, social movement into and out of more modest categories is at least as important and may throw more light on the character of a society than do dramatic leaps from rags to riches or equally dramatic falls in the opposite direction. The recent evidence is scattered, lighting up only a small portion of the antebellum social landscape. If it is neither abundant nor definitive, it is nevertheless useful, providing us a far more solid basis than we had earlier had for generalizing about the common man's social opportunity during the period.

Using occupations and residential locations by wards as his criteria for social position—useful but flawed indices, both, since occupations are internally differentiated and not necessarily responsible for the wealth levels associated with them in the census schedules, while wards contain within them streets and houses of diametrically opposed reputation—Stuart Blumin has done a substantial study of social mobility in Jacksonian Philadelphia. Tracing the social movement of random individuals over ten-year periods, between 1820 and 1860, Blumin's evidence discloses that what social movement took place was more marked between the lower than the higher of his five rungs. And when men did move upward, they did not move far, their motion occurring "between closely related occupations." Craftsmen or blue-collar workingmen rarely changed to the white collars of the middle classes. For the relatively few who did experience "vertical mobility," white-collar employees moved into slightly higher white-collar categories, with "manual workers moving into higher manual positions." Blumin concludes that "in purely quantitative terms, then, [social] mobility appears to have been fairly stable" rather than fluid or dynamic "in the four decades immediately preceding the Civil War." He attributes the rising amount of downward mobility to structural changes in the early industrial economy that were undermining the position of skilled craftsmen while sharply increasing the proportion of manual workers in the city.

Blumin's more recent study of a small community, Kingston, New York, concludes that "the chances for economic success for unskilled workers" there "were not very great" at midcentury. Working people in antebellum Kingston were much more likely to have been geographically rather than socially mobile, precisely as was the case in Boston. Richard Jones's study of the whaling and sealing center, Stonington, Connecticut, discloses an almost total absence of upward social movement in that small but not insignificant community. From one decade to another between 1820 and 1860, the minority who were property owners "were with [almost] no exceptions descended from fathers who had also owned property in the town." Only one unskilled laborer acquired taxable property in the borough during the 60 years before the Civil War. Becoming a property owner was difficult in Stonington "because the occupations by which property could be accumulated were not open to everyone on an equal basis." Success in the professions, for example, "required extensive education out of reach of all but the comfortable."

In a study that in a sense skips across the Jacksonian era, Gary Nash compared the social backgrounds of men becoming lawyers in Philadelphia in 1800 and 1861. The results are interesting because unusual, an oasis of increasing social movement in what seems otherwise a desert of social rigidity. The same small proportion of Philadelphians, 12 percent, entered the legal profession from the "lower classes"—"artisans, laborers, and [poor or small] farmers"—in each period. But where 72 percent of the 1800 sample belonged to the "upper class" of "wealthy landowners, merchants, and manufacturers, and prominent lawyers, doctors, and clergymen," with only 16 percent in the "middle class" of "prosperous, if not wealthy farmers, the less successful professional types, shopkeepers, minor officeholders, and bureaucratic functionaries," by 1860–61, 44 percent came of each of these two classes. The Phila-

delphia bar had become more accessible to middle—if not to working—class young men. The democratization of Philadelphia's legal
profession was somewhat akin to the changes that Richard E. Mitch-
ell has recently shown took place in the late Roman Republic's
bureaucracy, when "new men" were required to fill the places
created by conquest. Just as the newly ascendant plebeians occupied
the *lesser* magistracies in ancient Rome, so Philadelphia's new attorneys did not compete with the social eminences, the Whartons,
Merediths, Walns, and Peppers, who continued to dominate the
most lucrative and prestigious practices. As Maxwell Bloomfield and
William E. Nelson have recently shown, lawyers during the era
accepted and rationalized their own elite status, regardless of their
individual differences in background, with the law used increasingly
by large propertied elements as a tool designed to maintain their
ascendancy.

Colleges, even the smaller and less prestigious ones that proliferated in rural New England during the era, continued to be too
expensive for all but sons of the affluent. Yet institutional and
financial support did enable farm boys to attend in increasing numbers. While the achievement of a degree offered these young men
"no great material reward" as school teachers or ministers, it did
offer a favorable alternative to the labor that would otherwise have
been their lot.

Although not the product of a quantitative study, my own impression, drawn from an examination of the careers of many eminent
Jacksonians is that the era's political leaders, like Philadelphia's
lawyers, were increasingly men who had been born into the nation's
plebian orders. Of course to the constituents of the politicians, as to
the clients of the attorneys, the important question concerns the
present behavior and the social philosophies of these men rather
than their earlier socioeconomic status. If, as often happens, men
on ascending socially swiftly absorb the ideology of their new social
group and close ranks with its other members in defending its
interests, the social mobility experienced by the newcomers would
have little effect on the community's social structure.

Whatever the rates of social mobility—and they appear to have
been dramatically slight in Jacksonian America—they do not fore-
close the possibility that there was nevertheless equality of opportunity or what David Potter called "parity in competition" during the
era. For it is conceivable that the era's successful men reached the
top, not because of their inherited wealth, but because of their
talent and ability. The evidence, however, indicates that if dramatic
upward climbs were more fanciful than real in Jacksonian America,
competition was also marked by anything but parity. The absence of
legal disabilities did not mean that poor men started the race for
success on equal terms with their more favored contempararies.

According to Charles Astor Bristed, the young man who hoped to
gain entry into New York's upper one thousand was one who,
possessed of "fair natural abilities, adds to these the advantages of
inherited wealth, a liberal education and foreign travel." It need

hardly be pointed out that the travel and liberal education mentioned by Bristed were not available to most Americans. Rather, they were accessible to men such as Abram C. Dayton, son of "an opulent merchant" of New York City, who had "all the accomplishments that education, travel and wealth could give." They were available to Andrew Gordon Hamersley, who inherited from his father a fortune, which, by "judicious management," he succeeded in substantially enlarging. Like other of his golden contemporaries he never went into business, owing his success rather to his name, his original possessions, and his "entertaining conversation and courtly manner." They were available to John Collins Warren, Valentine Mott, David Hosack, and Philip Syng Physick, brilliant physicians all, who from childhood had moved in the most rarified circles, attending the greatest universities and studying with the most learned masters at home and abroad, accumulating much wealth largely because they had much to begin with. Means rather than need gave one access to the services of these eminences.

It is of course possible that innate ability or a fortunate genetic inheritance accounted for the success achieved by most of the era's socioeconomic elite. Such traits no doubt played a significant part in some cases. The biographical data indicate, however, that a material inheritance was the great initial advantage that enabled most of those fortunate enough to have it to become worldly successes. Dahl has contended that the era was marked by a "cumulative inequality: when one individual was much better off than another in one resource, such as wealth, he was usually better off in almost every other resource," including political influence. It is clear that almost all of the era's successful and wealthy urbanites had initially been much better off than their fellows in possessing the "resource" of wealth.

The race was indeed to the swift, but unfortunately the requisite swiftness was beyond the power of ordinary men to attain. For this swiftness was of a special sort. Unlike the speed of thoroughbred horses, which is a rare but a natural if inbred gift, the ability to cover great ground in the race for human material success appeared to depend less on the possession of innate abilities than on the inheritance of the artificial gifts of wealth and standing. During the "age of the common man" opportunity was hardly more equal than was material condition.

The egalitarian theory is also based on certain assumptions concerning social class and its role. It does not deny the existence of classes but stresses rather the easy fraternization that supposedly bound members of the different social classes together. There are almost as many definitions of class as there are scholars offering them, stressing such criteria as wealth, occupation, income, family, quality of education, the intangibles of prestige and standing, residential location, religious denomination, uses of leisure, and varying combinations of these and other variables. In Jacksonian America classes appear to have been differentiated from one another above all by wealth and the quality as well as the costliness of the lives they led. If their fortunes were of sufficient magnitude, men and families new to eminence usually earned quick acceptance into the highest social circles. Aristocratic upper crusts rate men not by wealth alone, yet it should be kept in mind that even the haughty English aristocracy of the Tudor-Stuart era treated the size of an individual's fortune as the vital qualification for determining whether he would remain within their charmed circle. We have seen that in contradiction to the claims of egalitarianism, the disparities between the classes were massive and the movement of individuals between them glacial during the antebellum era. Were close social relations between their members nevertheless commonplace?

The sociologist Harold M. Hodges, Jr., has observed that a class society manifests itself above all in the exclusiveness and the walls of separation it erects about such institutions as marriage, "friendship characterized by mutual entertainment in homes, common membership in 'social' organizations, and simply mutual visiting." Evidence drawn from diverse types of community in all parts of the country indicates that in Hodges' terms antebellum America was very much a class society. Wealthy and prestigious families everywhere constructed barriers designed to prevent social inferiors from entering the private world inhabited by the socioeconomic elite.

Contemporaries had not failed to detect evidences of class exclusiveness here. One informant told Tocqueville that rich Americans might be democratic enough to receive a man of talent but they would make him aware that he was not rich and refuse to receive his wife and children. Vigne found an "exclusive aristocracy in every city of the Union; and perhaps as many as four or five different sects or circles, notwithstanding their boasted equality of condition." Logan would have reduced the number of elite strata to three. Grund discovered that it was not simply that the fashionable would not mingle with the vulgar; in Boston, good society would not permit itself to be seen publicly. The "second society" of that city— itself unacceptable to the "first"—with a vulgarity peculiar to itself, was said in turn to display contempt for those below them. Nor was such repellant behavior confined to Boston. In *Home As Found*, Cooper wrote a biting satire directed against the varieties of class snobbishness practiced in American cities and villages. A number of visitors, while conceding the pretentiousness of Boston, gave the nod to Philadelphia as the most exclusive of cities. Bell was told that there were "nine or ten distinct ranks in the city, beginning at the lower class of traders and ending in the dozen or so who keep . . . a large establishment; each of these circles, repelling and repelled, carefully keeps itself apart, and draws a line that no one of doubtful status may pass." Murray believed that with the passage of time these lines were drawn more tightly than ever. Even Tocqueville made the uncharacteristic admission at the close of his second chapter that "the picture of American society has . . . a surface covering of democracy, beneath which the old aristocratic colors sometimes peep out." Evidence unearthed by recent scholarship suggests that the "old aristocratic colors" permeated the entire fabric of American society rather than merely "peep out" beneath the surface.

Modern sociologists agree that one of the most significant tests of "the 'openness' of social structure is the extent of marriages between persons of different social origins." For as Bernard Barber has observed, "marriage is the most complete and reliable expression of social intimacy and social equality." Data on the marital behavior of almost all families belonging to the northeastern socioeconomic elite and on their social equals elsewhere indicate that they married as though by a rule of social endogamy. During the second quarter of the 19th century wealthy families whose members entered into marriage did so almost without exception with partners whose own families possessed similar wealth and standing. Marriages uniting eminent families of different cities—such as the Boston Sargents and the Philadelphia Binneys, the New York Jays and the Brooklyn Pierreponts, the Boston Coolidges and the Virginia Randolphs—illustrated both the force of social considerations in the matrimonial choices made by the elite and their cosmopolitanism.

What Lawrence Stone has written about the English peerage of the early modern era appears to apply too to the upper classes in antebellum America: "they mostly married among themselves." It may be that to the upper crust here as abroad, "essentially marriage was not a personal union for the satisfaction of psychological and physiological needs; it was an institutional device to ensure the perpetuation of the family and its property. The greatest attention was therefore paid to the financial benefits of marriage." To the aristocratic Englishman's expression of surprise that elegant Americans married for money as often as did his own countrymen, Charles Astor Bristed has his fictional American reply: "They don't marry for anything else." Commenting on the marriage of a friend, Hone reported to his diary that the man on this day had "married 2 or $300,000." The mother of John Tyler's wealthy and aristocratic wife, Julia Gardiner, regularly admonished her daughters that "unless a young woman had a fortune in her own right," she should not "marry any man without means."

This is not to say that mercenary considerations were the sole or necessarily the predominant ones on the minds of the sons and daughters of the antebellum elite. Since novelists are like God—at least in their power over the characters they create—Jane Austen and Balzac could speak with certainty of the materialistic motives underlying the marriages they describe. Historians can only infer motives. My own view of the complex evidence is that idiosyncratic factors, romantic love, physical passion,—those assorted foolishnesses that compel one person to want another—combined with other, practical considerations in the thinking and feeling of elite individuals contemplating marriage. The precise balance of these ingredients doubtless varied with each case. Yet it would be unrealistic to discount sentiment and the element of personal desire in these matters. When a carefree son of a prestigious New York family broke up an elite marriage by stealing the affections of the wife, we can be fairly sure that financial gain was not solely on his mind and certain that it was not at all on hers.

The fair game in this pursuit was a woman of eminence as well as beauty. Recognition of the roles of youthful independence and the emotions in the marital choices made by the upper crust hardly refutes the interpretation that swells sought to marry swells. They may have wanted them for a variety of reasons but want them they did. For if the private social world of the elite was confined almost entirely to their own sort, great ardor if and when it erupted would be great ardor felt for social equals. And the record suggests strongly that the antebellum upper classes did inhabit a most exclusive social universe.

Those sociologists who interpret a social class as a stratum of society "composed of individuals who accept each other as equals" who are "qualified for intimate association," are particularly interested in how and with whom members of different classes spend their leisure time. Evidence of this sort for the Jacksonian era is understandably random and in short supply. For we are dealing here with private matters that do not lend themselves quantitative analysis. Fortunately, Philip Hone, retired New York City merchant and social lion, did record his social experiences in the amazingly detailed diary he kept between 1826 and 1851. Hone's descriptions of social visits, dinner parties, excursions to the country, summer holidays, sleigh rides, fancy balls, weddings, funerals, restaurant meals, fishing trips, boat rides, "cultural evenings," and informal parties better than any other source reveal not only the lifestyle of the urban elite but precisely which individual participated in shaping it. Our knowledge of the wealth and eminence of most of these persons makes it possible to know the ranking of each person present at the private gatherings of New York City's socio-economic elite. Almost without exception the persons with whom Hone dined or socialized over the course of the second quarter of the 19th century belonged to the wealthiest 1 percent of the community.

Hone emerges an increasingly crotchety but unfailingly honest diarist. Who can disbelieve him when he writes that he preferred some individuals to others because of their "agreeableness," good sense, and intellectual or social attractiveness? At no point did Hone refer to great wealth as a required characteristic of those with whom he would be intimate. Yet, as a very wealthy man himself, he like other rich men was part of a social set inhabited almost exclusively by those who had been similarly fortunate in worldly accumulation. The 60 persons who regularly mingled with Hone and belonged to families that intermarried with his were Astors, Brevoorts, Howlands, Livingstons, Schermerhorns, Ludlows, Minturns, Stuyvesants, Whitneys, and others of comparable eminence. All of these were not the very richest men or what I have called the "super rich" of New York City. Hone no more than other men chose his friends on the basis of a dollar and cents calculus. What is of great interest, however, is that almost all of the group indeed belonged on such a list, while the few who were not at the very top were not far below.

Hone's social life was of course not necessarily typical. It does not follow that persons on his social list similarly restricted their own circles. Yet a great deal of evidence gives us reason to believe that Hone's social orbit was similar to the one traveled by many other wealthy persons. The social world of his own intimates was similar to his in scope and values. Other notable diaries kept by leading men of New York and other cities tell stories similar to, if not nearly so full as, Hone's. Sidney George Fisher was no doubt right that wealth was not the only "passport to the best Philadelphia society," nor want of it a reason for exclusion. And yet the brilliant array whose company he kept, whose homes he visited, whose presence added luster to the balls and parties he attended, were almost invariably the upper stratum of Philadelphia society and wealth—Biddles, Walns, Willings, Gilpins, Whartons, Cadwaladers, Ridgeways, Mifflins, Binneys, Wistars, Merediths, and others of like reputation, all of them bound together for generations by a "great degree of intimacy."

Further reflecting the exclusive social habits and ideals of the antebellum rich were their social clubs. Elitist social organizations were not a new feature of American life. Socially restrictive clubs had come into existence even before the end of the Revolution. What was distinctive in the early 19th century was the sharp increase in the number of such groups and the more elaborate and formal structures they assumed. Informal gatherings, such as the "Hone Club" in New York City, the "Wistar parties" in Philadelphia, and the salons held regularly in the lavish home of Thomas Handasyd Perkins, Jr., in Boston, effectively screened out all but members of the upper crust. The only exceptions to this rule were men eminent in politics and such renowned cultural figures as William Thackeray, Baron von Humboldt, and Charles Dickens, with the latter the guest of honor at the inevitable "Boz Balls" that were given in his honor.

Some of the larger urban social clubs professed concern with public issues. Their constitutions, bylaws, and exceedingly high initiation fees and dues payments show that they were concerned more with restricting their memberships to the "fashionables" or "exclusives" as they were variously called. The Union Club of New York City is a case in point. Founded in 1836 by 12 leaders of the city's social elite, it was modelled after the upperclass clubs of London which, according to Hone, gave a "tone and character to the society of the British metropolis." The organizers sent out letters inviting membership only to "gentlemen of social distinction," families eminent in Peter Stuyvesant's day together with those whose wealth and renown were more recent. Wealthy and eminent persons in each of the great cities were eager to proclaim their standing as well as to emulate the style of an aristocracy in a society lacking in official or formal emblems of social hierarchy. The "primary function" of these clubs appears to have been the one ascribed by E. Digby Baltzell to Philadelphia's elite clubs—"the ascription of upper class status."

The residential behavior of the urban upper class offers yet another significant clue both to their social ideals and to the existence of class barriers in Jacksonian society. They not only lived in expensive homes, fitted out with sumptuous furnishings, as has been noted, but they lived among their own sort. In no city was there precisely the situation found by Floyd Hunter in 20th-century Atlanta, where almost every member of the "covert elite" that allegedly ran the city lived in splendor in one small enclave. The amazing thing is how similar to the modern Atlanta pattern was that of most antebellum cities. Two thirds of Brooklyn's wealthiest families lived on the streets of Brooklyn Heights, a charming neighborhood that covered a tiny portion of the total area of what was then the nation's seventh city. Most of New York City's rich lived on 8 of the city's more than 250 streets, concentrated near the southern tip of Manhattan and lower Broadway. More than one half of Philadelphia's leading families lived on a few blocks of Walnut, Mulberry, and Chestnut Streets. As for the elite of Boston—the families Oliver Wendell Holmes called "the sifted few"—most of them lived on 6 of the city's 325 streets in the Beacon Hill, Fort Hill, and Summer Street areas. That this pattern of exclusivity was not uncontrived is indicated by the pains taken by the wealthy residents on the southern slope of Beacon Hill to make it inaccessible to the poorer folk on the northern slope.

Nor was the attempt by the elite to isolate their homes from those of social inferiors confined to the northeast. In the smaller cities and towns of the other sections of the country the same trend was discernible. As Richard Wade has observed, "social lines could be plotted on a map" of the southern and western cities on the "urban frontier." In the "pre-horse car era" of the mid-19th century, Milwaukee's "upper classes sought residences near the central business district," away from the lower orders of the population. Houston's antebellum elite were rare, in scattering themselves throughout the city's wards; Kenneth Wheeler, modern historian of the city, believes this seeming "egalitarianism" may have been a shrewd move on their part that made it easier for them to exercise political control over the city. But in Galveston, as in most other communities in Texas and elsewhere, the "elite created an island for itself" in choice locations effectively closed off to all others.

Reducing slightly the pattern of elite housing concentration was the fact that many cities contained old families who were not about to tear down mansions going back generations because the neighborhoods were no longer fashionable. Elite enclaves did not follow smooth or obvious forms. A microscopic analysis of street maps shows that then as now many poor persons lived on plebeian alleys and streets that bordered the neighborhoods of the upper crust. Yet even when ordinary folk lived on the streets of the rich, they did not live on the same blocks with them. The elite were clustered together in contiguous rows rarely infiltrated by social or economic outsiders. Both the movement of their feet and their private comments indicate that an ideal of class exclusiveness influenced the rich and the eminent in their choice of residential location, precisely as it did in their choice of social intimates and marriage partners.

The Jacksonian upper classes were a group apart. Rather than mingle on terms of easy familiarity with the masses or the middling orders, as they were said to have done, they appear to have drawn an ever tighter circle about their own prestigious social world. As men of affairs, they unavoidably rubbed shoulders with other social types, charming observers on-the-run in the process, with what the latter regarded as a species of social levelling. The pursuit of success and social harmony compelled the upper orders to do business and maintain contact with the lower and middling. But in their private affairs, were they were free to indulge their personal feelings and deepest social values, the antebellum elite rejected egalitarianism for class exclusiveness.

The capstone of the egalitarian interpretation is that commoners controlled government, as they controlled most other forms of power, during the Jacksonian era. The expansion of the suffrage and other democratic political reforms were interpreted by Tocqueville's generation as a sign that in this country the people were sovereign. A "popular despotism" ruled America, said Chevalier. Unfortunately, as the experience of 20th century totalitarianism demonstrates, popular suffrage is not quite the same thing as popular power. Voting rights may go hand in hand with the political powerlessness of those who possess those rights.

In Jacksonian America the common (white) man's possession of the suffrage subjected him to much flattery by political leaders, for it is quite true that his votes decided whether this or that one would take elective office. An outpouring of modern studies reveal that regardless of party affiliation, the men elected to office in antebellum elections, whether in North or South, East or West, whether on the national, state, county, or town level were with few exceptions inordinately well-to-do and of high prestige occupation, rather than small farmers, clerks and workingmen. For all the differences in their political rhetoric, the major parties of the era were more like than unlike, not least in the extent to which their basic strategies and policymaking apparatus were controlled by relatively wealthy men.

How much power could the common man exercise when there was little real choice left open to him by the parties that counted? In the states, small groups of well-to-do insiders—"juntos," "regencies," machines by whatever name —had tight control over policymaking, with popular influence more nominal than real. Whether in New York or Mississippi, Pennsylvania or South Carolina, Michigan or New Jersey, Massachusetts or Florida, Tennessee or Ohio, Democratic leaders, more often than not, were speculators, editors, lawyers, the "land office crowd," coming from the "wealthier elements in the society," typically of the same economic background as their Whig opponents. For that matter, Andrew Jackson himself, not to mention the men who launched him in presidential politics, was uncommonly wealthy. As Robert V. Remini has noted, "it cost a great deal of money to enter politics." Jackson may have spoken in ringing terms of the common man's right to high office, as well as his ability to perform its tasks, but in point of fact Jackson, like his "aristocratic" predecessors, filled Cabinet and high civil service posts with men who possessed unusual wealth and social eminence. This is not to say that the era's leaders dealt with political issues primarily in terms of class interest. It is not farfetched, however, to interpret the lack of real issues on the national level in the decade of the 1820s, or the ambiguity of issues in the subsequent decades of the Jacksonian era, as due in part to the backgrounds of the era's leaders. (The era's politics and political issues are examined closely in subsequent chapters. The generalizations in this section are based on diverse primary sources and hundreds of older and contemporary studies.)

The political impotence of ordinary persons was particularly apparent in local communities, where wealth exerted power most directly. In cities throughout the country, mayors' offices were filed by an almost unbroken succession of wealthy merchants, men such as Philip Hone in New York, Harrison Gray Otis in Boston, James Hamilton and Robert Y. Hayne, who ran antebellum Charleston in the interests of the banks and railroads they represented. Nor was the socioeconomic status of city councilmen and aldermen significantly different from that of mayors. Local legislatures were composed of merchants, lawyers, men of affairs and eminence, and a sprinkling of successful artisan-entrepreneurs. Rarely present in these bodies were the journeymen mechanics and the laborers who constituted the majority in their communities.

More significant than the backgrounds of urban officeholders were the policies they pursued. The modern historians of antebellum urban politics speak almost with one voice. Jacksonian era cities were governed by the propertied for the propertied. As Michael Frisch reports for Springfield, Massachusetts, there was little public involvement in politics "beyond the election-time ballyhoo." Municipal budgets were minuscule because wealthy taxpayers were known to be unwilling to pay more. Wealth was notoriously underassessed because rich men insisted that it be. Public relief was administered by comfortably situated guardians, its scope limited by the parsimony of the great taxpayers, as the social message accompanying it reflected their conservative values. The history of each city contains numerous examples of the special sensitivity municipal governments showed their wealthiest constituents, whether in the form of lucrative and sometimes corrupt grants of property or in the general policy underlying public expenditures. As we have seen, little money was at first allotted to social services, in contrast to the lavish funding for projects of interest to the mercantile community; and the balance shifted only when that community decided it was necessary to change.

Their inordinate representation in all branches of local government enabled large property owners to promote their own varied interests. And yet when, as in Natchez and increasingly in other cities, the very richest and most eminent men chose to stand aloof from local politics, they could do so secure in the knowledge that their wishes would continue to be deferred to by the still substantial and uncommonly well-to-do men who held office.

If anyone reigned over the antebellum political world "as the Deity in the universe," alas, it was not the common people.

Power is manifested in a variety of other than political ways. Wherever one searches for it in antebellum America, he finds few if any traces of Tom, Dick, and Harry. Socially significant voluntary associations that often played a larger role than government in dealing with the most important local problems whether in Paris, Illinois, or Cincinnati, Ohio, were invariably controlled by wealthy managers and directors. Even in the "Burned-over district" of western New York State, a small elite—much more mercantile than "evangelical" in outlook—exercised leadership over "virtually every [community] endeavor." As with government, the policies of these organizations reflected the interests and values of the men and women who dominated them.

Power is in some instances impossible to measure, certainly not with precision. Antebellum workingmen, for example, when they struck for higher wages and shorter hours, were exercising their power to withhold their labor. Their numerous defeats and ephemeral gains testify to the relatively slight power they possessed before the Civil War. Great wealthholders, on the other hand, effectively exercised great power over the lives of entire communities through their control of banks and credit, industrial enterprises and employment opportunities, real estate and commerce. "Dominion follows property," wrote "Cato" in the 18th century. His observation appears to have retained its force a century later.

All of the chief assumptions underlying the egalitarian thesis are undermined by the evidence that has recently been brought to light. Great fortunes did exist in this country, hundreds of families living opulently even by European standards. An inequality that was marked at the beginning of the era became even more glaring at its end. Opportunity was no more equal than was material condition. With rare exceptions, wealthy and successful men were born into wealth and comfort, owing more to inherited advantages than to innate ability. Nor were more modest forms of upward social movement very much more prevalent during the era than was the leap from rags to riches. Instead of rising and falling at a mercurial rate, fortunes usually remained in the hands of their accumulators, whether in the long run or the short. Jacksonian America was very much a class society. Surface manifestations of easy mingling among diverse social orders may have given some European visitors the impression that class barriers were easily surmounted. In fact, rigid walls of separation divided the social classes from one another, with elite families choosing marital partners, neighbors, formal and informal social relationships, almost exclusively from among those of their own sort. Throughout the nation, in every kind of milieu and at every level of government, political power was commanded not by common men but by uncommonly well-to-do men of prestigious occupations and families. As for other forms of power, they were no more dominated by ordinary men than was politics.

The age may have been named after the common man but it did not belong to him. For he had very little of whatever it was that counted for much. Far from being an era of egalitarianism, the second quarter of the 19th century is more accurately described as an age of inequality, whether in material condition, status, opportunity, or influence and power.

6

JACKSONIAN CAPITALISM:
AGRICULTURE, LABOR,
AND INDUSTRY

Underlying all other developments during the Jacksonian era were changes in the nation's economy. Such social trends as the rise of urbanism, the growing exclusiveness of urban elites, the increasing class consciousness of organized workingmen, the population rise and particularly the vast upsurge of immigration from Europe, all rested on the new ways of producing and moving goods that marked the period. What after all was the greatest attraction to the armies of the Irish, Germans, and other Europeans who came here in the 1830s and 1840s but the promise of land or work? Opportunity meant above all economic opportunity.

An economic surge which by the end of the era catapulted the United States into a prominent place among nations, just behind Great Britain, accounted for the nation's greater weight and influence on the international scene. The era's great domestic political issues can be traced in almost every case directly to an economic development. Whether it was internal improvements, the Bank War, nullification and the tariff controversy, Indian removal and territorial expansion, or slavery, the substance of each of these political questions was essentially economic. The point is not that political leaders thought only about the economic aspect of issues. Like ordinary voters who identified with one or another political party or voted for one candidate rather than another for a variety of other than economic reasons, famous national figures were likewise motivated by diverse considerations. Such issues as slavery and nullification came to have subtle and emotional overtones that perhaps more than any other accounted for the bitterness of the men ranged on one or another side of them. But at bottom these issues had to do with a particular way of earning wealth.

The era was marked by continued economic growth, although modern economic historians are no longer certain its rate was unprecedented. Settlers spilled across the Appalachians converting the West into a region of unequalled agricultural abundance, the central and northern section moving rapidly to become the leading food producing area of the nation, the southern part taking the lead in cotton production largely because of its rich soil and its more businesslike system for managing production of the crop.

Agriculture continued to be the most important economic activity. Farmers outnumbered every other occupation by far at the end of the era as at its beginning. Agriculture earned twice as much wealth as any other activity, with transportation in second place only because of the movement of agricultural products within the nation. Farming accounted for the lion's share of the nation's exports, one crop, cotton, alone representing better than half of all exports during the era. Two of the three great geographical regions might be said to have been almost completely devoted to farming, while in what was ostensibly the commercial and industrial section of the nation was located its leading agricultural state.

Another significant characteristic of the Jacksonian economy was the growing importance of the factory system. The factories of one state, Massachusetts, by the era's end turned out close to one quarter of the cotton cloth that was the nation's leading industrial product. In 1840 the United States was behind only Great Britain in industrialization. Most modern economic historians, however, hold that a full-fledged industrial revolution was not yet under way. The consensus is that, during the pre–Civil War decades the problems of industrialization were solved, with the realization of the nation's potential for industrialization occurring only after the war's end. The third and fourth decades marked the "*significant beginnings* of the factory system rather than its full flowering, years of important experimentation and uneven development." The term "industrial revolution" has been given many definitions; what is a matured factory system to one scholar is only a maturing system to another. In the years between the opening of the Erie Canal and the nation's emergence from the Panics of 1837 and 1839 most of the nation's industrial goods were turned out, either in homes or small shops, by farmers and skilled journeymen or mechanics rather than by factory operatives, and the factory system was still confined essentially to the New England area in what used to be called the "Old Mill Zone." Yet it was then already understood by astute men as the wave of the future.

Constant experimentation in ways of improving the movement of men and goods also featured the era. This "transportation revolution" has been evaluated as perhaps the most significant of the era's economic developments. Among its other effects, it opened up great new markets for western produce, stimulated a vast interest in either the settlement or speculation in western lands, and bound the nation into something approximating a common market, accessible to any producer no matter how distant, so long as he produced cheaply, efficiently, and abundantly. Itself a lure to domestic and foreign capital, transportation moved into second place as an earner of income. New communities were opened up by canals and railroads, public support for some projects attaining a degree of enthusiasm that cannot be explained in economic or monetary terms alone. American traportation was so remarkable that even Mrs. Trollope praised it.

While in many respects it was an age of laissez-faire, perhaps a safer generalization would characterize the relationship between government and the economy during the era as flexible, governed by no strict doctrines, more inconsistent than certain strict-constructionist presidential messages make it appear. The Jackson Administration spent more money on internal improvements, which in theory it opposed, than the John Quincy Adams Administration which favored them. While a fairly imposing list of federal economic involvements can be drawn up featuring tariffs; patent laws; the sale of public land; Indian removal, which cleared the way for new settlements; a free immigration policy; and the national bank, the truth is that national government placed a very light hand on economic life during the Jackson years. Mayor Cornelius Lawrence, desperately seeking federal aid for a New York City gutted by the great fire of 1835, might describe the national government as "a large capitalist, with an overflowing treasury . . . whose duty is to promote the welfare and prosperity of the people," but his was an uncommon view of things best explained by the duress he was under. State governments played a much more important economic role. In many cases they not only granted charters to or sponsored corporations engaged in banking or transportation but they also subscribed heavily to the stock of others and owned outright a significant number of banks and enterprises of their own. In Missouri and Georgia, Massachusetts and Pennsylvania, there was no laissez-faire on the state level.

Visions of great killings in real estate or transportation lured masses of Americans during the era. A speculative spirit was everywhere noted, as real wealth, earnings, savings, coin, pieces of paper freely printed by the hundreds of state banks that suddenly sprang into existence—precisely in order to meet the demands for money—all were invested, and the fabulous profits of these investments reinvested, in the frenzied race for riches. The nation would not emerge from the ruin of the Panics of 1837 and 1839 until the middle years of the 1840s, the true end of the Jacksonian era, in economic terms.

As before, the economy was featured by private inheritance of wealth and by competition. During the era the market economy expanded, absorbing crops and goods that earlier had been either consumed by their producers or exchanged locally but which now were being shipped into the stream of national and international commerce. For all but a couple of years in the mid-1830s when the sale of public lands boomed as never before, the federal treasury was filled primarily with tariff dollars paid by the nation's merchant importers. Jacksonian Capitalism is a fitting label for the diverse, complex, dynamic, economic tendencies of the period.

Perhaps because with the passage of time an ever smaller proportion of Americans have made their living from farming, a great number of myths concerning antebellum agriculture have flourished. The chief among them emphasize the allegedly great differences between northern and southern agricultural practices. In the evolving folk wisdom of urban America, southern farmers used more wasteful methods, were more preoccupied with cash crops, raised far less food, and were much less concerned with the needs of the soil than were their northern brethren. In contrast to the family size farms that predominated north of the Mason-Dixon line, large plantations supposedly covered most of the area south of that boundary. The South would have been much better off had it taken Hinton R. Helper's advice and raised more hay and less cotton. Despite their awareness that hay was not particularly profitable, farsighted northern farmers planted it because they were ostensibly ready to sacrifice immediate gain for the good of their lands and the welfare of their animals. In view of its declining prices and the growing costliness of the slave labor that planted and picked it, cotton, like the South's other cash crops, was responsible for profits that were more illusory than real, burdening the South with a one-sided agricultural economy that was long believed to have made it dependent on the northwest for its food.

Actually farmers in all sections had a great deal in common, both in their motives or goals and in their methods of cultivation. Generally they sought to make money, northern farmers grudgingly raising hay and yielding as little labor and land to it as they could, precisely because it was not a great dollar earner. Toward the end of the era, when good statistics on crops and yields first became available, southern (border) states were in the lead in the production of corn and animals, while Virginia was among the top wheat producers. William K. Hutchinson and Samuel H. Williamson have recently confirmed Albert Fishlow's finding that in the two decades before the Civil War the "South was in fact self-sufficient and did not have to depend on the Western states for food supplies."

Northern farmers, like southern, used and misused the land for what it was worth, planting wheat—the great northern cash earner—year after year, to the detriment of the soil, treating the few scientific agriculturists in their midst like voices in the wilderness, just as did their southern brethren. All the evidence is not in, but recent studies also indicate that cotton was simply more profitable to raise in the South than hay, that there was a lot of life left in the area's ostensibly depleted lands, and that the appreciation in the value of slaves was by no means an unmitigated disaster either to the men who owned or dealt in them. The plantation system was influential, but most atypical in a section most of whose white farmers owned no slaves at all, the great bulk of what slaveowners there were owning fewer than 10 slaves, usually working the fields with them.

The transportation revolution, by opening up eastern markets to western producers of wheat whose richer lands enabled them to get either greater yields per acre or similar yields with much less labor than New Englanders with their thin and infertile soil over a granite base," did have the effect of promoting regional specialization and a degree of differentiation between the sections that is the basis of the myth as to their complete dissimilarity. Farming did not die in New England during the Jacksonian era, but clearly it was hard hit as the region's young men were drawn to points west, such as Wisconsin, where the wheat yield per acre was 30 times greater than in New England. The region fell back on sheep, as prices for wool were good even through the early years after the Panic of 1839, leading New England farmers to expand their flocks. At the end of the era Vermont and Massachusetts had also become major producers of dairy products. And the common potato proved a godsend, with yields ranging from 250 to 400 bushels per acre. Other responses of the region to the "western march of agriculture" (of corn, pork, wheat, and eventually wool) took the form of increased production of hay, fruits, vegetables, lumber, and maple sugar. Boys, who earlier might have become farmers, were now increasingly drawn toward factories as were, of course, the young women in Lowell, Waltham, and Chicopee.

The Middle Atlantic states thrived despite the rise of the West. New York, "the premier agricultural state," was first in hay production, the value of its livestock, and far ahead of all other states in dairy production. Even in wheat, Pennsylvania and New York were not supplanted by Ohio, Illinois, and Indiana so much as they were supplemented, as production figures for 1839 show. (Ten years later, in fact, Pennsylvania would replace Ohio as the leading wheat producer.) Increasingly compelled, however, to compete with and give ground before the new grain producing center, New York, Pennsylvania, New Jersey, and Delaware expanded their production of important crops and foods not planted in the West. The region became the center of a lucrative vegetable and fruit industry, now possible because of the emergence of urban markets, sufficient transportation facilities, and "the establishment of nurseries capable of providing budded or grafted stock."

The Ohio Valley was to become the nation's bread basket once improvements in transportation enabled it to send to the East, as well as down the Mississippi, the enormous yields made possible by its ideal soil and abundant rainfall. The population of Ohio which was 230,000 in 1810 by 1840 soared beyond 1.5 million. Cincinnati became "porkopolis," the nation's chief packing and distributing center of the swine and the beef cattle that thrived in the region. Corn was perhaps the most abundant crop, but in view of the low price it commanded most of it was not produced directly for cash but rather marketed through livestock. It could be raised cheaply and easily and, unlike wheat, harvested at the farmer's convenience. A saying popular in the North was that corn was fed to hogs there while in the South it was fed to humans. Closer to the truth is the statement that everywhere it was "the poor man's food, the pioneer's subsistence, the slave's usual handout, the feed of hogs, cattle, poultry, and horses. Corn pone, corn bread or johnny cake, corn mush, hominy and corn fritters were standard items in the farmers' diet." Paying no attention to voices of doom, farmers planted corn year after year. On one field in Ohio it was grown for 40 consecutive seasons. In the Northeast as elsewhere the prevailing mood seemed to be, the long view be damned, as farmers pursued "agricultural practices immediately profitable."

Wheat was the crash crop of the North. Western farmers tied themselves to this crop whose prices followed a zigzag course, affected among other things as they were by heavy speculation in the grain. The soil was badly damaged in many cases by repeated "cropping to wheat," but why put land and labor to corn or livestock when the price of wheat was right? Wheat required intensive labor, if for short periods, first to clear land and then for the harvesting which had to be done quickly since wheat when ripe could not stand for long without shedding its grain. Seasonal farm laborers were relied on heavily at such times by farmers who had planted beyond the capacity of their families to harvest. Western farms required much labor and at the beginning of the period its scarcity made it relatively expensive. By the time of the 160-acre farm "in well-established farming areas, the hired man had become almost as much a part of the agricultural pattern as . . . the milk pail or the hoe." Where they were not available, ambitious farmers who had sown many acres discovered that they had been overambitious farmers. Despite their favorable bargaining situation, farm laborers commanded low wages, the average in the 1840s coming to $10 to $15 per month, a very slight rise over what it had been two decades earlier. Constituting between one third and two fifths of the farm population of Ohio, Indiana, Illinois, Michigan, Wisconsin, and Minnesota, these workers typically put in 13- to 14-hour working days, were often unemployed during slack winter months, and in sum were engaged in what David E. Schob calls a "mediocre occupation."

By the end of the era New York spent more on farm machinery than any other state but the real home of mechanization was the new West. On the prairie plains, the "deeply penetrating, thick and coarse root structure of the . . . grass" required something better than the cast-iron plow that served so well in the older regions, the difficult soil resisting coulter and share, and clinging to the moldboard. Until John Deere's steel plow became available shortly after the close of the era, farmers in this region often had to depend on "custom plowers" who might get as much as $2 per acre. For a significant fact about the new machines was a relative costliness which placed them beyond the reach of many ordinary farmers. In view of the difficulties in producing it, wheat was the crop "which called forth the most continuous, concerted efforts . . . to improve the methods of production and reduce labor costs." Where one man with a sickle could cut one half to three quarters of an acre of wheat per day, with a cradle he could cut two to three acres daily and with a self-rake reaper, 12 acres. The use of the self-raker on such an area saved the labor of four men a day, a substantial saving in money to farmers notoriously short of the commodity. Of course the effects of machines were not uniformly beneficial since among other things they made farmers more dependent on credit, widened the gulf between wealthy and small farmers, and helped drive prices down to perilously low points. Yet there is no doubt that western prosperity owed much to the ability to reach distant markets with an abundance of produce that was made possible by mechanization.

While northern agriculture was marked by an essential equality, families typically working hard to produce their varied crops, some significant exceptions to the rule existed. The tendency of expensive machinery to widen disparities has been noted. On the prairie plains of Indiana, Illinois, Iowa and Missouri, unique natural conditions required special and costly solutions. "Men of small means," for example, "were not able to utilize the poorly drained prairie," since the cost of building the necessary drainage ditches was beyond them. A lack of lumber meant that fencing had to be bought. Peculiarly expensive plows were required. Gates' conclusion is that "farm making in the prairies, conditioned as it was by capital costs, attracted men of substantial means and tended to repel pioneers lacking resources. . . ." Another factor promoting inequality in land ownership was federal public land policy which fostered the growth of great land companies and the engrossment of the public lands by rich men.

In the South the diversity of agriculture was inspired above all by the goal of self-sufficiency. If acreage were the deciding factor then corn was king in the South. In 1849, for example, 18 million acres were planted to it, 5 million to cotton, 400,000 each to tobacco and sugar, and 70,000 acres to rice. Corn was raised not only in the border states but on Georgia plantations as well, even though the yield per acre for this crop in the deep South might be only one tenth of what it was on the northern prairies. In such cases self-sufficiency was less a realistic economic motive than an ideal, for it was not profitable. Northern advantages did not really manifest themselves significantly, however, until the very close of the period, for as late as 1839 approximately two thirds of the nation's corn was grown in the South. It was raised there by small farmer and larger planter alike. Before and after this date, every cotton boom was accompanied by a retrenchment in corn or other crops that would now be bought with the profits from cotton. Wheat was a significant crop in the border regions, with Virginia still one of the nation's leading producers in the early 1840s. The upper South also raised oats and rye, hemp and flax, and the sweet potato was a southern specialty. Georgia was famed for its peaches, but the only state active in garden vegetables and fruits was Virginia.

The South was the national leader in livestock, raising more oxen, swine, and cattle—exclusive of milk cows—than the rest of the nation. On the eve of the Civil War it had more horses than any other section. The quality of southern livestock lagged, however, in part due to insufficient hay, in part because of inattention. Farmers confronted by an array of ever more difficult problems simply left the animals to shift for themselves. Wild razorbacks did not make prime food, while the small number and qualitative deficiency of southern cows made for a diet lacking in butter and milk and almost completely devoid of cheese. The South had a near monopoly on mules. Raised in Kentucky and Tennessee, they were sold throughout the slave states. They were not things of beauty but they had many advantages over horses. In the words of one New England admirer, who may have thought he was developing an analogy with different types of human labor, "their life span and working period were longer; they were less subject to disease and accident; they consumed two fifths less food; the expense of shoeing them was less; they could stand up better to hard work in extremely hot weather; they recovered from fatigue more rapidly, pulled more consistently, required no shelter, and were one third less expensive."

The "aristocrats" of southern crops were rice and sugar. Their high cost of production tended to exclude small or middling farmers from their successful cultivation. Confined for this period to the coastal tideland swamp of the Carolinas and Georgia, rice required original outlays of from $50,000 to $100,000 in the 1830s and 1840s. Very few rice planters could approximate the wealth of John Burnside whose five estates occupied 7,600 acres, but practically every one of them owned a bona fide plantation. Imported oriental rice kept profits from soaring, however, and by the 1850s it was unable to meet the competition of cotton, as the rice belt moved to the southwest.

Sugar was another exotic crop, whose special requirements confined it to 24 parishes in southern Louisiana, on the lower Mississippi, where an unusually long growing season and a well-distributed precipitation of 60 inches" made successful cultivation possible. The difficult task of clearing a subtropical forest, digging out drainage ditches, laying roads, and constructing bridges; and the costliness of mills for grinding the cane and apparatus for evaporating the moisture, crystallizing the sugar, and purifying the molasses, made successful operation at least as expensive as for rice. Successful planters did extremely well during the era, profits reaching 17 percent in 1828 and almost 14 percent in 1844. For sugar as for rice, absentee ownership was the rule as planters sought escape from the unhealthy climate and found it in the "luxury of fine homes in Natchez, New Orleans and Charleston." Absentee ownership accentuated the evils of the southern staple economy: "the concentration upon one crop, mining of the soil, failure to build up a sturdy yeoman-farmer base, and dependence upon slave labor."

Whether or not it was a sturdy yeomanry is not certain—in terms of political influence of course it was not—but yeoman farmers predominated in the deep South as in the upper South. Typically they planted cotton and tobacco. The latter crop was destructive of the soil but it was popular for its high yield and good price relative to its bulk and acreage. In the Roanoke Valley great plantations were built by the successful planters of that region's "bright yellow tobacco." Samuel Hairston, for example, was worth several millions and in the 1850s owned close to 1,700 slaves. Usually, however, tobacco estates were not vast, since large planters had no important advantage over small. What tobacco culture required was neither expensive machinery nor elaborate and massive preparation by gangs of labor, but rather "a great deal of care and a high degree of agricultural skill to start the plants, set them, cultivate, harvest and cure the crop." A small farmer in charge of a few slaves could make the same per capita profit as the large planter with many slaves. Both also suffered from price declines that inevitably followed on the overproduction of the staple.

In his recent provocative study of economic growth, Douglass North makes cotton king not only for the South but for the entire nation. Eli Whitney's invention was the "major domestic innovation for the economy for the entire period," while the demand for cotton and the growth of the cotton textile industry were the "decisive" factors in the 30-year period after 1815. In North's view, the expansion of the cotton economy did not merely promote the growth of the West by a significant enlargement of its southern market; it *accounted* for the accelerated pace of westward migration." Cotton income was the "major independent influence on the evolving pattern of interregional trade." As went cotton prices so went the economy: "the vicissitudes of the cotton trade . . . were the most important influence upon the varying rates of growth of the economy during the period." The trade in cotton underlay the general economic acceleration and the beginnings of industrialism that marked the era, North concludes. Statistics on New Orleans' imports for the period do not bear out the suggestion that western crops suddenly poured into the South in greatly increased volume. But it is not necessary to subscribe to all of North's thesis to concede the very great importance of cotton in both the national economy and the international.

Since large outlays were required neither for preparing the land for cotton nor for gathering the crop when it was grown, cotton was raised by "squatters, tenants, mortgaged farmers, full owners, by yeoman farmers, medium planters, and owners of great estates." The absence of cotton-picking machinery made it economically easy for the yeoman farmer to compete with the large planter. If high prices spurred expansion of cotton acreage, lower prices "contributed to enlargement of the scale of operations." No wonder production just about doubled every decade, from 400,000 bales (of 50 pounds each) in 1820 to 750,000 bales in 1830 and 1,300,000 bales in 1840. The great movement in the latter part of the era was into the new southwest, where production costs were lower, plantations more specialized, in a sense the entire process more rationalized. That, with care, much depleted land could have been restored never occurred to men who, like their brethren to the northwest, were more interested in putting their labor into uses more immediately profitable. And so long as rich new lands were available, it made much better sense to the individual farmer to plant cotton on them than to struggle unprofitably to restore land for the planting of less valuable crops that northerners raised only because they had to. The north, worse luck for it, lacked the growing season that enabled a Tennessee farmer in the 1840s to get a return of $212 from four acres planted to cotton.

Slavery was the preferred labor system everywhere in the South. The slave population of slightly more than one and a half million at the beginning of the second quarter of the 19th century doubled by midcentury. Only one white southern family in four owned slaves. By the end of the era close to three fourths of the slaveowning families each owned fewer than ten slaves, while the slightly more than 10 percent of slaveowners each of whom owned 20 or more held most of the slaves. The South's "peculiar institution" was a most complex institution, economically as well as morally, emotionally, and politically. Perhaps 5 percent of the bondsmen and women were industrial slaves, many of whom enjoyed a surprising degree of freedom of action in the black sections of southern cities. (Recently Claudia D. Golden has presented data that challenge the assumption that urbanization was inimical to the flourishing of slavery.) The remainder were "agricultural slaves," roughly three fourths of whom labored in the fields, with the rest working in or near the house of their masters. Eugene D. Genovese's estimate is that about 20 percent of the latter group—or 5 percent of the total—constituted a slave elite of sorts. Like other groups in American life slaves too were "internally differentiated."

Frederick Law Olmsted, northern author of perhaps the most influential travel account of life and labor in the antebellum South, had written that "servile labor must be unskilled labor." In fact, many of the more than 100,000 industrial slaves were highly skilled men who worked as mechanics, machinists, printers, carpenters, cabinet makers, and in dozens of other crafts and in ironworks, lumber mills, fisheries, and sugar refineries as well as in canal and railroad construction. Roughly one fifth of these slaves were hired out by their masters to industrial employers for about $45 or $50 per year at the beginning of the era and three times that amount at its end. For all their skill and desirability as labor—with many employers finding them more efficient as well as more economical than whites—the working and living conditions ascribed to skilled black artisans in Robert Starobin's comprehensive recent study were not very much more attractive than those experiences by agricultural slaves. Unremitting toil, "filthy, crowded slave quarters [that] encouraged contagions," and an inadequate diet consisting typically of a weekly ration of "one peck of corn meal, three or four pounds of salt pork, and a quart of molasses," added up to a life that was "barely tolerable at best." Charles B. Dew's detailed examination of slave labor in southern iron works, on the other hand, while noting the significance of whipping in coercing slave labor, reports that the "central tendency was mutual accommodation" rather "than outright oppression," and it emphasizes the extent to which the masters' need for and readiness to give cash rewards to skilled labor produced "an environment in which [industrial slaves] could develop some sense of personal dignity and individual initiative."

The great majority of slaves worked in the fields, planting and picking cotton, and it is their work lives, families, and emotional and personality development that have been the center of much recent discussion. Most historians are skeptical toward Stanley Elkins' original and provocative interpretation which viewed the unlovely features of the Sambo personality ostensibly internalized by slaves as a development similar to the one which a generation ago turned inmates of Nazi concentration camps into docile and abject figures. In view of pervasive evidence of slaves' rebelliousness and eagerness to escape, it is not at all clear that the Sambo stereotype in fact describes the personalities of actual slaves. The ingratiating face the house slave showed his master has been recently interpreted as "a mask to hide his true feelings and personality traits." Slaves' own reminiscences and Lawrence W. Levine's fascinating recent study of black culture reveal the aggressiveness and hostility toward their masters lurking behind slave behavior that on the surface appeared to be totally deferential if not reverential. Slave attitudes and feelings, as Genovese has so masterfully shown, were hardly of a piece, covering a great range of seemingly contradictory beliefs and emotions. No single category or stereotype can contain them. George Rawick, John W. Blassingame, and most recently Herbert G. Gutman have reported a slave community in which the slaves' "distinctive culture" was far from crushed, a "durable family organization" functioned as "an important survival mechanism," and the slave remained an autonomous human being rather than a "total victim," his "creative instincts" intact. These are matters that are of course not directly related to the economic developments at the heart of this chapter. Since however the economic system of slavery rested after all on human labor, the moods and values of that labor are germane even to a discussion that is concerned primarily with its productivity and profitability.

White southerners, from the political economist Thomas Cooper in 1826 to the historian Ulrich B. Phillips almost a century later, had argued that in view of its costliness and its inefficiency, slave labor persisted in the antebellum South not because it was profitable or economically rational but rather because slaveowners felt that they had no alternative but to live with a system that maintained social controls and racial harmony. It *was* a tragic system, but not for its maltreatment of slaves who, according to Phillips, were well treated out of a combination of paternalism, good sense, and self interest. For why would planters stir up trouble by mistreating the labor they depended on? The real tragedy was in the great harm done the South by a system ostensibly so inimical to technological progress, industry, and the diversity necessary to regional prosperity. Using the statistical and mathematical approach that is the stock in trade of the new economic history, Robert W. Fogel and Stanley L. Engerman have recently argued that Phillips was at least partly right: slaves according to them were treated relatively well, their women rarely violated, both sexes seldom whipped, their housing and diet superior to that of free workers in the north. They depart from the traditional thesis in arguing that slaves were workers of such efficiency and productivity as to assure the system's profitability. (In 1958 Alfred H. Conrad and John R. Meyer had launched the new economic history in a pathbreaking essay that, on the basis of "counterfactual data" or evidence of things that never happened and the "statistical concepts of range and central tendency as applied to frequency distributions of data," found that slavery was profitable to sellers and purchasers alike as well as to the section in general.) A major problem with the findings of Fogel and Engerman, in addition to flaws in their data, mathematical errors, and lapses from logic that are apparent even to general readers, is the harsh critical reaction to their work by their fellow cliometricians, who have attacked the "persistent [theoretical] bias" in their study, its lack of a "scientific foundation," and its needlessly difficult and inaccurate equations, among other faults.

The burden of modern scholarly thinking is that slaves were indeed harshly used, often whipped or threatened with whipping, and cheaply housed, clothed, and fed. The system was indeed profitable, not impeding a rate of economic growth that in the decades before the Great War matched the 1.3 percent that prevailed in the north. Some students continue to argue that slavery fostered a distorted economic system whose masses lacked purchasing power and whose elite consumed too lavishly to permit the exemplary investments and capital formation that the section needed. To which a sophisticated refutation asserts that "skewed income distribution" does not necessarily inhibit capital formation, proof is lacking that the southern elite consumed more lavishly than the northern, and that modern evidence suggests that big spenders are big savers—who thus promote the "formation of capital." No consensus has been achieved, however, nor is one likely in the discussion of a question so intertwined with emotional ingredients.

Another feature of southern farming was the relative absence of machinery. Slavery of course has also been blamed for this lack. Statistics can be misleading for they seemed to show, for a later period just prior to the War, that in terms of expenditure per farm, the South spent almost as much on agricultural equipment as the North. Southern plantations and heavy expenditures on sugar refining and cotton ginning machines distorted the picture. When machinery *per acre of land* is used as the index, southern backwardness in this regard becomes apparent. The point is not that southern white farmers were congenitally antimechanical. Olmsted's famous assertion that much southern land had never felt a plow seems almost a moral judgment. The fact is that much southern land did not need a plow, a hoe being sufficient. As was also true of the North, many southern farmers were too poor to invest in machinery or too stubborn to give up the customary ways of farming, viewing all proposed innovations suspiciously. Since until recently cotton could be picked only by hand, there was no machine to invest in, even had planters wished to do so. For the crops or jobs that required machinery, heavy expenditures were made, as for the processing of cotton.

In sum the Jacksonian era was an age of transition for American agriculture. Important tendencies that came to fruition at a later date gathered momentum in the two decades after the completion of the Erie Canal. Farming became increasingly commercialized as improved means of transportation opened up new areas to cultivation, fostered regional specialization, created new markets for efficient producers, and started rearranging sectional relationships.

The Eighth Census of the United States lists the leading manufactures of the United States for 1860. In terms of the value added to the product by manufacture, the making of cotton cloth was the nation's leading industry, just as it had been during the latter part of the Jacksonian era. While the order of particular industries had changed since 1840, lumber, boots and shoes, flour products, clothing, iron products, machinery, woolens, carriages, and leather goods were the major products of the earlier era as they were at the end of the antebellum period. These products were made in a variety of ways.

Home manufacture was the most typical method of producing industrial goods during the early part of the period. In this country as in England the domestic system prevailed prior to the victory of the factory. Shoes were made by rural Massachusetts families which it used to be thought typically owned several pigs and a cow or two. Paul Faler has recently shown that while Lynn's shoemakers may have owned animals earlier in the century, by 1830 fewer than 10 percent of them did so, with less than half owning any kind of real property. Most other industries, including cloth, depended primarily on farm families taking in work to supplement their incomes. The system thrived above all in the new West where, apart from a few urban centers such as Cincinnati or St. Louis, it was unchallenged throughout the era. It flourished even in the middle Atlantic and New England regions, despite the competition afforded by factories and small shop production in the cities. Wages to farm families were notoriously low but they were nonetheless appreciated by a population which saw little cash otherwise. Where earlier, goods made in homes had been consumed or used by the families producing them, in the Jacksonian era they were fed into the stream of commerce. The developing market economy at first did not destroy the system of home manufactures so much as it modified it, if drastically.

The age of the transportation revolution had brought forward the merchant capitalist as a leading figure in the industrial as well as the commercial and financial life of the nation. In the face of the home producer's inexperience and lack of capital for marketing his product on a wide scale—disabilities shared by the skilled craftsmen who made goods in urban shops—the merchant capitalist came to the fore for he alone possessed the capital and the know-how to take advantage of the opportunities afforded by the new transportation network. The domestic workers' problem, of having "capital . . . so limited that they were forced to remain in idleness for want of raw material until they sold their finished product," was unknown to him. The new-style industrialist had easy access to the bank credit "necessary to finance a business on a large scale." If "the source of his power was the ability to size up markets for raw materials," as well as to dispose of finished products, it was also based on his increasingly greater ability to produce—or to have produced for him—these same products. Unable to compete with him, mainly because of his ability to cut costs and ultimately prices, the home producer was now absorbed into his system and in the process transformed, in an economic sense. From a relatively skilled craftsman who might work up a finished product from its original raw state, he now worked on raw material furnished by the merchant capitalist, "doing the less than skilled work" at piece-rate wages. By the latter part of the era, the household system was rapidly losing ground throughout the country. Historians of wool manufacture feel that in the industry 1840 was a turning point, the factory product thereafter essentially replacing homemade goods.

The second great industrial system was that of small shops located in the nation's towns and villages. Still very much guided by the medieval guild ideal, their skilled craftsmen in the late 18th and early 19th centuries were turning out homemade products if not for custom order then for the local market. Achievement of the status of master had been the great hope of journeymen artisans. That master and journeymen had similar interests is indicated by the fact that they both belonged to the societies that were organized in many of the nation's crafts. The ideology of the skilled worker is strikingly revealed by the typical goals of the early, pre-Jacksonian societies. In addition to the classic fraternal purposes of artisans' organizations, they often sought not higher wages but rather superior prices for the products jointly made by master and journeymen. The system of merchant capitalism changed all that. "The masters now became small contractors employed by the merchant-capitalists [who owned the raw material] and, in turn, employing one to a dozen journeymen [who owned most of the tools]." Though masters still "continued to work alongside their men," their reward was no longer the "profits of a capitalist," but "solely out of wages and work." The more work they could get out of the journeymen mechanics, the higher their own returns. "They played the less skilled against the more skilled, the speedy against the slow," reducing wages while "sweating" more work out of their labor force. Where possible they resorted to convict, child, female, or other unskilled labor in order to increase the capitalists'—and their own—profits. Wherever possible, as in shoemaking in Pennsylvania, masters drastically reduced the rates they paid mechanics. It was largely as a response to this new situation that the societies in the late 1820s and 1830s moved to confine their memberships to journeymen only, replacing the goal of a "uniform price list" with higher wages, shorter hours, an end to sweating, as to unfair competition from cheap labor. These demands were to be achieved by strikes or turnouts as they were then known.

In Philadelphia, New York, Boston, Baltimore, Newark, Pittsburgh, Cincinnati, Buffalo, Louisville, St. Louis, and New Orleans, as in small cities throughout the nation, skilled and semiskilled workers formed their separate journeymen's societies. Shoe workers (or cordwainers as they were then known), printers and compositors, blacksmiths and whitesmiths, leather makers, saddlers and harness makers, carpenters and housewrights, caulkers and coopers, bookbinders, chair makers and cabinet makers, gilders and carvers, bakers and soap makers, masons and house painters, comb makers and brush makers, tailors and hat makers, weavers and plasterers, jewelers and machinists, rope makers and sail makers organized, the movement at its height claiming a membership of 300,000.

To add to their resources and effectiveness, 16 journeymen's societies in Philadelphia merged in 1827 to form the "union of the trades" or the trades' union of Philadelphia, an event interpreted by the pioneer labor historian, John R. Commons, as the birth of the nation's first true labor movement. The movement caught on, as trades' unions sprang up in most of the nation's cities in the decade 1827 to 1837. Their members typically were not Karl Marx's proletarians but skilled men trying to resist the varied challenges to their status and conditions of work posed by the merchant capitalist on the one hand and the spreading factory system on the other.

If overwork was now a pressing problem, so paradoxically was insufficient work. As Bruce Laurie has shown for antebellum Philadelphia, workers experienced "alternating periods of feverish activity broken by slack spells," demoralizing periods during which a worker was "on his own, without work and unable to meet the day to day costs of running his household." For the new system of merchant capitalism did not always run smoothly, marked as it was by transportation irregularities, "discontinuous supplies," erratic deliveries of goods, and long layoffs, particularly in winter.

It seems clear that it was not working conditions alone that accounted for the growing restiveness of American artisans. Labor spokesmen resented pervasive expressions of scorn and hostility toward workingmen who would try to improve their lot. Such expressions made a mockery of the numerous assertions by influential men of their admiration for "noble labor"—in the abstract. Despite the absence in American statutes of a formal conspiracy doctrine pertaining to workingmen's attempts to organize unions and strikes, courts invoked that very doctrine in case after case, punishing American labor activity on the basis of dubious English precedents. (*Commonwealth* v. *Hunt* in 1842 was a landmark for in that case the highest court in Massachusetts for the first time held that a workingmen's society's attempt to induce "all those engaged in the same occupation to become members of it" was not an unlawful purpose and that a strike called to achieve that purpose was not necessarily a criminal means.)

This early union movement was a strange one by modern standards for its program was broad and its leadership most unusual. While many of the leaders were mechanics who had worked their way up from the ranks, equally representative were articulate men with little or no experience themselves as workers but possessed of reputations as reformers and friends to the workingman, men such as Charles Douglas and Theophilus Fisk in New England, Ely Moore and Levi Slamm in New York, Thomas Brothers and William English in Pennsylvania. A labor movement consisting of skilled artisans, ambivalent men who in some cases might still aspire to become masters even as they grew disenchanted with the changing social and economic order, saw no contradiction in conferring leadership on men of varied social background so long as they were champions of the workingman. Unions characteristically advocated abolition of imprisonment for debt, reform of a militia system which seemed to discriminate against the poor and the working class, land reform, improved educational opportunities for the poor and many other social reforms. Their interest in these reforms indicates that these early unions held to that broad concept of a labor movement's purpose which has traditionally inspired European unionism but which has become so alient to contemporary organized labor in this country. The Jacksonian unions were reform organizations, led by men who believed that labor's welfare could be truly achieved only through significant changes in American society that went beyond improved conditions in the shop.

While not restricting themselves to a narrow definition of unionism, the Jacksonian unions by no means neglected bread and butter matters. The societies had merged into unions primarily in order to enlarge their treasuries or "war chests." Their characteristic activity was the strike. In 1835 and 1836 hundreds of strikes were waged throughout the country, many for the ten-hour day, and even more for higher wages. Prior to the successful strikes for the reduction of the working day, workmen, like farmers, had put in a working day that lasted from sunup to sundown, more than 13 hours during the warm weather months. Those who argued that a reduction would lead to the debauching of the working class had no qualms about leaving workmen with whole days of free time during the cold weather months of little natural light, when to keep the shops going would have put employers to the expense of keeping them lighted. But by 1835, outside of New England, the long hours of labor that had prevailed "from time immemorial," had been lowered as a result of successful ten-hour-day strikes. A famous Philadelphia unionist, John Ferral, referred to the victory as the accomplishment of labor's "bloodless revolution."

The end of the short-lived depression of 1833 to 1834—"Biddle's depression," according to Jackson partisans, who blamed it on the policy of credit restriction followed by the head of the second Bank of the United States—was followed by an inflationary boom. In 1836 there were close to 200 strikes called by workers who found that wages lagged behind skyrocketing prices. Not only were skilled journeymen paid a wage, $1 to $2 daily, that did not permit most of them to maintain their families at a minimum standard of decent living, but they were often paid in paper currency that further lowered their actual wage by its depreciation. The gains registered in the strikes turned out to be ephemeral for following the Panic of 1837, wages were cut, jobs disappeared, as did most of the unions.

One of the more interesting developments of the era was the organization of a National Trades' Union in 1834. It too disappeared in the catastrophe of 1837 but prior to its demise it brought under one roof, at its annual conventions, the leading figures of the era's trade union movement. Its accomplishments were as modest as its membership was small, for transportation revolution or no, the time was not yet ripe for national labor organizations. (The attempts of the journeymen's unions of weavers, printers, carpenters, comb makers and cordwainers to organize nationally were also unsuccessful.) These conventions however did provide a sounding board for the attending representatives, and they thus give us an idea of what was on the mind of American artisans during the era. One of their central concerns was the factory system and its expansion.

The factory system was the remaining way of manufacturing industrial products during the era. Its evolution was a notable feature of the era. At the beginning it was essentially only a harbinger of things to come. For apart from sawmills, grist mills, and other neighborhood mills located throughout the country, factory operations were at first confined to a few places in New England. Francis C. Lowell and his associates in the Boston Manufacturing Company had followed up the successful establishment of Waltham in 1813 with factory towns in Lowell in 1822 and Chicopee in 1823; Samuel Slater had been well known and successful since the turn of the century; and apart from a few others, like Almy and Brown, that was all there was to the system at first. By the era's end, in the mid-1840s, factory labor was important in Pennsylvania and New York as well as in New England, the cotton cloth and woolen manufactures were dominated by the system, machine making and the iron industry significantly affected by it. But its standing should not be misunderstood. For as George Rogers Taylor has remarked, "though important for the future, factory manufacturing constituted, before 1840, a small fraction of total output."

In view of the system's expansion wherever a capitalistic society matures to a certain point, it seems clear that its victory in the United States was inevitable. Then it was not so apparent. English competition, technical difficulties, its high expense, the lure of higher rates of profit in other forms of enterprise, working class opposition, were all important obstacles to its growth. The nearest thing to "luddism"—or machine wrecking—in this country was the attack on machinemade yarn by rope makers boasting that their handspun product was more durable. If they could, some workers would have turned back the clock, but they confined their opposition to rhetoric rather than action.

By its superior division of labor, its integration of processes, and its ability to use cheap and unskilled labor to work its machinery, a factory could produce goods more efficiently, abundantly, and cheaply than any other system. In New England, plants which specialized in one product and whose entire output was sold to a single marketing agency, put the smaller producer at a great disadvantage. Their large capital requirements made it necessary to finance them through corporations. There was some question as to how well factories did. One modern estimate is that cotton factories made a most modest profit of 3 percent, which if true would explain the continuing reluctance to invest in these enterprises. In the early part of the era, on the other hand, the Boston Associates reached a profit of just under 20 percent, the kind of return that explains why capital derived from commerce and banking was invested in the system in increasing quantities, for all the hazards. As the system expanded, it became less dependent on capital from other activities, New England's textile mills, for example, expanding through reinvestment of their own earnings.

The major controversy concerned the welfare of labor in the new factories. Like the similar dispute in England, it has been waged by contemporaries and later scholars alike, although it has never become quite as acrimonious as the English argument. Many foreign visitors, like Chevalier and Miss Martineau, were charmed by the system's operations in Waltham and Lowell, and the many New England communities which imitated them, where the typical work force consisted of young women who lived in boarding houses supervised by the mill owners. Friends of the system saw clean houses, strict chaperoning, busy workdays of long hours, true, but work that was less than grueling and marked by the ballet-like quality of nimble fingers dancing over their machines. Critics saw a much darker picture. A number of modern studies appear to demonstrate conclusively that one cannot take at face value the rose-colored version of the boarding-house system that was depicted in the company-sponsored journal, *The Lowell Offering*.

The conditions and the price of boarding were fixed by the corporation which owned the factory. Rules were strict and they were strictly enforced. Woe to the girls "guilty of any improper conduct or [who were] . . . not in the regular habit of attending public worship." Overcrowding was "the chief problem," according to one factory girl. In Chicopee, "six girls often slept in one room, in three double beds." Pig pens, kept in the back yard of the tenements and "operated by each boarding house in the interests of economy," were responsible "during the early forties [for] . . . an epidemic of typhoid fever that was a record breaker." As for conditions within the factories, according to the testimony given by young women from the Lowell mills they worked from 13 to 14 hours a day, suffering from bad air, overcrowding, and lack of light. The Boston *Daily Times* agreed, reporting that the "young girls are compelled to work in unhealthy confinement for too many hours every day." In effect the women were contract labor, and breakers of the contract were subjected to an efficient blacklist. Weekly wages for all but a few unusually skillful operatives, ranged from $2 to $2.75 per week. Wages were paid at infrequent intervals, usually on a monthly basis, at some places quarterly or even semiannually. The working day hovered around 13 hours all during the period, in the late 1830s as in the early 1820s. Only three holidays during the year, and having to get up at 4:30 or 5:00 o'clock in the morning, were a regimen which permitted very few girls to take advantage of the vaunted cultural opportunities offered in the boarding-house type of factory towns. It seems clear that the young women who made up the bulk of the Massachusetts labor force during the era worked and lived under difficult conditions.

The other kind of factory system, sometimes known as the Fall River type, used the labor of entire families, provided no housing or other paternalistic features, and was prevalent outside of Massachusetts. Acceptance of employment by workers meant assent to harsh rules regulating in precise detail their hours of work—usually over 70 per week. There was excessive punishment for lateness or absence, and the strict discipline within the factorys walls, and the threat of forfeiture of wages to the operative who failed to give the required two weeks' notice prior to quitting. Workers, on the other hand, could be dropped without notice. Hours, wages, conditions were determined solely by management. A blacklist was enforced particularly against men suspected of union sympathies. Punishment of male adults was confined to heavy fines, even for five minutes' lateness, but children were often lashed and females sometimes mishandled. The wages of men dropped in the late 1830s and 1840s, seldom reaching more than $4 per week, more typically sinking to $3. Women and children at first made up more than half the labor force under the family system. In Pennsylvania it was estimated that one fifth of the factory workers were children under 12. The wages of women in that state "ranged from 50 cents per week to $2.62½ per week" in 1832, while children got a pittance.

Wages were hard to collect and when received in the form of bank notes, might depreciate by 10 percent. Even Harriet Martineau conceded that in America factory workers worked harder than their English cousins. Certainly they seemed to be more productive, one adult here performing work that it took two or three English workers to do. Against this background of overwork, low pay, long hours, overcrowding, excessive punishment and discipline, a factory owner reported to a state legislative committee inquiring into the evils of the system: "I know of no evil worth notice, except that which arises from the refractory, factious spirit of some of the men, and they are mostly foreigners." In fact, "foreigners" or Irish operatives did not become predominant until the 1850s. Harsh treatment reflected scornful attitudes toward factory labor. A New England supervisor told a visitor, "I regard my work people just as I regard my machinery. So long as they can do my work for what I choose to pay them, I keep them, getting out of them all I can."

Working people did not live for labor alone. The new labor history produced by Paul Faler, Bruce Laurie, Herbert Gutman, and others has thrown interesting light on how artisans and craftsmen spent their leisure time and the values implicit in this expenditure. Resisting a "new industrial morality" that, in David Montgomery's words, promised industrialists a "disciplined labor force, pacing its toil and its very life cycle to the requirements of the machine and the clock, respectful of property and order [and sober] in its demeanor," America's preindustrial workingmen asserted their independence and individuality. Whether skilled or unskilled, workers drank heavily during as well as after working hours, breaking up the day at regular intervals to "rob the mail." Required to do compulsory militia service, many artisans turned the occasions into "scenes of riot and disorder," scandalizing the champions of industrial discipline with their "disgusting and harmful" behavior. Artisans delighted in cockfights, roulette, circuses, shooting matches, hunting, and footracing, while the frequent "frolicking" of factory hands that "sometimes lasted for days, and uproarious Election and Independence Day celebrations plagued mill operators." Time off was considered a marvelous thing when it came at the worker's own insistence. As an old tailor in Philadelphia put it, "Pressure is well enough to be sure, as I can testify when the last dollar is about to be pressed out of me; but vacation is capital. It tickles one's fancy with the notion of choice. 'Nothing on compulsion' is my motto."

As was true of agriculture, industry too was in a state of transition during the era. The transportation revolution transformed domestic industry and small shop production. Internal relationships in both systems were drastically changed as their product increasingly was fed into the stream of national rather than regional commerce. The rapidly growing national market provided the impetus to the factory system, with its great productive capacity. By the end of the era the factory system was on the verge of breaking out of the geographical barriers that had contained it, ready to spread to industries other than textiles. Labor's lot may have been much superior to that of workers elsewhere but American working-men themselves felt dissatisfaction. Real wages appeared to stand still during the Jacksonian era. American labor spokesmen could argue with some justice that for all the talk of the common man's predominance here, American labor's status and influence were slight and its material conditions inadequate.

7

JACKSONIAN CAPITALISM:
TRANSPORTATION,
COMMERCE,
AND BANKING

Perhaps the most unique feature of American capitalism during the third and fourth decades of the 19th century was an aspect of its geographical situation. In contrast to European nations, whose economies evolved for the most part within territories that had been fixed for centuries, here the physical area within which the economy developed was a flexible one. The constant opening up of new western lands constituted the greatest pressure for the improvements in transportation that would make it possible to carry western products back to the older and more settled communities. For people, if they could not literally crawl or swim their way to the Ohio Valley or the Prairie Plains, could somehow manage to get there by virtue of effort, endurance, and other spartan virtues. But goods for sale could be moved feasibly only if the movement were swift or cheap. It was the transportation revolution of the era that moved the goods, created the markets, and spurred producers, whether of food or manufactured articles, to new heights of output in order to reach the new markets.

J. L. Hammond once observed of England that a nation, no part of which is more than 70 miles from the sea, could become great industrially without first requiring the building of an internal transportation network. Blessed with a much larger territory than our British cousins, the United States was not so lucky in this regard. Russian czars, ancient and modern, on the other hand, discovered that the industrial development of a vast territory was stifled until a sizable modern transportation facility had been perfected. The more fortunate United States, whose territorial expansion was a *gradual* one, was able to match its piecemeal physical enlargement with a corresponding step-by-step improvement of its transportation facilities. Unlike the Germanies of that era, which required a dramatic political measure, the *Zollverein,* to make a customs union or a single market out of territories previously separated by prohibitive internal tariffs, the United States—already a *de jure* customs union—required only technical advances in moving things.

America had some excellent natural advantages to help in accomplishing this goal. The nation was blessed with a number of marvelous river systems and countless small streams. Its most important highway was a natural phenomenon—the coastal waters of the Atlantic Ocean. Its human fauna, as was widely noted, were instinctive travelers, addicted to movement and as such ever ready to help nature along by improving on natural transportation facilities where improvement was needed. (In support of the latter thesis, perhaps, is the fact that those Europeans who came to settle in this country were obviously more footloose than their fellows in the first place.) The American traits of practicality and cupidity might also be invoked to explain an achievement that required the solution of difficult technical problems and which was inspired largely by visions of the lovely profits attending success. Very hard work was necessary because the ocean, the rivers, the streams, were insufficient, the waters for the most part running north and south. The facilities for using these waters at the start of the era were primitive. Since the high banks and the trees, which interfered with air currents, made sail impracticable on the Mississippi, for example, a variety of inadequate alternatives were used. Barges, flatboats, rafts, canoes, were all very slow. Downstream from Pittsburgh to New Orleans took six weeks. Upstream, if it could be done at all, took 17 weeks or more. It was no wonder many boats were broken up and sold for lumber at journey's end, after depositing their cargo at the southern port.

It was obvious that man-made improvements were necessary if the widely dispersed and expanding nation was to hang together as an economic unit. Realization of the great economic potential in its natural and human resources depended on a transportation network that would open up its most distant areas to its most efficient producers.

National government proved to be peculiarly unhelpful in dealing with the problem. The men who ruled the nation from Washington's time to Jackson's were quite aware of the importance to it of "internal improvements," regularly speaking out in glowing terms of the many benefits it would confer. In his message to Congress in December, 1815, Madison had stressed the "great importance of establishing throughout our country the roads and canals which can best be executed under national authority." To the consternation of those who thought that this statement demonstrated the President's sympathy with the earlier plan for a national system of internal improvements that had been put forward by Albert Gallatin, it developed that he meant no such thing. On March 3, 1817, he vetoed the Bonus Bill which provided that the funds owing to the Government by the new Second Bank of the United States were to be set aside for internal improvements. Thus the same President who had reversed his earlier position on the unconstitutionality of a national bank, despite the absence of language in the Federal Charter expressly giving Congress the power to establish one, did not waive his constitutional scruples concerning internal improvements merely because he had abandoned them with regard to the Bank. His veto message recognized the value of federal action, but in the face of the Constitution's silence, it advised that an amendment to the Constitution was necessary. Monroe's veto of the proposal to erect toll gates on the Cumberland Road, which was being built by the federal government, took the same constitutional ground. Jackson's veto of federal funds for the Maysville Road in 1830, although hinting at doubts about the legality of any federal support to internal improvements, essentially argued not the unconstitutionality of a federally sponsored national road system, but only of such aid to a project confined to one state. Cynics thought at the time that had the state been another one than Henry Clay's, the Presidential decision might have been different. In addition to constitutional objections, Jackson expressed concern about the likelihood of corruption in the execution of such projects, a view that had been shared by earlier leaders, perhaps with good reason.

Too much should not be made of Presidential scruples. The strict-constructionist messages were largely canceled out both by words of praise for internal improvements and more importantly by acts and expenditures that seemed to contradict them. As has been noted, Jackson's administration spent more money on them than John Quincy Adams'. The relatively little that was done, even by national administrations which had no legal reservations, seems to show that it was beyond the power of Presidents, no matter how disposed, to affect the issue significantly. Areas which improved transportation with their own funds came to oppose the use of their federal tax monies to help regions which had not made improvements. Southerners were wary of federal expenditures that would make high tariffs necessary. In this sense Presidential objections to federal internal improvement programs merely reflected concerns felt throughout the country, putting on a lofty theoretical and political ground opposition that was actually based on practical considerations.

During the so-called age of laissez-faire, municipal and, above all, state governments engaged in all manner of direct and indirect support to every variety of transportation project, running up debts for the purpose that were twice as great as all their other obligations combined. Pragmatism prevailed over abstract theories of nonintervention. The results were mixed. Chicanery, corruption, incompetence, short sightedness, greed, opportunistic politics, among other things, explained the failure of many projects. The era's economic graveyard was piled high with the bones of canal, turnpike, and railroad company failures. Heavily capitalized steamboats, one of the period's adornments, blew up at an alarming rate. Young Tocqueville almost lost his life as a result of one such disaster.

Track was laid and never used, productive only of profits to shrewd insiders and losses to everyone else. And yet with all the blundering, ineptitude, and occasional venality, an efficient transportation system was achieved during the Jacksonian era, that did well the job such a system is created to do. In the judgment of contemporaries it was the wonder of the world. It was not simply that by 1840 America had more railroad track than any other country. It was the relative efficiency of American transport, and the constant tinkering with ways of improving it, that were so amazing.

Improvements seemed to occur at a lightning rate. Tyrone Power recalled that he made his first journey from New York to Philadelphia in September 1833 "by steam-boat and railway, having cars drawn by horses." The trip took almost half a day. "In October of the same year [he] . . . did the same distance by locomotive in two hours." Francis Lieber made an observation that was more prescient than he knew: "When I first came to this country, I went from the Delaware to the Chesapeake in a confounded and confounding stagecoach. A few years later, I had to go again to Washington and found a canal cut through Delaware . . . , and a year or so later, I crossed the same state on a railroad; now I wait impatiently for a passage over the state, for aerial navigation is the next in order, all other means being exhausted." Dickens and other travelers were impressed, if not all of them favorably, by the egalitarian social conditions on board American public conveyances. Evoking a more universal accord from the visitors was the high efficiency if not always comfort of the young nation's means of transportation.

Unassuming country roads, a heritage of the Revolutionary era and even before, were still of great importance at the beginning of the period, providing "a continuous highway of sorts [that] extended from Maine to Georgia." For all their usefulness, they were woefully inadequate. Built by unskilled volunteer labor, from communities too poor to maintain the roads, they fell far short of the nation's needs. The War of 1812 had mercilessly exposed their weakness: during that conflict a wagon carrying cotton cards, drawn by four horses, took 75 days to go from Worcester, Massachusetts to Charleston, South Carolina. The glaring need for improved land travel sparked the turnpike movement of the early 19th century.

Turnpikes were toll roads. The turnpike boom had reached its height before 1825, the early part of the Jacksonian era witnessing a sharp curtailment of investment in these highways. In view of the short life of the boom as well as the poor quality of many of the turnpikes, it is easy to undervalue both the importance and the extent of the turnpike system. Certain statistics are instructive. By 1840, when canals were all the rage and after a decade of spirited railroad construction, the total mileage for each of these major forms was just over 3,325 miles. Yet by as early as 1830, New York State alone—which led in this as in so many other of the era's economic developments—had 4,000 miles of turnpike, and Pennsylvania better than half that amount. Of course mileage figures by themselves do not indicate the relative economic significance of a given means of transportation. For the humble country roads, if put end to end, would have outdistanced the turnpikes. Yet mileage figures are not totally devoid of meaning.

Some of the turnpikes, such as the great Cumberland Road of the national government, were well built, "on a solid stone foundation with a gravel dressing." Most of them were of lesser quality, consisting generally of nothing better than a layer of loose gravel and simple drainage ditches, with very little done to reduce steep grades, while the poorest "were little more than country roads kept in barely passable condition by the turnpike company." If freight deserted them for other means of transport during the era, they continued to hold their own in passenger traffic, a fact which bespeaks the hardiness of the American traveler by land. Tudor spoke for most of his fellow travelers when at the same time that he praised American transportation in general, particularly on the water, he complained that "the land carriage is a wincing and grimacing operation throughout," due to the poor condition of the roads.

Turnpikes promoted the economic well-being of the regions they served. Since this was a capitalistic society, their sponsors regarded them as profit-making ventures. Their financing and organization were diverse, typical of American arrangements for the capitalization and management of such enterprises during the era. In the North, where most of them were built, with the exception of Pennsylvania whose state treasury contributed about one third of the required funds, turnpikes were "financed almost exclusively from private investments." In the other sections, states typically invested heavily in the stock of privately-owned companies. South Carolina and Indiana were unusual in that the state governments completely owned as well as financed most of the turnpikes in their areas. The financial failure of turnpikes is a nice example of a free market rejecting a product it found somewhat wanting. Tolls, even when low, discouraged a freight typically "large in bulk, small in value." Reluctant travelers too often used "shunpikes"—roads near the toll gates—or simply waited till collectors went off duty. Operating expenses were high. The result was a net return that was "financially disappointing." Massachusetts turnpikes averaged a 3.1 percent profit over a 60-year period, while in Kentucky the value of turnpike stock by midcentury declined to about 25 cents on the dollar from its high point of decades earlier.

At the end of the era there was a short-lived craze for plank roads. Much cheaper than the turnpikes to build, they provided a smooth surface "on which heavy loads could be easily and quickly hauled to market." Thousands of miles of these roads were put together before it was realized that costs of maintenance were prohibitive and that they decayed much sooner than their enthusiastic promoters had expected.

The greatest single event in the transportation history of the times was the building of the Erie Canal. Its completion in 1825 was the signal for the start of a wave of canal building that swept over the land, the boom continuing throughout the Jacksonian era. Canals were more important than turnpikes because they carried far more freight, proving capable, in fact, of providing for the first time to western farmers a substantial bridge to the markets of the East. Peter B. Porter, who was later to become a member of the Erie Canal Commission, as early as 1810 stressed the need of western farmers on the Niagara frontier to have "a vent for their productions and thus break with subsistence farming." Prior to the completion of the great canals of the northeast, western products reached eastern cities by means first of a trip down the Mississippi to New Orleans, followed by the much longer voyage through the Gulf and up the Atlantic Coast. Eastern finished products in return moved slowly across the Appalachians and into western valleys via unsatisfactory land routes. The new canal network broke the barriers to the West, sparking a commercial revolution within the country. It did not occur overnight, for it was only at the end of the era in the middle and late 1840s, for example, that goods and crops from west of New York came regularly to outweigh the stuffs of western New York farmers in the journey from Buffalo to Albany. But well before that time, the trend was under way. It must be remembered that New York was a great agricultural state, whose predominance was not to be easily ended.

Work on the Erie Canal was approved in 1817, and commenced the following year under the sponsorship of the state and its governor, De Witt Clinton. (Martin Van Buren had shortly before used his considerable influence in the legislature to delay its beginnings, in the interests of his party and its prestige.) The idea of connecting the Great Lakes region with the Hudson appealed to the imagination of men, requiring a vision that transcended economic interest alone. George R. Taylor calls the building of the Erie Canal "an act of faith," while Nathan Miller writes that "the successful completion of the Erie and Champlain canals (the Champlain was a companion canal connecting Albany with Canada) filled Americans with wonder and amazement." Before the Erie, the country had perhaps 100 miles of canal altogether. The process of construction was very expensive and canal engineering was a relatively unknown science in America. The typical American transportation enterprise was "developmental" rather than "exploitative," traversing unsettled areas, and in the absence of assured profits depending heavily on government enterprise and subsidy or on "extraordinary illusions on the part of the original investors." In the case of the Erie, men of "moderate means" were the main subscribers, but in view of the excellent returns realized on the investment by as early as 1821 and continuing thereafter, it is clear that their hopes were more than illusions.

The commissioners, sensibly "confining initial construction to a fraction of the total project," demonstrated their ability both to solve technical problems and to complete serviceable portions of the entire work on a piecemeal basis, bringing immediate profit to the beneficiary communities. By 1821 English capital was being heavily invested in the enterprise and Langdon Cheves, then president of the Second Bank of the United States, invested $45,000 in its stock. That the Canal did well thereafter is understatement. Nathan Miller has shown that the resources of the Canal Fund became an important reservoir to be drawn on by the banks of the state and were of special importance during crises, such as the credit shortage in 1834, the Great Fire in 1835, and the resumption crisis after the Panic of 1837. The original investment was so quickly returned and profits on it so great, that for much of its early history the Canal and the men who managed it suffered from an embarrassment of riches. Great judiciousness had to be shown in the use of the "Fund," in order to placate different communities and interests within the state, sensitive to the slightest hint that Canal capital showed favoritism to interests other than their own. And from time to time critics accused its commissioners of bias in administration, not always unjustly. Such were among the wages of success.

When it was completed the Erie Canal was indeed a marvel of engineering. Its builders had somehow surmounted the large difficulties in the way of constructing a "great ditch, 363 miles long, crossing rivers, streams, and marshes on aqueducts, penetrating the lofty granite escarpment of Lockport, and surmounting the sharp rise in the terrain between the Hudson River and the Mohawk Valley." It had required 84 locks, was 28 feet wide at its bottom, 40 feet at the top, carried 4 feet of water, and had an 8-foot tow path for the draft animals which pulled its barges. At a cost of about $7 million it was a great bargain. Its economic effects were felt immediately. There are differing ways of reckoning costs but whichever way is used shows that the cost of moving one ton from Buffalo to Albany dropped to one twelfth of its earlier price. The West derived the greatest benefit, for although the price of western crops dropped sharply in the East, the prices of eastern goods fell even more drastically. Western flour could buy almost 50 percent more sugar, for example, in the period 1826 to 1830 than in 1816 to 1820. The rate of increase in western exports is indicated by the fact that, in 1835, 268,000 barrels of flour were shipped East on the Erie, while in 1840 the amount was over one million barrels. Freight left the turnpikes for the Erie Canal and its host of imitators.

A canal fever set in. New York State alone by 1838 had in addition to the Erie, the Champlain; the Oswego, which connected Lake Ontario to Syracuse on the Erie; the Chenango, connecting Binghamton on the Susquehanna to Utica on the Erie; the Delaware and Hudson binding the two rivers; a number of tiny canals in the west of the state; and, under construction, the Genesee Valley Canal and the Black River Canal. Pennsylvania's answer to the Erie was the famous Main Line, begun in 1826 and, when it was finished eight years later, connecting Pittsburgh with Philadelphia over a distance of 395 miles. More expensive to build than the Erie—it required more than twice as many locks, for example—it did well, though not nearly so well as its greater competitor. Elsewhere in the state, the contagion resulted in greater expenditures for canal construction than in any other state, although unfortunately, Pennsylvania was topographically poorly suited to canal building. Ohio was third in canal mileage. The state built and owned the two great canals that connected Cleveland with Portsmouth on the Ohio River, and Cincinnati with Toledo on Lake Erie. Additional state and privately run canals crisscrossed the state, for the most part doing a booming business. Virginia and Indiana were next in importance, the canals of the latter state turning out to be an unmitigated financial disaster. Other states which had relatively large systems included New Jersey, Maryland, and Illinois.

The enthusiasm for canals seemed to know no bounds during the 1830s. Citizens gave land, rights of way, labor, even the use of their slaves in an outburst of "local patriotism" that Carter Goodrich has called the spontaneous American equivalent to the attempts by a communist apparatus "to obtain [by regimentation and deliberate efforts] popular participation at the local level in the processes of economic development." Unfortunately the enthusiasm in more cases than not was overenthusiasm. For not only did no other canal come close to equaling the success of the Erie—at the end of whose line sat the nation's greatest commercial city—but most of them had a hard time breaking even. Of 102 millions invested in canals by New York, Pennsylvania, Ohio, Indiana, Illinois, Maryland, and Virginia, only 15 percent of the sum was profitably invested.

Goodrich, the leading authority on canals, has stressed three major weaknesses in the American internal improvements movement. These were the failure to develop a "workable criterion for the selection of projects," which led to poor choice of sites; the "failure to develop and apply criteria for the assignment of projects to different levels of government authority—federal, state or local," which manifested itself in faulty improvisation; and "the nature of the government agencies," lacking as they generally were in expertise and depending as they generally did on small staffs and budgets. The latter two shortcomings stemmed from built-in features of the American political system: federalism and weak government. State governments, the heaviest investor in the system, overextended themselves, running up huge debts in the process.

The term "canal madness" does not appear to be exaggeration in the face of the behavior of most state legislatures. No section was immune from the disease. Pennsylvania politicians, led by Thaddeus Stevens, sought popularity by promoting canals everywhere, securing credit—if not real money—for the purpose from Nicholas Biddle, who was astute enough to turn their lust to his gain. In the South, Alabama moved timidly because of lack of funds but other states were not so old-fashioned. The Carolinas spent far beyond their means on improvement projects; Virginia was dominated by a group "willing to vote for any internal improvement scheme, and to borrow any amount to carry it out." Large states and small, old ones and new, south of the Mason-Dixon line, tried to outdo one another and resorted to most dubious banking practices in the process. The West was even bolder. "The magnitude of the [not atypical] Illinois schemes," according to a close student, "exceeded the wants of the people in as great a degree as the estimated cost exceeded the resources of the state." The Illinois legislature had the marvelous idea of completing "the extensive improvements without any expense to the state." In fact, not one Illinois project was ever completed, although expense there was in abundance. Michigan had a "fanatical" plan but no more so than Ohio or Indiana. Reginald C. McGrane's conclusion was that the West, with its ill-planned and poorly managed internal improvement plans, contributed more than its share to the deceptive appearances of wealth within the nation prior to 1837.

But mainly in the high cost 1830s, the canals had to be paid for in the deflationary 1840s. There were too many of them and too often in poorly chosen areas. Construction costs were higher than anticipated. The cost of building the Susquehanna and Tidewater mounted to $80,000 per mile. Though the Chesapeake and Ohio's $60,000 per mile construction cost was partly defrayed by the federal government, it remained a losing proposition. Small canals proved unable to handle heavy traffic, while the expense of enlargement was prohibitive. The rub was that only a heavy traffic that utilized a canal close to capacity could head off failure. The slowness of movement, aggravated by the many locks; the irregularity of service, subject as it was both to droughts and floods; the incompetence and, as in Indiana, the "political log-rolling, and large scale peculation" indulged in by their managers, were additional causes of the movement's decline. By no means the least significant factor in its downfall was the rise of railroads, whose superiority made many canals "obsolescent even before they were opened for traffic."

The financial failures and the technical imperfections of many canals do not detract from their historical contribution. For what one contemporary said of the Blackstone Canal in Massachusetts applies to others as well: "The canal has been more useful to the public, than to the owners." Whether profitable to their investors or not, canal transport was very much cheaper than wagon haulage. Modern studies show that canals lowered transportation costs far more drastically than did railroads in their turn. Questions remain about the ultimate economic worth of canals, the *extent* to which they contributed to economic growth, whether in view of the waste and duplication of effort that characterized the building of so many of them, they were worth the cost. One can anticipate future studies hypothetically obliterating most antebellum canal mileage, subtracting the value of their investments from the nation's total, removing the freight they hauled either to a few older canals or to other forms of transportation, estimating the likely rate of profit for canal funds otherwise invested, and finally, guessing educatedly the likely economic effects on the communities so altered. The fact remains that canals were built in Jacksonian America by men who, as always, were variously motivated. The effects of the canal movement were mixed but there can be no doubt that goods flowed in much greater volume across the nation because of it.

Another major feature of the era was the continued development of the steamboat. The river steamboat came into its own during the era, from 1830 to 1850 becoming "the most important agency of internal transportation in the country." Steamboats "gave the first great impetus to western growth by making possible upriver trade and greatly reducing transportation costs up and down the [Mississippi] river." The steamboat made *possible* a vast increase in the export of cotton to the northwest. Timber, metals, and grains could now move downstream in great quantities. Of course there has recently been some question as to the extent to which the *actual* trade materialized.

In the northeast steamboats were used mainly to carry passengers. Tudor, who was so critical of American land travel, found them "admirable, and the mode of conveyance by them most commodious and delightful." The low-pressure engines of eastern steamboats made them safer than western boats, although their accident rate was also disconcerting. Western boats used a high-pressure engine which was cheaper, easier to operate, better suited to muddy western waters, and as noted, more dangerous. Great skill was needed to navigate western rivers with their ice, their fluctuations in depth, their ledges, rocks, sandbars, and worst of all, their snags. The captains who survived were indeed skillful men who knew every inch of the waters they navigated. The well-known boast of some Mississippi River captains that they could navigate in heavy dew was as doubtless an exaggeration but there is evidence they could manage in shallow water of only 22 inches in depth.

Steamboats contributed much to the legendry of a West where, as every reader of Mark Twain knows, the dream of every boy was to be a pilot or captain. Western steamboats also made a great economic contribution. Consider their effect on the price of goods moving upstream from New Orleans. Where in 1816 a resident of Cincinnati had to pay 16 cents more than his southern neighbor for a pound of coffee, by 1830 the steamboat had narrowed the difference to 2½ cents. Or consider their effect on the speed of travel. The 150 miles from New York to Albany, which took from two days to two weeks by sail and close to an entire day by coach, took only 8 to 10 hours by steamboat. Since the steam trip at five dollars cost only two thirds of the coach fare and was very much more comfortable, one can understand why travel thrived on the new medium.

As was true of other means of transportation, the financial picture of steamboats was not nearly so bright as their general value to the economy might indicate. They were very expensive to construct, their price ranging from $20,000 for western medium-sized boats to over $100,000 for larger eastern models. Corporations increasingly replaced individuals in their management and ownership. By the end of the era the return to investors had dropped to 6 percent. Repairs were expensive as was general maintenance, depreciation was rapid, and breakdowns were numerous due to faulty construction. By 1839 over 30 percent of the steamboats had been lost as a result of accidents. As was true of canals, steamboats too were hurt by the railroads, unable to match the flexibility, dependability, and above all the speed of the new carriers. The steamboats' greater comfort and their lower rates did, however, enable them to hold on to a significant portion of passenger traffic.

The place of railroads in the transportation spectrum of the Jacksonian era can be compared with that of factories in the industrial sphere. Both became significant factors during the era, while at its end they were poised to make dramatic strides forward that would soon enable them to outdistance their rivals in the transportation and in the production of goods. The rise of the railroads was much more swift, however, than that of factories. In 1830 the United States had only 13 miles of railroad track, laid by the recently established Baltimore and Ohio line. By 1840 there were 3,328 miles of track, exactly two miles more than the total length of canals. While traffic moved much more swiftly on rails than on any other medium, the very much lower cost of transportation on water continued to be an important consideration during the era. Where the roads charged from five cents to nine cents a mile to move freight, the charge on rivers and canals was only one cent. Railroads also provided more direct and reliable transportation, but essentially their triumph in areas already served by water routes awaited an expansion of productivity or a volume of trade that would make their greater expense worth the while of their users.

There were a number of obstacles to their development. Managers of other forms of travel threw up roadblocks. The legislatures of states such as New York, Pennsylvania, and Ohio tried at first to restrict them in an attempt to protect their heavy canal investments. Their excessive speed of 15 miles per hour was said to imperil health. Corruption in their management and a high accident rate in their performance were said to be characteristic. Yet their forward sweep was not to be checked, their admirers possessing an enthusiasm and determination not matched by their detractors. An optimistic era ready to give its all to improve transportation, could not fail to be attracted to this promising new method. Producers who stood to enlarge their markets, consumers to get more for their money, speculators to profit from enhanced real estate values, and government to derive increased revenues, were increasingly enthusiastic about the roads, giving them sweeping privileges in the form of rights, exemptions and real estate. Eastern cities such as Boston, Charleston, and Baltimore, lacking waterways to connect them with the hinterlands, were in the forefront of the new movement, with Baltimore and its famous road pioneering. By 1835 Boston was the hub of a railroad network connecting it with Worcester, Lowell, and Providence, which was to transform the economic life of that great New England city and its new suburbs. That such political enemies as David Henshaw, leader of the dominant wing of the Massachusetts Democrats, and Nathan Hale, Whig publisher and arch anti-Jacksonian, could sit together as directors of the Boston and Worcester Railroad, is a nice indication that sometimes political differences ceased at the railroad profits' edge during the Jacksonian era.

Most of the track was laid in New York and New England. It was not track of uniform width since the United States broke with the English gauge of 4 feet, 8½ inches. Fear and greed led the roads of different states or even of different companies within one state to choose different gauges, in order to "prevent diversion of traffic over other lines." That Pennsylvania and Ohio each had seven different track widths also had the effect of holding back the development of a national network. Yankee ingenuity, on the other hand, conceived a number of unique improvements that significantly abetted the development of the roads, including such devices as a lighter locomotive, an extra swivel track which permitted better negotiation of curves, the "cowcatcher," the replacement of the coach design of seating by the modern prototype, improved roadbeds, and spiking the rails to the ties. The steam locomotive carried the day after its introduction on the Charleston Railroad in 1830. Typically, roads were put up haphazardly, confirming just as much as did canals, Goodrich's judgment that poor site selection and questionable management were among the major weaknesses in American internal improvements.

Railroad expansion spurred the growth of the corporate form, since their heavy capital requirements and risks were beyond the capacity of individuals. As was noted earlier, corporate railroad charters were most liberal, typically less restricted than those of turnpike and canal companies. What restraints there were were generally ignored. Right of eminent domain, no restrictions as to types of securities, monopolies, tax exemptions, lottery privileges, were among the inducements held out to entrepreneurs by zealous state governments. In the West, where roads were regarded as the key to prosperity, local and state governments made great financial contributions to them. The federal government confined its aid during the era to a reduction of tariff rates on iron used in railroad construction. Vast land grants were a thing of the future. State governments, on the other hand, made lavish contributions, going so far in some cases as to require banks to buy their railroad stock, and by 1838 had run up $43 million in debts attributable to the railroads.

It has become impossible to consider the economic role of railroads in antebellum America without reference to the new economic approach to the issue, particularly the path-breaking studies by Robert W. Fogel and Albert Fishlow. Fogel set out to determine the validity of the proposition "that railroads were indispensable to American economic growth during the 19th century." The argument of indispensability is central to the well-known "take-off" thesis developed by Walt W. Rostow in his *Stages of Economic Growth*. The third of Rostow's five classic stages was the take-off, which allegedly occurred in the United States between 1843 and 1860, when an unprecedented leap in per capita output, accompa-

nied among other things by radical changes in production techniques, supposedly raised the entire economy to a new plateau from
which it would later and more gradually achieve the stages of
maturity and high mass consumption. Railroads play a decisive part
in Rostow's explanation of American take-off, at first for their alleged impact on eastern manufacturing and the stimulus they gave
such a specialized but vital industry as engineering, and subsequently by essentially opening up and vitalizing the great food-
producing region of the Middle West.

According to Fogel, the crucial aspect of the "axiom of [railroad]
indispensability" was the "implicit assumption that the economy of
the nineteenth century lacked an effective alternative to the railroad
and was incapable of producing one." Creating what one of his
critics called a "special and nonexistent world," Fogel proceeded to
hypothesize an antebellum America without railroads. What re-
moves his subsequent discussion from the realm of fantasy is the
fact that it is not simply a series of imaginative surmises. It is
indeed imaginative but it attempts to find factual answers to such
hard questions as the amount of traffic carried by railroads and
competitive forms; their comparative charges to users; the quantity
and value of the raw materials and manufactured products consumed by railroads, and the percentage these figures represented of
the total sales of the involved products; the cost of likely alternative
means of transport and the projected impact on economic growth of
the use of these hypothetical substitutes, or "the amount by which
the production possibilities of the nation would have been reduced if
agricultural commodities could not have been shipped by railroads."

This of course was an unhistorical and "unrealistic" if provocative
exercise. It has been asserted that the data both Fogel and Fishlow
use are at times of dubious accuracy, that in other instances their
work "is weakened by a serious data shortage," and that "assumptions central to their analyses were . . . at variance with reality."
They have not demonstrated precisely what the net benefits of railroads were to the national economy. With regard to the fault of
unreality, it is obvious that Fogel's "hypothetico-deductive" model of
a railless universe was constructed in order to help find the answers
to an important historical question. His own assumptions may be
questionable, his tables and choice of data selective and at times
inaccurate, for all one knows his motive may have been to down-
grade an institution that he hated. His work remains significant and
many of his conclusions interesting, if not unarguable. Peter
McLelland, one of the severest critics of this new interpretation of
railroads, concedes not only the landmark stature of its "application
of economic theory and statistical techniques to the problems of
economic history," but the value of its wealth of information on
railroads "and the multitude of strands that ran between this
single innovation and the fabric of American development." If no
final answer has been given concerning the very large question of
indispensability, light has been thrown on smaller but nevertheless
important questions.

It has been shown that transportation experts in the 1830s predicted that in the future canals would clearly continue [to be] the most advantageous means of communication" where moderate velocities were required. Although railroads won increased respect during the decade 1834 to 1843 their significance was greater to their own investors than to the economy at large. Fishlow found that "railroads influenced total expenditures [mainly in the form of railroad investment] long before they were a valuable asset for the transportation of goods." For all their attractiveness to investors their rate of return was disappointing. Their speed and comfort enabled the iron rails quickly to conquer passenger traffic but the victory they won in the competition for lugging freight became apparent only in the 1850s and was only "hinted at" even for the later years of the Jacksonian era.

The stimulus of railroads to industry was much smaller than had been believed. In contrast to Rostow's thesis, the vital emergence of specialized engineering firms owed far more to the earlier development of steamboats than to railroads. In fact "instead of creating an engineering industry, the rapid development of domestic production of locomotives in the United States can be explained by the existence of a prior level of skills and techniques upon which the [railroad] industry could call." The demand for rails, far from dominating the antebellum iron industry, represented only a small portion of that industry's output, in the 1840s not matching the iron consumed in making nails. Nor did railroads consume vast quantities of coal. The rise of iron and coal production in the 1840s was largely "independent of railroad demands." Crossties did not consume a substantial portion of lumber products. Insofar as the effect of railroads on manufacturing in general was concerned, the development of the latter owed little to the former. Fishlow's summation of this issue is that "one could write an independent history of manufacture and railroads in the 1840s." Modern research has also found wanting the old notion that the western economy and society of the United States "were, economically speaking, created by the railroad." Empirical evidence makes clear that "railroads were not constructed ahead of demand." Ohio's great growth and importance by the 1840s, for example, antedated its reliance on moving freight by rails. Fishlow concluded that since cheap *transportation* rather than railroads was "the necessary condition for the emergence of the North Central states as the granary of the nation," and since wagon and water transport "could have provided a relatively good substitute for the fabled iron horse," it was therefore likely that "even in the absence of railroads the prairies would have been settled and exploited." Paradoxically, it is in making this, one of its least questionable assertions, that the new approach sins most grievously. It is more than *likely* that the West would have been opened up without railroads. The fact is, however, that railroads *did* carry the day, ultimately. Their victory was determined by a market operating as impersonally in this case as it does in others. Investors, passengers, and finally movers of freight did choose them, and in view of the railroads' positive features the choice was hardly an inane one. But even if it was, what of it? Investors and for that matter entire nations have made much more terrible choices. With that caveat stated, it does now appear that the role of railroads was not as important in the Jacksonian era's economy as used to be believed prior to 1964.

The American economy was significantly affected by international trade. According to North's analysis, the "basic influence" on the American economy in the period 1815 to 1845 was the emergence of an international economy "in which the parts were interrelated by the forces of comparative prices of goods, services, and productive factors." American economic growth was "generated" or "induced" above all by the growing European market for American exports and partly by the flow of European products and capital into this country. The decisive influences on the timing, pace, and character of American development during the era were English and, to a lesser extent, French purchases of American cotton, with the rise or fall in cotton prices "the major element in any explanation of [American] economic change." This interpretation does not deny the significance of indigenous factors in accounting for the nation's economic growth. But it traces these factors ultimately to the international system which, at the same time that it drew American economic life into its orbit, was "making this country increasingly independent of the international economic context." If the export sector was the decisive one, imports had the significant effect on the American economy of protecting it against its own inflationary tendencies. By slowing down price rises within the country, they provided a subtle brake on expansion, thus lengthening and stabilizing the nation's prosperity. This view thus attributes decisive significance to international commerce, even crediting it with the rise of an internal economy, whose own dynamic growth would *subsequently* become the main stimulus to further expansion.

Many contemporaries would not have accepted this modern analysis. Champions of the protective tariff, of course, would have been indifferent to the argument extolling the virtues of a lower and therefore more sensible rate of profit for American manufactures. And while America's international trade thrived, expanding, for example, at a greater rate than Great Britain's, and fortunes continued to be made in overseas commerce, some astute persons felt that the balance was shifting from commerce to manufacturing, so far as opportunities for investment were concerned. Was it not merchant capital that was behind the growing factory system of New England? The victory of Nathan Appleton over Henry Lee in the 1830 election for congressional representative from Suffolk County in Massachusetts was widely interpreted as a victory for protection and the manufacturing interest over free trade and the commercial interest, at least in that section.

For most of the era the balance of trade was unfavorable. The relatively "primitive" nature of the American economy is also suggested by the fact that our chief exports were raw materials of great bulk and low price while our imports were finished products. English textiles continued to be very important despite the tremendous growth of American textile manufactures. The expansion of our enterprise and transportation depended heavily on English capital. For that matter American importers drew heavily on English banks. The outlines of the export picture are blurred by the sharp decline in cotton prices that marked the early part of the era. For example, the drop in the value of cotton exports between 1818 and 1830 occurred despite the fact that the number of pounds exported increased from 92 million to 298 million. A drop in price from 33.9 cents to 9.9 cents a pound explained the declining value of the exports. The tariff came to be an increasingly explosive political issue during the era. Economic historians tend to discount the economic importance of tariffs during that era, however, for there seemed to be no correlation between tariff rates and either the volume of imports or the acceleration of American production in the protected industries. The tariff nevertheless remained an explosive political issue.

The era was marked by an increasing division of labor in the merchant's function. Retailing was more clearly separated from wholesale dealings, with wholesalers gaining markedly in influence. Among importers there was a differentiation among shipping merchants who traded on a very large scale; smaller scale importers; jobbers who acted as middle men, purchasing in bulk from importers; and commission merchants or factors, favored by many planters. Auctions continued to be relied on by many importers to dispose of new merchandise, attractive because of their low overhead and quick sales. A lively re-export trade was another feature of the period, characteristically transferring English textiles from American ports in American ships to Mexico.

Domestic trade grew at a much more rapid pace than international during the era. It is arguable as to whether international factors were the *primary* impetus to growth. But there is no question that the growing British market for cotton, the increasing flow of European capital into the American economy (particularly into its transportation network), and the dramatic expansion of productivity in agriculture everywhere and industry in the North, were interrelated factors, each one of which played an important part in the growth of internal trade.

Inevitably, an economy as dynamic and speculative as this one needed money, far more money that it had ever had before. Banks sprang up everywhere to meet the need—some of them in places so remote that they were inhabited, so the saying went, only by wildcats. (It is useful to keep in mind Hugh Rockoff's conclusion that "both economic theory and the empirical evidence suggest that the quantitative impact of wildcatting was probably negligible.") Where in 1829 the nation had 329 state banks, by 1837 the number had risen to 788. The stock in trade of these institutions was note issue. Notes were not legal money since the Constitution explicitly barred the states, let alone private groups, from issuing money. Only the Congress could coin money and regulate the value thereof. Congress did coin money, but in such limited and inadequate supply that the American people brushed legal fictions aside and treated bank notes as money, despite their typical wording that they represented only promises to pay specie—or coins of gold and silver. Woe to those banks, had all their noteholders insisted on specie redemption. For that matter, woe to the nation, since when the banks' creditors did insist on getting coin at face value, and did so in large numbers, a greater or lesser financial panic threatened to set in.

The value of notes in circulation, which in 1821 had totaled $3 million, by 1833 had reached $10.2 million, and in 1837 had soared to $149.2 million. This was indeed the kind of increase that seemed to meet this dynamic nation's need for currency. Unfortunately, the currency was too often of dubious character and poor reputation, precisely the qualities which induced that lack of confidence on the part of its possessors that in turn led them to make their fateful runs on banks for a redemption the latter could not give. Everything would have been lovely if these "crises of confidence" had not arisen, if people had stilled their doubts and agreed to agree that the note in hand was truly worth what it claimed to be. But that was asking too much. Nor was the problem altogether psychological. When, for example, gold was drained from England because of grain purchases on the Continent made necessary by an English crop failure, a train of events was set in motion that had nothing to do with confidence as such but whose end result was repudiation by an American bank of notes it had promised to honor. Since English investments and purchases of American products accounted for a large and ever more significant proportion of what specie there was in this country, any event that led English banks and investors to slow down their American spending or, even worse, to demand payment, immediately confronted our banks with a grave problem. This is exactly what happened prior to the Panic of 1839.

American money, then, characteristically took the form of bank notes based on or backed by valuable metals worth a varying fraction of the notes' face value. This was unavoidable. It was also perfectly sensible, historically inevitable, in the case of a youthful nation whose real wealth, in the form of people, skills, raw materials, finished goods and services, far outpaced its possession of the gold and silver that were the basis of international trade. Peter Temin notes that during the era the gross national product was about ten times the stock of money and between 30 to 50 times the value of the country's specie. The nation got, by far, most of its specie in effect by converting its real wealth—mainly its cotton and secondarily the opportunity it offered foreigners to profit from its promising transportation ventures—into foreign gold. No knowledgeable man of affairs anywhere would have asked of currency that every last penny's worth of it be backed up by a specie reserve at 100 percent face value. (I exclude some of the extreme "hard money" and anti-bank theorists, who would get rid of almost all paper and, why not?, all banking, having convinced themselves that honest industry and honest commerce could manage better without the intervention of banking parasites. The only money they respected was real bullion. However adherents to such notions might be characterized, it seems safe to say that they were not knowledgeable men of affairs. Many of them, unhappy with good reason with the incredibly poor paper money circulated by fly-by-night banks of the time, lumped most paper money together as the allegedly dread evil of "rag money." They failed to see either the need for an elastic currency or that paper notes, when issued in moderation by banks not dedicated to quick speculative profits, could be a respected, stable, and most useful form of money.) The real problem it seems clear was not paper money versus hard money but rather the quality of paper money.

The old Jeffersonian, Albert Gallatin, became an admirer of the Second Bank of the United States because he believed that it was only during its existence and due to its ministrations that the United States had a sound currency. Although required by its charter to redeem its notes at face value and able to do so during its successful years in the decade prior to the removal of the government deposits, its typical practice was to have on hand a specie reserve of slightly better than 50 percent of the face value of its notes. This was not only effective practice; it was considered eminently sound practice. As American banks went it was highly unusual practice. More typical was a specie reserve for state banks that ranged from 25 to less than 10 percent of the face value of the notes issued. Many Americans wanted it that way. It is by no means as certain as monetary conservatives used to think it was that these Americans were wrong or, even worse, depraved. Excessively conservative bank practice, as William W. Freehling has shown for South Carolina, could be perhaps as hurtful to an economy in need of currency as a too reckless policy.

Had the nation been content to rely for money on its own specie and what it secured through trade or sale of its products abroad, there would have been few problems. There also would have been slow growth. Americans, as moralists such as Emerson noted, were greedy for quick gain. And as Tocqueville and others had observed, they were most optimistic about their chances. Men characteristically sought bank charters from state legislatures not in order to serve the community but to make large and quick profits. As William H. Crawford had put it, many banks had been incorporated "not because there was capital seeking investment [nor] because the places where they were established had commerce and manufactures which required their fostering aid; but because men without active capital wanted the means of obtaining loans, which their standing in the community would not command from banks or individuals having real capital and established credit." Directors of newly established banks commonly had "easy access" to loans from their own institutions at most favorable terms. Such bank managers invested as little capital as possible, issued as much paper money as they could get away with, speculated ceaselessly. Borrowers, even when they had to pay exorbitant interest or when they were aware of the flimsy nature of the notes they borrowed, acquiesced joyfully in the system, so long as they could get their hands on money, any kind, any value.   Many private bankers who themselves issued paper and made discounts, were like other men in their zeal to borrow as much as they could. In this sense, the picture was not one of bankers separated from the rest of a community whose needs they catered to, but rather of a single mass of profit seekers, all of them quite aware that the rise in their fortunes was based on an inflationary system. This was a dangerous system, obviously, but a marvelous one too, since by what other mechanism could fortunes be manufactured overnight out of little or nothing?

Moralists were appalled at illusory wealth begotten by near worthless paper. Looked at from the vantage point of economic development rather than morality, however, the paper money system presents an aspect that is not so unrelievedly dismal. Bankers and borrowers alike were gamblers to be sure, but they were gambling on the nation's economic future—its immediate future, in their locales. Investors in internal improvements and public or private real estate were gambling on sudden and vast increases in population, productivity, and commerce that would enable them to realize many times their investment—or gamble. Given this nation's vast land area, untapped resources, natural waterways, its magnetic attraction to European settlers as to European capital, the enthusiasm of the gamblers was not entirely misplaced. In the absence of sufficient gold or silver, Americans fell back on a fairly tried and true makeshift of western capitalistic civilization: paper money. That they put out too much paper is no doubt true. The terrible panics that punctuated the era were caused in part by excessive paper, although neither then nor now have we reached agreement as to the diverse and complex causation of these phenomena. Once it became part of an international system, the American economy simultaneously became subject to shifts and turns induced by factors over which it had no control. The severe drop in cotton prices, for example, was a problem that had little to do directly with the character of American money.

Paper money enabled the economy to *undertake* projects which otherwise could not have been attempted and which, as they came to fruition, in effect gave real value to the paper invested in them. That too many Americans then insisted on gambling their winnings in further domestic enterprises, backed by new quantities of paper, or on purchasing inordinate quantities of foreign luxury goods, was their privilege, albeit a very risky one. The fault was not with the system of paper money, as such, but with the people who pushed it beyond reasonable limits. Social and economic critics who seek the causes of social dislocations in institutions rather than chromosomes would blame "the system," but by that phrase mean speculative capitalism, rather than a particular device for promoting exchange and representing real values. Even Marx, who was at least as radical as William M. Gouge or Thomas Hart Benton—erstwhile hard-money champions of the era—would later attribute labor's plight to a general system that denied it the full product of its labor, rather than to rag money.

Workingmen paid in paper money whose value fluctuated wildly—seemingly always downward—understandably took a dim view of the stuff, some of them even responding to theorists like Gouge who regarded it as the root of all social and economic evil. Other people too were unhappy. Gallatin's praise of the Second Bank was representative of a widespread admiration for one of the few financial institutions whose notes were as good as gold. Arthur Fraas and other modern students agree that the Bank did well the job of providing a uniform national currency. Since BUS notes, while less than half the nation's total, were at times one quarter or more of it, they represented a not insignificant quantity whose quality enhanced the general reputation of American money, particularly abroad. Under the presidency of Nicholas Biddle the Second BUS also played a direct and vital role in maintaining the quality of state and private bank notes, operating effectively as a central bank. According to Bray Hammond, the Bank conducted the central banking function "in two ways, of which one was self-acting and one was discretionary. Controls were self-acting when the Bank, as it received the notes of state banks in the deposits of government collections and otherwise, required payment of them by the state banks. Save when the state banks would not or could not meet their obligations, this regulatory function proceeded in routine fashion; and its restraint upon the lending power of the state banks was comprehensive and effectual." Discretionary controls were exercised when the Bank chose to abstain from demanding payment, allowing the state banks to run into debt to it, thus qualifying the "automaticity" of the central banking function.

In other words the BUS could or it could not choose to compel state banks to pay in specie. This was what Biddle had in mind when he made the politically harmful remark to a Senate committee that, but for his forbearance, the BUS could have destroyed most state banks. His statement, which amounted to a truism in view of the charter provisions establishing the Bank as repository of federal funds, was seized upon by the Bank's enemies as a sign of its dangerous power. As a matter of fact, however, after he assumed the presidency of the BUS in 1823, Biddle, in the judgment of many contemporary and most modern authorities, used his discretionary power ably, promoting at one and the same time the real interests of the banks, their creditors, the Treasury, and above all the nation. Temin notes that the Second Bank was an "effective policeman," which was instrumental in preventing the reserve ratio of the nation's banks from falling during the 1830s. Prior to Jackson's veto of the bill to recharter the Bank, Biddle, in the words of one of his

severest modern critics, "placed a restraining influence on credit
expansion when trouble was coming"—by requiring redemption—
while "during the period of severe liquidation after the bubble burst
he wisely expanded loans, thus easing the impact of the crisis
[1825] on the financial and business community." He tried neither
to destroy competitors nor to enrich his own stockholders, many of
whom criticized him for being too concerned with the larger or
public consequences of the Bank's policies and insufficiently interested in large profits for them. Under Biddle's direction dividends
were typically limited to 7 percent. What to Jacksonian critics was
the "monster" of rag money was in fact the institution that was
responsible for keeping much of the nation's paper money honest—
or based on more specie than would otherwise have been the case.
As has recently been noted by Jean Wilburn, most banks, including
those in the South and Southwest, by 1831–32 very much appreciated the positive role the Bank played and wanted its charter re-
newed. Yet for all of Biddle's undoubted ability, one can understand
the resentment of some persons who had to answer to this less-than-
godlike eminence, himself fallible, and in their minds perfectly
capable of camouflaging erroneous or selfish policies in the lofty
language of the true national interest. As Joseph Dorfman has
pointed out, many knowledgeable men here felt toward the BUS as
did English critics toward the Bank of England, that it "was not a fit
regulator of the currency so long as it was at the same time a
commercial bank making discounts."

The story of the Second Bank's tribulations is a much-told tale.
Approved in 1816 after a change of heart by Jeffersonians who
earlier had let the charter of the First Bank lapse, nothing the new
Bank might do would shake the conviction of unrepentant agrarians
that it was a wicked engine for exploiting farmers and enriching
capitalists. Devotees of the yeoman myth clung to notions as anti-
quated as the Middle Ages, emotions disguised as beliefs, according
to which commerce and particularly finance were dishonest, para-
sitic, and downright evil. Diametrically unlike in their thinking,
although just a hostile to the BUS, were many local and state
bankers and the communities they served—at least prior to the
crucial years of the Bank War. Earlier historians made the point
that the latter, oblivious to ancient doctrine, sought cheap money
and resented the brakes occasionally placed on it by the Second
Bank. The BUS could do no right in the eyes of such bankers,
however, for when it followed an easy money policy it was hated as
competition and for its size and effectiveness. Its constitutionality
had never been universally accepted for all of John Marshall's
decision in *McCulloch* v. *Maryland*. It could be a respected repository of federal funds, disburse these funds with dispatch wherever
and whenever called on by government to do so, issue notes of
unmatched integrity, promote the economic welfare of the country,
not only by its central banking operations but by its own loans and
investments (which, during Biddle's tenure, stimulated western and

southern prosperity, among other ways by exchanging bills of exchange payable in the East or in Europe for western notes). It could do all these things and be pilloried nonetheless—particularly after the idolized Andrew Jackson decided it should be. Of course Mr. Biddle was not altogether angelic.

Even old Catterall, whose conclusion was that there were "few greater enormities chargeable to politicians than the destruction of the Bank of the United States," conceded that its record under Biddle was not spotless. If in his judgment it had not spent one dollar corruptly, it nevertheless had made loans to Congressmen under terms more charitable than they should have been. Biddle, who believed "money is neither Whig nor Tory," did not discriminate against Jacksonians in his appointments to the boards of branch banks. (Catterall adds the less than clinically detached observation that since Jacksonians for the most part were not intelligent business men, it followed that they would be underrepresented on these boards!) But Biddle did spend large sums, improperly, to buy a favorable press, manipulating the Bank's books to obscure his favors to those henceforth staunch anti-Jacksonians, the formidable Messrs. Webb and Noah of the New York *Courier and Enquirer*. Editors in Washington, Richmond, Philadelphia, and Boston were also accommodated by sizable loans at unusually permissive terms. The aim of these expenditures was to maintain or to win over friendliness. That, as Tocqueville and Abdy noted, other banks "bought" the press to attack the BUS, tells something of the common practice and the atmosphere of the day, but it does not exonerate Biddle, not even to Catterall. Biddle had too much power to dispose of funds at his own discretion. On at least one occasion, his "jobbing in public stock" placed the Bank in a position where it could not meet promptly the government's obligation of pay off holders of the public credit. Biddle was also charged with usurpation of the powers of the Bank's Board of Directors. While observing that the Board itself voluntarily gave up its own powers, Catterall grants that "under Biddle something like abuse can be detected."

After Jackson's veto turned the BUS into a lame duck, whose expiration date was 1836, the Bank had to be judged by new criteria. Just as Jackson himself and some of his supporters were undoubtedly sincere in their conviction that it was an illegal and unwholesome institution which had to be destroyed, so its supporters and above all its president were convinced that its continued life as a national bank was in the public interest. The Bank's policy of contraction, initiated in August 1833 and continued for more than a year, was undertaken by a man fighting fire with fire, ready to drive banks to their knees and bring economic activity to a halt, if to do so might compel the government to reconsider its policy. Both the effects of the retraction and Biddle's role in causing it have been exaggerated. Biddle's explanation to friends of why he would not relent displays his arrogance and at the same time the ingenuousness of his conviction that the Bank's welfare was the nation's

highest political and economic good: "But if, from too great sensitiveness, from the fear of offending, or the desire of conciliating, the
bank permits itself to be frightened or coaxed into any relaxation of
its present measures, the relief will itself be cited as evidence that
the measures of the government are not injurious or oppressive, and
the bank will inevitably be prostrated."

For all his acuity—and he was a brilliant man—Biddle lacked the
political astuteness to recognize how damning such a viewpoint
would appear to the many men who did not share his admiration for
the second BUS. Such views, which Biddle to his credit did not try to
hide, only seemed to confirm the charge of the administration that
this financial despot would sacrifice the welfare of the country in
the interests of his bank. After the removal of the deposits, when
hopes for charter resumption were buried, Biddle cast about for a
new charter, securing a most liberal one at the 11th hour from a
Pennsylvania Legislature for whose kindness he had paid liberally.
The risky and speculative policies adopted by the new United States
Bank of Pennsylvania, prior to Biddle's retirement in 1839, culmi-
nated in its ruin shortly thereafter, when a carefully planned
maneuver to withhold from the market some 50,000 bales of cotton
went astray. Biddle's detractors could now justify the government's
earlier attack as a necessary blow against this dangerous speculative institution. His supporters could with equal justice argue that a
private bank in pursuing profit was not subject to the limitations
and did not have the responsibilities of a quasi-governmental institution.

Most modern banking authorities tend to agree that on balance
the BUS, for all its flaws, served the economy and the nation well,
providing the best banking system the country was to have prior to
the Federal Reserve. Unfortunately Biddle lacked the political
touch, alienating many conservative men of affairs who evidently
resented his cocksureness, what one writer calls his intellectualism,
what was usually called his arrogance. Biddle, of course, was himself convinced that a bank such as the BUS was the truest friend to
labor. "What laboring people want," he once wrote, "is labor, work,
constant employment. How can they get it? In building shops and in
building houses; in coal mines; in making roads and canals; and
how are all these carried on except by credit in the shape of loans
from banks. If it were not from such credits, nine tenths of all the
works which give wages to labor would be at an end. Banks may
sometimes be badly managed," he conceded, thinking no doubt of
other banks, "but good banks are the support of industry. . . . The
greatest misfortune to the laboring classes would be to banish the
system of credit" made possible by good banks such as his. This is
not a bad argument. In practical terms it makes perhaps better
sense than the utopian notions of a Skidmore or Gouge. But Biddle
did not know how to make people listen, and in a democracy that
was fatal. He could convince himself that he cornered cotton in
order to aid the planters and the country by driving up the price of

the nation's leading commodity and acquiring invaluable specie thereby. But to much of the country, his actions were nothing but speculation. It does seem clear, however, that the demise of the Bank was due essentially neither to his nor its faults. Once Andrew Jackson, for reasons of his own, decided to destroy it, its days were numbered. For Jackson's influence and popularity were such that even politicians who obviously favored the Bank, voted to uphold his veto.

Most of the nation's money was issued by banks either operated by state governments or, more typically, whose state governments had granted charters to the corporations which ran them. Many of the newer banks were speculative ventures pure and simple, whose managers were operators in the worst sense of the word. They should not be confused with some of the older banks in the great cities, whose notes commanded as much respect as those of the BUS. In New York, men like Maltby Geltson and Robern White of the Manhattan Company; Preserved Fish and William H. Falls of the Tradesmen's Bank; Lynde Catlin and Walter Mead of the Merchants' Bank; Jacob Lorillard and John Fleming of the Mechanic's Bank; Cornelius Heyer and A. P. Halsey of the Bank of New York; or John Pintard, Peter Jay, and Philip Hone of the Bank for Savings in the City of New York, were not primarily get-rich-quick operators. Conservative men, pillars of the community for the most part, they frowned on the irresponsible practices that were becoming current. Since New York's capitalists were primarily interested in commerce, Moses Beach long ago and Robert G. Albion more recently concluded that few of them were engaged in finance. As men of diverse affairs most of them in fact were heavily involved in the activities of the cities' incorporated banks. Others, like Isaac Bronson, were champions of private banking or "free banking" that could be carried on without the necessity of state charters of incorporation. According to Bray Hammond, they hoped to bring about the downfall of the BUS and thus replace Chestnut Street with Wall Street as the nation's financial capital. Actually, some of New York City's leading bankers refused to support Jackson's war on the Bank; while in Boston, too, some of the leading figures in the mercantile community had no objections to a national bank whose branch in their city discounted their notes liberally.

After noting the conservative practice of some of the nation's state banks, it remains true—as the statistics of banking expansion make clear—that sobriety was not the keynote of the era. Bank failures were disturbingly common. The "Safety-fund" system introduced by New York State in 1829, itself imperfect in its indirect punishment of banks that were responsibly capitalized, was atypical for the era. Banks elsewhere did not relish putting aside a portion of capital, no matter how slight, for rainy days. Not that the system prevented bank failures in New York.

The difficulties presented by the circulation of a chaos of currencies, some of them backed by a prayer—as was literally a Morman bank established in Ohio in 1837 with hardly any capital—and subject to drastic depreciation, are indicated by a European visitor:

> The greatest annoyance I was subjected to in travelling was in exchanging money. It is impossible to describe the wretched state of the curency—which is all bills issued by private individuals; companies; cities and states; . . . All the bills are at a discount, varying from ten percent to fifty percent; and such rags of bills, too! In some of the states they issue bank notes for as small as three pence sterling; and in all of them the bills are as low as one dollar. . . . Some of these bills promise to pay in specie; . . . some promise to be paid on demand in current bank notes which are as bad as their own; some bear a promise to be received in payment of a ride on a railway; all sorts of notes—some bearing interest. But all are depreciated below the specie standard.

In the South and West banking was carried on most irresponsibly. In Mississippi "mystery and concealment" were the characteristic features of the banking processes of the state. Directors contributed capital in the form of notes borrowed; or they borrowed the entire capital; or they gave themselves heavy discounts; or "proceeded from one bank to another, extending their credit and increasing their property at an enormous price," until the whole system collapsed. Mississippi's 17 banks circulated more than $6 million with $303,000 of specie in their vaults. The malefactors came of both major parties, for all the anti-bank rhetoric practised by the Jackson supporters. Florida banks made loans secured by slaves—enumerated by their first names. Recipients of state charters in Georgia borrowed specie for a few days in order to meet the legislature's requirements and then returned the specie to its rightful owners once the banks were open for business! "Laxness in banking practices" was the rule in the West, with Michigan, Ohio, and perhaps Illinois vying with one another as to which state was the most likely to penalize lenders and depositors.

Had bank defaults wiped out the recently made paper profits of their own directors or of speculators only, there might have been poetic justice discernible in them. But they also wiped out the hard-earned savings of "unsuspecting farmers and mechanics," whose small contributions were simply used as a basis for further speculation by bank managers, as was the case in Michigan. When state banks failed throughout the nation in 1841 and 1842 it was due not only to economic forces beyond their control but in many cases to such practices as those described or even to more flagrant fraud. In 1843 a writer in the respected *Hunt's Merchants' Magazine* could say of western banks, "the capitalist cannot repose confidence in [them] . . . because, monthly and weekly for the past three years, explosions have taken place disclosing fraud and mismanagement of the most astounding nature." Banking fraud and mismanagement helped bring on the Panic of 1837, the terrible price paid by the people of the Jacksonian era for their lack of restraint during the previous decade.

The clearest thing about it was its terrible effects, felt in all sections. In view of the privation they suffered, it is hard to doubt that the working classes suffered the most, even if they did not lose the most. A study of the tax assessments for the late 1830s indicates that Boston's wealthiest capitalists almost without exception became richer during the years of the crisis, at the same time that from one third to one half of working people suffered unemployment for substantial periods, some of them petitioning government "to ameliorate the sufferings of those whose families depend entirely on weekly earnings for support."

The causes of the crash were diverse. Trade Jacksonians blamed Biddle; agrarian Jacksonians blamed banks; Whigs blamed Democrats or Jackson, in general, and the Bank War, the removal of the deposits and the Specie Circular, in particular. Fatalists blamed the Great Fire that devastated New York City. Abolitionists blamed slavery. Sensible eclectics, while inevitably assigning different weights to different causes, would include the rage for improvements, the era's bank practices, the speculation in land, the economy's great reliance on a European capital over whose removal Americans had no control, the too great reliance on one crop as the means of raising foreign specie, the Hessian fly for its effect on American crops, and in sum the abandon with which too many Americans had pursued wealth during the era. In his provocative recent interpretation, that stands on their heads many earlier interpretations of the Panic and its causes, Temin concludes that while Jackson's policies "did not help the economy," they were not the "prime mover in the inflation, the crises, or the deflation," less influential than was the Opium War in accounting for the era's economic difficulties. Yet it is hard to avoid the conclusion that the policies of the Democratic administrations, particularly Andrew Jackson's, were instrumental in hastening the cataclysm. (Van Buren's subtreasury idea was too little, too negative, and surely too late.) The BUS may have been unconstitutional, its president dictatorial, its advantages over its competitors too great, its European stockholders too many. All of the other two dozen or so bad things Amos Kendall, Roger B. Taney, and other advisers got the President to say about it in his veto message may have been true. Yet in refusing to recharter this bank, the government did destroy a major check on the inflationary propensities of the state banks. By placing the deposits in the pet banks, the administration further promoted speculation, granting that this was not its intention. The administration's distribution of the surplus and its essentially know-nothing policy towards the fraudulent actions committed by its land offices were not helpful. The Specie Circular came too late. Jackson himself knew what land speculation was all about, for, as he told the Congress, "the banks let out their notes to speculators, they were paid to the receivers, and immediately returned to the banks to be sent out again and again, being merely instruments to transfer to the speculator the most valuable public lands. Indeed, each speculation furnished means for another." Coming when it did, however, the Circular—which required that henceforth payment for the public lands be in specie—was followed by a contraction as disastrous in its way as had been the previous expansion. John McFaul has noted that the issuance of the Circular produced a "scramble for specie between banks . . . which had a disastrously disruptive effect on the nation's financial affairs." The government's refusal to accept bank notes exposed their weakness, led to the disappearance of specie, and further advantaged speculators, more likely to have cash than were small farmers. The government was compelled shortly to repudiate its attempt at a hard money policy. Its unwitting revelation of the speciousness of the nation's money created still new problems for Democratic administrations whose own policies had helped create a situation that further deteriorated on exposure.

In the wake of the Panic and the public outcry that followed the wave of bank failures, states resorted to new measures curbing note issues and loans to be granted by banks, and limiting the debts to be run up by state governments. The federal government divorced itself from banking. Diverse social panaceas flourished in an atmosphere of economic stagnation. In the classic manner of the 19th century, the resumption of prosperity awaited the clearing away of the debris thrown up by the excesses of the past.

8

THE NEW POLITICAL SYSTEM
OF THE JACKSONIAN ERA

The politics of no era in American history were as fascinating or dramatic as those of the two decades commencing with the election of John Quincy Adams by the House of Representatives in February 1825. Political colossi—Andrew Jackson, Henry Clay, John C. Calhoun, and Daniel Webster—towered over the scene, while such figures as Martin Van Buren and John Quincy Adams occupied a scarcely less prominent place on the national political stage. Bitter political warfare raged, marked by drama, bombast, spleen, demagogy, vituperation, the threat—and sometimes the actuality—of violence. The level of rancor was not at all diminished by the absence of real issues in a number of the contests. Opportunistic men who lust for office are capable perhaps of even more amoral tactics than men of principle.

In the 20th century, Claude Bowers and Arthur M. Schlesinger, Jr., have written lively comprehensive accounts of the era's political battles while more recently Glyndon Van Deusen has done a more impartial if brief version of the great national contests. In view of the many studies that have been published on politics at the state level, on particular presidential elections, and on the careers of political personages, the purpose of the following chapters on politics is not to retell the events, but rather to try to explain them and perhaps to offer some insights into the political character of the era that do justice to the new evidence and interpretations.

149

The Jacksonian era was in a political sense an age in transition. Generalizations applicable to Jackson's first administration do not apply to Van Buren's. At the beginning of the era, for example, national political contests were waged between individuals ostensibly of the same party, good Jeffersonians all, to hear them tell it. But within ten years of John Quincy Adams' victory, two major parties, each distinctive and well-organized, controlled the field. A regular supplement to Democrats and Whigs were third parties, usually created in behalf of one principle or interest, in contrast to the more amorphous major parties.

Political campaigning, particularly in the great national contests, became far better organized and more expensive than it had been early in the era. It was the campaign of 1828 that taught politicians the unforgettable lesson that an attractive candidate is likely to do very well if his friends and supporters spend money lavishly, have dozens of partisan newspapers scattered all over the union, concert their actions in Congress with the end in view always of promoting his chances in the next election, and span the country with a fine network of committees that are capable of organizing the campaign, disseminating propaganda, and dispensing the vital ingredients in liquid or solid form that were assumed to be the way to the voter's heart.

It is a myth that most obstacles to the suffrage were removed only after the emergence of Andrew Jackson and his party. Well before Jackson's election most states had lifted most restrictions on the suffrage of white male citizens or taxpayers. Jackson was the beneficiary rather than the initiator of these reforms. During the Jacksonian era some further extension of the suffrage took place, the electoral system was changed in a number of states, and a new system for nominating candidates gained wide popularity.

National elections—at first seemingly issueless contests between ambitious personalities—were transformed into contests over such significant matters as banking, public land policy, internal improvements, tariffs, Indian removal, and territorial expansion. The progression was by no means a clear-cut one. The early campaigns of the era were not altogether devoid of issues, in the ordinary meaning of that term. In 1824, for example, Mississippians preferred Jackson to Clay in part because the Old General's career indicated that he would be better on the Indian question than his rival. Proslavery voters knew Adams was not their man. The issues as posed in party campaign rhetoric were not necessarily the issues as understood by the electorate. For election issues are not simply a matter of planks in a platform, formally approved by the candidate and his party. Of course the absence of a platform, particularly when it is accompanied by a candidate who utters not one word likely to betray a viewpoint toward a significant issue, leaves the impression that the party is trying to evade. The Whig Party candidate in 1840, William Henry Harrison, earned the derisive nickname "General Mum," for his own and his party's silence on issues.

It was an age of pragmatism and opportunism. The major parties and their leading figures—both the charismatic standard bearers and even more the gray eminences who operated behind the scenes—seemed interested in political principles primarily insofar as talking about them was likely to attract voters. Candidates and and their parties paid lip service to the right and the just but their behavior indicated that it was office above all that they yearned for. Ambition, not ideology, was the prime mover. That is why the pervasive theme in the adult careers of so many of the era's political leaders was flip-flop: reversal of previously held positions in order to capitalize on new opportunities, win the support of a new constituency, or hold on to the support of an old one which, as in the case of Calhoun's South Carolina from the early 1820s on, had itself undergone a change of heart because of a change of interest. That is why Jackson himself and his heir apparent, Martin Van Buren, managed to be so many things to so many men. Van Buren delighted in telling stories about his own artful ambiguity. Jackson lieutenants explained that the Old General was pro- or anti-tariff, pro- or anti-internal improvements, depending on which state they happened to be in. There was, however, a natural limit to such disingenuousness that even the astute Jackson managers could not transcend. Whatever else they might be able to do, they could not make the General out to be an antislavery man or a supporter of Indian rights derived from treaties with the federal government.

It was an age of increasing democracy if by that term is meant broadening of the suffrage, and the replacement of indirect methods, for nominating and voting for candidates, by direct methods. As has been indicated, the important changes in the suffrage antedated the appearance of Jackson and his party. In most cases, in fact, they owed nothing to them while in New York State in the early 1820s it was necessary to overcome the opposition of the party that later became the Jacksonian Democrats. By 1824 important restrictions on the vote of white adult males still obtained only in Rhode Island, Louisiana, Mississippi, and Virginia. In the years before 1824 a number of electoral reforms expanded the political role of ordinary citizens. *Viva voce* voting was steadily replaced by the printed ballot; an increasing number of positions became elective rather than appointive and the secret ballot spread in favor. On the other hand, voice voting continued to be the rule in many states while official ballots remained unknown. Ballots printed in the different colors of the competing parties were not fully "secret." Confusing the issue were the differing suffrage requirements for local, state, and national elections in some states.

Although the franchise was extended during the Jackson era, important limitations remained. In Louisiana, for example, the electorate was still roughly only one half of the white adult male population by as late as 1840. A Virginia reform of 1831 while extending the franchise to some leaseholders and householders as well as to freeholders, thus appreciably increasing the electorate, left about one third of the white population voteless. Rhode Island would have to go through the ordeal of the Dorr War in the 1840s and not even then attain manhood suffrage. A Mississippi Constitutional Convention in 1832 introduced a prohibition on property qualifications both for officeholding and the suffrage. Matters in that state were most complicated, since the supporters of the democratic change, who were more or less divided between Jackson men and their opponents, refused to permit the electorate to vote on the revised constitution, while "aristocratic" opponents of the measure urged a popular referendum. A slight property requirement persisted in other states during the era, though unfortunately there is no precise information as to its extent.

While some conservatives here as in Europe feared that universal white male suffrage would be followed by social leveling, others had learned to accept the reform with equanimity. For one thing, restrictions on the suffrage created problems. As Chilton Williamson, the modern historian of suffrage reform, has pointed out, "a taxpaying qualification encouraged numerous frauds at the polls." Conservatives more than other people disliked fraud. In New York suffrage extension was thus as much promoted by opposition to fraud or the desire to surmount such difficulties as determining how much taxation voters paid as by democratic ideals or theories. The fact is, too, that changing suffrage requirements in many cases had little effect on the numbers voting. A "democratized" suffrage in Massachusetts had less effect on voter turnout than did interest in election issues. In some cases electoral requirements were neither clearly written in law nor consistently enforced. The (N.C.) *Fayetteville Observer* in 1837 complained at the lack of uniformity in the decisions of election inspectors: "the practice is not only different in different counties, but in different parts of the same county, and even in different periods in the same place."

The early 19th century movement to end suffrage restrictions was hardly due to the democratic influence of the frontier, as Frederick Jackson Turner had held. Western states borrowed ideas from the older eastern models. For that matter some early western constitutions were no more liberal than those of the East. In Missouri, western elements, far from struggling for democratic electoral reform, fought against democratic reapportionment that reduced the advantage of the less populous frontier counties. A far cry indeed from the Turner thesis.

Even in the days when property qualifications loomed large on paper or in theory, they did not always succeed in preventing the voting of many persons theoretically disfranchised. Enacted reforms that "democratized" the suffrage, on the other hand, did not always produce the desired effect. The freehold requirement, a truly formidable and significant barrier to manhood suffrage, had been removed in most states before the age of Jackson, early in the century. The less difficult taxpaying qualification was erased early in the Jacksonian era in Mississippi and New Jersey and toward its close in Connecticut and Louisiana. It remained an issue in Ohio, Pennsylvania, Delaware, New Hampshire, Massachusetts, and Rhode Island, particularly in local elections. Yet it is a fair generalization that something approximating white manhood suffrage had been achieved in most American states prior to 1824 and that during the Jackson era the franchise for white males was extended in the few states which still restricted it.

The democratization of the suffrage was a significant reform which seemed to make all things possible. Writing in 1843, the young Karl Marx interpreted the "suppression of private property" as a voting requirement as "great progress," a "political emancipation" which he defined as the final form of human emancipation within the framework of the prevailing social order." As has been noted, Tocqueville and many of his contemporaries concluded that their possession of the ballot gave the enfranchised masses power over American politics.

The facts of Jacksonian political life do not bear out this notion. Possession of the suffrage did not give the men who had it real control of the great parties that came into being. South Carolina's democratic constitution, for example, required only two years of residence from white male adults to qualify them as voters. But, as William Freehling notes, essentially they could vote only for state legislators who in turn elected almost all other officials. In view of the high property qualification required of legislators, "the lower class [was kept] outside the statehouse. Political power . . . was uniquely concentrated in a legislature of large property holders, which set state policy and selected the men to administer it." The system of apportionment "made even more sure that those with a stake in society would continue to rule." Calhoun's state provided a good example of the truth that despite a democratic suffrage, government in fact could be in the "complete control of upper-class planters."

As Seymour Martin Lipset has recently observed, the citizenry may show a "high rate of voter turnout, and yet have little or no influence on policy." The actual measures selected for enactment by party members in Congress or in a state legislature were not decided on by the voters. In this sense major party leaders who had in effect rejected the Burkean conception of party, as a group dedicated to fundamental political principles, adhered to his more congenial notion that the representative owes his constituency not his industry but his talent. Congressmen could thus flout their electorates and repudiate campaign promises. Modern historians have raised some questions about the average voter's astuteness, inferring that even had he wished to rule and been able to do so, he lacked the capacity to understand his own interests. In one version, his vote was largely a response to the sensual stimuli directed at him by the parties. In another, he voted out of a complex of emotional, nonrational impulses. Richard P. McCormick has shown that in New York and North Carolina regardless of how little wealth the voter might possess himself, his vote on candidates and issues was essentially similar to the one cast by his wealthier neighbor. Given the opportunity to vote for the first time in state contests previously barred to them by a stiff property requirement, poorer voters in New York and North Carolina responded by voting in great numbers, indeed. But their ballots showed "that there was little reason for the more substantial voters to fear the consequences of entrusting the masses with the franchise." The electorate in these states was oblivious to Madison's dictum that differences in property create divergent interests.

What Walter Hugins has recently written of New York might be said of other states: "the lower orders of society, the 'labouring classes,' had discovered . . . that the right of suffrage alone was no panacea. . . ." Disraeli perceived this truth a generation later in England. The fault, if fault there was, lay not with the suffrage, of course, but with a party system that for all its flattery of the common man effectively insulated him from the sources of power and decision making. In his *Notions of Americans*, Cooper wrote that rich Americans were not taking the road that led to political office, evidently out of discouragement with the allegedly prevalent egalitarianism. The fact is, however, that the cost of running for office, estimated as roughly $3,000 for a congressional seat in 1828, was prohibitive to all but rich men or men with rich friends. And as Sidney Aronson has shown, Andrew Jackson's appointments to high federal posts went to the inordinately well-to-do, not the poor. Jacksonian rhetoric stressed the importance of the common man but Jacksonian practice ignored him.

Changes in the suffrage were accompanied by other important electoral changes. States replaced the split district system in presidential elections with the general ticket system. By 1828 only five states still permitted their electoral votes to be divided among more than one candidate. These developments were not particularly democratic but they were undoubtedly significant. They added to the influence of large and populous states. They promoted the growth of major parties capable of attracting broad sections of the public and obversely worked against the candidates or parties of limited and special appeal. They thus combined with other tendencies to foster a party system that would be dominated by pragmatic coalitions—"major parties"—that would be more clearly vote-getting machines than anything else, and therefore inevitably conservative and unideological. In consonance with the American habit of making a virtue of necessity, the latter characteristic has been much praised as a sign both of good sense and the evident social justice and equilibrium in our society: good sense in choosing a political system that muffles tensions rather than exacerbates them; social harmony according to the belief that were social evils important their victims would somehow have erupted in powerful parties of protest. Excesses committed in the modern era by ideological parties come to power offer a confirmation of sorts to these notions.

A different conclusion can be drawn, however. The muffling of issues is essentially a device for perpetuating the status quo. The many instances of popular acquiescence in misery refute the view that unbearable strains somehow beget organizations of doctrinaire dissent. So-called unideological parties are based on social concepts of their own, ideologies, as the term has come to be used, but bland rather than pointed ones. Blandness may be less a sign of good sense than of selfish interest, smugness, or blindness.

Democratization of the state judiciary was an important development of the period. By midcentury one half the states had followed the example of Mississippi, which in 1832 adopted a contitutional provision calling for the popular election of state judges for limited terms. Most of the remaining states moved to indirect election of judges by the legislature, rather than retain the system of executive appointment and lifetime tenure. Complementing what Maxwell Bloomfield calls "the expansion of the spoils system to the bench went a curtailment of judicial power over jury trails." Laws enacted in a number of states "made the judge little more than a passive moderator in his own court, forbidden to comment on the evidence or otherwise to assist the jury in reaching a verdict."

Another democratic innovation of the era had to do with the manner for electing presidential electors. In 1800 they were elected by popular vote in only two states. Prior to Jackson's nomination in 1824 a movement had gathered force and had succeeded in transferring the selection from legislatures to the voters in all but six states. Between 1824 and 1828, New York, Vermont, Georgia, and Louisiana also adopted the new measure. Before Jackson's election, Delaware was added to the list, leaving South Carolina as the only state which had not adopted the procedure by 1832. It is instructive to note that a bitter struggle broke out in New York, where a People's Party appeared in 1823 in order to accomplish this reform, against the opposition of Martin Van Buren's Regency which dominated the legislature. The New York Democracy fought the reform not out of a deep-seated aversion to democracy but from an expedient wish to assure William H. Crawford of the Empire State's votes. The Regency's tactics disclose, however, that in their scale of values democratic reform was subordinate to expediency.

Another vital change was fully realized by the end of the era. By 1842 single-member congressional districts had everywhere replaced the system of congressmen-at-large or multiple member districts, which had been common earlier. The new system, like its companion reform in the method of counting state electoral votes, worked mightily to turn the congressional district into a battleground between *likely winners*—plurality gatherers—and therefore candidates of pragmatic party organizations. Some political scientists see the American two-party system as the offspring of this modification. It is a good question as to whether we developed our unique major parties as a consequence of procedural reforms or whether the reforms were devised to bring about the party system. One thing is clear. Such reforms resulted not from any ground swell of public opinion but rather as a result of the maneuvering of astute men.

In sum these electoral changes produced what McCormick has called a "hidden revolution." For realistic party leaders understood clearly the benefits to be derived from a transformation in the "electoral environment." Far from being passive beneficiaries of an unplanned design that happened to reward opportunists at the expense of the principled, they had "early discovered that by changing 'the rules of the game' they might achieve advantages over their opponents and this consideration, among others, was influential in stimulating change." Once accomplished, such a change as the new system for choosing presidential electors "gave a popular dimension to the presidential contest, created or enhanced the need for state party machinery, weakened the political authority of legislative caucuses, occasioned the development of national party conventions, and made the presidential election the dramatic focal point of American politics." Parties seeking high office now had "to undertake to mobilize a mass electorate," and they proceeded to do so. The new political structure has been called by McCormick the central feature of the politics of the Jacksonian era.

It is unsound to attribute too much significance to structure, to the field on which and the ground rules by which the game of politics was played. For one thing, preoccupation with *models* of political structure can rob a discussion of the vitality that the clash of personalities gives to politics, making both the politics and their discussion unnecessarily bloodless. There can be little question, however, that the new procedures when supplemented by the new frankness in turning appointive office over to the party faithful, paved the way for the unique American party system that has flourished since Andrew Jackson's time.

In 1831 the Antimasonic Party, in national convention assembled, named William Wirt as their candidate for the presidential election of the following year. Thus was born—on a national party level—a new system of nomination that was almost immediately taken up by the supporters of the major candidates. In American political mythology, the overthrow of King Caucus represented a great victory for popular government, since it replaced the secret designation of candidates by a small, entrenched political elite with public nominations by elected representatives of the people. The mythological description is an accurate one of course. Its weakness lies in its failure to convey the true spirit of Jacksonian politics.

In many states before 1828 and in most of them after that date, politics in general, nominations to office, dissemination of propaganda, publication of programs, and courting of the electorate, in particular, were controlled by small numbers of men organized into tightly knit groups best described as political machines. Typically, apart from inevitable references to certain shared principles that appeared in party propaganda, only cursory attention was actually given them. The working hours of machine members were devoted to more prosaic and practical matters: winning office; enforcement of strict discipline on party activists; using office, once in, to enact legislation or support policies of interest to party leaders or which were likely to win the support of more influential portions of the party's constituency. Machines regarded caucuses or conventions as mere devices, one, like the other, easily controlled by party insiders who in either case managed the nomination process.

On the state level it was the New Hampshire machine run by Isaac Hill, who became one of Jackson's leading advisers, that was the first to use a convention. Once Hill's party gained power it reverted to a caucus. In New York the Regency was devoted to the caucus. Van Buren long professed to believe the device an article of the true Jeffersonian Republican faith but it seems clear that his Bucktails admired it for more realistic reasons. It made nominations, gave official sanction to party policies, "was a whip to hold together an otherwise lax majority in the Assembly and Senate," in effect enforcing party discipline. The Regency leaders, William L. Marcy and Edwin Croswell, put their case for insistence on strict adherence by party members to caucus decisions in a succinct statement to their colleague, Azariah C. Flagg: "an opposition on the ground of principle [if permitted] will be used to authorize an opposition on the ground of caprice." A model of party efficiency, their machine did not bother with a convention because there was no need for it. In Pennsylvania, on the other hand, the Jackson machine had no objections to the innovation since it changed nothing and was good public relations. In that state, county committees, consisting of officeholders, kept the party together by their careful handling of the mundane tasks of correspondence, publication of journals, organization of celebrations, and of vigilance committees to keep an eye on anti-Jackson activities. "They also assumed the leadership in making nominations for offices. The procedure was simple and informal. They would issue the call for a meeting now termed a convention, but differing little from the traditional caucus which was in bad repute with the public, prepare a ticket in advance, and usually secure its acceptance from the assembled party members." New Jersey Jacksonian leaders supplemented the nominating convention with a legislative caucus that "dispensed state patronage and dictated party positions on legislation."

In their actual operations state conventions in the West and South were no more democratic than they were in the northeast. Illinois Jacksonians found them a convenient device for "concentrating their actions," useful above all for organizing the party and getting out the vote. In Missouri the convention system was made to order for what Robert Shalhope calls the "oligarchic style of politics" that prevailed there. Men of "social prestige and influence" became "masters of convention technique," if anything strengthening their control over "men and measures" under the new system. The earlier masters of Maryland politics manipulated conventions to abet their search for new constituents. Jackson's political friends in Tennessee were very much in favor of the renunciation of the caucus system, but for reasons having nothing to do with democratic principle. In the late 1830s Alabama's Democrats and Whigs came to recognize the convention as a "powerful, well-controlled engine" that promoted party unity. A critic charged that conventions tended "to 'steal power from the many to the few'—to impair if not to destroy the independence and purity of the elective franchise." His complaint was understandable in view of the role of "a few active individuals" in running conventions in Alabama.

A short history of the state convention would show that the system swept all before it in the states in the northeast between 1824 and 1832, had scattered success in the West during the same period and took root more slowly in the South. By the end of the era it was well established there, too. It was the "standard device for party management" everywhere in the new states as parties were formed.

Conventions *were* more democratic than the legislative caucus. In view of the manner in which the new system was typically manipulated by party insiders during the era, one is tempted to say of it that it was democratic in theory only. But such a comment would be inaccurate. A political form, after all, does not contain within itself assurances that it will accomplish the goals its idealistic admirers anticipate. An expanded suffrage is a democratic reform even though in Bismarck's Germany it might have little effect. A system requiring candidates to be nominated by elected delegates is simply more democratic than one that assigns the function to officeholders or to self-appointed elites. But the experience of the Jacksonian era shows that hard political realities—in this case, that party managers were as able to control the new system as they did the old—can negate a democratic innovation, reducing it to little more than a token that if anything is the more unattractive for being deceitful.

The convention system spread for three reasons, essentially. Supporters of a candidate unlikely to win the vote of the legislature or a caucus, hoped that a meeting of the friends of their man could give an authority and sanction to his nomination that would otherwise be lacking. In this sense the convention was the device favored by the "outs." Pro-Jackson men, aware that the Republicans in Congress would not nominate a man the revered Jefferson regarded as dangerous, naturally gravitated toward the convention. Having swung over to Jackson before 1827, Van Buren now had no further objection to a convention, seeing in it, too, the possibility of reorganizing and purifying the Republican party—or assuring that a convention would be composed entirely of pro-Jackson men. The state convention was popular with party leaders also because, as was demonstrated conclusively in 1828, it could efficiently generate party discipline and loyalty. Conventions fashioned the apparatus that locked the state parties together in a national organization. The final practical reason for the popularity of the new system is revealed in a comment made by Van Buren, as to why a convention might be preferable to a caucus after all. It would be "more in union with the spirit of the time." In an age of popular suffrage the masterful New Yorker understood well the political rewards to be derived by the party that convinced the voter it sought to turn nominations over to him.

The convention system also affected oratory since politicians now were compelled to proclaim their undying devotion to the citizens who ostensibly controlled the nomination process. And it fostered versatility since it required politicians to master new and difficult skills of organization and manipulation. They proved to be more than equal to the challenge.

In Illinois, prior to the election of 1836, Democratic opponents of Van Buren charged that the convention system was a transparent device designed to assure his nomination. The convention was "destructive of the freedom of the elective franchise, opposed to the republican institutions, and dangerous to the liberties of the people." Supporters of the system there, on the other hand, were impressed at how effectively Democratic party managers elsewhere had used the system in "managing elections successfully." In Mississippi, the maverick radical Franklin Plummer, denounced the convention as an "insidious revival of the discredited caucus system," after friends of the notorious speculator and occasional pro-Jacksonian, Robert J. Walker, had used the system to win the Jackson party nomination for Walker in the Senate race of 1834. The Jackson faction, intent on ousting Old Hickorys' one-time friend and now deadly enemy, George Poindexter, were not fastidious about how they did so. McCormick's study of conventions in every state where they were in operation concludes that they "did not have precisely the functions that they appeared to have. Ostensibly they were decision-making bodies. In actuality they seem to have had a cosmetic function. That is, they gave the appearance of representing party sentiment whereas, in fact, they usually did little more than follow the dictates of party leaders. Made up in large measure of officeholders and party activists, they were readily susceptible to manipulation and control." In the Jacksonian era the great new parties that came into being were dominated in every important respect by small cliques as much under the new convention as under the old caucus system. As James Staton Chase has noted, it was not the elected delegates but small committees which truly governed conventions. "The delegates were only asked to approve a choice made by the inner circle of party leaders." Only rarely were such choices rejected. Chase concludes that conventions were "manipulated no less than caucuses."

A new political atmosphere is discernible in the Jacksonian era. This is not to say that gentility was the earlier rule. In the age of Jefferson and Hamilton, national and local political battles were hard fought; public party warfare was disfigured by almost unbelievable invective. The state contests of the early 19th century, before as during the so-called era of good feelings, were oftentimes viciously waged, with the interim between campaigns witness to incessant thrust and counterthrust by rival factions burning for office and amoral about the tactics they employed in seeking it. De Witt Clinton's biographer has written that modern political struggles are not "half as fierce or as devious or as riddled with slander and self-seeking. Government in his [Clinton's] time . . . was an almost impenetrable maze of double-dealing in which an honest man found it hard not to lose his way." New York State was by no means unique in that regard. The point then is not that the atmosphere of politics was completely transformed in the new time but that its most unlovely characteristics were accentuated, tending to become the rule where earlier they had been considered excessive. There is little question that the cult of the common man—who was universally regarded by political managers as a simple fellow more responsive to hokum than to straight talk about issues—was responsible for the falling off.

Demagogy of the most transparent sort became the practice. Always aware that the ordinary man had the vote, the politician "tried to identify himself with the common people, to wear old clothes, to claim a log-cabin origin, and conceal his superior education." After plying their audience with free whiskey, politicians would "speak grandiloquently of 'the sovereign people.'" Such well-to-do men as Andrew Jackson, Henry Clay, Daniel Webster, and William Henry Harrison proclaimed their humble origins and poor present circumstances. Whether it was the military academy at West Point or a licensed medical academy, institutions that trained or would train a small number to do a specialized service became fair game for politicians so in love with the people they could not abide such elitist establishments. "Tom, Dick, and Harry: office-holders, officers, and doctors, with or without training," seemed to be the slogan of the astute democrat. According to one sour contemporary, a defeated political party had only to brand its opponents "aristocrats" in order to regain office in this era in which "George Washington could not . . . compete with Amos Kendall," the astute and changeable Jacksonian strategist. Lee Benson has called attention both to the democratic fondness for invoking a political rhetoric "designed to sound something like class war," and the Whig response of attacking this alleged Democratic agrarianism as though for all the world it was authentic. This was an inept response indeed, helping to fix an impression of Democratic affinity for radicalism. The judgment of the modern not unsympathetic historian of the New York Regency is that their public statements to the effect that the 1828 national contest was between rich and poor, aristocracy and democracy, were "superheated partisan rhetoric, almost totally devoid of truth." But it was of infinite value to politicians because it was "invariably appealing and persuasive."

Demagogic speechmaking was everywhere supplemented by a kind of showmanship which added a "dramatic function" to politics. A series of theatrical devices were used to stimulate mass enthusiasm, featuring parades, rallies, barbecues, and lavish dispensation of hard liquor. Fastidious or serious persons who clung to the notion that political campaigns should devote themselves to issues were shouldered aside by keener realists who understood better the American electorate's taste. The new hoopla did not necessarily preclude the consideration of real issues or the merits of rival candidates. What was feared, however, and with some reason, was that contests conducted in such an atmosphere subordinated real issues or camouflaged them. Since this was precisely the effect of some of the era's electoral measures, as well as of the new frankness in turning government office over to the party faithful, political theatricality can be said to have been in harmony with the more "serious" political changes introduced during the era. Like them it fostered the relatively issueless campaigns and pragmatic parties that have become so characteristic of American politics. Buncombe in other words was no less serious in its consequences than electoral reform.

The reign of political pragmatism resulted in a lower tone of politics. This tone, "which had begun to show signs of wear in the 1820s, deteriorated steadily" in subsequent decades as parties which "sought victory by avoiding issues and men of conviction," fell prey to drunkenness, violence, gambling, and a general deterioration both in the quality of political discourse and political behavior. Congressional debate more and more took the form of vicious attacks on personalities and physical assaults on persons. The news of Chief Justice Marshall's death was greeted by a New York Democratic newspaper as "a cause for rejoicing." Elections were typically followed by duels. A Clay supporter was killed by Sam Houston in a duel growing out of the 1824 contest. Duff Green, at the time Jackson's publisher in the Capital, threatened to assault with a bludgeon the pro-Adams men who challenged his right to appear on the floor of Congress, while Green's associate assaulted President Adams' son as the latter was performing government business. The prestige of the Congress understandably declined in the face of the corruption and excesses of too many of that Body's members. Drunkenness during debate, misuse of funds, misrepresentations "on the travel allowance of members, as in the use of the franking privilege," were widespread. A sympathetic historian of the Van Buren party found consolation in the fact that they were "*not often charged with gross corrution!*" [Italics mine]

One dismal by-product of the spoils system was a deterioration in the quality of government service. The amazing peculations committed by the head of the New York Customs Office were too exorbitant to be typical. Samuel Swartwout had been installed in the high post by Jackson over the objections of advisors who had warned of the man's unreliability. Not everyone could steal over $1 million from the public treasury, or count on subordinates who held their tongues in the face of massive theft, convinced that their loyalty was owing not to the government but to their individual superior. There seems little question that part of the price the nation had to pay for the politics of expediency took the form of regular petty corruption and, occasionally, massive corruption. A political system flourishing within a speculative society populated by materialistic seekers after the main chance would inevitably bear such fruit from time to time.

The leaders of New York's Regency "exchanged the higher offices and honors among themselves," oblivious to the charge of corruption. In 1836 one of their leaders, John A. Dix, wrote Van Buren, "the legislation of the whole winter has been a matter of bargain and sale. [A spirit of speculation] has taken possession of too many

of our political friends; and it is not to be disguised that their
conduct is more under the regulation of pecuniary considerations
than motives of a higher origin and character." In Mississippi during the same period, the Democratic party was rocked by scandals.
One defaulting receiver of public lands was replaced by another
who proved to be equally culpable, while John H. Mallory, the state
auditor, was proven to be $50,000 "short in his accounts."

The great presidential elections provide the richest examples of
the new campaign tactics and the general political spirit of the age.
Since they involved the most conveted of all political prizes, they
evoked the choicest specimens of the new political behavior. After
the completion of Monroe's second term, the absence of an heir
apparent turned the election of 1824 into a wide-open contest.
William H. Crawford of Georgia, the choice of the Republican
caucus in Congress as of Martin Van Buren in New York; John
Quincy Adams, Monroe's Secretary of State; Henry Clay, beloved of
many in the West and the possessor of a national reputation;
Andrew Jackson, Indian fighter par excellence and above all, the
Hero of New Orleans; and, for a time, the inordinately brilliant and
ambitious John C. Calhoun, were active candidates. An early
debacle in Pennsylvania, where Jackson swept all before him, at
least for the moment, convinced Calhoun that his alleged strength
there was an illusion and led him to withdraw. (He settled for the
Vice Presidency from which office he discovered himself later to be
strategically situated for the purpose of destroying the future hopes
of his President, while furthering his own.) Issues were not totally
absent from the contest, the nation's newspapers stressing slavery,
the tariff, the Indian question, sectionalism, and other issues. The
rub however is that voters interested in the issues had a hard time
knowing where the candidates, particularly Andrew Jackson, stood
with regard to them.

A subsequent chapter will deal with Andrew Jackson's earlier
career and the clues and insights it offers into his Presidency. His
record and comments on most issues prior to 1824 had been sufficiently inconsistent to permit his managers in different states to
make contradictory claims. When Jackson did speak, as on the issue
of the tariff, he let it be known that he favored the *judicious*
protection of our domestic manufactures. Jackson took seriously the
advice of his close advisor, John Eaton, that he neither "commit
[his] opinions" nor permit "malevolence to drag [him] . . . into
any newspaper controversy." According to Adams, all that the Jackson people had to do was to cry "8th of January and the Battle of
New Orleans." In Pennsylvania it was Jackson's character, his
"power to command implicit confidence [that] overcame any general desire to investigate seriously his ideas" on such a subject as the
tariff. In New York State he attracted support from conservatives
who had opposed the popular election of presidential electors. In
Mississippi "personalities overshadowed issues in the election of
1824," the electorate displaying little interest in Jackson's earlier
pro-tariff position, cited by his opponents in that state as reason to

oppose him. In Ohio his supporters created a picture stressing his "energy, patriotism, courage, decisiveness rather than more abstract virtues." Voters in Ohio appear not to have been issue-oriented. Former debtors of the Second Bank of the United States showed no animus at the polls toward Clay, for example, despite his role as the Bank's attorney in suits pressed against them. Compared with the bitterness generated by the House's election of a President after the failure of any candidate to win an electoral majority, the actual campaigning had been relatively old-fashioned. Many people even favored a ticket uniting the two leading candidates:

> John Quincy Adams,
> Who Can Write,
> and Andrew Jackson
> Who Can Fight.

The campaign of 1828—one of the most vicious in the nation's history—really began almost immediately after the House's choice of Adams as President in 1825. Jackson himself set the tone for he never accepted the verdict, certainly not its legitimacy. On the basis of no better evidence than the adverse vote in the House, he immediately charged that cheating, corruption, and bribery were responsible for denying him his rightful place at the head of the nation and defeating the will of the people. Of course Jackson had won a plurality both of the electoral and the popular vote but Adams was a close second. In any case the constitutional provision that the House choose from among the top three candidates in the absence of a majority for any one, made it clear that the House's action was to be construed as a new election rather than an automatic conferring of the Presidency on the leading vote-getter. Jackson's disappointment at the subsequent result was understandable, but his accusations, while in perfect accord with his lifelong tendency to impugn the motives of any critic, were unfair, not least because in rejecting him the House majority was only agreeing with his own earlier estimate that he was not fit for the job. Adams was not particularly pleased at his manner of election, although his comment that he would have resigned were it possible to do so loses some if its force in view of his knowledge that it was not. Jackson's friends, in Congress and out, proceeded to act on the assumption that the General's accusations were valid and they managed to poison the political atmosphere for the next four years.

"Corrupt bargain!" charged the Jacksonians. Their attack was directed against Clay, primarily, for intriguing to win the House vote for Adams in return for the promise of the highest office in the Department of State—the stepping stone to the Presidency—and at Adams for consenting to the low proposition. Unfortunately for Clay's reputation the charge stuck. It would be raised even in the campaign of 1844, haunting Clay as it had throughout the previous two decades. One understands his rueful admission in 1842 that his acceptance of the Secretaryship was perhaps his greatest political blunder. This was an admission not that moral wrong had been done or that the Jacksonian charge was true, but that false though it was, the charge had worked politically. It badly hurt, if it did not destroy, Clay and conveyed to the nation the impression that the guileless Hero had been deprived of his rightful victory, done in by an unholy alliance of charlatan and hypocrite. Nothing Clay, his supporters, or even some of Jackson's friends might say, had much effect. Actually Clay had intended to use his influence against the election of Jackson well before the office of State was offered him. Thomas Hart Benton and Francis P. Blair, ardent Jackson admirers at the time they said it, stated that to their personal knowledge Clay had indicated he would support Adams over Jackson *before* the issue was placed before the House. But "the violence of party," to use Benton's phrase, would not permit so effective a smear to be withdrawn merely because it might be unfounded.

Clay of course was an old critic of Jackson. The Kentuckian, for example, had publicly attacked Old Hickory for his notorious Florida actions in 1818—in contrast to Calhoun who confined his criticisms to the secrecy of Monroe's cabinet meetings and who thereafter lived in some dread that his support of censure might one day be brought to Jackson's attention. On other grounds of public policy, not to mention the understandable unwillingness of one western luminary to build up the political career of another, Clay had excellent reason to have used his influence in the election as he did. At worst Clay was charged with the kind of opportunism that as a matter of fact described the past behavior of many prominent Jacksonians including Amos Kendall, Robert J. Walker, Francis P. Blair, and even Martin Van Buren, who also shifted political allegiances in return for the promise of political advantage. Even before Clay had accepted the alleged reward, Jackson characteristically told his friend and adviser, William B. Lewis, on the basis of nothing more than a rumor, that "the Judas of the West has closed the contract and will receive the thirty pieces of silver." The Hero was undoubtedly sincere but there is reason to believe that the cooler heads, who in 1825 induced the erratic George Kremer to make the original public charge of "Bargain" and in 1826 got Duff Green to revive it, cared not at all about its truthfulness but only of its effectiveness.

Jackson in 1827 came up with a variation in which he now charged that Clay, desperate for office at any price, had on the eve of the House election sent an emissary to sound Jackson out on the possibility of a cabinet post for Clay. Unfortunately for Jackson the alleged emissary—the good Jacksonian, James Buchanan—while conceding that he had indeed talked with Jackson about Clay, stated that he had done so on his own responsibility and as a friend to the General. Nor was his version ever shaken or evidence adduced to challenge it. (Old Hickory, whose memory was long, later banished Buchanan to Russia, after the embassy post in that cold place had first been turned down by another of Jackson's new political enemies.) Obviously Buchanan's ground for contradicting the Jackson tale was something other than self-interest. What was characteristic of the new low tone of politics was not the substantive wrongs attributed to Clay and Adams by the corrupt bargain charge but the charge itself, the fact that it was made and how it was reiterated and used.

In Congress the Jacksonians devoted themselves to no loftier goal than ruining the Adams Administration. To have sought to turn issues to the advantage of their candidate for 1828 would have been one thing. What is dismaying in the behavior of the 20th Congress was the frank dedication of the Jackson men who controlled it to blocking "all constructive legislation that might redound to the credit of the Administration," and to framing legislation "with the single purpose of ousting Adams from the presidency and replacing him with Andrew Jackson." The Congress toyed in partisan fashion with the President's plan to send an American delegation to the Hemisphere Congress at Panama, although some of Jackson's southern supporters may well have been sincere in professing an aversion to having Americans "forced to sit with delegates of mixed blood." The notorious "Tariff of Abominations," it has recently been noted, was not devised by Van Buren to be beaten, as was believed for so long. But it was indeed created with the end in view of mortally weakening the administration and was a nice example of the subordination of principle to party.

The Jacksonians even sought to commandeer art to their political purposes, urging that a congressional committee "inquire into the expediency of having an historical picture of the Battle of New Orleans painted and placed in one of the panels of the Rotondo [*sic*]." Kremer sarcastically recommended the substitution of the "secessionist" Hartford Convention as an historical event more pleasing to those congressmen whose opposition blocked the proposed artistic tribute to the Hero's great victory over the British. A low point prior to the election year was reached in the Jacksonians' slander of John W. Taylor, the pro-Adams House speaker, whom they ousted from the office to the accompaniment of accusations that he had committed "sexual irregularities." Taylor, whose offense consisted of having been on a coach trip in the company of two women whom he evidently did not know, interpreted the attack as "part of a system to calumniate and vilify every man in distinguished station connected with the present administration." The Taylor case was but a foretaste of 1828.

There have been many nastly elections in American history but a good case can be made for the view that the election of 1828— about which Edward Channing wrote that it was more honorable to have lost it than won—was the dirtiest of all. According to Robert V. Remini, its most recent student, it "splattered more filth in more different directions and upon more innocent people than any other in American history." The pro-Adams convention in North Carolina that said the contest was "not a conflict between opposing principles, but a conflict between opposing men," was close to the mark. In New York it was said no one in the Democratic caucus that nominated Jackson knew precisely what his principles were. One

Pennsylvanian wrote to another, "the great mystery of the case to me is that the South should support General Jackson avowedly for the purpose of preventing tariffs and internal improvements and that we should support him for a directly opposite purpose." But it was no mystery to the men in Jackson's home state of Tennessee and elsewhere who had organized the General's masterful campaign.

It was Jackson against Adams and as might have been expected, the cry of "Bargain!" was heard throughout the land. For all the high moral tone of their standard bearer, the Adamsites proved themselves adept at the art of mud-slinging. They went through Jackson's career with a fine eye for scandal. That much valuable information was in the public record was no credit to the men who used it.

The old adultery story was exhumed. Thirty years before, Jackson had evidently believed himself married to Rachel Robards when in fact she had not yet been legally divorced from her first husband. The couple had subsequently had to go through a second ceremony several years after the first. Henry Clay may have lived as long as he did only because he convinced Jackson's friend, John Eaton, that he had had nothing to do with the publication of the story of these events by Clay's friend Charles Hammond, editor of the *Cincinnati Gazette*. One marvels at the intrepidity of Thomas D. Arnold, candidate for Congress from East Tennessee, who actually published a handbill calling Jackson a wife-stealer. Before shackles had been placed on him by his candidacy, Jackson had killed Charles Dickinson for less. That he had killed others as well was unsubtly suggested by John Binns, the editor of the Philadelphia *Democratic Press*, in his notorious "Coffin Handbill." This document was featured by the coffins of the 12 men allegedly murdered by Old Hickory, with less than detached accounts of the details in each case. In addition Jackson was called son of a prostitute and a Negro, usurper, gambler, cockfighter, brawler, drunkard, illiterate, unfit for high office. His friends, after first exhorting him to restraint and, if possible, silence, gave back blow for blow.

The Jacksonian press in Pennsylvania charged that Mrs. Adams was born out of wedlock. Duff Green countered the adultery story with the charge that not only was it a falsehood but that Adams himself had lived illicitly with his wife prior to marriage. To Jackson's credit he immediately intervened, warning he would not tolerate a war on females. His admonition had no great effect, however. Isaac Hill shortly published the slander that Adams was a panderer, a charge soon taken up by western Democrats who professed now to understand better the diplomatic success that had been enjoyed by "the pimp of the coalition." It was said Adams had bought the presidency, was opposed to American institutions, was an "aristocrat who had squandered the people's money in lavishly furnishing the East Room of the White House after the fashion of Kings," and had misspent public funds to buy a billiard table for his home. Nor was Clay spared. The villain of the bargain charge was now damned as a traitorous ally of Aaron Burr, whom he had defended before a Kentucky Grand Jury. He was also accused of instigating the assassination of William Morgan, in order to prevent the exposure of Freemasonry! Some Jacksonians evidently believed these slanders for in a private leter he wrote Van Buren after the victory was assured, William B. Lewis could actually refer to the "triumph of virtue and republican simplicity over corruption and an unprincipled aristocracy."

It may not have been a victory for virtue but it was a victory for the South. The returns show that but for the huge popular and electoral margins run up by Jackson in Virginia, North Carolina, Georgia, Alabama, Mississippi, Tennessee, and Missouri, the Hero would not have been swept into office. Adams had an electoral and close to a popular majority of the votes of the states of the other sections. Van Buren's gamble with regard to the Tariff of Abominations had paid off, for he had anticipated continued Southern support of the Southern candidate, the slaveholder and cotton planter, Andrew Jackson, no matter how unhappy Southerners might be with the tariff prepared by his friends. As Ronald Satz has noted, Southerners also applauded Jackson's "enthusiastic support of Indian removal." The total vote, while more than double that of 1824, hardly constituted the mighty outpouring of the masses that historians had long insisted it was. As a close study noted, instead of a "mighty democratic outpouring" there was in 1828 a voter turnout that approached—but in only a few places matched or exceeded— the maximum levels that had been attained before the Jacksonian era. For all the clamor and the propaganda directed at them, American voters did not rush to the polls to install the alleged great champion of popular rights. It is more accurate to say that Jackson's election was assured by the votes of men convinced he was sound on the issue of slaveowners' rights. In this sense the American voter, particularly in the South, was more thoughtful than he is given credit for being. In a campaign which had bombarded him with irrelevancies and hullabaloo, he never lost sight of a most serious issue indeed. Jabez Hammond more than a century ago, Edward Channing 60 years later, and Richard Brown more recently all made the point that Jackson's party was a Southern party. The voting statistics for 1828 provide persuasive evidence that they were right.

Unlike Southerners, Pennsylvanians evidently voted with little regard to issues, in part, undoubtedly, because the issues that concerned them lacked the emotional, not to mention the economic, significance of slavery. One can nevertheless share the view that their performance in 1832 was incredible: "Jackson opposed internal improvements, . . . the second BUS, refused to uphold the protective tariff, and allied himself with Van Buren. Pennsylvania's voters desired internal improvements, favored the Bank, insisted upon the protective system and hated Van Buren. Yet these same voters without blinking an eye, were ready to drop Jackson ballots into the box." The cult of personality prevailed, voters voting issues for local and congressional candidates but not for Presidential. If this behavior is compared with southern voting in 1828, the paradoxical conclusion can be drawn that while in 1832 many voters ignored real issues despite party insistence on their importance, in the earlier election voters insisted on reading issues into a campaign that party managers wanted devoid of them.

The American voter was at times clearly a most unpredictable fellow. The Bank veto and Jackson's Indian Policy had the wholesome effect of tending to subordinate scandal to matters of policy in 1832. But not altogether. An anti-Jackson newspaper in Boston described the President as "the wretched object who impersonates the Chief Magistrate of the country!— . . . broken down in health and intellect . . . the slave of the profligate creatures of both sexes by whom he is surrounded." The ever reliable Isaac Hill listed in his *New Hampshire Patriot,* two months before the election, 21 reasons why Clay should not be President. The 21st was "because . . . he spends his days at the gaming table and his nights in a brothel." Nothing Harry of the West might do, not even his exemplary home life, could undo the effects of rumor or of the kind of comment made by Adams about Clay's alleged vices when both were commissioners at Ghent in 1814. The Democracy organized a "colorful campaign of noise and nonsense" that won a decisive victory for the popular President—albeit, when compared with the 1828 returns, not really so sweeping as general accounts have long suggested. In fact, as James Curtis has recently observed, Jackson is "the only president whose re-election to a second term was marred by a decline in popular approval."

In 1836 some Democrats showed a short memory, arguing among other things that Harrison, one of a number of sectional Whig candidates, was unfit for the highest office because his life had been spent in the military. The campaign was decidedly "one of personalities and not of issues." Van Buren, Jackson's handpicked political heir, had no trouble defeating a Whig party whose support was hopelessly splintered behind four major candidates, although Van's popular majority was slight. In Tennessee a vigorous campaign waged by the supporters of Hugh L. White against Van Buren succeeded not only in winning the state for White, but in drawing more than twice as many Tennesseans to the polls than had the 1832 contest.

The canvas of 1840 was a lively one in the new style, the Whig Party recovering from its fragmentation of four years earlier. They struck political gold in the candidacy of their own military hero and as the party of the "outs" they derived great political profit from the economic depression that had devastated the economy. Clay bemoaned his fate as that of a man nominated in difficult elections but bypassed when victory seemed certain. The Whig party's pragmatists knew what they were about, rejecting their party's true leader for Old Tippecanoe, a man of no known views. According to William H. Seward, "General Harrison's strength lay in the fact that he was the most unobjectionable and therefore the most suitable candidate." Once nominated, pains were taken to make him "General Mum." And of course the party had a field day turning the Democratic reference to hard cider to its advantage. Andrew Jackson wrote scornfully of Whigs misleading the people, "worshipping coon and sour sider [sic.]. . . [attempting] to degrade the people to a level with the brute creation." The editors of the *Democratic Review,* with a more accurate memory of tactics used to elect Jackson in earlier campaigns, ruefully conceded, "We have taught them to conquer us!" Wealthy Whigs put on "cowhide boots, felt hats and homespun coats," in order to register their humble circumstances and thus woo the voters more successfully. Whig editors sneered at their General's critics as "Eastern officeholder pimps." Nor did the new masters of demagogy neglect their opponent, little Van. If Harrison was the "Cincinnatus of the West," Van Buren was "a man who wore corsets, put cologne on his whiskers, slept on French beds, rode in a British coach, and ate with golden spoons from silver plates when he sat down to dine in the White House." In Thurlow Weed's thoughtful language, Van was a "grovelling demagogue" who had "slimed himself into the Presidency." Van Buren understandably attributed his defeat to the "instrumentalities and debaucheries of a political Saturnalia, in which reason and justice had been derided." In a startling reversal of party name-calling, the Democratic candidate was called the symbol of a "bloated aristocracy." Issues were avoided and the Whig victory was decisive.

Clay's nomination in 1844 was assurance that the campaign would not be a pretty one. Democratic slander reached new depths, campaign literature depicting the Great Compromiser as immoral, a duelist, a pro-abolitionist—a charge regarded by ordinary citizens in pretty much the same way the charge "Communist" would have been regarded in the days of Senator Joe McCarthy. A pamphlet reminded "Christian voters" of Clay's alleged gambling, profanity, Sabbath-breaking, dueling, cursing, cruelty toward his slaves, and sundry other offenses. Friends of the "old coon"—one of Clay's many nicknames—sang, that

> high on a limb that "same old coon,"
> was singing to himself this tune:—
> Get out of the way, you're all unlucky;
> Clear the track for old Kentucky!

But it was not to be. A southern wind blew in Polk's direction, while the dissatisfaction of abolitionists with Clay's evasive stand on Texas helped cost him the votes in New York that would have enabled him to realize his dream. Vindictive enemies "deluged [him] with letters of insult and hung skinned coons . . . from trees along main traveled ways."

Too much significance should not be attributed to the new atmosphere of politics. For while it *affected* the results and even more the tone of the era's political battles, it did not totally obliterate issues of real significance or their consideration by voters. It did, however, help obscure them. In terms of their real political effect, then, demagogy, barbecues, concentration on personalities, slander and insult had the serious role of fostering a political system dominated by major parties that follow expediency rather than principle. In this sense all of the era's important political changes were of a piece. Together they combined to usher in the modern American political system.

Certainly the system corresponds closely to the spirit and the genius as well as to the condition of the American people. Its emphasis on practicality, shrewdness, success at almost any price, the avoidance of intellectually tough or ethically austere principles and alternatives, its liveliness, exuberance and vitality is in accord with the traits and values attributed to the American people by contemporaries. In effect this people seemingly created a politics that beautifully reflected their own personalities.

If, however, the job of the historian is not merely to describe and explain but also to appraise or evaluate, it becomes impossible to avoid making critical judgments. While the system worked and comes off well by relativist standards, it has important deficiencies when subjected to a stricter test. Evading issues serves the interests of some but not of others. The politics of expediency provided a cover for charlatans, contributed to miseducating the public about specific issues, and propagated dangerously simplistic notions about complex problems. It has fostered the dubious notion that thorny problems are easily solved. A system catering to simplistic nationalism better explains the American public's tendency to understand international issues in terms of their wrong and our right. Perhaps these are weaknesses of democracy. But precisely the greatest weakness of the new politics was that for all its talk of democracy and its flattery of the common man who allegedly ruled under it, its definition of democracy was concerned not with the common man's rule, but with his voting opportunities, while its practice effectively denied him either great influence or any realistic chance of exercising it.

9

THE NEW MEN OF POLITICS

While the electoral and other changes that transformed politics during the Jacksonian era were of high importance, the political life of the times was created not by a system but by men. Structural changes had fashioned a new political milieu governed by new possibilities and limitations. But changed rules of the game provide no sure clue as to how, in fact, the game will be played. It was the political actors, particularly those in the first rank of the great battles, who determined the issues to be fought out and gave precise direction to political events, fleshing out the bare bones of political structure and breathing life, vitality, and the charm of human foible into them.

The great figures were unique individuals, of course, each possessing a singular intelligence and personality. The quality of Henry Clay's mind was most unlike John Caldwell Calhoun's. Integrity meant something different to John Quincy Adams than it did to Daniel Webster. Frankness was one thing to Andrew Jackson, another to Martin Van Buren. But innate personal differences, since they are always present, are unrevealing about the *particular* period in which they appear. Brilliance, one suspects, was in as short supply in Cicero's time as in Emerson's, and if it was not, can only be explained as Rome's good fortune.

The striking fact about the political leaders of the Jacksonian era, for all their diversity of intellect and character, was the large degree of similarity in their backgrounds, values, and behavior, both before and after they attained prominence. Such sameness is of special interest since it is unlikely that the political leaders of a time will share acquired traits unless the characteristics in question correspond somehow to the requirements of their era. The traits may

171

have been useful or popular, but in either case they are reflective of the political and, for that matter, the general atmosphere in which they flourished. Certainly nothing affords a clearer insight into the nature of Jacksonian politics than what was common to the back-grounds, methods, and goals of its leaders.[1]

The political leaders were not poor men. The line between be-ing rich and well-to-do is not always a clear one but typically the leaders were one or the other, possessing either an in-come or wealth that was not approximated by most men. Jackson's fortune fluctuated. At one low point, early in his career, he suddenly found himself in debt, due to the failure of a Philadelphia merchant and speculator whose notes Jackson had accepted as payment for land, and in turn used in large purchases of his own. Such were the risks typically run by accumulators and capitalists in the age of speculation. But Jackson extricated himself from the near dis-aster and went on to become planter, large landowner, sometime merchant, owner of fine race horses, as well as of perhaps the most imposing residence in Tennessee. When in 1818 funds ran out for the payment of a newly formed brigade of New Orleans veterans, Jackson, like Augustus, drew from his private purse the necessary sum—in this case $4,000—to pay the troops. He was one of that small number of inordinately large slaveowners who owned over 100 slaves. He had that number at the Hermitage alone, which was only one of his properties. He may have been a paternalistic master but he advertised for runaways, kept captured slaves in chains, and always was on the alert for bargains for purchase or unusu-ally high prices for purposes of sale.

Clay, his great political enemy, was born of a well-to-do father who owned 21 slaves and over 400 acres, and a mother who herself owned half as much as her husband. Clay used his gifts to become lawyer for the wealthy, himself becoming rich in the process, own-ing slaves, plantation, fine home, and having diversified interests in agricultural and commercial enterprises. From youth on, the golden-tongued Webster had developed a taste for money so sharp that he came to desire it "as an addict craves [his] drug." His ability, combined with his flexible scale of values, enabled him to satisfy the lust. In the 1820s he was reputedly the highest paid lawyer in the country.

---

[1] The following discussion is based for the most part on the entire careers, through the Jacksonian era at least, of the men under consideration. Arthur M. Schlesinger, Jr., makes a good point when he notes that nothing Jackson did before he took office "can be a substitute for the facts after 1828." But to those of us who wish better to understand why Jackson acted as he did after 1828, the events of his earlier career are most germane, indeed. These earlier incidents were not the history of an adolescence but carried him through the 61st year of his life, after all. They are illustrative of patterns of thinking and acting that were well formed if not rigidly hardened. In any case, I have tried to confine my discussion to those aspects of Jackson's past which are most helpful in explaining his subsequent behavior as President.

Most of the country's rich men were probably Whigs during the party battles of the 1830s, but most leaders of the Democratic Party were as inordinately wealthy and successful as their Whig counterparts. Van Buren had turned a "modest competence" into an "ample fortune," and the Regency he presided over, like its great opposition, contained men of substantial wealth who typically enjoyed close and profitable ties with the business community. It used to be thought that the Whig Party had a much larger reservoir of rich men to draw from in New York City than the Democrats. But both were led by "solid men." Such Democratic leaders as Duff Green, Samuel Ingham, Isaac Hill, Amos Kendall, Francis P. Blair, and C. C. Cambreleng were business men who were already wealthy or well on the way to becoming wealthy through their political influence. James K. Polk's father was a successful planter and speculator, able to send the young Polk to college at Chapel Hill, while Polk himself became a successful lawyer and politician who moved in the most elegant circles of his state. The privileged son of a substantial property owner, Louis McLane in the 1830s moved freely between the most prestigious positions in Andrew Jackson's cabinets and lucrative presidencies of some of the nation's premier canal and railroad companies.

The New York Jacksonian, William L. Marcy, was the son of a large landowner. Marcy's father-in-law, Benjamin Knower, another Regency stalwart, was successful banker, speculator, and man of diverse investments. Thomas Hart Benton, like his father, was a slaveowner and an intermittently successful speculator in real estate lots, for all his well-known identification with cheap or free public lands, opposition to paper money, and support of the principle of *demos krateo* or majority rule. Roger Brooke Taney, another famous Jacksonian "radical," was a slaveowner and bank investor who was born into a Maryland family of substantial estate as well as Federalist principles. Thomas Ritchie, leader of the Virginia Junto that combined with the New York Regency to forge the national coalition that swept Jackson into the presidency in 1828, inherited a "considerable fortune" from a merchant father whose imports and exports made him "the chief businessman of his community" and who moved "in the best social circles" of Virginia.

Studies on the state and local level bear out the contention that there was an essential similarity in the social and economic circumstances of leaders of both major parties. Ohio Jacksonians like their opponents included "large proportions of merchants, manufacturers, bankers, business men and professionals." The state's cultural elite did not like Old Hickory, but the men who organized a party in his name in Pennsylvania were themselves of the upper economic orders. New Jersey's Jacksonian leaders were among the wealthiest men in the state, their wealth grounded in land, manufactures, canals, and banks. No social or economic differences can be discerned among the relatively wealthy men who led both parties in Michigan. Florida's democratic leaders may have sounded ideological themes that differed from their opponents' but their substantial

wealth and high status did not. Georgia congressmen and governors
of whatever party background were almost without exception well-
educated members of the legal profession. The leaders of both
parties in Mississippi had an affinity for slaves, banks, and speculation. The extremely detailed modern studies of Alabama politics
reveal that for the leaders of one major party as for the other, the
status of planter, slaveowner, or professional was the rule in a
community most of whose members by far were yeoman farmers
who owned no slaves. Jackson's supporters in Massachusetts were
often split among themselves. David Henshaw, the leader of one
faction, was a wholesale druggist, a bank and a railroad director,
while Theodore Lyman, the leader of the other, was a "shipowning
aristocrat." Vermont's Jacksonians were led in 1828 by Ezra Meech,
"one of the largest landowners and wealthiest farmers in the state."
The New York Regency included in its leadership Thomas W.
Olcott, Erastus Corning, Charles E. Dudley, and Benjamin
Knower—bankers all—while the Tammany leadership "included
many members of the 'privileged aristocracy'—bank directors, leading merchants, lawyers, and prominent physicians." It is clear that
leaders of the one or the other great organizations that dominated
Jacksonian political life were atypically wealthy men.

If the growing costliness of political campaigning effectively excluded ordinary men from running for office, the increasing vulgarity of politics appears to have discouraged patrician types. Whether
it was due to vulgarity or not is one of those questions that does not
lend itself to confirmation by quantitative studies. The evidence is
fairly conclusive however that for whatever the reasons, the sons of
the nation's most prestigious families did not aspire to high public
office. National political leaders were commonly self-made men. If
they were not born poor, neither were they born to lavish comfort.
Ambition was the great spur. Their ambition was not the type that
yearns for those great achievements whose absence in America was
so disquieting to a Michel Chevalier. Rather it was the more
mundane sort whose goals are material or emotional aggrandizement. In the Jacksonian era men of such worldly ambition found
politics one of the surest roads to prestige, influence, power—and
wealth. The high-minded William Henry Seward had "boundless
ambition"—to achieve personal success through politics. David
Henshaw of Massachusetts, William Marcy and Thurlow Weed in
New York, Samuel Gwin and Robert J. Walker in Mississippi,
Thomas Hart Benton in Missouri, Isaac Hill in New Hampshire,
Francis P. Blair and Amos Kendall in Kentucky, Roger B. Taney in
Maryland, and their like in other states, were not inspired by a noble
vision. The dreams they dreamed were of personal gain. Lynn
Marshall, Kendall's recent biographer, has written, "Kendall
suffered no confusion or painful ambivalence about values and
goals. However doctrinally ambiguous, Kendall remained quite
steadfast, throughout a long and eventful life, about values and
goals. His values were pragmatic and his goals material." Of
Edward Livingston, Jackson's masterful legal adviser, a modern

student reports that "he seemed incapable of thinking in terms of anything but his own advantage, his own enrichment, his own fame, or his own convenience." Louis McLane has been adjudged as "almost sinfully ambitious" for worldly gain. As for the Bay State Jacksonian leader David Henshaw, his life has been recently interpreted as "the record of a man who knew what he wanted and how to get it. Ambition consumed him; his goals were wealth, power, and influence." Idealistic dreamers in Jacksonian America were found not in the leadership of the major parties but in Emerson's circle, in reform and utopian movements, or in truly radical and therefore short-lived labor parties.

Worldly ambition seems to have urged on the great political figures as much as it did the less than great. Jackson himself was never explicit as to what drew him into a political career but it is the judgment of the most uncritical of his comprehensive biographers, Marquis James, that an urge to enhance his fortune beckoned him on. This same man who professed his disinterest in the Presidency, suddenly became a subscriber to 20 newspapers from all over the nation. One cannot doubt the sincerity of his regular assurances in letters to his beloved Rachel in the years just before the Presidency, that he wished more than anything that they were not so often separated. Yet what but ambition drove him precisely to the regular separations made necessary by his poltical career? It is hard to subscribe to a simple economic explanation of Jackson's ambition: it seemed to be compounded of a number of elements. Social idealism does not appear, however, to have been one of them.

Henry Clay advised History that he would rather be right. Many contemporaries however agreed with his admirer, Senator A. T. Mason, who wrote that "disgusting vanity and inordinate ambition were fast destroying" Clay's opportunities as a public man. In 1837 dwellers in the nation's capital were regaled by the story that Clay went to the White House "to examine the premises, and to satisfy himself whether they would be likely to be in a tenantable condition about three years hence," when the Democrats would be ripe for defeat. Nor can there be any question as to why the Kentuckian earlier had turned down Adams' offer of a place on the Supreme Court. Webster's constant but forlorn hope that the highest office might yet be his, obviously accounted for his amazing reconciliation with Jackson and his politic tour of the West in 1833—all done under the watchful eye of Van Buren, whose own ambitions would not permit the unlikely marriage of the Bank's heroic enemy and the Bank's heroic champion to be consummated. The discerning Harriet Martineau found the godlike Daniel's eloquence expended not out of principle but "from ambition for office and for the good opinion of those who surround him." His modern biographer writes of Polk's "intense ambition" and again of his "burning ambition," no exaggerations in the description of a man who pursued political success so feverishly.

Ambition sometimes did strange things to the judgment of men. The normally sagacious William Wirt, on receiving the Antimasonic nomination for the Presidency for 1832, actually began to tremble in delight and perhaps fear, at the significance of the great event. Ambition led Calhoun, Vice President under Adams, to repudiate and work against his President. It drove Van Buren in 1824 to try desperately to assure the election of a stricken man probably incapable physically of performing the duties of the Chief Executive. It helps explain why a romantic democrat such as George Bancroft affiliated with Jackson's party as he did, convinced, as he wrote Polk, that it was the likely winner, the party which would enable him to rise.

They were not necessarily social climbers in the sense of subordinating their personal desires to the pursuit of status, but it is a fact that a number of the era's leaders made marriages that were most useful either in increasing their wealth or broadening their opportunities. The list of these fortunates included such luminaries as Calhoun, Clay, Polk, and Crawford; and such lesser lights as McLane, W. L. Marcy; the Democracy's great intellectual, George Bancroft; John A. Dix of the Regency's ruling echelon; and Jackson's intimate adviser and organizer of victory in 1828, William B. Lewis. Jackson's own marriage was not a bad one. No one climbed more single-mindedly than Webster, although he relied on means other than marriage.

Jacksonian politicians characteristically had materialistic values. Webster's taste for the good things was great but by no means unique. His early apprenticeship under the wealthy Christopher Gore taught him in addition to the fine points of the law, a love of good wines and gourmet foods that remained more fixed than did his political beliefs. At Ashland, his 513-acre estate, Clay indulged his expensive tastes. In addition to his romantic enthusiasm for the people, Bancroft had an aristocratic fondness for fine wines that made his stay at St. James all the more pleasurable. Polk had to have the very finest and costliest of carriages. Old Hickory's early reputation for pursuing the high life led a modern admirer to write an article with the charming title: "Jackson's Loose Living Common Sin of the Period." In his maturer years he eschewed the livelier activities of his youth but although his health imposed a simple diet, he by no means became a consumer content with coarse or utilitarian fare. His expenditures included large sums for fine wines, expensive furnishings, hand-painted wall paper, various *objets d'art* and costly cut glass. This materialistic planter was a rude child of the soil only in the speechmaking of party propagandists.

In common with many other ambitious office seekers, Jackson's chief interest in land was not in working it but in accumulating as much as he could. He was ever ready to buy or sell, with an eye out for high profits. A taste for speculation was a ruling passion of the era. Not that this or the other traits were unique. As T. P. Abernethy long ago showed, the Founding Fathers were rapacious speculators. But if no single trait was unique to the Jacksonian era or its political leaders, the combination of them under consideration here was distinctive. In any case, speculation occupied Jacksonian political figures at least as much as it did earlier ones. Jackson himself speculated throughout his adult career not excluding his years in the White House. In 1817 a land company in which he had invested made a killing by buying a vast territory below the Muscle Shoals of the Tennessee River. Collusive bidding assured that no one submitted a bid higher than Jackson's minimum bid of $2 an acre for cotton land that shortly after sold at 40 times the price. The following year he used his official capacity in connection with the Chickasaw Treaty to engineer a most favorable land deal, acting in a manner variously characterized by historians as corrupt and shady. The Panic of 1819 hurt him because he was deeply involved in Alabama land speculations. One of his many bitter quarrels was with Thomas Kirkman over a speculation in Indian lands. It is true that his speculations were paltry in comparison to those of some of his intimates, such as William Blount, John Overton, William Polk, and John McLemore. These men were virtuosi of speculation whereas Andrew Jackson had other preoccupations. The point in any case is not that Jackson was one of the era's greatest speculators, but rather that the significant speculations that attracted him throughout his career throw a revealing light on his values, as they also relate him to his many contemporaries who were similarly occupied.

Robert J. Walker, who became a Jacksonian leader after he defeated Jackson's enemy George Poindexter in the Mississippi senatorial race of 1834, was so notorious a speculator that it was said that "suspicion of involvement in the schemes of moneyed men hung over him like a cloud." Clay's financial gambles were not notorious, but from his view, much better: they were successful. Thomas Hart Benton—"Old Bullion," as he liked to be called, in recognition of his opposition to a paper money system—speculated his way to a small fortune even before he reached his 21st birthday. Seward, like his father, speculated in lands. Edwin Croswell, the influential editor of the Albany *Argus*, the official journal of the New York Regency, was heavily involved in bank and other speculations as was Benjamin Knower. Polk collaborated with his father in a number of speculations, even if on a modest scale. According to one of Webster's modern biographers, "no one was more virulently infected . . . with the speculative fever of the time, and no one did more to stimulate it." Webster's agents in 1836 "avidly bought prairies and timberland and town sites in Ohio, Michigan, Wisconsin and Illinois." Alas, the gains proved illusory to him and the army of lesser political figures who like him were shortly to suffer through a panic brought on in part by their own mania for speculation.

Gambling in one form or another attracted many of the leaders. The harsh characterization of Clay that Adams in 1820 inserted in his memoirs—that "in politics, as in private life, Clay is essentially a gamester"—was unfair, primarily for its political judgment. Nor was Clay the dissolute fellow described in Democratic propaganda. But he did gamble. On one not unusual evening in 1821 he lost and then won back $8,000 from Poindexter, at that time still much admired by Jackson for his defense of the Hero's Florida raid. Betting on elections was a common practice and one which, in view of his political perspicacity, regularly provided nice bonuses to Van Buren. Jackson bet heavily on his race horses in the decades before he came to Washington, plunging heavily on his beloved Truxton, whose successes earned him over $20,000. His stay in the White House modified his habits only to the extent that his stable was now ostensibly in the hands of his ward, young Andrew Jackson Donelson, one of his prime favorites among the many young people he had drawn close to his bosom after the tragic miscarriages of Mrs. Jackson.

The leaders were uncommonly bright men. Their chief mental quality, shrewdness, is demonstrated over and over again in their political acts as well as in their comments, whether about politics or about one another. The political acuity of the men described, as of the man describing them, is nicely revealed in Calhoun's comments on his two chief rivals, a few years before the 1840 election: "the two prominent candidates for [President], Mr. Van Buren and Mr. Clay naturally come together on all questions in which North and South come into conflict. One is a southern man relying on the North for support, and the other is a northern man relying on the South. They of course dread all conflicting questions between the two sections, and do their best to prevent them from coming up, or when up, to evade them." Calhoun's mind was uncharacteristic in the sense that it had an affinity for theoretical abstractions and a gift for expounding them. That the ultimate shrewdness of his changing political stances can be questioned does not detract from the practical wisdom he brought to the analysis of political relationships and of political events. Of Jackson it might be said that he shrewdly cultivated an impression that he was both too honest and too rash to be shrewd. This elemental force who, in John William Ward's interpretation, somehow personified Providence, Nature, and Will, obviously was beyond guile.

His temper was indeed hot, displayed most uncontrollably when a disappointment, a criticism, or an attack caught him off guard, as John Spencer Bassett long ago noted. But when he anticipated a situation, he was capable of controlling it, not least by simulating an emotional explosion that he contrived rather than felt. He even fooled Van Buren with his pretended rage at Nicholas Biddle's supporters. When the time was ripe he gave Calhoun the impression that he, Jackson, was shocked at Crawford's recent disclosure to him that Calhoun had 12 years before urged Monroe's Cabinet to censure Jackson for his Florida raid. All these years, he implied, he had believed otherwise. Yet he had been told the facts two years earlier, by Sam Houston, had actually seen a confirming document which made his hair stand on end "for an hour," he wrote his then friend, Hugh White. Houston's disclosure came early in 1828 when Jackson's friends were not only wooing Calhoun to accept the second place on a ticket with the General, but dropping hints that the sickly old man would surely not live long beyond his inaugural. In any case, the irascible Jackson permitted himself to be conciliated then. When the time came, after the notorious Peggy Eaton controversy, and at the climax of the bitter struggle for the succession between Calhoun and Jackson's self-designated political heir, Van Buren, he suddenly confronted the South Carolinian with the dread question. He was delighted at the Vice President's "confusion." (Calhoun himself had reason to know at least two years earlier that Jackson no longer believed that Calhoun had tried to defend him in the Monroe Cabinet.) Calhoun's alleged crime is a most interesting one. It consisted of a cabinet member proposing a criticism of a commander who in violating his instructions had brought his country to the edge of war with one nation and possibly with another, the most powerful in the world. Of course Calhoun had subsequently taken great pains to prevent Jackson's knowing the truth, just as later he tried desperately to exonerate himself. This was character weakness, perhaps, but it was induced by understandable fear of a man who as President could regard Calhoun's perfectly defensible earlier position as sufficient ground for breaking off personal relations.

Another manifestation of Jackson's shrewdness was the quality of the men he came to rely on when in office: in Lynn Marshall's words "the practical, the shrewd, the opportunistic, and the efficient." Both during his Presidency as well as before, Jackson in effect tried to strew the historical record with seeming evidence tending to justify, put in a better light, or at worst show the sincerity of some later action. The Bank War, people were told, was waged by a man who had once written a friend that he had long distrusted banks ever since he had read an account of how 100 years before a Britisher had defrauded Frenchmen too greedy for speculative profits! The Rhea "letter"—which even sympathetic historians cannot credit—was mentioned in a Jacksonian reference made late in his first term to justify his amazing Florida invasion. According to Jackson the letter had been sent by President Monroe, transmitted through Congressman Rhea, and had approved in advance his subsequent actions. Unfortunately the letter had been burnt—per Monroe's instructions. More unfortunately, Monroe denied ever sending, and Rhea denied ever transmitting, the alleged communication. Jackson was no more embarrassed at this lack of confirmation than he was at Buchanan's denial of his charge that Clay had sent him to sound out Jackson about a Cabinet position for Clay. These Jacksonian allegations were not very convincing but the President was clever enough both to see the political need for them and to profit from them, for despite their phantom quality they were accepted outright by his partisans and discussed seriously by critical students at later times.

Clay's quick mind was capable of most artful disingenuousness. Who else could patiently explain to a southern audience as he did in 1830 that "the tariff was a national necessity which had raised the price of southern cotton and lowered the cost to the South of manufactured goods"? A few years later he quickly saw in Webster's opposition to the compromise tariff he had prepared to conciliate the Nullifiers, the opportunity to convince the South that this opposition by the mouthpiece of protectionism was the surest sign that Clay's tariff was pro-Southern. To prevent the disaffection of Webster during the Bank War, he artfully offered him an irresistible political plum. In the manner of a Polonious, late in his life he addressed the following advice to a new speaker of the House: "Decide, decide promptly, and never give your reasons for the decision. The House will sustain your decisions but there will always be men to cavil and quarrel about your reasons." The great disappointment of the era to this masterful man and his army of admirers was that all his astuteness could not win him the presidency he so coveted. They consoled themselves that he was too pure and took principles too seriously in an age dedicated to expediency.

When it came to political shrewdness, Van Buren was widely regarded to be the master. Interestingly enough, once he became President he displayed less of the trait than did the ostensibly guileless Jackson. But in the years in which he laid his plans for his own ascension to the highest office, as he contrived to win Jackson over to support his own ambitions, to destroy Calhoun yet attract the South, and to put down the pretensions of such powerful rivals as Webster, his artfulness was envied if not acclaimed by his fellow politicians. His successor in the Department of State, Edward Livingston, spoke of the State Department as the place where the "great magician brewed his spells." His earlier career as head of the Regency was a legend of political wizardry. In one outstanding example of the art of manipulation, in 1826 he got his machine to nominate for governor a man it did not particularly approve. The candidate, William B. Rochester, was, in fact, associated with the Adams Administration, which on the national level the Regency sought to destroy. Van Buren anticipated, accurately, not only that Rochester would draw votes away from and thus defeat De Witt Clinton, the Regency's mortal enemy, but that Clinton's subsequent attacks on the Adams men would lead to their desertion of Clinton and the collapse of his party. Van Buren's record as state leader is replete with evidences of his mastery of the game of politics.

American political leaders typically were more shrewd than profound and for the most part neither learned nor well-educated men. Calhoun was exceptional as well for his Yale degree as for his gift for theorizing. Detractors have challenged the originality, and even more the consistency, of his arguments in behalf of the concurrent majority, nullification, or the superiority of the slave to the wage system. One need not agree with his views, however, to recognize in them intellectual creativity, force, and learning. The Harvard-trained John Quincy Adams was also a man apart in this as in other respects. He could not bring himself to witness the conferring by Harvard of an honorary degree on Jackson in 1833 for, as he confided to his diary, as "an affectionate child of [his] . . . Alma Mater he would not be present to witness her disgrace in conferring her highest literary honors upon a barbarian who could not write a sentence of grammar and hardly could spell his own name."

The comment was unfair, for Jackson's correspondence—better than his state papers written by other men—shows that he could often transmit his ideas with some force. In James Curtis's phrase, Jackson "mangled words but seldom minced them." But of course he was not learned. He wrote of "parsomony," "confidents," "vissit," "betalions," and "youthood." According to Parton, an early biographer, it was doubtful that he had completed the reading of any secular book besides *The Vicar of Wakefield* or that he had even attempted to learn something of law, history, or political science. Parton passed on the report that Nicholas Trist had been told by a member of Jackson's family that "the General did not believe the World was round." Jackson's disinterest in books was shared by others, notably Clay. This disinterest was indicative not of mental deficiency of course. Every one of the major figures had an unusually good, certainly a quick, mind. It spoke more of lack of training and, most of all, of values in which the place of learning was not an exalted one.

Almost without exception the political careers of the leaders were models of opportunism. Adams' marvelous—if possibly unfair—appraisal of De Witt Clinton could have been applied to many other men: "His own aggrandizement has been the only test of his party attachments, and he has, consequently, been a mere man of coalitions." Adams himself was occasionally bitten by the bug of expediency. In his own memoirs he draws a frank and at times chilling self-portrait, but of a man who in being reserved, austere, and forbidding, even misanthropic, is obviously meant to be understood as a man of strong principles who is beyond considerations of petty personal advantage. Yet he sometimes lapsed. At the height of the early antimasonic frenzy, Adams proposed "to help tear off the veil that sheltered such fraternities" by exposing the harmless secrets of Phi Beta Kappa. But usually this complicated patrician lacked the flexibility that was one of the era's major requirements of party leadership. He did not even understand the obligation of replacing efficient government servants with party hacks, writing that he saw no reason "sufficient to justify a departure from the principle with which [he] . . . entered upon [his] . . . Administration, of removing no officer for merely preferring another candidate for the Presidency." He even admitted to Clay that officials like John McLean, the Postmaster-General, were actively working to undermine his administration. Yet, like Richard II, he contemplated incipient disaster reflectively, fortified by his conviction that his path was the moral one. Undoubtedly, that is an important explanation of why his administration was not only short-lived but was constantly on the defensive. Adams' political opponents of course had no such scruples.

The politics which placed success over principle was practiced by the leaders of the two major parties. For much of the era Democrats were more adept at it, but National Republicans and Whigs, if they succeeded only once with General Mum, failed not for lack of trying. The name of Thurlow Weed, one-time Antimasonic and later Whig party chief tactician, came to be synonymous with opportunism. In opposing Van Buren's Bucktails in New York, Whig leaders fought fire with fire, using the tactics made famous by their opponents. In Van Deusen's words, Seward was a "shrewd politician" who sought reforms always with an eye toward gaining votes. The greatest Whig of them all was more than once drawn toward political marriages likely to feed his own ambition. Having determined on a reconciliation, Clay after 1833 went to some lengths not to antagonize further Calhoun, who himself, though less than thrilled at the prospect of a political alliance with Harry of the West, also timidly approached it. Clay managed to be absent from the Senate vote on the Force Bill, citing ill health as his excuse. In the era's election seasons when as often as not he was likely to be running, at least for his party's nomination, Clay was most likely to trim his sail to the political winds. He sincerely liked the Second Bank of the United States not least because of its liberal personal loans to him. It seems clear that he fought the Bank War as and when he did for purely political reasons. It was believed by many that 1832 was chosen as the year for recharter more in the hope of electing Henry Clay President—forlorn though Clay knew his chances were—than of saving Mr. Biddle's institution. On more than one occasion, Henry Clay, hemp entrepreneur, had stood to profit from the high tariff policy advocated by Congressman Clay. His 1844 position on that contest's main issue, Texas, has been described as "consistent throughout—a consistent straddle." With terrible irony history repaid his expedient attempt to propitiate the South by denying him the northern votes that might have given him the election. How many times he seemed to be falling to destruction only to land on his feet. Jackson, exulting at Tyler's vetoes of Clay's measures, told Van Buren, "the old coon is really and substantially dead, skinned and buried—Clay's political career is closed forever." Of course he was wrong.

Calhoun's career is fascinating not least because of its admixture of doctrinaire zeal with the most calculated self-interest. His switch from strident nationalim to championship of states' rights was obviously due to his constituency's change of heart. In the contest between Adams and Jackson he offered himself to both men and served the winner until he found it impolitic to do so. In 1837 he deserted Clay and Webster for Benton and Van Buren "not so much because of principle as because of expediency." Few men were more crassly opportunistic than Webster. Attacked for allegedly saying that Congress should look after the rich who in turn would look after the poor, he assured the press he had said no such thing and believed rather that "all legislation . . . is especially bound to pay particular respect to the earnings of labor, . . . the source of comfort and independence," and so on. His reversal from free trade to protection was diametrically opposed to Calhoun's, but was due to the same general reasons: his new master spoke with a different voice than the old. In Benton's phrase, Clay and Calhoun attacked Webster's pro-Jackson stand on nullification because "his motives as well as his actions [were signs of] . . . subserviency to the President for the sake of future favor." The pots were calling the kettle black. Webster's short-lived political romance with Jackson came to nothing and is significant mainly as still another example of the era's fondness for subordinating principles to personal interests. Perhaps his most unlovely act, worse even than his reminder to Biddle that his additional political service to the BUS would be withheld until his retainer was forthcoming, took place toward the end of the era during the Maine boundary negotiations. Webster was Tyler's Secretary of State at the time, his continuation in the Cabinet itself suspect after Tyler's betrayal of the Clay program. Lord Ashburton (Alexander Baring), the British minister with whom Webster conducted the crucial negotiations, was a partner in the great English banking house of Baring Brothers, a firm that Webster himself had earlier served. The two men knew one another. Their ultimate plan for settling the issue conceded to Britain most of the territory she claimed. Webster's concessions were based on a map whose markings—drawn from memory by his friend Jared Sparks—were supposed to be similar to those made by Franklin in Paris in 1783. Sparks' memory was at fault. The markings on the original map would have shown that the United States was entitled to most of the territory in dispute. The damning judgment of Webster's recent biographer is that he not only did not know of the discrepancy but that "he did not care." His goal was a successful negotiation.

Van Buren's opportunism was on constant display, related as it was to his cleverness. In 1824 he appealed both to Clay's ambition and his ego in assuring him that his acceptance of the Vice Presidential nomination on a ticket headed by Crawford would relieve Van Buren's friends "from much of their apprehensions on the score of Mr. Crawford's health." This delicate suggestion, that the likely death of the President-elect made it worth an astute man's while to accept second place for the time being, was taken up four years later by Jackson men trying to seduce Calhoun. Little Van gallantly offering an arm to Peggy Eaton when the wives of Calhoun men were snubbing her was a commonplace example of the Albany magician's instinct for the main chance. He had not contrived to be a widower at that juncture: one suspects that a Mrs. Van Buren would have received Mrs. Eaton as though she were Martha Washington. After the "Eaton marlaria" had run its course, Van Buren suddenly felt that Eaton's presence was no longer necessary to the War Department—now that the Calhounites were on their way out of the Cabinet.

During the course of a political career dedicated almost fanatically to his personal advance, Polk managed to remain silent when either friends or an earlier position of his came under attack by Jackson. He improperly collected and used damaging information against a congressional opponent, tried to promote the senatorial candidacy of a man whose only qualification was his support of Polk's ambition to become Vice President, and in general displayed "disingenuousness and preference for devious manipulation." Benton "inveighed against unsound banking" at a time, early in his political career, when he was active in the affairs of the Bank of Missouri. As for the famous George Bancroft, it is hard to say from his statement to Edward Everett that "the man of letters cannot have brilliant success except on the popular side," whether he was drawn to that side out of concern for principle or out of the hope for brilliant success. Another eminent Jacksonian, Roger B. Taney, won his first renown, as well as Old Hickory's acclaim, by the stand he took during the Bank War, but there is reason to believe that his position on that issue was somewhat influenced by his personal interest in a Maryland bank. Amos Kendall's reputation for opportunism owed much to the circumstances by which he became a Jacksonian. In 1824 this able publisher was heavily in debt to Clay. After advising Clay that he would be happy to support him against both Adams and Jackson and would "take some pride in vindicating [him] . . . from the aspersions with which [Clay's] . . . enemies would overwhelm [him]," Kendall insisted on $1,500 instead of the $1,000 offered by Clay. In view of Clay's adamance, Kendall's *Argus* shortly thereafter commenced its bitter attacks on Harry and its lavish praise of Jackson.

Jackson, no less than the astute men who launched his national campaign for reasons of their own, was touched with opportunism. Neither in the years immediately prior to his election nor during his administration, was he simply used by others. He sensibly let men more skilled than he in the job of organizing victory perform their tasks, but he remained his own man. He permitted his name to be used because he wanted to be President. He himself double-talked on the tariff and internal improvements, or permitted others to do so for him, obviously because he cared more about his personal success than he did about the issues involved. This is not to say that he had no convictions. For every one of the great figures had certain beliefs that might be called principles. Yet they were essentially opportunists, dedicated above all to their own success, ready to pursue devious political courses if necessary to attain it.

The typical pattern of their political careers was inconsistency as they moved in zigzag fashion from one strongly held conviction to another. Of course when, as was often the case, the leaders assumed principles that were the opposite of their earlier ones, disquieting questions are raised about the depth of conviction in either instance. It seems evident, to paraphrase Mr. Dooley, that our Jacksonian politican leaders' views both followed the election returns and shifted in anticipation of them. Southern politicians, according to Van Buren, showed a "remarkable consistency" in their political positions, due to the alleged superiority of their pure republican principles. It seems more likely that it was slavery that promoted an unusual degree of stability of thought, at least about matters relating to its defense. But for the most part consistency was as rare in one latitude as in the other.

Many minds changed on the subject of Jackson's fitness for the Presidency. When he was first apprised that he was under consideration, Jackson himself denounced the idea in a characteristic outburst: "Do they think I am such a damned fool! No sir; I know what I am fit for. I can command a body of men in a rough way; but I am not fit to be President." Van Buren thought him "unsafe" in 1824 but the chief of the New York Bucktails was less concerned about the country being led by an unqualified man than at the "terrifying" prospect that Jackson might give De Witt Clinton, Van's mortal political enemy, a high office. Clinton's death shortly thereafter led Van Buren to see Jackson in a new light. Francis P. Blair who wrote Clay in 1825 that he hoped "Jackson's prospects had been cut off forever," became a Jacksonian when it became clear they had not. More flexible than most, Robert J. Walker first gave, then withdrew, then once more offered his support to the Old Hero. In 1826 Walker believed that "Nature has stamped upon him [Jackson] the seal of moral and intellectual preeminence," and in addition to his undoubted energy, granted him "more prudence, foresight and judgment, than have ever coexisted in any man but Washington." Not ten years later, after the removal of the deposits, Jackson had "proved himself a fool and a tyrant," to his former admirer, a judgment that was reversed in less than a year when once more Jackson became a genius, the removal of the deposits "in every point of view, one of the wisest measures of the government." More transparently than was the case with most of his contemporaries, Walker's shifting attachments were occasioned by considerations of interest rather than passion. Louis McLane, who would later catch Jackson's fancy, in 1824 said "they might as well think of turning the Capitol upside down as persuading me to vote for Jackson." It took no such upheaval to induce a change in the feelings of McLane and the numerous others who found Jackson's abilities and qualities marvelously enhanced as the old man's performance at the polls improved.

Jackson reversed himself as much as any man. As senator he voted "consistently in favor of internal improvements," although he previously had congratulated Monroe on his veto of the Cumberland Road Bill in 1822. The same man who vetoed the Maysville Road measure signed internal improvement bills fully as local as that one. With regard to the ticklish issue of the tariff, the protectionist senator became the evasive presidential candidate whose position depended on what state he happened to be appealing to. Jackson was a firm opponent of partisan political appointments, denouncing them in 1798, again in 1816 when he urged Monroe to disregard partisan considerations in making cabinet selections and to choose "characters most conspicuous for their capacity without any regard to party," and in 1825 during the first year of the Adams administration. As the whole world knows, when he became President he adopted an actual policy of appointments that totally contradicted his earlier professions, cleverly justifying his reversal by stressing the democratic implications in the expulsion of officeholders. His thinking on this issue was not static. By 1835 he was convinced that the President "must give direction to his administration" by appointing his political supporters; for "it is as true in politics as in morals that those who are not for us are against us." Like his master, Amos Kendall too repudiated an earlier position condemning partisanship in federal appointments, once he was given power himself to make them. Jackson's position on the distribution of the treasury surplus to the states was both for and against before he "grudgingly" approved a measure he probably helped steer through the Congress.

Jackson's disparate policies with regard to the power of the federal government seemed to be based not on any conviction about the matter but upon the likely substantive results of the exercise of federal power in a particular case. The same President whose Proclamation to the People of South Carolina advised them that the laws of the United States must and would be executed, earlier that same year professed federal impotence to protect Indian rights and territory against the state of Georgia. Marshall's decision in *Worcester* v. *Georgia,* that the national government had exclusive jurisdiction over Indian lands and that Georgia lacked authority to extend its laws over them, may not have provoked the remark Greeley claimed he heard, concerning Marshall enforcing his own decision. But Jackson did write that the federal government was too weak to protect Indian rights, his words and actions alike encouraging nullifiers to think that his position of national weakness was based on convictions rather than—as they were shortly to discover—on his approval of Indian removal.

Van Buren's inconsistencies in his years as Regency chieftain and Jacksonian intimate have been alluded to. As President during a great depression, he and his Party felt compelled to jump through new hoops in order to capture public favor. The despised Locofocos —the dissident New York Democrats whose antibank and generally radical views had made them anathema to the Regency, subjecting them to denunciation in its *Albany Argus* as "Jack Cades," "Carbonari," and other species of monster—were suddenly courted by the Democratic machine in New York. When President Van Buren visited New York City, "he attended the Bowery theatre in company with Alexander Ming, but recently despised as the 'agrarian' candidate for mayor." Van Buren's alleged adoption of Locofoco principles amounted essentially to nothing more than a new way of storing public monies, a device that only a vivid imagination, Democratic Party oratory, and what Whigs believed to be their shrewd refutation, could somehow distort into a radical measure smacking of spoliation.

In addition to his fluctuating views concerning federal appointments, Amos Kendall's other opinions were so mercurial that his biographer calls him "the very personification of inconsistency in formal theory." He had "managed simultaneously to espouse both hard money and paper money; he had shifted adeptly from preaching the preeminence of the federal government to that of the states and back again; he had even switched sides on the national bank issue itself." This man, who authored the politically persuasive Bank Veto message, had earlier kept changing his grounds for opposing the BUS. Political chameleon was the name for Amos Kendall as it was for other Democratic figures of the time. Polk believed one way and then another with regard to internal improvements, expansion, the Force Bill, hard money, and the Independent Treasury.

As was true of other traits, one party did not monopolize this one. Jackson's three great rivals were no models of consistency. Calhoun's famous switch from loose to strict construction is too well known to warrant more than brief reference. In view of his later identification with a relatively abstruse reading of the Constitution in order to justify state sovereignty, there was irony in his famous assertion of February 4, 1817, that he was "no advocate for refined arguments on the Constitution. The instrument was not intended as a thesis for the logician to exercise his ingenuity on. It ought to be construed with plain good sense." His views concerning tariffs, internal improvements, the power of the Federal Government, the BUS, first went this way and then that. After he moved back to the Democracy in 1837 he even found it within himself to speak of Jackson as "the great and remarkable man." Webster's reversals, as have been noted, were in an opposite direction from Calhoun's. The magnificent orator from New Hampshire was never at a loss, espousing a new cause dictated by interests of pocketbook with as much fervor and eloquence as would have been devoted to a change inspired by deep conviction. The great champion of the Union and federal power in the Debate with Hayne, 16 years earlier had argued "the solemn duty of the state governments to protect their own authority" against unconstitutional usurpation on the part of the national government, by interposing "between their citizens and arbitrary power." But that was when he was opposing military conscription for a war most unpopular with his constituents. Later he of course attacked nullification, although almost simultaneously first denouncing and then approving Jackson's firm stand against it.

Harry of the West was a great admirer of consistency. He was evidently convinced that he had sinned against it only once. Reviewing his career before a Lexington audience in 1842, Clay held that his reversal of his stand on a national bank after the War of 1812 was the only blemish on his record. This is debatable. When he first conceded the switch, in 1816, he argued that his earlier anti-BUS stand in the Senate had been based on instructions from his state. Yet in 1825 he disregarded his state's instructions that Kentucky's vote go to Jackson in the House balloting on the Pesidency. The explanation he later gave at Nashville, that the only instructions that would have been binding on him in 1825 would have had to have come from his congressional district of Fayette, Woodford, and Jessamine counties, was not convincing. This commanding man did not regard himself as the mere mouthpiece of his constituency's viewpoint. The man who once said that "to preserve, maintain and strengthen the American system, he would defy the South, the President and the devil," in 1838 let it be known "the American system was an abandoned issue"; he had modified all his positions. New times and the perennial lure of the White House led him to part even from the great idea with which he was so clearly identified by the American people.

The swtiching of allegiances was a characteristic theme in the political behavior of lesser figures as of the giants. In Rhode Island William Sprague "ran for the governorship in 1832 as an Antimason, was elected to Congress in 1835 as a Democrat, and became a Whig governor in 1838. John Brown Francis, after serving several terms as a Democratic governor, was subsequently elected to the Senate as a Whig. D. J. Pierce . . . shifted his allegiance in 1833 from the Whig to the Democratic party. The redoubtable Thomas Dorr was a Whig in 1835, a Constitutionalist in 1837, and a Democrat in 1839." Francis Grund, who in 1834 championed the Whigs, in 1835 switched to Van Buren, in 1840 campaigned for Tippecanoe, in 1844 swung over to Polk, a few years later went back to Clay, only to reverse himself again and support Buchanan. It is no wonder that he has recently been likened to a "political weathervane." Contemporaries fastened the name "General Weathercock" on the "not altogether atypical" Mississippi politician who was a Democrat in 1834, a Whig in 1835, a Democrat again in 1836, a Whig in 1837, and once more a Democrat in 1840. In view of the changing circumstances of American life, a rigid consistency by political leaders would have indeed betrayed small minds. The evidence, however, indicates that their reversals were induced less by the desire to serve better the interests of community and nation than to promote their own and their parties' political chances. As clever men they had no difficulty in explaining the latter motives in terms of the former.

Ambitious and opportunistic men whose views were tentative could be easily embarrassed, particularly when they were forced to take a stand that might hurt them politically. Evasiveness was a useful defense some of the leaders developed. Van Buren was its most perfect exponent. Phrenology is more than pseudo science if the visiting phrenologist, George Combe's description of the Van Buren head was not influenced by what others might have told him: "the head is large, the anterior lobe is of ample dimension. . . . The base of the brain is largely developed; the coronal region is both broad and high. Secretiveness, cautiousness, and love of approbation are very large. . . . Acquisitiveness and ideality are fully developed. . . . Conscientiousness is . . . the smallest of the moral organs. The combination of great cautiousness and firmness relatively less, will produce a tendency to prefer indirect to direct means of accomplishing an end. In difficult situations dexterity . . . will be more relied on than manly courage and an apparent expediency will sometimes be preferred to justice."

Van Buren had managed "to be on circuit" when a large meeting was called in Albany to endorse the prohibition of slavery in Missouri, during the controversy over that state's admission. Thus a northern man with Southern principles could retain support of men on both sides of the ticklish issue. Of the explanation he gave in his autobiography for not being present for the decisive tariff vote in 1827—that his absence was "occasioned by a promise he had given to accompany a friend on a visit to the Congressional Cemetery"—a sympathetic biographer concedes, "the excuse is hard to believe." Ever fertile of resource, he evaded John Bell's persistent attempt to elicit from him his position in regard to internal political divisions in Bell's home state of Tennessee in 1834, by suddenly developing a severe toothache that "compelled [him] to decline the conversation and to retire almost immediately." That Andrew Jackson could call this artful dodger "frank, open, candid and manly," suggests something of the General's quality of discernment. Others, including Clay, missed votes and side-stepped tough questions but none with the dexterity and aplomb of Van Buren.

At worst, ambition, expediency, evasiveness, and inconsistency combined to produce hypocrisy or downright dissimulation. The same Van Buren who in 1828 denied that "he either opposed the Tariff [of Abominations] or voted for it solely in compliance with the wishes of his state," was to swear years later "that he had been forced to support the measure on orders from the New York legislature." The latter statement was intended to mollify the South but indubitably it contradicted his own earlier version of his motives. Polk's reference—made "somewhat disingenuously," according to his modern biographer—to his alleged "passive part" in trying to secure the Democratic Vice Presidential nomination in 1840, invites incredulity in view of the forceful and even machiavellian tactics he used in trying to get the coveted place. On the one hand, this intensely ambitious man had let it be known that in return for the nomination he would renounce a contest for either of the two highest posts in 1844. On the other, he was not above intimating to Van Buren that crucial Southern support for Van's 1840 race would not be forthcoming unless Van Buren urged the party to name Polk as his running mate. During his last year in the presidency his reputation was forever sullied by Alexander H. Stephens' bitter label—"Polk the Mendacious"—and its variation, "James K. Polk— a man whom none could believe." Seward denied that he had ever planned to veto a voter registration law, when in fact he actually had written the veto message—only to tear it up. Jackson's uncharacteristic hesitancy to speak of the Rhea "letter" until 13 years after the event, his failure to pursue the matter in the press after Monroe's denial of Jackson's assertion, raises questions about Jackson's own convictions on the matter. With regard to his 1827 exchange, denied by Buchanan, that the latter had been sent to him by Clay, Jackson's delay in making the accusation and the repudiation of it by the one person directly involved explains better why "there were many who [said] . . . in the words of James Stevenson of Pittsburgh, "Why, by God, I will believe Buchanan in preference to General Jackson.' "

Hypocritical seems to be the word for Webster's professed sympathy for the laboring poor, as well as for President Van Buren's report to Congress that the United States Indian policy had been "just and friendly throughout; its efforts for their civilization constant, and directed by the best feelings of humanity; its watchfulness in protecting them from individual frauds unremitting," at a time when thousands of Cherokees were dying due to their forcible removal by General Winfield Scott, acting under orders of the Van Buren Administration. Clay's explanation that he would pursue the Presidency only by means "reconcilable to the nicest sense of honor and the strictest propriety," meant, so far as he was concerned, that he could not make a college commencement address in 1838 at Franklin College in Athens, 'Georgia; but "strictest propriety" appears exaggerated as a description of the tactics he did employ in pursuit of the highest office. The like claims made by Jackson, Calhoun and their adherents as to the fastidiousness of their campaign styles were equally disingenuous.

Demagogy was another characteristic of the political behavior of the era's party leaders. It is not always easy to detect, since in one form it manifests itself in promises to the people by men intent more in profiting from the promises than in keeping them. In such cases the sincerity of the politician is in question and sincerity is a devilishly elusive phenomenon, perhaps impossible to track down. Another more manageable type of demagogy involves behavior transparently at odds either with the views or the ways of the man manifesting it. Professing to be aghast at Whig "trickery and flummery" in their successful Presidential campaign of 1840, Polk had not been above rolling out a barrel of whiskey to his followers on the street in the gubernatorial campaign of the preceding year. Certainly the Harrison campaign was demagogic. So were the comments of partisans who implied that their own party was above the low tactics used by the Whigs, partisans who themselves used similar tactics in other elections. Hyperbole, gross oversimplification of complex issues, identification of the Whigs as abolitionists or Federalists—in areas where those terms were political death—were other forms of Democratic political craftsmanship practiced in Tennessee.

Amos Kendall's bank veto message, signed by Andrew Jackson, was an inspired piece of political demagogy, successful beyond the calculations of the men who profited from it; but demagogic it was, particularly in its hints that the nonrenewal of the charter of an agency that kept and transferred public monies would somehow help the nation's poor and was a blow against "the rich and powerful [who] too often bend the acts of government to their selfish purposes." The Whig attack on the alleged radicalism of the theory expressed in Van Buren's presidential message of 1838—his allusion to "the anti-republican tendencies of associated wealth"—is a nice example of the kind of exaggerated response to demagogic talk that helped foster a widespread belief in the sincerity of such talk. The Independent Treasury harmed none of those associations of wealth in New York State or in the South which had provided such a solid underpinning to Van Buren's career. It is not to discredit entirely Benton's early land proposals to note that their reputation for radicalism was somewhat misplaced, providing as they did for sale at a special low price or "donation" only of that land which went begging at public auction. They met with the enthusiastic approval of urban merchants on the western "frontier." The enactment of such measures would not quite have indicated that the government was now "working for the poor," as Benton claimed. George Bancroft wrote that the "common mind" or "the people" were "wiser than the most gifted individual; the decision of the many is to be preferred to the judgment of the enlightened few," even with regard to intellectual or artistic judgments. Bancroft was a romantic and possibly believed his statement. The astute men who used it and others like it give the impression that they believed it only when common preferences were similar to their own.

Demagogy of course was a game played by both sides. Daniel Webster's performance in telling an 1840 audience that "it did not happen to me to be born in a log cabin; but my elder brothers and sisters were born in a log cabin, raised amid the snowdrifts of New Hampshire," and then weeping—as he had been wont to do since the Dartmouth College case—itself evokes smiles rather than tears. Clay was fond of dwelling in his later years upon his humble background, convincing his earlier biographers that he was "an orphan boy brought up amid poverty and ignorance." But as Van Deusen observed in his comprehensive biography, "the facts present a somewhat different picture." Clay's father had actually left him an inheritance, a small one to be sure but one that was assurance against poverty. Some of Clay's followers felt that his failure to win the Presidency was due to the fact that he was "too pure a patriot to win in [those] . . . demagogueing times," in which "we must mix up a little 'humbugging' with our glorious Whig creed before we can expect a victory." Humbugging certainly helped produce victory in 1840. It also made Clay unhappy that his party had stooped to imitate the Jacksonians, for as he wrote Crittenden, "I lament the necessity, real or imaginary, which has been supposed to exist, of appealing to the feelings and passions of our countrymen, rather than to their reasons and judgments." The question has occurred to many people however whether Clay would have been so unhappy had he rather than Harrison been the beneficiary of the low campaign style he found so offensive, a style it might be noted that his party and its National Republican predecessor favored before and after 1840, when Clay himself was running.

In view of their unlovely traits and values, Abraham Lincoln in the 1830s could define politicians as "a set of men whose interests are aside from the interests of the people and who [are] as a class, at least one long step removed from honest men." This caustic appraisal cannot of course be taken literally. The burden of my argument to this point is that the leading political figures of one or another of the Jacksonian era's major parties were astute realists, largely of similar background, mental habit, and values. Ambitious for material gain, worldly success, and prestige, they improvised in politics as some of them speculated in lands, forsaking old supporters and beliefs for new, always with an eye for the main chance. The era's truest examples of men on the make capable of rising through their own efforts were not Tom, Dick, and Harry but rather the essentially amoral men whose flattery of the common man was simply one further testimony to their mastery of the new political realities. Yet one hesitates to call them pragmatists devoid of political, social, or philosophical conviction.

As men attached to the major parties, they of course identified themselves with greater or lesser vehemence to the programs espoused by their organizations. Some historians take seriously, others dismiss as claptrap, the formal appeals and policy statements put forward by the parties. Certainly the issue is an important one and shall be dealt with in the subsequent discussion of the Jacksonian parties. My suspicion that flexible pragmatists though they were, they nevertheless held to certain beliefs—in some cases they can be called convictions—is based not on their or their parties' electioneering statements and propaganda. Rather it stems from an evaluation of their adult careers and on those of their utterances whose tone and circumstances give them the ring of sincerity. Even political opportunists retain the complexity attendant on their membership in the human species. Their beliefs may seem to have little influence on their behavior and yet it is rare that the career even of a political chameleon is marked by *total* unscrupulousness or by actions, no matter how self-interested, bearing no relation whatever to the sympathies of the actor.

If attention is turned not to their tariff ideas, or their choice of federal or state monies for financing transportation improvements—or what might be called the tactics and the mechanisms or the procedures of politics—but is focused instead on their beliefs concerning the proper order of society, or to the interrelationship of its constituent elements, the era's chief political figures again exhibit a notable similarity. They were conservative in their beliefs about these fundamental matters. They believed in private inheritance of wealth and the sanctity of private property. They accepted a hierarchical social system and the enormous social and economic disparities prevalent in their era—for all the oral thunder directed against inequality in their party pronunciamentos. Their acceptance of the broadened suffrage was more politic than enthusiastic, although their flexibility enabled them to adjust to, even to thrive on, the new system, for all the aversion to it expressed by a Chancellor Kent or for that matter, Martin Van Buren early in his career. As Disraeli and Bismarck discovered later in the century, popular suffrage was not necessarily unsettling to an ordered society based on social distinctions, for all the fears of some conservatives that it would be.

Some applauded or profited from, others reviled and had nothing to do with, slavery; but almost every one of them accepted it. The explanation that this was in accord with the spirit of the times explains nothing and overlooks the many citizens who devoted themselves to eradicating the system. Such citizens it goes without saying were not leaders of the major parties. Of course Whig and Democratic parties had distinctive positions concerning the issue. It is no accident that a Polk and a Jackson who entertained few if any qualms about the system were in one party, while Clay who had many, was in the other. But qualms were not opposition. If the leaders became interested in relief for debtors it was usually only when they themselves or their venturesome friends were affected, debtors not from poverty but from excessive speculative zeal. In word and even more clearly in deed they revealed themselves to be friends to the established order of things. Opportunists tend to have an ideology of sorts, an unspoken one, that is manifested in their behavior. In devoting themselves to personal advance *within* the system rather than to challenging or changing it, they display acquiescence in, or support of, its underlying social arrangements.

Evidence concerning the profoundest beliefs of the political leaders bears out this suggestion. Edward Everett appealed to Webster's admirers in Boston to raise a trust fund of $100,000, explaining that having Webster in Congress was necessary to protect "our friends in Boston . . . their houses, their land, their stocks." Webster may not have said, as the Democratic press charged he did, that if Congress took care of the rich, the rich would take care of the poor. But he did not believe in the stake-in-society theory, in 1833 arguing that "to be safe depositories of political power, they [the people] must be able to comprehend and understand the general interests of the community, and must themselves have a stake in the welfare of that community." Calhoun's affinity for a hierarchical social system is well known, his fear of the white industrial masses of the North surpassed only by his dread of their black brethren in his own section. Clay's economic philosophy, it has been observed, "favored the rich and the able at the expense of the masses." In principle he subscribed to a paternalistic credo which held that men of all sections and interest were "bound up and interwoven together, united in fortune and destiny." In practice he was unconcerned with the problems of working people, devoting his skill in law to the service of the rich. His anti-Jacksonian position on the Indian issue made him seem humanitarian by comparison with his opponents. A relatively liberal attitude toward the Indian and Negro minorities was no sign of social radicalism, however. Clay's success in prosecuting defaulting debtors was due in part to his devotion for the task. He had no sympathy with debtors or with the movement in his state to abolish imprisonment for the crime. He moved with ease in the highest social circles of his community in part because he shared the values of its members.

Van Buren's early opposition to the granting of full white male suffrage betrayed fears similar to Webster's. At the New York State

Constitutional Convention in 1821 he warned that "the character of the increased number of voters would be such as would render their elections rather a curse than a blessing." He, like his political machine, had no use for the radical ideas they attributed to the Locofocos, although perfectly willing to appropriate some of their rhetoric in behalf of the Subtreasury proposal. Amos Kendall even at his most demagogic alluded to the inevitability of social distinctions. His idea was neither that the rich be disturbed in their riches nor the poor in their poverty, but only that national government bestow none of the few favors available to it on the one or the other. The Kentucky Relief movement of the 1820s which enlisted his support was no poor man's movement, had no sympathy with the general notion of repudiation, committing itself "to debtor relief not on principle but because [its leaders] . . . felt a practical need for it, and their attachment to it lasted only as long as their need." Polk was more interested in reforms, such as broadened educational opportunity, than most high-placed Jacksonians, but he was hardly a firebrand. In voting against granting firewood to the Georgetown poor in 1831, "lest it develop a lamentable tendency on the part of the poor people to look to the government for relief," he betrayed above all a zeal for frugal government and strict construction. At the height of the depression following the Panic of 1839, his fellow Democrats, James Buchanan and Robert Walker, warned that wages were too high.

"The feud between the capitalist and the laborer, the House of Have and the House of Want, is as old as social union," thundered George Bancroft. But unlike a Thomas Skidmore or a George Henry Evans, Working Men's leaders, who would end the feud by abolishing the inequalities which produced it, Bancroft concluded that the conflict "can never be entirely quieted." As a practical politician himself, who rose to the Collectorship of the Port of Boston and later to a position in Polk's Cabinet, he was critical of "the radical who makes war upon everything in which he can discern a fault." Struggle against abuses was unnecessary since, according to Bancroft's consoling philosophy, "evil and injustice were temporary, and . . . the inevitable flow of events brought remedy in time."

Neither in word nor action did Jackson reveal a consistent interest in, let alone sympathy for, democracy and democratic social change, during the first 62 years of his life. One of the things that appealed to him about his early position as attorney general in Tennessee was that it was "independent of the electorate." An important difference that arose between him and Governor Blount had to do with the method for designation of field officers of the militia, Blount favoring "the old and popular method of election by the men," Jackson insisting on appointment by the commander. His own earlier election as Major-General of the Tennessee militia was due not to any popular ground swell in his behalf, but to the vote cast for him by his friend, Governor Archibald Roane, against Jackson's enemy, the democratically minded John Sevier. Richard

Hofstadter, in questioning the view that Jackson believed strongly in democratic principles, notes that he was of that small number of frontier rich men who were regarded as "natural leaders," and to whom "political offices fell like ripe fruit." According to Hofstadter, "such beneficiaries of popular confidence developed a stronger faith in the wisdom and justice of popular decisions than did the gentlemen of the older seaboard states." The thesis may have general application but in Andrew Jackson's case, the posts he gained whether in Tennessee or in the national government, prior to 1828, were appointive for the most part, and when elective were based not on the votes of the people, but on the legislature or a handful of friends in the militia. His relative popular success in the national canvass of 1824, on the other hand, did make him more sympathetic both to white manhood suffrage and to the direct election of presidents by the people. Yet his political *beau ideal* was the military dictator, Napoleon Bonaparte.

In the economic and social conflicts that racked Tennessee in the decade before he became President, Jackson aligned himself with the most conservative groups in his state. It was not only a matter of being out of sympathy with reform movements. Jackson fought for the right of absentee claimants to the lands of Tennesseans, he and Patrick Darby trying unsuccessfully "to eliminate the Tennessee statute of limitations which protected land occupiers of long standing." Jackson and his friends fought against the democratic and liberal reforms urged by William Carroll during the era. His first cases in law in Nashville had involved him on the side of creditors against debtors, while his subsequent practice was "largely concerned with landowners' interests." His habits of thought, particularly as he himself became a member of their class, came to be those of the men he had served. When the Panic of 1819 turned a mass of formerly prosperous men into debtors, Jackson was one of the few prominent men in Tennesses who opposed repudiation, stay laws, or other forms of debtor relief. He himself brought suit against 129 of his personal debtors, while in politics he fought against the Relief Party. A prominent part was played in the latter group by Nashville merchants and "wealthy and influential speculators [who] had plunged recklessly and dragged the whole community to ruin with them." But that Tennessee's Relief Party was evidently no more principled or poor than its counterpart in Kentucky, does not make its enemies, Colonel Edward Ward or General Andrew Jackson, any the less conservative. There is no reason to doubt the sincerity of the letter Jackson sent to his adopted son, later, from the White House, in which he wrote, "nothing can be more disgraceful, or more injurious to a man's standing in society, than the charge truly made that he has promised to pay money at a certain day, and violating that promise." The social values here upheld are private property and the sanctity of financial obligations. And in the famous message vetoing the bill to recharter the Second Bank of the United States, Jackson identified himself with the view not only that inequality was inevitable and beyond the power of government to prevent, but that the rich owed their fortunes to their "superior industry, economy, and virtue."

For all their similarity, the era's political giants were each of a unique mold. They would not have attained the heights they did had they not been blessed with a flair that brought them to the attention of party managers or that appealed to the voter. Webster's matchless oratory, his command of at least three distinctive styles, depending on the issue or the occasion; Clay's vast charm, beguiling to the humble and mighty alike, the evident delight taken in a man of so many nicknames—"Gallant Harry of the West," "The Cock of Kentucky," "The Western Hotspur," "The Western Candidate," "The Western Star," "The Mill-Boy of the Slashes," "The Old Prince," "The Sage of Ashland,"—unhappily, —"The Judas of the West,"—and, as he tenderly referred to himself, the "Old Coon"; Adams' uncompromising crustiness; Calhoun's almost terrible intensity; Van Buren's charm and subtlety; and Old Hickory's fierce determination, physical courage, fighting ability, proneness to violence, and even the mighty ego that identified his own opinions with God, assumed the rascality of his critics, and was fed by the continuous presence of a court painter required only to paint, endlessly, portraits of the old man and his family; none of these can be conveyed in a study of the important similarities of these disparate figures. But distinctive personal characteristics, as was mentioned at the outset of this discussion, are true of any era, while unusual ability is almost always present in men who are leaders.

The particular similarities in background, beliefs, traits, and values of the Jacksonian era's political leadership were not a chance occurrence, but seem obviously to have been in accord with the spirit of the times. Certainly the rampant opportunism of the leaders was precisely the trait likely to bring them success under the "new rules of the game" that were transforming politics during the era. That their values were like those of the electorate that honored them was an important element in their success, not least because it conveyed to the people the comforting feeling that its leaders were not only for them but of them. Their oneness with the larger community, in the sense that is was cultivated, was but another example of the uncommon cleverness and ability that enabled the political leaders to realize their ambitions more fully than did lesser men. These were the Jacksonian era's true self-made men, moving freely up the ladder of their political society, ideally suited to command the great pragmatic party organizations of their time.

10

THE RISE OF MAJOR PARTIES: DEMOCRATIC AND WHIG THEORY AND PRACTICE

Great national parties reemerged during the era of Andrew Jackson. If, as Edmund Burke had said, a political party is "a body of men united for promoting by their joint endeavor the national interest upon some particular principle in which they are all agreed," the Democratic and Whig organizations would hardly qualify. Only the parties of principle such as the Liberty or antislavery party, the Working Men, the nativist groups that organized under a variety of names, and the Antimasonic party—at least at the beginning of its career—met the Burkean standard. In Lord Acton's phrase, the major parties endeavored to get advantages rather than realize ideals.

But of course party is as party does. In the late 1820s the United States gave birth to a new kind of political party not dreamed of in the political theory of earlier thinkers. It was capable of appealing to all manner of men, standing for diverse things to its different constituencies and organized and led by men united above all in behalf of no loftier principle than winning office for themselves. The modern American major party was thus born during the period.

At the beginning of the era there were no distinct national parties—or there was only one party. The political effect was the same in either case. The disappearance of the Federalists left the field to the Jeffersonian party as was illustrated by the near unanimous election of Monroe in 1820. The claim was put forward once more, as it had been in the early days of the first Washington Administration, that "party division was bad and that a one-party system best served the national interest." Of course what was the orthodox party in 1820 had been the heterodox 30 years earlier. Thus the contest of 1824 was ostensibly among good Republicans all. Jackson supporters were unabashed at the repudiation of the Hero by Jefferson. For that matter, all of William H. Crawford's opponents repudiated what until that point had been considered a major principle of pure Republicanism: the support of the presidential candidate nominated by the party's congressional caucus. Van Buren had referred to the caucus as the mainstay of the Republican faith. But the ambitious candidates would not permit mere traditions to frustrate their drive for high office, insisting all the while on their devotion to Jeffersonian ideals. The electorate in effect sustained their claims. The bitter contest of 1828 was between Jacksonians who referred to themselves either as Republicans or Democrats and the followers of John Quincy Adams and Clay—Republicans or National Republicans.

For all the continued insistence by both sides on their good Republicanism, the fact is that midway through the Adams administration a new political party was formed—by its opponents. Masterfully organized in Congress by Van Buren, and throughout the country by friends of Old Hickory, the new party reiterated its devotion to the principles of the Sage of Monticello, but its practice effectively separated out supporters of Andrew Jackson from his critics. At its birth it was the Jackson party and so it remained until the Hero's death, its leaders consulting and paying attention to his wishes after his departure from the White House, as they had followed them during his residence there.

Jackson's opponents responded to the formation of a national Democratic party by creating a National Republican party. This group attempted to imitate the skillful organization, the committee network, and the hard-hitting party press of the Democrats, but it succeeded only in part. While strong elsewhere in the country it failed altogether to build a base in the South. It did not last very long beyond the decisive electoral defeat it suffered in 1832. In 1834, however, a formidable major rival to the Jacksonian Democracy emerged in the form of the Whig party. This new party was strong in all sections. Led by Henry Clay, it was able to mount powerful political campaigns on the national and state levels all during the 1830s and 1840s, while the Whig share of the nation's electorate roughly equaled that of their Jacksonian opponents. The belief was widely held then as later that the constituencies of the two parties were as different in wealth and social status as the parties were believed to be unlike in philosophy and program. In any case, the nation once again as in the days of the Washington administrations had two great political organizations competing for control of government.

There was not then or is there now agreement as to the reasons for the reemergence of a two-party system. Jackson's congressional partisans naturally enough liked to emphasize their dedication to democratic beliefs that were ostensibly jeopardized by the Adams administration. On the state level the factions that jumped on Old Hickory's bandwagon had as little difficulty in justifying their affiliation on the high ground of political principle. But that the early organizers of the Democracy found it politic to explain the origins of their party in lofty terms is no indication that their argument was anything more than self-serving propaganda. In view of the mystery surrounding Jackson's own opinions, the fact that some of his supporters had seemed to shop around for a candidate—any candidate—who seemed capable of winning in 1828, and the total disregard for ideological matters shown by the Tennessee realists who launched Jackson's national campaign, it is hard to credit the theory that the national Democratic party was called into being in order to achieve the political convictions of its founders. The champions of Andrew Jackson seemed to be inspired mainly by the dream of electoral success for their candidate and the political rewards that would be earned accordingly by his loyal supporters.

The emergence of a national organization dedicated to the election of Andrew Jackson as President profoundly affected state politics. On the state level there had never been an era of good feelings. Bitter wrangling among opposing political factions was as much the rule during the reign of Monroe as it had been in the days of John Adams. Opposing state leaders were not averse to labeling their own cliques "Republican" or "Jeffersonian" or even "Democratic." State politics had been characteristically a sordid business, preoccupied with the pursuit of office by any means, nepotism, and partisan legislation. Parties there were but, as in New York State, they "continued more from memory and habit than from calculated differences of interest." A Martin Van Buren or a De Witt Clinton in New York, a William Blount in Tennessee, or an Isaac Hill in New Hampshire was followed not for what he believed in but for what he could deliver. These men and others like them transferred their affections to Andrew Jackson for similarly amoral reasons.

A kind of coattails politics became the rule, state friends of Jackson obviously hoping to become the local beneficiaries of a national landslide for the Hero. Some clusters of office seekers insisted they were truer Jacksonians than others. Where rival Jacksonian factions arose, as in North Carolina, the split was caused not by ideological differences but by competition for office. Radicals and conservatives were present in both groups. Pennsylvania's Democrats were badly split—as they had been before they became Jacksonians—and for reasons that continued to have nothing to do with political or social philosophy. In New York, on the other hand, what became the Democratic party was a monolith that brooked no opposition. This of course was the Regency, created in the early 1820s to gain and hold political power for Martin Van Buren and his friends. Andrew Jackson's great lure to this pragmatic machine had little to do with political principles. In the Empire State, in fact, the General's new supporters commented that they did not quite know where their candidate stood on the important issues of the day. Political profit seemed to be the explanation of their attachment to the Hero. Jackson's early popularity in Missouri derived from his heroic military reputation, not his beliefs. His party won overwhelming political victories in that state throughout the era by attracting the votes of thousands of Missourians who were in fact opposed to its well-known national "principles." For Maryland, Mark Haller has noted that the Jackson party developed primarily as a coalition of dissident politicians, "composed of former Federalist leaders, personal friends of John C. Calhoun, Republican followers of William H. Crawford, and ambitious younger politicians. Jackson leaders in Maryland, as they were painfully aware, had no distinctive economic issues or legislative program to rally their supporters. . . . They were, in short, united chiefly in a desire to secure the victory of Old Hickory and of his loyal followers in Maryland." As Peter Levine drily reports, "parties developed in New Jersey in the late 1820s as agencies designed to elect men to office and to reward loyal party workers," an explanation that applies as well to Michigan and Louisiana.

If the Jackson party organizers were essentially astute realists rather than democratic or radical firebrands, they were not totally lacking in political convictions. Certainly the Democracy was very much concerned if not preoccupied with defending slavery from political attack. The Virginia-New York alliance that was the bedrock of the Jackson party rested on the southerners' dedication to preserving and insulating from political attack the "peculiar institution" and Van Buren's sympathy for their position. It was no accident that the national leader of the party was Andrew Jackson, slaveowner and friend to slavery. Northern Democrats tended to be more proslavery than their political opponents in that section. Free Negroes knew this and voted—where they could vote—accordingly. The English visitor Edward Abdy "never knew a man of color that was not an anti-Jackson man." While Democratic ardor for slavery indicates that the new party was not entirely a creature of expediency, it hardly constitutes support for the old theory first popularized by Jacksonians themselves that theirs was the party of the common man. The principle of laissez-faire discernible in the stance of some Jacksonian congressional leaders at the party's inception is similarly hard to equate with an ideological interpretation of the party's origins.

Convictions of any sort had little to do with it. The Democratic party was conceived in lust for political office by men who had in common mainly their desire to replace John Quincy Adams with Andrew Jackson. At its birth it was a heterogeneous catchall whose great national leader had taken pains to avoid committing himself on the important issues.

The short-lived National Republican party seemed much more concerned with principles than were their Democratic opponents. While it too was a broad coalition, it was not all things to all men. Its national leaders, John Quincy Adams, Henry Clay, and Daniel Webster, favored a degree of federal involvement in the economy that was frightening to many Jacksonians. Since Andrew Jackson's popularity was so manifest in the years after his first election to the Presidency, it might seem that the failure to jump on his bandwagon attested to his opponents' convictions. For all their diversity the National Republicans appeared to share certain political beliefs, which they took seriously enough to jeopardize their own chances, particularly on the state and local level.

To a *national* figure such as Clay, the American System was an astute concept in the sense that it had the effect of exalting his ambition and personal hostility to Jackson into a position seemingly grounded in principle. But the local personages who courted election defeat by supporting internal improvements, a high tariff, or the Second BUS, obviously found these issues important in their own right. Support of internal improvements, however, hardly betokened doctrinaire zeal in behalf of an abstract political theory. The farmers, millers, and speculators who favored canal expansion by whatever means did so because it enhanced their real interests or because they thought it did. Jackson's inconsistency on the issue was matched by that of his local followers: Jacksonians were by no means inveterate enemies of improvements. Nor were the early National Republican supporters of federally financed transportation projects the stuff of martyrs. Ordinarily, if such sentiments were strong in a given locality, it was likely too that they were popular at the polls. No more than the Democrats was the National Republican party a manifestation of a consistent political theory firmly subscribed to. That differences over what Shalhope calls "doctrinal issues" were not totally absent in party formation in such states as Missouri and Ohio hardly constitutes proof that the era's major parties were inspired essentially by great principles. These differences suggest rather that in a democracy the politics of pragmatism will not be totally devoid of some elements of principle, at least on the level of rhetoric.

The great political organization that fought against the Democrats for most of the period and which, like the Jacksonians, proved capable of attracting massive support in all sections of the country was the Whig party. There is no agreement as to how the party came to be named. Clay used the term Whig in a Senate speech on March 14, 1834, attacking the removal of the deposits. Two years earlier nullifiers in South Carolina and Georgia had applied it to their cause. The eminent New York merchant, Philip Hone, and James W. Webb, publisher of the New York *Courier*, each claimed the honor of having been the first to conceive the name for the new anti-Jackson party. Actually, the term "Whig" had been used in American politics since the days of the Revolution. If there is some doubt as to how the Whig party came to be named, there is little or none as to what accounted for its appearance. What called the Whig party into being was not a classical principle of politics or society. At its birth its discordant elements were united by one thing above all: their opposition to the political behavior of Andrew Jackson. "King Andrew" they thereafter called him. Their choice of name explained what the creators of the new party thought they were about.

According to John Quincy Adams the Whigs at birth were a

heterogeneous coalition of five distinct groups, united only by their opposition to the election of Jackson's heir apparent, Martin Van Buren. These were "part of the southern democracy: deserters from Jacksonism in two divisions [Calhoun nullifiers and Hugh White Tennesseans]; Clay Democrats; the 'Webster Federalists'; Antimasons; and a disgruntled segment of the Pennsylvania Democrats." "It is needless to say of these parties," he wrote to A. H. Everett, "there are no two that would hold any great political principles in common. Most of them call themselves Whigs, only for the sake of calling their adversaries Tories." Even the early 20th-century historians of Whiggery who, in the fashion of their time, interpreted the party as the ideological opposite of the Democrats, conceded that at its birth the Whig party lacked a distinct ideological identity. Its leaders "often had entirely opposite opinions and sentiments upon every important question . . . preceding the formation of the Whig coalition." They could agree only on a name and on what they opposed.

The new crystallization of anti-Jacksonian political sentiments sharply affected state politics. Whig parties came into being in the states or, to put it another way, the Whig label was, after 1834, affixed to state coalitions at least as diverse and as unconcerned with agreement on a "particular principle" of politics as were their Congressional counterparts. In Tennessee, for example, the impetus for creating the new party was said to have come from a number of men grown disenchanted with Andrew Jackson and in every case for personal reasons rather than principle: Colonel John Williams who resented his defeat by Jackson in the Senatorial contest of 1823; Jesse Benton, who never forgot nor forgave his humiliation by Jackson in their brawl 20 years earlier; James Jackson, aggrieved at being left out on a limb by the Chickasaw land deal in 1828; Andrew Erwin, the father-in-law of the young man Jackson killed in a gambling quarrel; and Newton Cannon, who had incurred Jackson's wrath for once voting, as a juror, for the acquittal of one of Jackson's enemies. And James Edward Murphy has recently expanded this list of influential Tennesseeans who "all bore animosity toward Andrew Jackson." Out of such a mixture of hatreds, ambitions, jealousy, and a "modicum of principles," the Whig party took shape in the spring of 1834.

In a state such as Missouri, in which political opposition to Jackson was utterly unrewarding politically, a formal Whig party emerged only after The Hero vacated the White House. The new party's relatively few stalwarts seemed readily identifiable as former National Republicans pure and simple. Local issues could also account for Whig organization. Thus citizens in a number of Michigan cities were evidently moved to create a formal party structure by their fear of the alleged corruption that would follow an extension of the suffrage to foreign Catholics. The new Whig party in the states of New York and Pennsylvania had little to do with one another but they had much in common, particularly in the goals they pursued. According to Van Deusen, New York's original Whigs were a strange amalgam, consisting of "states' righters and nationalists, Masons and Antimasons, pro- and anti-Clay men, pro- and anti-Bank men, merchants and manufacturers, farmers and laborers"—united in opposition to Jackson, Van Buren, and the Regency. So heterogeneous a coalition could easily fall into disarray. Later Greeley would rail against the "dirty, disgraceful, miserable . . . faction" that alone prevented sweeping Whig successes in New York. Opposed to the Regency largely out of expediency, New York's Whigs had as "their immediate and chief objective . . . control of the state." The motley groups which created Pennsylvania's Whig party had similarly realistic ambitions, but found at first they "could not advance a concrete program because this would cause the coalition to dissolve."

For all their realism, however, the Whigs no less than their opponents did believe in certain principles. Opposition to Andrew Jackson was an expression, albeit an indistinct one, of political beliefs of sorts. The Whig charge of executive tyranny, if taken at face value, was made by men who believed in the Lockean and Jeffersonian concept of legislative dominance. Some skeptics have wondered whether Whigs would have been so opposed to a strong President had his name been Clay rather than Jackson. There is little reason to believe that any man but Jackson would have been capable of the enormities both of style and substance that he, in fact, committed as the nation's Chief Executive. Whig theories of the Executive were consistent and probably sincere expressions of constitutional convictions. It was not Andrew Jackson's person that most Whigs objected to, but his official acts. Thomas Hart Benton, who had as much reason as his brother to hate Old Hickory, did not become a Whig, after all. He belonged to that legion of men who had no fault to find with arbitrary means used to accomplish ends with which they were in sympathy.

Whig objections were not to mannerisms but to concrete policies. The precipitating issue that impelled the Administration's diverse opponents to coalesce was the removal both of the deposits as well as of the Secretaries of the Treasury who would not go along with it. No doubt some Whigs found this issue a convenient pretext essentially which might help them win office. The banking issue, for all the flaming rhetoric used to describe it, was not an ideological issue in the common meaning of the term. Rich men were on both sides of the issue and for good reason. If poor men were largely on one side of it, it was not because they should have been but rather, as Thurlow Weed had pointed out in 1832, because the demagogic phrases in Kendall's veto message had captured their imagination. Jacksonian leaders in a number of states had believed Biddle's Bank an excellent institution but not so excellent as to lead them to jeopardize their personal political careers by supporting it, after 1832. The views of the first Whig leaders were thus not fundamentally unlike those of their Democratic opponents in the sense that

Jacobin principles differed from Monarchist, or English Tory from English Whig. But if the differences between the American major parties were more over means than ends, they were real differences nonetheless.

While the new parties seem to have sprung into existence for reasons having little to do with classic principles or convictions, their subsequent behavior has been widely interpreted as proof of their fundamentally dissimilar character. Of course the parties were different—in program, style, propaganda, and in the kinds of support they attracted. But the question is: were they opposed in the sense that Arthur Schlesinger, Jr. suggested? Was one the party of the people, devoted to a truly radical program, followed by a motley mass of have-nots and underprivileged? Was the other a party of wealth, committed to a conservative program that was justifiably supported by the established orders?

That the era's leading political figures were cut from the same cloth, regardless of party affiliation, suggests the similarity of the political organizations they led. But to *suggest* is not to *establish*. Parties led by similar types can themselves be unlike. A comparison of the Whigs and Democrats, if it is to be fruitful, must be based on their actual performance. Fortunately the historical record has been examined intensively in recent years, resulting in scores of rewarding studies of Jacksonian politics, particularly on the state and local level, that make possible a modern synthesis. It is not to give the story away to note at this point that the recent work deals in nuances, in shades other than black and white. The truths concerning Jacksonian parties are more subtle than the contemporary partisan rhetoric or, for that matter, the scholarly controversy of a few decades ago, might suggest.

Many contemporaries seemed convinced that party clashes in this country were similar to the conflicts that divided men on the Continent and in Great Britain. Writing of the Democrats and the Whigs, Emerson said "one has the best cause, and the other contains the best men." According to him, the former party stood for reform, democracy, and "facilitating in every manner the access of the young and the poor to sources of wealth and power," while the Whigs, for all the moral superiority of their members, were "timid and merely defensive of property." Emerson was one of that sizable group of contemporaries who believed not only that the major parties were different but that the differences concerned precisely the bedrock issues that classically separated men into opposing parties. In Virginia the story was told that John Syme, asked if a Democrat could be a gentleman, "was wont to tap his snuff box significantly, and reply, 'Well, he is apt not to be; but if he is, he is in damned bad company.'"

The painters, sculptors, poets, essayists, and novelists proudly claimed by the Democracy, particularly in Massachusetts, did in fact identify themselves with the Jackson party in inordinate numbers. In Harriet Martineau's phrase, "the men of genius were with the Democracy." Of course men of genius were not necessarily gifted in political analysis. George Bancroft's romantic notion that the popular judgment is never wrong in artistic matters raises questions about his own political acuity. Then as later, creative men innocent of the ways of politics could hold to views that grossly oversimplified the political warfare of their time. Some writers may have been Democrats because of the jobs offered them. Those who felt contempt for "inferior races" found the Jackson party altogether congenial. Whatever the reasons, the fact remains that many creative figures subscribed to the Emersonian thesis that the one party was more democratic and radical than the other.

Since a popular belief is itself an important historical fact, regardless of its wisdom or accuracy, contemporary conceptions—or misconceptions—about the nature of Jacksonian Democracy cannot be entirely discounted. Yet it is significant that much of the contemporary comment stressing the alleged gulf separating the parties came from interested or partisan rather than disinterested sources. As early as 1828, on the occasion of Jackson's visit to New York City, the editor of the *American* referred contemptuously to the crowd that surrounded the Hero as a mob made up of mechanics rather than the city's "most respected inhabitants." During the bank war, a Boston journal charged that the "spirit of Jacobinism" was "the same that pervaded in France during the worst period of the Revolution." Florida's Whigs joined Webster in excoriating Democratic Jacobinism, leveling, and revolutionary agrarianism. Traveling in New York during the years of the Van Buren Administration, John S. Buckingham heard the Democrats denounced as "atheists, infidels, agrarians, incendiaries, men who were without religion and honesty, who desire to pull down all that is venerable in the institutions of the country, to seize the property of the rich, and divide it among the poor," among other things. It was precisely such Whig charges that helped produce Van Burens' victory, for as William H. Seward wrote Thurlow Weed, just prior to the 1836 election, "the people are for him. Not so much for him as for the principle they suppose he represents. . . . It is with them the poor against the rich." In view of his own party's insistent repetition of this theme, Seward thought it only natural that common men would identify with the Democrats.

The Democrats gloried in the charge—to the extent that it was politically useful. Revolutionary agrarians, they assured the nation, they were not. But as true champions of the lowly was it not to be expected that they would be outrageously abused by the sycophants of aristocracy? The Regency leader, Michael Hoffman, saw the early party battles in terms of "the aristocracy and the democracy arrayed against each other." In the aftermath of the bank war, a New England Democratic organ found it fitting that "farmers, mechanics, laboring men . . . the true bone and sinew—the virtue, honesty and patriotism of the country," were aligned with the party of Jackson. The years of the bank struggle were particularly productive of this kind of discussion. Radical editors who now found themselves in harmony with the Democracy they heretofore had criticized, contributed their flair for polemics to the cause. George Henry Evans' labor journal, *The Man,* ran jingles explaining that aristocrats and "such as Hartford Feds oppose the poor and Jackson," while its columns charged that if the "Tory Whigs had their way, the poor would be placed in a complete state of vassalage." Tory Whigs! They also hinted at Whig management of the burning down of the Ursuline Convent.

Sometimes fiery Democratic language camouflaged most moderate Democratic thought, as in the case of a Boston *Post* election year editorial urging keener community appreciation of the working classes. Success and esteem, according to the Democratic editor, were to be won by mechanics through "industry, temperance and frugality"—precisely the roads to lower class upward movement that were traditionally urged by the most timid defenders of the status quo. Of course if party propaganda was read and heard, it is likely that it was neither listened to with great care nor read with an eye for nuance. On the other hand it does seem clear that many voters did not discount altogether the mutual recriminations showered down by the great parties on one another. Whig leaders obviously thought it good politics to brand the Jacksonians revolutionist, while Democrats hoped to profit in turn from labeling their enemies aristocrat. Observing that the poor outnumbered the rich, Seward had misgivings about the astuteness of his party's diatribes. National election results for the era confirm his wisdom. Politically astute or no, the Whig "interpretations" and the Democratic responses to them, were also to foster oversimplified notions about the major parties, leaving the impression in the minds of later generations that the great parties of the age of Jackson were, as their zealous protagonists described them, representatives of conflicting interests in American society.

A surprising number of contemporaries, however, thought otherwise. Some of them were themselves Jacksonians. The eminent anti-Bank radical, Robert Rantoul, in the midst of the controversy over the Second BUS, confided to his memoirs his belief that "our party contests have not that intrinsic importance with which the lively fancies of the heated partisans often invest them; . . . they are often in a great degree struggles for office. . . ." Even the editors of the *Democratic Review,* the Jackson party organ, conceded that "the violence of the party warfare in which we are perpetually engaged" obscured the basic agreements and the common "democratic sentiment and spirit" of members of both parties. To Francis Baylies, a former Massachusetts Federalist visiting New York in the mid-1830s, "with the Whigs and Van Burenites it is a contest of office and nothing else," between these two "miserable" parties. Franklin E. Plummer, champion of Mississippi's lower classes, in 1834 denounced the Democratic party of his state as no better than the

Whigs and, like them, "lacking any real concern for the interests of the major class," the workers. At the time he spoke he continued to support the Bank Veto. Plummer's views were similar to those expressed by labor leaders throughout the country, before and after the Bank War.

The accusation made first in Philadelphia in 1828 by the *Mechanic's Free Press*, that the Democrats were more dangerous to the working classes because more deceitful than their opponents, was repeated regularly in the labor press during the following decade. Such leaders as John Commerford of the New York Trades' Union counseled labor that the major parties were frauds: "Stand aloof, remember we have no alliance with either of the humbugs," he advised. The Pennsylvania labor veteran, John Ferral, hoped that workers would not permit themselves to be duped by the shrewd politicians in control of both parties. Lesser known labor correspondents warned that "designing demagogues [had] . . . set themselves up as political reformers under the name of Democrats . . . and Whigs, and a catalogue of names used as baits" to lure mechanics "into the nets of political fishers of all parties." To the prolabor dissidents who broke with the New York Democracy in 1836, "the leaders of the two great political parties under which the people have arrayed themselves are selfish and unprincipled; the objects of both are power, honors, and emolument." Nor were these criticisms atypical. They were representative of a persistent denunciation by Working Men's party and trade union leaders alike of the major parties as of the political system the latter ostensibly dominated. From the other end of the social spectrum came similar judgments. In New York City the *Journal of Commerce* observed that Whigs and Democrats "agree upon all the questions in debate" between them, "except that greatest of all questions, who shall have office."

Less embattled figures also agreed that political hyperbole only masked the basic similarities of the major parties. Tocqueville had concluded that America lacked great parties in the absence of great issues; "and if her happiness is therefore considerably increased, her morality has suffered." No party seemed "to contest the present . . . course of society," while all the shouting was over differences and issues so slight as "to be incomprehensible or puerile." He was no doubt influenced by what John Latrobe and Jared Sparks had told him. Latrobe had said, "realistically speaking, there are no parties in the United States: everything is reduced to a question of men; there are those who have the power and those who want to have it, the people in and [the people] out." According to Sparks, "there were no political parties properly so called: only local interests and personal rivalries." For all the clamor, "their differences were those of personal preference, rather than of principle." Several years later, when party bitterness was at its height, Francis Lieber observed that "however great the excitement may appear, on paper or in words, the people know very well that their lives and property are not in jeopardy; that whatever party may come in or go out, the broad principles of the whole system will be acted upon, the general laws will be preserved." Harriet Martineau found it "remarkable how nearly [the] . . . positive statements of political doctrine [of Whigs and Democrats] agree, while they differ in almost every possible application of their common principles."

Many influential persons thus saw through—or thought they saw through—the sham nature of the era's party battles. Their voices however were muted if not drowned out by the sounds of partisan political trumpeting. The fact remains that if contemporary opinion was not equally divided between those who took party rhetoric seriously and those who did not, a significant number of respected persons dissented from the Emersonian view of the parties.

The school of thought which finds the Whigs and the Jacksonian Democrats dissimilar, makes much of the allegedly contrasting philosophies and beliefs of the parties. This is both understandable and sensible. What the parties and their spokesmen said obviously throws some light on the character of the parties. The question is: how much light? In answering this question, at one extreme stand historians who appear to take party statements at face value. At the other stand those who would discount them entirely. Most of us stand between these two polar positions, convinced that professed beliefs cannot be totally discounted as a clue to actual convictions. The question of course is how much insight they afford. The answer requires close investigation of the context in which party statements are uttered.

The search for the parties' true beliefs is a most difficult one. There is the insoluble problem of determining the weight to be affixed formal party pronunciamentos on the one hand and the more informal remarks by individuals on the other. The two are very different kinds of statement. How seriously can one take policy statements which were admittedly not binding either on the men who made them or on those to whom they were addressed? What is "party thought" when party leaders think contradictory thoughts about a given problem? How distinguish between a demagogic comment, motivated only by a desire to sway voters, and a sincere revelation of a true conviction? These are some of the problems that attend a discussion of party philosophy and principles.

In the case of parties as dedicated to winning office as were the Jacksonian Democrats and the Whigs, it is hard to take their platforms seriously as expressions of true belief. For that matter, national platforms were avoided until 1840 when the beleaguered Democracy tried to explain away its role in causing the depression. The Whigs waited until 1844, in that year building a platform for Henry Clay that alas proved a mite too broad and not sufficiently solid. It had more to do with gathering votes than anything else. No doubt many Democrats sincerely wanted to put down the Second Bank of the United States. But their willingness to replace it by dozens of other banks as repository for federal funds is hardly convincing evidence of the anticapitalistic animus attributed to them by some scholars. The age of popular suffrage called forth demagogic party pronouncements in behalf of socially mild programs. That one party, the Whigs, typically eschewed such propaganda, while the other, the Democrats, relied on it enthusiastically, reveals a difference in tactics as in the public image sought, rather than in fundamental beliefs.

When scrutinized carefully, the meaning in much Democratic oratory turns out to be extremely conservative, for all the flamboyance of the rhetoric cloaking it. The great principle espoused by the national party organ *The Democratic Review* was laissez-faire. Professing to fear that governmental "attempts to operate directly or indirectly on the industry and prosperity of the community" would lead to corruption and "the most pernicious abuse," its editors reminded a nation reeling from the effects of the Panic of 1837 that "the best government is that which governs least." "Strict economy in public spending" was the political end devoutly sought by Senator Isaac Hill in New Hampshire, Governor Thomas Reynolds in Missouri, Congressman Clement L. Vallandigham in Ohio, and Mayor William Frederick Havemeyer in new York City—good Democrats all. Jacksonian denunciation of governmental meddling in "those private affairs and relations between man and man, which . . . ought to be left to the individual citizen himself" must have been most reassuring both to large merchants in the North and slave-owning planters in the South. As Michael Wallace has shown for New York State in the 1820s and Ronald P. Formisano for Michigan in the 1830s, party orthodoxy and "adherence to regular nominations," not social justice, came to be viewed by Jacksonians in these and other areas as a "sacred and inviolable principle." William Gouge's 1833 tract on banking became the Democratic bible on the issue during the Bank War, winning a radical reputation for its attack on incorporated banks of note issue. Gouge would not end banking operations but turn them over to private individuals—"men of large fortunes." Fabled accumulators such as John Jacob Astor and Isaac Bronson heartily agreed. The "little compassion for the poor and the helpless" attributed by his recent biographer to the Jacksonian editor and poet William Cullen Bryant differed little from the values guiding Democrats of more conservative reputation.

The belief in Jacksonian radicalism nevertheless persists. Glyndon G. Van Deusen, a modern authority on the era, while denying that the Democracy was "in any real sense a party that actually arrayed or sought to array the masses against the classes," judges that it moved in that direction. Like many other historians he detects a transition that significantly altered this one-time opportunistic coalition: "six years after Jackson had entered the Executive Mansion, the party could still be described as moving slowly and spasmodically to the left." Obviously, the definition assigned the term "left" determines the validity of this view. Right-wing usage has tried to make the term as inclusive as possible, the better to stigmatize liberals in a society suspicious of the term. As used by scholars, however, the left has traditionally stood for a radical position calling for drastic modification if not abolition of a system of private property; far-reaching social reforms; and the subordination of liberty to equality if necessary to accomplish its goals. While parties of the left have made much of expanding the suffrage, like the English Chartists they applauded the reform as the necessary precondition for rearranging society in the interests of have nots. When the term is thus defined, no significant leftward movement can be detected in the Democratic party's behavior either in the later years of the Jackson or in the Van Buren administrations.

The one Locofoco doctrine that the party took over was neither left nor right: it was a currency policy capable of earning support from conservatives and bankers for the good reason that it had no appreciable effect on property. The party's antitariff views were not beloved of manufacturers but they were hardly a radical, pro-consumer position, supported as they were by wealthy merchants and planters. Cheap public land did mean a reduced starting price at public auction yet it did not seriously interfere with speculation. Many Democrats favored revision of "aristocratic" corporation laws that in effect gave monopolies to the privileged recipients of special charters. Democratic opposition to freer incorporation laws could also be made to appear downright anticapitalistic. In New York it was a tactic used in an attempt to maintain the privileges of Democratic bankers—prior beneficiaries of the special acts of incorporation passed by Regency-dominated state legislatures. If these mixed Democratic attitudes do not cancel each other out, certainly they raise doubts as to the actual crucial nature of the issue, for all the marvelous rhetoric used in public discussion of it. Even the famous rulings of the Taney Court, most of whose members had like Taney himself been appointed by Old Hickory, are not quite the egalitarian decrees some exaggerated comments make them out to be.

Roger B. Taney of Maryland was a former Federalist of conservative monetary and social beliefs. He had endeared himself to Jackson by the unswerving support he gave to the Hero's war on the Second Bank of the United States and by what even Taney's sympathetic chief biographer regarded as his "sycophantic" behavior in the controversy that arose within the administration over the removal of the deposits. Taney won Jackson's heart when he agreed to replace as Secretary of the Treasury the recalcitrant William J. Duane, who was unwilling to order the removal of the deposits and who was summarily dismissed for his obstinacy. Duane himself had replaced Louis McLane, whose "promotion" to the State Department had evidently been planned prior to and perhaps in anticipation of McLane's refusal to remove the deposits. Taney's great claim to fame of course was his decision in the Dred Scott case. That ruling was not inconsistent with the principles underlying his and his court's important decisions during the Jacksonian era.

Chief Justice Taney was a champion of states' rights and the rights of creditors, was reverential toward property in land, persons, and mortgages, and had a pragmatic but respectful attitude toward corporate rights. He was strict or loose constructionist depending on the ends he sought. Staunch hard-money man though he was, he was capable, as in *Briscoe* v. *Bank of the Commonwealth of Kentucky,* of supporting the right of a state government to issue paper money in violation of the Constitution. In *New York* v. *Miln,* in 1837, the Taney Court upheld a state law designed to prevent entry into the state by unwanted indigents, and did so on the basis of what Kent Newmyer calls an erroneous reading of earlier high court decisions. Taney showed no sympathy whatever for debtors or for relief legislation. In *Brownson* v. *Kinzie,* in 1843, he held for the Court that Illinois laws "interfering with foreclosures impaired the obligation of contracts, and were in violation of the contract clause of the Constitution." Justice Story, a great conservative, was delighted with this decision. Taney's ruling in this case was consistent with his private belief that debt must be paid regardless of the circumstances of the debtor. He was a great believer too in the sanctity of contracts. What has caused confusion was his unwillingness to support the doctrine of *implied rights,* that was urged by some corporate champions as justification for extending corporate privileges that had no specific basis in any state charter. But if the privilege or right had been expressly conferred by a contract, Taney held "the state bound by the contract clause of the Constitution, even though the grant had been unwisely made" or corruptly granted. The decision of the Taney Court in *Louisville Railroad Company* v. *Letson,* in 1844, that gave corporations "the right to remove cases from state to federal courts when suing or being sued by citizens of other states than those in which they had been created," has been judged as "more friendly to corporations than the position of Chief Justice Marshall had been."

The decision that is chiefly responsible for the radical reputation of the early Taney Court is the one Taney delivered in 1837 in the case of the *Charles River Bridge Company* v. *Warren Bridge Company.* In this undeniably liberal and liberating ruling, Taney brushed aside the theory that a toll bridge company had an implied right not to have competition in the form of a free bridge built over the same river. "In a country like ours," he argued, "free, active, and enterprising, continually advancing in numbers of wealth, new channels of communication are daily found necessary both for travel and trade; and are essential to the comfort, convenience, and prosperity of the people." The advocates of the entrepreneurial theory of Jacksonian Democracy have no stronger documentation than the Charles River decision, for in it the Jacksonian Court ruled not against private property or capitalism, but in favor of an expanding capitalistic society and the free competition necessary to assure it. As Stanley Kutler has observed, the decision could have been written by John Marshall, was in its own time supported by conservative Federalist judges, and was consonant with Taney's dictum that the "rights of private property must be sacredly guarded." There was nothing radical in the decision except some of its language. In implying that no interest was equal in weight to the community's, the Court suggested to some overwrought people that it was prepared to impair contracts or acquiesce in attacks on property. Such newspapers as the Boston *Daily Advertiser* and the New York *Commercial Advertiser* lamented the alleged "subversion of the principles of law and property" and the threat to corporate investments inherent in the decision. Two years later, when in *Bank of Augusta* v. *Earle*, Taney once again stated his opposition to an implied right—this time however against the State of Georgia— arguing that although a corporation was not a citizen and could not emigrate to where it was not wanted, "the principle of comity . . . in the absence of a clear prohibition [by the state, means] the right to do business ought to be assumed," he was now attacked by many Democrats for his "surrender" and "betrayal." It is difficult to dis- agree with the judgment that Whig unhappiness and near hysteria in the one case, like the Democratic reaction in the other, were due to misinterpretation of their significance.

If "Jacksonian thought" or "Democratic thought" is what repre- sentative Jacksonian leaders believed about social and economic issues, a most discordant blending it would be, albeit one whose essential conservatism would shine through. Its heterogeneity mir- rored the diversity of the party's following. There were Democrats and Democrats. Such amoralists as Henshaw, Samuel Swartwout, Samuel Gwin, and Robert J. Walker were most unlike Marcus Mor- ton, William Leggett, and Richard M. Johnson. Further clouding the issue was the tendency of Jacksonian publicists to frame public statements in a language that was more useful in giving an impres- sion of Democratic egalitarianism than in clarifying their beliefs. Particularly misleading has been the readiness of some scholars to treat the writings and speeches of men of unusual articulateness and even more atypical radicalism as though they were *representa- tive* of Jacksonian thinking.[1] Historians who are convinced that the Jacksonian coalition was dedicated to drastic alteration of American capitalistic society, will understandably search for the intellectual foundations of this radical movement and find them in the work of noted dissenters. The prosaic actual achievements of the Demo- cratic party, nationally and within the states, however, best explain why collections of such writings constitute Jacksonian thought only

---

[1] "Social Theories of Jacksonian Democracy" is thus a rubric applied to a popular collection of some two dozen statements, whose authors include James Fenimore Cooper, William Leggett, Benjamin F. Hallett, Walt Whitman, Stephen Simpson, Theophilus Fisk, Frances Wright, Ely Moore, Orestes A. Brownson, Langdon Byllesby, and Thomas Skidmore. Skidmore? Signs of a connection between this uncompromising advocate of a periodic redistribution of property and the Jackson party are nonexistent. That the rest of the list consists largely of nominal Jacksonians at best, or of persons who opposed the Jacksonian party or its dominant pragmatic wing within their states, is not as significant as the fact that it is made up of men and a woman whose influ- ence on the Democratic party was slight, confined mainly to the party's rhetoric rather than its actual policies. See Joseph L. Blau, ed., *Social Theories of Jacksonian Democracy*, New York 1947. That Blau's anthology is interest- ing and useful is another matter.

in the sense that the ideas contained within them were expressed while Andrew Jackson was alive.

Democratic policies which contradicted Democratic pronouncements do not inspire respect for the latter as serious statements of intentions. At the same time that Democratic leaders took up the cry against monopolies, Democratic legislatures approved monopolistic charters "as if propelled by steam power," according to the Regency leader, Azariah Flagg, conferring them naturally enough on deserving Democratic entrepreneurs. "Untrue to their own principles!" charged the Locofocos. New Jersey Democrats were perfectly capable of attacking monopoly in general while bending all their energies in the state legislature to assure a continued monopoly over the route from New York to Philadelphia for the Camden and Amboy Railroad they controlled. Developing an interesting division of labor, "in national contests the party adopted an anti-monopoly ideology . . . but in the state the party balked at carrying through an anti-monopoly campaign because of the close connection between many of the party leaders and New Jersey corporations." Their anti-monopoly slogans were meaningless in the judgment of their leading student.

Florida's Democrats espoused a philosophy more democratic and radical than that of their opponents, favoring expansion both of the suffrage as of business opportunities. However, "a gap of varying proportions between the party's philosophy and its pronouncements, on the one hand, and the party's practices and its activities on the other," has been discerned. Specifically, Jacksonians in Florida talked up popular sovereignty while they opposed the wishes of their own electorate on the statehood issue. They talked of aid to debtors but passed legislation that helped planters. For all their talk of the common man, labor turned to the Whigs in view of Democratic inaction. In a sense, of course, Democratic negativism was a rare example of the concord of their theory and practice. President Van Buren's first message to Congress reminded the people that "all communities . . . are apt to look to government for too much. . . . But this ought not to be," he admonished. His philosophy was one that actual Democratic policy closely followed.

It is hard to pin down a formal Whig program. In its first presidential campaign, in 1836, the party ran a number of favorite sons, who jointly subscribed only to the hope that they could beat Van Buren by forcing the contest into the House. In 1840 General Harrison kept mum, slogan makers extolled log cabins and hard cider, Whig leaders concentrated on the Van Buren depression. And the following campaign was marked by Clay's unsuccessful attempt to avoid committing himself and his party to controversial policies. For most of the period formal statements were forthcoming from state or local groups rather than national. And as in the case of the declaration of Whig principles supported by a Massachusetts meeting in 1840, they were uninformative documents: they show that the Whigs wished to be considered more sensible than their "agrarian" opponents, whose penchant for revolution ostensibly jeopardized all hard-earned wealth. A resolution passed by a meeting of Philadelphia Whigs, affirming the interdependence of classes, or an editorial in the *National Intelligencer*, were not binding, not indicative of anyone's viewpoint but the particular individual or group responsible for it, even in the latter sense requiring some discounting of its language.

Given the paucity, the hyperbole, and the small force of so-called party statements, historians of Whig thought have sensibly paid little attention to them, focusing instead on the utterances of Clay, Webster, Weed, Hone, Greeley, White, Mangum, Crittenden, Bell, dozens of little-known publishers and the better known Gales and Seaton, and sundry other individual Whigs. "Whig thought" turns out not to be the party's formal beliefs but a kind of blending of the thinking of diverse individuals. Obvious problems arise. For example, were Calhoun's ideas Whig ideas for the less than five years that he aligned himself with the party? What does give validity to the exercise of the scholars, however, is the fair degree of consistency and agreement on social, economic, and political beliefs among the men who called themselves Whig.

In our era of striking revisions and reinterpretations of history, older versions of Whig thought have been modified to an amazingly small extent by new. American historians in the early 20th century were drawn toward a New History whose scope was broad, whose spirit was critical, and whose goals were humane and democratic. Brave new historical thought *circa* 1915 was excited at its discovery that American history, like European, was racked by social and class conflict, and that powerful economic interests here as elsewhere sought to control politics to their own advantage. Working in this intellectual atmosphere, such scholars of Jacksonian politics as Dixon Ryan Fox, Arthur C. Cole, E. Malcolm Carroll and their students concluded not only that bitter social and economic conflict marked the Jacksonian era, but that the great opposing interests were represented politically by the two major parties. In this view the Whigs were the party of property. Their beliefs and philosophy were profoundly conservative. They viewed with alarm all evidences of social disorder. They liked to think that the interests of all social classes were similar. Interestingly, a modern study of Whig thought, that is out of sympathy with the assumptions that governed the work of earlier students, revises only slightly their views of Whig conservatism. It is evidently impossible to make radicals out of the party of Clay and Webster. The Whig, Edward Everett, *was* opposed to labor parties. The Whig editors of the Boston *Courier*, *were* convinced that men of affairs should run society.

In contrast to the historians of Charles Beard's day, recent reappraisals of Whig theory stress the similarity of aims of the major parties. According to Glyndon Van Deusen, Whigs "sought the prosperity of the people as a whole, and both parties oriented, just as the two major parties do today, around a middle-class norm." Their divergences "were more over means than ultimate ends." At his hands the Whigs emerge not so much as the party of conservatism as the party of energy, optimism, nationalism, constructiveness, and humanitarianism, ready to use government to build roads, canals, schools, and promote the welfare of the poor and the indigent. He is by no means the only historian who finds that both in theory and practice the Whigs approached the spirit of the New Deal more closely than did the Jacksonian Democrats.

In William Shade's reading, Whigs in the northwestern states regarded government action as "potentially a positive force in structuring the society of the future." In contrast to Democratic do-nothingism in the face of depression, Whigs argued the government's obligation to act during periods of distress, Thurlow Weed asking, "for what purposes was government instituted, and why are its burthens borne, but to secure for its constituencies, protection and relief under all circumstances?"

Whig thinking on such matters was neither rigid nor altogether consistent. In an interesting examination of changing Whig thought that focuses on New York State, Elliott Barkan discerns three chief themes in "Whig conservatism:" concern over "rapid and/or radical alterations in political and social institutions"; emphasis on "the harmony of the classes," accompanied by repudiation of the rhetoric that before 1837 expressed disgust if not contempt toward the masses; and support for the pre-1828 "structure [of] federal government" combined with "strong hostility toward the new highly organized party structures." Whigs could be found who of course took the opposite of each of these positions.

Some earlier judgments were harsher than the facts warranted. Aware that new immigrants tended to become Democrats, Whigs in a number of states did cooperate with nativists. Yet such leaders as Seward, Weed, and Greeley wished foreigners to be received on an equal footing with old settlers, their concern springing "from an honorable and sympathetic spirit." Many Missouri Whigs frowned at the policy of some "pragmatists" in their party to harmonize their efforts with nativists, a cooperation that hurt the Whigs at the polls. For that matter Whigs had more humane views than their major opponents with regard to most issues involving race. They championed the rights of Indians, urging that treaty guarantees of these rights be upheld. In the North their attitude toward free Negroes was more liberal than that of Democrats. Many southern Whigs either opposed the gag resolution or actually supported old Adams' fight against it. Surely it is no accident that of 60 New England abolitionists examined by David Donald—"not merely the leaders but their followers as well"—all but one were members of the Whig party. An admirable attitude on racial matters is neither conservative nor radical but that fact detracts not at all from the significance of the attitude. There are other ways of classifying beliefs, after all, than in the terms used by economic determinists.

Southern Whigs in the early 1840s by and large stood for "honest banking and sound finance." In Georgia and Mississippi they opposed "the flood of relief measures" that came before the legislatures and rejected repudiation. In Kentucky and Louisiana, Whig

governors refused to call special sessions to consider such legislation, emphasizing instead the responsibility of national government.
If such Whig practice was timid it was certainly in accord with the
ideas of that monetary conservative, Andrew Jackson. Conservative
banking practice of course has no connection with conservative
social philosophy: many speculative Jacksonian practitioners of
wildcat banking were firm supporters of a class society.

If beliefs are displayed in actions, Whigs were occasionally radical. It was Thaddeus Stevens who led the fight for free unstigma-
tized public schools in Pennsylvania. In New York state in 1839 it
was a Whig governor who cleared the jails of antirenters, while
"Whig legislators did not as a group oppose the measures by which
the ancient privileges of the great landlords were diminished one by
one." A realistic critic noted that Whigs "were as willing to attract
five thousand voters as were the Democrats." The trouble with so
hard-boiled an interpretation is not only that it is hard to prove but
that it seems to leave out altogether the possibility that some element of conviction may be present in political behavior. The Whig
farmers who sacked the office of the Mayville land agent, give every
evidence of having been quite sincere. The anti-Jacksonian mayor of
Boston in 1832 showed a greater sensitivity to the needs of commoners than had his Jacksonian opponent.

Too much should not be made of the philosophy of a party whose
own leaders said, as did Thurlow Weed in 1839, that anyone who
believed that the Democrats should be driven from office because
they were responsible for hard times "is a Whig no matter by what
name he has been called or is called." Earlier studies of "Whig
theory" were usually undertaken by men convinced that the parties
were fundamentally different and that their words were to be taken
seriously. The present era's greater skepticism toward political
mouthings may not merely be a reflection of a changed political
atmosphere but simply a truer appraisal. To a generation which
better than any other seems to understand the *complexity* of truth,
party statements can neither be taken at face value nor dismissed
out of hand. So-called Whig theory was not really that. It was the
oftentimes contradictory notions of diverse men, many of whom
were well explained in Weed's simple, almost cynical, definition of a
Whig. In common with the other major party, Whigs accepted the
fundamental institutions of their society. While they favored economic and political policies that differentiated them from their opponents, neither the Whig nor the Jacksonian measures represented
the kind of social cleavage suggested in the more overwrought
oratory of the times.

F or all the undeniable importance of their theory and beliefs,
clearer insight is afforded into the character of the major parties by their behavior than by their propaganda. Whig practice—inevitably disparate—was seldom in full accord with Whig

preachments. And yet there was often a large degree of consistency between the two. Whig affirmations of the value of sound banking, a strong Congress, vigorous economic intervention by national government, internal improvements or the rights of Indians and Negroes, were not mere lip service, to judge by the actions of Whig legislators on the national and state levels.

Joel Silbey's detailed study of every Congressional vote taken discloses that in the latter part of the era Whigs in the 27th and 28th Congresses overwhelmingly supported a new Bank of the United States, a high tariff, distribution of land revenues to the states, relief legislation to mitigate the effects of the depression, and federal reapportionment of House seats. The latter was from the Whig standpoint a lovely measure, easily and perhaps arguably described as promoting more just representation, but certain to assure more Whig representation. Whigs were as united in their opposition to the Independent Treasury, an aggressive foreign policy, and expansionism. The latter votes also signified opposition to the spread of slavery. Although Congressional Whigs did favor internal improvements in the period 1841 to 1845, sectional and other factors accounted for a fairly even division of votes on this issue.

These were significant measures. Whig cohesion in dealing with them shows just how important they were in the eyes of the party's Congressional leadership. If some of these proposals reveal a pro-business spirit, it can with equal justice be said they were designed to restore prosperity. They reflect above all a belief in the principle of federal responsibility for promoting the public welfare. If another of these bills was transparently motivated by the desire to enhance the chances of Whig success in congressional elections, the plan nevertheless strengthened the two-party system. The other proposals display Whig dislike of slavery and imperialism. Major Wilson's recent reading of political statements made by the era's party leaders offers an interesting explanation of Whig hostility to expansion. It holds that Whig leaders, concerned with improving the *quality* of American freedom, looked to the future in contrast to Democrats, ostensibly satisfied with the freedom already achieved in the present, who therefore had little interest in the future and stressed the need for territorial expansion. Whatever the final explanation of Whig performance, it would be farfetched to try to make of these admittedly important measures class legislation in the ideological sense. The near unanimity achieved in the roll calls shows that for the congressmen of the early 1840s party loyalty was a stronger force than sectional background or interest. But party loyalty is something that pragmatic parties of moderate program can achieve quite successfully—as the machines of Martin Van Buren, Isaac Hill, and Samuel Gwin demonstrated during the era. It is significant that Whig parties in the states paid little attention to the great national issues.

William Shade and Herbert Ershkowitz have more recently done for the state level what Silbey did for the national. Examining Whig as well as Democratic roll calls in New Hampshire, Pennsylvania, New Jersey, Ohio, Virginia, and Missouri for the years from 1833 to 1843, they report that in state legislatures as in Congress Whigs and Democrats voted as blocs, almost diametrically opposed to one another on most issues. In these states "there were few differences between the parties on the issue of internal improvements." While "Democrats were even more willing than Whigs to charter transportation corporations," Whigs consistently gave more support to all other forms of corporation, were much more sympathetic to the concept of limited liability, as well as toward the incorporation of banks, and were against "encumbering (bank) charters with hostile amendments" and restricting the issue of small notes. Whig state legislators showed much greater support than did their Democratic colleagues for such "humanitarian issues" as militia reform, abolition of capital punishment, temperance, the expansion of prisons and asylums, and educational reform. John McFaul has recently suggested that, in opposition to this author's contention, Whig views and behavior on racial matters did not differ significantly from Democratic policies. The fact is however that "on every occasion" in state voting, "a higher percentage of Whigs voted the antislavery, pro-Negro position than did Democrats." Clearly Whigs voted differently on issues than did Democrats, while at the same time supporting roughly similar policies in all sections. Yet Whig consistency was not as great as their legislative behavior suggests. As Shade has himself pointed out for Northampton County in Pennsylvania, Whigs and Democrats "took strikingly similar stances" toward many "traditional and economic issues." In Michigan as elsewhere it is hard to find differences in major party policies on these issues.

A glance at the variegated Whig practice on the state and local level should dispel any impression that after its formative period the party became a kind of monolith. Not only did Whig behavior vary from one state to another, in some cases a united Whig party showed itself capable of policy reversals best explained by opportunism or lust for office. Whigs cooperated with local nativists, or even with Democrats or particular factions of Democrats, against other Whigs. While some Whig politicians evidenced that ineptness and lack of zeal for party organization that, according to a recent interpretation, accounts for the party's "stillbirth," other Whigs in states as far removed as New York and Georgia demonstrated remarkable political know-how. In Cumberland County, North Carolina, Whig leaders feigned "anti-partyism" as a tactic which they swiftly abandoned when they no longer found it useful. Some Whig parties were led by high-minded zealots, others by children of expediency. The party program in some states was identical with the national attitudes displayed by Whigs in Congress, in other states was largely antithetical to national Whig policy, and in still other states a program was either nonexistent or extremely hard to discern.

In examining party behavior in the states, it should be kept in mind that state governments touched the lives of citizens much more directly during the era than did national governments. Whether the issue was business, banking, credit, internal improvements, voting requirements, public welfare, or taxes, state and local governments bore greater and more direct responsibility for them than did national government.

In several southern states Whig difficulties seemed to stem not from the party's mistakes or any intrinsic deficiencies but from external circumstances it could not control, particularly the vast popularity of the frontiersman war hero, friend to slavery, and Indian remover, Andrew Jackson. Whig policy in such states was the policy of losers. What can cast a greater blight on a party of nonzealots than their foreknowledge of certain defeat? For most of the years between 1840 and 1848 Missouri's Whigs failed to put up either congressional or gubernatorial candidates. George Sibley, who ran for the Senate in 1844, was regarded by his fellow Whigs as a "foolish idealist" for so doing. The party's perennial hope was for a Democratic split which would enable it to support the lesser evil. But let the Whigs nominate their own candidate and hostile Democratic factions united to crush him.

The party had gotten off on the wrong foot when Clay refused to modify the land provisions of his American System. This was a deadly blow in a state whose rule was: "he who would carry Missouri must espouse a generous land system." The party was further hurt by the almost total lack of concern for its welfare shown by Whig national figures, the dalliance of one Whig faction with nativism, the snobbishness, distaste for campaigning, and ineptness in propaganda displayed by its leaders. The negative Whig image in the state was largely due to effective Democratic propaganda in the handling of such issues as suffrage extension and the length of the working day. The Whigs were pilloried for allegedly opposing important suffrage reforms and attacked for hostility to labor. The suffrage issue was exaggerated. And in an overwhelmingly Democratic State Legislature in 1841, St. Louis' few Whig delegates in fact voted as a bloc to support the "radical ten-hour principle" that was buried by the vote of the rest of the legislature. While Whigs had a pro-business outlook, they were not indifferent either to the interests of small farmers or good sense, coming out in 1840 for "any" land policy likely to promote settlement. Missouri's Whigs often cooperated with the anti-Benton faction of the Democracy. The nonideological character of Missouri politics was best illustrated in St. Louis during the era. There the parties fought with some vigor—on the verbal level. In actuality campaign issues were trivial, personalities overshadowed issues, and the sensible men who comprised the urban leadership of the two parties cooperated more often than not. At the state capitol Whigs and Democrats also "tended to vote solidly on St. Louis matters."

Georgia's Whigs, descended from the George M. Troup party and the State Rights party, were like their Missouri counterpart in emerging relatively late under the Whig label, and in their position of weakness in the great contest for votes. The Georgia Whigs were distinctive, however, both for the cleverness of their tactics as for many of their positions. Their antagonism for much of the era to educational and prison reform, to paternalism in general, to internal improvements, and the Central Bank of Georgia, seemed most unWhiggish. A Whig-dominated legislature finally killed the Bank in the early 1840s, charging graft and "financial oppression!" Even more unique was this Whig party's strong affirmation of states' rights. Georgia's Whigs felt little of that great awareness Alabama's party had of "broad national interests" or of the need for the federal government to promote them. Prosperity *was* to be encouraged but the Georgia Whig party was not quite certain and kept shifting its ground in trying to find out precisely how. The party combined flexibility with realism, changing to a high tariff stance once its leadership became convinced that low cotton prices compelled Georgians to develop their own manufactures. Their liberal land policy was not mere lip service: a Whig legislature in the 1840s overruled opponents who would sell instead of give lands to Georgia citizens. Whigs proclaimed their intellectual, educational, moral, and ethical superiority to the Jacksonians in the state, a boast a critical historian finds valid. The Whigs of Georgia never bothered particularly to defend themselves against the inevitable charge of "aristocracy," although they were in fact at least as "democratic" as the party that bore the latter name. The main difference found between the major parties in Georgia was that where Whigs appealed to the "intelligence and patriotism" of voters, Democrats appealed to prejudice. But the Whigs of Georgia were not naive idealists. They built an excellent organization, campaigned well, masterfully sidestepped tricky issues, and were not "oversolicitous about principles." Driven by hunger for public office, "the compelling aim of the [Whig] party was to get [and maintain] control of the existing machinery of government." Increasingly preoccupied with mobilizing the electorate to win Georgia's closely contested elections, Whigs like Democrats "suppressed [issues] which threatened the primary goals of predictability and stability."

Louisiana's Whigs characteristically supported a political program more positive and in some respects more democratic than the one offered by their opponents. Whigs there as elsewhere championed improved education and also urged a homestead exemption law and an elective judiciary, to complement their advocacy of state railroads and banks. As James Roger Sharp has recently noted they played an influential role in winning passage of "the most progressive bank law of the period," requiring that cash liabilities be liquid at all times. Hardly a monolithic group, some Whig leaders would in 1844 extend the vote to the propertyless, others would hold back, with both factions concerned more with the likely results than the abstract merit of such reform.

Most unlike the worldly Whiggery which flourished south of the Mason-Dixon line, the Whig party which emerged in the new West after 1835 in many respects appeared to be a special form of evangelicalism. At least this seemed to be the case with the Whig party of Michigan's most important county in the late years of the Jackson era. While a Michigan territorial convention of the Whig party went on record against any suffrage restrictions, Wayne County's Whig party arose out of a suspicion of "aliens," particularly Catholics, who were regarded by many of the party's founders as an alleged threat to the Presbyterian version of "cultural homogeneity" they had brought with them from New England. Ronald P. Formisano finds that the political program of the urban and suburban Whigs of Michigan was to a large extent biblical in both tone and substance. This was the party of temperance, maintenance of strict laws on adultery and fornication, respect for the Sabbath. It was not merely opposed to sin; it politicked against it. In some respects it appeared to be a political arm of the great benevolent crusade carried by New England Calvinists into the northwest. If it was not a very effective political agent, that too was largely due to the values of its zealous members.

Evidently equating efficient party organization with a sordid secularism and with the abhorred Democrats, many Whigs felt a revulsion toward party politics that no doubt explains some of their failures. Their political rallies resembled camp meetings, the speeches of their leaders, revival sermons. Zeal is not always a negative political trait but the Michigan Whigs would have benefited from a spirit of compromise. Yet even in this high-minded organization, pragmatists replaced evangelical types as leaders in the late 1830s. The new men were "interested less in ideology and more in getting elected." Whig voters may have harbored hostility toward aliens, but Whig leaders would deny them the vote because they were certain their party would derive no benefits from such ballots. As for Whig economic policies in Michigan, they mirrored those of Democrats.

For all the evidence that Whigs and Democrats opposed one another in the roll calls of some states, Shade's close look at politics in Ohio, Indiana, Illinois, Wisconsin, and Michigan shows that on most social and political issues—including their willingness to gerrymander "under the guise of reform"—there was little to choose between the major parties. They did divide on banking policies but their stands even on this issue were more complex than the voting tallies by themselves suggest. During the Van Buren administration and after, western Whigs "were not uncritical defenders of all banks," opposing their excessive proliferation. In Indiana, as James H. Madison has recently shown, Whig leaders agreed with the Democrats that a branch of the state bank was corruptly administered, but it was the Whigs who instituted the necessary reforms, not only curbing abuses in the granting of loans but putting an end to the partisanship that excluded Democrats from the board of directors. Rodney Davis's complex portrait of the Illinois Whigs projects an organization that was relatively "antiparty," moralistic, humanitarian, as it has been found to have been in some other states, but that was led at times by pragmatic men indifferent to the ideals that so affected some of their co-workers.

Whiggery on the state and local level in the northeast was a mixed baggage. The inept and unprincipled performance of New York City's Whig Administrations in the early 1840s infuriated Horace Greeley, whose public denunciations themselves illustrated the existence of factions as well as of honest difference of opinion within the party. Like their allegedly venal Democratic opponents, Whig city councilmen were not above granting contracts of dubious legality to party stalwarts who fulfilled only their responsibility for being paid. New York's Whigs as a whole may have been less hostile than Democrats to black suffrage but John L. Stanley finds the party's leaders split on the issue in the mid-1840s. As was true of the Democrats in the state, Pennsylvania's Whigs were capable of supporting diverse positions. In Northampton County the party combined support of temperance, abolition of imprisonment for debt, and banning Sunday mails, with opposition to Jackson's removal of the Cherokees. It exhibited greater sympathy for working-men's right to organize and to lay first claim to employer payrolls than was shown by the Jacksonians.

Not all northeastern Whigs were afflicted with the aversion to party building and organization that constrained Whigs elsewhere. From Jackson's administration through Polk's, New Jersey's Whigs maintained an internal discipline and dispensed patronage quite as ably as did their opponents. In New York and Pennsylvania on the other hand, for much of the era Whigs displayed the chronic Whig indisposition to organize political campaigns efficiently, at a time when the Democracy's mastery of the art approached genius. In such a New England state as Massachusetts, however, the issue of tactics hardly arose, for there Whig strength was so great that between 1834 and 1848 the party never lost a Senate race and seldom any other. The classic blend of social conservatism, nationalism, and hostility to racism sufficed to assure Whig predominance in that milieu of merchants, millowners, Yankee farmers, and high-minded Protestants, even though the party's "system" of nominating candidates and organizing campaigns left much to be desired. When a split ruptured the Bay State party in the mid-1840s it was occasioned not by a class issue but a racial and moral one. For all the diversity of Whig political behavior on national, state, and local levels, there is a significant degree of congruence between the party's theory and practice during the era. The case of the Democrats is very different.

Decried by the Whigs as the party of the rabble, Democratic spokesmen were better able to depict themselves the party of the people. Until recently most scholars seemed inclined to accept their estimate. If modern critics have done more violence to the Democratic image than to the Whig, it is because the old version of the Jacksonian party was so much more susceptible than that of their opponents. Who ever claimed that the Whigs were a great party of commoners and democratic reformers? The Democratic fall has been dramatic because they had so great a distance to fall.

In Congress Democrats united to vote against what Whigs favored and, with the exception of perhaps one measure, to support what Whigs opposed. The Jacksonian positions on the great national issues of the early 1840s were not so much anticonservative as anti-Whig.

The practice of local and state Democratic parties is most revealing. Tightly run machines tolerating no deviations from policies hammered out from above, or vying factions struggling for control, seemed equally the rule, with all factions proclaiming the superiority of their "principles." That in some cases they may have meant what they said would not make false notions any truer. In New England states, the Democratic party usually followed the politics of personality rather than principle. David Henshaw in Massachusetts and Ezra Meech in Vermont controlled their party machines for reasons that had little to do with ideology. In Rhode Island, Democrats played a most tricky game. On the one hand they tried to pose as the champions of manhood suffrage in the election of 1840. On the other, a prominent Democratic politician, James Fenner, stepped forward shortly afterward as the leader of the anti-suffrage movement at a time when feeling had turned against the Dorrites and their great reform. Not idealism but cynicism characterized Democratic behavior in this state.

For most of the era the New Hampshire Democracy was ruled by a machine controlled by the amoral Isaac Hill. A confirmed spoilsman, Hill told a friend that now that the Jacksonians had come to power Adams men or the "barnacles" would have to be scraped off the ship of state. Partisan removals in New Hampshire were wholesale. Most Democratic leaders there were "moderate pragmatic reformers" who, not uncharacteristically for Jacksonians, at times argued that slavery was a positive good, and more surprisingly, chartered almost 200 corporations in the decade after 1828. While Hill was the governor in the mid-1830s he pulled strings to secure federal funds for his own bank and railroad. The demand of some alleged radicals to limit note issue and confine it to bills of ten dollars or more was supported by the state's bankers, hopeful thus to "free them[selves] from dependence on Boston banks." When "radicals" finally did take over the state government in the early 1840s, their tenure turned out to be a short one. Although they opposed limited liability for corporations, they also showed great solicitude for the interests of private railroads. Their economic policies were above all anachronistic, in the judgment of Donald Cole causing a "disastrous lag in the growth of the New Hampshire economy."

The Massachusetts party, dominated by Henshaw during the years of the Jackson administrations, came to be torn by factionalism as a rival group headed by Marcus Morton and Bancroft arose to contest his control. They did not succeed in wresting power from

him until 1838. Henshaw was a self-made man, who rose from druggist's apprentice denied entry into Boston society and into the anti-Jackson party, to wealth and memberships on railroad and banking directorates. Shortly after Webster brushed him off, he hitched his wagon to Jackson's star. After much infighting, commencing with a war against the ex-Federalist Jacksonian, Theodore Lyman, Henshaw was in 1828 rewarded by his designation by Old Hickory to the strategic Collectorship of the Port of Boston. This selection gave Henshaw control of the party. It was this opportunist, not idealistic radicals, who was master of the Democracy for most of the era. His machine had its own press to lay down the line, keep the membership together, and organize campaigns. The following description by Arthur Darling of its system of operation in Boston after 1834 is suggestive of its less than egalitarian tone and of its efficiency:

For all who wished to maintain close touch with the most recent developments in party affairs there was a common meeting place in Boston. It was the banking room of the Commonwealth Bank, designated by Jackson as a government depository. . . . Here gathered all loyal Democrats, especially those from outlying towns who came to Boston for the sessions of the legislature. From the office of the Commonwealth's president, J. K. Simpson, set out the individual missionaries—called by their enemies "mercenaries" or "minutemen"—who conducted street-corner conversations and watched over certain sections of the city or the state and the political frame of mind therein. Henshaw possessed many such henchmen, ever on hand to act as secretaries or to take occasional trips through Broad Street and across the tide-flats to South Boston to spread whatever opinion might be desired.

The wealthy Henshaw was regularly attacked by some enemies as a dangerous radical in his own right. A renegade from his machine charged that Henshaw sought to get his supporters from the dregs of the population, "the tenants of poor-houses and penitentiaries." From another extreme in his own party, he was denounced by Morton and Bancroft as the spokesman of the few Democrats who had no interest in the party's great principles. Henshaw in fact commanded wide support from all elements in the party, for when Bancroft challenged his power in the gubernatorial contest of 1835, Bancroft got no votes to speak of. The Massachusetts Democracy did move in a liberal direction, however. After Morton was elected governor he put forward a program that was undeniably democratic. In addition to administrative reforms, it opposed the militia system for its discrimination against the poor, would liberalize the legal system, reduce the number of capital offenses, enact universal suffrage and a secret ballot, and reapportion the legislature on the basis of population rather than property. Even Henshaw had regularly declaimed against "toll bridges, imprisonment for debt, and the creation of soulless monopolies and corporations." (Evidently his own corporations had soul.) Henshaw's "radical" critics within the party were as interested as he was in winning the patronage and the advantages that went with it. Yet the worst construction that can be placed on the behavior of the dissidents is that they too used down-to-earth tactics to try to win power. Their program remains a popular and democratic one. The shrewdness of the men who devised it against the party of family and old merchant and new industrial wealth, does not detract from its liberal quality.

In the middle states the Jacksonian Democracy practiced the politics of amorality. In New York State the Democratic party was synonymous with Van Buren's Regency, masters in the art of political management. Their cardinal rule was that office and influence were to be granted only to those who worked within the framework of their machine and who accepted without question the authority of its leadership. Those who would challenge Regency control were removed from appointive office and barred from patronage. Judgeships went not to the qualified but to the loyal. Loyalty was defined not in terms of principle but in subservience to Van Buren, Croswell, Flagg, and others of that clique who ran the Bucktail machine.

It was hard to know what the substantive goals of the New York Democracy were, not least because it shifted its ground so often. Immediate political profit and the success of the machine—whatever its present line—were always the primary considerations. The leaders of the New York City Jacksonians supported abolition of imprisonment for debt, in the judgment of Peter Coleman "not so much because they cared particularly about imprisoned debtors but because they shrewdly sensed that it was expedient to do so." After first supporting internal improvements, the Albany *Argus* came to regard them with "aversion and horror." The party chieftains later reversed themselves on banking and other issues, "to suit the changing temper of the times," managing so well that "down to the disastrous panic of 1837 they provided their opponents with no 'burning issue.'" The habit of the party's leaders in justifying their policies in the language of democracy and egalitarianism tells much more about their skill in oratory than of the quality of these policies.

Dissident reform movements that emerged during the era usually arose out of protests against the Democratic machines in the state and in New York City, typically charging that the party had betrayed its principles—whatever they happened to be at the moment. This was the case with the People's Party and the Antimasons of the 1820s as with the Working Men's party and the Locofocos in the 1830s. The "infected district's" farmers became anti-Democrats largely because they identified oppressive bankers with the Van Buren party. As Lee Benson has pointed out, "Jacksonians did not serve as leaders of the movement [against monopolies] but as its targets." "Far from responding favorably to the reform movements taking political shape in 1829 to 1830, . . . the Regency's 'Republican State Convention' in 1830 ignored demands for abolition of licensed monopolies, abolition of imprisonment for debt, and establishment of a system of equal education for all." The *Argus* attacked those who would divide the community into classes, displaying an attitude that has been identified as one of the more conservative of Whig beliefs. Just as Working Men cooperated for a time with the

Antimasons in 1830, so six years later Locofocos united with Whigs against the party "which had connected itself almost indissolubly with the system" of banking monopolies. It was well understood at the time that Regency bankers had profited most from the system which restricted banking only to those granted charters by special acts of the state legislature—usually controlled by Van Buren's faction.

In New York State, the principles which Jacksonian leaders there seemed to take most seriously, such as "pure Republicanism," states' rights, limited government, and the like were not the stuff of reform politics, nor was the Democratic determination, as late as midcentury, to maintain the property requirement for free black voters. New York City's Democratic machine devoted itself mainly to winning office during the 1830s and 1840s. It disregarded its own reform proposals, rewarded unqualified individuals with patronage, overlooked conflicts of interest, all the while stigmatizing internal critics of its own derelictions as bribed agents of sinister banking interests. The Tammany promise made late in the era to change its ways came "too late to convince many skeptical voters."

The Pennsylvania Democratic party was like its New York counterpart only in the unideological bent of its major figures. A state Democratic party largely dominated by supporters of a high tariff and the Second Bank of the United States naturally had very special problems in view of the position that was ultimately taken by the occupant of the White House. That it managed as well as it did was a tribute both to its leaders' ability to walk a political tight rope and to their essential unconcern with Jackson's beliefs. Unlike the New Yorkers, however, the Pennsylvania Democracy was torn by factionalism, rival "families" waging a near incessant civil war for control of the party. Identification with the Old Hero and masterful demagogy enabled this strange amalgam of hostile elements to win the highest state offices more often than not.

The New Jersey Democratic party was a pragmatic political machine whose low practice constantly contradicted its lofty pronouncements. Its leaders' political actions were governed not by principle but by their diverse investments and economic interests. For a while known as the canal party, they even raided the state's school fund to finance pet projects from which they stood to profit, in "a brazen disregard of the public welfare." Despite the antibank and anticorporation talk by some Democratic orators in New Jersey, Jacksonian legislatures approved more bank and corporate charters than had any group in the state's history. The central fact illuminating the character of the Jersey Democracy was its connection with the Delaware and Raritan Canal Company in the 1830s and later with the Camden and Amboy Railroad. During the earlier phase, "the leaders of the Jackson party built their legislative policies around protection for the Delaware and Raritan, while the . . . canal company used its great financial resources to promote the interests of the Jackson Party. Indications of this cooperation occurred at every legislative session following the creation of the company in February 1830." Political principles were important primarily as a means of flavoring speechmaking to the New Jersey Jacksonians.

Peter Levine's thoughtful recent study discloses that between 1829 and 1844 New Jersey Democratic and Whig legislative policies were controlled by officeholding cliques who alone decided on the candidates for office and the "legislative business" to be acted on. This "business" was rarely concerned with anything but "special legislation" designed to benefit the private interests influential in party councils. While the major parties usually found it useful to align themselves on opposite sides of the issues they chose to contest, their legislative programs were devised to promote the electoral success and the preservation of the parties rather than to enact "comprehensive programs of public policy."

The Democratic parties in the western states and territories were hardly organizations of political firebrands. Prodded by Jackson's national policies to pay an unusual amount of attention to the banking issue, they characteristically divided into what James Roger Sharp calls "hards," who opposed "monopolistic" bank charters, small notes, and even note issue, "softs" who opposed hards, and those in between. While the hard line that became increasingly influential after the Panic of 1839 could be made to sound radical, it was actually a position favored by many conservative capitalists, particularly by those who profited from private banking. In Ohio softs compelled hards to accept a compromise that reformed rather than put an end to the state's banks, calling for enlarged specie requirements and officer liability for mismanagement or loss of capital. The Ohio Democracy was also devoted to the principle of gerrymandering.

The antibank stance became so popular in Iowa that a student of the state's politics finds it "not so much ideological as it was expedient." There as in other western states and territories the "radical wing" of the Democratic party had by midcentury succeeded in banning entirely banks of issue, putting an end to incorporated banks of any sort. The results were the emergence of dozens of unincorporated private banks which easily got around the prohibition on note issue and the flourishing of strange devices for issuing the "queer mess of stuff" that circulated as money in the area. That several allegedly radical "antibank" Jacksonians themselves became private bankers throws interesting light both on their earlier motives as on the unideological nature of the banking issue.

"In an effort to frighten voters," Indiana's Jacksonian leaders "fabricated a monster, a junto of businessmen united to deprive the people of their economic and political liberties." Madison's recent study concludes that this Democratic campaign "was no more than the thin rhetoric of partisan politics." While Illinois Democrats could display "something like issue-orientation" in their banking policies, they appear to have placed greater emphasis on "relatively safe non-issues which might have voter impact," in their determination to achieve their primary objective: "control of the government."

Michigan's Democratic party characteristically combined idealistic rhetoric with opportunistic practice in the late 1830s and 1840s. At the same time that the Jacksonians were denouncing banks and banking, they harbored more bankers in their party than did the Whigs. Formisano finds that with the exception of a debt exemption law for workers and debtors that was favored by some Jacksonians, "Democrats showed little interest in the poorer classes." His examination of Michigan politics "failed to discover any Democratic 'radicalism,' [disclosing] rather a lack of vital differences between the two parties."

Essentially the Democracy was more pragmatic and far better attuned to the new political realities than its opponents. Democrats had a penchant for party organization and were masterful in constructing "balanced tickets" likely to attract minority ethnic groups. A critic discerns "some 'melting pot' idealism" in the Democratic approach to low prestige minorities but characteristically it did not apply to blacks. The Michigan Democracy was adept at the Jacksonian art of urging extended suffrage in one breath and opposing Negro suffrage in the other.

In the southern states the Democratic parties were characteristically even less concerned with ideology than were their realistic northern counterparts. The Jacksonian party in Virginia and for that matter in the state legislature itself was for most of the era the "Richmond Junto," a disciplined group whose "power . . . purposes . . . opinions and wishes could supplant those of the whole people." Guided by Thomas Ritchie, publisher of the Richmond *Enquirer,* and a select number of eminent, wealthy, and influential Virginians, the Junto laid down the party line, dispensed patronage, and punished disaffection. A student notes that the machine maintained its power through such techniques and "also by methods less associated with Jacksonian Democracy: family influence, minimal rotation in office, a centralized and irresponsible judiciary, and the weight of corporations, especially banks." Where John McFaul finds that before the Panic of 1837 the Democrats' banking position "sought to occupy the middle ground between those who favored an unlimited expansion of state banking and those who opposed all banks," with the *Enquirer* calling for a "careful and reasonable addition to banking capital," James Roger Sharp notes that in the wake of the panic most Democrats imitated their brethren in other states in assuming a "radical [banking] position." Joseph H. Harrison Jr. reports that the Junto's increasing opposition to a national bank may have reflected "the position of Dr. John Brockenbrough, original cashier of the Bank of Virginia and its president from 1811 to 1843." Kentucky Jacksonians were equally masters of anti-Clay and antibank oratory, on the one hand, and nepotism, on the other.

Like Pennsylvania's Democrats, Mississippi's Jacksonians "championed the Old Hero more often in spite of his policies rather than because of them." Democratic leaders were "essentially practical politicians who had hitched their wagon to Old Hickory's star and realized that their personal advancement depended upon their unequivocal support of him in all controversies." It is not known whether Robert J. Walker actually had made the comment sometimes attributed to him: "had General Jackson recommended the recharter of the Bank, we should all have been good Bank men"; certainly his actions were in accord with the sentiment. Wiley P. Harris of that state confessed, "I found myself a Democrat without being able to explain why I was of that party." Mississippi's answer to Van Buren was Samuel Gwin, "the guiding spirit of the state Regency." Gwin was an out-of-stater whose designation to federal office by Jackson had infuriated George Poindexter and initiated the terrible feud between "old Poins" and Jackson. The Mississippi prototype of the era's machine politician, Gwin had "mastered the art of manufacturing public opinion" and he worked indefatigably at strengthening the Democratic party. He took charge of correspondence, organized meetings, and like Henshaw "dispatched couriers to insure that they were well attended; he supervised the printing and distribution of presidential messages, handbills and ballots; and he rallied the 'sovereigns' to exercise their franchise on election day." Newspapers were used assiduously and in recognition of their vital role, "leading Democratic editors were rewarded with state or federal offices." Democratic masters of speculation became veritable Locofocos after the Panic of 1837, astutely joining in the popular clamor against banks. Democratic support of hard money, however, was due more to concern for world cotton prices than to agreement with such a hard money theorist as William Gouge. Jacksonian antibanking policy in Mississippi blended antisemitic rhetoric, fear that paper money would "weigh down the planting and commercial interest," and the intense dislike of banks felt by speculators who themselves had obtained substantial loans from, and were therefore heavily in debt to, the banks. The elements of principle that bound Mississippi Democrats to Jackson were their views on slavery and Indian removal, "principles" that do little service for the ideological interpretation of Jacksonian Democracy.

Florida's Democratic-Republican convention in 1839 went on record against "abolition incendiarism," in the course of building a remarkably efficient party organization. A "pyramidal structure" of local, county, and district organizations was firmly guided by the principle of democratic centralism. Nominations for delegates to county conventions were made not from the floor or by elected groups but by a committee appointed by the party leaders in charge. Utilizing its efficient machine, the press, the beneficiaries of national patronage, barbecues, flowing alcohol, astute positions on local issues, and indifference to social reforms, the party did remarkably well at the polls in the early 1840s. In contrast to the situation in Mississippi and Pennsylvania, Jackson's name counted for little in Florida, in part because of his checkered pre-Presidential career in that territory. Democrats in need of a great personal symbol invoked the name of the Sage of Monticello.

North Carolina's Democratic movement regularly shifted its ground during the era but not for ideological reasons. Party battles there "were not a reflection of any broad crusade for social justice or for freedom of enterprise." As in New York, Democratic leaders were "satisfied with the economic, social, and cultural condition of the state," in contrast to the Whigs, who favored an "active, paternalistic government." But Jackson's name and influence counted heavily in a state where Willie P. Mangum, who in 1832 believed the Bank "an indispensable necessity," nevertheless voted against recharter in order to stay in the President's good graces. Jackson won many supporters from among strict constructionists for his Bank veto message and from the many Unionists for his firm position on nullification. Much of this support was withdrawn after the issues responsible for it receded. While these issues were of high importance they had nothing to do with haves and have-nots. Nor did they clearly separate the parties, since most of North Carolina's anti-Jacksonians were themselves Unionists. Emerson to the contrary notwithstanding, in North Carolina a modern Jacksonian sympathizer finds that the Democrats had the better men, the Whigs the better program.

It matters not whether the Tennessee Democratic party is appraised by critic or admirer of the Jacksonians. In either case it emerges as an organization dominated by cliques of wealthy, uncommonly powerful men, seeking personal advantage above all, using the name and prestige of Jackson for all it was worth, resorting regularly to demagogy. Polk trimmed his sails to the political winds, regarding only Jackson as a fixed star from which he could never stray no matter the inconsistencies he might be thus forced into. The Democratic principles of limited government, thrift, strict construction, preference for one banking system over another, defense of slavery and expansionism, were hardly a program for the common man.

For most of the era the Democratic party of Missouri was dominated by Thomas Hart Benton, erstwhile enemy to "aristocratic banking" and the so-called worthless paper it issued, and friend to the small farmer and poor settler. Certainly this was the reputation he himself assiduously sought to promote. Benton in fact presided over one wing of the Missouri Jacksonian party, the faction that prevailed for most of the era. Its ascendancy rested largely on the fact that it was composed of the state's wealthiest slaveholders, as well as on Benton's considerable prestige and political prowess. His vaunted bullionist principles were loyally supported by men who in some cases saw the wisdom of a flexible currency but joined the Democratic ranks because "that was the sensible place for an ambitious Missouri politician to be." Many Missouri Jacksonians supported banks, *the* Bank and internal improvements, total converts to the American System whose great leader they carefully opposed in the prints and at the polls. Missouri's Democrats were gifted in denouncing corporate wealth, but a Democratic legislature toward the end of the era approved more corporate charters in one session than had been approved at any time during the previous decade. The one "corporate monopoly" the Bentonites consistently opposed was a Bank of the United States. At the beginning of its career, in 1828, the party did urge the popular election of circuit court judges and their rotation in office. Yet after it had been in power for more than a decade, the Democratic State Legislature refused to enforce a federal redistricting law. Benton feared that no matter how gerrymandered, a new districting system would benefit his party's opponents. This consideration was sufficient to justify what a modern student calls nullification of the congressional law. For all its presumed radicalism, Benton's hard money position was enthusiastically supported by the state's greatest slaveholders who were evidently oblivious to its agrarian implications. The evidence is strong that the conservative man of affairs, Thomas Hart Benton, emphasized the banking issue to the extent he did primarily because in so doing he could most effectively perpetuate his own influence over his party. The great preoccupation of the "Boonslick" faction, to which a modern student finds that even Benton was beholden, was party unity and the purging of dissident or "impure" elements from Missouri Republicanism. Their avowal of Jeffersonian principles did not preclude their establishing in 1837 what Robert Shalhope calls a "republic-style state bank" that they of course dominated as officers and directors.

In Louisiana, Martin Gordon, collector of the customs in New Orleans, was the great power, having convinced Jackson that "he was the Jackson party in Louisiana." Political principles mattered little to Democratic leaders who not only supported the Second Bank of the United States for the ready credit and other valuable services it had provided, but who were for the most part active bank directors. Joseph Tregle finds that political affiliations in Louisiana were determined by ego rather than ideals: "each Louisiana politico was an issue in himself." Domination by cliques of ambitious opportunists was, as Edwin A. Miles has observed, also the rule elsewhere in the South. Power in Georgia's Jacksonian movement was divided between the Troup and Clark factions. Newer territories such as Arkansas were particularly conducive to the politics of personality. In its territorial period the Arkansas Democracy was in the hands of a clique variously known as the "Family Combine," the "Bourbon Dynasty," and "Sevier's Hungry Kinfolk," led as they were by Jackson's old crony, Ambrose H. Sevier. Following statehood, Sevier's clique continued to rule the state, while distributing "the loaves and the fishes" to the party faithful. Forced, in the phrase of a modern student, to play "catch-up," Arkansas' poorly-organized Whigs managed only once to elect a candidate to state office in the period 1836–1850.

On the state level the major parties were devoted largely to attaining "the very practical goal of controlling the government of the several states," rather than the realization either of principles of the famous national programs they knew so well how to praise. Since all the evidence is never in, it is not impossible that future historical expeditions into the Jacksonian past may turn up material that compels a reevaluation of the state Democratic parties. But the modern studies offer little support to the view put forward by the Jackson partisans that theirs was the party of the common man. Evidence on the theory as well as the practice of the Whigs and the Jacksonian Democracy does not bear out earlier notions that these great parties were deeply split along ideological lines.

Discovering that the parties usually took different positions on the issues that came before the state legislatures, a recent study reports that from their voting behavior "one could generally differentiate a Democrat from a Whig": the major parties were thus not mere "electoral machines." No organized political group is ever a *mere* electoral machine. No matter how cynical and amoral its leadership, the presence of a powerful opposition leaves them no alternative in a democracy but to appeal to the electorate and to do so in terms of lofty principles that are *distinguishable* from the lofty principles proclaimed by their opponents. For even the most simple-minded and gullible voters are unlikely to respond favorably to a party naïve enough to proclaim frankly its dedication to pelf and power. Knowing this fundamental fact of political life in America, the astute men who controlled the major parties during the Jacksonian era struck dissimilar stances on the issues they chose to contest. Nothing about their inevitably contrasting party lines and voting records, however, can disguise the fact that their supreme interest seems to have been in winning office and, once in, using it to reward themselves and their most loyal and influential followers, while doing what seemed likely to prolong their tenure.

11

WHO WERE THE DEMOCRATS? WHO WERE THE WHIGS? THE MAJOR PARTIES' DIFFERENCES EVALUATED

Those who find striking contrasts in the beliefs and actions of the major parties tend to believe the Whigs and Democrats appealed to unlike constituencies. In this view, Democrats were led by plebeians, Whigs by aristocrats. The Democratic rank and file, whether in city or countryside, were allegedly much poorer than their Whig counterparts. Whiggery flourished where soils were superior. In the South it was most popular in the black belt, where plantations prevailed or where slaveownership was greatest. The religious diversity of the party memberships was also believed to reflect the social gulf dividing them. Denominations of high prestige thus aligned themselves with the party of Clay while their social inferiors chose Jacksonian Democracy. And where poor or ordinary folk voted Whig, as millions of them obviously did, a traditional interpretation explained the phenomenon in terms of an "economic dependency" that drew the lower orders to support their overlords.

According to the popular interpretation of American history that stresses the twin themes of continuity and struggle, the Jackson party took up where the Jeffersonians had left off in the never ending fight of the people against the privileged few. The Democratic party of Franklin Roosevelt's time would later fight the same good fight that had been waged a century earlier by the partisans of Old Hickory. The enemies of the people—whether Federalists, Whigs, or Liberty League—were also judged to be spiritually akin. Certainly Jacksonian campaigners regularly referred to their opponents, whether Whig, Antimason, or other, as "Federalists." There is no doubt the charge was an effective one, what with the deteriorating reputation of Washington's and Hamilton's old party after the War of 1812. What the student of history wishes to know is whether the charge was accurate.

233

That the Jacksonians cared only about the political capital to be derived from the charge and not at all about what Arthur M. Schlesinger, Jr., has called the "class-conflict doctrines" of Federalism or any other of its actually complex doctrines, is revealed by how assiduously the Democrats themselves wooed Federalists and how well they rewarded them following Jackson's election in 1828. The Jacksonians' courtship of Federalists was a subtle affair marked by evasiveness, half truths, occasional dissimulation, much coyness, and from time to time straightforward almost blunt embraces— even if the latter went unaccompanied by the frank, joyous words that thrill the hearts of innocent lovers. But eager partners in an illicit relationship understand the necessity for veiled public discourse. They are also quick to recognize the true passion that sometimes lurks behind seemingly bland phrases. When Jackson let it be known during the 1824 campaign that he would proscribe or deny office to no man "on account of his political opinions," Federalists understood and were delighted. For all the blight that had fallen on the one-time great party, its supporters had not disappeared from the earth. The split introduced into the Republican party by the Missouri controversy, and the repudiation by the ambitious presidential candidates in 1824 of the congressional caucus method of nominating Republican candidates, gave to old Federalists new opportunities. In an inevitably close contest, opportunistic presidential candidates were sure to seek assistance from any quarter. In politics support requested is support rewarded.

The Jacksonians were not alone in soliciting Federalists' aid. A rough division of labor saw the John Quincy Adams' men going after blocs of Federalists whereas the Jacksonians cleverly tended to recruit them as individuals. And many thousands were recruited. After Adams' election a favorite Jacksonian tactic was to stigmatize Adams' administration as "Federalist," while the General's party "at the same time . . . adeptly gathered their own legion of Federalist auxiliaries." "Former Federalists" from every section flocked to the party of the great popular hero. Many of them disliked Adams for his earlier apostasy, and they became increasingly disenchanted with his administration for its few appointments of Federalists to office as well as for its policies on tariffs and internal improvements. They supported Jackson on the basis of their estimate of his character, and for his and his party's obvious willingness to let bygones be bygones or "to forgive any man's past sins if he would swear loyalty" to Jackson. Martin Van Buren in his autobiography made the politically motivated statement that "Jackson had lost all his Federalist friends by 1828." Van Buren had possibly forgotten his own artful political seduction of influential southern Federalists at the time. Actually as Shaw Livermore, Jr., the modern historian of declining Federalism has demonstrated, "there were probably as many men who had acted with the Federalist party in Jackson's corner as in Adams'."

The roster of the Jackson party's "former Federalist" supporters constituted a who's who of both parties. The Jacksonians fished for Federalists from states in every section, succeeding in hauling in such luminaries as Theodore Lyman, Jr. and Timothy Pickering in Massachusetts, James A. Hamilton, Chancellor Jones, and Josiah Hoffman in New York, much of the top Federalist leadership in Connecticut and New Jersey, James Buchanan, Henry Baldwin, and Horace Binney in Pennsylvania, Louis McLane and James Bayard in Delaware, Roger Brooke Taney, Vergil Maxcy, and Benjamin Latrobe in Maryland, John A. Cameron, Littleton W. Tazewell, William Drayton, William Polk, and John Berrien elsewhere in the South, and many others of like eminence. In Robert Remini's phrase, "one quick rub with Republican cloth and they were as good as loyal Democrats."

After his election Jackson appointed more Federalists to office than had all of his Republican predecessors combined. Collectorships and such a new post as "Solicitor to the Treasury"—expressly created for Maxcy—as well as cabinet positions went to Federalists. Both Samuel Ingham and John Branch had "acted with" the old party and John Berrien had been active in it. Livermore's estimate that Federalists were evenly split in 1828 may be a modest one, for his detailed study specifically excludes the South, whose Federalists evidently went over "*en masse*" to Old Hickory and his party. Herbert Ershkowitz's subsequent study of New Jersey indicates that ex-Federalists in that state were perhaps more pro-Jackson than had been believed. Practically every major leader of the New Jersey Jacksonian party from its beginnings until the Panic of 1837, was a former Federalist. Maine's Federalists played an increasingly important part in Democratic success *after* Jackson's election. The Regency never let up on the charge that first its Clintonian opposition, and later the National Republicans and the Whigs, harbored ex-Federalists, while true Jeffersonians had gravitated toward the Democracy. Actually, as Whig campaigners effectively demonstrated in 1840, six of the surviving seven Jeffersonian electors of 1801 were in their party while numerous Federalists were high in the state Democratic administration.

If it is not surprising that a party of political realists was happy to obtain political support from any quarter, such behavior was hardly the stuff of the politics of principle. Democratic opportunism, however, does not by itself contradict the thesis that the Jacksonians were the party of commoners. The old question still stands: were the memberships of the major parties dissimilar in their social and economic backgrounds?

It is very difficult to discern any significant differernces in the social composition of Democratic and Whig party leaders. Of course the situation varied from state to state. The men at the helm of the Jacksonian party in Massachusetts, for example, were outsiders, politically, and of lower status than their opposite numbers in the other party, socially, in part because the wealth of Democratic leaders was in some cases only recently come by. Yet there were Bay State Whig leaders who were also *nouveau*. The "Conscience Whigs," who emerged with the heating up of the slavery issue and who became Free Soilers after the Mexican War, were for the most part of older family and higher social status than their more expedient Whig fellows. In that state the inveterately successful Whigs reigned as the party not only of old wealth but of practically every other social stratum as well. The slight but signifi-cant differences in the social tone of major party leadership there were due essentially to the domination of state politics by one party. Whether *parvenus* or not, David Henshaw and his circle,—typically bankers or members of the boards of directors of railroads and other businesses—were not poor men. New Hampshire's Jacksonian leaders, like their National Republican counterparts, may have rep-resented poor constiuents but they were not poor themselves. They "did not make fortunes, but they did make good."

The Albany leadership of the Democratic party were hardly commonfolk. Martin Van Buren belonged to the upper one percentile of wealthholders and his chief lieutenants, as well as the "middle grade" leadership, were men of wealth and high status, the social and economic equal of their Whig opposite numbers. Ev-idence from localities in other parts of the state points in the same direction. About two-thirds of Kingston's party leaders were men of high prestige occupations. The major party leadership of the vil-lages in Genessee County in western New York—"the burned-over district"—was similar in socioeconomic character to the political elites of more placid communities. Since few of the farmers who predominated in the region "enjoyed the financial resources or control of time needed for involvement in county politics," they sanctioned a leadership that Kathleen Kutolowski finds "remarkably unlike themselves in major social characteristics." In the mid-1830s political offices were filled and Genessee's parties led by men two-thirds of whom were successful professionals and businessmen, the same sort of men who ran the area's temperance and benevolent associations, its lyceums and school boards. In a county almost notorious for the evangelical Congregationalism and Presbyterian-ism of most of its population, more than two-thirds of the major party leaders belonged to the socially prestigious Episcopalian Church. The increasing participation by farmers and commoners late in the era was confined to "ceremonial posts" at the "outer edge" of leadership. As for New York City's Democratic leadership, their reputation as "'Bank Democrats'" was well founded in view of the wealth of Gideon Lee, Preserved Fish, George Templeton Strong, Walter Bowne, Jonathan Coddington, and most other Tammany leaders during the era. Whether in poor neighborhoods or wealthier ones, ward committees of both major parties were overwhelmingly controlled by wealthy merchants and property holders. In the other middle states the Democratic leadership was similarly in the hands of men of unusual wealth and prominence in business affairs.

In Michigan's strategic Wayne County, leaders of the two major parties, whether of the top, middle, or intermediate grades were essentially alike in their social and economic backgrounds. Lawyers and businessmen were to be found in roughly equal numbers in the Democratic and Whig top echelons. That they evidently mingled socially without regard to party suggests something of their view of the "great" party battles in their community. Differences there were in the elites of the parties but they had to do with religion, ethnic origins, the geographical backgrounds of the native-born, and how long they had lived in their Michigan residences, not with wealth or occupation. In contrast to Kentucky, Democratic leaders were less foot-loose than their Whig counterparts. In common with other states, Michigan Whig leaders were more likely to be New England-ers and of that section's predominant Protestant denominations, less likely to be foreigners or Catholics than the Democrats. In contrast to Alabama, youth was no more a characteristic of the leadership of the one party than of the other.

The socioeconomic status of Jacksonian and Whig leaders has been most fully investigated for the southern states. Of course scholars of different persuasion will either interpret the same evidence differently or focus on different facts. Thus one study notes that Whig members of the Tennessee lower house were more than twice as likely as Democrats to be lawyers. A more recent examination of Tennessee's Congressmen finds that for all their ideological differences, the men of both parties were of roughly equal wealth and professional attainment. Despite the inevitable differences in viewpoint of the men engaged in the modern research, its most amazing feature is the essential similarity it discloses in the occupations, wealth and status of Whig and Jacksonian leaders. Ralph Wooster's comprehensive overview of governors, judges, legislators, and county officials in the lower South states of South Carolina, Georgia, Florida, Mississippi, Alabama, Texas, and Louisiana at midcentury reports the inordinately professional and merchant occupational backgrounds, the lofty social status, the substantial property and slave holdings of Whigs and Democrats alike. In some states "a higher percentage of Whigs possessed real property and slaves," in others Democrats "had a higher median in real property than did Whigs." For the section as a whole, "as perhaps nowhere else in America, with the possible exception of Virginia, political and social power remained in the hands of the rich and well born."

The social standing of party leaders was not much unlike that of their candidates and officeholders. The Richmond Junto that ruled the Virginia Democracy during the era was at one and the same time "an urban-centered group, consisting mostly of business and professional men," that was also "essentially representative of the planters." Active in the Junto were members or relatives of the Old Dominion's great families—Carters, Braxtons, Nicholsons, Carys, Burwells, Fitzhughs, Harrisons, Nelsons, Pages, and Randolphs. In Jacksonian Maryland "the common man appeared isolated from the fruits of political preference." Democrats and Whigs both relied heavily on the "cultivated, well-to-do" among the state's mercantile and professional orders, with their leaders also sharing common religious denominational as well as socioeconomic standing. The struggle for power that broke out between the "old" and the "new" Jacksonians "did not represent the eclipse of the elite and a triumph

of the masses in the governing of the party," but a form of inter-
necine conflict between two elitist factions. There was little to
choose between Whig and Democratic congressmen and governors
in Georgia, with 92 percent of the former and 89 percent of the
latter from the legal profession. North Carolina's Jacksonian
leaders in the early 1830s were substantial eastern elements rather
than the frontiersmen and westerners who earlier had been influential. In Cumberland County in that state, during the 1830s
Whig and Democratic leaders were similar in socioeconomic status,
each of them between three and four times as wealthy as the
average farmer in that community. Harry L. Watson II finds that
while the base of the Jacksonian party's activists was enlarged by
new rural elements of modest property, the truly influential
Democratic leaders were primarily wealthy Fayetteville residents of
prestigious occupation. "In spite of their rhetorical appeals and
differing constituencies," he concludes, "Whigs and Democrats drew
their most important leaders from the same elite social circles."

Florida's party leaders have been examined closely. The
Democracy's chieftains may perhaps have owned less land and
fewer slaves than their Whig colleagues. Yet the "nucleus," which
constituted the original Jacksonian coalition of the early 1830s, was
composed of speculators, planters, bankers, and professionals.
True, many of these men later deserted the Jacksonian party for the
Whigs. But the residue were not poor men. The Democratic party of
1838 to 1845 was made up of farmers and planters, large and
small, with merchants, rural capitalists, and village entrepreneurs
having "considerable weight" in its affairs. As in Massachusetts,
newer and smaller merchants were more likely than the well-established ones to be Democrats. Yet 150 Democratic leaders in Florida,
when subjected to a detailed analysis, proved to be unusually
wealthy men. There were "a disproportionate number of them
lawyers, relatively few yeoman farmers—fourteen percent—in
contrast to planters who made up close to forty percent of the
group, while merchants and manufacturers constituted twenty-five
percent." For all the Whig demagogy and Democratic counter-
demagogy about Jacksonian leveling and affinity for the poor, the
"Democratic movement in Florida was certainly no lower-class
manifestation of radicalism."

An exhaustive study of the socioeconomic and family backgrounds of the more than 1,000 Alabama congressmen and state
legislators for the period 1835 to 1856 found no important differences between Democrats and Whigs. A larger percentage of
Democrats had gone to college; 47.6 percent of Democrats were
planters in contrast to 34.5 percent of the Whigs. Slightly more
than half of the representatives of each party were lawyers. The
percentage of businessmen was about equal. A "slightly higher
percentage of Whigs than Democrats" were professional men. As
for religion, Methodists and Baptists abounded: there were "few
Episcopalians in either party." A subsequent study of several
hundred Whig and Democratic local activists in Alabama found a
remarkable similarity in their situations. Occupations and religious

denominations were alike while they owned equal amounts of real estate and were "strikingly similar in their pattern of slaveowner-ship."

There is little doubt that the Whig Party in the South became increasingly preoccupied with banking and business issues or that its leadership included many wealthy merchants, bankers, and professional men. As the historians of an earlier day suggested, it was also a party dominated by the planter and slaveholder, in the language of one memorable characterization, "the broad cloth and silk stocking party." A stunning word picture of a later time depicted the typical Whig leader as the man in a silk hat nearby a Negro on a cotton bale. But the painstaking modern studies of Alabama and other southern states indicate that broadcloth and silk stockings were the badge not only of *Whig* party leadership; "the man in a silk hat nearby a Negro on a cotton bale was by no means necessarily a Whig."

In Missouri, too, the Jackson party leadership contained more slaveholders as well as the men who owned the largest numbers of slaves. Practically no Whigs owned more than 20 slaves. While Democratic leaders were wealthier and of higher status than the average Missourian, the leaders of the Whig party of that state were typically richer, more likely to be lawyers, slightly more likely to be businessmen, and while less likely to be farmers, more likely to claim large farms than the Jacksonians. Among the top leaders of the party, more than twice as many Whigs on the average had attended college—although the rate of college attendance among the Democracy's prominent figures was between 500 and 1,000 times the national average. In the city of St. Louis both parties typically put up extremely wealthy men for mayor and middle-class persons for the council, although Democrats did on occasion also nominate artisans to that body. On the level of "vigilance commit-tees" or poll watchers, essentially similar patterns prevailed, al-though when tavern keepers and brewers are ranked as "businessmen," there is little to choose between the party faithful. The Democracy's local activists included 21 tavern keepers or brewers while the Whigs had none. Differences there were in the social and economic positions of Missouri's party leadership, but as John Vollmer Mering has observed, they were hardly those separat-ing an "aristocracy" from a "proletariat." More recently Shalhope has reported that most Missouri Democrats during the era accepted "political leadership by the social elite." They got exactly that, since the "Boonslick" politicians after their "conquest of the 1835 nomi-nating convention . . . began to tighten their control of the party," were "the leading planters and merchants of their respective counties."

Jacksonian leaders in Louisiana matched Whigs in wealth and education as well as in the number of their bank directorships. Nor was there anything to choose between major party leaderships in the city of New Orleans. Not only did Whig and Democratic leaders come from "an American-Creole upper class," but they shared "identical political philosophies," conducive to "an accelerated capitalistic development in the city." Because of the existence of a viable Whig opposition in the state, Brian G. Walton prefers to call the Democratic leadership of Arkansas a "dynasty," rather than a "machine," but no matter how labelled it was a group composed of uncommonly well-to-do and influential men "related to one another by birth or marriage." A recent study, based on the 1850 census, reports that Whig leaders in Arkansas were on the average wealthier and more likely to be large slaveowners than were Democrats. According to Sam Houston, Texas in the late 1840s had only six Whigs, "one of whom was a horsethief—another a black-leg—a third a landgrabber, and the other three were the mere tools and understrappers of the first three." Actually, the Whigs won close to one-third of the new state's votes in the presidential balloting, with the party's leaders predominantly of "commercial-related or professional" occupations. In an admirably thorough recent investigation of antebellum Texas major party leadership at all levels from county office through membership in the United States Senate, Richard Lowe and Randolph Campbell reveal that the important differences in the social profiles of these leaders were not those distinguishing Whigs from Democrats but rather the glaring dissimilarities between political leaders of whatever party and their constituencies. "Political leadership in antebellum Texas was provided primarily by an economic elite," men several times as rich as the people they represented, whether in slaves or other forms of wealth.

The significance of the remarkable similarities in the socioeconomic backgrounds of Whig and Democratic leaders should not be overestimated. Their public behavior as political men was more important to their constituencies than were their social characteristics. That political leaders held inordinate wealth and prestigious occupations did not preclude their laboring for the welfare of the mass of propertyless persons. The fact that major party activists were cut of the same social cloth did not mean that their political philosophies and policies necessarily had to be similar. As a matter of fact their programs, as has been noted, were different. And yet the unrepresentative social profiles of the leading Jacksonians and their opponents, the striking differences between the leaders and the citizenry whose votes they solicited, was not devoid of larger meaning.

The conservative social philosophies underlying the legislative actions—and inaction—of Whigs and Democrats spoke to the interests of the social, economic, and occupational groups represented by their leaders. The seeming disinterest of the major party leaderships in ascertaining from the "common people" they so praised in their rhetoric what these people actually wanted in the way of legislation doubtless has a complex explanation. Certainly an important element in the explanation of why commoners went unconsulted by Whig and Democratic policy makers was the absence of commoners from the positions of command. It is hard to avoid the related conclusion that the essential blandness of major party legislative policies and enactments in the states, their preoccupation with corporate matters and with catering to influential private interests owed much to the fact that the men who formulated Whig and Democratic policies and bills were themselves most comfortably situated men.

V aluable investigations have also been undertaken of the rank and file memberships and the kind of voters attracted by the major parties. In answer to the question, what manner of man supported the one or the other party, scholars who once went about the investigation in the manner made famous by Charles A. Beard—that is by focusing on economic data—have more recently employed methods that a Freudian might approve. One recent analysis has even posited a Whig personality type: pompous and stuffy. Jackson himself offered a psychological interpretation of sorts but unfortunately it was lacking in clinical detachment. According to Old Hickory a Whig was a man "devoid of principle and honesty, a man completely untrustworthy." Emerson would have thought that Jackson's definition applied better to Democrats. It now seems clear that Whig voters were apt to be relatively disinterested in liquor. Could this explain the heavier emphasis by Democratic campaigners on the free dispensation of large quantities of the stuff? Horace Greeley thought his party contained ten times as many truly moral men as the Democrats but his, like Jackson's, was an undocumented impression. Lee Benson's study concludes that New York State's Whig voters "were more likely than Democrats to share puritanical attitudes" such as piety, sobriety, thrift, steady habits, and book learning. Democrats on the other hand had their greatest success among New Yorkers "who bragged about their fondness for hard liquor, fast women, and horses, and strong racy language."

While modern history has invoked emotional and psychological criteria in the search for the distinctive types who made up the constituency of the one or the other major party, the examination of wealth, occupation, and social background of party members has by no means been forsaken. This is as it should be since it is obvious that the social complexion of a party's supporters is a most important clue to its true nature. Too much should not be made, however, of the correlation between a party and its voting support from a distinctive socioeconomic group.

There seems to be a widespread assumption that a party supported overwhelmingly *by* the poor or by whatever class, is the party *of* the poor or of the class that does support it. If this is taken to mean—as I think it often is—that a so-called party of the poor either truly serves them or that it deserves their support, then I think it is a false notion. It does not take into account the power of demagogy or the gullibility of voters. To cite a drastic example, the fact that Hitler's party may have been supported by the German workers would hardly make the Nazis the party of the poor. American history, fortunately not yielding examples so dramatic as

German, also affords illustrations of the point. McKinley's party would not be the party of the poor no matter how well it might do in working class electoral districts. The determination that the Democrats were the party of this or that group must finally be made not on the basis of the degree of electoral support the Democracy got from the group in question, but according to an *evaluation* of the party's behavior.

Neither demagogy by the parties nor gullibility of the voters can be assumed, however. Particular facts must be studied. A correlation between the vote of a particular income group and one of the parties *might* be due, at least in part, to the party's performance. And in contrast to an historian's interpretation, which can turn out to be all wrong if not altogether valueless, correlations—even at worst—are factual relationships that become available building blocks for the construction of theories or interpretations. V. O. Key, Jr., in *A Primer of Statistics for Political Scientists*, has cautioned that "statistical procedures only identify relationships," proving nothing; correlations must be subjected to scholarly *evaluation* if they are to be made meaningful. All of which is to say that if socioeconomic information on voting does not by itself explain the patterns it identifies, it nevertheless remains important.

If the traditional view did not stress the poverty of Democratic party members, it noted their relative lack of affluence. Yeoman farmers, owners of no or few slaves, small planters, and other noncommercial types predominated in the South; Indian fighters and small farmers in the West; "country folk, fishermen, and the poorer classes generally," in New England and the North. Their country folk came of the poorer soils or from counties of lower land values, their urban dwellers from "the less prosperous towns," more likely to be debtors than creditors. These were the economic components of the Jacksonian Democracy. Its chief ethnic elements were Scotch-Irish in the back country, the new immigrants in the East, Irish in the cities, Germans in rural towns or settled communities. Presbyterians, Baptists, and Methodists predominated, supplemented by Catholics in the cities.

The traditional portrait of the Whig constituency recently redrawn by Glyndon Van Deusen, its leading student, holds that "New England and Middle State Whigs numbered industrialists, commercialists, and much of native labor in their ranks, together with a respectable number of conservatively minded farmers. In the Ohio Valley, the pushing, ambitious, go-ahead bankers and businessmen, canal promoters, land-owning interests, lawyers with an eye to the main chance, and farmers anxious for internal improvements were more apt than not to be found in the Whig ranks. In the South, one source of Whig strength lay in the urban commercial and banking interests." The "economic dependents" of the latter, who followed them from Democracy to Whiggery, were "the big cotton, tobacco, and sugar planters who owned perhaps two thirds of the slaves in the South." These groups when supplemented by individuals who personally disliked Jackson and his party or who had special reason to fear its policies, "were the elements which constituted the Whig party."

Certain aspects of Whig support are so obvious as to be beyond dispute. Election returns for the period establish that the party commanded support from all of the major sections of the country, a backing so massive that it could not have materialized had the party not been able to dip into all economic strata as well as every kind of geographical region. Poor tactics helped explain defeat in an 1836 election in which the Democratic popular majority was slight. In 1840 the Whigs won, while in 1844 they lost by a hair. There were not nearly enough rich men or wealthy planters or big city dwellers or direct beneficiaries of the American system in America to account for Whig success at the polls. The party had the allegiance of social and economic types whose interests, according to the traditional view, were not truly represented by it. Roger B. Taney assured Jackson that workers, in voting Whig, "sold their freedom" in return for economic favors. The later variations on Taney's theme, according to which poor Whig voters acted on the basis of the "friendship bred by dependence," assumed as did he that the common man votes essentially by bread alone. It did not occur to the authors of this theory that voters might vote as they do largely out of conviction or a sense of right.

Historians are very much affected by the climate of opinion or the intellectual atmosphere of the era in which they work. When the assumptions of Progressivism held sway, depicting as they did a Jacksonian era whose politics reflected the struggle of the people against the interests, studies of Whig and Democratic electoral support focused on their differences. Somehow Jackson's party was found to attract poor voters, Clay's and Webster's party, the wealthy. The work done more recently by scholars of different mood more often discloses marked similarity in the socioeconomic backgrounds of Whig and Jackson voters.

It is not subjective factors alone, however, that account for the recent emphasis on the social heterogeneity of each of the major parties. The modern research has relied on a methodology that is very different from that used in an earlier time. Some of the newer findings are superior to the old because they rest on methods that are far more exacting and sophisticated than those used in the past. A brief comparison of methodologies is illuminating if not indispensable to an understanding of the changing viewpoints.

The conclusion that Whigs rather than Democrats attracted the great slaveowners' vote was based on research that plotted out the presidential vote by counties whose slave populations had been determined. What gives weight to the modern refutation is not its recency but the impressive research and the sensible methodological scheme that guided it. Doing a far more detailed examination of the socioeconomic character of small communities than was dreamed of by Arthur C. Cole a half century before, Grady McWhiney found little or no correlation between wealth, soil fertility, and the extent of slavery, on the one hand, and voting, on the other. "In only three of the sixteen [Alabama] counties where over half of the population was slave did Whig candidates receive a majority in every election." But the Democrats won in three similar counties. "The other ten . . . were inconsistent in their loyalties, and frequently the contests were close . . . a shift of five per cent in the vote would have brought defeat in nearly half of the Whig and in thirty-six per cent of the Democratic victories." In view of the fact that some of the largest majorities given Whigs were polled in counties where there were few slaves, and some of the largest majorities given Democrats were polled in counties where there were many slaves," it could be said that "Whig strength was not based solely upon planters."

A subsequent study of Alabama, penetrating well beyond the presidential vote for counties, examined the smallest electoral units or "beats" for their general socioeconomic character and voting behavior. Thomas B. Alexander and the other scholars who employed this comprehensive approach did find that in the hill country of Tuscaloosa, "the eastern, poor-soil beats of the county were controlled by Democrats . . .; the southwestern half of the county, containing some of the most productive soils, was strongly Whig." But the affinity of poorer soils for Democracy was not typical, occurring in only two elections. While there was a "tendency for Whiggery and the plantation system to appear together," no correlation could be detected between manufacturing, commercial, professional, or educational preeminence and Whig voting. Their evidence was equally devastating to traditional notions as to the religious denominations drawn to the great parties. "If the aristocratic Whig was supposed to be Episcopalian or Presbyterian, his humble Democratic counterpart Baptist or Methodist . . . Tuscaloosa County must have been an exceptional place. There Democrats were just as likely as Whigs to be Episcopalian and much more likely to be Presbyterian. About the same proportion of each party group was Baptists, and more of the Whigs were Methodist." The Alabama citizens who voted Democrat during the Jacksonian era subsequently have been found to have been not the poor but the young. A man's economic status was not an insignificant factor in accounting for his vote but it was no more influential than other factors. As in other states, communities voted in large part as they had voted earlier, no matter the explanation of their original choice.

The scholars who study a particular community or state generally concede that the patterns they have disclosed may not be true elsewhere, although characteristically they suspect that they may be. My own suspicion is that what is unique about Alabama of the middle period is not the fascinatingly complicated picture presented by its painstaking analysts, but the fact that it has been examined in such detail. One suspects that other communities subjected to equally sensitive treatment would reveal unique but similarly complex patterns and relationships, profoundly disquieting to the either-or version of Jacksonian Democracy.

Other detailed studies of voting in Georgia, Maryland, North Carolina, Michigan and New York, counties in Pennsylvania and Tennessee, and of townships in New Jersey, also suggest that the relative wealth or poverty of citizens had little to do with their party preferences. Poorer voters divided their votes among the two major parties in almost exactly the same proportions as did their wealthier neighbors. Donald DeBats' regression equations indicate insignificant correlations between the socioeconomic composition of Georgia voters and their party preferences in the years from 1833 to 1850. And when Georgia voters made up their minds to support one or the other major party they rarely changed thereafter: "Intense competition, high turnout, and political stability were the hallmarks of Georgia's party period." Wayne Smith's close examination discloses similarly insignificant correlations between wealth and party preference in Maryland. "Neither party in Maryland represented class interests," he observes. "Both parties drew from the wealthier classes for their leaders and depended upon the common folk to fill out their ranks." Whitman Ridgway has more recently found that in the moderate slaveholding region of rural western Maryland, "the yeoman farmers divided their allegiance between the two competing parties" during the era.

Michigan voting late in the Jackson era, certainly in the towns and villages of Wayne County, sharply contradicts the older version of the nature of the major party electorates. Middle- and lower-class persons who made up the great bulk of the electorate divided their votes, without reference to class, more or less equally among Democrats and Whigs. That towns were populated either by "rural lower classes" or by large proportions of "prosperous, middle-class farmers" was no clue to their political preferences. Towns with similar social patterns differed sharply in their voting behavior while towns whose social elements were markedly unlike nevertheless exhibited similar voting patterns. No discernible correlations existed between economic status and party choice. In Virginia in 1828 both the Tidewater and Piedmont, "strongholds of conservative views," went heavily for Jackson. In North Carolina the Democratic party's social and geographical bases did not conform to the traditional ideas about them. Democratic strength in that state was not on the frontier but in "the North-Central counties and in the East." Democratic majorities were large in districts where slavery was most prominent. In Arkansas, on the other hand, the Whig congressional candidate in 1836 and their presidential candidates in the 1840s appear to have received slightly heavier, if not majority, support in "those counties containing a large majority of slaves" than they received elsewhere in the state. In a word, voting patterns were varied, sometimes contradictory, and give little support to the theory that clear-cut class lines divided Whig from Jacksonian voters.

The economic factor as correlate of party preference does seem to work to this extent: as Frederick Jackson Turner long ago suggested, economically developed communities usually preferred the Whig party. In such communities the Whig appeal cut across class lines, with men of dissimilar wealth and occupation equally embracing the anti-Jackson party, precisely as in counties of another sort the Democracy attracted near universal support. It was not solely a matter of the economic state of such communities that determined whether they would lean in the one political direction or the other. Otherwise how explain the fact that through all manner of fluctuation between prosperity and depression or changes in the socioeconomic status of their electorates, some counties reported exactly the same distribution of Whig and Democratic votes at the end of the period as at its beginning? Jacksonian electoral support at first came from the old Republican—if not necessarily poor—districts of Baltimore and the western counties. Even T. P. Abernethy, as sharp a critic of the progressive interpretation of Jacksonian Democracy as any historian of the 20th century, conceded that in the Tennessee gubernatorial election of 1839, the "focal points of Whig strength . . . tended to radiate along the lines of communication." The Whig constituency in Florida lived in the "rich, earlier-settled, plantation areas" of middle Florida, while Democrats were in the "new, frontier, small farmer region of East and South Florida." The commercial centers, however, leaned toward the Democracy.

Less than one-fifth of Missouri's 108 counties consistently voted Whig in presidential elections between 1836 and 1852. The Whigs of Thomas Hart Benton's state were inveterate losers who as often as not chose not to run candidates. If one can therefore speak of characteristic Whig counties in such a state, he would note that they were relatively old or long-established, touched the Missouri or Mississippi river, contained unusually large farms, and were the more populous counties. (Of course many Democratic counties, in a state controlled by the Jacksonians, had similar traits.) That the Whig vote was high where slaveholding was great, does not substantiate the old Phillips-Cole thesis: John Mering, the modern historian of the Missouri party, cautions that "slavery and the interests it generated do not explain a Missouri county's Whiggery."

This tendency of relatively well-established, commercially active, "go ahead" communities to vote against Jackson has also been found by Donald Cole to have been true in New Hampshire, at least in the presidential election of 1832. A "typical" Clay town in that state was old, prosperous, populous, connected to the outside world by many roads, near the ocean, possessed of a lively newspaper, great buildings, and a couple of Congregationalist churches. Jackson towns— and one had recently changed its name from Adams to Jackson!— were isolated, poor, "out of the mainstream" of New Hampshire life, sparsely populated, and had no church or perhaps one church, the Free Will Baptist. Small upland villages on poor soil worked by small farmers, voted overwhelmingly for Old Hickory, with the exception of one district of 16 towns whose Clay vote has recently been interpreted as due to its relative prosperity and its proximity to the world outside and to areas of former Federalist influence. The correlation between religious denomination and voting appears to have been greater than any other. For in addition to the "exceptional" Clay upland towns running from Sullivan to Amherst, the next to the poorest town in the state voted for Clay, while the second wealthiest went for Jackson by two to one. But the latter were exceptions to the New Hampshire pattern. For that matter any anti-Democratic voting seems to have been exceptional in a state whose "Concord Regency," led by the redoubtable Isaac Hill and Levi Woodbury, "had been electing Democratic Governors and Congressmen by wide margins since 1829."

In Virginia "the more urbanized and commercialized areas were strong in their support of the Whig party," whereas Democratic counties were located in "the declining agricultural area south of the James River," and in "sparsely settled areas in the mountains of the Trans-Alleghany section." Democratic strength in the "wealthy tobacco region in the southern Piedmont" may have been due to the heavy concentration of pro-Jackson German families living there. In Georgia, Whig strength was greatest in counties "where investment in primary types of manufacturing and commercial ventures supplemented cotton growing." In the Tennessee gubernatorial election of 1839, the "focal points of Whig strength . . . tended to radiate along the lines of communication." If Florida's commercial centers were surprising in their preference for the Democracy, the Whig constituency was unsurprisingly concentrated in the "rich, earlier-settled, plantation areas" of middle Florida, whereas Democrats were in the "new, frontier, small farmer region of East and South Florida." Mississippi's wealthiest counties were most likely to vote heavily for Whig presidential candidates in 1836, 1840, and 1844, while poorer counties—with the exception of very poor and strongly pro-Whig Perry County—voted Democratic. That Whig support came from the "better-informed areas" likely to have a newspaper or a periodical was no doubt interpreted by the party's stalwarts as proof that the more voters knew the more likely that they would vote intelligently. In Kentucky Jackson did particularly well in "counties with high rates of population growth" and with men who had been active in the old Relief movement: the latter movement, it should be remembered, was led by many well-to-do men who became repudiationists out of temporary need rather than from compassion for poor debtors.

James Roger Sharp concludes that "typical Whig constituencies were those that were fully participating in the market economy," ranging from "areas heavily involved in commercial agriculture to urban centers of industry and commerce." Democrats were not the poor but rather citizens of all classes who lived in communities that intellectually and socially, as well as economically, were different from those conducive to flourishing Whiggery.

I t is not their economic status but their ethnic identity and their religious or denominational affiliations that best explain the political preferences of voters: this at least is the argument of the "ethnocultural" interpretation that has been put forward by a number of modern historians. Discovering from his examination of New York voting records of 1844 that the correlation between the ethnocultural characteristics of certain communities and their party choices was greater than the correlation between the occupations of their residents and their voting preferences, Lee Benson reports that "at least since the 1820's, when manhood suffrage became widespread, ethnic and religious differences have tended to be *relatively* the most important sources of political differences." Several scholars have drawn similar conclusions from the electoral evidence afforded by other states. The "primary importance" of ethnocultural factors "in the 19th century becomes increasingly clear with each new study," proclaims one of Benson's disciples. The evidence does not quite sustain this claim.

In New York State, according to Benson, Irish Catholics and French Canadians gave 95 percent of their vote to the Democrats, while "New German" and French immigrant voters gave almost as large a proportion. The Whigs attracted almost all Negroes' votes, 90 percent of the votes of Scots, Welshmen, and Protestant Irishmen, and 75 percent of English votes. "Yankees" voted Whig by a slight margin but "Penn-Jerseyites," "Old British," "Dutch," and "Old German" voters preferred the Democracy by roughly three to two. The Progressive historian Dixon Ryan Fox had a generation earlier produced evidence for several cities in New York State between 1828 and 1840 indicating that "where the property per capita was relatively large" or where a ward was heavily populated by "merchants, manufacturers, and professional men," Whigs drew an inordinate proportion of the vote. "Conversely, where mechanics made their home, Democratic candidates were generally certain of election." Looking beyond economic data to the places of birth, the ethnic identities, the religious affiliations, and the sense of group membership of voters, as well as their alleged psychological states and their feelings toward "negative reference groups," Benson reads the New York evidence very differently. The Jacksonians' main support, he asserts, came not from "farmers, mechanics, and 'working classes,'" but from "relatively high-status socioeconomic groups in the eastern counties, and relatively low-status ethnocultural groups" in all sections of the state. In Benson's provocative interpretation, gamblers, bohemians, the free thinking, and the free swearing adopted the Democracy, their more puritanical neighbors chose the Whigs.

Ronald Formisano finds voting alignments in late Jacksonian Michigan quite similar to those Benson found in New York. No discernible relationship existed between voters' economic statuses and their political preferences. But striking correlations were found between ethnicity, lifestyle, religion, and party choice. Yankees, for example, while decisively pro-Whig were not nearly so likely to support Clay's party as were Yankee *Presbyterians*. Evangelicals were overwhelmingly Whig; Catholics, whether Irish or French, were Democrats. And as in New York, hedonists were Jacksonian, the God-fearing, Whig. From his reading that in Northampton County, Pennsylvania, "devotionalist" Moravians and Presbyterians "tended to support the Whigs, while the 'doctrinally orthodox' members of Catholic, Lutheran, and Reformed churches voted for the Democrats," Shade too argues that "religious orientation" was the great clue to political behavior. As early as 1824, heavily Jackson counties in Ohio outside the Cincinnati region contained "large numbers of Scotch-Irish or German settlers from Pennsylvania." By the late 1830s and early 1840s Whig counties in Ohio were "populated mainly by New Englanders," self-reliant, sober, and prudent men, who gave the area "an ethnocultural homogeneity that no other section in the state could match." And a close study of Greene County, Illinois, reveals that "while individual voters' wealth and occupation bore some slight independent relation to party preference," their "cultural background and religion were far more predictive of party."

Partisans of the new approach argue that ethnocultural factors were not only most "predictive" of voters' party preferences but that they also throw the greatest light on the political issues of the era as well as on the voters' preceptions of these issues. As James E. Wright has observed, the correlations that they have discerned have led the "ethnoculturalist historians" to conclude that "the real issues of politics have been those most significantly related to lifestyle and values": issues such as prohibition, sabbatarian laws, public funding of sectarian schools, "efforts to hasten or retard ethnic assimilation."

While the ethnocultural interpretation is interesting and provocative, it is weakened by a number of flaws. Any claims it might make to universality are undermined by contemporary evidence that points in an opposite direction. The political behavior of New York City's merchants, whatever their denominations or national origins, was totally at odds with what the theory holds it should have been. In rural Cumberland County, N.C., ethnicity was "irrelevant to party choice." In wealthy Davidson County, the political preferences of the elite, who were divided almost equally between Whigs and Democrats, showed no particular relationship either with religion or ethnicity. Kathleen Neil Conzen has shown for antebellum Milwaukee and Jay Dolan for New York that thousands of Catholics enrolled in a "holy crusade" against intemperance, the issue that supposedly divided anti-Jacksonian "evangelicals" from Democratic—largely Catholic—latitudinarians. Impressionistic evidence, such as that supplied by Henry Conklin, a farmer in upstate New York, challenges assertions alleging bitter emnity between members of dissimilar churches and denominations.

The most serious deficiencies of the ethnocultural interpretation concern its assumptions and its methodology. Benson's admitted assumption that "men tend to retain and be far more influenced by their ethnic and religious group membership than by their membership in economic classes or groups" is based on his unwarranted because undocumented assumption that there was "high social mobility" in the United States. His further assumption, that men are more influenced by a durable characteristic, such as "their ethnic and religious group membership," than by a supposedly newly acquired characteristic, such as membership in a new "economic class," runs counter to a weight of evidence afforded by the sociological literature on the enthusiasm of recent converts either to a faith or to a social class. In arriving at figures for the alleged ethnic and religious composition of particular communities and the correlations between these figures and the division of votes between the parties, he and other scholars have at times relied on secondary sources for their ethnocultural breakdowns of populations, on impressionism and surmise for their conclusions about the beliefs and emotions of voters, and on inspired guesswork as to how individual voters voted.

It is disconcerting to be told that a group of men were free thinkers on the basis of nothing better than a few scattered and undocumented allusions or that it is *assumed* that there were differences in the "psychological makeup" of men in different industries. Aggregate data on group affiliations and identities do not reveal the breakdown of votes by individuals. The headcount of denominational memberships that the ethnoculturalists rely on—or, as John V. Mering remarks, the seat count, when they use numbers of pewholders—does not come close to justifying their assertions about the alleged depth of religious conviction in the statistical units they use. Nor are such surmises much strengthened by the random, impressionistic evidence some ethnoculturalists adduce to supplement their tabulations; that Charles G. Finney swept through a community did not quite make it the hotbed of evangelicalism one ethnoculturalist says it was—as Finney himself would have conceded. And as a host of critics of the ethnocultural interpretation have noted, even if the correlations it posits between ethnocultural identity and party preferences rested on better evidence, they would still not have the significance that has been attributed to them. That a mass of Congregationalists, Methodists, or Irish Catholics voted this way or that, even with regard to so-called symbolic or noneconomic issues, could have been due to complex considerations nowhere hinted at in the quantitative evidence. V. O. Key has reminded us that correlations are not causal relationships. As David Thelen has observed, unwarranted religious determinism is no better than the economic variety. And a number of religious sociologists have produced evidence showing that while religious affiliation is important, it is "seldom dominant" in influencing political behavior. Some members were only "marginally" attached to their churches and almost all church members had "other roles and statuses," including economic roles and statuses, that affected their behavior.

It does appear likely that the ethnic origins, religion, and values of some individuals strongly influenced their political actions. But no study yet done and no interpretation yet offered clearly establishes why men voted as they did. And it is doubtful that such a study of interpretation will be forthcoming. For what is more complicated than the mind of the voter? The eminent statistician Samuel Richmond concludes that "no statistical procedure can explain why any individual does anything."

I n the first edition of this book I wrote that "one important traditional belief appears not only to have withstood modern revi-
sionism but to have been confirmed by recent findings. Rich
men were evidently pro-Whig." All the evidence is of course not
in, but the most recent research suggests that my earlier comment
needs to be modified. The point is not that the rich have now been
shown to have been ardent Jacksonians but rather that their margin
of preference for the Whigs appears not to have been nearly so
great as had been thought.

A recent analysis of the political affiliations of the most "prominent" men of antebellum Davidson County, Tennessee, reveals an
almost even split, with the Democrats among the top 100 outnum-
bering the Whigs by one. Composed almost entirely of planters,
businessmen, lawyers, and a sprinkling of journalists, physicians,
and ministers, Nashville's elite probably included the community's
wealthiest as well as its most eminent citizens. Burton W. Folsom II
finds that Davidson County leaders "maintained their social cohesion despite" what he calls "the deceptive rhetoric of party
struggle," as friendships "transcended party allegiance." Party
loyalty among the elite was "generally rigorous," since not "even one
prominent [man] switched his party affiliation" in the period from
1835 to 1855. The much vaunted "radicalism" of Jacksonian
policies during and after the Bank War was evidently taken in stride
by elitist Democrats.

In Michigan, according to Formisano, wealthy men gravitated
toward both parties because Whig and Democratic programs "never
threatened the distribution in society of property or power." An
earlier study revealed that the social and economic elite of Michigan's Wayne County preferred Whigs to Democrats by a margin of
slightly better than two to one. About 85 percent of the merchants
and lawyers were Whigs, while landowners—a smaller number of
the county's rich men—were decisively Democratic and the few
bankers slightly pro-Jacksonian. The total number in this Michigan
sample was only 100. Much more substantial and systematic evidence has been gathered on the political preferences of the rich in
New York City.

Contemporary opinion was divided. Joseph Scoville, onetime
secretary to John C. Calhoun and author of an interesting, intimate,
but unreliable group biography of the city's merchants, claimed that
"Democratic merchants could easily have been stowed in a large
Eighth Avenue railroad car." Horace Greeley and other Whig leaders disagreed, arguing that the state's wealthiest landlords and
many of the city's leading merchants were Democrats: "The rich
men are divided," they declared. Modern scholarship also speaks
with two voices on the issue.

Discovering that roughly equal percentages of New York State
Whig and Democratic leaders were present in an 1845 edition of
Moses Yale Beach's "Wealthy Citizens" listings, Lee Benson implied
that the earlier Whig suggestion that the city's rich men as a whole
were equally divided between the two major parties was therefore

well founded. But as Frank Otto Gatell observed, it did not follow from the fact that a few dozen party leaders were roughly equal in wealth that a much larger number of rich men were equally divided in their party preferences. Using Beach's list of the 1,000 New Yorkers each ostensibly worth $100,000 or more as his source of New York City's rich men, Gatell reported finding evidence for about 70 percent of the group. His conclusions sharply refuted Benson's surmise and Greeley's claim.

According to Gatell, 84.3 percent of "the rich" were Whig. And the richer they were the more likely were they to be. Those who were each worth $400,000 were 92 percent Whig; millionaires were 94.1 percent Whig. Since he found a significant increase in the percentage of rich men who became Whigs in the years after the commencement of the Bank War, with about one third of those who earlier had been Democrats ostensibly deserting the party, Gatell concluded that the wealthy by no means dismissed the reigning political issues as mere "claptrap." By the early 1840s "monied men" in New York City and elsewhere thought that the Whig party "better served their interests and better calmed their fears than did the Democracy." As for the ethnocultural political affinities posited by Benson, they did not hold up for wealthy New Yorkers. Their wealth better than their religion or national identity explained their party choices.

Brian J. Danforth's recent investigation of New York City's wealthiest merchants finds too that their ethnocultural character-istics betray no significant connection with their political behavior. But for the rest, his findings are sharply at odds with Gatell's. Gathering detailed evidence on the political affiliations of about 700 of the city's wealthiest merchants for the period 1828–44, Danforth found "an almost even division" among them: 52 percent were Whigs, 48 percent were Democrats. If these wealthy merchants engaged in a "high level of political activity," such activity "coin-cided with a high degree of political consistency." Since only 2 percent of the group "crossed party lines during the period," and only one-tenth of these did so during the Bank War, Danforth is skeptical toward "the thrust of Gatell's thesis" that rich men fled to Whiggery in great numbers because of that issue.

The differences in the findings of these scholars may be ex-plainable at least in part by the differences of their sources. Gatell reports on New York City's "rich," Danforth on its wealthy *mer-chants*. The Beach list that Gatell relied on has subsequently been exposed as unreliable, a piece of guesswork put together by an erratic man whose claimed intimacy with the city's elite of wealth appears to have no basis in fact; it is not hinted at in the private papers of hundreds of the city's wealthiest families. In contrast, more than one half of Danforth's merchants were actually among the 1 percent of the city's citizens assessed for wealth of $45,000 or more. The evidence on the political activities of the merchants was drawn from diverse contemporary sources, spelled out in much detail.

One of Danforth's most interesting conclusions is that "the main determinant" in the political behavior of New York City's wealthiest merchants "was economic realism." Economic subgroups of the heterogeneous merchant class tended overwhelmingly to identify themselves politically with the party whose policies were most favorable to the interests of their particular subgroup, whether auctioneers, wholesalers engaged in the southern trade, or any other.

It is possible that future investigations may yet disclose that unlike the wealthy men of New York City and Nashville, rich men elsewhere did prefer Clay's party to Jackson's by a decisive margin. If such evidence should materialize, its significance should not be misconstrued. That rich men, if they were to influence politics, had to belong to one major party or the other, would not prove that their choice of one by an overwhelming *margin* is likewise a sign of overwhelming *fears* on their part. Particular banking schemes or a special plan for storing public monies could divide men and provoke substantial opposition from businessmen convinced that these measures would have detrimental effects. But Independent Treasury up or Independent Treasury down, American society, private inheritance, and the American business system would continue on their erratic course. If the issue of one kind of money rather than another were in fact the main explanation of the rich man's politics during the later years of the Jacksonian era, it would seem to be a most powerful argument that both major parties were essentially consoling to monied men, whose choice of one party over another was dictated by such a matter. All the inflammatory rhetoric in the world could not transform the deposit of federal funds in many banks instead of only one into a dread act of confiscation. The wealthy Missouri slaveholders who ardently supported "hard money" were neither radical nor lunatic. Since businessmen, as Samuel Johnson once suggested, are not necessarily astute about anything but business, it is quite possible that some of them were as gullible as their fellows in other classes, as prone to become excited at fiery language that bore little relationship to reality. It is also likely that in preferring Whigs to Democrats, many merchants understood as did Tocqueville, Francis Lieber, and Harriet Martineau, that the alternatives were not greatly different. Interestingly, rich men who divided politically with few exceptions maintained close social relations. Their party differences did not mean nearly so much to them as their social kinship.

The remaining question concerns the behavior of working men. Did labor support Jackson? A number of scholars, including the influential Beard, had regarded the Jacksonians as a farmer-labor party whose success was in large part due to the support it got from urban mechanics. But until 1945 most informed discussions stressed the rural and western character of the Jacksonian coalition. Arthur M. Schlesinger Jr.'s *The Age of Jackson*, published at the end of World War II, was not simply a brilliantly written account of the era but in itself an event of historical significance. More than any other single factor it was that volume that led a generation of historians either to view the era as did its author, or to argue the issues in terms posed by him. In Schlesinger's version, "during the Bank War, laboring men began slowly to turn to Jackson as their leader, and his party as their party." The "labor thesis" rests on the conviction that Jacksonian policy earned or deserved workingmen's votes. That judgment is of course arguable. Less controversial is its belief that the Jacksonians got *much* labor support. The clear implication of the theory is that *most* workers supported the Democratic party.

New England's voting behavior for the era does not substantiate this notion. In the presidential election of 1832 in New Hampshire, factory towns in an otherwise Jackson state divided their vote evenly, with Clay evidently getting most of the workers' vote in the eight largest industrial towns. Isaac Hill showed little interest in workingmen. A more detailed study done for Boston tried to locate working class districts. In the face of such evidence as the city's wards' assessed valuation of property per capita, their populations, the number of wealthy persons living in them, and their comparative expenditures for poor relief, it seems clear that the "laboring poor" of the city were concentrated in 5 of its 12 wards or electoral units. Election returns from these wards during the years of Andrew Jackson's presidency show that Boston's poor consistently voted against Andrew Jackson and his party, whether in presidential, congressional, gubernatorial, or local elections. In 1828 much of what little support Old Hickory got came from among the have-nots and disgruntled elements of the upper classes—ambitious merchants and disappointed Federalists. In only one of the working class wards did he receive more than one third of the vote. In the state elections of 1830 Democratic candidates fared even worse. Two gubernatorial elections in 1831, made necessary by a change in the state election laws, were marked by the nonsupport of the Democrats by the poor in each. The lack of success irked Henshaw for in a fit of pique he charged that Boston Working Men were the enemies of Democracy.

While Jackson continued to run a poor second, even in working class wards in the 1832 presidential contest, the great number of new voters in all wards who voted for Jackson suggests that the Democracy was becoming more acceptable to all classes throughout the city. Democratic gains were registered among the city's poor in the elections of 1834 but they did not match the party's advance on a state-wide scale. In 1835 although the party continued to be decisively beaten in the poorer wards, its regular candidate for governor did manage to win a majority in one of them. Interestingly, the "radical" George Bancroft, who was put forward by some Jacksonian dissidents, got no support. With Jackson's retirement from the scene, the Democratic party scaled new heights in Massachusetts during the presidential election of 1836 and actually won majorities in three of the five poor wards if not a majority of the combined total.

This refutation of the Jackson urban labor thesis was almost immediately challenged by Robert T. Bower. In view of the influence attained by the challenge, its argument warrants a brief review. It held that in a predominantly Whig city, "it is not too illuminating to discover that even the relatively poor areas often voted over fifty percent Whig." With the "whole climate of opinion so much in favor of one party we would expect that any section within the city would still tend to lean toward the Whigs, regardless of its social composition." It advised students to disregard the absolute vote and rather to pay attention to the relative vote, "as it varies from ward to ward in correlation with the richness or poorness of the wards." When this was done, it argued, a significant correlation was established between the socioeconomic status of the wards and their party preferences. Despite his party's failure, therefore, to win majorities in working class wards during Jackson's Administrations, it concluded that "Jackson and his political allies *did* get their support from working-class groups."

While the stress on the importance of a city's "climate of opinion" was useful, as was the reminder that the pattern of working class voting changed during the era, the validity of the Jackson-labor thesis was not proven by this critique.[1] That some socioeconomic groups in Boston may have been even more opposed to Jackson than were workingmen, does not transform the workers into the man's supporters. The only question that the original study attempted to answer was this one: did most of Boston's workers support Jackson? Simple arithmetic provided the answer: they did not. If Jackson's minority vote from Boston's workers were part of a larger picture in which workingmen in other cities showed him an unusual degree of support, then this Boston working class support he got— even though it came from a minority—would take on heightened significance. But the evidence from other cities discloses no such pattern of unusual affinity of workers for the Hero. Overlooked in the critique of the Boston study was the vital fact that although the

---

[1] In trying to establish the socioeconomic status of the wards, Bower relied *only* on assessed valuation of property. Carl N. Degler among others has noted the weakness of this method as an index to the wealth or poverty of a community. Bower did not establish that the workers who voted for Jackson did so because they were workers. He seemed unaware of the points subsequently made by V. O. Key, Jr., that "correlations do not necessarily mean anything in themselves"; that checking voting against only one variable, as Bower did, establishes no causal connection between the two; and that finding "the magnitude of (the) . . . square" of a coefficient of correlation is highly important in trying to interpret the latter (*A Primer of Statistics for Political Scientists*, 117, 123, 130–31, 145). Bower did not attempt to "square the magnitude" and thus find the *coefficient of determination* from the coefficient of correlation he arrived at. Professor Adam Abruzzi, a statistician, pointed out to me that a coefficient of determination that was 0.5 or higher could be considered significant, even though it did not prove causality. The highest coefficient of determination between Jackson voting and wards of low assessed valuation of property was .3136.

poorer wards showed an increasing preference for the Democrats between 1828 and 1836, Boston's wealthy wards also showed a rate of increase in their Democratic vote that was almost identical to that evidenced by the working-class wards.

It is of interest that in the base year, 1828, the poor districts, although very much against Jackson, nevertheless gave him a larger proportion of their vote than did the wealthier wards. Even the strongest supporters of the labor thesis concede that prior to the Bank War—and certainly in 1828—Jackson and his party had taken no substantive position justifying unusual labor support. It is quite possible therefore that this early relatively greater support shown him by the "lower orders" was due to his military reputation or any number of other factors having nothing to do with class interest. But thereafter, particularly after the Bank crisis, the urban labor theorists argue that Jackson's party began to attract inordinate support from the poor. The Boston evidence indicates rather that his party's appeal was heightened for all classes. As for Massachusetts as a whole, it was long ago demonstrated that the Democracy's great success was not with the workingmen of the cities but rather with the farmers of the western and southern counties. In the urban areas, the Democracy was above all assured of the Irish vote.

The urban labor thesis has also been tested for the middle states. The New Jersey evidence is inconclusive. Certainly the state's labor movement formed no lasting ties with the Jacksonians. Its supporters regularly voted against both major parties. Democratic support in New Jersey came most clearly from voters of German, Dutch, and Scottish extraction. Philadelphia has been examined in detail by William A. Sullivan. In the election of 1828, Jackson, whose popularity ran high in the city and throughout the state despite his reticence on issues, won a sweeping victory in the poorer as well as in the other wards. But the returns from working-class wards for all subsequent contests down to 1840 constitute a clear-cut refutation of the labor thesis. The results showed that "the workingmen of Philadelphia gave their votes far more consistently to the Whigs than to the Jacksonian Democrats. Moreover, it was prior to the Bank War and not during it that the working-class districts revealed any inclination to follow the lead of Jackson and his party." The Democracy blamed its poor showing on intimidation by the "monster bank" and its subject manufacturers and on the importing of voters into the city on election day. There is no evidence substantiating the latter charge. Though it was impossible to determine the causes of the Jacksonians' failure, one thing was certain: "the inability of the Democrats to hold the labor vote which they had captured in 1828 led to their ultimate defeat in the city."

New York City's voting during the era permits no clear-cut conclusions. Metropolitan Democratic politics was a most tangled skein. In the city *as a whole*, the Democracy won decisive victories over its major opponents in elections on all levels from 1828 through 1832. Congressional, local, and state elections from 1834 through 1838, on the other hand, were extremely close, the Whigs in fact doing slightly better than the Jacksonians. But how did the laboring poor vote?

New York City's annual election returns hardly substantiate the labor thesis. In 1828 the rough two-to-one preference for the Democrats shown by the poorest wards only matched the results in five much wealthier districts. That the city's three wealthiest districts voted by a slight margin against the Jacksonian electors was, of course, due to factors other than Old Hickory's beliefs. In 1829 the Jacksonians got their strongest support from the richer wards. In 1830 the support given by working-class wards to the Democrats was if anything slightly less than that demonstrated by wealthier districts. That candidates of the recently formed Working Men's party diverted Democratic votes may explain the Jacksonians' failure but it does not alter the fact. For that matter, the Working Men came into existence largely because their organizers were convinced that the Democrats, no more than their opponents, deserved labor support. The poorer wards in 1832 provided a degree of Democratic support that was matched by all but the three wealthiest wards. In 1834, however, the Democrats did do much better in the wards of low assessment than elsewhere. The gain was an ephemeral one. In 1835 half the working-class wards were split between the two major parties, while the only ward in the city that went *overwhelmingly* Democratic was among the wealthiest. Economic factors obviously had little to do with it. The 1836 and 1837 results are inconclusive although in the gubernatorial election of 1838 Tammany fared much better in the poorer wards than in the wealthier. In sum, then, in the elections of only two years did Democrats do inordinately well in poorer communities. In the late 1830s and in the 1840s New York City's Democracy evidently owed its close victories not to the votes of the working class, but to the votes of foreign-born Catholics. As for the other cities in the Empire State, there was no homogeneous working-class vote and a variety of factors seemed to account for the electoral behavior of laboring men.

It is not at all certain that an economic interpretation of the labor vote or the vote of any other class has been refuted. For while the modern studies show that the working-class vote was divided, it is within the realm of possibility that in any given election voters may indeed have consulted their economic interests—or their own possibly misguided notions of their economic interests—and have voted accordingly. A subsequent split vote might indicate not that voters gave no thought to economic interests, but rather that they had different conceptions of where their economic interest lay. It is more likely than many individuals, then as now, voted for a great variety of reasons mixed with emotions that even the voters themselves were not aware of. Undoubtedly many voters responded to issues and parties in terms of what they believed to be the right and the true, without a thought to self-interest, as men sometimes do. For as V. O. Key noted, in what in 1966 he called his "perverse and unorthodox agrument," "voters are not fools." There is reason to believe that the voter is "a reasonably rational fellow." The political scientist Arthur S. Goldberg has more recently used contemporary game theory persuasively to argue the rationality of voters.

Many scholarly conclusions as to why men acted or voted as they did are nothing more than inferences based on statistical correlations. There is nothing wrong with making such inferences: it may well be the scholar's duty to do so. But it must be remembered that the causes of an individual's behavior are not proven when evidence is afforded that others who behaved or voted similarly had either the same kind of job, soil, religion, nationality, prejudices, drinking habits, or vocabulary as he. Only one thing is certain. The bulk of American voters of all classes divided their support more or less equally among Whigs and Democrats.

F or all their similarities in theory, practice, and the social composition of their constituencies, the Whigs and the Jacksonian Democrats *were* different. Even the iconoclastic studies of class and suffrage, where they disclose a slightly greater predilection toward wealth, usually reveal that it applies to the Whigs rather than to the Democrats. On the other hand this kind of difference hardly sustains the Jacksonians' own notion that theirs was the party of the common people. That in New Jersey the Jacksonians championed the Camden and Amboy Railroad, and their opponents the rival New Jersey Railroad, is a difference that is really a similarity. That Democratic businessmen in a few places were not as well established as their Whig counterparts is a most subtle distinction that offers little comfort to believers in the traditional theory of party differences.

The Whig party was above all the practical political organization devoted to the defeat of Andrew Jackson and his supporters. It attracted men interested in no loftier objective than that, and other men who seriously opposed both the arbitrary methods of the President and the specific policies and programs of the Jacksonians. It seemed to command vast support from businessmen throughout the country, for a number of reasons. Many men of affairs were concerned, quite sensibly, about the effects of Jacksonian financial policy on the economy. What is bad for business is not necessarily good for the country. Some of them were undoubtedly affected by the political rhetoric of the times. Others, without necessarily believing that Democrats were the idealistic radicals they claimed to be or the revolutionary agrarians Whigs charged they were, simply felt more at home within a party not tainted by such unpleasant allegations. On the state level, northern antislavery men who disapproved the tactics, the low status and the low morality attributed to members of the Jacksonian coalition, would themselves have no part of it.

Some modern scholarship, attempting to break with the socioeconomic stereotypes and preoccupations of the past, has sought to fathom the emotional sources of the Jacksonian appeal and the subtle factors that distinguished the followers of Jacksonian Democracy from their opponents. Jacksonian leaders have been adjudged as socially obscure, not particularly attractive, almost faceless men, their traits indicative of their commonness and the democratic cast of their party. In this reading, their party, more truly a child of the new egalitarian times, was better able to break with old forms of political organization and campaigning. In contrast to its tradition-encrusted rivals, it appealed directly to the common people. A "Jacksonian persuasion" has been located somewhere between the best and the worst of the Democrats' public talk, consisting of a set of beliefs that approximated the public professions of the men who shared it. Thus Jacksonians were not necessarily right or even admirable, but they *were* sincerely fearful of the America growing up around them, a world of commercial wheeling and dealing. Their alleged Jeffersonian economic notions may have been archaic, but they were also humane and somehow democratic, at least in the sense that a precapitalist society dominated by a yeoman ideal is innocent of the vast disparities in power, as well as in wealth and status, that accompany an age of exploitation. A new analysis finds Jacksonian spokesmen preoccupied with the present. Convinced that they had achieved the essential qualitative dimensions of freedom in their own time, they ostensibly sought to expand liberty by expanding the territory of the nation. To the Whigs, who "had a far more positive appreciation of the qualitative dimensions of time, . . . qualitative change through time rather than quantitative growth across space marked the true destiny" of the nation. If none of these interpretations is altogether convincing, they represent praiseworthy attempts to try to approach the Jacksonian era in new terms.

In consequence of the tireless propaganda of both major parties, it seems to me that the word "Democratic" came to take on an aura of humanity and even frailty, akin to what some Byzantologists seem ready to ascribe to the "Greens" as against the "Blues" in the party warfare of that ancient metropolis, Byzantium. (The former color is indubitably *warmer* than the latter, modified as it is by the yellow of the sun.) Democratic parties, in tying their fate to Andrew Jackson, found it necessary to explain away the violence and the contempt for law displayed by the Hero in his earlier career. They capitalized most astutely on the antiaristocratic implications in their leader's traits. Demagogic references to Providential preference for Old Hickory and common people, succeeded beyond the expectations of party managers in drawing the latter to the former. Jackson's elemental nature was opposed to the artifice and intellectualism of his enemies: the learned George Bancroft was there to demonstrate that the people's untrained instinct was a surer judge than any other, in politics as in all other spheres.

It is likely that continued investigation by imaginative scholars will disclose still further—if subtle—distinctions between the parties and their adherents. These variations in nuances, however, should not blind students to the very large areas of agreement and the fundamental similarities of the Democratic and Whig parties. For all their unique styles of operation, they were alike great vote-getting machines, "primarily concerned," according to the political scientist E. Pendleton Herring, "not with framing issues and drawing up distinctive programs, but in trying to discover some way of bringing together . . . as large a proportion of the voters as possible."

12

THE IDEOLOGICAL PARTIES OF
THE JACKSONIAN ERA:
THE MINOR PARTIES
REVISITED

A number of "third parties" flourished during the Jacksonian era. They are significant both for their impact on American political life and as an indication that the major parties were too opportunistic for the tens of thousands of Americans who participated in these dissident movements. For unlike the pragmatic Jacksonian and Whig coalitions, each of the important minority parties came into being to dramatize either a single issue or the interests of a particular group or class in American society. It is tempting to generalize about all of these parties as a whole; to note, for example, the enthusiasm of their organizers or that whatever success they achieved usually came early, at their inception, as thereafter their programs were absorbed by the major blocs and their councils infiltrated by designing schemers. Or to make the obvious point that their characteristically short life and small electoral success illustrate the aversion of the typical voter to ideological parties on the European model. For all the sameness in their histories, however, these parties for the most part were utterly dissimilar. To be understood they must be dealt with singly.

The most fascinating as well as the most influential of the offbeat political movements was the Antimasonic party. Starting in 1826 in the western counties of New York State—previously known as the "infected district" or, as Charles G. Finney called it, the "burned-over district"—antimasonry spread like wildfire throughout New England and across the northern middle states into Ohio and Michigan, quickly achieving in some places an amazing political success that startled even its own organizers. The movement maintained a position of political influence for the better part of a decade. Such master figures as Thaddeus Stevens, Thurlow Weed, William H. Seward, Horace Greeley, and Millard Fillmore first learned the art of politics in this strange movement which blended religious zeal, hatred of aristocracy, and, above all, fear of the secret order of Freemasonry. According to its first historian, the antimasonic movement "furnished the first solid basis for the Whig movement of the future."

Antimasonry antedated the election of Andrew Jackson, in this country going back at least to the 1790s when some New England enemies of the Masons charged that its members had conspired to spread the terrorism, anarchy, and atheism attributed to the French Revolution. Suspicion of Freemasonry was evidently based not only on the pledge to secrecy exacted of members in the order, but on a belief that they were an aristocratic lot who threatened to control all society by their power to reward one another. The suspicion had some basis in fact. In Vermont, "Masonry exerted a strong appeal to men high in the affairs of the state." The lists of lodge members in that state "resembled a roll call of the Legislature and the Bar." But after the "antimasonic madness" had broken out, the fact that the signers to a petition defending the order were men of place does not substantiate the frequency broached charge that "Masonry composed an aristocratic body in a political democracy." Aristocracy even in a broad sense is not evidenced by the mere existence of an organized group of wealthy or successful men. For if it were, then every major party committee, not to mention the Congress of the United States, was an aristocratic body. In Massachusetts too, when Masons felt compelled, prior to the election of 1832, to proclaim that "they were under no obligations to Masonry at variance with morality and loyalty to their citizenship," the signers of the statement included such successful men as Henshaw, A. Peabody, and J. T. Buckingham. Their conflicting political backgrounds gave credence to their statement "that Masonry did not hinder freedom of religious belief or political preference."

The Masons of western New York State are of particular interest in view of the fact that the antimasonic movement was born in the region. Members of Masonic lodges in Warsaw and Batavia were inordinately active in political, professional, and voluntary associational affairs, holding offices "out of all proportion to their numbers." Of course, this influence may have been due as much, if not more, to their personal statuses as to their Masonry. For in Genessee County, more than 90 percent of whose residents were small farmers, close to 90 percent of the Masonic brothers "were engaged in non-farm occupations such as merchandising, tavern keeping, manufacturing, law, and medicine." Although they were not among the richest men, at least not in Batavia, Masons were disproportionately present in the most socially prestigious Episcopalian church. To judge from the bylaws of the western New York Masons, they sought to proscribe "indecent or improper conduct, malice, slander, and intoxication" among their members. "Masonic morality," according to Kutolowski, emphasized such Christian virtues as "temperance, industry, harmony, patience, meekness, and obedience to civil and religious authority." In view of the social calibre of the men Masonry's high status enabled it to attract, there appeared to be no problem in their conforming to the injunction that they should "earn enough for works as charity as well as for their families." If one can believe the public statement of Masonry's Grand Master in Vermont, the order's purpose was the "great work of reforming and happifying [sic] the world," through "enlightening the understanding, cultivating the mental faculties and improving the moral virtues of men, and teaching them their duties and relations to each other, in connection with their religious obligations." Unfortunately for the order, their enemies did not believe them, particularly after the disappearance of William Morgan in western New York.

Morgan's abduction after he was released from a Canandaigua jail on the night of September 12, 1826, "by a person pretending to be his friend," was the spark that lighted what was to become a great conflagration. The fact that Morgan, a stonemason, had announced his intention of publishing a book exposing Masonic secrets and that he had subsequently been hounded and only one day before his disappearance imprisoned on petty charges—trumped up charges! cried the suspicious—when added to his evident kidnapping set in motion a political storm. Before it was spent it would destroy the Masonic order in much of the Northeast, compelling thousands of lodges to give up or their members to quit, and fatefully influence state and national politics. In Vermont and Pennsylvania, the political party organized in the name of the antimasonic cause actually held power for a number of years, while in both Massachusetts and New York it won significant local victories and at times held the balance of power. Antimasonic votes elected the governor in Rhode Island in 1833 and congressmen two years later.

The entire Masonic fraternity was implicated in the Morgan crime, according to a contemporary historian, only because, as the investigation of the foul deed proceeded, "it was found that all those implicated in the transaction were Masons; that with scarce an exception, no Mason aided in the investigation; that the whole crime was made a matter of ridicule by the Masons, and even justified by them openly and publicly; that the power of the laws was defied by them, and committees tainted with their inability to bring the criminals to punishment before tribunals, whose judges, sheriffs, jurors, and witnesses were Masons; that witnesses were mysteriously spirited away, and the committees themselves personally vilified and abused for acts which deserved commendation, the impression spread and seized a strong hold upon the popular judgment, that the Masonic fraternity was in fact responsible for the crime." By this less than detached and undocumented rendering, not only was the antimasonic fury *caused* by Masonic duplicity in the wake of the Morgan affair but it was a justifiable response.

Recent work by Formisano and Kutalowski on the origins of the antimasonic movement in western New York State, which argues convincingly that the investigation of Morgan's disappearance was in fact glaringly obstructed by partisans of the secret fraternity and was so perceived even by moderate Masons themselves as well as by many detached observers, has led me to retreat from the view expressed in the original edition that antimasonry was a "movement conceived in hysteria" and that a conspiracy to prevent the solution of the Morgan mystery was "alleged only by antimasonic partisans." While the sincerity of many of the earliest antimasonic zealots appears to be beyond question, the fact remains that an actual Masonic *conspiracy*, whether to cover up the Morgan abduction or to control the state and society, was not proven. Antimasons may well have believed that in denouncing Masonry they were protecting a Republicanism "threatened by a secret society's ability to cover up dark deeds and thwart justice," yet in subsequently demanding the wiping out of an organization they detested and in justifying its destruction on the ground that the people insisted on it, antimasons, even if unwittingly, manifested their contempt for the Constitution they were allegedly defending from its aristocratic enemies. That some antimasons were unaware of the inconsistency, or others kept quiet about it, is understandable: the former were fanatics, the latter opportunists.

Antimasonry sprang into existence as a political movement in the year following Morgan's disapearance, first, among the hill folk who lived south of Rochester, along the Genesee River. Zealots took the "blessed spirit" into other sections of the state, over most of New England, southern New Jersey, western Pennsylvania, and northeastern Ohio. It thrived first of all among farm folk. Masonic lodges were generally found in the towns. The movement to destroy them, at least in New York, has been described as "an early evidence of rural jealousy towards urban superiority, or at least towards the controlling middle class of the larger villages and country towns. Clearly . . . it had an agrarian cast in that it aligned leaseholders and renters against the resident agents of absentee landlords." While New York City's antimasons claimed that "the sturdy yeoman, the vigorous mechanic, the honest countryman," were the backbone of the movement, in fact the city's antimasonic ranks "were filled by people from all classes." In Massachusetts its strength was "among the ultra-religious country folk who were already antagonistic toward the urban classes." In Pennsylvania, "antimasonry was . . . allied with hatred of Philadelphia." The Address to the People put out by the powerful Antimasonic party of that state during the gubernatorial election of 1829 frankly proclaimed that "the country has generally looked upon the city as overweening, arrogant, and dictatorial." Their candidate for governor, Joseph Ritner, was a champion of the West. In Vermont, where the movement won its greatest successes, it also "waxed strong in country districts . . . and proved relatively weak in the cities, where a more sophisticated, less emotional attitude prevailed."

The antimasonic movement was largely a rural phenomenon but of a special sort. It appears to have flourished "everywhere that the New England conscience was present to receive it," not in all country districts but those "where the revivalists had won so many converts," or where "the evangelistic churches . . . held more complete sway" than elsewhere. It seemed to appeal more to the supercharged emotional and evangelical sects than to any other. In Vermont "the Methodists were less receptive to anti-masonry than their evangelical Baptist brethren." Sects "which had arisen as a protest against hyper-Calvinism embraced anti-masonry and incorporated it into their creeds."

Interesting questions have recently been raised about the antimasons of New York State's "burned-over" district. An earlier surmise had found antimasonry's appeal greatest among farm people whose "most striking attribute" was "moral intensity;" to whom "emotional religion was (hyperbolically) a congenital characteristic, present at birth." Kathleen Kutolowski's recent quantitative investigation of Genessee County's antimasons casts doubt on the thesis that they were "rural evangelicals who rose up against an urban elite." Antimasonic leaders there were "village attorneys and non-evangelicals," most of them Episcopalians, the others Congregationalists and Presbyterians. Including in their hierarchy former Bucktails as well as Clintonians, antimasonic leaders "interacted" closely with the mercantile leadership of the Democracy that they supposedly detested.

The "conscience" of the early antimasons may have been a more revealing characteristic than their denominational affiliations. Antimasons were characteristically do-gooders, if of a peculiar cast. They were ardent temperance men, bitter toward Masons in part because of the "rumored alcoholic excess" in the ceremonies of the latter. Vermont was not unique in the fact that "many of . . . the leaders and practically all of the newspapers championing antimasonry soon engaged in denouncing another venerable institution which denied the equal rights of man—American Negro slavery." The youthful William Lloyd Garrison really began his public career as an antimasonic journalist, in 1829 writing that once the sons of Vermont see "the path open before them, and duty bids them onward, they move with the rapidity of light." Antimasonry also contained a strong ingredient of democratic and egalitarian feeling. As has been noted, its rural constituency hated the city for its wealth and power as well as for its alleged immorality. In Pennsylvania, "the democratic Scotch-Irish and the independent farmers and mechanics who considered one man as good as his neighbor discovered that in the Masonic Order the abstract idea of aristocracy took a peculiarly tangible form." New York's Protestants resented a

Masonic movement which among other things had five times as many ministers as laymen in it. The Masonic Order was regarded as the secretive agency through which the rich and the powerful conspired against the people. The antimasonic movement was motivated not only by democratic social and political objectives but by ethical ones. The major issue seemed to be one of morality. Masons were "believed to have committed a crime"—namely of putting their secret vows "ahead of their duty to state and society"—as well as other primarily moral offenses.

The Antimasonic *party* that played so decisive a role in northeastern politics had little to do either with attacking Masonry or with the religious and moral characteristics of the rural Protestants who predominated in its original rank and file. Having a substantial base of numerous and dedicated persons, the party quickly attracted ambitious men much more interested in achieving personal political success than the victory of antimasonic principles. Like a Roman cynic who had said to the Church, "make me bishop of Rome and I will become a Christian," William Wirt, the Antimasonic Presidential candidate chosen in 1831, had himself been a Mason and was a critic of the new movement right up to the time it tendered him the nomination. He converted to the new party at the 11th hour. His letter of acceptance made clear he had not forsaken his earlier criticisms of the handling of the Morgan affair nor would he participate in attacks on Freemasonry. Uninterested in their doctrinal positions, he "appeared enraptured by their opposition to the Jacksonians." The young Seward also aligned with the party for its anti-Jacksonianism. Other opportunistic men, eager to do battle with the Jacksonians for the rewards of office, and having few compunctions about the tactics or the human material they would use, had little difficulty in assuming positions of leadership in the new movement. The early career of Thurlow Weed appears to fit this description. Weed was by no means devoid of principle. He shared a number of the feelings of the antimasonic farmers. But above all he was a politician, a master manipulator, a typical pragmatist of the era. Apprised shortly after the disappearance of Morgan that a body had been found, Weed was rumored to have said, "It is a good enough Morgan until after the election." Principles were subordinate to expediency in the operational ethics of this antimasonic editor, later chief Whig organizer in New York State, and gray eminence of that party on the national level.

It was not true in every state but as a general rule political antimasonry was anti-Jacksonian by the election of 1828, remaining that way until its demise or absorption into the Whig party after 1834. The antipathy was probably not due to the fact that Jackson was a Mason. Andrew Jackson *was* a Mason—but so was Henry Clay. Of course the national party—which was little more than the 1831 convention—would not back Clay, although Wirt's background and views were similar to Clay's. In Michigan the Jacksonian leader, Lewis Cass, was a Grand Master of the Masonic

Lodge. In western New York where the movement started, the hated landlords were generally Regency men. Since Van Buren's party turned Jacksonian, as did the maligned Tammany machine in New York City, what alternative was left the sincere antimason but to oppose Andrew Jackson's party nationally as he fought its representatives on the state level? The sincere antimason, emotional firebrand though he may have been, was not altogether innocent of considerations of self-interest. Pennsylvania antimasons liked Ritner—a "political antimason"—for governor because he was a champion of the wool growers and a high tariff, as well as of the abstractions they fancied. Jackson's shilly-shallying on the tariff issue left them cold. Similarly Vermont, antimasonry's most successful political base, was a "wool-growing region which depended on sound currency, good transportation and a high protective tariff for its economic welfare," programs which inevitably made it difficult if not impossible for the Democrats to have much success with the new faith. Once the new party's national sympathies—or antipathies—became clear, the Albany *Argus* had no trouble in identifying the new movement: it was made up, oddly enough, of "Federalists."

The swallowing up of most of the Antimasonic party by the Whig was no accidental act. On the pragmatic level it was explained by their joint desire to replace Jacksonians in positions of power. On the level of principle both groups favored a basically similar set of economic policies for national government and they also had somewhat similar feelings about such issues as slavery, excessive use of liquor, traditional morality. On the level of state politics, the Antimasonic party very early went the way of the Jacksonians and devoted itself to no loftier objective than securing office, all the while, to be sure, proclaiming its undying devotion to the ideals of equality and opposition to aristocracy. It is not clear why professions of love for the "sovereign people" are any the less "claptrap" when uttered by antimasons than when spoken by Democrats.

With Freemasonry on the run, if not altogether routed, the new party if it were to remain alive had to broaden its program and appeals. Its leaders never had any intention of giving up merely because its ostensible purpose was achieved. In addition to the American System, they came out for such reforms as abolition of imprisonment for debt, repeal of the inequitable militia system, and other issues that were high on the list of reformers in all parties. Astute men, they made alliances with other opponents of the Democracy and when, as in New York in 1830, they made common cause with one faction of the youthful Working Men's party of that state, they sought to make political capital of the latter party's comprehensive reform program. An alliance with a dubious group of alleged "Workingmen," who as a matter of fact had been charged with insincerity by the zealots whose platform they mouthed, no more made radicals of New York's Antimasons, however, than it did six years later of Whigs who coalesced with Locofocos. There is much to recommend the judgment that "the original emphasis of the western New Yorkers," if it never entirely disappeared, was "eclipsed" after 1834 by the more practical platform of the Whig party.

In Pennsylvania many Masons jumped on the bandwagon of the new party as its success spread! In the Keystone State, according to Philip S. Klein, antimasonry was based on "a solid nucleus of conscientious voters whose personal religious scruples guaranteed their allegiance. This nucleus came under the leadership of stranded politicians who used it and built it up for purposes quite outside the object of crushing the Masonic Order in America." Those purposes were eminently practical. On the other hand Thaddeus Stevens, the dominant figure in Pennsylvania antimasonry was no expedient antimason. In 1831 he scourged the secret order mercilessly as a "prostituted harlot," led by a "feeble band of lowly reptiles" who drank wine out of human skulls and conspired among themselves to keep secret the treason and murders they committed. This was characteristic Stevens' style although he may have been more overwrought than usual in view of the Masonic response to his own charges that they had murdered and drowned Morgan. They retorted by insinuating that Stevens had murdered a Negro woman he had made pregnant.

In 1835 and 1836, long after the frenzy had gone out of political antimasonry and indeed after even the more political form of the movement was dormant elsewhere, Stevens was still flaying the hated order in the Pennsylvania state legislature, subpoenaing Masonic leaders to testify on his bill to suppress secret societies. The eminent former Masonic Grand Master, George M. Dallas, refused to betray the secrets of the order, asserting that the investigation was "utterly inconsistent" with the Constitution. "I can not, without a sense of treachery and degradation which would embitter all my future life, prove false to my promise," he eloquently continued. "Better by far endure the penalties of alleged contumacy, be they what they may." Stevens and company purported to interpret the defiance of the committee by Dallas and other Freemasons of "considerable public stature" as "incontrovertible evidence of their awesome secret power." The "Buckshot War" in 1838 in a sense punctuated the career of Pennsylvania antimasonry but that fiasco had much more to do with Thaddeus Stevens' political ambition and the bitter opposition it evoked than with antimasonic or any other principles.

Massachusetts politics were very much complicated by the antimasons' policies and strategy. The new party there was riddled with inconsistencies in program and tactics. Emerging as an influential force just about the time when Henshaw and Morton had managed to unite the supporters of Jackson into one party, the new cause "attracted many of the more radical spirits away from the cause of [the] Democracy." A convention held prior to the 1832 election was dominated by anti-Clay "Old Democrats," despite the new party leader's strong support of Old Kentucky. Their Boston leader, Benjamin F. Hallett, was a radical of sorts who after the birth of the Whig party "tried to carry antimasons with him into the Democratic party"—the Henshaw clique—"to oppose the 'money power.'" The fact was that Hallett's own newspaper, the *Advocate*, "was financed by antimasons, some of whom also happened to be bankers." When a Boston trades' union was created in 1834 this inveterate enemy of "secret societies" managed to attack it mercilessly on the grounds that like Freemasonry it was a secret and privileged organization that threatened freedom and practiced unusual cruelties on its members!

Vermont's Antimasonic party won the governor's office for four consecutive terms, commencing with 1831. Apart from his "recommendation of the abolition of extra-judicial oaths" and his plea for appointments of officials "who were unshackled by an earthly allegiance," Governor William A. Palmer urged no measures which could not be found in the National Republican platform. In view of their program for 1832 one can better appreciate the chagrin of Clay's partisans at the Antimasonic snubbing of their idol. By 1836, although the party held its own convention, it approved a slate of officers identical with that of the Whigs and thereafter disappeared as a separate entity. The membership went into both major parties, although the majority followed their leaders into the Whig party. In Rhode Island antimasons cooperated with Democrats for partisan purposes.

Political antimasonry in New Jersey in the late 1820s and early 1830s has been judged "futile because of the state's early formation of balanced parties." It flourished for a while in Morris and Essex counties ostensibly because of "opportune party situations" there—the split of the Adamsites and the "anemic nature of the Jacksonians." In other states too historians have related the strength of the Antimasonic party to the weakness or the splintering of the major parties.

As has been the fate of most minor parties in American history, the Antimasonic party for all its dynamism had a relatively short life. Yet in a sense it is amazing that a party ostensibly of such single purpose could last as long as it did. But of course it was antimasonic in name only. Starting as a coalition of the religiously zealous and socially discontent, it was quickly taken over by men who knew the game of politics. The original constituency, given the power of their emotions, compelled the new leaders to keep the party's program within certain circumscribed limits. Since the party's new leaders were never themselves zealots, they had no difficulty in aligning themselves when the time was ripe with a more powerful because less dedicated political movement. Even then, principles were not entirely forsaken, however, since antimasonry was for the most part absorbed by the party dedicated to the defeat of that King of Masonry, Andrew Jackson, as to the overthrow of his negative economic program.

Another new party that emerged shortly after the appearance of the antimasons was the Working Men's party. The closest thing to a classic ideological party in the entire antebellum period, the Working Men burst forth like a political meteor only to fall to earth in the space of a few years. Following the creation of the Philadelphia Working Men's party in 1828, groups sprang up all over the country. The modern discussion, focusing as it does on a few major cities, has perhaps obscured what Helen Sumner, one of the pioneer labor researchers working with John R. Commons, long ago discovered: the ubiquitousness of the movement. In fact recent investigations show it to have been even more widespread than Miss Sumner imagined. Operating under a variety of names, "Working Men's Parties," "Working Men's Republican Associations," "People's Parties," "Working Men's Societies," "Farmers' and Mechanics' Societies," "Mechanics and Other Working Men," and just plain "Working Men" appeared in most of the states of the Union. Critics had other names for them, including "mob rabble," "Dirty Shirt Party," "Tag, Rag, and Bobtail," and "Levelers." The new organizations took shape in such communities as Carlisle, Pennsylvania; Glens Falls, New York; Caldwell, New Jersey; Zanesville, Ohio; Dedham, Massachusetts; Lyme, Connecticut; and Calais, Vermont; as well as in such centers as New York City, St. Louis, Boston, Newark, and Philadelphia.

Many questions have been raised about the Working Men's party, the most important having to do with its authenticity. "Decayed Federal dandies!" not true workingmen, charged a New England journal, while at other times proto-Whig editors bitterly stamped the new organizations a mere front for the Democracy. Modern scholars have been skeptical and with good reason. For as one of them wrote, after noting the great wealth of the Philadelphia Working Men's candidates for office, "to believe that [such] a party . . . was really devoted to solving working class problems in the interests of the workers would seem to lay a heavy tax on credulity." And yet the record is clear: the Philadelphia Working Men's Party was no misnomer.

The party arose out of a decision by the city's Mechanics' Union of Trade Associations to enter into politics, in order to promote "the interests and enlightenment of the working classes." There can be no question of the authenticity of this latter group, "the first union of all the organized workmen of any city." Consisting of individual unions—or societies as they were than called—of journeymen bricklayers, painters, glaziers, typographers, house carpenters, and other craftsmen, its main purpose was to provide financial support to journeymen striking against their masters. An amendment to this Mechanics' Union's constitution, in 1828, provided that three months prior to the forthcoming elections, the membership should "nominate as candidates for public office such individuals as shall pledge themselves . . . to support and advance . . . the interests and enlightenment of the working classes." Shortly thereafter the *Mechanic's Free Press*, edited by a young Ricardian socialist, William Heighton, reported that "at a very large and respectable meeting of Journeymen House Carpenters held on Tuesday evening, July 1st . . . the Mechanics' Union of Trade Associations is entering into measures for procuring a nomination of candidates for legislative and other public offices, who will support the interest of the working classes." Thus was born the Philadelphia Working Men's party, in the promise made by journeymen workers to support at the polls individuals sympathetic to—not necessarily members of—the working class.

New York City's Working Men made their appearance in 1829 when their candidates for the State Assembly made a remarkable showing. Some contemporaries and later scholars alike explained this new party as nothing more than anti-Tammany dissidents, born out of "the bitter internal dissensions and schisms that were wrecking the Republican party of New York." The fact remains that the decision to run candidates on a separate Working Men's ticket was made at a meeting of mechanics on October 19, 1829, in agreement with the proposal by the executive body—the "Committee of Fifty." A number of journeymen's meetings held in April had created this Committee. Its purpose was to combat "all attempts to compel journeymen mechanics to work more than ten hours a day." It would seem that at least in its origins the New York Working Men's party was indubitably a response of workers to a threatened attack on their working conditions.

For Boston the evidence is not clear, for all the press unhappiness with the new party or the impressionistic recording by a journalist present at early meetings of the Working Men's party in the summer of 1830. He wrote that they were attended by large numbers of men who, "from appearance, were warm from their workshops and from other places of daily toil, but who bore on their countenances convictions of their wrongs, and a determination to use every proper means to have them redressed." Two years later New England workingmen and their friends formed the New England Association of Farmers, Mechanics, and Other Working Men, described as a "new type of labor organization, in part economic and in part political." This interesting organization was preoccupied with trying to achieve for New England's workers what remained a will-o'-the-wisp for most of the era—the ten hour day. Its failures do not detract from its authenticity.

Logic as well as the historical record suggest the essential validity and independence from other political groupings of the Working Men's party—at least at its birth. The new party was a form of rejection by its members of both the Jacksonians and their major opponents. The Working Men stood for programs and called for changes in American society not dreamed of by the pragmatists at the helm of the major parties. And in view of the relatively small followings of the new organizations for all their idealism—or was it because of it?—it strains credulity to attribute to shrewd Jacksonian manipulators the formation of ostensibly single-class political organizations that exasperated both the business community and those many Americans of whatever class who under no circumstances wished to think of themselves as workers.

Much of the problem concerning the wealth of the new party's leaders arises from a confusion of terms. For example, it has been found that only 10 of 100 of the Philadelphia Party's candidates were workingmen. But of course the party's interest was not in the wealth but in the attitudes of its candidates toward education and the other issues that concerned them. The backgrounds of the men who actually *ran* the Philadelphia Working Men reveal that better than 75 percent were workers or artisans. Noting that Boston's Working Men also nominated primarily wealthy candidates—40 of the party's 68 nominees belonged to the wealthiest segment of the community (the top 2 percent in value of property owned)—as recently as 1963 I wrote that I am "now not so sure of what I wrote [in 1949] . . . , that these figures 'do not imply anything fraudulent': . . . doubts as to the actual nature of the party are indeed raised by such figures," I concluded. My own doubts about the Boston group are allayed by the realization that the wealth in question belonged not to the party's leaders but to its *candidates*. In New York on the other hand, 10 of the 11 candidates who made the strong electoral showing of 1829 were journeymen as were the great majority of the general executive committee. Most of the committee's members belonged to the "laboring element in the community." The early New York party had an unusually uncompromising attitude, since one of its leaders, George Henry Evans, tried to restrict leadership to journeymen mechanics. His lack of success was one of the factors that drove the zealous Thomas Skidmore out of the party, convinced that it was being taken over by rich men. When Skidmore first made that charge even Evans joined the scoffers. But subsequently Evans agreed with the firebrand.

The parties' leaders are best studied not for their social and economic backgrounds, which were in fact diverse, but for their ideas and personal force, which actually accounted for their leadership. Unlike their contemporaries in the major parties these men were indeed radicals, certainly for this phase of their careers. There was nothing politic in adhering to essentially socialistic doctrines that most of the press savagely denounced. Beliefs such as theirs, going beyond the patent demagogy of the day, could find no expression in the programs of the era's major parties. As to the party's rank and file constituency, apart from the sparkling successes achieved in Philadelphia and New York in 1829, it does not seem ever to have been very great. On the other hand, particularly in the latter city but in Boston, too, what electoral support it got did come primarily from poorer or working-class wards. In New York City its candidates got close to 50 percent of the vote of the five poorest wards while averaging only about 20 percent in the wealthier districts.

Their program was amazingly similar, with substantially the same measures advocated in most of the western and southern cities that were advocated in Philadelphia and New York. The original Philadelphia demands became the nucleus of the Working Men's program everywhere. They called above all for free, tax-supported school system of high quality to replace the stigmatized "pauper schools." Stephen Simpson, brilliant and unreliable one-time Jacksonian, was nominated to office by the Philadelphia Working Men and became a leading figure in the movement mainly because of his advanced educational ideas. In addition, the masthead of the *Mechanic's Free Press* urged abolition of imprisonment for debt; abolition of all licensed monopolies; an entire revision or abolition of the prevailing militia system; a less expensive legal system; equal taxation on property; no legislation on religion; and a district system of elections. The paper's columns also pressed vigorously for a mechanics' lien law to assure workers first claim to their employers' payroll, shorter hours, better working conditions, and constantly urged improved housing for workers. The major parties were regularly denounced as were city fathers who administered the city by a double standard, failing either to provide sufficient "hydrant water for the accommodation of the poor" or "to clean the streets in the remote sections of the city where the workingmen reside." Political action was not considered at odds with economic, by the Working Men's leaders, for they strongly favored creation of unions. Nor does this exhaust the list even of the Philadelphia issues.

The movements in other cities added dozens of other grievances. The New York party went so far as to call for "equal property to all adults" in its early stages when the radical Thomas Skidmore was its leading figure. When he was cashiered out of the party at the end of its first year by the opportunists who had infiltrated it, with the acquiescence of the more innocent Robert Dale Owen and George Henry Evans, even the latter continued to insist, in the party's official organ, that it continued to stand for Skidmore's principles; it had only modified its tactics for achieving them. The Owen-Evans faction of the party stressed the need for a revamped educational system featured by "state guardianship" or the boarding out of working-class children in publicly-supported schools. Regional variations might call for a reform in land tenure laws or, as in the case of the New England Association, insistence on factory legislation. Abolition of capital punishment and prison reform were popular demands everywhere. In sum, Working Men's parties were champions of a great variety of political, social, economic, and educational reforms. That much of the program was not of a "bread and butter" character or that the victims of some grievances were not confined to the "laboring poor" are not valid grounds for skepticism. For it would be a most doctrinaire economic determinism indeed that insisted that authentic labor organizations confine their programs to economic issues. In that era when the diverse and youthful American labor movement was very much influenced by the radical English model, and when American workmen were as much concerned with enhanced status and educational opportunity as with material gains, organizations speaking for labor quite naturally reflected this breadth of interest. Short-term, pitifully organized affairs for the most part, a major function of the new organizations was not to win elections so much as to call attention to the gamut of abuses bearing most heavily on the nation's working people.

The Working Men were essentially independent of the major parties although from time to time they cooperated with them. Certainly in choosing candidates they paid little attention to the previous political preferences of a nominee who was sound on an important Working Men's principle. At times, particularly during the Bank War, they cooperated closely with the Jacksonians. Stephen Simpson's refusal to issue a blanket condemnation of the "monster bank" infuriated many of his one-time admirers. The regular support given the Democracy by the Newark Working Men, their tendency, if not to hold joint nominating conventions, then to hold them on the same date and in the same town, and to approve closely similar lists of candidates, did not fail to draw the condemnation of the anti-Jacksonian press.

The New York City party broke into three pieces shortly after its 1829 success, the largest splinter supporting and subsequently being absorbed into the New York State Democratic party. New England's Working Men in 1833 threw their support in the gubernatorial campaign to Samuel Clesson Allen, champion of Andrew Jackson and enemy to Nicholas Biddle. Evidence of Working Men's collaboration with anti-Jacksonians however, as in Philadelphia, is as easily come by. When the New England Association again nominated Allen in 1834 it condemned the candidates of both major parties. Working Men of most New Jersey towns and cities typically had as little to do with Democrats as with their opponents, while even in Newark the romance was not a lasting one. It was punctuated finally by a falling out in 1836. The Working Men's party of Maryland rose in 1833 out of the defection of "blue-collar Jacksonians." Most of the Working Men's leaders even when cooperating with the Democrats on a particular issue, never ceased warning that the Jackson party was no different from the Clay, no more concerned with the real problems of working people.

Future studies of the Working Men's party are likely only to accentuate what previous work has disclosed: how hard it is to generalize about the movement as a whole. For as I have elsewhere noted, "there were Working Men and Working Men. The origin of some was obscure; of others, dubious. Some arose out of economic struggles, others out of concern for status. Some came to be dominated by opportunists, others by zealots." The significant common feature of the movement as a whole was its authenticity—at least for part of its history. I regard it authentic because the parties seem to have been formed by workers and men devoted to their interests, and concerned themselves with the cause and welfare of workers, hoping to goad or influence the major parties into like concern. Of course the parties contained many men who by present standards would not qualify as workers. The definition of that day was less restrictive. George Henry Evans for example seemed to regard only "lawyers, bankers, and brokers as disqualified for membership." The equally radical William Heighton advised his Philadelphia party that "an employer [who] superintends his business" but "works with his own hands is a workingman." A movement in need of all the membership it could get would not permit a Skidmore to narrow down further its small chances for growth by establishing uncompromising standards for participation. The typical resolution of this problem was to ask few questions about the social position of any individual who in Heighton's words, was "willing to join us in obtaining our objects." But of course such an approach created additional problems.

In New York City, for example, by 1830 elements which not only were not themselves of the working class but which had little sympathy with its aspirations succeeded in taking over the party by the use of money, intrigue, and extralegal tactics that denied the floor to opposition, all the while paying lip service to the party program. There was nothing to prevent special pleaders from calling meetings designed to further their objects while masquerading under the banner of the new party. Much of the nation's press, Democratic and National Republican alike, nevertheless persisted in taking a dim view of a party whose own press constantly reminded its readers that this was a class society. "The very pretension to the necessity of such a party is a libel on the community," protested the editors of the Boston *Courier*. Shortly afterwards Edward Everett pressed home the point that rich and poor alike, all are workingmen. What need was there for a separate Working Men's party? Parties nevertheless insisted on forming, in the City of Brotherly Love obtaining the ballance of power by their second electoral try, in New York winning better than 6,000 out of 21,000 votes cast in their initial effort. And yet their success was decidedly ephemeral.

Most of the Working Men's parties disappeared within five years of their birth. Among the many factors responsible for their downfall, newspaper denunciation, internal dissensions in some cases introduced by infiltrators intent on taking over the party, doctrinal squabbles by party zealots, the hostility of the major parties, the increasing prosperity which, according to Miss Sumner, turned the attention of workers from "politics to trade unionism," the inexperience of their leadership, and not least the absorption of some of their program by the major parties, all played their part. Parties which sharply delineated the social and economic cleavages and disparities besetting American society on the one hand were offensive to those Americans used to more cheerful assessment, and on the other were inevitably attacked by men, newspapers, and political parties possessed of far more money, experience, and influence. And a political system which rewarded only winners of majorities or pluralities was not conducive to the perpetuation of such a movement.

The Working Men's parties were an interesting phenomenon, playing an important part in the achievement of a number of the era's reforms. Particularly outstanding was their contribution to the movement for a democratic and public educational system. They agitated not only for broadened opportunities for the poor but for surprisingly sophisticated modifications in curriculum and teacher training. A final significance of the movement was its indirect testimony that even in the age of optimism, speculation, and major party demagogy, a small number of Americans were disenchanted with their society and responsive to the voice of radical dissent.

To all practical purposes the New York Working Men disappeared as a separate political entity after 1832 even though the indefatigable George Henry Evans and his *Working Man's Advocate* went on. But in the fall of 1835, or more precisely on the evening of October 29, 1835, a spiritual descendant of sorts was born amidst the glow of tallow candles lighted up by the matches— loco focos, they were called—used by antimonopoly Democrats who stayed on at a Tammany meeting that evening, after the old guard declared the meeting adjourned. The Locofoco party was thus at birth a movement of dissidents from Tammany.

Drawing their inspiration from William Leggett, editor of the New York *Evening Post,* the Locofocos were the enemies to banks, paper money, and the "monopolies" conferred by state legislatures on favored entrepreneurs. They regarded both the Tammany-dominated Democracy of New York City and the Regency as a "monopoly aristocratic" party, although they went to some pains to avoid criticizing the Jackson Administration. The dominant conservative wing of the Jacksonian party had for some time prior to the actual split made clear its suspicion of the "Utopian" dissidents. Bitterness had been generated over the attack led by Leggett and George Henry Evans on the "ferry monopoly" that was protected by Tammany, and above all over Leggett's criticism of the Democratic policy of denying the free use of the mails to abolitionist literature. Leggett was no abolitionist and most of his antimonopoly supporters were even less so, but the administration actions both in the capital and in New York were too much for him to swallow. The regular party press accused him of encouraging abolitionism and in effect read him out of the party. Although in a sense the abolitionist literature issue was thus the last straw that finally led to an open rupture, the original resolutions passed by the rebels show that other things were on their mind.

In addition to their opposition to special bank charters granted by states, the Locofocos opposed any circulating medium but gold and silver, the Bank of the United States, monopolies, laws infringing the "equal rights and privileges of the great body of the people," and they recommended that "all distinctions but those of merit" be *discouraged.* They came out in favor of rotation in office, direct election of the President and Vice President, deference by elected officials to the views of their constituents, the present administration, and the Presidential nominations made by the National Convention.

This was hardly firebrand. The wealthy private banker Isaac Bronson admired Leggett for his free banking as well as his free trade principles. Yet, almost immediately the Democratic party press denounced the antimonopolists as "Carbonari," "infidels," "Fanny Wright men," "nasty brawlers," "scum of politics," "agrarians," and of course the "Locofoco party." When Fitzwilliam Byrdsall, the first secretary of the group, published his short history of the Loco Foco party in 1842, he wrote, "how dim-sighted were the Albany *Argus*, the Richmond *Enquirer*, the Washington *Globe*, and the other Democratic Republican editors, that they could not foresee that all the charges of 'agrarian spirit,' 'Jack Cadeism,' destructiveness, and so on, which they invented and so liberally applied to the Equal Rights Democracy, would come home to themselves with accumulated interest in future years!" Byrdsall himself could not foresee the extent to which the "monopoly Democracy" would win an undeserved radical reputation from such charges.

Before a year had passed the more militant members of the new group had declared themselves the Equal Rights Party. The new organization did not even claim to be a separate party. Since many of the original Locofocos refused to separate from the mother party, those who felt Tammany was beyond repair four months later proclaimed the party of Equal Rights. And yet even as they did, their Declaration of Principles stated: "we utterly disclaim any intention of instituting any new party, but declare ourselves the original Democratic party, our whole object being political reformation by reviving the landmarks and principles of Democracy." It is no wonder that the new movement confused many observers in its own and later times. It made poor electoral showings and gave up the ghost in two years, when most of its members crawled back to Tammany saying with less than burning conviction that they discerned a great change in the old machine. The principled minority, now scornfully referred to as "the Rump" by their one-time fellow idealists, refused to reunite with a Democratic party whose "vicious system virtually [gave] . . . to a few a despotic and irresponsible power." Despite its brief and unsuccessful hsitory, the new movement gained much notoriety.

"Slamm, Bang, and Company!" they had been dubbed by some opponents, in part because their second secretary was Levi Slamm, militant unionist and aggressive intriguer, and in part because of their allegedly radical views. Yet Carl Degler did not exaggerate when he wrote that "wedded to private property and profits as they were, the Locofocos were no socialistic opponents of capitalism like the Owenites or Brook Farmers." The legend of their radicalism has flourished side by side with its companion notion that after 1837 their strident principles were taken over completely by the Democratic party not only in New York State but in other states, and even on the national level by Martin Van Buren. As economic conditions worsened early in 1837 the poor staged flour riots that were blamed on Locofocos despite the fact that not one member of the faction was among the more than 50 rioters arrested. And as Van Buren sought to maintain his party's popularity with the common man, he had no objection whatever to being "smeared" by Whig critics for an alleged softness toward Locofoco "agrarians" whom less than a year before he had snubbed. His adoption of the Independent Treasury scheme, so in accord with Locofoco antibanking strictures, in Dixon Ryan Fox's memorable phrases "made the Locofocos orthodox," and the Tammany Society and the Regency "were forced to listen to their homilies with at least the affectation of respect."

In 1836, well after the Democratic Party's Bank War had, according to one view, won workers and radicals over to it, the Locofocos delivered a stinging rebuke to Democrats and Whigs alike, charging "the leaders of the two great political parties under which the people have arrayed themselves are selfish and unprincipled . . . ; they are the enemies of the equal rights of the citizens." But the Locofocos, too, it turned out had no permanent friends or enemies, only permanent attachment to their principles.

What these principles were is not clear. According to the most influential national Whig journal, a Locofoco was "a man not satisfied with anything that exists; but is in favor of an equal distribution of property." The *National Intelligencer* may have been overimpressed that the son of Thomas Skidmore's one-time collaborator and publisher was prominent in the group. In any case the characterization remains ridiculous. To judge from the behavior of their elected New York State Assemblymen, their main concern was to curb paper money, credit, and banking. Their principles were deflationary. William G. Sumner admired the Locos' "strict insistence upon fidelity to the principles of laissez-faire." Their own early statements of principles stressed a broad program that does clearly reveal their kinship to the earlier Working Men. Thus they favored an "extended, equal and convenient system" of public education; no restoration of imprisonment for debt; a more effective mechanics' lien law; legal recognition of trade unions; the popular election of judges; and short terms in office; in addition to opposing the circulation of small bank notes under $10 in value, and special acts of incorporation. On the latter issue, of course, their position was similar to that of the Whigs, though it does not thereby follow that theirs was anything more than a marriage of convenience in 1836. Locos were not above tactical cooperation with nativists. Their radical reputation may rest, too, on the fact that some of the highly articulate earlier Working Men's leaders and such unionists as Slamm and John Commerford were active too with the Friends of Equal Rights. But it is necessary to keep in mind that no matter what the private beliefs of some of its leaders may have been, the stated purpose of the Locofocos was to restore the New York Democratic party to an "antimonopoly" position. In actuality, they rejoined Tammany not in triumph, but after a crushing electoral defeat in 1837 forced them to swallow their pride and accept half a loaf.

Their composition is not in question. Their identifiable leaders included artisans and mechanics, primarily, and relatively few lawyers, although the deficiencies of the data do not preclude the possibility "that many leaders counted as artisans and mechanics were actually employers or self-employed." Their leaders "were predominantly small craftsmen, shopowners, and workers, rather than lawyers, manufacturers, and merchants," men whose careers were characterized by a "high incidence of social and occupational mobility." Neither proletarian nor radical was this short-lived movement. It arose as a protest against conservative control of the New York State Democratic party yet paradoxically helped fasten an egalitarian reputation on that party both nationally and in New York, despite the continuation within it of the same leadership that had provoked the Locofoco protest in the first place.

An unlovely but important phenomenon of the decade 1835–45 was the intermittent political success enjoyed by nativism in a number of the nation's cities. The contemporary historian of Locofocoism derided nativism as a movement based on "one *little* idea." This "basic idea," according to an early student of nativism in New York, "was that a person whose primal sympathies or interest lay outside the American body politic could not be in real sympathy with the American system, and must therefore, be a danger to that system." From not in "real sympathy" to "absolute menace" was less than a logical progression but then the "basic idea" of nativism was an emotion only masquerading as a theory. For "when the idea of nativism was applied more specifically it took two chief forms. It declared, first, that any person of foreign birth was unfitted for citizenship [for a long period] . . . and any person in the Roman Catholic church was unfitted for citizenship because obedient to an extraterritorial ruler." In even plainer language, nativism was anti-Irish as well as anti-Catholic. When its leaders spoke of the dangerous immigrant whose strange ways threatened our culture and its institutions, they invariably had Paddy in mind. Nativism was strongest in cities of the seaboard and of the West which were centers of immigration. New York City was the chief center of nativism and "nativism in New York City from first to last was mainly an expression of antagonism toward the clannishness of Irishmen and Irish ways." The alleged "Irish clannishness" cited by nativists was more a rationalization than a real reason. The movement also took political form in such widely separated places as New Orleans, St. Louis, Boston, and Philadelphia, and managed to make some small inroads in the West as well as the seaport towns where it thrived best.

Political nativism came to the surface on two distinct occasions late in the Jacksonian era, first in the mid-1830s, when it won a dramatic but short-lived success, and again in the early 1840s. In 1835 a New York Protestant Association was organized by voters of the 14th ward under the prodding of a series of 12 anonymous letters by "Brutus" that had appeared in the New York *Observer* the previous year. Brutus was in fact Samuel F. B. Morse, Van Buren Democrat, now well launched on his career as man of science and anti-Catholic fanatic. A series of anti-Catholic meetings were followed by violence and when two aging Revolutionary War veterans were fired from their city posts, ostensibly to make way for foreigners, nativists had all the pretext they needed to form the Native American Democratic Association. The new party was organized to deal with a limited number of issues. It was opposed to "pauper and criminal immigration," "office-holding by foreigners," and to the Catholic Church. The party did extremely well in its first electoral effort in 1835, winning more than 8,000 votes for each of its candidates, only 2,000 less than the Democrats got. Morse, who ran for Mayor in 1836, after Philip Hone refused the new party's nomination for the office, did very poorly, capturing only about 7 percent of the vote. In 1837, however, the new party registered a spectacular success when Aaron Clark, its candidate for mayor, was elected. He was swept in with the overwhelming support of Whig voters.

Democrats denounced the alliance. C. C. Cambreleng told Van Buren that he found the spiritual ancestry of nativism in the Federalist party, this new movement, like the old, allegedly dedicated to persecution and intolerance. Actually, according to a modern student of the Native American Democratic Association, Democratic involvement in it was "undoubtedly larger than is generally supposed," even if not as great as Whigs counter-charged it was. Consisting mainly of middle-class persons from the trades, small business, and the professions, this early nativist party had itself split shortly after its emergence. The striking victory of 1837 was due largely to the fact that the dominant faction in the new party was more interested in playing the political game successfully than in harping on anti-Catholic or antiforeign themes.

The great Whig leaders in New York State took a dim view of the nativists. In fact it was Seward's 1840 gubernatorial message that perhaps more than any other factor set off a second wave of political nativism. The latter was a reaction to its call for the use of tax monies to support "the establishment of schools in which they [the children of foreigners . . . too often deprived of the advantages of our system of public education, in consequence of prejudice arising from difference of language or religion] may be instructed by teachers speaking the same language with themselves and professing the same faith." But there was a division of labor among New York Whigs. High-minded state leaders like Seward, Weed, and Greeley spoke one way. Local chieftains such as the influential publisher, James Webb, who had been the chief organizer of the new party in 1835, acted another. Although the Whig-nativist relationship in some ways appeared to be a natural affinity, it was due primarily to amoral considerations. Whig leaders did not hesitate to make political capital of an alliance that Democratic lieutenants feared to duplicate only for fear it "would lose them . . . the Irish-Catholic vote." If Whig politicos coalesced with nativism for what appeared to be purely pragmatic considerations, Whig voters seemed to be moved by sincere fears and prejudice. What is more sincere than prejudice? The evidence of the polls, in Lee Benson's words, shows that "although sympathy for [nativism] . . . cut across class and ethnocultural lines, a large majority of its adherents apparently were urban, native Protestants of skilled worker, mechanic, or lower middle-class socioeconomic status, who resented competition and contact with immigrants of 'strange' cultures, faiths and languages." This was the ethnic and occupational stuff of Whig voting. But the coolness toward nativism shown by New York Whig leaders probably more than any other factor accounted for the demise first of the Native Democratic Association and then its replacement, the American Protestant Union, the latter group appearing shortly after the Association was born in 1841.

The history of nativism in St. Louis in the early 1840s paralleled events in New York in a number of respects. The St. Louis Native American Democratic Association like its eastern counterpart was not a monolithic organization. Western nativism also drew much political support from Whigs while it alienated other Whigs. The critical Whigs were convinced that their party was hurt politically by its identification with nativism. Election returns indicate the critics were right.

Nativism came alive again politically in New York City in 1843. This movement was much stronger than its predecessor had been. It spread to rural counties in the southeast of the state and to Albany and was paralleled by the emergence of similar movements in a number of the eastern states. It had a decisive impact on the election of 1844 and gave birth to a national party in 1845 that claimed over 100,000 supporters in 14 states. Then, in part because of the *hubris* of its leaders, in part because of their misinterpretation of the sources of their strength, the party fell as quickly as it had risen, once again to experience a recrudescence in the 1850s, this time as Know-Nothingism. But that is another story.

The American Republican Party at its birth in June 1843 in New York City was bipartisan. In fact it drew more heavily at first from the Democracy than from the Whigs. It seemed to have been precipitated by the policy of the heavily Democratic common council to grant "unusual favors in the way of market licenses and petty offices," to Irish Catholics as a reward for their support of Tammany. When "American meat sellers found themselves . . . with Irish competition and subject to oversights by Irish clerks, weighers, and watchmen, . . . nativism at once sprang into new life in the markets." If the pretext for the reemergence of political nativism in 1843 was the alleged Democratic bias in favor of Irish Catholics, the amazing political success it won in New York City in 1844 had relatively little to do with "ideological" fervor or the nativist beliefs or voters. Ira M. Leonard's recent study stresses above all the ineptness and outright corruption of Whig and Democratic municipal administrations early in the decade. In view of the dereliction of the major parties, voters in the metropolis responded enthusiastically to the appeals made by a new nativist party that cleverly muted its anti-

Catholic and anti-Irish doctrines, promised reform and efficient government, and let voters know it had no objections if they remained Whigs and Democrats with regard to the great national issues. The new party knew the game of politics better than did its predecessor, creating an efficient party organization in the wards and in the city as a whole that was modeled on the structures of the major parties.

Although nativist ideology was soft-pedalled by the American Republicans, it was by no means completely de-emphasized. The new party at first made four demands on its candidates. They had to support a 21-year residence law for aliens who would become citizens and the repeal of the New York City School law providing public funds for Catholic school; oppose the selection of foreigners to office; and accept no nominations from any other party. In 1843 when Democratic and Whig candidates got roughly 14,000 votes each, the nativists got close to 9,000 votes. (Something is told of the white New Yorker's scale of political values by an antislavery vote of about 70 in the same elections.) By 1844, however, the American Republican party was able to take control of the politics of the metropolis.

Its leaders saw the wisdom of broadening its program for the Presidential year, as they took up the cry of "reform," particularly of the police system. They also saw the political capital in calling for reduced government expenses. The nativist leaders knew the game of politics quite as well as did the antimasons before them, and like their predecessors understood that success in politics required a realistic supplement to the burning issue that was sufficient only to the zealots—inevitably a small minority of the voters. They played a deep political game with the Whig party in 1844 in Pennsylvania and above all in New York.

Despite the unremitting hostility of Seward and Weed, local Whig leaders and the Whig press throughout the latter state carried on a lively flirtation with the American Republicans. Ostensibly out of a desire not to hurt Clay's chances, New York City's Whig candidate for mayor was kept in the field. But in fact Whig journals supported James Harper, the American Republican mayoralty candidate, who subsequently won with almost 25,000 votes to slightly over 20,000 for the Democrat, and 5,000 for the official Whig candidate. In view of these figures, contemporary and later estimates that perhaps 60 percent of Harper's vote came from regular Whig voters, seem modest. The defection of Whig voters from the party's approved candidates had fateful consequences. Clay's loss of the state—and with it the Presidency—was perhaps as much due to Whig defections to nativism in New York City as to antislavery in the counties. Furious, Seward declared war on the American Republicans but too late to help Harry of the West.

Nativism gone pragmatic conquered New York City. But it was unable to hold the great prize. The new leaders of the movement discovered that they, no better than the older parties, could satisfactorily deal with the city's growing problems. And as the gulf between American Republican performance and promise became wider, voters became increasingly disenchanted. James Harper, the eminent publisher, was intelligent and sincerely interested in reform but he lacked the political skill necessary to accomplish it. As did the Jackson party, American Republicans seemed to define reform as the replacement of the bad fellows—inevitably of other parties—with their own stalwarts. Unlike the Jacksonians, Harper and his administration would close saloons on Sunday and enforce other unpopular ordinances. Since the party's virulent anti-Irish Catholicism was never completely submerged, the seeming support the editor of its main New York City journal gave to a call for violence, and even for the blood of foreigners, frightened moderates. George Templeton Strong, himself scornful of his era's "new immigrants," was shocked by the tone of the *New York Citizen and American Republican*. In view of the obvious decline in the party's popularity, its leaders in 1845 "threw off their cloak of reform and made a last-ditch nativist appeal for support." But to no avail. The party lost the 1845 municipal elections and within two years had ceased to be a force in the city.

The publicized successes in New York City and elsewhere in 1844 resulted in the emergence of new nativist parties in South Carolina, Delaware, and Maryland as well as in New England. Over the objection of New York's representatives, who favored the name American Republicans, 141 delegates who met in Philadelphia on July 4, 1845, to form a national party, christened it the Native American Party. Claiming 48,000 voters in New York, 42,000 in Pennsylvania, 14,000 in Massachusetts, 3,000 in New Jersey, 1,000 in Delaware, and 2,000 in nine other states, the party by its choice of name opted for narrowness, strict adherence to "principles," and—unbeknownst to its delegates—oblivion. Where the antimasonic movement appealed to the emotions and prejudices of rural citizens against an alleged plot directed by an urban elite from "without," nativism was strong in the city, stirring up the emotions of urban voters against a religious plot allegedly being hatched from within. More socially genteel than the earlier movement, nativism's villains came not of the upper orders but the lower, resented not for their present power as for their future menace. According to nativists, two evil propensities—one of Irish Catholics to multiply, the other of politicians to cater to the foreigners—had to be frustrated. It is a tribute to the major parties of the Jackson era that protagonists of such doctrine ultimately had to go elsewhere to find a political home.

In 1840 the same "infected district" of New York that had earlier been the breeding ground for political antimasonry gave birth to the Liberty party. Simultaneously the party sprang up in Massachusetts and the West. The "antislavery" party it was called but it attracted few opponents of slavery at the polls. James G. Birney, its presidential candidate that year, got perhaps 7,000 votes in a nation which had over 1,500 antislavery societies. Antislavery men hated the South's "peculiar institution," of course, but to judge from the bitterness of their intermural quarrels, they seemed to dislike one another almost as much. The influential Garrisonians wanted no part of separate political action that might free the major parties from pressure to take positions hostile to slavery. Garrison himself considered the organization presumptuous, referring to its leaders as "restless, ambitious men, who are determined to get up a third party, come what may—in the hope, doubtless of being lifted by it into office." If the great abolitionist meant what he said—and he generally did—he was here accusing Myron Holley, Alvan Stuart, and Gerrit Smith, the organizers of the party in New York State, of incredible optimism.

Abby Kelley, who was a follower of Garrison, told a leader of the new organization that his party was "dirty, dirtier, dirtiest." What she meant exactly is not clear but it does appear that she wished to convey her dislike. Most abolitionists preferred to rely on moral suasion. Abolitionists who favored political action, would call on the states rather than the federal government. Others professed to have great expectations from poor Harrison as President. For whatever the reasons, the new antislavery party of 1840 got less than one tenth of 1 percent of the Presidential vote. Four years later, of course, its 15,814 votes in New York alone were regarded by many as the decisive factor that cost Clay the victory. The ninefold increase, however, while bringing the total Liberty party vote to slightly above 62,000, still constituted a very small percentage of the persons opposed to slavery and an even tinier fragment of the nation as a whole. The main significance of the Liberty party derived from something other than its numerical following.

The versatile Jabez Hammond, historian, political activist, "lawyer and reformer of Cherry Valley," was one of the first to propose the formation of the new party, as far back as 1836, seconded shortly afterwards by John Greenleaf Whittier. They brought the idea before Gerrit Smith who was later to become a founder of the party as well as the man who gave it its name. But at first he turned them down. Smith's influence at the time was due more to his wealth than to any reputation either for brilliance or zeal. The owner of one million acres which prior to the Panic of 1837 had netted him close to $100,000 per year, Smith had become a kind of bankroll to the New York antislavery movement. His sincerity impugned by a zealot, Smith's idea of a proper rejoinder was to remind his critic that he was no fly-by-night abolitionist: he had contributed $50,000 to the cause! He had come to antislavery relatively late, after 1831, and for a number of years thereafter favored nothing more drastic than colonization of African slaves, criticizing the American Anti-Slavery Society for its indiscriminate attacks on all slaveowners including "our young Christian brothers at the South." But after he joined the Society in 1835, his views rapidly became more radical. A decade later he would attack the "liberal constitution" of New York State for its discriminatory property requirement for Negro voters and also urge that a portion of the homestead of all farmers be exempt "from the grasp of creditors."

New York State's antislavery movement veered toward politics in 1838. The convention of the Anti-Slavery Society voted to put three questions to the gubernatorial candidates and their running mates. Where did they stand on the right of fugitive slaves to trial by jury? Did they favor repeal of all distinctions in the state "founded solely on complexion"? Would they work to repeal the law permitting slaves to be kept by their visiting masters for nine months in the state? The Democratic answers were completely unsatisfactory. While Seward's answers were "fairly good," his straightforward— and unsatisfactory—response to the second question cost him the convention's support. It was decided to back only his running mate, Luther Bradish. A national movement came even closer to formation when the following year the Albany convention approved a resolution that its supporters vote only "for candidates who favored immediate abolition." This was not yet a call for a separate party, since many leaders still agreed with Lewis Tappan that "an abolition party would be a real evil." Tappan's position toward the new party softened thereafter, as he voted for its candidates even though he remained convinced that he functioned more efficiently by remaining outside the party. The subsequent difficulties experienced by Tappan's American and Foreign Anti-Slavery Society, set up after 1840 as a rival to the Garrison-dominated American Anti-Slavery Society, helped induce the eminent New Yorker and many of his disciples to change their minds about the Liberty party. In any case, Smith's call for a national nominating convention of a "Liberty Party" for April 1, 1840, at Albany, successfully launched the anti-slavery party in politics.

Abolition and antislavery meant a variety of things. To the founders of the new party they meant something a good deal short of the immediate emancipation of all slaves in the United States. The original convention, attended by delegates from six northeastern states, was less than precise. The delegates nominated James Birney of Kentucky, husband of Smith's sister-in-law and former slaveowner himself, as candidate for President but adopted neither a platform nor an official name for their party. By 1843 progress was made, for the Buffalo convention of that year hammered out a platform for Birney to stand on the following year. It demanded "the absolute and unqualified divorce of the general government from slavery." What did this mean? According to the party's leaders it meant that Congress could establish slavery neither in the District of Columbia nor the territories; and that the three-fifths clause and fugitive slave acts were unconstitutional. The principles of the later Free Soil party flowed naturally out of the Liberty party program. Practical men like Salmon P. Chase of Ohio, intent on broadening the appeal of the party, even hoping to "win over the middle-minded men of the South," would not condemn slavery in that section. Chase's idea was not to overthrow slavery in the states, but rather the power of its masters in the national government. When subsequent to the elections Gerrit Smith proposed that the party declare slavery in the states unconstitutional, his motion was voted down.

What manner of men supported the Liberty party? "Disgruntled Whigs who used the abolition label as a means of making trouble for the Democrats," said a disgruntled Democratic editor. There is reason to think that northern Democrats who believed Polk's nomination "an abandonment of principles," also swelled its totals in 1844. In Vermont, "members of the recently organized Wesleyan Methodist church were arrayed solidly behind the Liberty Party." Whig rank and file voters, unhappy with their party's "neglect on the *absorbing* question" in their state, increasingly tried to "abolitionize the Whig Party." No such thing happened but Vermont's Whig leaders were clever enough to put up an antislavery slate in the state elections, "while the national ticket was dominated by the proslavery element." For New York Benson's close study supplemented the earlier suggestions made by Ralph Harlow and Whitney Cross: "political abolitionists' hammer blows struck responsive chords in central, western, and northern New York communities containing few Negro inhabitants, or in cities serving these communities—and in these areas almost exclusively." His Liberty party voters were typically of "small, moderately prosperous Yankee farming communities," "shared a common set of 'radical religious beliefs,'" their political abolitionism being "only one manifestation of religious ultraism." Since they were men who believed it proper that the community and government act to set wrong things right, they were likely to have been of the Whig party which held to a like notion of the state's positive responsibility toward the community welfare, in contrast to Democratic negativism. In Michigan, towns that gave no votes to Birney were invariably Democratic towns while Liberty party voters came from Whig strongholds.

The era's third parties reveal among other things that the Empire State was preeminent in more than just wealth and political influence. For every one of the third parties examined here, with the exception of the Working Men, was born in the state. The ample and diverse culture of the great state provided fertile ground for dissent based on social envy, economic inequality, religious zeal, ethnic bigotry, and racial idealism. Rural New York was the original locale of both antimasonry and political abolitionism, the former movement combining religious fundamentalism with social underprivilege, the latter religious zeal and social stability. Nativism and the Working Men's movement were urban manifestations, as was the short-lived Locofoco movement. The Workies and the Locos were unique for while they, too, were formed by zealots, the inspiration urging on their faithful was secular rather than moralistic.

On the national level, particularly in 1844, and on the local and state levels throughout the era, a number of the third parties at times held the balance of political power. In view of the nearly equal followings of the great major parties, a minor party whose own voting support was minuscule could nevertheless manage to determine the outcome of an election. The major significance of the dissenting parties however was in other things than their occasional fateful effect on the party battles between the giants. Their very existence highlighted the nonideological nature of the Democracy and Whiggery. The absorption of parts of their program and their memberships by the major parties was one more revelation of the political know-how of the latter. Small memberships and highly localized centers of support testified to the indifference most American voters felt toward the politics of principle and zeal. For if the very existence of third parties showed that the Jacksonian consensus was not universally subscribed to, the most revealing feature of the situation was how few Americans dissented from it.

13

REFLECTIONS ON THE POLITICAL ISSUES OF THE JACKSONIAN ERA

The issue that most occupied Andrew Jackson during his first administration was both unusual and fascinating. It had to do with a beautiful woman—the wife of his friend the Secretary of War—and the fact that many prominent persons in the capital, particularly the wives of Cabinet members, would not accept her socially. A truly loyal friend to those who remained loyal to him, Jackson not only refused to give ground but he insisted finally that either the snubs cease or he would oust from his Cabinet the husbands of the offending prudes. His zeal was in part due to his conviction that the attack on the lady—the notorious Peggy O'Neale Timberlake Eaton—was akin to the hateful smear that had earlier been directed against his beloved Rachel for living in adultery with him prior to their legal marriage. "She is chaste as a virgin!" he admonished his first Cabinet after summoning all of them except Eaton to what was to be their last meeting, there to hear the President refute allegations discrediting Mrs. Eaton's character. It was widely believed then and later that Van Buren rather than Calhoun became the nation's eighth President because the little bachelor ostentatiously accompanied the vivacious Peggy to social functions that Floride Calhoun avoided. Jackson himself explained the affair as an attempt by Calhoun "to weaken me . . . and open the way to his preferment on my ruin." Ironically he offered this interpretation in a letter to Emily Donelson, wife of Rachel's nephew, who herself had refused to receive the woman and had accordingly been required to leave the White House. Pleading with Mrs. Donelson to return and be kind to Peggy Eaton, the lonely old man failed to see that Emily's own behavior seemed to contradict his notion that the scorning of Mrs. Eaton was a plot gotten up by the nefarious Calhounites. The fact is that Mrs. Sarah Polk and much of Washington society closed their doors to the notorious lady well before Andrew Jackson appointed her husband to the Cabinet.[1] But like so many other people, Andrew Jackson liked to read a larger significance into a personal squabble.

By the time the issue came to a head the President and Calhoun were indeed far apart but for reasons that had nothing to do with social etiquette. The "Eaton malaria" widened the breach. But knowing Jackson's character as we do, it is hard to avoid the conclusion that this stubborn, self-righteous man was simply furious at an affront to his crony's wife that had intimations in it of *lesè-majesté*. Even the Tennessee Congressional delegation had requested that Eaton not be appointed to the Cabinet because they feared that his wife would become an issue. But Andrew Jackson would not dream of being deflected from his course by such a consideration. Jackson evidently wanted Eaton in his Cabinet in part to help execute his planned Indian policy. In any case, once the deed was done not only would he not retract, but it was in character for him to attribute evil intentions to the wicked enemies responsible for the scandal.

To make such charges and not so much to have them believed as *to have it believed that he meant them,* had the positive effect for his reputation of turning the sordid affair into a controversy based on larger principle. For Jackson could not have been ignorant of what John Overton's nephew had written to Jackson's old friend: "public opinion does not sustain him in relation to Mrs. Eaton. . . . This is a game too insignificant for a President." The weight of the evidence suggests that the main principle involved in the affair was the power of the nation's Chief Executive to make something close to a fool of himself as he involved leading figures in government in a clash that had not the remotest connection to the real issues confronting the nation.

Who is not for us, is against us! was a rule of Jackson's thought. His idea of enemies however was not men warring on his or his party's program so much as men who thwarted him or who would impair his reputation, challenge his veracity, or frustrate a scheme of his—a scheme typically devoid of ideological content. Even to call some of his minor acts "petty schemes" is to read into them an element of design or of fitting into a larger pattern which they lacked. He seemed to hate Calhoun because the Carolinian had once favored censuring Jackson's incursion into Florida. He hated Poindexter after the latter insisted that civil service posts in Mississippi not be filled by Jackson's Tennessee cronies. Jackson could conveniently "forget" if not forgive, as his reconciliation with Benton

---

[1] Peggy Eaton was a young woman, who, before she was 15, had driven men to duel over her and one man to suicide. John Eaton, who met her when she was Mrs. Timberlake, "pulled wires to send Timberlake to sea" and to send him back when he returned. That she was unacceptable to Washington society is indicated by the fact that Mrs. Monroe had advised her not to attend receptions which, as a naval officer's wife, she was eligible to attend. At age 60, her granddaughter's dancing master, 19, married her, took her fortune, and then eloped with the granddaughter.

showed, but it took an overriding selfish interest to induce him to do so.

Rejecting what he calls a Victorian interpretation, Richard H. Brown has argued brilliantly that the bitter struggle for power between Jackson and Van Buren on the one side and Calhoun on the other, cannot be explained by reference "to whores or to the unbridled pursuit of ambition." Such explanations accorded with a "simple view of history"—shared unfortunately by most historians—"and the Jacksonians got both barrels, one through the beguiling story of Peggy Eaton, the other through the notion of a sterile and essentially meaningless struggle to succession between Van Buren and Calhoun." Brown's way of rendering the struggle vital and meaningful is to transform it into a warfare over the disposition of the nation's most crucial issue—slavery. Earlier historians, whether of the Jacksonian or other eras, made American history vital by metamorphosing its seemingly personal or petty controversies or its disputations about political theory into class struggles. The clash of mighty impersonal forces thus truly explained what was going on—even though the mere human actors in the drama might themselves be oblivious to the fact. A well-known example of this approach applied outside the sphere of American history is the unwillingness of some to treat the assassination of tens of thousands of men of diverse beliefs by a paranoiac dictator as merely a species of insanity and rampant dictatorship: large policies must be involved. The banishment of one would-be despot by another must connote conflicting interpretations of revolution by the two men. Otherwise, it would seem, it is feared that history becomes sterile.

It is a good question as to which history is more lively, the one that notes a clash of personalities and treats it respectfully, curiously, searching out its nuances of feeling and action; or the one that dismisses the "trivia," impatient to get at the *real* meaning, the fundamental issues that must be lurking behind or be represented by the mere events. Why must they? Human affairs are what they are. Of course human events are complicated and without doubt are never entirely unreflective of larger issues. An historian whose aim is not narrative but rather interpretive history would be expected to be sympathetic to a historical method that strains to find the deeper significance of human actions. But the elusive truth that is the interpreter's quest is not necessarily achieved when large or fundamental socioeconomic issues are invoked. The complexity of truth suggests that at times in history, personality prevails over ideology, petty and subjective motives account for the behavior of mighty men, entire nations are turned this way or that by actions more accidental than designed. Significant issues *were* touched on by every act of the Jackson administration. But they are not exclusively the great issues of class, property, distribution of wealth, or social status.

My own reading of Jacksonian politics is that the great major parties and their leaders almost instinctively anticipated the views later expressed by the great English conservative, Walter Bagehot. Fearing the consequences of the newly granted democratic suffrage which enfranchised the English working class, Bagehot in a new introduction he wrote in 1872 to his *The English Constitution,* advised statesmen how they could allay the dangers:

They have to guide the new voters in the exercise of the franchise; to guide them quietly, and without saying what they are doing, but still to guide them. The leading statesmen in a free country have great momentary power. They settle the conversation of mankind. It is they who, by a great speech or two, determine what shall be said and what shall be written for long after. . . . The common ordinary mind is quite unfit to fix for itself what political question it shall attend to; it is as much as it can do to judge decently of the questions which drift down to it, and are brought before it. . . . And in settling what these questions shall be, statesmen have . . . a great responsibility. If they raise questions which will excite the lower order of mankind; if they raise questions on which those orders are likely to be wrong [i.e., questions concerning the distribution of wealth]; if they raise questions on which the interest of those orders is not identical with . . . the whole interest of the state, they will have done the greatest harm they can do. . . . Just when it is desirable that ignorant men, new to politics, shall have good issues, and only good issues, put before them, these statesmen will have suggested bad issues. They will have suggested topics which band the poor as a class together; topics which will excite them against the rich. . . . [While statesmen cannot "choose with absolute freedom what topics they deal with,"] statesmen [do] have great power; when there is no fire lighted they can settle what fire shall be lit.

The evidence does not suggest that Jackson and his great political rivals contrived to keep such paltry matters as Mrs. Eaton's social acceptance, or whether a Tennesseean or a Mississippian would have the Land Office of Mississippi, in the public spotlight, as "good" issues not likely to disturb the status quo. But both the electoral system and the major parties that thrived under it were geared, if not to avoid the great issues altogether, then to deflect or muffle them. And men like Amos Kendall, Isaac Hill, and Francis P. Blair were perfectly capable of transforming a good issue—in Bagehot's terms, one that would have no other real effect on American society than to unsettle its currency or to offer several dozen wealthy Democratic bankers an opportunity to become still wealthier—into a revolutionary act of confiscation. But that Democratic rhetoric was capable of alchemy was not taken seriously, sometimes not even by the masterful men who uttered it—except as a means of getting and holding office. Of course to men who live for office, nothing which threatens their hold or their chances is paltry. Once Peggy Eaton has become an issue, image and prestige become involved in her fate, the future behavior of voters is likely to be affected even if slightly by their reactions to the affair. The remark attributed to Clay, that "age cannot wither nor time stale her infinite virginity," becomes a tactical coup that can cost votes in 1832. There was an issue, too, in the fact that the American political system permitted its Chief Executive the latitude it did to determine the fate of grown men over such matters.

Too much can be made even of the lower key, subtle issues I have been trying to discern. Political affairs are sometimes issueless in the ordinary sense precisely because they are the affairs of men and thus reflect the fascinating perversity and irrationality of the species. The fate of Calhoun during the first Jackson administration is a case in point. Suddenly, inexplicably, early in 1831 the same Jackson who has coldly advised Calhoun that he knows the truth about his stand on Jackson's Florida raid, who has interpreted the Eaton embarrassment as a Calhoun plot, and who has made definite plans for Van Buren rather than Calhoun to be his heir, announces that "the whole affair was settled," Calhoun is to dine at the White House, harmony has been restored! Seeing a marvelous opportunity to deal a death blow to Van Buren's chances, Calhoun, with the aid of Duff Green, publishes a long document that puts himself in the light of aggrieved and true friend of an Andrew Jackson whose mind had been poisoned by the machiavellian Martin Van Buren. The document, which included the correspondence with Old Hickory on the Florida matter, was modified in accord with the suggestions made by Eaton, to whom it was shown, and it was published on Calhoun's understanding that Eaton had shown it and in effect cleared it with the Old Hero. When the pamphlet came out, however, Jackson responded with fury. "They have cut their own throats," he said of Calhoun and his editor, whose *Telegraph* praised the pamphlet lavishly. What had happened? The melodramatic answer given by a Jackson biographer in this instance seems apropos: "John C. Calhoun's long and precariously sustained attempt to ride the Jacksonian tide into the Presidency was over. So soon as they could assemble their wits, Calhoun and Green learned the simple cause of their downfall. John Henry Eaton had not so much as mentioned the existence of the manuscript to Andrew Jackson: a humiliated husband's revenge." Grant that Marquis James, Jackson's sympathetic modern biographer, perhaps makes too much of the incident. Grant that old Parton was right in judging that Jackson "would have been glad of any pretext for breaking with" Calhoun. A question still stands: why did John Eaton act in the matter as he did? What "issue" drove him later to search the Washington streets, dueling pistols in hand, for a chance to revenge himself on Samuel Ingham, a Calhounite in Jackson's first Cabinet?

The warfare over issues during the Jacksonian era dominates the political histories of the era. My intention therefore is not to write a narrative account of the struggles but to approach them from a different angle, essentially by posing the issues that were fought over by the politicians, against the issues truly facing the country. James Bryce long ago dealt with American politics in the era of Grover Cleveland in this manner. His conclusions were as critical as they were because he found the parties wanting. They emerged as mere vote-getting machines, "ins" v. "outs," because in his judgment the issues that did engage them were not the issues that should have engaged them. And when they did deal with the latter, they did so ineffectually.

Such an approach to politics it might be argued is highly unrealistic. It would measure the actuality against a standard of perfection that although ostensibly absolute is in fact the subjective standard of the one doing the judging. At the least, however, it does serve the reader by converting the author's unspoken assumptions into criteria explicitly set forth, the better to be judged thereby. Furthermore, notions as to the nation's true problems need not be the source of controversy a rigid relativism might suggest they would be. Hamiltonians and Jeffersonians, Freudians and Pavlovians, would all agree I think that slavery was a major issue in Jacksonian America.

No other issue presented the nation the terrible moral, psychological, economic, and political dilemmas of slavery. But William Lloyd Garrison notwithstanding, the United States faced a number of other great issues. An incomplete listing that does not pretend to rank order of importance, would include economic growth. Although the phrase and the concept as presently understood were not yet part of discourse, the expansion of productivity and commerce, both domestic and foreign, were crucial to the nation's development. Improvements in transportation were necessary if the nation were to realize its economic potential. Economic stability was a vital need, particularly to a nation whose citizens seemed perennially in the throes of get-rich-quick delusions. An effective currency—I hesitate to say "sound currency" because of the pro-creditor bias historically associated with the phrase—was central both for stability and growth. The material situation and the status of various underprivileged groups inevitably were problems. Economically: the poor, urban workers, small farmers, the growing body of factory labor; socially: the newer immigrants, the "lower orders," the outsiders who could not break through the narrow circle enclosing elites which monopolized prestige and influence in the cities of every section in the nation; biologically: by sex, females; by skin color, Indians, Africans and their known descendants; by congenital traits, the insane and the sick. The society had a great need for an educated citizenry and from the point of view of underprivileged individuals, they deserved something better than stigmatized schools of low quality. For that matter thoughtful Americans like Ralph Waldo Emerson and James Fenimore Cooper were convinced that the low quality of American life and the sordid values of the people were as significant as any other problems. Political issues abounded. Domestically, the nation needed efficient government in order to deal effectively with the inevitable increase in governmental responsibilities. If democracy were to be more than a mere token, manhood suffrage would have to be supplemented by popular control of parties and political institutions. Sectional divergences of interest would have to be both reflected and effectively reconciled by the political system. Internationally the ancient verities applied. Peace and the respect of other nations were the goals. A related question concerned the territorial expansion of the nation in the face of opportunities presented by contiguous land areas in the possession of weak or distant European states.

How do the era's major parties and their leaders come off when their actions are measured against the "real issues" that faced the nation? That they will be found wanting goes without saying. For as Mr. Madison wrote in the 51st *Federalist,* men are not angels nor do angels govern men. The question is, how short did they fall?

The Whig party had what amounted to a built-in advantage over the Democracy, since its leaders accepted a general theory of governmental activism that contrasted with the laissez-faire or negativistic notions of most Jacksonians. The former principle at least held out a promise of useful or ameliorative action that seemed to be missing from the latter. But theoretical predilections were as little binding on the behavior of men in the Jacksonian era as at other times. Not theory but practice must be consulted in order to answer the last question. Limitations of space compel us to paint in broad strokes.

It would be more than utopian to expect that government would have done anything important about some of the nation's problems. A society cannot be made great by legislative enactments. The quality of American life, disappointing though it might have been to Emerson, Cooper, Tocqueville, and Mrs. Trollope, was beyond the power of statecraft to alter. It is just as well that this was so since there are few prospects more chilling than politicians dedicated to uplift. "That government is best which governs least," was not an official American maxim but limited government came close to being, thus assuring that serious governmental assaults against fundamental problems were not likely. Certainly the needs of the underprivileged got short shrift from Jacksonian administrations.

Five years after the Philadelphia unionist, John Ferral, wrote exultantly that American labor had accomplished a "bloodless revolution"—the replacement of the sunup to sundown work day in urban shops by the ten-hour day—the Van Buren Administration in 1840 issued an order establishing ten hours as the work day on federal public works. Jackson himself had earlier established the rule for the Philadelphia Navy Yard. Perhaps this cancelled out Andrew Jackson's earlier breaking of a strike of workers employed on a canal corporation headed by John Eaton, in an unprecedented display of federal force whose legality was highly problematical. But for all the lavish oratory professing sympathy for labor and concern for its plight, the Democratic record was otherwise barren of achievements that directly aided workingmen. The war on the Bank was of course explained as a struggle of the poor against the rich, but the Democratic argument was no more compelling than the Whig case for a high tariff's allegedly beneficent effects on native labor. A recent survey of his private correspondence discloses

Jackson's monumental indifference to the problems faced by urban workingmen. Democratic inaction in this instance corresponded closely with the social sentiments displayed by Democratic leaders.

Nor were the Jacksonians or their Whig opponents great champions of the small western farmer—that is, when their political behavior rather than their public speeches is examined. Richard Latner has recently discerned important western influence on Jackson in the fact that Old Hickory depended so heavily on the advice of the "westerners," Amos Kendall and Francis P. Blair. Malcolm Rohrbough thinks the label "western man" is not misapplied rather because "the general had long been a land speculator, interested in the public domain as a field for profitable investment," and also because of his profound dislike for Indians" and his craving for their large tracts of land suitable for white cultivation." To the chagrin of those who believed him a friend to squatters, Old Hickory not only proposed no legislation favorable to them during his first term, but in 1830 issued a proclamation threatening the forcible removal of the "many uninformed and evil disposed persons" who had settled on the public lands in Huntsville, Alabama. After a preemption act was passed in 1830, its administration by land commissioners and officers infuriated the settlers and squatters who had "so vociferously supported" passage of the law. The pattern of Jacksonian land policy throughout the era was consistent: laws were passed, the language of which was often as populistic as had been the language supporting them; these laws were then administered in a manner that made a mockery of their language.

Triggered by amazing appreciation in the market value of western land, federal land offices sold more than 32 million acres in 1835 and 1836, an amount more than 300 percent greater than the norm of earlier years or for the years following the Panic of 1837. Wealthy speculators based in the east as well as the west, who "saw public lands in the West [as] a profitable form of investment for surplus capital," brought up vast quantities of these lands, typically resorting to collusive bidding that "defrauded the government out of much of its expected profit." Delighted at the opportunity to get theirs, corrupt land officers placed no obstacles in the way of such practices, thus making a mockery of the concept of public auction.

Thomas Benton's program for the public lands was adopted ultimately by the Van Buren Administration and eventually produced the famous preemption acts which safeguarded squatters' rights— at least on paper. Unfortunately, however, it did little for small settlers. On the one hand, "it was not evidence that Congress placed settlement above revenue," for accompanied as it was by a "distribution" scheme which emptied the Federal treasury of net proceeds from public land sales (by dividing the money among the states according to population) it assured that land prices would remain high. And "it did not retard the engrossment of land by speculators." The practice of Democrats in state land offices negated the abstract theories of Thomas Hart Benton.

So far as the needs of the nation's various underprivileged groups went, it was precisely the do-nothingism of national administrations that accounted for the flourishing of the diverse reform associations of the period 1830 to 1850. Individual Jacksonians such as Edward Livingston, Robert Rantoul, Jr., and John L. O'Sullivan were active in the movements for prison reform and abolition of capital punishment, but they were atypical. Men and women concerned over the situation of the insane, the poor, the disinherited, women, child labor, social and economic inequality, the plight of the dark-skinned whether slave or free, had to look elsewhere than to national government. Such men and women were rarely supporters of the Democratic party. Even Jacksonians with a reputation for radicalism, such as William Cullen Bryant and Walt Whitman, commonly harbored beliefs in the innate inferiority of other peoples.

Jacksonian Democracy did have a program for American Indians, one which it carried through forcefully, in one of the few instances where its theory and practice were not in conflict. The policy was to separate Indians from their lands. To accomplish this purpose the Hero in the White House in effect pleaded federal impotence to implement Indian rights guaranteed by federal treaties when these rights came under attack from the states. Federal potency was reserved for the actual physical removal of Indians from their lands, federal troops providing the indispensable element in the process.

Jacksonian Indian policy was a blending of hypocrisy, cant, and rapaciousness, seemingly shot through with contradictions. Inconsistencies however are present only if the language of the presidential state papers is taken seriously. "The language of Indian removal was pious," observes Michael P. Rogin, "but the hum of destruction is clearly audible underneath." In Ronald Satz's phrase, such language provided a "convenient humanitarian rationale" for a policy of force. When the lofty rhetoric is discounted and viewed for what it was—sheer rationale for policy based on much more mundane considerations—then an almost frightening consistency becomes apparent. By one means or another the southern tribes had to be driven to the far side of the Mississippi. For as Mary E. Young has pointed out, by 1830 "east of the Mississippi, white occupancy was limited by Indian tenure of northeastern Georgia, enclaves in western North Carolina and southern Tennessee, eastern Alabama, and the northern two thirds of Mississippi. In this 25-million acre domain lived nearly 60,000 Cherokees, Creeks, Choctaws and Chickasaws." The Jacksonians invoked alleged higher laws of nature to justify removal. Thomas Benton spoke of a national imperative that the land be turned over to those who would use it "according to the intentions of the creator." Jackson himself referred to the march of progress and civilization, whose American manifestation was "studded with cities, towns and prosperous farms, embellished with all the improvements which art can devise or industry execute, occupied by more than 12 million happy people and filled with all the blessings of liberty, civilization and religion," before which "forests . . . ranged by a few thousand savages" must give ground.

In Miss Young's laconic words, "such a rationalization had one serious weakness as an instrument of policy. The farmer's right of eminent domain over the lands of the savage could be asserted consistently only so long as tribes involved were 'savage.' The southwestern tribes, however, were agriculturists as well as hunters." The obvious proof that the federal government did not take seriously its own justification for removal is the disinterest it displayed in the evidence that Cherokees, Choctaws, and Chickasaws were in fact skilled in the arts of civilization. That "the people it now hoped to displace could by no stretch of dialectic be classed as mere wandering savages," would have given pause to men who sincerely believed in their own professions that it was the Indians' alleged savagery that primarily justified their removal. There is every reason to think that the Jacksonians were fully aware that their doctrine—specious and arrogant at best, with its implication that a people living a "superior" life had the right to take the lands of "inferiors"—was all the more specious because its assumption of Indian savagery was untrue.

White speculators and politicians in the southern states had little interest in *theories* of removal. They wanted removal, however rationalized, and were not fastidious as to the means used to accomplish it. No issue was more important, certainly not in Mississippi, where "to most residents . . . the most salient event of 1833 concerned neither the tariff nor nullification," but the fact that that autumn "the first public auctions of the Choctaw lands were held." According to Edwin Miles, Mississippians were so "grateful to Old Hickory for making these lands available to them [that] . . . they were inclined to disregard differences of opinion that he might entertain on issues of less importance." That happy day came to pass in Mississippi and elsewhere only because of the total cooperation shown by the Jackson administration in helping the southern states separate the tribes from their lands. The federal government had to display tact, cunning, guile, cajolery, and more than a hint of coercion. That it proved more than equal to the task was due in no small measure to Andrew Jackson's dedication to it. His performance was not that of responsible government official deferring to the will of constituents but rather that of a zealot who fully shared their biases and rapacity.

Before Jackson became President he had urged that the tribes not be treated as sovereign nations, and when he assumed the highest office he continued to feel that Indians were subjects of the United States, mere hunters who occupied land under its sufferance. A major difference between Jacksonian Indian policy and that of his predecessors lay in this fact. From Jefferson through John Quincy Adams, while national administrations had *desired* the removal of the southwestern tribes and countenanced threats and unlovely inducements to accomplish it, they had continued to treat the tribes "as more or less sovereign nations and to respect their right to remain on their own lands." And where Secretary of War Calhoun, for example, had hoped to accomplish Choctaw removal by "educating" the Indians to see the need for it, Jackson relied on more forceful means certain to work more quickly. In his first inaugural message he promised Indians a humane, just, and liberal policy, based on respect for Indian "rights and wants." A little more than one year later, Secretary of War Eaton induced the highly civilized Choctaws to sign a treaty removing them from their ancient homeland in Mississippi. Eaton succeeded through the use of hypocrisy, bribes, lies, suppression of critics, and intimidation, in securing approval of a treaty that, according to Colonel George Gaines who was present during the negotiations, was "despised by most of the Indians."

Jackson bypassed William Wirt for John Berrien as Attorney-General because he distrusted Wirt on Indian removal. When Wirt subsequently became the lawyer for the Cherokees, Jackson denounced the "wicked" man. He removed the knowledgeable Thomas L. McKenney as head of the Bureau of Indian Affairs because McKenney, as a "warm friend of the Indians," had to be replaced by someone of sounder feelings. (Among McKenney's other flaws, he had been too close to Calhoun and served the Adams Administration too well.) Jackson regarded the practice of negotiating treaties with Indian tribes as an "absurdity" and a "farce." On more than one occasion the President reverted to the practice of his Indian-fighting days, personally dealing with "reluctant tribes" in order to bring about their acquiescence to an agreement detrimental to their interests. He hated Crawford in part because the latter had exposed the inequity and fraud in the Creek Treaty Jackson had negotiated in 1814. In the judgment of one modern student, Jackson, prior to the Supreme Court decision in the case of *Cherokee Nation* v. *Georgia* in 1831, "threatened the Supreme Court with a refusal to enforce its decree." The Court in that case sidestepped the issue of the constitutionality of Georgia's Indian laws. But when the following year the Court ruled, in *Worcester* v. *Georgia* that the State of Georgia had no right to extend its laws over the Cherokee nation, the Indian tribes being "domestic dependent nations," with limits defined by treaty, the President refused to enforce this decision. Unfortunately for the Cherokee, some of their best friends in Congress and on the high court now urged them to sign a removal treaty. Jackson's failure to direct federal troops to exclude intruders from Indian lands either in Georgia or Alabama was construed by ardent states' righters as a sign of federal permissiveness in the face of state repudiation of unpopular federal laws. How could nullifiers know that Old Hickory acquiesced in state violations of federal statutes only when he himself shared the violators' dislike for the repugnant laws? Many men understandably did not anticipate so chameleon-like an approach to his nation's fundamental charter by the official chiefly responsible for enforcing it. Several scholars have pointed out the legal technicalities that would have posed problems for

Jackson even had he wished to enforce the Marshall court decision. In view of his character and his previous history, however, can anyone seriously suggest that Jackson deferred to these legalistic barriers because of his respect for law or that he would not have contemptuously brushed them aside had he been so inclined?

The actual procedures used to accomplish the desired end were numerous, ingenious, and effective. Simple force was eschewed, "forbidden by custom, by conscience, and by fear that the administration's opponents would exploit religious sentiment which cherished the rights of the red man." But as Miss Young points out, "within the confines of legality and the formulas of voluntarism it was still possible to acquire the much coveted domain of the civilized tribes." A kind of squeeze was directed against the Indians. On the one hand state governments refused to recognize tribal laws or federally assured rights, bringing Indians under state laws which dealt with them as individuals. Only Indians who chose to become citizens could hold on to what their skill and industry enabled them to accumulate and develop. The federal government continued the earlier policy, begun late in the Madison Administration, of offering reservations or allotments to individual Indians who cultivated their lands and wished to become citizens, while encouraging the trans-Misssisippi migration of the others. When a Congressional measure appropriating $500,000 and authorizing the President to negotiate removal treaties with all the eastern tribes was under debate in 1830, even administration critics agreed that the "Indian's moral right to keep his land depended on his actual cultivation of it." In some cases the removal treaties were negotiated after sufficient pressure had been exercised by private individuals or government officials, who resorted to physical threats as well as to more subtle means. Jacksonian emissaries carried money and liquor in ample quantities.

In the case of the Creeks, who refused to agree to emigration, their chiefs were persuaded in March, 1832, to sign an allotment treaty. Ostensibly depriving the tribe of none of its Alabama territories, in fact by allotting most acreage to heads of families, it not only reduced the tribal estate but it made the individual owners prey to thieves and corruptionists in civil or public garb, who took advantage of Indian innocence and ignorance concerning property values and disposal. Advised that speculators were defrauding the Indians, among other ways by simply "borrowing" back the money they had paid for individual allotments without any intention of paying back the "loans," Secretary of War Lewis Cass enunciated the interesting doctrine that the War Department had no authroity to circumscribe the Indian's right to be defrauded.

The deception practiced by the government in the Creek Treaty may have been as much self-deception as anything else. Certainly many federal agents were honest. Nor was the government's objective profit through fraud. From the Indians' viewpoint however, as from that of moralistic critics, the federal purpose was even more terrible. Mere corruptionists could have been bargained with;

zealous believers in their own superiority and their God-given right to Indian lands, could not. In any case, "the disposal of Creek reserves exhibited an ironic contrast between the ostensible purposes of the allotment policy and its actual operation. Instead of giving the tribesmen a more secure title to their individual holdings, the allotment of their lands became an entering wedge for those who would drive them from their eastern domain."

If cunning, bribery, and guile were the main tactics used to assure Indian prior agreement to removal, brute force and cruelty were employed to execute the policy. The war that drove the Seminoles out of Florida was largely caused by broken American promises, and in the actual fighting the Indians were often lied to. The Creek War, begun after the murder of some whites in retaliation for the "orgy of fraud" perpetrated on the tribe, was described by one Alabama newspaper as a "humbug," a "base and diabolical scheme" to justify still further crimes against the Indians. In the case of the Creeks, the government contracted with private companies to effect their removal west. In addition to the miserable rations and conditions administered by the profit-seekers in charge, "one decrepit steamboat sank through mishandling and 311 Creeks drowned." Earlier, the Choctaws were forced out of Mississippi in the dead of winter, crossing the great river thinly clad and "without moccasins." "Force, terror, and fraud" were used to drive the Seminoles from their rich Florida lands to the west. Probably the worst treatment of all was reserved for the Cherokees. They had balked at moving to a region their own surveyors described as "nothing but mountains and [a] huge bed of rocks." In 1838 General Winfield Scott began their systematic removal, more than 4,000 out of 15,000 of them dying, according to one estimate, in the course of "the Trail of Tears." One judgment is that "at their worst the forced migrations approached the horrors created by the Nazi handling of subject peoples."

Men like Edward Everett and Emerson recoiled in horror, the New England press was sickened at the reproach to our national character in this "abhorrent business." But not Andrew Jackson. In his last message to Congress, he complimented the states on the removal of "the evil" that had retarded their development. He also expressed pleasure that "this unhappy race— . . . the original dwellers in our land—are now placed in a situation where we may well hope that they will share in the blessings of civilization and be saved from the degradation and destruction to which they were rapidly hastening while they remained in the states." This bewildering combination of sentiments seemed to mean, as John W. Ward has observed, that "America would save the Indians for civilization by rescuing them from civilization." Jackson's certainty that "the philanthropist will rejoice that the remnant of that ill-fated race has at length been placed beyond the reach of injury or oppression," may have been warranted although one suspects that this monument of self-deception might have been chagrined to discover philanthropy's estimate as to the true source of Indian oppression.

Henry Clay and other Whigs opposed particular removal treaties on constitutional and humanitarian grounds. And yet the Whig party position should not be misconstrued. For, as Satz observes, while the Whigs "found it expedient to condemn the Jacksonian removal policy when they were struggling to gain political control of the government," once in power they followed the very same policy. The Harrison and Tyler administration did not allow "Indians still east of the Mississippi River to remain there." In 1842 it was to a Whig Administration that the War Department reported that in the North as in the South, there was no more Indian land "east of the Mississippi, remaining unceded, to be desired by us." As was true too of the "spoils system," a policy begun by the one major party was continued by the other. Individual Whigs may have been more sensitive than their Democratic counterparts but the policies of their parties were at times remarkably similar.

J acksonian Democracy was proslavery and antiblack. In fact as the respected English visitor, Edward Abdy, observed, free Negroes everywhere voted against the Jacksonians for they knew who their enemies were. It was the Van Burenites in New York, for example, who took the lead in modifying the State Constitution to make it close to impossible that any citizen of color would vote. In Ohio, Pennsylvania, and elsewhere the great champions of restrictive "black laws" and other deprivations of Negro rights were invariably Jacksonians, with Whig legislators split or opposed. In supporting slavery, Jacksonians were not unique of course. Whigs were themselves split even before the "Conscience Whigs" separated from the party. Few leading Whigs were abolitionists of any variety during the era. Yet many New England Whigs detested Tyler, the "acting President" of the United States to them, as much for his slaveowning as for his betrayal of the American System. The Democratic party did, of course, contain some antislavery elements. In Massachusetts, for example, the party would ultimately founder precisely on that issue. It is understatement, however, to conclude that critics of slavery had no visible influence on the national party's treatment of the peculiar institution. John McFaul's observation that "the Jacksonians did not consider slavery a legitimate political issue," even if true, is not a refutation of the judgment that they were proslavery, but only an attempt to explain their position. That they may have interpreted "antislavery demands as disguised efforts to provoke disunion," tells us more about the Jacksonians than about abolitionists' motives.

Characteristically, Van Buren was not prepared to attribute idealism to antislavery. The motives of northerners who took the issue up were in his judgment, "rather political than philanthropical." A fellow New York Jacksonian defined abolitionists as "niggerloving and white-men hating fanatics." Jackson, a large slaveowner and seller and purchaser of slaves, was not prepared to entertain attacks on the system that served his personal needs so well. The circulation of abolitionist literature was to him both "unconstitutional and wicked," and he recommended legislation to prohibit the circulation in southern states of "incendiary publications intended to instigate the slaves to insurrection." He urged that the names of those southerners who wished to receive this "inflammatory mail" be publicly listed in order to "have them exposed." As for the "monsters" who had composed the pamphlets, Jackson thought they "ought to be made to attone [*sic*] with their lives." The president acquiesced in the policy of his postmaster general Amos Kendall permitting southern postmasters to violate the law on the ground that Kendall's first duty was to an alleged "higher" obligation. The issue had arisen after 1835 in the wake of the campaign launched by the American Anti-Slavery Society to swamp influential persons, North and South, with abolitionist pamphlets. Calhoun's opposition to federal control, as an undue extension of Congressional power, prevented the passage of a federal law. He would assign the power to the states. But the split between the two great Southerners was purely a procedural one. Ultimately, Kendall, decided the issue by so interpreting the Post Office Act of 1836 as to permit southern justices of the peace to brand a particular piece of received mail as abolitionist and to fine the local postmaster who did not immediately burn the inflammatory literature. The mails were thus kept free, the government avoided censorship, "incendiary publications" became literally that, and southern eyes were spared the painful sight of printed antislavery material. To leave nothing to chance, Kendall advised federal postmasters in the South to obey the state laws dealing with abolition material. In New York Samuel Gouverneur, the Jacksonian Postmaster, on his own had decided not to permit the mails to be used for abolitionist purposes, earlier decreeing that such literature was to be sorted out and held in the New York Post Office. Jacksonians obviously would have disagreed with historian Bertram Wyatt-Brown that the antislavery movement was "a greater expression of egalitarian idealism than Jackson ever dreamed of."

Looked at one way, the party in power for most of the period was, as in Jefferson's day, an alliance between Virginia and New York, between southerners who, regardless of their moral and philosophical sensitivities and unhappiness over chattel slavery, would brook no challenges to the system, and "northern men of southern principles." Strict construction was the very first article of faith to these "pure Republicans" largely because a loose construction of the Constitution could lead to federal interference with the institution of slavery in the states. Loose construction had already justified the two Banks of the United States, internal improvements and, according to some critics, tariffs for the improper purpose of protection rather than the constitutional one of raising revenue. It enabled the national government to swell its powers, inevitably at the expense of the states. It appears obvious that most southern opponents of Hamiltonian loose construction were motivated more by fear of its unlovely substantive consequences than from any abstract preference for small government over large. The thing above all that a local government in a slaveholding region could be counted on to do was to protect slavery. In the abolition-mails controversy Calhoun spoke for that sensitive slaveowning South, which was so fearful of what a *future* federal administration might do to slavery if it had too much power over other matters, that he would not entrust the solution of the immediate issue to a federal government that was perfectly sound on it. The only differences among prominent national Jacksonians with regard to slavery were tactical ones. Polk did not please some southerners who feared that a war with Mexico might ultimately jeopardize slavery in general, or be harmful to the particular interests of slaveowning states on the Atlantic seaboard. But there could be no question, as there was none about Old Hickory or little Van, that the head of the Democratic party during the Jacksonian era was dedicated to the preservation of slavery.

An ultimate judgment must go even further. For Jacksonian Democracy explicitly avowed or tacitly assumed not only the rightness of slavery within the states, but the propriety of committing the nation to diplomatic or military action that would spread the institution to new territories. Jackson's last official act had this intent. Silas Wright would complain later that Jackson had a mania on the issue of Texas annexation. Finally, the Jacksonians were not simply critical of the antislavery argument. They also impugned the motives of the men who made it and preferred not to refute them so much as to shut them up altogether. It is hard to disagree with Richard Brown's assessment that "from the inauguration of Washington until the Civil War the [proslavery] South was in the saddle of national politics. This is the central fact in American political history to 1860. To it there are no exceptions, not even in that period when the 'common man' stormed the ramparts of government under the banner of Andrew Jackson." That it was only a supposed "storming" by the common man is another matter. What is not in question is the Southern orientation and character of Jacksonian Democracy. The Dred Scott decision was not accidentally the handiwork of one of its chief figures.

Inspired—if that is the word—by laissez-faire notions, the national government did not attempt to do much about economic problems. Significant neomercantilistic measures were reserved during the era to the states. But within the limits of its negativistic theoretical assumptions about the lack of federal responsibility in the economic area, the Jacksonians did set forth policies whose effects both on growth and stability were by no means negligible. It is impossible to measure its precise effects, but the famous *Charles River Bridge* decision of the Taney Court was justly if not always accurately celebrated. It was not anticapitalistic. For all its general assertions about the supremacy of the public interest, there was nothing in it that smacked of confiscation or hostility to private property. Overwrought Whig responses to it, when they were not contrived, showed mainly how much even men of affairs are influenced by the excessive rhetoric that features the propaganda warfare of their day. And yet, after all that is said, the decision remains a liberating one. By denying to vested or established interests additional implicit powers that might enable them to engross the field of their enterprise, it opened wider the door of entrepreneurial opportunity, answering perfectly the needs of a youthful, vigorous, expanding capitalistic society. Democratic state legislatures that would prevent the replacement of special acts of incorporation by general or which tried to perpetuate the monopolistic system so dear to Jacksonian propaganda because so rousingly attacked in it, worked at cross purposes with the spirit of *Charles River*. The party faithful in the state capital were not disposed to give up a good thing under which they decided who got what. Fortunately for the development of the corporate form, ultimately they did not have their way.

Protective tariffs according to their supporters were the preeminent means of promoting the nation's economic growth. Free traders of course disagreed. The consensus of modern scholarship in economic history is that the significance of the tariff in American economic development in the 19th century has been much overrated. Significant correlations have not been found between tariff levels and the growth of the industries affected by them. Political interest in the issue was nevertheless intense, customs duties normally providing by far most federal funds, except for the few years of booming land sales prior to the Specie Circular and the Panic of 1837, and all administrations had to tread carefully in this area. Certain manufacturers and raw materials producers were convinced they needed it; increasingly, as in South Carolina, partisans of an unprotected economy came to be convinced that Congressional enactment of such partial legislation raised the question as to whether continued adherence to a union so governed was in their interest. But in politics men may be ready to resort to extremes over issues that reflective observers of a later time judge insignificant or inflated. That Jacksonian tariff policies were inconsistent and politically motivated is one of the less controversial assertions one can make of the era. In view of the mixed consequences, even of a consistent tariff policy, it is hard to draw any firm conclusions as to the role federal policy had in the nation's economic growth other than that it was slight.

Government on the state level played a vital role in expanding and improving the nation's transportation network. Private capital, insufficient at best and made even more unlikely by the risks attendant on investment in "developmental" projects running through underdeveloped areas, could not have done the job of binding the expanding Union together. State intervention was the necessary ingredient that made possible a form of common market in which superior producers of an industrial or agricultural commodity could dispose profitably of their product in the most distant corners of the nation. The social price paid, in the form of poor construction, mismanagement, speculation, and downright corruption, cost more than the achievement warranted, according to some critics. But that kind of question is never resolved. Whether worth the cost or not, state support to the transportation revolution was indispensable.

Federal support of "internal improvements," for all the hulabaloo and controversy it engendered, was inconsistent, spasmodic, and mired in politics. Since it was a cardinal principle in Clay's American System, Jacksonians acted as though they had no alternative but to take a less than enthusiastic stand on the issue. Jackson's views changed after he moved to the White House, but too much should not be made of the Maysville veto in view of the fact that Old Hickory approved greater expenditures of internal improvements, including those purely local in character, than all previous administrations combined. Many internal improvements champions had no qualms about such vetoes. Like Cyrus King, who said, "the post roads of New England are now good . . . if they are not so elsewhere let those concerned make them so," they would not have their tax monies used to pay for projects not of direct benefit to their own states.

Attitudes toward the issue were most complex. Mississippians who eagerly sought federal assistance were dismayed but not discouraged by Maysville. Despite their disappointment at the "betrayal," many voters remained loyal to a Democracy and a Hero who pleased them in other, not always rational, respects. But Marylanders were evidently discountenanced by Jackson's veto of a bill that provided for a turnpike from Washington to Frederick. Significant defections from the Jackson party's leadership, and a decline in its voting strength, followed the veto, in a state where federal aid for internal improvements was taken seriously. In South Carolina, Virginia, and Georgia, however, strong constitutional scruples accounted for an opposition to federal roads that in some cases were badly needed. In Joseph Harrison's words, Jacksonian and particularly Van Buren's opposition to internal improvements, "however agreeable to the constitutional susceptibilities of the Southern Atlantic States, did little for their badly deficient systems of communications." Jackson's actual approval of such measures was not popular in the South, but "since its worst enemy could not accuse it [the Jackson administration] of systematic planning . . . the South was accordingly comforted."

If national government did little for economic growth it had a much greater effect on economic stability. But its role was largely negative. Jacksonian policy and practice, in contrast to Old Hickory's rationales for them, fostered not stability but its opposite. For all the brave talk in Jacksonian utterances in praise of hard work, honest industry, frugality, modest rewards to sober enterprise, and all of the other canons of the old agrarian faith, actual Jacksonian measures either did nothing to thwart speculation or they abetted it. The Specie Circular of 1836 tried too late to call a halt to a process whereby government land offices themselves had encouraged dangerous speculation in public lands. The sudden federal refusal to accept as payment local bank notes whose overissue its own previous policy had encouraged, aggravated rather than stabilized the situation. As Harry N. Scheiber has noted, "by casting doubt on the solvency of some banks, Jackson contributed to public distrust of all banks and increased the tendency of private persons to hoard specie." Whether done grudgingly, as Jackson indicated it was, or not, the decision to distribute the federal surplus to the states only fed more fuel to the fires of inflation, promoting overextension of improvement projects as of state banks and the paper notes some of them printed in ever greater quantities. Jackson's great war on the Second Bank of the United States was the federal policy that more than any other touched on the issue of stability. Since I have dealt earlier with other aspects of the Bank struggle, the following discussion will try to focus on the issue of stability.

In his first message to Congress, Jackson charged that since the Bank had "failed in the great end of establishing a uniform and sound currency," therefore the Congress and "the people" might begin to consider whether another agency could be devised to replace it. Even a most sympathetic modern critic considers Old Hickory's currency ideas "weird." Less than three years later the Hero struck down the bill to recharter favored by the people's representatives, who obviously disagreed with him about the effect of Mr. Biddle's Bank on the nation's currency. Was Jackson's criticism valid? It is not even certain that *he* thought it was. According to Matthew Bevan, President Jackson had told him the Bank "was a blessing to the country, administered as it was, diffusing a healthful circulation, sustaining the general credit without partiality of political bias." It is altogether possible that intending to destroy the BUS for reasons having more to do with politics or prejudice than anything else, he simply criticized it on grounds he and his political managers thought would be best accepted by the electorate. Old Hickory himself, to use an old expression, did not put his money where his mouth was. At the same time that he attacked the Bank, Jackson "continued to keep every dollar he owned in the [Bank's] Washington and Nashville branches." As James Curtis has recently observed, "Jackson did not hate all paper money, only the excessive note issues that threatened to depreciate his holdings."

Apart from Democratic politicians, few knowledgeable contemporaries agreed with the President. And the motives and anti-Bank behavior of Jacksonian leaders and officeholders should not be misunderstood. Prior to Jackson's veto it appears that most Democrats favored the Bank. "Only then," as Bruce Ambacher notes, "did Jacksonians have to choose between Jackson and the Bank." Not surprisingly they deferred to their leader. It is hard to disagree with McFaul's recent assessment that their responses are best explained by "political necessity rather than ideological commitment."

Gallatin thought the Bank's own notes were as good as gold. William David Lewis, cashier of the Girard Bank of Philadelphia, who would subsequently be one of the beneficiaries of the removal of the deposits from the BUS when his own bank was designated an official repository of federal funds, himself had no doubts about the reliability of Biddle's notes. No modern economic historian, not even Thomas P. Govan, finds Biddle's performance as banker altogether blameless. Yet the one point banking specialists seem to agree on is that the notes of the Second Bank of the United States were the soundest money not only of their own time but perhaps of the entire period prior to the Federal Reserve.

The ratio of specie or coin to the face value of the Bank's notes was generally higher than one to two, a far higher ratio than was typical for the era's money. One of the severest critics of the Second Bank's performance gives it plus marks for helping to "create a sound national currency . . . by maintaining specie payments on its own notes." That its own eastern branches accepted notes from western branches at a discount of 1 percent or less in order to avoid being stripped of specie by the needier western outlets, was sensible and sound, although it "gave critics of the Bank an opportunity to accuse it of not maintaining a uniform currency." But such a charge was politically motivated rather than soundly based. The eminent John McLean, who commanded great respect from the Jacksonians, could not believe "the adversaries of the Bank in good faith," however. The Bank's effects were "obviously excellent, especially in the West where it furnishes a currency that is safe and portable." Detailed studies by modern banking specialists find that the second Bank provided a currency of high quality, its notes frequently preferred to gold. Based on ample specie reserves and domestic bills of exchange for the most part, its notes were far more sound than those of most other American banks, on the one hand, while the Bank's currency policy has been found more conducive to growth and therefore more in the national interest than the rigid hard money ideas of a Thomas Hart Benton, on the other.

The Bank's role in maintaining the stability of the notes of other banks was perhaps even more important in promoting a sound currency for the nation than was its policy with regard to its own notes. For as McLean observed of the BUS, "aside from its other advantages it has that of preventing the establishment of bad banks. It refuses to take their notes and in this way discredits them on the spot." He was describing a variation on the procedure that was later called a "self-acting" way of conducting the central banking function. As the repository of government funds, the Bank, as has been pointed out earlier, accumulated the diverse notes used in payment to customs collectors and government land offices. When the Bank of the United States required payment from the state banks which had issued the notes, in effect it compelled them to "be honest." And by punishing banks too free to print paper whether or not they had specie to back it up, the BUS certainly was forcing them in the direction of issuing a more trustworthy currency and thus indirectly working to stabilize the economy. Inflationists and wildcat bankers, who could not care less about stability, took a dim view of the "monster" institution which thus interfered with their undisciplined schemes.

But Biddle did not inveterately insist on specie payment, thus qualifying "the automaticity of the [central banking] function." For when in his judgment it was to the interest of the nation, the economy and the BUS to loosen up credit, perhaps because specie had been drained either from the nation as a whole or from a particular section, he would exercise his discretion by simply abstaining from the demand for payment. Of course these were only technical functions capable of being performed well or badly, depending on the ability of the man at the controls. The consensus of the cognoscenti is that Nicholas Biddle was a virtuoso. He was a brilliant man and also an arrogant one, impatient, even contemptuous of the criticism directed at him by those he considered ignorant. But he was not venal. His main concerns prior to 1832 seemed always to be the interests of the economy as a whole rather than the highest possible profits for the BUS stockholders. The modest 7 percent profit that was the norm during his tenure in fact brought on his head the censure of some stockholders. He had a flair for central banking and seemed to delight in playing the game, deciding when to go easy, when to crack down. The important thing is that he played the game well. Under his guidance the BUS came close to being the "balance wheel of the banking system" that Biddle and his friends liked to think it was. In any case one can understand the contemporary viewpoint that "destroying the national bank to expel paper money was like killing the cat to keep the mice away." After the "war" was begun, Biddle hit back, launching the famous contraction of 1833 to 1834 that was designed, among other things, to demonstrate the indispensability of his Bank. That this tactic failed is another matter; modern research indicates that the so-called Biddle depression was slight and hardly due to his policies at all. The modern econometrician Peter Temin, whose overall interpretation betrays no particular sympathy for Biddle, concludes that his policy of contraction was an understandable response to a series of "provocations," and that far from hurting the economy, Biddle's actions stimulated the flow of European specie into the country, thus increasing its specie reserves. Edward Abdy had discerned that "though President Jackson and his organs of the press . . . are declared enemies of paper money, yet his chief supporters not only maintain the system he attacks" but they perpetuate "what he professes to detest." Later critics found a terrible irony in this Jacksonian policy.

Abetted by Amos Kendall's marvelously effective Veto message, which even Jackson's warmest modern admirer concedes was essentially demagogy, the Hero succeeded not only in frustrating the Congressional majority which favored renewing the charter of the BUS, but in winning warm popular approval for his anti-Bank campaign. Certainly this was the construction he placed on his decisive electoral victory in 1832. He now decided that his next contribution to a sound currency would take the form of gradually replacing the BUS as the repository for federal funds with state banks chosen for the purpose. In his first message to Congress after his reelection, his language was reflective, questioning: in view of the Bank's abuse of its powers, might it not be wise for Congress to investigate whether the deposits of the government were safe in such an institution? Jackson's subsequent behavior shows how little these words can be credited. For when the House three months later approved a majority report by the Ways and Means Committee that an investigation had indeed established the safety of the government's deposits, Jackson was dissuaded not at all, confiding to Taney, his Attorney General, his wish to discuss "the problem of finding safe places of deposit for the government funds."[2] Taney proved his mastery of human nature by responding with a letter that heaped sycophantic praise on the old man, reminding him of his heroic military and political victories but evincing concern about the effect removal would have on his reputation. Since Secretary Duane was unwilling to authorize the removal, he, Taney, unqualified though he was, would stand beside his great chieftain and accept the Treasury portfolio—if the Hero thought it would be helpful. But in view of the great political risks attendant on such a policy, should Jackson jeopardize his splendid reputation? Of course, Taney hastened to assure his master, only he could slay the monster, but was the risk worth taking? One can guess Jackson's reaction!

McLane, in refusing, had argued that "no adequate reason existed for the removal." After he was moved upstairs to the State Department, William J. Duane likewise refused to be Jackson's puppet and authorize the removal of the deposits, rightly insisting that under the law he, not the President, had the responsibility for the deposits.[3] He refused to give a removal order, citing among other objections, his belief that "the state banks, fearing the vengeance of the Bank of the United States, would not dare to accept deposits from the government." That was all the excuse Jackson needed to send Amos Kendall on a tour of the eastern seaboard cities, to visit banks in Baltimore, Philadelphia, New York, and Boston to find out if this was so. It was not. Kendall reported back that "a considerable number of banks [were] eager to have the deposits." In view of

---

[2] Some pro-Jackson historians have ridiculed the majority report that found in favor of the BUS, one of them even noting that the minority report was a longer document! I find it hard to interpret Jackson's deposits policy as a sincere response to a real danger. Suddenly government deposits were no longer safe; the discerning man in the White House, who knew best, could not wait until he safeguarded the national interest by turning the deposits over to Thomas Ellicott and company. Knowing Charles Sellers' general view that Jacksonian Democracy was in fact a movement of and for the people, led by their true champions, I find very creditable his observation that "Jackson was impatient for the [Congressional] investigation, which he counted on to give him a *pretext* for removing the deposits" (*Polk*, I, 196). [Italics mine.] Sellers quotes Charles Wickliffe of Kentucky who had predicted that "the government deposites are to be withdrawn, they are wanted elsewhere! State banks are to be enlisted as soldiers in the next campaign, The Government deposites are wanted to pay the bounty" (ibid., 189, 190).

[3] The law establishing the second Bank stated: "The deposits of the money of the United States . . . shall be made in said bank or branches thereof, unless the Secretary of the Treasury shall at any time otherwise order and direct. . . ." Later the Supreme Court in *Kendall* v. *Stokes*, 1838, took a position similar to Duane's, arguing that an appointed official was *not* a mere creature of the Executive.

their great joy, Kendall was here uncharacteristically guilty of understatement. Having used the pages of the *Globe* to inform the public that commencing October 1 new deposits would be placed in designated state banks, Jackson removed Duane one week prior to October 1, as was his right. He replaced him with the complaisant Taney.

Of course a storm broke out. This was not the first time deposits were to be made in a state bank, for in 1831 Lewis Cass's intervention had helped secure federal deposits for the Bank of Michigan. But that had been a most exceptional decision, not part of an anti-BUS policy. Clay compared the "daring usurpation" to the same "spirit of defiance to the Constitution and to all law" shown by Jackson "during the conduct of the Seminole War." John Derby, heretofore an ardent Jacksonian, wondered what "temporary illness and imbecility . . . persuaded [the President] to lay violent hands on the public treasure and transfer it." Mississippi Democrats for once sided with old Poins. In New York a number of mercantile Democrats defected. A Cincinnati Whig wrote to Jackson: "Damn your . . . soul, remove them deposites back again, and recharter the bank or you will certainly be shot in less than two weeks and that by myself!!!" But such language, it goes without saying, only encouraged a man who needed no encouragement to stay on the course he had decided to follow. Told of a rumor that a Baltimore "mob" intended to "lay siege to the Capitol until the deposits were restored," Jackson said, "I shall be glad to see this mob on Capitol Hill. The leaders I will hang as high as Haman to deter forever all attempts to control the Congress by intimidation." Only one man in America obviously had the right to control Congress. But political controversy aside, what effect did the removal have on economic stability in general and monetary stability in particular?

Horace Binney told the House of Representatives that the new administration policy would bring in its wake "paper missiles shooting in every direction through the country" and a "further extension of the same detestable paper" that the Democracy professed to abhor. This of course was not Jackson's intention. If a powerful wing of his party hoped that Biddle's defeat opened up profit-making opportunities for the new depositories, the hard money faction thought of the removal as a "first step toward more fundamental reform."

Jackson and his lieutenants established a standard that the new depositories would ostensibly have to meet. Security would be required to assure the safety of the funds; regular reports would be made to the Secretary of the Treasury; the banks' books would be open to government examination at all times; the deposits could be withdrawn at will by the government. In practice, however, the criterion a bank had to meet was not financial or banking reliability so much as political loyalty. "Those which are in hands politically friendly will be preferred," said Amos Kendall. Good banks of ample resources and excellent reputation were bypassed for banks whose only virtue was the Democratic politics of their officers. Levi Woodbury, Secretary of the Treasury in 1836, actually "had to explain to irate Democrats that several 'enemy' banks in Ohio began receiving deposits after 1836 because there were not enough friendly institutions in the state." Frank Otto Gatell's investigation of the political ties of the presidents, cashiers, and directors of the banks chosen prior to 1836, shows that of the more than 200 men identifiable, 78.8 percent were Democrats, 21.2 percent were Whigs. Somehow Amos Kendall had been able to ferret out Democratic bankers from amongst those common folk who alone belonged to the Jacksonian party. "Pet" banks indeed! During this period as new deposit banks were named, "the political and personal bias . . . became more pronounced, and many recently chartered banks began to receive deposits." Not only politics but nepotism or personal connections were "determinants for selection." Banks selected by such standards tell better than all the political rhetoric what the removal of the deposits was about. Of course Jackson, Kendall, and Taney would have been delighted had the "pets" performed well. But their methods of selection, like the initial decision to remove the deposits from the BUS, show that sound banking performance was not the major consideration.

The choice of the Bank of Manhattan Company, the Bank of America, and the Mechanic's Bank as the New York City pets, lent color to the charge that the Jacksonian policy served the interests of Wall Street. McFaul's conclusion is that Secretary of the Treasury Levi Woodbury's "management of pet banking operations depended upon cooperation between the Washington Treasury and Wall Street bankers." While there is no evidence that Wall Street called the administration's tune, there is ample indication that such New York City financial luminaries as Isaac Bronson, Nat Prime, James Gore King, and William B. Lawrence abandoned their earlier policy of support for Biddle, accommodating themselves to the changing flow of events.

The Bank of the Manhattan Company, under the control of good Democrats, was selected as one of the first of the pets in New York City. The same administration that opposed the BUS on the ground, among others, that undue foreign ownership of its stock was unfair to American citizens and would in wartime constitute a greater threat to us than the presence of foreign armed forces, managed to overlook the fact that "Irish landlords and British noblemen" held most of the Manhattan Bank's stock. For that matter Taney selected Thomas Ellicott's bank as a pet although its charter was soon to expire, despite the fact that the "impending charter expiration had been a principal argument used ugainst the Bank of the United States."

As might have been expected, the banks receiving the deposits were not thinking of stabilizing the economy. In Mississippi during the height of the "flush times" in 1836, "the Planters' Bank and the Agricultural Bank, which as 'pet' banks were entrusted with the proceeds from the record land sales of that era, were discounting recklessly." The closing of the BUS branch at Natchez, "conferred a sense of urgency to the movement for new banking facilities," and the legislature responded by chartering new banks to feed the speculative boom. Banks sought the coveted status of pets not for the honor but for the greater profits likely to result. The new system by replacing one comparatively conservative depository with dozens of more speculative ones inevitably escalated the paper inflation the Administration professed to dread. Thomas Hart Benton, dismayed at the scene, uttered his famous plaint: "I did not join in putting down the Bank of the United States to put up a wilderness of local banks." When Thomas Ellicott, the president of the Baltimore pet, the Union Bank, embarrassed the Administration by speculating recklessly with the deposits as soon as he received them, helping to bring on a bank panic in the city, Ellicott was helped out of his difficulties by Roger B. Taney, a stockholder in the bank, who "promised to support him fully—even to the extent of transferring government funds from other cities, despite the political dangers involved." Taney was irked with his old friend but the administration had to stand by its pets, for political if for no better reasons.

It is true that after the Deposit Act of 1836, which both enlarged the system, calling for a depository in each state, and which tried to strengthen it, by requiring of deposit banks ample specie reserves, confining government deposits to an amount three quarters of the value of a bank's paid-in capital and forbidding depositories to issue notes smaller than $5, new banks were selected on other than political grounds. In Harry Scheiber's careful language, "there were significant deviations" from the system of selecting pets by the politics of their directors, in the banks selected after 1836. In Ohio in 1836 and 1837 Whigs outnumbered Democrats by 66 to 20 on the directorates. (As was indicated above, the administration felt compelled to apologize to Democratic partisans.) By this time the system had not long to live. The Deposit Act stated that no bank that suspended specie payments could continue to hold government deposits. By May, 1837, the suspension of payments by all but five of the depositories marked the practical end of the experiment.

When Jackson had broached the plan to remove the deposits to his Cabinet, he had been warned that it might turn public opinion against him. According to Taney he had responded, "never fear, the people will understand it, and if we do right Providence will take care of us." There is more than enough in Jackson's 18 words to yield a modish discussion of his faith in the people or his conviction that he was the Lord's anointed. A more mundane explanation may suffice. While Jackson was as free as the next man in invoking Providence, it is hard to believe that this astute man of affairs seriously believed God preferred David Henshaw to Nicholas Biddle. Jackson's words seem to mean: "Never fear. The people can be made to agree with our explanation that a politically inspired move that actually threatens government funds is really part of the eternal struggle of the poor and the virtuous against the rich and the wicked." Certainly Jackson had no objection to receiving Providential support. But in such matters he was used to answering to himself alone. It seems clear that he had initiated the Bank War not at the behest of Wall Street or any other group but because he had decided to destroy the BUS.

As for the Independent Treasury, that old Calhounite idea which became law late in the Van Buren Administration, while it took the government out of banking, it did little either for financial stability or a sound currency. Despite its provision that government disbursements be only in gold, silver, or notes issued under government authority, Benton sadly noted the fact that "paper money and even broken bank paper money" continued to be paid out to the government's creditors. Indifferent to warnings, such as Isaac Bronson's to Gulian C. Verplanck, that "to separate Bank and State, [was] about as practicable [as] to make the waters on one side of a stream run in an opposite direction from the waters on the other," the Democrats enacted precisely such a separation. The best that a sympathetic modern economic historian can say for the independent treasury is that it "was of little economic importance" in its own time.

Gallatin charged that Jackson "found the currency in a sound and left it in a deplorable state." For all the inevitably lofty explanations they gave for destroying the second Bank, the Jacksonians appear to have been motivated largely by partisan political considerations in pursuing their policy. Removal must be undertaken, argued Amos Kendall, because a Democratic party ostensibly plagued by "doubt, hesitation, and discouragement," needed "some decisive act to reunite and inspirit them." It is not surprising that a policy whose architects appear to have given little thought to the welfare of the country should have had minimal, if not negative, effects on that welfare.

An important political issue concerned the efficiency and honesty of government. The Jacksonian and subsequent administrations undertook policies which bear directly on these twin issues. But even more pointedly than in the case of other problems, the question arises: was the federal influence constructive? During Jackson's first administration probably nothing incensed his critics more than his policy on appointments. The Spoils System his policy was named, and the Spoils System it remained, particularly in the treatment by James Parton and Whig historians who regarded it as the main blemish on Jackson's record. Progressive historians stressed the democratic implications in more rapid turnover of federal offices and the new policy's effects in fostering pragmatic parties held together by the contributions of officeholders—a party faithful whose loyalty was not to ideals but to the organization whose victory brought tangible rewards. In the higher civil service, among the officeholders whose positions were traditionally not protected by tenure, Andrew Jackson was no more democratic or an admirer of the common man than his aristocratic predecessors. Jackson's words

in his first annual message, that "the duties of all public officers are
. . . so plain and simple that men of intelligence may readily
qualify themselves for their performance," and that "no one man
has any more intrinsic right to office than another," clearly implied
that common men would be selected. For he did not say that public
office required educated men. Native intelligence, not learning, was
the qualification and in the Jacksonian canon who were more intelligent than Tom, Dick, and Harry? But Jackson's actions once more
belied his words. For in contrast to what most historians had believed, Old Hickory's choices were about as atypically rich, educated,
and of the most prestigious ethnic and social elites as those of the
Adams and Jefferson administrations.

Instead of reopening the question of whether the Jacksonians
truly initiated the Spoils System, a more fruitful line of enquiry is to
examine their actual policies for their effects on government. Jackson initiated no clean sweep, an 1832 report in the *Globe* showing
that 919 of 10,093 officeholders were removed up to 1830, with
slightly more than 10 percent of all officeholders replaced during
Jackson's tenure. Old Hickory grew understandably cynical about
the constant stream of office seekers who besieged him, observing of
those who appeared to turn against him only because he could not
satisfy their clamor for jobs, "if I had a *tit* for every one of these *pigs*
to suck at they would still be my friends." What critics called a
wholesale turnover was only retail to disappointed placemen. For all
the criticism of the new policy, the Whigs once in office proceeded
to administer it with as much enthusiasm as had their opponents.
As the Whig governor of New York in 1838, Seward asked one
question of a prospective candidate for office: "Is he a Whig?"
Clearly the rule answered to the mood and needs of the major
parties.

If Jackson's first message provided a lofty rationale, William
Marcy's blunt statement much better described Democratic practice.
Marcy had said that successful politicians "claim as a matter of
right, the advantages of success. They see nothing wrong in the
rule, that to the victor belong the spoils of the enemy." Trained in
the realistic atmosphere of New York State politics, Marcy had once
written his fellow member of the Regency, Azariah Flagg, "Don't be
too fastidious; where party feeling is strong almost anything that is
done is right." To him as to other Jacksonian pragmatists, the Spoils
System was old hat, unique after 1828 only in the larger number of
jobs to be given away and the larger expanse over which they were
distributed. In the elections that year Jackson editors explained
removals as a necessary "reform" of government, but by reform they
meant removal of political enemies. Language similar to Marcy's
was used by Reuben Whitney who, after 1832, became an ardent
Jacksonian, influential in the deposits controversy. "Those who
fought the battles are entitled to the spoils of victory" was to be the
standard for determining depositories. "The barnacles shall be
scraped clean from the ship of state; every 'traitor' must go," roared
Isaac Hill's organ. John Quincy Adams' diary recorded shortly after

Jackson's inauguration that "the only principles yet discernible in the conduct of the President were to feed the cormorant appetite for place, and to reward the prostitution of canvassing defamers."

Adams' sour words were written by a man who had been unable to bring himself to fire John McLean *merely* because he knew that McLean as Postmaster General was opposed to him, politically. Jackson was very different. When McLean, who had more patronage at his disposal than all other officials combined, told Jackson he would fire pro-Jackson as well as pro-Adams postmasters if he must kick men out for political activity, the General answered with a direct question. "Mr. McLean, would you accept a seat on the bench of the Supreme Court?" Four days later the malleable William T. Barry had replaced McLean and the wholesale "reform" began. According to L. D. White, the something new contained in Jacksonian appointments policy was neither the fact nor the number of replacements, but rather the reasons for them. Where "none of Jackson's predecessors had used the power to remove subordinate officers . . . for other reasons than well-justified cause, excepting Jefferson's removals in 1801 and 1802 to secure a party balance . . . Jackson and every one of his successors to 1861 reversed this rule and deliberately removed or sanctioned removal . . . for personal and partisan reasons." After the election of old Tippecanoe in 1840, Whig job seekers now "rushed pell-mell to Washington, every man with a raccoon's tail in his hat."

It was theoretically possible that partisan appointments might have gone to the most qualified of the party faithful. That was not the way it was done however. "In building his civil administration Jackson tended to judge men by their political faith and personal loyalty, not by their executive talent." Barry was designated because he had opposed Clay. A Federal judgeship was awarded the nonentity, Senator Powhatan Ellis of Mississippi, whose claim to the job consisted of his opposition to Poindexter. It was said of Ellis in the Senate that he had "attracted no further notice than an occasional expression of wonder how he ever got there." Nepotism, not personal ability, was the rule, as "personal friends, relatives, and party hacks multiplied on the public payrolls." In Massachusetts Jackson even went over the head of Henshaw, his own appointee to the strategic Collectorship of the port of Boston, to make sure that the Federalists who had supported him in the Bay State got their rewards.

Jackson would brook no opposition to appointments he had decided to make. He broke with Poindexter, his indefatigable champion in Mississippi during the 1828 campaign, over a patronage squabble. Their bitter feud began when Poindexter, a senator from Mississippi, protested the nomination to the land office of that state of a "Tennessean, a neighbor of the Hermitage," who had once served one of Jackson's cronies.

To the Jacksonians the main function of officeholders was not to do their jobs well but to contribute to the party and bring in voters on election day. To assure achievement of the former purpose, offices were "bought and sold to subordinates by a regulated annual stipend." By the end of the era, Tammany had lists in the New York Customs House containing "a scale of contributions according to the nature and income of the job." In Matthew Crenson's phrase, major party appointees had come to regard office "less as opportunities for public service than as sources of private profit."

One of the fruits of the new policy was corruption. The Post Office under Barry was tincured with scandal. Land office agents in the South and Southwest openly speculated with government funds. Jackson probably did not appreciate the irony in a finding by the Senate Committee on Public Lands in 1835, under the chairmanship of old Poins, that speculation and fraud were practised on "a large scale in Alabama, Mississippi, and Louisiana." Charged as the greatest offender was Samuel Gwin, whose appointment by Jackson had caused the rupture in the Mississippi Democracy. Officials of the Indian Bureau, like those in the land offices, were not above actually filling their pockets with government revenues. The most notorious crimes took place in the New York Customs House. Samuel Swartwout, distrusted by many but liked and therefore chosen by Jackson, embezzled not quite $1.25 million in what Philip Hone called "the most appalling account of delinquency ever exhibited in this country." His successor, Jesse Hoyt, was as troublesome if not as successful, his deficiencies enlivening the Van Buren years. If it has not been demonstrated quantitatively that the incidence of political corruption actually increased during the era, much evidence suggests that it did so. Attempts to blame the falling off on the spread of democracy and to an alleged deterioration of values seem misguided. Americans, as Henry Clay discovered, were not ready to forgive even the hint of "corruption," nor is there persuasive evidence that business and professional values were changing for the worse. Increasing venality seems to have been due more to the rise of peculiarly pragmatic political parties than to changes in the people and their values.

The efficiency of the public service sharply declined. The devaluation of prestige that accompanied the impairment of efficiency tended to create a vicious cycle in which able men increasingly avoided government service. The picture, however, was not totally negative. The continuation of "a nucleus of permanent clerks who knew what had to be done" was a positive factor. Not all appointments were bad. Amos Kendall turned out to be an able administrator in the Post Office. The public service was enlarged and some of its functions expanded, while in the nonappointive positions, earlier traditions of ethical deportment and efficiency continued to be observed. Crenson credits Jackson with beginning "to erect a formal bureaucratic structure which was designed to produce mechanical adherence to some of the old standards of decency." A modern admirer of Old Hickory who finds that "his efforts resulted in a substantial improvement in the performance of Federal business," concedes that "unfortunately, the techniques Jackson employed to bring about that improvement were susceptible to serious abuse in the hands of lesser men."

Much has been made by some analysts of the democratic tendencies of a Spoils System which rewarded not an aristocratic elite but faceless commoners required only to help fill the party coffers. A case can also be made for a different viewpoint. If one of the real political issues of the era was the fact that popular influence in the major parties was more nominal than real, it can be argued that the new appointments policy worsened rather than improved the situation. Creation on a national scale of the kind of tight groups of officeholding elites, similar to those which earlier had managed to make state political machines essentially impervious to popular control, represented not so much the democratization, as the commercialization of politics.

J ackson's own behavior as Chief Executive became one of the era's most bitterly disputed political issues. Supporters and admirers liked to stress the allegedly democratic or egalitarian substance of the campaigns he waged, on the one hand, and the democratic implications of his rough, emotional, forceful style, on the other. His weaknesses, in being weaknesses shared or easily understood by the people, were thus really strengths. Political scientists who have succeeded in establishing Jackson as one of the handful of men accepted as great Presidents emphasize his affinity for the people, his bold and strong leadership, and above all his dynamic administration of the office whose powers he significantly expanded. Critics spoke of his demagogy and "executive tyranny." Temporarily commanding a majority in the Senate in 1834, Whig opponents proposed a formal censure of the President. They charged that he had "assumed upon himself authority and power not conferred by the Constitution and laws, but in derogation of both." Clay's detailed censure resolution ranged over Jackson's "unconstitutional" removal of the deposits, his abuse of the removal and appointive powers, his disregard of the high court's decision in *Worcester* v. *Georgia,* and a misuse of the veto power that was turning the republic into a tyranny. When the Senate by 26 to 20 voted to censure the President, Jackson immediately sent back a protest that warned of a "senatorial oligarchy." While the Senate debate was on, Jackson wrote his adopted son, "the storm in Congress is still raging, Clay reckless and as full of fury as a drunken man in a brothel, his abuse and his coadjutors pass harmless by me." The actual censure vote however stung the Hero sharply. Neither he nor his political friends could not rest until another Senate in 1837 voted to undo the indictment by writing the word "expunged" heavily across the offending passage while Whig critics charged mutilation of the Senate's record. Modern observers seem to have as much trouble in being neutral or detached about the man as his contemporaries.

The Whig defense of Congressional prerogatives owed as much to practical considerations as to theoretical ones. "Executive usurpation!" was the transparently political war cry of the party out of power—or at least out of the Presidency. After Jackson was no longer in office, Clay lucidly explained why the expansion of the executive power was inevitable, no matter who or what kind of personality wielded it: "the executive branch was eternally in action; it was ever awake . . . its action was continuous and increasing . . . like the tides of some mighty river and removed every frail obstacle which might be set up to impede its course." That Whig accusations against "King Andrew" were obviously expedient does not automatically negate their validity. Jackson's claims to greatness are not established by the fact that his critics were partisan. His own performance must be evaluated.

Approve of his measures or no, there is no denying the strength of Andrew Jackson as President. The fact that his manner—a blend of forthrightness, simplicity, stubbornness, self-righteousness, controlled anger, fearlessness, and more subtlety than met the eye—had great appeal for the American people was hardly a fault. I suppose I have made fairly clear my own disenchantment with his traits but I have no doubt I would find them more attractive if I thought better of his and his party's behavior. At his best this man did indeed show how a leader could lead, and how force of personality might not only enable a man to prevail over opponents or discover previously unknown powers in the executive office but also could promote the national interest. The nullification controversy is a case in point. Certainly Jackson's conduct was not blameless. His treatment of *Worcester* v. *Georgia did* encourage the nullifiers. His—or Edward Livingston's—Proclamation to the people of South Carolina was regarded by Democrats as well as by Henry Clay as "too strongly biased on the side of consolidation." In the battle of the toasts, at the famous Jefferson Day Dinner, there is much to be said for the moral superiority of Calhoun's, "The Union—next to our liberty the most dear." His hatred of Calhoun seemed to affect the President's tactics. Oversimplifying and distorting the motives of the nullifiers, whom he interpreted as demagogic conspirators, Jackson overreacted in a manner that Richard Latner holds "strained the loyalties of his party's southern wing."

Yet Jackson's conduct in this case was effectively designed to achieve the goal proclaimed in his own toast: "Our Federal Union. It must be preserved." A chief executive's first obligation is not to achieve noble abstractions but to deliver the realm intact to his successor. When his performance is contrasted with Buchanan's, a quarter of a century later, it becomes all the more luminous. Jackson *did* preserve the Union—if for the time being and not by himself alone. Old Hickory was tactful as well as firm in dealing with this most thorny of problems. For all the toughness of the Force Bill, he had the flexibility to permit South Carolina to save face as it withdrew and Clay to solidify his reputation as great compromiser. Jackson's near deathbed utterance that his two great regrets were that he had not hanged Calhoun and shot Clay were only honest expressions of *private* feelings, fortunately.

Jackson's own personality made a particularly sharp impress on foreign policy. "Shirtsleeve diplomacy" was the affectionate and admiring description of Jackson's informality, honesty, and pugnaciousness in dealing with the sophisticated embassies of the old world. It reflected so well the people and the nation it represented, in its candor, crudeness, vigor, and disrespect for traditional forms. And it seemed to work. The self-praise heaped on the administration by its gray eminence, Kendall, during the campaign of 1832, seemed not altogether unjustified. Colombian depredations had ceased, Turkish waters had been opened to American shipping, a suspended treaty with Mexico was put into operation, and indemnity claims collected from Denmark. More significantly, the long overdue French spoliation claims that traced back to Napoleon's attacks on American shipping were finally collected, mainly as a result of Jackson's forcefulness; and the vital British West Indies trade finally opened to us, the controversy "untangled with skilful diplomacy." Paradoxically, the latter achievement was due more to guile than bluster, although threats were made by the President when he felt the British were dragging their feet. In April 1830 he proposed a nonintercourse law to be applied against Canada, with provision for enforcement by revenue cutters, advising his Secretary of State that the United States must act "with that promptness and energy due to our national character." But in fact Van Buren succeeded in winning a West Indies treaty only after what has been called a "humiliating disavowal of Adams and Clay, in the name of the American people." Where the Adams administration had indeed been tough, insisting on most-favored-nation status for Americans trading in the Indies, the Jackson Administration went hat in hand, asking less, promising not to repeat the errors of the past, behaving in a manner described by Webster as "derogatory to the character and honor of the United States." Even George Dangerfield, as uncritical an admirer of Jacksonian political behavior as any historian one can encounter, concedes that perhaps Webster was right.

The problem with Jacksonian diplomacy was the extent to which the tactics it pursued reflected the personal idiosyncracies of the Chief Executive rather than the needs of the nation. As the West Indies negotiations indicated, Jackson did not conduct all the nation's foreign affairs in a rage. A modern historian concludes that Jackson came close to living up to his boast that his administration "had no agency . . . in the steps resorted to by the people of Texas to establish for themselves an independent government." (Critics charged that Jackson was indifferent to the smuggling of men and supplies across the United States border into Texas in violation of the Neutrality Act of 1818.) Political considerations may have prevented Jackson from moving rashly to annex Texas, since as Frederick Merk has noted, he feared that such a move might threaten Van Buren's chances in 1836. They did not however inhibit Jackson from privately advising the Texans to claim California territory "in order to paralyze the opposition of the North and East to annexation." In a recent analysis of Jackson's foreign policy, Robert Charles Thomas concludes that many Americans *rightly* feared that "Old Hickory's temper, dare-deviltry, and xenophobia would embroil the United States in difficulties with other nations." In the references to the foreign claims disputes that were sprinkled through his annual messages, Jackson left no doubt that the American cause was invariably and "irrefutably just, and not subject to further consideration."

Jackson's admirers may take comfort from the fact that the president did not distinguish between small nations and large in his highhandedness. In 1830 he intimidated Denmark with a veiled threat of force in connection with an American claim of Danish violations on the high seas. In 1832 American Marines killed more than 100 Malaysians, mainly civilians, in Sumatra in retaliation for an incident the previous year that cost the lives of three American seamen. In fairness to Jackson, his orders that force follow only on unsuccessful negotiations were reversed; yet Congressional Democrats successfully prevented public disclosure of the President's correspondence with the American commander. Jackson hurled "insulting and threatening" demands against the Kingdom of the Two Sicilies, threatening to back them up with force. Thomas concludes that "the success of such a policy of threats must have influenced Jackson in his opinion of how to deal with France."

Some ardent nationalists were delighted that Old Hickory brought the nation to the brink of war over the dilatoriness of the French *Chambre* in appropriating the 25 million francs French negotiators had earlier agreed to pay in settlement of American claims. Even Jackson's critic, old Philip Hone, thrilled at the manliness of the Jacksonian determination to resort to force—"reprisals upon French property"—in case the French government delayed further. When the French finally did agree to pay the sum, the final deterrent to payment was in fact the Jacksonian language that was unacceptable to a great European state. All's well that ends well is not a bad standard for appraising international controversies. But it is a fact that Andrew Jackson unnecessarily brought the two nations to the edge of a war that easily *could* have broken out.

That the successful resolution of the dispute in 1836 was a "feather in the cap" of the Democracy was a political fact, due in large measure to the restraining influence of Clay and Congressional Whigs and Democrats alike who early in the dispute went on record to assert that although our claims were justified, it was "inexpedient to threaten reprisals." But how can one give passing grades to a "diplomacy" that is almost a contradiction in terms; which provokes a war atmosphere by undiplomatic language or usages that, in addition, are utterly gratuitous? It is not effective diplomacy to invoke measures and run risks whose vast dimensions bear no relationship to the small problems they ostensibly would solve. Unwise bellicoseness would be bad enough if it conformed to a rational design in the mind of the Administration that resorted to it. It becomes frightening when it rather seems to be due to the temper and personality of the man in the White House.

A year later, in the face of a stalemate over another claims controversy, Jackson threatened Mexico with "immediate war" that according to him would have been justified "in the eyes of all nations." By what a recent biographer calls his fair and honest behavior, Van Buren convinced the Mexicans to settle the claims dispute. Contrasting Van's performance with Jackson's, James Curtis concludes that "at no time did [Van Buren] indulge in the irresponsible behavior that so often marred the diplomacy of his predecessor."

The character of Andrew Jackson was a political issue because so much of his political behavior seems to be explained by it. A fellow Tennesseean described him as one of "those fighting characters [who] are never at peace unless they have something to quarrel with." Jackson seemed to concur, when at the beginning of his presidency he said, "I was born for a storm and calm does not suit me." Several modern historians discern an "intense and inner turmoil" in the man from childhood on, a byproduct of emotional and physical disorders that engulfed him after the early death of his parents, manifested in "traumatic early speech difficulty," a melange of physical ailments, and erratic social behavior. Whatever their ultimate causes—and none of the recent psychoanalyses are fully persuasive—Jackson's public actions, like his private, seem to have owed more to his inner rage than to the nature of the events leading up to these actions. That same readiness to resort to violence which led this man, prior to his accession to the Presidency, to threaten or actually to inflict physical punishment or death on almost every man who thwarted him or who had offended him with some fancied insult, was brought into play in his dealing with foreign governments as with domestic issues and personages. There may have been something democratic in his total unconcern with the stature of the men he challenged—although he was southern aristocrat enough to distinguish between pistol whipping, caning, or dueling, depending on the status of his enemy. But there was something infinitely disturbing in the judgment that could distort picayune differences literally into issues of life and death. He killed one man over a racetrack argument, threatened to kill two others for calling him ambitious, and a Secretary of War for advising him, accurately, about rumors that connected him with Burr. In 1817, in his 50th year, he challenged General Winfield Scott, calling him a "hectoring bully" and one of the "intermeddling pimps and spies of the War Department," after Scott advised him that while he had not *written* that Jackson committed an act of mutiny in ordering disobedience by his troops of direct commands of the War Department, he had privately called Jackson's behavior mutinous and a reprimand to President Monroe.

Jackson took criticisms of his acts as personal attacks. Hugh White's preference for Clay's tariff bill over his, in 1833, was, in

Jackson's words, "an insult to me." Jackson was a good son, for his mother's last letter had urged him, "sustain your manhood always. Never bring a suit at law for assault and battery or for defamation. The law affords no remedy for such outrages that can satisfy the feelings of a true man." Jackson certainly seemed to equate true manhood with violence and a refusal to accept criticism. He told volunteer troops in 1812 that through war they would "reestablish the national character." In the face of challenges, whether in national or international politics, he invoked the same standard of response that earlier he had fallen back on in a personal quarrel over land or women. The contempt for authority and law that characterized his youthful and early adult life in Tennessee is clearly discernible in his later acts. Florida boundary, War Department orders, Marshall Court decisions, Congressional resolutions, all got equally short shrift. The arrogance, the disingenuousness, the cruel disregard for the rights of Indians, the highhandedness, the egotism bordering on egomania, the intolerance, the joy in hating, the emotionalism, the pettiness, the vindictiveness, that mark his career before 1828 continued to manifest themselves afterwards. Obviously a President's official performance will be influenced by his personality. That is unavoidable. In Jackson's case a special point need be made of this truism not so much because the *gestalt* of his traits was unique, but rather because they were so dangerous and so productive of conflicts that should have been avoidable.

There is no denying that this commanding personality transformed the Presidential office. Brushing aside traditional restraints and usages, constitutional precedents, Supreme Court decisions, federal treaties, and laws of Congress, Andrew Jackson substituted what the great constitutional historian Edward Corwin called presidential domination for the legislative authority that had prevailed earlier. The same man who ridiculed South Carolina's right unilaterally to set aside a law it found unconstitutional, himself, according to Corwin, claimed the "right to refuse to enforce both statutes and judicial findings on his own independent finding that they were not warranted by the Constitution." His "removal of subordinates for personal and partisan reasons" expanded the power of the presidential office, according to L. D. White, "to proportions hitherto unknown or unthought of"; for this unprecedented "capacity to remove could be used to induce almost universal compliance among officeholders, either by its exercise or by mere threat or expectation of its use." Opponents attacked Jackson for reducing Cabinet ministers to clerks if not ciphers, with Democratic supporters protesting his failure to hold formal cabinet sessions and urging him to consult more frequently with department heads. Recently disclosed evidence indicates that at least after 1831 Jackson held cabinet meetings fairly regularly. There are no signs however that his new practice was anything but an astute maneuver designed as "window dressing."

In vetoing more congressional bills than had all previous presidents combined, Jackson did not of course violate the Constitution. What he did repudiate was a tradition of executive restraint that had been heavily influenced by the clear intention of the Founding Fathers. As Alexander Hamilton recognized in *The Federalist*, the veto was a power associated with the British monarchy, an undemocratic and unpopular power that Hamilton assured the American people would be used only in those rare instances when congressional legislation either threatened to reduce the powers of the presidency or was flagrantly at odds with the Constitution. Unlike his predecessors, who refused to invoke this power merely because they were presented with bills that, were they congressmen, they would have voted against, Jackson vetoed measures that for whatever reasons he opposed, in the process making the president the *legislative* equal of roughly one-sixth of congress. And by that rhetorical alchemy of which they were masters, Jacksonian propagandists turned what two generations of Americans had considered a monarchical power—the veto—into a "great expression of the popular will."

The strong Presidency owes as much to Andrew Jackson as to any man. But this fateful contribution was a mixed blessing. Without a doubt it has made possible quicker responses both to domestic and international crises. But even those who approve the wars strong Presidents have led the nation into, must give pause to the upsetting of the traditional constitutional balance that has accompanied these adventures. And what happens when a "strong President" leads the nation along a dismal path—or at least one that is dismal in the judgment of most knowledgeable men—but manages through artful propaganda and news management to convince the mass of the electorate that this policy is morally good and pragmatically sound? My own reading of Jacksonian politics is that Jackson accomplished something very close to that, as he appealed to the people over the heads of his—and therefore their—enemies, oversimplifying complex issues and fighting the good fight against the forces of darkness, even though in fact the warfare was largely confined to the field of rhetoric.

14

CONCLUSION

The era that bears his name was not really the age of Jackson. The label has been attached too long for it to be torn off, however, and it continues to be most satisfactory to a people who like to think their history was made by mythic figures of heroic stature who imposed their will on their times. Were the name of an era determined by a scholarly process that assigned a proper weight to all the relevant factors that shaped it, it would be apparent that no individual, not even Andrew Jackson, dominated the period 1825 to 1845. Certainly he was not the typical man of the time. For all his towering personality, his own and his party's influence even on the politics of the period have been exaggerated. That in hundreds of places the name Jackson was invoked by men eager to win office bespeaks not real influence so much as the power of propaganda and popular hero worship. The notion that the era was his has also rested on a belief that an indissoluble bond connected the Hero and the common man, to whom Jacksonian Democracy ostensibly gave power. But in fact Jacksonian Democracy gave power not to Tom, Dick, and Harry but to the shrewd, ambitious, wealthy, and able politicians who knew best how to flatter them.

Nor was it the age of the common man. If talk alone determined the character of an era then there would be much reason to think that it was. Politicians who sought the common man's vote bombarded him with praise. Romantic artists, whether using pen or brush, extolled his simplicity and his innate wisdom. The American style of life, for all its unloveliness, seemed to be shaped by his mannerisms, his interests, his limitations. Scandalmongering journalism, coarse public manners, the frenzied pursuit of things, the indifference to learning and unconcern with quality, were only some of the characteristics of American civilization that bore the stamp of the ordinary man. Since it was primarily the surface aspect of things that he influenced most—precisely those phenomena that caught the eye of outsiders passing through—visitors understandably concluded that here the common man was sovereign. But he was not.

Political authority belonged not to him but to the uncommon men who typically controlled the major parties at every level. It goes without saying that unusual men will emerge as leaders, even in the most democratic society conceivable. The era's political leaders were distinctive, however, not only in their ability but also in the possession of status and wealth that were unrepresentative of the mass of men. The seats of power in society and the economy were also filled by men whose origins and outlook were not plebeian. Self-made men may have been in greater abundance here than in the Old World. In the 1830s as before, individual Americans of whatever origins might move to positions of eminence that in Europe were unattainable to men of like background. But their numbers were not legion. The weight of the evidence is that family ties and a form of nepotism played an important part in singling out fortune's favorites. Andrew Jackson's own political appointments were heavily influenced by such considerations.

The era's egalitarianism was more apparent than real. American farmers and working men *were* better off than their European counterparts. Their material condition was superior, as were their opportunities, their status, and their influence. Yet this remained a class society. The small circles that dominated the life in the great cities of the East as well as the new towns of the West, lived lives of relative opulence, while socially during the Jacksonian era they became, if anything, more insulated against intrusion by the lower orders. Social lines were drawn even tighter in the slave states. For all the era's egalitarian reputation, evidence is lacking that movement up the social ladder was any more commonplace than it was in subsequent periods of American life; eras whose reputations for social fluidity have been largely deflated by modern empirical studies that characteristically reveal that the race was to the well born. Tocqueville's influential insight that the American rich man was typically born poor was not a conclusion drawn from evidence but an undocumented inference, characteristic of the brilliant French visitor's flair for generalizing from unproven assumptions. James Fenimore Cooper and Michel Chevalier were among the contemporaries who observed that money increasingly tended to be concentrated in relatively few hands, widening the gulf between classes for all the brave talk to the contrary.

It is impossible to know whether people believed that their chances for success were as great as some contemporaries claimed they were. Certainly many Americans seemed to throw themselves into the race for gain, undeterred by religious enthusiasms which cheerfully approved worldly success. Materialism and a love of money were perhaps their most noticeable traits. An ambivalence may be detected in the fact that while the nation participated in a speculative orgy whose goals were selfish and material, reform movements designed to enhance the quality of American life and end social injustice, also flourished. But the two "movements" had different memberships. The movements to uplift slaves, the poor, and the conditions of the weak have caught the eye of scholars—themselves relatively perfectionist when their values are compared to those of more unreflective men. The reform cause was not insignificant. But it was led and kept alive by unusual men and women whose values were outside the mainstream of American life. The mass of Americans seemed far more interested in personal enrichment than in moral uplift.

The depression that followed the great panic at the end of the 1830s temporarily halted the economic growth that had moved the young nation into a prominent place in the world economy. It also dampened if it did not completely suppress the exuberant mood that characterized the earlier period. Optimism had by no means been totally misplaced. The great enhancement of profit-making opportunities only reflected solid advances in the nation's technology, its agricultural and industrial capacity, and above all in the scope and quality of its internal transportation system. Currency was a problem to a country whose opportunities far outstripped its gold supply and whose urge to profit was so overwhelming. Americans, said by discerning observers to value quantity over quality, were content to use vast amounts of paper currency as though it were solid coin. In the absence of sufficient precious metals, the system was not without redeeming social value. Yet it was a precarious one. In a sense, the great Bank War represented the brushing aside of an agency that would restrain the flood of paper desired by the community of profit seekers, although Jackson had not intended such a result.

The nation's modern political system was born during the era, reflecting beautifully the traits of the people it served. Dominated by pragmatic parties which placed electoral success above principle while managing to remain distinctive from one another—in part because of differences in policy as well as in style—it was marked by extravagant campaign techniques, sordid manipulation, brilliant organization, marvelous rhetorical flourishes and a degree of popular participation that were unknown on the Continent. Yet it was not as democratic a system as it seemed. Not only were large numbers denied the suffrage by virtue of sex or color, but astute party managers devised ways of confining real control to small cliques of insiders, just as corporate managers would later use widespread stock ownership as a means of tightening their control over business organizations. While the rhetorical excesses of demagogues had little relationship to their parties' actual achievements, real issues were not altogether avoided, in part because of the clamor of dissenters. Characteristically the great parties dealt with the great issues not by meeting them squarely but by indirection.

Tocqueville thought that the American people were essentially conservative. For all their restless temper, their hunger to change both their lot and their locales, they had no interest in drastic alteration of their society. They loved change [in their personal status] but dreaded revolution. The American exceptions to this rule were fascinating but in view of their small numbers and unrepresentativeness, their influence was slight. The dominant values, like the dominant political, economic, and social tendencies of the Jacksonian era, were essentially conservative. Moralistic dissenters, unhappy with the era's prevalent opportunism, like social radicals displeased with its inequality, got equally short shrift.

It is undoubtedly too late to try to change the name of the Jacksonian era. If it could be done, my idea of a new label would not be a catchy one. For one thing the era was too heterogeneous to be captured by any simple rubric. If the attempt were made nevertheless to capture its spirit in a phrase, there is something to be said for calling it an age of materialism and opportunism, reckless speculation and erratic growth, unabashed vulgarity, surprising inequality, whether of condition, opportunity, or status, and a politic, *seeming* deference to the common man by the uncommon men who actually ran things.

BIBLIOGRAPHICAL ESSAY

There was a time when a bibliographical essay on the Jacksonian era meant a discussion devoted almost entirely to Jacksonian parties and politics. That time is past. Antebellum politics retains its importance but we have become increasingly aware that economic, intellectual, artistic, religious, and social events and developments throw at least as much light on Jacksonian America as do the era's famous party battles. For that matter, it has become clearer too that understanding of politics is immeasurably enhanced by understanding of the other than political context of party warfare. While there is a vast and proliferating literature on these diverse matters, considerations of space dictate that this essay be confined to writings that were or are unusually influential, illuminating, or interesting.

Bibliographical discussions of varying comprehensiveness can be found in several recent collections of contemporary sources. The most substantial of these anthologies is Edward Pessen, *Jacksonian Panorama*, Indianapolis 1976. *Jacksonian America: 1815–1840: New Society, Changing Politics*, Englewood Cliffs 1970, edited by Frank Otto Gatell and John M. McFaul; and *The Nature of Jacksonian America*, New York 1972, edited by Douglas T. Miller, are slim, brief treatments. Useful surveys of the literature on particular topics, such as politics, are cited below in the discussion of these topics. While contemporary sources, such as private papers, are indispensable to all who would understand history, space requirements again dictate that I confine myself to a general injunction to the reader to consult such evidence rather than discuss or even list the hundreds of such sources I have relied on.

In view of the great outpouring of scholarly writings during the past decade and the relatively full treatment accorded earlier publications in the original bibliographical discussion in *Jacksonian America* and in other sources, *this essay pays particular attention to the recent work.*

Society and Social Developments

Social history is an expansive topic, here organized at least as arbitrarily as it is elsewhere. Many social themes defy categorization, touching as they do on diverse aspects of antebellum life. A charming and humorous contemporary reflection of American life is A. B. Longstreet, *Georgia Scenes*, Augusta 1835. The *Report to the Committee of the City Council Appointed to Obtain the Census of Boston for the Year 1845*, Boston 1846, by Lamuel Shattuck, the father of the American statistical profession, offers revealing insights into the life of a city that transcend the mass of information contained between its covers. The life and times of an ordinary lawyer are interestingly conveyed in "The Diary of Henry Van Der Lyn," *New York Historical Society Quarterly* (hereafter *NYHSQ*), 55 (April 1971), 119–152. G. R. Taylor, introduction, " 'Philadelphia in Slices' by George A. Foster," *Pennsylvania Magazine of History and Biography* (hereafter *PMHB*), 93 (January 1969), 23–72, offers unusually revealing glimpses into an antebellum city's seamier side by a newspaper man who was familiar with it. A good example of the "new social history," with its emphasis on new, more analytical approaches, "neglected" often sociological—themes, and the lives of the obscure is *Anonymous Americans: Explorations in Nineteenth-Century Social History*, Englewood Cliffs, 1971, edited by Tamara K. Hareven. William J. Rorabaugh, "The Alcoholic Republic, America 1790–1840," University of California at Berkeley doctoral dissertation 1976, is a stimulating if not fully persuasive attempt to explain the unprecedented "national binge" between the presidencies of George Washington and Andrew Jackson. While I have not been able to work out a satisfactory rubric to contain Richard Slotkin's *Regeneration Through Violence: The Mythology of the American Frontier, 1600–1860*, Middletown 1973, what is not in question is the book's originality, vitality, and passion.

The accounts of American society written by European visitors are indispensable. Of the hundreds of such reports, a small number stand out for their discernment and/or influence. These include Frances Trollope, *Domestic Manners of the Americans*, London 1832; Harriet Martineau, *Society in America*, London 1837; Michel Chevalier, *Society, Manners and Politics in the United States*, Boston 1839; Charles Dickens, *American Notes*, London 1842; Captain Basil Hall, *Travels in North America in the Years 1827–1828*, Philadelphia 1829; Captain Frederick Marryat, *A Diary in America*, London 1839; Thomas Hamilton, *Men and Manners in America*, Philadelphia 1833; Edward Abdy, *Journal of a Residence and Tour in the United States*, London 1835; J. S. Buckingham, *America*, London 1841; Francis Grund, *Aristocracy in America*, London 1839; Godfrey T. Vigne, *Six Months in America*, Philadelphia 1833; Francis Lieber, *The Stranger in America*, London 1835; and above all, Alexis de Tocqueville, *Democracy in America*, New York 1835 (Part I), 1840 (Part II).

For all his flaws as a reporter, Tocqueville's study stands in a class by itself. The basic work on his American trip remains George W. Pierson, *Tocqueville and Beaumont in America*, New York 1938, a book that covers the itinerary of Tocqueville and his companion in minute detail. William J. Murphy, Jr., "Alexis de Tocqueville in New York: The Formation of the Egalitarian Thesis," *NYHSQ*, 61 (January/April 1977), 69–79, reveals that Tocqueville's New York informants were almost without exception among the wealthiest men in the city. Other rewarding discussions are Cushing Strout, "Tocqueville's Duality: Describing America and Thinking of Europe," *American Quarterly*, 21 (Spring 1969), 87–99; Lynn L. Marshall and Seymour Drescher, "American Historians and Tocqueville's *Democracy*," *Journal of American History* (hereafter *JAH*), 55 (December 1968), 512–532; Drescher, "Tocqueville's Two *Démocraties*," *Journal of the History of Ideas*, 25 (April/ June 1964), 201–216; Edward T. Gargan, "Some Problems in Tocqueville Scholarship," *Mid-America*, 30 (January 1959), 3–26; and Marvin Zetterbaum, *Tocqueville and the Problem of Democracy*, Stanford 1966.

Many Americans reacted strongly to the sharply critical tone taken by some of the visitors, accusing them of bias. Not too many years ago Allan Nevins could still describe Mrs. Trollope as a "censorious harridan"; Nevins, ed., *America through British Eyes*, New York 1923. Such judgments are a matter of taste. I agree with Henry T. Tuckerman that Mrs. Trollope had remarkable powers of observation and that objections to her criticisms "should have been reconciled by her candor"; *America and Her Commentators*, New York 1864. In two recent essays Helen L. Heinemann contrasts Mrs. Trollope's knowledgeable reports on Cincinnati, where she spent much time, with the hearsay she sometimes transmitted when passing through other communities. Heinemann nevertheless concludes that "even when not completely objective," Mrs. Trollope's book "never degenerated into mere vituperative polemic"; Heinemann, "Frances Trollope in the New World," *American Quarterly*, 21 (Fall 1969), 544–559; and " 'Starving in the Land of Plenty': New Backgrounds to Frances Trollope's *Domestic Manners of the Americans*," *ibid.*, 24 (December 1972), 643–660. An interesting commentary on the political opportunism of one of the best of the European reporters (who decided to stay on when he fell in love with this country) is Holman Hamilton and James L. Crouthamel, "A Man for Both Parties: Francis J. Grund as Political Chameleon," *PMHB*, 97 (October 1973), 475–484. Older but still useful are Jane Louise Mesick, *The English Traveller in America, 1785–1835.* New York 1922; and Max Berger, *The British Traveller in America, 1836–1860*, New York 1943.

Vintage specimens of truly unreliable reporting governed by spleen and outrage toward all things American are Richard Weston, *The United States and Canada in 1833*, Edinburgh 1836; and Thomas Brothers, *The United States of North America As They Really Are*, London 1840. The former book alleged that aristocrats and swindlers controlled this caste society, while the latter was a one-sided collection of every manner of atrocity. For a discussion of the factors that led its author from enthusiasm for America to his later jaundiced state, see Edward Pessen, "Thomas Brothers," *Pennsylvania History*, 24 (October 1957), 321–330.

For influential appraisals of the American character and personality for the era see Frederick J. Turner, "The Significance of the Frontier in American History," American Historical Association, *Annual Report for 1893* (Washington 1894), 199–227; David M. Potter, *People of Plenty*, Chicago 1954; George W. Pierson, "The M-Factor in American History," *American Quarterly*, 14 (Summer 1962), Supplement, 275–289; Potter, "The Quest for National Character," in *The Reconstruction of American History*, ed. by John Higham, New York 1962; Henry Steele Commager, *The American Mind*, New Haven 1950, ch. 1; and David Riesman, Nathan Glazer, and Reuel Denney, *The Lonely Crowd*, New York 1953. For an informed criticism of the tenuous historical foundation of Riesman's character study see Carl N. Degler, "The Sociologist as Historian:

Riesman's *The Lonely Crowd*," *American Quarterly*, 15 (Winter 1963), 483–497. For examples of social scientists' treatment of the issue see the collection by Michael McGiffert, ed., *The Character of Americans*, Homewood 1964. McGiffert's "Selected Writings on American National Character and Related Subjects to 1969," *American Quarterly*, 21 (Summer Supplement 1969), 330–349, is a useful compilation. Also worthwhile are David E. Stannard, "American Historians and the Idea of National Character: Some Problems and Prospects," *American Quarterly*, 23 (May 1971), 202–220; and Richard D. Brown, "Modernization and the Modern Personality in Early America, 1680–1865: A Sketch of a Synthesis," *Journal of Interdisciplinary History*, 2 (Winter 1972), 201–228, for all the speculative character of Brown's generalizations.

In view of the great number of antebellum Americans, well known and obscure, whose writings have influenced my thinking about American values and character, this essay will settle for this general allusion to the fact of their influence, rather than cite the publications of Ralph Waldo Emerson, James Fenimore Cooper, and many dozens of their countrymen.

A modest revolution in the thinking of historians has in the past decade increased their sensitivity to and interest in the place of women in antebellum life. Barbara Welter's *Dimity Convictions: The American Woman in the Nineteenth Century*, Athens, Ohio 1976—the title is drawn from a phrase in Emily Dickinson—is a brilliant essay, vastly informed, nuanced, ironic, devilishly witty, unsentimental, piercingly intelligent, simply a pleasure to read. It contains Welter's much-anthologized, "The Cult of True Womanhood: 1820–1860," (*American Quarterly*, 18 (Summer 1976), 151–174), and discussions of anti-intellectualism and the American woman, the feminization of antebellum religion, and medical views of American women, among other topics. The medical issue is interestingly treated too in Ann Douglas Wood, "'The Fashionable Diseases': Women's Complaints and Their Treatment in Nineteenth-Century America," *Journal of Interdisciplinary History*, 4 (Summer 1973), 25–52; and in Carroll Smith-Rosenberg and Charles Rosenberg, "The Female Animal: Medical and Biological Views of Woman and Her Role in Nineteenth-Century America," *JAH*, 60 (September 1973), 332–356. Anne Firor Scott, *The Southern Lady: From Pedestal to Politics 1830–1930*, Chicago 1970, is an outstanding contribution which, among other things, dispels myths concerning the allegedly indolent life led by "delicate" Southern ladies. John C. Ruoff, "Frivolity to Consumption: Or, Southern Womanhood in Antebellum Literature," *Civil War History*, 18 (September 1972), 213–229, is interesting and informative. Useful on the life of more plebeian southern women is Jerena East Giffen, "'Add a Pinch and a Lump': Missouri Women in the 1820's," *Missouri Historical Review*, 65 (July 1971), 478–504; as is William R. Taylor, "Ante-Bellum Southern Women," in Barbara Welter, ed., *The Woman Question in American History*, Hinsdale 1973. Other valuable offerings include two essays by Carroll Smith-Rosenberg, "Beauty, the Beast, and the Militant Woman: A Case Study in Sex Roles and Social Stress in Jacksonian America," *American Quarterly*, 23 (October 1971), 562–584; and "The Hysterical Woman: Sex Roles and Role Conflict in Nineteenth-Century America," *Social Research*, 39 (Winter 1972), 652–678; Charles E. Rosenberg, "Sexuality, Class, and Role in Nineteenth-Century America," *American Quarterly*, 25 (May 1973), 131–153; Ronald W. Hogeland's good, if impressionistic, articles, "'The Female Appendage': Feminine Life-Styles in America, 1820–1860," *Civil War History*, 17 (June 1971), 101–114, and "Coeducation of the Sexes at Oberlin College: A Study of Social Ideas in Mid-Nineteenth Century America," *Journal of Social History*, 6 (Winter 1972–73), 160–176; Robert E. Riegel, "Changing American Attitudes Toward Prostitution (1800–1920)," *Journal of the History of Ideas*, 29 (July–September 1968), 437–452; Kathryn Kish Sklar, *Catharine Beecher: A Study in American Domesticity*, New Haven 1973; and Gerda Lerner, "The Lady and the Mill Girl: Changes in the Status of Women in the Age of Jackson," *Midcontinent American Studies Journal*, 10 (Spring 1969), 5–15. Good introductions to the topic are provided by Lerner's "New Approaches to the Study of Women in American History," *Journal of Social History*, 3 (Fall 1969), 53–62, and her impressively researched and inventively organized collection, *The Female Experience: An American Documentary*, Indianapolis 1976. Unfortunately, Nancy F. Cott, *The Bonds of Womanhood: Woman's Sphere in New England, 1780–1835*, New Haven 1977, and Ann Douglas, *The Feminization of American Culture*, New York 1977, came to my attention when the book was in production.

The antebellum free black population has been the subject of increasing scholarly attention. Ira Berlin, *Slaves Without Masters: The Free Negro in the Antebellum South,* New York 1974, is marvelously comprehensive and detailed, exploring a great variety of topics touching on all aspects of the peoples' lives. Leon Litwack, *North of Slavery: The Negro in the Free States, 1790–1860*, Chicago 1961, is a valuable if not nearly as full account of the situation in the North. Jack E. Eblin, "The Growth of the Black Population in antebellum America, 1820–1860," *Population Studies*, 26 (July 1972), 273–289; Ira Berlin, "The Structure of the Free Negro Caste in the Antebellum United States," *Journal of Social History*, 9 (Spring 1976), 297–318; and John L. Stanley, "Majority Tyranny in Tocqueville's America: The Failure of Negro Suffrage in 1846, *Political Science Quarterly*, 84 (September 1969), 412–435, are informative discussions of broad themes. Worthwhile studies of particular communities include James Oliver Horton, "Generations of Protest: Black Families and Social Reform in Ante-Bellum Boston," *New England Quarterly*, 49 (June 1976), 242–56, and an unpublished paper Horton presented to the ninth Annual Conference on History at Brockport in October, 1976, "Black Migrant Adaptive Mechanisms in Ante-Bellum Boston"; Judith Polgar Ruchkin, "The Abolition of 'Colored Schools' in Rochester, New York: 1832–1856," *New York History* (hereafter *NYH*), 51 (July 1971), 377–393; Rhoda G. Freeman, "The Free Negro in New York City in the Era Before the Civil War," Columbia University doctoral dissertation 1966; Lee Calligaro, "The Negro's Legal Status in Pre-Civil War New Jersey," *New Jersey History*, 85 (Fall–Winter 1967), 167–180; Theodore Hershberg, "Free Blacks in Antebellum Philadelphia: A Study of Ex-Slaves, Freeborn, and Socioeconomic Decline," *Journal of Social History*, 5 (Winter 1971–72), 183–209; Harry C. Silcox, "Delay and Neglect: Negro Public Education in Antebellum Philadelphia, 1800–1860," *PMHB*, 97 (October 1973), 444–464; Leonard Erickson, "Politics and Repeal of Ohio's Black Laws, 1837–1849," *Ohio History*, 82 (Summer–Autumn 1973), 154–175; Harold B. Hancock's somewhat thin, "Not Quite Men: The Free Negroes in Delaware in the 1830's," *Civil War History*, 17 (December 1971), 320–331; Dorothy Provine, "The Economic Position of Free Blacks in the District of Columbia, 1800–1860," *Journal of Negro History*, 58 (January 1973), 61–72; Letitia Woods Brown, *Free Negroes in the District of Columbia, 1790–1846*, New York 1972; and Donald D. Bellamy, "Free Blacks in Antebellum Missouri, 1820–1860," *Missouri Historical Review*, 67 (January 1973), 198–226.

Excellent on the two groups mentioned in its title is Jay P. Dolan, *The Immigrant Church: New York's Irish and German Catholics, 1815–1865*, Baltimore 1975, which better than do studies of an earlier time reveals the diversity present within the Catholic community. Still invaluable are Oscar Handlin, *Boston's Immigrants*, Cambridge 1941; and Robert Ernst, *Immigrant Life in New York City, 1825–1863*, New York 1949. Also useful are Gilbert Osofsky, "Abolitionists, Irish Immigrants, and the Dilemmas of Romantic Nationalism," *American Historical Review* (hereafter *AHR*), 80 (October 1975), 889–912; William E. Rowley, "The Irish Aristocracy of Albany, 1798–1878," *NYH*, 52 (July 1971), 275–304; A. B. Faust, *The German Element in the United States*, Boston 1909; William V. Shannon, *The American Irish*, New York 1963; and Earl T. Niehaus, *The Irish in New Orleans, 1800–1860*, Baton Rouge 1965. Many of the recent urban histories (considered below) deal with ethnic—particularly Irish and German—factors. Good examples are Kathleen Neils Conzen, *Immigrant Milwaukee, 1836–1860: Accommodation and Community in a Frontier City*, Cambridge 1976; Stephen F. Ginsberg, "Above the Law: Volunteer Firemen in New York City: 1836–1837." *NYH*, 50 (April 1969), 165–186; James F. Richardson, *The New York Police: Colonial Times to 1901*, New York 1970; and Thedore Hershberg, Michael Katz, Stuart Blumin, Lawrence Glasco, and Clyde Griffin, "Occupation and Ethnicity in Five Nineteenth-Century Cities: A Collaborative Inquiry," *Historical Methods Newsletter* (hereafter *HMN*), 7 (June 1974), 174–216.

The "new urban history" has arisen in the past decade, witness to some historians' twin beliefs that detailed examination of local communities can yield significant insights into American life and that the themes and approaches associated with sociology and statistics can be fruitfully appropriated by historians. While both contain essays on antebellum America, Stefan Thernstrom and Richard Sennett, eds., *Nineteenth-Century Cities: Essays in the New Urban History*, New Haven 1969, is more accessible to the reader than the collection by Leo F. Schnore, ed., *The New Urban History: Quantitative Explorations by American Historians*, Princeton 1975. A bibliographical essay of exemplary comprehensiveness is Raymond A. Mohl, "The History of the American City," in William H. Cartwright and Richard L. Watson, eds., *The Reinterpretation of American History and Culture*, Washington 1973, 163–205. Useful studies of particular cities and towns, some of them traditional in approach, some "new," others a blending of the two, include Michael H. Frisch, *Town Into City: Springfield, Massachusetts, and the Meaning of Community, 1840–1880*, Cambridge 1972; Stuart M. Blumin, *The Urban Threshold: Growth and Change in a Nineteenth-Century American Community* (Kingston, New York), Chicago 1976; Sam Bass Warner, Jr., *The Private City: Philadelphia in Three Periods of Its Growth*, Philadelphia 1968; Edward Pessen, "A Social and Economic Portrait of Jacksonian Brooklyn," *NYHSQ*, 55 (October 1971), 318–353; Richard S. Alcorn, "Leadership and Stability in Mid-Nineteenth Century America: A Case Study of an Illinois Town," *JAH*, 61 (December 1974), 685–702; Richard C. Wade, *The Urban Frontier*, Cambridge

1959 (about five antebellum southern and western cities); Irwin F. Flack, "The Growth of Urban Government in the Antebellum Period: Cincinnati as a Case Study, 1820–1860," an important paper presented at Duquesne University, October 29, 1975; D. Clayton James, *Antebellum Natchez*, Baton Rouge 1968; Robert C. Reinders, *End of an Era: New Orleans, 1850–1860*, New Orleans 1969; and Kenneth W. Wheeler, *To Wear a City's Crown: The Beginnings of Urban Growth in Texas, 1836–1865*, Cambridge 1968. Michael B. Katz, *The People of Hamilton, Canada West: Family and Class in a Mid-Nineteenth Century City*, Cambridge 1975, is about a small Canadian city but its striking judgments are illuminating too for the country south of the Canadian border. Essays that touch interurban themes include Leonard P. Curry's valuable "Urbanization and Urbanism in the Old South: A Comparative View," *Journal of Southern History*, 40 (February 1974), 43–60; Edward Pessen, "The Social Configuration of the Antebellum City: An Historical and Theoretical Inquiry," *Journal of Urban History*, 2 (May 1976), 267–306; Thomas Bender, "James Fenimore Cooper and the City," *NYH*, 51 (April 1970), 287–305; Samuel P. Hays, "The Changing Political Structure of the City in Industrial America," *Journal Urban History*, 1 (November 1974), 6–38; and George R. Taylor, "The Beginnings of Urban Transportation in Urban America," *Smithsonian Journal of History*, 1 (Summer and Autumn 1966), 35–50 and 31–54.

Good studies on the related issues of crime, violence, and police reform, in addition to James F. Richardson, *The New York Police*, are Roger Lane, *Policing the City: Boston 1822–1885*, Cambridge 1967; Stephen F. Ginsberg, "The Police and Fire Protection in New York City: 1800–1850," *NYH*, 52 (April 1971), 133–150; David Grimsted, "Rioting in Its Jacksonian Setting," *AHR*, 77 (April 1972), 361–397; Leonard L. Richards, *"Gentlemen of Property and Standing": Anti-Abolition Mobs in Jacksonian America*, New York 1970; Theodore M. Hammett, "Two Mobs of Jacksonian Boston: Ideology and Interest," *JAH*, 62 (March 1976), 845–868; Michael Feldberg, *The Philadelphia Riots of 1844: A Study in Ethnic Conflict*, Westport 1975; John Runcie, " 'Hunting the Nigs' in Philadelphia: The Race Riot of August 1834," *Pennsylvania History*, 39 (April 1972), 187–218; David Montgomery, "The Shuttle and the Cross: Weavers and Artisans in the Kensington Riots of 1844," *Journal of Social History*, 5 (Summer 1972), 411–446; Elizabeth M. Geffen, "Violence in Philadelphia in the 1840's and 1850's," *Pennsylvania History*, 36 (October 1969), 381–410; and Vincent P. Lannie and Bernard C. Diethorn, "For the Honor and Glory of God: the Philadelphia Bible Riots of 1840," *History of Education Quarterly*, 8 (Spring 1968), 44–106.

The resurgence of interest in urban history has been accompanied by increasing research in the diverse social and cultural life of antebellum cities. For discussions of the local voluntary associations concerned with uplift of one sort or another see Richard D. Brown, "The Emergence of Voluntary Associations, Massachusetts, 1760–1830," *Journal of Voluntary Action Research*, 2 (April 7, 1973), 64–73; Robert S. Pickett, *House of Refuge: Origins of Juvenile Reform in New York State, 1815–1857*, Syracuse 1968; W. David Lewis, *From Newgate to Dannemora: The Rise of the Penitentiary in New York, 1796–1848*, Ithaca 1965; Raymond A. Mohl, "The Humane Society and Urban Reform in Early New York, 1787–1831," *NYHSQ*, 54 (January 1970), 30–52; three essays by M. J. Heale: "The New York Society for the Prevention of Pauperism, 1817–

1823," *ibid.*, 55 (July 1971), 153–176; "The Formative Years of the New York Prison Association, 1844–1862: A Case Study in Antebellum Reform," *ibid.*, 59 (October 1975), 320–347; and "From City Fathers to Social Critics: Humanitarianism and Government in New York, 1790–1860," *JAH*, 63 (June 1976), 21–41; William W. Cutler, III, "Status, Values, and the Education of the Poor: The Trustees of the New York Public School Society, 1805–1853," *American Quarterly*, 24 (March 1972), 69–85; Ronald Story, "Class and Culture in Boston: The Athenaeum, 1807–1860," *ibid.*, 27 (May 1975), 178–199; Edward Pessen, *Riches, Class, and Power Before the Civil War*, Lexington, Mass. 1973, ch. 12; and Walter S. Glazer, "Participation and Power: Voluntary Associations and the Functional Organization of Cincinnati in 1840," *HMN*, 5 (September 1972), 151–168.

David J. Rothman, *The Discovery of the Asylum: Social Order and Disorder in the New Republic*, Boston 1971, is a provocative and original if not always persuasive analysis of the motives and achievements of the local reformers. Interesting recent discussions of education include Michael B. Katz, *The Irony of Early School Reform*, Cambridge 1968; Raleigh A. Suarez, "Chronicle of a Failure: Public Education in Antebellum Louisiana," *Louisiana History*, 12 (Spring 1971), 109–122; Stanley K. Schultz, *The Culture Factory: Boston Public Schools, 1789–1860*, New York 1973; and Carl F. Kaestle, *The Evolution of an Urban School System: New York City, 1750–1850*, Cambridge 1973. Calling attention to paradoxical elements in the motives and policies of educational reformers, the interpretations in these studies differ from the more roseate perceptions found in the work of earlier historians of education. A modest but useful book on a lightly treated subject is David F. Allmendinger, Jr., *Paupers and Scholars: The Transformation of Student Life in Nineteenth-Century New England*, New York 1975. Also useful are William G. Shade, "The 'Working Class' and Educational Reform in Early America: The Case of Providence, Rhode Island," *Historian,* 39 (November 1976), 1–23; Ronald Story, "Harvard and the Boston Brahmins: A Study in Institutional and Class Development, 1800–1865," *Journal of Social History*, 8 (Spring 1975), 94–121, and Story's "Harvard Students, the Boston Elite, and the New England Preparatory System, 1800–1870," *History of Education Quarterly*, 15 (Fall 1975), 281–298; and Stanley M. Guralnick, *Science and the Ante-Bellum American College*, Philadelphia 1975, which emphasizes the curriculum rather than the social context. On scientific developments see George H. Daniels, *American Science in the Age of Jackson*, New York 1968; and Donald Zochert, "Science and the Common Man in Ante-Bellum America," *Isis*, 65 (December 1974), 448–473. Russel B. Nye, *Society and Culture in America, 1830–1860*, New York 1974, says little about society but offers informed if often unanalytical coverage of the life of the mind. Rush Welter, *The Mind of America, 1820–1860*, New York 1975, is a sprawling, dense, at times turgid, at other times most rewarding examination of a great variety of American ideas offered by little known as well as eminent individuals. James L. Crouthamel, *James Watson Webb: A Biography*, Middletown 1969, illuminates antebellum newspaper publishing and the technological changes that transformed it. David Grimsted, *Melodrama Unveiled: American Theatre and Culture, 1800–1850*, Chicago 1968, is informed, perceptive, and brightly written.

A bold, lively, brilliant essay on the interaction between Jacksonian Democracy and art is Oliver Larkin, *Art and Life in America*, "Jacksonian Ferment," New York 1949, chs. 13–15. Its strengths and its weaknesses derive from its author's treatment of art as social barometer and his acceptance of simplistic notions concerning the common man's alleged domination of the era. Reflecting, in a sense, the contemporary retreat from both stances are Neil Harris, *The Artist in American Society: The Formative Years, 1790–1860*. New York 1966; David P. Handlin, "New England Architects in New York, 1820–40," *American Quarterly*, 19 (Winter 1967), 681–695; Lillian B. Miller, "Painting, Sculpture and the National Character, 1815–1860," *JAH*, 53 (March 1967), 696–707; and Miller, *Patrons and Patriotism: The Encouragement of the Fine Arts in the United States, 1790–1860*, Chicago 1966. Also useful are Harold E. Dickson, *Arts of the Young Republic: The Age of William Dunlap*, Chapel Hill 1968; George R. Neilsen, "Painting and Politics in Jacksonian America," *Capitol Studies*, 1 (Spring 1972), 87–92, on partisan attempts to exploit politically the selection of art works for government buildings; and William Cullen Bryant II, "Poetry and Painting: A Love Affair of Long Ago," *American Quarterly* 22 (Winter 1970), 859–882.

Interesting work has recently been done on the related subjects of medicine and public health. Valuable overviews are Richard H. Shryock, *Medicine and Society in America, 1660–1860*, Ithaca 1960; Joseph F. Kett, *The Formation of the American Medical Profession: The Role of Institutions, 1780–1860*, New Haven 1968; and Charles E. Rosenberg, *The Cholera Years, The United States in 1832, 1849, and 1866*, Chicago 1962. Invaluable on mental illness are Norman Dain, *Disordered Minds: The First Century of Eastern State Hospital in Williamsburg, Virginia, 1766–1866*, Williamsburg 1971; and Gerald N. Grob, *Mental Institutions in America: Social Policy to 1875*, New York, 1973. Dain and Grob effectively counter Rothman's denigration of antebellum mental institutions. Charles E. Rosenberg, "Social Class and Medical Care in Nineteenth-Century America: The Rise and Fall of the Dispensary," *Journal of the History of Medicine and Allied Sciences*, 29 (January 1974), 32–54, is good on the social implications of medicine as are Kett, Dain, and Grob.

The literature on changing theories and ideas of medicine includes John Rickards Betts, "American Medical Thought on Exercise as the Road to Health, 1820–1860," *Bulletin of the History of Medicine*, 45 (March–April 1971), 138–152, which shows that jogging and physical fitness are hardly new fads; Russell M. Jones's excellent "American Doctors and the Parisian Medical World, 1830–1840," *ibid.*, 47 (January–February 1973), 40–65, on the great influence exerted by French medical theory and practice; Martin Kaufman, "Edward H. Dixon and Medical Education in New York," *NYH*, 51 (July 1970), 395–409; James O. Breeden, "Thomsonianism in Virginia." *Virginia Magazine of History and Biography* (hereafter *VMHB*), 82 (April 1974), 150–180, on the spread of the "natural medicine" fad; and John S. Haller, Jr., "The Negro and the Southern Physician: A study of Medical and Racial Attitudes, 1800–1860," *Medical History*, 16 (July 1972), 238–253. John Duffy, *A History of Public Health in New York City (1625–1866)*, New York 1968, is a magisterial factual study. Duffy's "Nineteenth Century Public Health in New York and New Orleans: A Comparison," *Louisiana History*, 15 (Fall 1974), 325–337, is sketchy but interesting. Also good on public health are Gert H. Brieger, "Sanitary Reform in New York City: Stephen Smith and the Passage of the Metropolitan Health Bill," *Bulletin of History of Medicine*, 40 (September–October 1966), 407–429; John H. Ellis, "Businessmen and Public Health in the Urban South During the Nineteenth Century: New Orleans, Memphis, and Atlanta," *ibid.*, 44 (May–June 1970), 197–212; David R. Goldfield, "The Business of Health Planning: Disease Prevention in the Old South," *Journal of Southern History*, 42 (November 1976), 557–570.

As I indicate in the text, I focus more on the social aspects and implications of antebellum religion than on the theological. Fine overviews are T. L. Smith, *Revivalism and Social Reform: American Protestantism on the Eve of the Civil War*, New York 1957; and Jay P. Dolan, *The Immigrant Church*. Useful older studies of the evangelicalism of the second quarter of the 19th century include William G. McLoughlin, Jr., *Modern Revivalism*, New York 1959; Perry Miller, *The Life of the Mind in America*, New York 1965 (Book I, "The Evangelical Basis"); and Whitney R. Cross, *The Burned-Over District: The Social and Intellectual History of Enthusiastic Religion in Western New York, 1800–1850*, Ithaca 1950. Mario De Pillis, "The Social Sources of Mormonism," *Church History*, 37 (March 1968), 50–79, questions Cross's view of the society of the "burned-over district." Other worthwhile recent studies include Ann C. Loveland, "Evangelicalism and 'Immediate Emancipation' in American Antislavery Thought," *Journal of Southern History* 32 (May 1966), 172–188; James E. Johnson, "Charles G. Finney and A Theory of Revivalism," *Church History*, 38 (September 1969), 338–358; Major L. Wilson, "Paradox Lost: Order and Progress in Mid-Nineteenth Century America," *ibid.*, 44 (September 1975), 352–366; and Richard Cawardine, "The Second Great Awakening in the Urban Centers: An Examination of Methodism and the 'New Measures'," *JAH*, 59 (September 1972), 327–340. Social factors behind denominational splits are profitably discussed in Donald G. Mathews, "The Methodist Schism of 1844 and the Popularization of Antislavery Sentiment," *Mid-America*, 51 (January 1969), 3–23; and in two studies by Robert W. Doherty, *The Hicksite Separation: A Sociological Analysis of Religious Schism in Early-Nineteenth Century America*, New Brunswick 1967; and "Social Bases for the Presbyterian Schism of 1837–1838: The Philadelphia Case," *Journal of Social History*, 2 (Fall 1968), 69–79.

Facets of religious benevolence are instructively examined in Lois W. Banner, "Religious Benevolence as Social Control: A Critique of an Interpretation," *JAH*, 60 (June 1973), 23–41; Timothy F. Reilly, "Parson Clapp of New Orleans: Antebellum Social Critic, Religious Radical, and Member of the Establishment," *Louisiana History*, 16 (Summer 1975), 167–191; Carroll Smith-Rosenberg, *Religion and the Rise of the American City: The New York City Mission Movement 1812–1870*, Ithaca 1971; Bertram Wyatt-Brown, "The Antimission Movement in the Jacksonian South: A Study in Regional Folk Culture," *Journal of Southern History* 36 (November 1970), 501–529; Clifford S. Griffin's excellent *Their Brothers' Keepers: Moral Stewardship in the United States, 1800–1865*, New Brunswick 1960; Charles C. Cole, *The Social Ideas of the Northern Evangelists, 1826–1860*, New York 1954; John R. Bodo, *The Protestant Clergy and Public Issues*, Princeton 1954; and Charles I.

Foster, *An Errand of Mercy: The Evangelical United Front, 1790–1837,* Chapel Hill 1960. Valuable treatments of neglected themes are Stuart M. Blumin, "Church and Community: A Case Study of Lay Leadership in Nineteenth-Century America," *NYH,* 56 (October 1975), 393–408; and particularly, Michael S. Franch, "The Congregational Community in the Changing City, 1840–1870," *Maryland Historical Magazine,* 7 (Fall 1976), 367–380, a most informative discussion of social differentiation and its influence within the parish.

There are a number of fine studies of antebellum legal developments. Maxwell Bloomfield, *American Lawyers in a Changing Society, 1776–1876,* Cambridge 1976, is a series of unusually thoughtful essays which, among other things, refutes the widely asserted but slightly documented thesis that standards were deteriorating in the profession during the period. Elizabeth Casper Brown, "The Bar on a Frontier: Wayne County, 1796–1836," *American Journal of Legal History,* 14 (April 1970), 136–156, is also good on this score. William E. Nelson, *Americanization of the Common Law; The Impact of Legal Change on Massachusetts Society, 1760–1830,* Cambridge 1975, although it focuses on the earlier years, is particularly useful for its account of the increasing sympathy toward debt and debtors. R. Kent Newmyer, "Justice Joseph Story on Circuit and a Neglected Phase of American Legal History," *American Journal of Legal History* 14 (April 1970), 112–135, is clear as crystal on the operation and significance of circuit courts. Newmyer's *The Supreme Court Under Marshall and Taney,* New York 1968, gives informed and succinct appraisals of the important cases and the legal principles they epitomized. Also good on the high court is Gerald T. Dunne, *Justice Joseph Story and the Rise of the Supreme Court,* New York 1970. Indispensable on the crucial Charles River Bridge case are Newmyer, "Justice Joseph Story, the Charles River Bridge Case and the Crisis of Republicanism," *American Journal of Legal History,* 17 (July 1973), 232–245; and Stanley I. Kutler, *Privilege and Creative Destruction: The Charles River Bridge Case,* Philadelphia 1971. Joseph C. Burke, "What Did the Prigg Decision Really Decide?" *PMHB,* 93 (January 1969), 73–85; and Donald Roper, "James Kent and the Emergence of New York's Libel Law," *American Journal of Legal History,* 17 (July 1973), 223–231, are admirable studies. Garry B. Nash, "The Philadelphia Bench and Bar, 1800–1861," *Comparative Studies in Society and History,* 7 (January 1965), 203–220, discusses changes in public attitudes toward the bar and in the backgrounds of lawyers.

A number of modern studies have uncovered a great wealth of data, much of which undermine the influential "egalitarian thesis" articulated by Tocqueville and other contemporaries. Edward Pessen, "The Egalitarian Myth and the American Social Reality: Wealth, Mobility, and Equality in the 'Era of the Common Man,'" *AHR,* 76 (October 1971), 989–1034, subjects central elements of the thesis to "the empirical test it had previously been spared," by gathering evidence from the greatest cities of the northeast. A fuller statement of Pessen's case is given in his *Riches, Class, and Power Before the Civil War.* Although the latter book relies heavily on quantitative data, its author's decision to eschew esoteric statistical techniques has been criticized by one reviewer as a sign that "although Pessen is not a narrative historian . . . he arrays himself fully within the humanists' tradition," and by another for its preference of sentences to scatterograms. Impressionistic but useful discussions of antebellum poverty, in addition to Handlin's *Boston Im-*

migrants and Ernst's *Immigrant Life in New York City, 1825–1863*, are Raymond A. Mohl, *Poverty in New York 1783–1825*, New York 1971, and Benjamin J. Klebaner, "The Home Relief Controversy in Philadelphia, 1782–1861," *PMHB*, 78 (October 1954), 413–423. Wendell Tripp, ed., *Through "Poverty's Vale": A Hardscrabble Boyhood in Upstate New York, 1832–1867*, Syracuse 1974, is a fascinating diary account of the life of a desperately poor rural New Yorker and his family and neighbors. Peter J. Coleman's authoritative *Debtors and Creditors in America: Insolvency, Imprisonment for Debt, and Bankruptcy, 1607–1900*, Madison 1974; and Emmet J. Mittlebeeler, "The Decline of Imprisonment for Debt in Kentucky," *Filson Club Historical Quarterly*, 49 (April 1975), 169–189, throw useful light on debtors as well as on the movement to improve their legal situation. Douglas T. Miller, *Jacksonian Aristocracy: Class and Democracy in New York, 1830–1860*, New York 1967, is a lively but impressionistic account of growing inequality in New York State.

The most comprehensive study of the distribution of wealth is Lee Soltow, *Men and Wealth in the United States, 1850–1870*, New Haven 1975, a detailed examination of national census data. Edward Pessen, "The Distribution of Wealth in the Era of the Civil War," *Reviews in American History*, 4 (June 1976), 222–229, reports the strengths and weaknesses of Soltow's important but excessively undecipherable study. Also valuable is Soltow, "The Wealth, Income, and Social Class of Men in Large Northern Cities of the United States in 1860," in James D. Smith, ed., *The Personal Distribution of Income and Wealth*, New York 1975. Other examinations of antebellum wealth distribution for particular communities include Gavin Wright, " 'Economic Democracy' and the Concentration of Agricultural Wealth in the Cotton South, 1850–1860," *Agricultural History*, 44 (January 1970), 63–94; George Blackburn and Sherman L. Richards, Jr., "A Demographic History of the West: Manistee County, Michigan, 1860," *JAH*, 57 (December 1970), 600–618; Richard Lowe and Randolph Campbell, "Slave Property and the Distribution of Wealth in Texas, 1860," *ibid.*, 63 (September 1976), 316–324; Robert E. Gallman, "Trends in the Nineteenth Century: Some Speculations," in Lee Soltow, ed., *Six Papers on the Size Distribution of Wealth and Income*, New York 1969; Robert H. Doherty, "Property Distribution in Jacksonian America," an unpublished paper on New England presented at the annual meeting of the Organization of American Historians on April 19, 1971, in New Orleans; Pessen, "The Egalitarian Myth and the American Social Reality"; and Harold Hurst, "The Elite Class of Newport, Rhode Island: 1830–1860," New York University doctoral dissertation 1975. Evidence on the distribution of wealth in mid-19th century Hariss County, Texas, has been furnished me by M. Susan Jackson, author of "The People of Houston in the 1850s," Indiana University doctoral dissertation 1975. Also valuable is Randolph B. Campbell, "Planters and Plain Folk: Harris County, Texas, as a Test Case, 1850–1866," *Journal of Southern History*, 40 (August 1974), 369–398.

While the "new social history" has evinced much interest in the poor, the rich and elite have by no means been neglected. Pessen's *Riches, Class, and Power Before the Civil War* examines the lifestyles and uses of leisure, as well as the backgrounds, the wealth, and the influence of the northeastern socioeconomic elite. Touching on these themes are Pessen's two essays, "Philip Hone's Set: The Social World of the New

York City Elite in the 'Age of Egalitarianism,'" *NYHSQ*, 56 (October 1972), 285–308, and "The Lifestyle of the Antebellum Urban Elite," *Mid-America*, 55 (July 1973), 163–183. Hurst's "The Elite Class of Newport, Rhode Island" is a comprehensive quantitative study of a small but interesting community. Jane H. Pease, "A Note on Patterns of Conspicuous Consumption Among Seaboard Planters, 1820–1860," *Journal of Southern History*, 35 (August 1969), 381–393, is an interesting impressionistic study which challenges the notion of highly elaborate, unique consumption patterns of planters. Nicholas B. Wainwright, "Andalusia, Countryseat of the Craig Family and Nicholas Biddle and His Descendants," *PMHB*, 101 (January 1977), 3–69, describes the residential style of a famous social light. Also useful are E. Digby Baltzell, *The Protestant Establishment: Aristocracy and Caste in America*, London 1965: Frederic Cople Jaher, "Nineteenth-Century Elites in Boston and New York," *Journal of Social History*, 6 (Fall 1972), 32–77, much of it on a later period; and Paul Goodman's sensitive "Ethics and Enterprise: The Values of a Boston Elite, 1800–1870," *American Quarterly*, 18 (Fall 1966), 437–451.

For all the recent interest in social mobility, little research has been published to date on Jacksonian manifestations of the phenomenon. Useful unpublished work includes Alexandra McCoy, "The Political Affiliations of American Economic Elites: Wayne County, Michigan, 1844–1860, As a Test Case," Wayne State University doctoral dissertation 1965; Richard M. Jones, "Stonington Borough: A Connecticut Seaport in the Nineteenth Century," City University of New York doctoral dissertation 1976; Hurst, "The Elite Class of Newport, Rhode Island"; Brian J. Danforth, "The Influence of Socioeconomic Factors Upon Political Behavior: A Quantitative Look at New York City Merchants, 1828–1844," New York University doctoral dissertation 1974; and Stuart Mack Blumin, "Mobility in a Nineteenth-Century American City: Philadelphia, 1820–1860," University of Pennsylvania doctoral dissertation 1968. Blumin, "Mobility and Change in Ante-Bellum Philadelphia," in Thernstrom and Sennett, *Nineteenth-Century Cities*, 165–206, reports the fruits of his study of intergenerational occupational and residential mobility. Although Peter Knights, *The Plain People of Boston, 1830–1860: A Study in City Growth*, New York 1971, is primarily a severely statistical study of physical rather than social mobility, it does consider vertical as well as geographical movement. Edward Pessen, "Did Fortunes Rise and Fall Mercurially in Antebellum America? The Tale of Two Cities, Boston and New York," *Journal of Social History*, 4 (Summer 1971), 339–357, examines intragenerational wealth mobility, while Part II of his *Riches, Class, and Power* considers varied aspects of social mobility. Garry B. Nash, "The Philadelphia Bench and Bar, 1800–1861," contrasts the social backgrounds of lawyers of Jefferson's and Lincoln's time. Edward Pessen, ed., *Three Centuries of Social Mobility in America*, Lexington, Mass. 1974, discusses the varied meanings and significance of social mobility.

The Economy and Economic Developments

Valuable surveys include George R. Taylor, *The Transportation Revolution, 1815–1860*, New York 1951, a detailed, descriptive, and comprehensive account of nonagricultural developments; Douglas C. North's slim but original *The Economic Growth of the United States, 1790–1860*,

New York 1965; Stuart Bruchey, *The Roots of American Economic Growth, 1607–1861*, New York 1965, a series of capsule summaries and evaluations of secondary sources; and Peter Temin, *The Jacksonian Economy*, New York 1969, an informed, opinionated, not always persuasive, provocative essay by a bright cliometrician. Other useful overviews include Stanley Lebergott, *The American Economy: Income, Wealth, and Want*, Princeton 1976; Thomas C. Cochran, "The Paradox of American Economic Growth," *JAH*, 61 (March 1975), 925–942; and Jeffrey G. Williamson, "American Prices and Urban Inequality Since 1820," *Journal of Economic History* (hereafter *JEH*), 36 (June 1976), 303–333.

The era's economic developments have recently been illuminated by practictioners of the "new economic history." Particularly valuable examples of the new approach for subjects relevant to the Jacksonian era include Alfred H. Conrad and John R. Meyer, "The Economics of Slavery in the Ante Bellum South," *Journal of Political Economy*, 66 (April 1958), 95–130; Robert W. Fogel, *Railroads and American Economic Growth: Essays in Econometric History*, Baltimore 1964; Albert Fishlow, *American Railroads and the Transformation of the Ante-Bellum Economy*, Cambridge 1965; and Fishlow, "Antebellum Interregional Trade Reconsidered," *American Economic Review*, 54 (May 1964), 352–364; Paul A. David, "The Growth of Real Product in the United States before 1840: New Evidence, Controlled Conjectures," *JEH*, 27 (June 1967), 151–195; Jacob P. Meerman, "The Climax of the Bank War: Biddle's Contraction, 1833–1834," *Journal of Political Economy*, 71 (August 1963), 378–388; Roger L. Ransom, "Canals and Development: A Discussion of the Issues," *American Economic Reviews*, 54 (May 1964), 365–376; and Peter Temin, "Steam and Water Power in the Early Nineteenth Century," *JEH*, 26 (June 1966), 187–205.

Some of the leading practitioners of the new methodology have offered the most perceptive criticisms of it. These include Lance E. Davis, "And It Will Never Be Literature: The New Economic History: A Critique," *Explorations in Entrepreneurial History*, 6 (Fall 1968), 75–92, which faults its preoccupation with methodology; Albert Fishlow and Robert W. Fogel, "Quantitative Economic History: An Interim Evaluation, Past Trends, and Present Tendencies," *JEH*, 31 (March 1971), 15–42, which criticizes its "narrow focus"; Peter D. McClelland, "Railroads, American Growth, and the New Economic History: A Critique," *JEH*, 28 (March 1968), 102–123; and Douglas C. North, "Beyond the New Economic History," *JEH*, 34 (March 1974), 1–7, which faults the new method's failure to hold the interest of students and general readers, among other weaknesses. Balanced appraisals of the new, by practitioners of an older approach, are Fritz Redlich, " 'New' and Traditional Approaches to Economic History and Their Independence," *JEH*, 25 (December 1965), 480–495; and Thomas G. Cochran, "Economic History, Old and New," *AHR*, 74 (June 1969), 1561–1572. Robert W. Fogel and Stanley L. Engerman, eds., *The Reinterpretation of American Economic History*, New York 1971, offers examples of the new approach.

Government economic intervention during the era meant state government intervention, essentially. Landmark studies are Louis Hartz, *Economic Policy and Democratic Thought: Pennsylvania, 1776–1860*, Cambridge 1948; Oscar and Mary F. Handlin, *Commonwealth: A Study of the Role of Government in the American Economy: Massachusetts, 1774–1861*, New York 1947; James N. Primm, *Economic Policy in the*

Development of a Western State: Missouri, 1820–1860, Cambridge 1954; and Milton S. Heath, *Constructive Liberalism: The Role of the State in Economic Development in Georgia to 1860,* Cambridge 1954. Also valuable are Carter Goodrich, *Government Promotion of American Canals and Railroads, 1800–1890,* New York 1960; Goodrich, ed., *The Government and the Economy: 1783–1861,* Indianapolis 1967; Harry N. Scheiber, "State Policy and the Public Domain: The Ohio Canal Lands," *JEH,* 25 (March 1965), 86–113; and Scheiber, "Government and the Economy: Studies of the 'Commonwealth' Policy in Nineteenth-Century America," *Journal of Interdisciplinary History,* 3 (Summer 1972), 135–154. Malcolm J. Rohrbough, *The Land Office Business: The Settlement and Administration of American Public Lands, 1789–1837,* New York 1968, is caustic, knowledgeable, and indispensable. The gap between government pronouncements and its actual land policies inevitably evokes a skeptical scholarly stance. Other important studies are Roy M. Robbins, *Our Landed Heritage: The Public Domain 1776–1936,* Princeton 1942; Helene S. Zahler, *Eastern Working Men and National Land Policy, 1829–1862,* New York 1941; Robert P. Swierenga, *Pioneers and Profits: Land Speculation on the Iowa Frontier,* Ames 1968; and Peter D. McClelland, "New Perspectives on the Disposal of Western Lands in Nineteenth Century America," *Business History Review,* 43 (Spring 1969), 77–83.

A good recent introductory overview of antebellum agriculture is Paul W. Gates, *The Farmer's Age: Agriculture 1815–1860,* New York 1962. Older standards are Louis C. Gray, *History of Agriculture in the Southern United States,* Washington 1933; and Percy W. Bidwell and John I. Falconer, *History of Agriculture in the Northern United States, 1620–1860,* Washington 1925. Of the ample literature, Donald B. Marti, "In Praise of Farming: An Aspect of the Movement for Agricultural Improvement in the Northeast, 1815–1840," *NYH,* 51 (July 1970), 351–375; David W. Francis, "Antebellum Agricultural Reform in *DeBow's Review,*" *Louisiana History,* 14 (Spring 1973), 165–178; Robert E. Gallman, "Self-Sufficiency in the Cotton Economy of the Antebellum South," *Agricultural History,* 44 (January 1970), 5–24; Hugh Hill Wooten, "A Fourth Creek Farm from 1800 to 1830," *North Carolina Historical Review,* 30 (April 1953), 167–175; Robert H. George, "Life on a New Hampshire Farm, 1825–1835," *Historical New Hampshire,* 22 (Winter 1967), 3–16; Richard H. Abbott, "The Agricultural Press Views the Yeoman: 1819–1859," *Agricultural History,* 42 (January 1968), 35–48; William K. Hutchinson and Samuel H. Williamson, "Self-Sufficiency of the Antebellum South: Estimates of the Food Supply," *JEH,* 31 (September 1971), 591–612; and Stanley L. Engerman, "A Reconsideration of Southern Economic Growth, 1770–1860," *Agricultural History,* 49 (April 1975), 343–361, usefully explore aspects of the general theme. David E. Schob, *Hired Hands and Plowboys: Farm Labor in the Midwest, 1815–1860,* Urbana 1975, is valuable but at times frustrating because of its unanalytical and unsystematic examination of a largely ignored but important matter.

There would be little point in trying here to appraise the vast literature on slavery. The recent general works that have most informed my thinking are Kenneth Stampp, *The Peculiar Institution,* New York 1956, invaluable above all for its description of conditions on large plantations; Eugene D. Genovese, *Roll Jordan Roll: The World the Slaveowners Made,* New York 1974, a flawed but magnificently sensitive study of the interaction between slave and master and how this interaction affected the spiritual and emotional as well as the material lives of both; Lawrence W. Levine, *Black Culture and Black Consciousness: Afro-American Folk Thought from Slavery to Freedom*, New York 1977, worth many times its price for its reporting of marvelous examples of black thought and feeling alone; John W. Blassingame, *The Slave Community: Plantation Life in the Antebellum South*, New York 1972, an impressionistic but broad study which fulfills its promise to describe and analyze "the life of the black slave, his African heritage, culture, family, acculturation, behavior, religion, and personality"; and George P. Rawick, *From Sundown to Sunup: The Making of the Black Community*, Westport 1972, which distills ex-slaves' own reminiscences about the workings of the peculiar institution. Herbert G. Gutman, *The Black Family in Slavery and Freedom, 1750–1925*, New York 1976, is a book of high importance, which accumulates massive data to underpin its argument that slaves strived heroically and with surprising success to maintain family life in the face of monumental obstacles. Eugene D. Genovese savagely criticizes the book in "Solidarity and Servitude," *The Times Literary Supplement*, February 25, 1977, 198–199, in a review that is less than detached. Subsequent expert reviews are likely to be more sympathetic to Gutman's heroically researched and forcefully—perhaps too forcefully—argued study.

There has been a lively controversy over the economics, particularly the profitability, of slavery. Robert W. Fogel and Stanley L. Engerman, *Time on the Cross: The Economics of American Negro Slavery*, Boston 1974, is the most recent and most provocative major contribution to the literature on the subject. Ridiculing Stampp's and other studies for their wrongheaded reliance on what they deride as unrepresentative data, the authors of *Time on the Cross* utilize the methods of the new economic history to argue the profitability of slavery, the high productivity of slaves, and the surprisingly good treatment, clothing, housing, and food they enjoyed, setting forth their essential argument in one volume and their data base and methodological explanations in another. Their tour de force, while swiftly hailed in the media, has been devastatingly attacked by specialists, above all by their fellow cliometricians. "The problem," write Paul A. David and Peter Temin, "is that the second volume . . . simply does not set out the bushels of footnotes" one had expected to find for a text "unencumbered by documentation." See David and Temin, "Slavery: The Progressive Institution," *JEH*, 34 (September 1974), 739–783. *Time on the Cross* has inspired two book-length denunciations, in addition to many shorter ones. Richard Sutch, *The Treatment Received by American Slaves: A Critical Review of the Evidence Presented in Time on the Cross*, Berkeley 1975, which attempts "to replicate the results of [the book's] experiments" by using the procedures adopted by its authors, concludes that *Time* is a failure because of "many errors in computation," its selective use of data, misrepresentation of sources, faulty and biased procedures, evidence that "does not withstand close scrutiny," and "distorted" conclusions. Herbert G. Gutman, *Slavery and The Numbers Game: A Critique of Time on the Cross*, Urbana 1975, if anything savages the book even more mercilessly—and effectively—since the fact that Gutman does not speak the language of cliometrics makes his argument easier to follow than the criticisms written by Sutch, Temin, David, and others of the new men. Hardly obsolete is the pathbreaking econometric essay by Alfred H. Conrad and

John R. Meyer, "The Economics of Slavery in the Ante Bellum South," not to mention such older works as Ulrich B. Phillips' famous volumes, *American Negro Slavery*, New York 1918, and *Life and Labor in the Old South*, New York 1925. Rejecting Phillips' racial premises, while trying to synthesize his economic interpretation with that of Conrad and Meyers, is Genovese, *The Political Economy of Slavery: Studies in the Economy and Society of the Slave South*, New York 1965.

Slavery was not confined to plantations. Richard C. Wade, *Slavery in the Cities: The South 1820–1860*, New York 1964, is informative and well written. Critical of Wade's argument that cities were ultimately incompatible with slavery is Claudia Dale Golden, "Urbanization and Slavery: the Issue of Compatibility," in *Schnore, The New Urban History*, 231–246. Indispensable on industrial slavery are Robert S. Starobin, *Industrial Slavery in the Old South*, New York 1970, and Charles B. Dew, "Disciplining Slave Ironworkers in the Antebellum South: Coercion, Conciliation, and Accommodation," *AHR*, 79 (April 1974), 393–418.

The fullest general accounts of antebellum labor were written more than a half century ago. John R. Commons and Associates, *History of Labour in the United States*, New York 1918; Commons, ed., *A Documentary History of American Industrial Society*, Cleveland 1910; and Norman Ware, *The Industrial Worker, 1840–1860*, Boston 1924; all of which remain indispensable. A recent overview of the first half of the 19th century is Edward Pessen, "Builders of the Young Republic," in Richard B. Morris, ed., *The American Worker*, Washington 1976. The dozens of journals which constituted the labor press are discussed in Commons' *History*, vol. 1, and in Edward Pessen, "*La Première Presse du Travail: Origine, Role, Idéologie*," in J. Godechot, ed., *La Presse Ouvrière, 1819–1850*, Paris 1966, a study of the labor press of the industrial nations. Richard B. Morris, "Labor Controls in Maryland in the Nineteenth Century," *Journal of Southern History*, 14 (August 1948), 385–400, is instructive on an interesting issue. The antebellum trade union movement is considered in Commons' works; Edward Pessen, *Most Uncommon Jacksonians: The Radical Leaders of the Early Labor Movement*, Albany 1967; and Louis Arky, "The Mechanics' Union of Trade Associations and the Formation of the Philadelphia Working Men's Movement," *PMHB*, 76 (April 1952), 142–176. For conditions of factory labor see William A. Sullivan, *The Industrial Worker in Pennsylvania, 1800–1840*, Harrisburg 1955; Thomas Dublin, "Women, Work, and Protest in the Early Lowell Mills: 'The Oppressing Hand of Avarice Would Enslave Us.' " *Labor History*, 16 (Winter 1975), 99–116; Vera Shlakman, "Economic History of a Factory Town: A Study of Chicopee, Massachusetts," *Smith College Studies in History*, 20 (1934–1935); H. M. Gitelman, "The Waltham System and the Coming of the Irish," *Labor History*, 8 (Fall 1967), 227–253; and Hannah Josephson, *The Golden Threads*, New York 1949. The tricky issue of wages of labor is fruitfully considered in two articles by Donald R. Adams, Jr., "Wage Rates in the Early National Period: Philadelphia, 1785–1830," *JEH*, 28 (September 1968), 404–426, and "Some Evidence on English and American Wage Rates, 1790–1830," *JEH*, 30 (September 1970), 499–519; Stanley Lebergott, *Manpower in Economic Growth*, New York 1964; Dorothy S. Brady, "Relative Prices in the Nineteenth Century," *JEH*, 24 (June 1964), 145–203; Walter B. Smith, "Wage Rates on the Erie Canal, 1828–1881," *JEH*, 23 (Summer 1963), 298–311; Robert F. Martin, *Na-*

tional Income in the United States, 1799–1938, New York 1939; and Robert Layer, *Earnings of Cotton Mill Operatives, 1825–1914*, Cambridge 1955.

The "new labor history" has emerged simultaneously with "new histories" of other subjects, stressing, among other themes, the impact of expanding capitalism and industrialism on working people's values, lifestyles—in and out of the shop—and the factor of ethnicity. Good examples of the new approach are Herbert G. Gutman's sprawling but valuable "Work, Culture, and Society in Industrializing America, 1815–1919," *AHR*, 78 (June 1973), 531–588; Bruce Laurie, " 'Nothing on Impulse': Life Styles of Philadelphia Artisans, 1820–1850," *Labor History*, 15 (Summer 1974), 337–366; Paul Faler, "Cultural Aspects of the Industrial Revolution: Lynn, Massachusetts, Shoemakers and Industrial Morality, 1826–1860," *ibid.*, 15 (Summer 1974), 367–394; and John Modell, "The Peopling of a Working-Class Ward: Reading, Pennsylvania, 1850," *Journal of Social History*, 5 (Fall 1971), 71–95. A review copy of Alan Dawley, *Class and Community: The Industrial Revolution in Lynn*, Cambridge 1976, reached me too late for consideration.

An important discussion of legal aspects of corporations is James Willard Hurst, *The Legitimacy of the Business Corporation in the United States 1780–1970*, Charlottesville 1970. Margaret Walsh, *The Manufacturing Frontier: Pioneer Industry in Antebellum Wisconsin, 1830–1860*, Madison 1972, is a clear, informative discussion. Industrial developments and the expanding factory system are also discussed profitably by Victor S. Clark, *History of Manufactures in the United States*, New York 1929; Arthur H. Cole, *The American Wool Manufacture*, Cambridge 1926; George S. Gibb, *The Saco-Lowell Shops, Textile Machinery Building in New England, 1813–1949*, Cambridge 1950; and Thomas R. Smith, *The Cotton Textile Industry of Fall River, Massachusetts*, New York 1944. Marvin Fisher, *Workshops in the Wilderness: the European Response to American Industrialization, 1830–1860*, New York 1967, is an interesting if not always convincing discussion of the visitors' reactions to and evaluations of the factory system. Rolla M. Tyron, *Household Manufactures in the United States, 1640–1860*, Chicago 1917, is the single standard on a not insignificant topic that badly requires an updated study.

Biographies offer some of the best discussions of antebellum business. Particularly worthwhile are Elva Tooker, *Nathan Trotter, Philadelphia Merchant, 1787–1853*, Cambridge 1955, which better than almost any other source describes in detail the operation of what John R. Commons called the "merchant capitalist" system; Carl Seaburg and Stanley Peterson, *Merchant Prince of Boston: Colonel T. H. Perkins, 1764–1854*, Cambridge 1971, thinly descriptive but written with verve; Kenneth W. Porter's massive *John Jacob Astor, Businessman*, Cambridge 1931, a multivolume account not of Astor's life but of his business activities alone; Porter, *The Jacksons and the Lees: Two Generations of Massachusetts Merchants, 1765–1844*, Cambridge 1937; Edwin J. Perkins' authoritative *Financing Anglo-American Trade: The House of Brown, 1800–1880*, Cambridge 1975; Henry Cohen, *Business and Politics in America from the Age of Jackson to the Civil War: the Career Biography of W. W. Corcoran*, Westport 1971; Frances W. Gregory, *Nathan Appleton: Merchant and Entrepreneur, 1779–1861*, Charlottesville 1975, detailed but unanalytical; Philip L. White, *The Beekmans of New York in Politics and Commerce, 1647–1877*, New York 1956, thorough and fact-filled; and Richard Lowitt, *A Merchant Prince of the Nineteenth Century: William E. Dodge*, New York 1954, evocative of the mundane details of commercial life in antebellum New York City. Also valuable on commerce are Robert G. Albion, *The Rise of New York Port, 1815–1850*, New York 1939, a delightful descriptive account; James Mak, "Intraregional Trade in the Antebellum West: Ohio, A Case Study," *Agricultural History*, 46 (October 1972), 489–497; Jacques M. Downs, "American Merchants and the China Opium Trade, 1800–1840," *Business History Review*, 42 (Winter 1968), 418–422; and Bennett D. Baack and Edward J. Ray, "Tariff Policy and Income Distribution: The Case of the United States 1830–1860," *Expl. Eco. Hist.*, 11 (Winter 1973–74), 103–122.

The best single volume on commerce and transportation is Taylor's *The Transportation Revolution*. The most valuable work on canals has been done by Carter Goodrich and his students. Particularly good are Goodrich, ed., *Canals and American Economic Development*, New York 1961; Goodrich, "American Development Policy: the Case of Internal Improvements," *Journal of Economic History*, 16 (December 1956), 449–460; Jerome Cranmer, "The New Jersey Canals: A Study of the Role of Government in Economic Enterprise," Columbia University Doctoral Dissertation 1965; Roger L. Ransom, "Canals and Development: A Discussion of the Issues," *American Economic Review*, 54 (May 1964), 365–376; Ransom, "Interregional Canals and Economic Specialization in the Antebellum United States," *Explorations in Entrepreneurial History*, 2nd Series, vol. 5 (Fall 1967), 12–35; Ralph D. Gray, *The National Waterway: A History of the Chesapeake and Delaware Canal. 1769–1965*, Urbana 1967; and Harry N. Scheiber, *Ohio Canal Era: A Case Study of the Government and the Economy, 1820–1861*, Athens, Ohio, 1969, excellent above all for its treatment of technical engineering problems. There are two fine modern accounts of the Erie Canal: Nathan Miller, *The Enterprise of a Free People: Aspects of Economic Development in New York State during the Canal Period, 1792–1838*, Ithaca 1962; and Ronald E. Shaw, *Erie Water West: A History of the Erie Canal, 1792–1854*, Lexington 1967; the former more analytical, the latter descriptive. I have also profited from Peter Temin, "Steam and Water Power in the Early 19th Century," *Journal of Economic History*, 26 (June 1966), 187–205.

A lively controversy over Jacksonian railroads followed the publication of two brilliant and original works; Robert W. Fogel, *Railroads and American Economic Growth;* and Albert Fishlow, *American Railroads and the Transformation of the Ante-Bellum Economy*. Peter D. McClelland, "Railroads, American Growth and the New Economic History," offers the best criticism of their approach. Stanley Lebergott, "United States Transportation Advance and Externalities," *Journal of Economic History*, 26 (December 1966), 437–461, argues the superiority of railroads to canals in freight-carrying capacity relative to costs. Harry N. Scheiber effectively demolishes Lebergott's methodology in a brief rebuttal; *ibid.*, 462–465. Also bearing on the latter issue is Julius Rubin, *Canal or Railroad? Imitation and Innovation in the Response to the Erie Canal in Philadelphia, Baltimore, and Boston*, Philadelphia 1961; and Stephen Salsbury, *The State, The Investor, and The Railroad: The Boston and Albany 1825–1867*, Cambridge 1967, which criticizes the "analytical technique" of Rubin's study. A useful factual survey is Merl E. Reed, *New Orleans and the Railroads: The Struggle for Commercial Empire, 1830–1860,* Baton Rouge 1966.

Andrew Jackson's war on the second Bank of the United States (BUS) has focused scholarly attention on banking and finance. The literature of the Bank War is discussed below, with other political issues. An interesting interpretive introduction to banking in general is Fritz Redlich, *The Molding of American Banking: Men and Ideas,* New York 1947. James Sloane Gibbons, *The Banks of New York,* New York 1858, is an invaluable contemporary description of how discounting and other technical banking operations were handled, written by an insider. J. Van Fenstermaker, *The Development of American Commercial Banking, 1782–1837,* Kent 1965; Paul B. Trescott, "An Old Look at American Monetary History," *Explorations in Entrepreneurial History,* 6 (Spring–Summer 1969), 254–267; Hugh Rockoff, "Money, Prices, and Banks in the Jacksonian Era," in Fogel and Engerman, *The Reinterpretation of American Economic History;* and Richard H. Timberlake, Jr., *Money, Banking, and Central Banking,* New York 1965, are worthwhile modern supplements to the earlier general studies, Davis R. Dewey, *Financial History of the United States,* New York 1934; and W. J. Schultz and M. R. Caine, *Financial Development of the United States,* New York 1937. Valuable studies which emphasize the economic more than the political aspects of the Second BUS are R. C. H. Catterall's classic, *The Second Bank of the United States,* Chicago 1902; Walter B. Smith, *Economic Aspects of the Second Bank of the United States,* Cambridge 1953; and Arthur Fraas, "The Second Bank of the United States: An Instrument for an Interregional Monetary Union," *JEH,* 34 (June 1974), 447–467. Profitable discussions of the era's financial panics include Reginald C. McGrane's richly factual *The Panic of 1837: Some Financial Problems of the Jacksonian Era,* Chicago 1924, "old-fashioned" in a very nice sense of that term; Richard W. Timberlake, Jr., "The Specie Circular and the Distribution of the Surplus," *Journal of Political Economy,* 68 (April 1960), 109–117; and Temin, *The Jacksonian Economy,* provocative and very new-fashioned indeed.

Some of the most interesting work has been done on banking in the states and local communities. An excellent older study is Robert E. Chaddock, *The Safety Fund Banking System in New York 1829–1866,* Washington 1910. I have been influenced too by Alan L. Olmstead, "Mutual Savings Bank Depositors in New York," *Business History Review,* 49 (Autumn 1975), 287–311, which challenges older notions about the allegedly important role played by marginal investors in the mutual banks of the early 19th century; also by Olmstead, "Investment Constraints and New York City Mutual Savings Bank Financing of Antebellum Development," *JEH,* 32 (December 1972), 811–840; Donald R. Adams, Jr.,"The Bank of Stephen Girard, 1812–1831," *ibid.,* 841–868; Grant Morison, "Isaac Bronson and the Search for System in American Capitalism, 1789–1838," City University of New York doctoral dissertation 1973, which is instructive on private banking operations; Harry N. Scheiber, "Public Canal Finance and State Banking in Ohio, 1825–1837," *Indiana Magazine of History,* 65 (June 1969), 119–132; Dean A. Dudley, "Bank Born of Revelation: the Kirtland Safety Society Anti-Banking Company," *JEH,* 30 (December 1970), 848–853, about a bank founded by Mormons in 1837; Erling A. Erickson, *Banking in Frontier Iowa, 1836–1865,* Ames 1971; James H. Madison, "Business and Politics in Indianapolis: The Branch Bank and the Junto, 1837–1846," *Indiana Magazine of History*, 71 (March 1975), 1–20; and J. Mauldin Lesesne, *The Bank of the State of South Carolina: A General and Political History*, Columbia 1970. The informed writings by Bray Hammond, Frank O. Gatell, John McFaul, James Roger Sharp, William G. Shade, and others, that emphasize the political implications and overtones of banking are discussed in the section on political issues.

Parties and Politics

The Jacksonian political literature is exhaustive. Useful introductions to it include Ronald P. Formisano, "Toward a Reorientation of Jacksonian Politics: A Review of the Literature, 1959–1975," *JAH*, 64 (June 1976), 42–65, a fair-minded and thoughtful interpretive discussion of recent writings by a scholar himself identified with one of the influential modern schools; Alfred A. Cave, *Jacksonian Democracy and the Historians*, Gainesville 1964, which clearly summarizes some of the leading interpretations of the past century; Edwin A. Miles, "The Jacksonian Era," in Arthur S. Link and Rembert W. Patrick, eds., *Writing Southern History*, Baton Rouge 1965, an informed, thorough, and judicious appraisal of the literature on Jacksonian politics in the South; and Glyndon G. Van Deusen, *The Jacksonian Era, 1828–1848*, New York 1959, the bibliographical essay of which is informative on national political issues. Perhaps the most interesting of these discussions is Charles G. Sellers, Jr., "Andrew Jackson versus the Historians," *Mississippi Valley Historical Review*, 44 (March 1958), 615–634, a clearly organized and provocative essay, which relates scholars' changing judgments of the Jacksonian era to the changing intellectual atmospheres in which they were written. At times, however, Sellers explains historians' interpretations he does not approve by reference to biases whose existence he does not demonstrate. In his introduction to the Harper Torchbook version of James Parton's *The Presidency of Andrew Jackson*, New York 1967, Robert V. Remini shows that Parton's criticisms of Old Hickory were hardly due to the "patrician bias" attributed to Parton by Sellers. It is also doubtful that it is the "personal origins and sympathies" of both Arthur M. Schlesinger, Jr., and his Columbia University critics that account for what Sellers calls the urban emphasis in their views or for their alleged criticism of agrarian elements in American history. Some of these historians were country boys.

Frank O. Gatell's bibliographical essay, "The Jacksonian Era, 1824–1848," in Cartwright and Watson, *The Reinterpretation of American History and Culture*, 309–326, is slim and not as up-to-date as Formisano's *JAH* article. Recent collections of modern political interpretations are Edward Pessen, ed. *New Perspectives on Jacksonian Parties and Politics*, Boston 1969; and Joel H. Silbey, ed., *Political Ideology and Voting Behavior in the Age of Jackson*, Englewood Cliffs 1973.

The private papers and correspondence, published and unpublished, of the great and not so great are a fundamental source that has been mined intensively by biographers. Current projects will result in the publication of the papers of Daniel Webster, Jackson, and Martin Van Buren, among others. Such earlier collections—space forbids alluding to more than a handful—as John S. Bassett, ed., *Correspondence of Andrew Jackson*, 7 vols., Washington 1926–1935; Charles F. Adams, ed., *Memoirs of John Quincy Adams*, 12 vols., Philadelphia 1874–1877;

Calvin Colton, ed., *The Life, Correspondence and Speeches of Henry Clay*, 6 vols., New York 1864; and such first person accounts as *The Autobiography of Amos Kendall*, Boston 1972; John C. Fitzpatrick, ed., *The Autobiography of Martin Van Buren*, Washington 1920; William H. and Frederick W. Seward, eds., *William H. Seward: An Autobiography*, 3 vols., New York 1891; and *Autobiography of Thurlow Weed*, Boston 1883—are of course invaluable. Another important source are contemporary reflections such as Thomas Hart Benton, *Thirty Years View, 1820 to 1850*, New York 1954; Ben Perley: Poore, *Reminiscences of Sixty Years*, Philadelphia 1886; or James A. Hamilton, *Reminiscences of Men and Events*, New York 1869, by the good Jacksonian and son of the first Secretary of the Treasury.

Good biographies offer uniquely valuable insights into men and affairs. Biographies that are outstanding in my judgment include Carl B. Swisher, *Roger B. Taney*, New York 1936; Samuel F. Bemis, *John Quincy Adams*, 2 vols., New York 1956; Russel B. Nye, *George Bancroft*, New York 1964; William N. Chambers, *Old Bullion Benton, Senator From the New West*, Boston 1956; Charles M. Wiltse, *John C. Calhoun*, 3 vols., Indianapolis 1944–1951; Glyndon G. Van Deusen's comprehensive accounts of the leaders of Whiggery—*The Life of Henry Clay*, Boston 1937; *Horace Greeley, 19th Century Crusader*, Philadelphia 1953; *Thurlow Weed, Wizard of the Lobby*, Boston 1947; and *William Henry Seward*, New York 1967; Charles G. Sellers, Jr., *James K. Polk, Jacksonian, 1795–1843*, and *James K. Polk, Continentalist, 1843–1846*, Princeton 1957, 1966.

James Parton, *Life of Andrew Jackson*, 3 vols., New York 1861, is the most faultfinding of the major works on Old Hickory. Marquis James, *The Life of Andrew Jackson*, Indianapolis 1938, is almost embarrassingly uncritical, managing to explain away almost all foibles, but it is richly detailed and makes for better reading than John S. Bassett's more scholarly, *The Life of Andrew Jackson*, 2 vols., New York 1911. Students will find Robert V. Remini's recent *Andrew Jackson*, New York 1966, compact, readable, scholarly, and adulatory. James C. Curtis, *Andrew Jackson and the Search for Vindication*, Boston 1976, is an unusually sensible and well-reasoned "psychobiography."

Other political biographies that are valuable are Elbert B. Smith, *Magnificent Missourian: The Life of Thomas Hart Benton*, Philadelphia 1958; William E. Smith, *The Francis Preston Blair Family in Politics*, New York 1933; Philip S. Klein, *President James Buchanan*, University Park 1962; Margaret L. Coit, *John C. Calhoun: American Portrait*, Boston 1950; Clement Eaton, *Henry Clay and the Art of American Politics*, Boston 1957; Dorothy Goebel, *William Henry Harrison*, Indianapolis 1926; Marquis James, *The Raven: A Biography of Sam Houston*, Indianapolis 1929; William G. Sumner, *Andrew Jackson as a Public Man*, Boston 1882; Leland W. Meyer, *The Life and Times of Colonel Richard M. Johnson*, New York 1932; Ivor D. Spencer, *The Victor and the Spoils: A Life of William Marcy*, Providence 1959; Oliver Chitwood, *John Tyler*, New York 1939; Edward M. Shepard, *Martin Van Buren*, New York 1889; James Shenton, *Robert J. Walker*, New York 1961; Claude M. Fuess, *Daniel Webster*, 2 vols., Boston 1930; George T. Curtis, *Life of Daniel Webster*, 2 vols., New York 1870; Richard N. Current, *Daniel Webster and the Rise of National Conservatism*, Boston 1955; John Garraty, *Silas Wright*, New York 1949; George Rawlings Poage, *Henry Clay and the Whig Party*, Chapel Hill 1936; Chase C. Mooney, *William H.*

Crawford, 1772–1834, Lexington, Ky. 1974; John A. Monroe, *Louis McLane: Federalist and Jacksonian*, New Brunswick 1973; Holman Hamilton, *Zachary Taylor: Sword of the Republic*, Indianapolis 1941; Charles Henry Ambler, *Thomas Ritchie: A Study in Virginia Politics*, Richmond 1913; and Herman J. Viola, *Thomas L. McKenney: Architect of America's Early Indian Policy, 1816–1830*, Chicago 1974.

Not all worthwhile biographical accounts take the form of full-length studies of the giants. Useful articles on lesser figures include Philip S. Klein, ed., "Memoirs of a Senator from Pennsylvania: Jonathan Roberts, 1771–1854," *PMHB*, 62 (July 1938), 361–409; J. E. Rea, "William Lyon Mackenzie—Jacksonian?" *Mid-America*, 50 (July 1968), 223–235; John M. Martin, "William R. King: Jacksonian Senator," *Alabama Review*, 18 (October 1965), 243–267, an interesting discussion of the dilemma of a loyal Jackson supporter; Jean E. Friedman and William G. Shade, "James M. Porter: A Conservative Democrat in the Jacksonian Era," *Pennsylvania History*, 42 (July 1975), 189–204; Gordon T. Chappell, "John Coffee: Land Speculator and Planter," *Alabama Review*, 22 (January 1969), 24–43; James Earl Moss, "William Henry Ashley: A Jackson Man with Feet of Clay," *Missouri Historical Review*, 61 (October 1966), 1–20; and Brian G. Walton, "Ambrose Hundley Sevier in the United States Senate, 1836–1848," *Arkansas Historical Quarterly*, 32 (Spring 1973), 25–60.

A Retrospective Glance at the Modern Jacksonian Controversy

The last part of the bibliographical essay in the original edition of this book was set aside for "The Modern Jacksonian Controversy"—essentially a discussion of Arthur M. Schlesinger, Jr., *The Age of Jackson*, Boston 1945, and the lively scholarly debate that seminal book provided. It is a fair statement that most of the important political literature on the period written in the 20 years following publication of Schlesinger's book dealt explicitly or by indirection with the issues it raised. I have decided to reorganize the political discussion because the many new departures of the past ten years, if they do not reduce to obsolescence the argument over the alleged radicalism of Jacksonian Democracy or the "aristocratic" character of its opponents, nevertheless suggest the wisdom of treating the recent discussion as something more than mere postscript to the earlier controversy. For, as Ronald P. Formisano has recently observed, "it is unlikely . . . that parties in the period will be fitted to a liberal-conservative schema or that Jackson and his opponents will be divided again into radical democrats and aristocrats." It now appears to me most fruitful to discuss the literature along topical lines that are carved out naturally by the history of the period, rather than by categorizing the varied contributions according to whether they were published before or after 1945 or interpreted the Jacksonian political movement this way or that. Of course, no matter how an essay on ante-bellum politics is structured, Schlesinger's book must occupy a central place in it.

The Age of Jackson occupies a special niche as perhaps the most influential of the large or overarching interpretations of Jacksonian politics. In a sense it represents a culmination of the Progressive interpretation put forward earlier by Charle A. Beard and Frederick Jackson Turner in a number of their writings and by Arthur M. Schlesinger, Sr., in *New Viewpoints in American History*, New York 1922. The elder

Schlesinger had suggested that poorer urban elements belonged to the Jacksonian coalition that the Progressive view had peopled almost entirely with rural and western masses who owned modest property. Complementing this view of the Democracy were such Progressive perceptions of the Whigs as Arthur C. Cole, *The Whig Party in the South*, New York 1914, and E. Malcolm Carroll, *Origins of the Whig Party*, Durham 1925. *The Age of Jackson* was the most vigorous and comprehensive statement of the thesis that Jacksonian Democracy was a class rather than a sectional phenomenon. According to the younger Schlesinger, eastern workers constituted a significant part of the Jacksonian coalition, urban ideological radicals—unless they were perversely doctrinaire—were influential in its leadership, with Old Hickory keenly sympathetic to the plight of the former and responsive to the thought of the latter. Jackson's chief opponents were ostensibly the masters of eastern capitalism, whose political instruments became first the National Republican and then the Whig party, both arrayed against the party of the working classes and the have-nots—Jackson's Democratic party. In Schlesinger's version, the Jacksonian movement continued the good fight in behalf of the "people" and against "the interests" that had been begun earlier by Jeffersonian Democracy and was ostensibly continued a century later by Franklin D. Roosevelt's New Deal. Adding to the book's persuasive power was its verve and flair.

Charmed by its version of history, the author of this essay was himself inspired to become an historian, never dreaming that his early professional career would subsequently be spent in challenging its assertions. Many of the assertions in *The Age of Jackson* are indeed challengeable: "The people called him [Jackson], and he came, like the great folk heroes, to lead them out of captivity and bondage," it states at one point. The unsuspecting would never guess from this phrase that the Jacksonians were ardent supporters rather than opponents of the *actual* system of slavery in antebellum America. Almost all of the central points of *The Age of Jackson* have been challenged or devastatingly refuted by Bray Hammond, Lee Benson, Richard P. McCormick, Joseph Dorfman, Richard B. Morris and the "Columbia School" of critics, and numerous other historians. While the debate has no doubt been a fruitful one that, among other things, stimulated a great interest in the period, it inevitably has resulted in the propagation of oversimplifications in which devils and angels are everpresent, while issues and events are colored black or white.

Parties and Politics–Continued

Although no other author has presented so ambitious and comprehensive an interpretation as the Schlesingerian supplement to Progressivism, a number of original and influential analyses have been offered. John W. Ward, *Andrew Jackson: Symbol for an Age*, New York 1955, is a strikingly original study of the emotional sources of Andrew Jackson's popular appeal, which holds that The Hero came to personify elemental natural forces to his countrymen.

The so-called entrepreneurial school argued that Jacksonians were dedicated to the main chance, inspired not by a radical or anticapitalistic animus but by a vision of expanded opportunities for personal profit within capitalism. Representative writings would include Bray Hammond, "Jackson, Biddle and the Bank of the United States," *JEH*, 7

(May 1947), 1–23; Joseph Dorfman, *The Economic Mind in American Civilization*, New York 1946, vol. 2, ch. 24; and Richard Hofstadter, *The American Political Tradition*, New York 1948, ch. 3. Marvin Meyers, *The Jacksonian Persuasion*, Stanford 1957, is a subtle modification of the entrepreneurial thesis, which argues that while Jacksonians indeed sought the main chance, they yet clung in their hearts to anticommercial beliefs. If Meyers would not go quite so far as Schlesinger in accepting the sincerity of Jacksonian oratory, he insisted nevertheless that it could not be dismissed out of hand. Bearing on this issue is Perry M. Goldman, "Political Rhetoric in the Age of Jackson," *Tennessee Historical Quarterly*, 29 (Winter 1970–71), 360–371.

Glyndon G. Van Deusen, whose *The Jacksonian Era, 1828–1848*, is a balanced description of national politics, in "Some Aspects of Whig Thought and Theory in the Jacksonian Period," *AHR*, 63 (January 1958), 305–322, argued the essential similarity of the two parties, certainly in their goals, a point even more sharply developed by the "Columbia School" in their studies showing that Andrew Jackson was no special friend to labor and that working men whether organized or unorganized were in their turn no champions of the Democracy. Representative studies include Richard B. Morris, "Andrew Jackson, Strikebreaker," *ibid.*, 55 (October 1949), 54–68; and the following essays by Morris's students: William A. Sullivan, "Did Labor Support Andrew Jackson?" *Political Science Quarterly*, 62 (December 1947), 569–580; Walter Hugins, *Jacksonian Democracy and the Working Class*, Stanford 1960; and Edward Pessen's two essays: "Did Labor Support Jackson? The Boston Story," *Political Science Quarterly*, 64 (June 1949), 262–274; and "The Workingmen's Movement of the Jacksonian Era," *Mississippi Valley Historical Review*, 43 (December 1956), 428–443. For a critical analysis of this author's interpretation, developed in these and subsequent writings, that the major parties were largely indifferent to the massive inequities disfiguring antebellum America, see Donald M. Roper, "Beyond the Jacksonian Era: A Comment on the Pessen Thesis," *NYH*, 56 (April 1975), 226–233.

Richard P. McCormick, *The Second American Party System: Party Formation in the Jacksonian Era*, Chapel Hill 1966, has provoked a lively debate for the good reason that it is a forceful statement of a crystal clear thesis based on impressive evidence intelligently evaluated. Examining the emergence of Jacksonian and opposition parties in every state but South Carolina in the years after the disputed election of 1824, McCormick finds that the pragmatic hope of exploiting the "presidential question" rather than lofty or ideological principles animated major party organizers. For McCormick's response to the criticism by Robert E. Shalhope, "Jacksonian Politics in Missouri: a Comment on the McCormick Thesis," *Civil War History*, 15 (September 1969), 210–225, see the correspondence in *ibid.*, 16 (March 1970), 92–95. Obliquely critical of McCormick's thesis—which in my judgment they oversimplify—are Herbert Ershkowitz and William G. Shade, "Consensus or Conflict? Political Behavior in the State Legislatures during the Jacksonian Era," *JAH*, 58 (December 1971), 591–621, a useful survey of roll calls in six states between 1833 and 1843 which reads more into the inevitably opposing legislative stances adopted by the major parties than is warranted by the evidence. For as Peter Levine has effectively shown in his "State Legislative Parties in the Jacksonian Era: New Jersey, 1829–1844," *JAH*, 62 (December 1975), 591–608, pragmatic no less than ideological parties find it necessary to identify themselves with distinctive legislative programs that contrast with those of their opponents, finding little difficulty in publicly explaining their postures in the loftiest terms.

In *The Concept of Jacksonian Democracy: New York As a Test Case,* Princeton 1961, Lee Benson dismissed Jacksonian party pronouncements as "claptrap." Focusing largely on 1844 election returns in upstate New York communities, Benson's interpretation of the tallies has attained wide influence that extends beyond the Jacksonian era. Ingeniously manipulating data on ethnic and racial identity, denominational affiliations, psychological and sociological concepts, and the lifestyles and values of major party supporters, to document his thesis that voters were complexly motivated, influenced more by economic than by other social class considerations, Benson concluded that the concept "Jacksonian Democracy" should be discarded as an obstacle to a true understanding of the era's politics. This "ethnocultural" interpretation has been most effectively applied by Ronald P. Formisano, *The Birth of Mass Political Parties: Michigan, 1827–1861,* Princeton 1971, a book readers will find valuable on a number of levels, even should they feel it strains to fit the major parties into "evangelical" and nonevangelical molds. Much less persuasive is William G. Shade, "Pennsylvania Politics in the Jacksonian Period: A Case Study, Northampton County, 1824–1844," *Pennsylvania History* 39 (July 1972), 313–333, which draws unwarranted inferences concerning individual voting behavior from inappropriate aggregate data. The latter weakness has been discerned too by many critics in the influential ethnocultural studies of a later period: Richard Jensen, *The Winning of the Midwest: Social and Political Conflict, 1888–1896,* Chicago 1971; and Paul Kleppner, *The Cross of Culture: A Social Analysis of Midwestern Politics,* New York 1970. Of the many critiques published to date the methodology—and therefore the conclusions—of the ethnocultural school, the most effective are Richard L. McCormick, "Ethno-Cultural Interpretations of Nineteenth-Century American Voting Behavior," *Political Science Quarterly,* 89 (June 1974), 351–377, all the more devastating for its meticulous fairness and its applause of the virtues it detects in the approach; J. Morgan Kousser, "The 'New Political History': A Methodological Critique," *Reviews in American History,* 4 (March 1976), 1–14; James E. Wright, "The Ethnocultural Model of Voting: A Behavioral and Historical Critique," *American Behavioral Scientist,* 16 (May/June 1973), 653–674; and Richard B. Latner and Peter Levine, "Perspectives on Antebellum Pietistic Politics," *Reviews in American History,* 4 (March 1976), 15–24.

Challenging Benson's surmise that men of wealth were equally divided in their major party preferences because Whig and Democratic leaders in New York State were—according to the evidence of one of Moses Yale Beach's lists of New York City's wealthiest men—roughly of equal wealth, Frank O. Gatell used the same list in his, "Money and Party in Jacksonian America: A Quantitative Look at New York City's Men of Quality," *Political Science Quarterly,* 82 (June 1967), 235–252, to argue that wealthy New Yorkers overwhelmingly preferred Clay's party to Jackson's, particularly after the commencement of the Bank War. Brian J. Danforth, "The Influence of Socioeconomic Factors Upon Political Behavior: A Quantitative Look at New York City Merchants, 1829–1844," is a powerful refutation of Gatell's thesis, made all the more compelling by the diverse and detailed evidence Danforth cites to document his conclusions that the city's richest men were almost evenly split in their political allegiances before, during, and after the Bank War. (Danforth does agree with Gatell on one point: the significant correlations between voter's ethnocultural identities and their party preferences, found by Benson for New York State, did not obtain in New York City.) Edward Pessen, "Moses Beach Revisited: A Critical Examination of His *Wealthy Citizens* Pamphlets," *JAH*, 58 (September 1971), 415–426, discloses the unreliability of Beach's lists; Pessen's "The Wealthiest New Yorkers of the Jacksonian Era," *NYHSQ*, 54 (April 1970), 145–172, presents new lists based on the tax assessment data for 1828 and 1845. Robert Rich, " 'A Wilderness of Whigs': The Wealthy Men of Boston." *Journal of Social History*, 5 (July 1971), 263–276, argues that Gatell's thesis is valid too for Boston but does so on the basis of a few scattered and unrepresentative instances.

The above survey far from exhausts recent interpretations. I find Major L. Wilson, *Space, Time, and Freedom: The Quest for Nationality and the Irrepressible Conflict*, Westport 1974, an awkward, unpersuasive, often perverse, yet ultimately provocative and stimulating discussion, which contrasts Democratic proccupation with expanding across space an allegedly satisfactory society, with Whig determination to focus rather on improving the society qualitatively. Lynn L. Marshall, "The Genesis of Grass-Roots Democracy in Kentucky," *Mid-America*, 47 (October 1965), 269–287, finds the restless and the footloose drawn toward the Democracy, while his "The Strange Stillbirth of the Whig Party," *AHR*, 72 (January 1967), 445–468, discerns a connection between Whiggery and stuffy, pompous men. Although Marshall makes neither case convincingly, let alone conclusively, his ideas are interesting. Richard B. Latner, "A New Look at Jacksonian Politics," *JAH*, 61 (March 1975), 943–969, reasserts the old thesis that Jacksonian Democracy was essentially a western phenomenon, but does so on the basis of the tenuous argument that two of Jackson's chief advisers were, among other things, westerners. Richard H. Brown, "The Missouri Crisis, Slavery, and the Politics of Jacksonianism," *South Atlantic Quarterly*, 65 (Winter 1966), 55–72, fixes the defense of slavery as the primary ideal of Jacksonian Democracy in a perhaps overdrawn but brilliant essay that is challenged by John M. McFaul, "Expediency vs. Morality: Jacksonian Politics and Slavery," *JAH*, 62 (June 1975), 24–39. McFaul's article is in my judgment unconvincing, lightly documented, and explains away more than it explains Democratic motives. Some of my colleagues evidently find the substance of Michael H. Lebowitz's "The Jacksonians: Paradox Lost?" in Barton Bernstein, ed., *Towards A New Past: Dissenting Essays in American History*, New York 1968, 65–89, as interesting as I find its title. Richard J. Moss, "Jacksonian Democracy: A Note on the Origins and Growth of the Term," *Tennessee Historical Quarterly*, 34 (Summer 1975), 145–153, offers a footnote to the discussion of the popular rubric. James Sterling Young, *The Washington Community, 1800–1828*, New York 1966, has been much praised for its originality and unconventionality, although I must admit to being perplexed by its undocumented view that the "Jacksonian revolution" represented a political movement designed to satisfy the "popular demands" of an "aroused and demanding citizenry."

My discussion of the new structure and atmosphere of politics has been influenced by Leonard D. White, *The Jacksonians: A Study in Ad-*

ministrative History, 1829–1861, New York 1954; McCormick, *The Second American Party System;* Robert V. Remini's lively description of the new politics, *The Election of Andrew Jackson,* Philadelphia 1963; and James Staton Chase, "Jacksonian Democracy and the Rise of the Nominating Convention," *Mid-America,* 45 (October 1963), 229–249. Chilton Williamson, *American Suffrage from Property to Democracy, 1760–1860,* Princeton 1960, is indispensable and authoritative, although—as I am certain its author would agree—it would be strengthened if modified by recently disclosed evidence on diverse local practices.

As has been indicated, broad overviews have been provided by Arthur M. Schlesinger, Jr. and Glyndon G. Van Deusen, and earlier by Claude G. Bowers' rousing and Manichean Progressive tract, *Party Battles of the Jacksonian Period,* New York 1929, and Frederick J. Turner, *The United States, 1830–1850,* New York 1935. Robert V. Remini, *Martin Van Buren and the Making of the Democratic Party,* New York, 1959, interestingly, combines descriptive material, much of it antithetical to the Schlesinger thesis, with interpretive comment that is not. Charles G. Sellers, Jr., author of an outstanding biography of Polk, has written a series of influential essays, maintaining that the parties *were* fundamentally different, particularly in the South. According to him the Whigs were a party of finance and capitalism, the Democrats essentially a party of the yeomanry; Jackson may have been surrounded by unprincipled types, but Old Hickory himself had begun to move toward the politics of principle in the years before he became President. Sellers makes these points in "Who Were the Southern Whigs?" *AHR,* 59 (January 1954), 335–346; "Banking and Politics in Jackson's Tennessee, 1817–1827," *Mississippi Valley Historical Review,* 41 (June 1954), 61–84; and "Jackson Men with Feet of Clay," *ibid.,* 62 (April 1957), 537–551. James C. Curtis, *The Fox at Bay: Martin Van Buren and the Presidency, 1837–1841,* Lexington, Ky. 1970, is a judicious and excellent discussion, very much superior to William G. Carleton, "Political Aspects of the Van Buren Era," *South Atlantic Quarterly,* 50 (April 1951), 167–185. For a swift evaluation of Van Buren that, considering its source is surprisingly sympathetic, see Edward Pessen, "The Modest Role of Martin Van Buren," in Harry Sievers, ed., *Six Presidents From the Empire State,* Tarrytown 1974. In his comments on Pessen's essay, in the same volume, Richard P. McCormick makes an interesting point about Van Buren's deft handling of the South.

My discussion of politics and parties has been influenced by discussions that transcend the Jacksonian era. Important studies include Walter Dean Burnham and William N. Chambers, eds., *The American Party Systems,* New York 1967; Roy F. Nichols, *The Invention of Political Parties,* New York 1967; Richard Hofstadter, *The Idea of a Party System: The Rise of Legitimate Opposition in the United States, 1780–1840,* Berkeley 1969, which is of course bright and thoughtful but also disconcertingly oblivious to social contexts; Maurice Duverger, *Political Parties,* New York 1954; E. E. Schattschneider, *Party Government,* New York 1942; and Frank J. Sorauf, *Political Parties in the American System,* Boston and Toronto 1964. Focusing more closely on the Jacksonian period are Shaw Livermore, Jr., *The Twilight of Federalism: The Disintegration of the Federalist Party 1815–1830,* Princeton 1962, a book to which I am heavily indebted; Michael Wallace, "Changing Concepts of Party in the United States: New York, 1815–1828," *AHR,* 74 (December 1968), 453–491; and two interesting essays by Ronald P. Formisano: "Political Character, Antipartyism, and the Second Party System," *American Quarterly*, 21 (Winter 1969), 683–709; and "Deferential-Participant Politics: The Early Republic's Political Culture, 1789–1840," *American Political Science Review*, 68 (June 1974), 473–487.

The legislative behavior of major party congressmen is illuminated by a number of studies. Joel H. Silbey, *The Shrine of Party: Congressional Voting Behavior, 1841–1852*, Pittsburgh 1967, shows that late in the era congressmen felt a stronger attachment to party than to section. Thomas B. Alexander, *Sectional Stress and Party Strength: A Study of Roll-Call Voting Patterns in the United States House of Representatives, 1836–1860*, Nashville 1967, modifies Silbey's verdict; its last sentence states that the "elaborate game of musical chairs" played by congressional Whigs and Democrats attested to "real and persistent sectional differentials in interests and attitudes." Of course Alexander's study includes the pre-Civil War decade. Also useful is David J. Russo, "The Major Political Issues of the Jacksonian Period and the Development of Party Loyalty in Congress, 1830–1840," *Transactions of the American Philosophical Society*, 62 (May 1972), 1–51.

Good discussions of voter behavior are V. O. Key, *The Responsible Electorate*, Cambridge 1966; and Arthur S. Goldberg, "Social Determinism and Rationality as Bases of Party Identification," *American Political Science Review*, 63 (March 1969), 5–25, which argue persuasively that for all the complexity of voters' motives, they may not be as indifferent to rational considerations of self-interest as in recent years it has become modish to say they are. Richard P. McCormick, "Suffrage Classes and Party Alignments: A Study in Voter Behavior," *Mississippi Valley Historical Review*, 46 (December 1959), 397–410, shows that in state elections in antebellum North Carolina and New York, differences in the wealth of voters appear to have had little effect on their voting behavior.

Good on particular elections are Paul C. Nagel, "The Election of 1824: A Reconsideration Based on Newspaper Opinion," *Journal of Southern History*, 26 (August 1960), 315–329; Everett S. Brown, "The Presidential Election of 1824–1825," *Political Science Quarterly*, 40 (September 1925), 384–403; Florence Weston, *The Presidential Election of 1828*, Washington 1938, which is superseded by Robert V. Remini, *The Election of Andrew Jackson*, Philadelphia 1963; Robert Gray Gunderson, *The Log-Cabin Campaign*, Lexington 1957; Samuel R. Gammon, Jr., *The Presidential Campaign of 1832*, Baltimore 1932; and Donald B. Cole, "The Presidential Election of 1832 in New Hampshire," *Historical New Hampshire*, 21 (Winter 1966), 32–50. An important essay on comparative voter turnouts in the era's elections is Richard P. McCormick, "New Perspectives on Jacksonian Politics," *AHR* 65 (January 1960), 288–301.

The political ideas of Whig and Democratic leaders are of course treated in many of the writings discussed above. Robert Kelley, *The Transatlantic Persuasion: The Liberal-Democratic Mind in the Age of Gladstone*, New York 1969, is an interesting comparative study. Benjamin G. Rader, "William M. Gouge, Jacksonian Economic Theorist," *Pennsylvania History*, 30 (October 1963), 443–453; Edward K. Spann, *Ideals and Politics: New York Intellectuals and Liberal Democracy, 1820–1880*, Albany 1972; and John R. Wennersten, "Parke Godwin, Utopian Socialism, and the Politics of Antislavery," *NYHSQ*, 60 (July/

October 1976), 107–127, all throw light on the erratic and inconsistent quality of Democratic "radicalism." Whig thought is the chosen subject of a number of thoughtful essays. It is dealt with indirectly in a sprawling, factually invaluable, but analytically deficient study of the major Whig newspaper, William E. Ames, *A History of the National Intelligencer,* Chapel Hill 1972. Van Deusen, "Some Aspects of Whig Thought and Theory in the Jacksonian Period," finds that Whigs differed with Jacksonians over means, not ends. Edwin A. Miles, "The Whig Party and the Menace of Caesar," *Tennessee Historical Quarterly,* 27 (Winter 1968), 361–379, is an excellent study which ingeniously surveys congressional debates and the private papers of public men to reveal that Whigs came to identify themselves with senators of classical Rome, defending the republic against a demagogic tyrant. Elliot R. Barkan, "The Emergence of a Whig Persuasion: Conservatism, Democratism, and the New York State Whigs," *NYH,* 52 (October 1971), 367–395, is a fine essay which argues convincingly that ideas are as much a part of history as events, and intelligently separates different strands of Whig thought. Kinley J. Brauer, *Cotton Versus Conscience: Massachusetts Whig Politics and Southwestern Expansion, 1843–1848,* Lexington, Ky. 1967, effectively portrays an important split in Whig thinking. Also worthwhile are Alfred A. Cave, *An American Conservative in the Age of Jackson: The Political and Social Thought of Calvin Colton,* Fort Worth 1969; a number of studies of Webster's ideas and public actions: Melvyn Dubofsky, "Daniel Webster and the Whig Theory of Economic Growth 1820–1848," *New England Quarterly,* 42 (December 1969), 551–572; Sidney Nathans, *Daniel Webster and Jacksonian Democracy,* Baltimore 1973; Robert F. Dalzell, Jr., *Daniel Webster and the Trial of American Nationalism, 1843–1852,* Boston 1973; and Norman D. Brown, *Daniel Webster and the Politics of Availability,* Athens, Ohio 1969; and John V. Mering's perceptive discussion of a later period, "Persistent Whiggery in the Confederate South: A Reconsideration," *South Atlantic Quarterly,* 69 (Winter 1970), 124–143.

The literature on the minor parties remains sparse. A useful introduction to antimasonry is Lorman Ratner, *Anti-Masonry: The Crusade and the Party,* Englewood Cliffs 1969. Frank Gerrity, "The Masons, the Antimasons, and the Pennsylvania Legislature, 1834–1836," *PMHB,* 99 (April 1975), 180–206, is good on the role of Thaddeus Stevens in invigorating the legislative assault on masonry. Philip A. Grant, Jr., "The Antimasons Retain Control of the Green Mountain State," *Vermont History,* 34 (July 1966), 169–187, describes but does not explain the party's success in the 1834 elections. Also see Frederick M. Herrmann, "Anti-Masonry in New Jersey," *New Jersey History,* 90 (Autumn 1973), 149–165. Unfortunately, Kathleen Kutolowski's excellent "Freemasonry in New York: The Case of Genesee County, 1809–1847," a social profile of masonic lodges in upper New York state, is not yet in print. Older studies that remain useful are Charles McCarthy, "The Antimasonic Party: A Study of Political Antimasonry, 1827–1840," American Historical Association, *Annual Report for 1902,* Washington 1903, 1, 365–574; Jabez Hammond, *History of Political Parties in the State of New York,* New York 1846; Whitney R. Cross, *The Burned-Over District;* and David H. Ludlum, *Social Ferment in Vermont, 1791–1850,* New York 1939. Ronald P. Formisano with Kathleen S. Kutolowski, "Antimasonry and Masonry: The Genesis of Protest, 1826–1827," *American Quarterly,* (Summer 1977), 139–165, which came to my notice at the eleventh hour, persuasively argues that at least in its inception, organized antimasonry was by no means a totally hysterical movement.

The Working Men's party and the substantial literature it has evoked are dealt with at length in Pessen, *Most Uncommon Jacksonians*, chs. 2 and 5. Studies of particular interest are Helen Sumner, "Citizenship" (1827–1833), in Commons and Associates, *History of Labour*, vol. 1, 169–332; and Seymour Savetsky, "The New York Working Men's Party," Columbia University Master's Essay 1948. Walter Hugins' *Jacksonian Democracy and the Working Class* is invaluable both for the Working Men and the Locofocos.

Still the fundamental source on the Locofoco movement is Fitz-William Byrdsall, *History of the Loco-Foco or Equal Rights Party*, New York 1842. Other valuable studies in addition to Jabez Hammond's and Dixon Ryan Fox's accounts of New York State politics, are Carl N. Degler, "The Locofocos: Urban 'Agrarians,'" *JEH*, 16 (September 1956), 322–333; Richard Hofstadter, "William Leggett, Spokesman of Jacksonian Democracy," *Political Science Quarterly*, 58 (December 1943), 581–594; William Trimble, "The Social Philosophy of the Loco Foco Democracy," *American Journal of Sociology*, 26 (May 1921), 705–715; and Leo Hershkowitz, "The Loco-Foco Party of New York: Its Origins and Career, 1835–1847," *The New-York Historical Society Quarterly*, 46 (July 1962), 305–329, interesting but at times excessively speculative.

The nativist political movement has also been examined in the broader political studies, most notably in recent years by Lee Benson and by John Vollmer Mering's *The Whig Party in Missouri*, Columbia 1967. The major studies of the Whig party and its leaders are valuable on this issue in view of the characteristic flirtation between anti-Catholics and anti-Jacksonians. The fullest and most useful account remains Lewis D. Scisco, *Political Nativism in New York State*, New York 1901. Also good are Ray A. Billington, *The Protestant Crusade, 1800–1860;* Carroll J. Noonan, *Nativism in Connecticut, 1829–1860*, Washington 1938; Leo Hershkowitz, "The Native American Democratic Association in New York City, 1835–1836," *NYHSQ*, 46 (January 1962), 41–59; Richard J. Purcell and John F. Poole, "Political Nativism in Brooklyn," *Journal of the American Irish Historical Society*, 32 (New York 1941), 10–56; Ira M. Leonard, "New York City Politics, 1841–1844: Nativism and Reform," New York University Doctoral Dissertation 1965; and also by Leonard, "The Rise and Fall of the American Republican Party in New York City, 1843–1845," *NYHSQ*, 50 (April 1966), 151–192.

For the Liberty party I have relied primarily on Ralph V. Harlow, *Gerrit Smith*, New York 1939; and T. C. Smith, *The Liberty and Free Soil Parties in the Northwest*, New York 1897. Also useful are Julian P. Bretz, "The Economic Background of the Liberty Party," *American Historical Review*, 34 (October 1928), 250–264; Kinley J. Brauer, *Cotton Versus Conscience: Massachusetts Whig Politics and Southwestern Expansion, 1843–1848*, Lexington 1967; George W. Julian, *The Life of Joshua R. Giddings*, Chicago 1892; and Louis Filler, *The Crusade against Slavery, 1830–1860*, New York 1960.

Accounts of the famous national political issues are of course the meat and drink of the general histories of the era. A good short introduction to the Bank War is Robert V. Remini, *Andrew Jackson and the Bank War*, New York 1967, a fair-minded and succinct exposition of the issues. Bray Hammond, *Banks and Politics in America From the Revolution to the Civil War*, Princeton 1957, is a brilliant and informed discussion by a one-time member of the Federal Reserve Board but it is less than a balanced account. Thomas P. Govan, *Nicholas Biddle, Nationalist and Public Banker*, Chicago 1959, is another important interpretation of the Bank War that views it essentially through the eyes of Biddle. Jean Alexander Wilburn, *Biddle's Bank: The Crucial Years*, New York 1967, refutes the idea, propagated by the Jacksonians, alleging the unpopularity of the BUS. In making a case that is persuasive, although flawed by her uncritical use of some of her data, Wilburn shows that at least for 1831–32 this was not so, with the people, their congressional representatives, and many local bankers evidently appreciative of the services performed by the bank stigmatized by the Jacksonians as "The Monster." Frank O. Gatell, "Sober Second Thoughts on Van Buren, the Albany Regency, and the Wall Street Conspiracy," *JAH*, 54 (June 1966), 19–40, effectively challenges the idea first put forward by Biddle's supporters and more recently by Hammond that Wall Street's desire to replace Chestnut Street as the nation's banking capital explained the Jackson administration's policy. As a fair-minded as well as informed historian of this issue, Gatell's "Spoils of the Bank War: Political Bias in the Selection of Pet Banks," *AHR*, 70 (October 1964), 35–58, discloses that Wall Street bankers were indeed among the important beneficiaries of a Jacksonian policy of selecting new depositories that was motivated largely by nepotism and the hope of political gain. Gatell's "Secretary Taney and the Baltimore Pets: a Study in Banking and Politics," *Business History Review*, 39 (Spring 1965), 205–227, suggests that neither a devil nor an angel theory can explain the administration of the new deposits policy. In a nice example of the new economic history, Jacob Meerman, "The Climax of the Bank War: Biddle's Contraction, 1833–1834," *Journal of Political Economy*, 71 (August 1963), 378–388, in effect subtracts the BUS's measures from the financial picture to discover that both the "panic" and Biddle's role in it had been much exaggerated. The most detailed and informed treatments of the financial operations of Biddle's Bank are Catterall, *The Second Bank of the United States*, and Walter B. Smith, *Economic Aspects of the Second Bank of the United States*. Other worthwhile discussions are David A. Martin, "Metallism, Small Notes, and Jackson's War with the B.U.S.," *Explorations in Economic History*, 11 (Spring 1974), 227–247, which interprets the "war" as a metallists' attempt to reform the money supply; John M. McFaul and Frank O. Gatell, "The Outcast Insider: Reuben M. Whitney and the Bank War," *PMHB*, 91 (April 1967), 115–144; Harry N. Scheiber, "The Pet Banks in Jacksonian Politics and Finance, 1833–1841," *JEH*, 23 (June 1963), 196–214; Philip A. Grant, Jr., "The Bank Controversy and New Hampshire Politics, 1834–1835," *Historical New Hampshire*, 23 (Autumn 1968), 19–33; John M. Behohlavek, "Dallas, the Democracy, and the Bank War of 1832," *PMHB*, 96 (July 1972), 377–390; Bruce Ambacher, "George M. Dallas and the Bank War," *Pennsylvania History*, 42 (April 1975), 117–135; and three recent books, all of them important: William G. Shade, *Banks or No Banks: The Money Issue in Western Politics 1832–1865*, Detroit 1972; and above all, James R. Sharp, *The Jacksonians versus the Banks: Politics in the States After the Panic of 1837*, New York 1970; and John M. McFaul, *The Politics of Jacksonian Finance*, Ithaca 1972, both of which delineate well the complexities and ambiguities of the issue.

Scholarly interest in the Indian tribes and the Jacksonian policy of forcibly removing the southern tribes west of the Mississippi has height-

ened in recent years, reflective no doubt of the nation's greater sensitivity to racial injustice. Three important modern studies are Herman J.
Viola, *Thomas L. McKenney: Architect of America's Early Indian Policy*,
Chicago 1974, which helps unravel the "not entirely unselfish" motives
of this "sincere humanitarian"; Michael Paul Rogin, *Fathers and Children: Andrew Jackson and the Subjugation of the American Indian*,
New York 1975, a brilliant, passionate, and provocative condemnation
of Jackson's policy that is marred by its unsubstantiated flights into
psychoanalysis and some of its tenuous historical judgments; and Ronald N. Satz, *American Indian Policy in the Jacksonian Era*, Lincoln
1975, a criticism of Jacksonian policy that is all the more effective for
its attempts to deal as fairly and sympathetically as possible with the
administration's own rationalizations and arguments. Standing in lonely
splendor in its favorable appraisal of Jacksonian policy is Francis Paul
Prucha, "Andrew Jackson's Indian Policy: A Reassessment," *JAH*, 56
(December 1969), 527–539, an essay I find altogether unconvincing, if
reflective of the gentlemanly traits of its author. Donald Grindle, Jr.,
"Cherokee Removal and American Politics," *Indian Historian*, 8 (Summer 1975), 33–42, 56, concludes that "Andrew Jackson was an unprincipled man in his dealings with the Cherokee Nation." Interesting for
the light it throws on *General* Jackson as negotiator is Thomas D. Clark,
"The Jackson Purchase: A Dramatic Chapter in Southern Indian Policy and Relations," *Filson Club History Quarterly*, 50 (July 1976), 302–
320. Mary E. Young's "The Creek Frauds: A Study in Conscience and
Corruption," *Mississippi Valley Historical Review*, 47 (December 1955),
411–437, and her "Indian Removal and Land Allotment: The Civilized
Tribes and Jacksonian Justice," *AHR*, 64 (October 1958), 31–45, are
outstanding. Young carefully notes Jackson's own unhappiness with
corruption practiced by government agents. Her indictment is no less
damning for the fact that peculation was discouraged from above.
Jacksonian Indian policy may not have been venal—although venality
by private citizens went unpunished if it was not actualy encouraged—
but it was harsh, arrogant, hypocritical, and of dubious legality. Excellent on the legal niceties attendant on the Indian issue are Joseph C.
Burke, "The Cherokee Cases: A Study in Law, Politics, and Morality,"
Stanford Law Review, 21 (February 1969), 500–531; and Edwin A.
Miles, "After John Marshall's Decision: *Worcester* v. *Georgia* and the
Nullification Crisis," *Journal of Southern History*, 39 (November 1973),
519–544. Also useful on this point is Anton-Herman Chroust, "Did Presi-
dent Jackson Actually Threaten the Supreme Court of the United States
with Nonenforcement of its Injunction Against the State of Georgia?"
American Journal of Legal History, 4 (January 1960), 76–78. Good full-
length treatments of the southern tribes and removal are Grant Foreman, *Indian Removal: The Emigration of the Five Civilized Tribes of
Indians*, Norman 1953; Arthur De Rosier, *The Removal of the Choctaw
Indians*, Knoxville 1970; and Grace Steele Woodward, *The Cherokees*,
Norman 1963. John K. Mahon, *History of the Second Seminole War,
1835–1842*, Gainesville 1967, is a detailed and informed treatment of a
neglected tragedy; and Cecil Eby, *"That Disgraceful Affair," The Black
Hawk War*, New York 1973, throws light on popular white attitudes that
help explain that western Indian war.

Surprisingly few special studies have been undertaken of Jacksonian
foreign policies. (I use the plural knowingly, in the absence of evidence
demonstrating a coherent single policy.) Robert Charles Thomas, "An-

drew Jackson Versus France: American Policy Toward France, 1834–1836," *Tennessee Historical Quarterly*, 35 (Spring 1976), 51–64, is a splendid analysis which shows what little account Jackson took of other men's ideas in this sphere. Informative and interesting is Jack E. Bauer, "The United States Navy and Texas Independence: A Study in Jacksonian Integrity," *Military Affairs*, 34 (April 1970), 44–48, which gives Old Hickory high marks. John M. Belohlavek, "Andrew Jackson and the Malaysian Pirates: A Question of Diplomacy and Politics," *Tennessee Historical Quarterly*, 36 (Spring 1977), 19–29, is a clearly written account of a fascinating episode. Older studies are Lee Benns, *The American Struggle for the British West Indies Carrying Trade, 1815–1830*, Bloomington 1930: and Richard A. McLemore, *Franco-American Diplomatic Relations, 1816–1836*, Baton Rouge 1941. A number of biographies are good on this subject, particularly Sellers' second volume on Polk and Curtis' discussion of the Van Buren Administration.

Andrew Jackson's own behavior, both before and after he became president, was itself an important issue—certainly to his army of contemporary critics. The Hero comes off well in Albert Somit, "Andrew Jackson, Legend and Reality," *Tennessee Historical Quarterly*, 7 (December 1948), 291–313; Major L. Wilson, "Andrew Jackson: The Great Compromiser," *ibid.*, 26 (Spring 1967), 64–78; and Robert Kelley, "Presbyterianism, Jacksonianism and Grover Cleveland," *American Quarterly*, 18 (Winter 1966), 615–636. Much more critical are Richard Hofstadter, "Andrew Jackson and the Rise of Liberal Capitalism"; James C. Curtis, *Andrew Jackson and the Search for Vindication;* and Richard R. Stenberg's essays: "Jackson's 'Rhea Letter' Hoax," *Journal of Southern History*, 2 (November 1936), 480–496; Jackson, "Anthony Butler and Texas," *Southwestern Social Science Quarterly*, 13 (December 1932), 264–286; and "The Texas Schemes of Jackson and Houston, 1829–1836," *ibid.*, 15 (December 1934), 229–250, studies in vitriol, all. On the issue of the "Corrupt Bargain," see William G. Morgan, "John Quincy Adams versus Andrew Jackson: Their Biographers and the 'Corrupt Bargain' Charge," *Tennessee Historical Quarterly*, 26 (Spring 1967), 43–58; Morgan, "The 'Corrupt Bargain' Charge Against Clay and Adams: An Historiographical Analysis," *Filson Club Historical Quarterly*, 42 (April 1968), 132–149; and Stenberg, "Jackson, Buchanan, and the 'Corrupt Bargain' Calumny," *PMHB*, 58 (January 1934), 61–85.

The magisterial study of the issue of Jacksonian appointments and political administration remains L. D. White, *The Jacksonians: A Study in Administrative History, 1829–1861*, New York 1954. An older book that views Jacksonian innovations more sympathetically is Carl R. Fish, *The Civil Service and the Patronage*, New York 1905. Matthew A. Crenson, *The Federal Machine: Beginnings of Bureaucracy in Jacksonian America*, Baltimore 1975, is a rewarding if not altogether persuasive interpretation that attempts to connect changes in the civil service to the alleged breakdown in the professions that has been posited unconvincingly in a number of thesis-ridden secondary sources. James C. Curtis, "Andrew Jackson and His Cabinet—Some New Evidence," *Tennessee Historical Quarterly*, 27 (Summer 1968), 157–164, is factual, interesting, and provocative. Interesting information is presented in Ari Hoogenboom and Herbert Ershkowitz, "Levi Woodbury's 'Intimate Memoranda' of the Jackson Administration," *PMHB*, 91 (October 1968), 507–515; and in Leonard Tabachnik, "Political Patronage and Ethnic Groups: Foreign-born in the United States Customhouse Service, 1821–

1861," *Civil War History*, 17 (September 1971), 222–231. Also relevant are Erik M. Erikson, "The Federal Civil Service under President Jackson," *Mississippi Valley Historical Review*, 30 (March 1927), 517–540; Albert Somit, "Andrew Jackson as Administrative Reformer," *Tennessee Historical Quarterly*, 13 (September 1954), 204, 208; Richard P. Longaker, "Was Jackson's Kitchen Cabinet a Cabinet?" *Mississippi Valley Historical Review*, 44 (June 1957), 94–108; Thomas P. Govan, "John M. Berrien and the Administration of Andrew Jackson," *Journal of Southern History*, 5 (November 1939), 447–467; and an illuminating work by a sociologist, Sidney H. Aronson, *Status and Kinship in the Higher Civil Service: Standards of Selection in the Administrations of John Adams, Thomas Jefferson and Andrew Jackson*, Cambridge 1964, that demonstrates the gulf between Jackson's "appointments ideology" and his practice.

The issues of the tariff and internal improvements are illuminated in Carter Goodrich, "Internal Improvements Reconsidered," *JEH*, 30 (June 1970), 289–311; Robert V. Remini, "Martin Van Buren and the Tariff of Abominations," *AHR*, 63 (July 1958), 903–917; Carlton Jackson, "The Internal Improvement Vetoes of Andrew Jackson," *Tennessee Historical Quarterly*, 25 (Fall 1966), 261–279; and John D. Macoll, "Representative John Quincy Adams' Compromise Tariff," *Capitol Studies*, 1 (Fall 1972), 41–58. Nullification, near the center of all overviews on the national politics of the era, is of course singled out for special attention in studies of Calhoun and South Carolina. Particularly valuable is William H. Freehling, *Prelude to Civil War: The Nullification Controversy in South Carolina*, New York 1966, a first-rate study which holds that nullificationists were motivated by diverse fears, some of them having nothing directly to do with the tariff that on the surface seemed the chief irritant. Paul H. Bergeron, "The Nullification Controversy Revisited," *Tennessee Historical Quarterly*, 35 (Fall 1976), 263–275, ably uses demographic data to disclose the "shaky factual foundations" for Freehling's argument that tension over blacks and slavery was a decisive consideration to the nullifiers. Also valuable are Richard B. Latner, "The Nullification Crisis and Republican Subversion," *Journal of Southern History*, 43 (February 1977), 19–38; George C. Rogers, "South Carolina Federalists and the Origins of the Nullification Movement," *South Carolina Historical Magazine*, 71 (January 1970), 17–32, if slightly; and William H. and Jane Pease, " 'Money, Class, and Party': Charleston's Nullification Politics, 1830–1833," a stimulating paper presented at the Ninth Annual History Conference, October 1976 in Brockport. Light on the Jacksonians' attitudes toward blacks is thrown by Gerald S. Henig, "The Jacksonian Attitude Toward Abolition in the 1830's," *Tennessee Historical Quarterly*, 28 (Spring 1969), 42–56; Julius Yanuck, "The Force Act in Pennsylvania [1833]," *PMHB*, 92 (July 1968), 352–364; and Alexander Saxton, "Blackface Minstrelcy and Jacksonian Democracy," *American Quarterly*, 27 (March 1975), 3–28.

There is an abundant literature on the major parties and political warfare in the states. McCormick, *The Second American Party System*, is an excellent starting point. Donald B. Cole, *Jacksonian Democracy in New Hampshire, 1800–1851*, Cambridge 1970, is first-rate, although its notions of Jacksonian "radicalism" might not be universally shared. Other New England studies that warrant examination are Marvin E. Gettleman, *The Dorr Rebellion: A Study in American Radicalism, 1833–1849*, New York 1973; Philip A. Grant, Jr., "The Election of 1834 in

Essex County, Massachusetts," *Essex Institute Historical Collections*, 106 (April 1970), 126–141; Arthur B. Darling, *Political Changes in Massachusetts, 1824–1848*, New Haven 1925; Philip A. Grant, Jr., "Party Chaos Embroils Rhode Island, 1833–1835," *Rhode Island History*, 26 and 27 (October 1967 and January 1968), 113–125, and 24–33; Peter J. Coleman, *The Transformation of Rhode Island, 1790–1860*, Providence 1963; and Peter J. Parish, "Daniel Webster, New England and the West," *JAH*, 54 (December 1967), 524–549.

Recent additions to the study of Jacksonian politics in the middle states include Kim T. Phillips, "The Pennsylvania Origins of the Jackson Movement," *Political Science Quarterly*, 91 (Fall 1976), 489–508, a thoughtful but unconvincing attempt to fathom Jackson's appeal prior to 1824; Peter Levine, "The Rise of Mass Parties and the Problem of Organization: New Jersey, 1829–1844," *New Jersey History*, 91 (Summer 1973), 91–107; and Herbert Ershkowitz, "Samuel L. Southard: A Case Study of Whig Leadership in the Age of Jackson," *ibid.*, 88 (Spring 1970), 5–24. Also valuable are Dixon Ryan Fox, *Decline of Aristocracy in the Politics of New York, 1801–1840*, New York 1919, a classic of Progressive interpretation; Philip S. Klein, *Pennsylvania Politics, 1817–1832*, Philadelphia 1940; Charles M. Snyder, *The Jacksonian Heritage: Pennsylvania Politics, 1833–1848*, Harrisburg 1958; Robert V. Remini, *Martin Van Buren and the Making of the Democratic Party;* Henry R. Mueller, *The Whig Party in Pennsylvania*, New York 1922; Alvin W. Kass, *Politics in New York State, 1800–1830*, Syracuse 1965; and of course Lee Benson, *The Concept of Jacksonian Democracy*.

For the western territories and states, Donald J. Ratcliffe, "The Role of Voters and Issues in Party Formation: Ohio, 1824," *JAH*, 59 (March 1973), 847–870, claims more than it proves but is nonetheless instructive; M. J. Heale, "The Role of the Frontier in Jacksonian Politics: David Crockett and the Myth of the Self-Made Man," *Western Historical Quarterly*, 4 (October 1973), 405–423, has a few interesting thoughts; and Rodney O. Davis, "Partisanship in Jacksonian State Politics: Party Division in the Illinois Legislature, 1834–1841," in Robert P. Swierenga, ed., *Quantification in American History*, New York 1970, 149–162, is a noteworthy discussion. Kermit L. Hall, "Andrew Jackson and the Judiciary: The Michigan Territorial Judiciary as a Test Case, 1828–1832," *Michigan History*, 59 (Fall 1975), 131–151, gives Jackson high marks for blending "the need for a competent judiciary with national political priorities," while avoiding a "betrayal of public service to crass politics." Stephen C. Fox, "Politicians, Issues, and Voter Preference in Jacksonian Ohio: A Critique of an Interpretation," *Ohio History*, 86 (Summer 1977), 155–170, criticizes Ratcliffe and Sharp for their methodological deficiencies. Indispensable for Michigan and suggestive for other places is Formisano, *The Birth of Mass Parties*. Useful older discussions are Harry R. Setvens, "Henry Clay, the Bank and the West in 1824," *AHR*, 60 (July 1955), 843–848; and Stevens, *The Early Jackson Party in Ohio*, Durham 1957.

Perhaps because of Jackson's own origins, antebellum politics in the South and southwest have attracted the most scholarly attention. Burton W. Folsom, II, "Party Formation and Development in Jacksonian America: The Old South," *Journal of American Studies*, 7 (December 1973), 217–229, is an interesting but unconvincing test of the McCormick thesis. Ralph A. Wooster, *The People in Power: Courthouse and State-house in the Lower South 1850–1860*, Knoxville 1969; and Robert M.

Ireland, *The County Courts in Antebellum Kentucky*, Lexington 1972, are fine studies. Joseph H. Harrison, Jr., "Martin Van Buren and His Southern Supporters," *Journal of Southern History*, 22 (November 1956), 438–458, is useful; Arthur C. Cole, *The Whig Party in the South*, remains a Progressive classic.

In view of the voluminousness of the literature, it is perhaps best organized by states and territories. Good recent treatments of the Chesapeake region include Whitman H. Ridgeway, "A Social Analysis of Maryland Community Elites, 1827–1836: A Study of the Distribution of Power in Baltimore County, Frederick County, and Talbot County," University of Pennsylvania Doctoral dissertation 1973; Ridgway, "McCulloch vs. the Jacksonians: Patronage and Politics in Maryland," *Maryland Historical Magazine*, 70 (Winter 1975), 350–362; and Joseph Harrison, Jr., "Oligarchs and Democrats—the Richmond Junto," *Virginia Magazine of History and Biography*, 78 (April 1970), 184–198. Also worthwhile are W. Wayne Smith, "Jacksonian Democracy on the Chesapeake: Class, Kinship and Politics," *Maryland Historical Magazine*, 63 (March 1968), 55–67; Smith, "Jacksonian Democracy on the Chesapeake: The Political Institutions," *ibid.*, 62 (December 1967), 381–393; Mark Haller, "The Rise of the Jackson Party in Maryland, 1820–1829," *Journal of Southern History*, 28 (August 1962), 307–326; and Henry H. Simms, *The Rise of the Whigs in Virginia, 1824–1840*, Richmond 1929.

Harry Legare Watson II, " 'Bitter Combinations of the Neighborhood': The Second American Party System in Cumberland County, North Carolina," Northwestern University doctoral dissertation 1976, presents very interesting material on rural politics. Harold J. Counihan, "The North Carolina Constitutional Convention of 1835: A Study in Jacksonian Democracy," *North Carolina Historical Review*, 46 (October 1969), 335–364; and Max R. Williams, "The Foundations of the Whig Party in North Carolina: A Synthesis and a Modest Proposal," *ibid.*, 48 (April 1970), 115–129, are slight additions to the literature. More substantial is William S. Hoffman, *Andrew Jackson and North Carolina Politics*, Chapel Hill 1958. Diane Cook Norton, "Social Composition of the South Carolina Political Elite of the 1830's," is a useful paper that was presented at the April 1972 Chicago meeting of the Organization of American Historians. Indispensable for South Carolina are Charles Wiltse's biography of Calhoun and William H. Freehling, *Prelude to Civil War*. A good, yet unpublished, paper is Donald DeBats, "Political Elites and the Structure of Ante-Bellum Georgia Politics," presented November 1976 at the meeting of the Southern Historical Association in Atlanta. Also useful are Jack N. Averitt, "The Democratic Party in Georgia, 1824–1837," University of North Carolina doctoral dissertation 1956; and above all, Paul Murray, *The Whig Party in Georgia, 1825–1853*, Chapel Hill 1948, which is excellent. Lynn L. Marshall, "The Genesis of Grass-Roots Democracy in Kentucky," *Mid-America*, 47 (October 1965), 269–287 is interesting. For Florida there are good studies by Herbert J. Doherty, "Andrew Jackson's Cronies in Florida Territorial Politics," *Florida Historical Quarterly*, 34 (July 1955), 3–29; and Arthur W. Thompson, *Jacksonian Democracy on the Florida Frontier*, Gainesville 1961.

Good recent studies of Tennessee include Paul H. Bergeron, "Politics and Patronage in Tennessee During the Adams and Jackson Years," *Prologue: Journal of the National Archives*, 2 (Spring 1970), 19–24; Burton W. Folsom II, "The Politics of Elites: Prominence and Party in

Davidson County, Tennessee, 1835–1861," *Journal of Southern History*, 39 (August 1973), 359–378, which shows that the prominent were equally divided in their major party preferences; Brian G. Walton, "The Second Party System in Tennessee," *Eastern Tennessee Historical Society Publications*, 43 (1971), 18–33; and James Edward Murphy, "Jackson and the Tennessee Opposition," *Tennessee Historical Quarterly*, 30 (Spring 1971), 50–69. Almost a half-century old but enduringly trenchant is Thomas P. Abernethy, *From Frontier to Plantation in Tennessee*, Chapel Hill 1932. See also R. Beeler Satterfield, "The Uncertain Trumpet of the Tennessee Jacksonians," *Tennessee Historical Quarterly*, 26 (Spring 1967), 79–86; and Milton Henry, "Summary of Tennessee Representation in Congress from 1845 to 1861," *ibid.*, 10 (June 1951), 140–148. Charles G. Sellers, Jr., "Banking and Politics in Jackson's Tennessee, 1817–1827," and his "Jackson Men With Feet of Clay," discussed above, are invaluable. The best study by far of Missouri is John V. Mering, *The Whig Party in Missouri*, Columbia 1967, which is superb. Robert E. Shalhope, "Thomas Hart Benton and Missouri State Politics: A Re-examination," *Missouri Historical Society Bulletin*, 25 (April 1969), 171–191, is rewarding if not thoroughly convincing. See also Hattie M. Anderson, "The Jackson Men in Missouri in 1828," *Missouri Historical Review*, 34 (April 1940), 301–334.

Edwin A. Miles, *Jacksonian Democracy in Mississippi*, Chapel Hill 1960, is excellent. A number of fine studies have illuminated Alabama politics. These include Grady McWhiney, "Were the Whigs a Class Party in Alabama?" *Journal of Southern History*, 23 (November 1957), 510–522; Thomas B. Alexander, et al, "Who Were the Alabama Whigs?" *Alabama Review*, 16 (January 1963), 5–19; and Alexander et al, "The Basis of Alabama's Ante-Bellum Two Party System," *ibid.*, 19 (October 1966), 243–276. J. Mills Thornton III, "The Growth of Elitism in Alabama Politics, 1840–1860," a paper presented at the November 1976 meeting of the Southern Historical Association, contains some useful information. Joseph G. Tregle, Jr., "Louisiana in the Age of Jackson: A Study in Ego-Politics," University of Pennsylvania doctoral dissertation 1954, is very good. William H. Adams, III, *The Whig Party of Louisiana*, Lafayette 1973 (which I read in its dissertation form) is useful. Richard Lowe and Randolph Campbell, "Wealthholding and Political Power in Antebellum Texas," *Southwestern Historical Quarterly*, 79 (July 1975), 21–30, is a statistically refined and thorough quantitative study of the social and economic characteristics of Texas political leaders. See too Campbell, "The Whig Party of Texas in the Elections of 1848 and 1852," *Southwestern Historical Quarterly*, 74 (July 1969), 17–34; and for Arkansas, Lonnie J. White, *Politics on the Southwest Frontier: Arkansas Territory, 1819–1836*, Memphis 1964; Brian G. Walton, "The Second Party System in Arkansas, 1836–1848," *Arkansas Historical Quarterly*, 28 (Summer 1969), 120–155, and Gene W. Boyett, "Quantitative Differences Between the Arkansas Whig and Democratic Parties, 1836–1850," *ibid.*, 34 (Autumn 1975), 214–226, which although useful is sketchy and imprecise.

Although many of the state studies and several of the broad surveys touch on local politics, historians have only recently sought to discover the sources of power in towns and cities, as political scientists have for some time sought to trace such power in contemporary communities. Floyd Hunter's study of mid-20th century Atlanta, *Community Power Structure: The Study of Decision Makers*, Chapel Hill 1953, located power in a small socioeconomic elite. For the "pluralist" refutation of Hunter, see Robert A. Dahl, "A Critique of the Ruling Elite Model," *American Political Science Review*, 52 (June 1958), 463–469; and Nelson W. Polsby, "How to Study Community Power: The Pluralistic Alternative," *Journal of Politics*, 22 (August 1960), 474–484. Thomas J. Anton, "Power, Pluralism, and Local Politics," *Administrative Science Quarterly*, 7 (March 1963), 425–457, analyzes these approaches. For the Jacksonian period see Edward Pessen, "Who Governed the Nation's Cities in the 'Era of the Common Man?'" *Political Science Quarterly*, 87 (December 1972), 591–614; Pessen, "Who Has Power in the Democratic Capitalistic Community? Reflections on Antebellum New York City," *NYH*, 58 (April 1977), 129–156; Kathleen Kutolowski, "American Political Elites: A Case Study of Local Power, 1803–1860," a valuable paper on the "burned-over" district presented at the April 1976 meeting of the Organization of American Historians in St. Louis; Whitman H. Ridgway, "Community Leadership: Baltimore During the First and Second Party Systems," *Maryland Historical Magazine*, 71 (Fall 1976), 334–348; Robert A. Dahl, *Who Governs? Democracy and Power in an American City*, New Haven 1961, a classic study of New Haven from colonial times to the present; and Maximilian Reichard, "Urban Politics in Jacksonian St. Louis: Traditional Values in Change and Conflict," *Missouri Historical Review*, 70 (April 1976), 259–271, which suggests the imperviousness of local politics to the slogans and issues of the major party warfare fought on state and national battlegrounds. For a recent study that attempts to go beyond both "elitism" and its pluralist refutation, see Edward Pessen, "Who Rules America? Power and Politics in the Democratic Era, 1825–1975," *Prologue: Journal of the National Archives*, 9 (Spring 1977), 5–26.

Political historians have told us a great deal about the kind of men who were active in party politics in antebellum America. It would be useful if in the future they try to throw additional light on what party leaders did and did *not* do, and on the consequences of their action and inaction. Another fruitful line of future inquiry would explore further the relationship between the social and economic context and politics, in order to achieve deeper understanding than we now have of the effect of the one on the other. The proliferating studies of that context make possible investigations that will permit us to go beyond the undocumented assumptions that some of us relied on in the past.

INDEX

This book has been set in 10 and 9 point Primer, leaded 2 points. Chapter numbers are 54 point Palatino and chapter titles are 18 point Palatino. The size of the type page is 27 by 52 picas.